Classical Conditioning

3rd Edition

Classical Conditioning

3rd Edition

Edited by

Isidore Gormezano
University of Iowa

William F. Prokasy
University of Illinois-Urbana-Champaign

Richard F. Thompson
Stanford University

LEA LAWRENCE ERLBAUM ASSOCIATES, PUBLISHERS
1987   Hillsdale, New Jersey   London

Lawrence Erlbaum Associates, Inc., Publishers
365 Broadway
Hillsdale, New Jersey 07642

Library of Congress Cataloging-in-Publication Data
Classical conditioning.

Rev. ed. of. : Classical conditioning II : current
research and theory. 1972.
Includes indexes.
1. Classical conditioning.   2. Neuropsychology.
3. Rabbits — Psychology. I. Gormezano, Isidore.
II. Prokasy, William F. (William Frederick), 1930-
III. Thompson, Richard F.   IV. Classical conditioning II.
BF319.C573   1987   612'.8   86-6253
ISBN 0-89859-507-X

Printed in the United States of America
10 9 8 7 6 5 4 3 2 1

Table of Contents

Preface

This book is devoted to behavioral, neurophysiological, and neurochemical methods and findings in classical conditioning. It is devoted to a set of model Pavlovian, or classical conditioning, preparations in the rabbit. Although primary emphasis has been placed on the nictitating membrane response (NMR), the set includes, in addition, eyelid, eyeball retraction, jaw movement, and heart rate responses.

It has been evident since Pavlov's time that the classical conditioning paradigm has had the potential of helping us to understand the functioning of the nervous system, the neural substrate for functional units of behavior, and behavioral systems. Nonetheless, prior to the 1960s there was a paucity of research in Western laboratories based upon preparations reliable enough to go very far in reaching that potential. In part, the relative neglect can be attributed to Watson's use of the term *classical conditioning* to refer not only to a method but to a functional unit, or building block, of behavior. Unfortunately, Watson's speculative use of the term *classical conditioning* created the illusion that its laws had been specified fully by Pavlov's conditioning research. In addition, through the year methodological difficulties were encountered with many of the response system and species selected for study with classical conditioning procedures. For example, although extensive methodological work had removed many measurement difficulties in human eyeblink conditioning, the data still displayed considerable variability and the human preparation was clearly inappropriate for physiological intervention. This was further complicated by the fact that such data were frequently interpreted in terms of "volitional" processes despite the physicalistic and deterministic nature of conditioning theory dating from Pavlov. Furthermore, in both humans and animals other prominent conditioning preparations (e.g., GSR and salivary) suffered from noise levels introduced by response characteristics not attributable to the associative processes of interest.

Some 25 years ago the senior editor and his associates undertook the development of rabbit conditioning preparations in an attempt to remedy some of the deficiencies and difficulties of the sort just mentioned. In particular, attention was paid to the objective determinants of conditioning and to the acquisition of data robust enough to address both physiological and theoretical questions about learning and memory. This meant the development of more suitable animal preparations. Patterson and Romano (Chapter 1) provide a detailed account of the 25-year development and modification of these preparations.

We referred previously to a set of model rabbit preparations. Few preparations become "model" preparations. To be sure, they must be preparations through which enduring, and important, questions can be asked. At the same time they must be (relatvely) economical to employ; they must be duplicable with relative ease in many laboratories; and their basic empirical characteristics must be highly reliable. Of considerable importance, a model preparation must also exhibit properties that are not entirely unique to the particular experimental circumstances. It also is essential that the results not be entirely species specific. As the sophisticated nature of modern ethological research makes clear, if we are to understand a species there is no substitute for extensive laboratory and field research on that organism. We are, however, confronted with a fact: Many properties (e.g., physiological, neurological, and behavioral) are common to sets of organisms beyond the single species. It is that commonality with a focus on understanding behaving organisms that is the focus of study for psychologists. Thus, the value of the model rabbit preparations is not only in what we can learn about the rabbit as a species but, as well, is in the identification and elucidation of more general properties of organisms.

The extensive use made of the rabbit preparations over the past 25 years reflects their "model preparation" status. In that sense, the NMR preparation, particularly, parallels such model preparations as those of the fruit fly in genetics, the squid in the study of the nerve cell, and the pigeon in instrumental learning. Many studies have been conducted to refine and extend the nictitating membrane preparation and to provide better controls and increased generality. We now have substantial information on the basic behavioral properties of the preparation, and it is clear that many of these properties appear in other species and preparations. Beyond these basics, however, the preparation has been used extensively in the development of broader theorizing about conditioning and about the neural and biochemical substrates of both the reflex system and the necessary and sufficient conditions for an organism to learn to respond to altered environmental contingencies. In certain respects that is not surprising. In the past 2 decades behavioral scientists have been concentrating less on behavior as a level of analysis unto itself and more on brain-behavior correlates on the one hand, and the (cognitive) systems that yield the behavior on the other. Though it could not have been predicted 25 years ago, the NMR preparation happens to have been admirably suited to addressing theoretical issues implicit in these developments.

The rabbit classical conditioning preparations have been employed in the study of many important questions in, for example, behavioral adaptation, associative learning and the underlying neurophysiological and neuro-chemical processes, and as a source of axioms in theories of learning. How-ever, the label *classical conditioning* also has been applied to a broad aggre-gate of paradigms each of which has its own virtues in the study of associative processes. They include, principally, such "transfer of control" (or "classical-instrumental") procedures as taste aversion learning and conditioned sup-pression as well as discriminative instrumental anticipatory approach activ-ity. In these, as well as in more general instrumental conditioning paradigms, the target response is usually outcome-defined (e.g., press the bar) and there-fore allows a wide variety of different movements to yield the required out-come. It is precisely here that what we call the CS-CR paradigm, as reflected in the model rabbit preparations, is distinct and merits further comment.

As first recognized by Karl Lashley in 1916, it is the precision of control over CS and US presentations, their characeristics, and their relationships, together with the precision of response measurement that makes the CS–CR paradigm a particularly attractive vehicle for the study of the neural sub-strates of learning and memory. As noted, the paradigm is very well suited to permitting the identification of stimulus antecedents (CS/US) of the target response (CR/UR) and thus of learned associations. All of the rabbit prepa-rations fall into the class of CS–CR procedures and, under appropriate con-trol contrasts, have revealed remarkably low levels of nonassociative re-sponding. Moreover, the class of behaviors studied with the CS–CR para-digm have an anatomically defined set of movements or secretions mediated by a relatively small group of muscles and/or glands. Because the target re-sponse system is elicited by the US, it has been possible to identify effector pathways outside the conditioning situation that permits the observation of changes in the activity of those pathways from the start of conditioning. Consequently, from among the set of conditioning paradigms, the CS–CR paradigm uniquely allows for the potential identification of neural path-way(s) for the target response.

One of the editors (RFT), of a physiological persuasion, early recognized and argued for the extraordinary value of the nictitating membrane/eyelid response conditioning preparation in the rabbit as a mammallian model sys-tem for the localization and analysis of the neurobiological substrate of basic associative learning. Since then, a number of laboratories, including those of the editors and their former students and postdoctoral fellows, have pursued this approach to brain mechanisms of learning and memory. Indeed, over the past 18 years, this preparation has proved to be the most productive mammalian model system for understanding the biological bases of memory. Much of the essential memory trace circuitry has been identified and the exact localization of the memory traces may soon be determined. Then, for the first time, it should be possible to analyze the neurobiological mechanisms of memory storage and retrieval in the mammalian brain.

The chapters in this book reflect, albeit more in selective than systematic fashion, ways in which the CS–CR paradigm and model preparations have been used to theoretical and empirical advantage. The chapters begin with a description of the preparations and their properties and then progress through an examination of the response systems, stimulus controls, neural and biochemical correlates, models, and more general theory. Our intent is to illustrate some of the many theoretical and experimental advances that have been made in the past 25 years. In turn, these advances have sharpened and informed many enduring questions about the nature of the behaving organism and, as well, have provided some provocative questions of their own.

1 The Rabbit in Pavlovian Conditioning

Michael M. Patterson
Anthony G. Romano
*College of Osteopathic Medicine
and Department of Psychology
Ohio University*

The rabbit has long been a favorite subject for neurological research and for many types of medical and cosmetological testing. Although the animal has been long used in these fields, it has, until relatively recently, been relatively little used in various behavioral studies, the preferred subjects generally being the rat, pigeon, dog, cat, and various primates. In the early 1960s, Gormezano and his students began a search for a preparation that would embody the best physical properties of the animal subject with the advantages of the classical conditioning or Pavlovian situation to produce an optimal model system for the study of Pavlovian conditioning. The animal would have to accept restraint, provide a convenient response system that was easily measured, be available at low cost, be easily cared for and have a low genetic variability. These traits would allow exact stimulus placement and delivery, accurate response measurement over successive trials and sessions, and large numbers of subjects to be run with minimal variability and low cost. These factors were necessary to fully exploit the particular advantages of the Pavlovian conditioning paradigm that include invariant stimulus delivery, well-defined stimulus–response relationships, and complete experimental control of event timing. The New Zealand white breed of rabbit fit the specifications for low genetic variability because it is an albino, readily bred and available, is docile (we have, over many years of handling the rabbit, been nipped at only once), and is not expensive in most locales. To this list of positive features can be added the fact that the rabbit can, after behavioral studies, be used as a food source by underpaid graduate students. Over a period of 1–2 years, Gormezano's group developed the techniques for restraining the rabbit and for presenting stimuli to, and recording various responses from, the restrained animal. The initial report of this preparation was presented in *Science* in 1962 (Schneiderman, Fuentes, & Gormezano, 1962) in a study showing classically conditioned eyelid responses in the rabbit. This was soon followed by a report (Gormezano, Schneiderman, Deaux, & Fuentes, 1962) showing conditioned responding of the nictitating membrane (NM) response and later (Deaux & Gormezano, 1963) by a study of classical conditioning of eyeball retraction in the rabbit. Over the next decade, the rabbit preparation was refined by Gormezano and his students, and used by others for similar studies, with the result that a great deal of data was collected from the preparation. Other preparations have followed. For example, in 1969, Rubin and Brown detailed the use of the rabbit in a Skinnerian conditioning situation, using lever pressing with the teeth as a response, and Swadlow has described another operant conditioning method (1970).

Following the phenomenal success of the rabbit as a subject in the behavioral paradigm, Thompson and his colleagues (e.g., Cegavske, Thompson, Patterson, & Gormezano, 1976) began utilizing the rabbit classical conditioning preparation in studies of the neural correlates of classical conditioning, an endeavor that has also been very productive, as can be seen in other chapters of this volume.

The present chapter is devoted to presenting the characteristics of the rabbit as a subject in Pavlovian conditioning, its care and preparation, the behavioral techniques useful in the preparation, and the basic neurophysiological methods used in working with the rabbit. In many cases, descriptions of techniques are not exhaustive but given in sufficient detail to allow an assessment of whether they are useful for the interested experimenter, who may then consult the primary references given.

THE RABBIT

Characteristics

The rabbit most often used in classical conditioning studies is the New Zealand white breed, although other strains such as the Belgian have also been used. The New Zealand White is an albino strain, thus insuring a reasonably pure genetic character. The albino rabbit has a nonpigmented eye, resulting in somewhat less visual acuity than pigmented animals, a characteristic to be considered in any studies involving visual processing. The usual New Zealand White can be used for conditioning and neurophysiological studies when it is about 2.0 kg in weight but will grow to a weight of 8–10 kg over a year or two. In general, this rabbit is fairly docile, being easily carried by the scruff of the neck with a hand supporting the abdomen, and accepts restraint well as described later. The animal is readily available from breeders in most locations and is usually not overly expensive, ranging from $5 to $25 per animal at the 2.0 kg weight. There can be some variability in temperament among animals, a trait that seems to depend on both animal stock and breeder. If the animals obtained from a supplier seem overly excitable, obtaining different breeding stock often results in more docile animals. However, the manner in which the animals are raised, for example, crowding conditions, sanitary care, and general environmental stimuli, can affect the subject's behavior. Thus, the animal supplier should be checked for overly harsh breeding and housing conditions if the animals supplied are overly excitable. It is optimal to house the animals for several days after receipt and prior to an experimental use to allow adaptation to the new environment and thus further minimize between-animal variability.

Housing and Identification

The minimal housing and identification standards for rabbits have been set by the United States Department of Agriculture. These standards, at this time, specify that rabbits up to about 2.3 kg (5 lbs) must have 180 sq in. of floor space when housed individually. If housed in groups, each must have 144 sq in. of floor space. For animals from 2.7 to 3.6 kg, each animal must have 360 sq in. of floor space if housed individually, and 288 sq in. if in groups. The figures are 540 sq in. and 432 sq in. for animals of 4 kg and go to 720 sq in. for animals of 5.4 kg if housed individually. In each case, the cage must be of sufficient height to allow normal postural adjustments and have no dangerous protuberances. Food and water receptacles cannot overhang applicable floor space. In point of fact, most caging supplied by commercial vendors meets or exceeds minimal standards, although care must be taken to acquire caging meant for the size animal to be used. It is preferable to obtain stainless steel cages with removable waste pans and partial solid side walls, rather than full bar or screen walls. The rabbit tends to spray urine, sometimes above the height of the rabbit's back, and occasionally a rabbit has been known to urinate on an experimenter or the caretaker with seemingly calculated regularity and accuracy, especially if the animal is housed at head level in a cage rack, thus making the partial solid side walls even more attractive. Rabbit urine is quite strong, making stainless steel caging the choice rather than galvanized, for longer life and ease of cleaning. Cages should be washed regularly, at least once every 2 weeks, and waste pans cleaned at least once a week or more often if needed. A bed of cedar chips in the waste pans keeps odors and cleaning to a minimum. Rabbits should be kept in a comfortable environment of about 68°F and will not perform well in experiments if the environment is above 75–78°F.

Animal identification is an important part of rabbit use. From the standpoint of USDA regulations, the experimenter must have proof of purchase of his or her animals and keep records of each animal's origin, use, and disposal. It is a necessity to maintain identification of each subject during experiments. For this purpose, writing in the ear with an indelible marker is minimally satisfactory as the marker fades over a few days. It is better to attach a metal tag through the very outer tip of the ear and best to use a veterinarian tattoo machine to permanently mark the animal's ear with a number that can then be used to track the animal in all care and experimental records. Such a tattoo machine can be obtained from The Anacare Corporation, 47 Manahasset Avenue, Manahasset, Long Island, New York 11050.

Feed and Water

Rabbits should be maintained on ad lib feed and water schedules unless deprivation is necessary for experimental procedures. Commercial rabbit chow is sufficient for most diets and can be supplemented by hay or lettuce scraps if desired. Hay supplement to a chow diet will often avoid bouts of diarrhea that sometimes occur with a change of environment from breeder to experimental colony. Food deprivation as an experimental procedure has been reported to be very difficult, taking long periods of severe deprivation to reduce body weight, but water deprivation is routinely used and can be achieved with a 22-hr deprivation schedule (Rubin & Brown, 1969).

Common Diseases and Injuries, Natural and Experimental

A normal, healthy rabbit should appear alert and have bright eyes and a smooth glossy coat. Rectal temperature is normally 40°C. The average heart rate is 205 beats per minute and may vary between 125 and 305 beats per minute. Respiration rate is normally 39 beats per minute. Diseased animals appear listless, have dull eyes and a rough, lusterless coat, and often exhibit a loss of appetite. The problems that are most likely to be encountered in laboratory rabbits include ear mites, conjunctivitis, broken backs, and intestinal disorders.

Ear mites are a common problem in rabbits. The mites bite the inner surface of the ear causing serum to ooze and eventually harden. Unless the mites are removed, they will reproduce beneath the surface of the crusted serum and will continue to be a source of irritation to the animal. Furthermore, a sufficient build-up of the hardened exudate may impair hearing and, as a result of secondary infections, may damage the inner ear and subsequently affect the CNS. Rabbits infested with ear mites often exhibit head shaking, ear flapping, and attempts to scratch the ear with a hindpaw. Upon delivery by the supplier, and prior to the start of an experiment, each animal should be inspected for ear mites. If possible, affected animals should be isolated from the colony because the mites are easily transmitted to adjoining cages.

The recommended procedure for treating animals infested with ear mites consists of first removing the crusted exudate with cotton soaked in dilute hydrogen peroxide and then swabbing the area with a mixture of one part Canex to three parts mineral oil. The treatment should be repeated 6 to 10 days later.

Rabbits are susceptible to two unrelated intestinal disorders. Intestinal coccidiosis is a parasitic disease brought on by the ingestion of fecal pellets containing the oocysts of one of four protozoans: *Eimeria perforans, E. magna, E. media,* and *E. irresidua.* Symptoms of intestinal coccidiosis consist of an inability to gain weight, loss of appetite, pot-bellied appearance, and a tendency toward soft droppings and diarrhea. If intestinal coccidiosis is suspected, a fecal sample should be obtained and examined microscopically for oocysts. Infested animals should be isolated and treated with sulfaquinoxaline at .10% in their feed continuously for 2 weeks.

Hepatic or liver coccidiosis has been attributed to *E. stiedae.* In severe cases, diarrhea, anorexia, and a rough hair coat are observed and enlargements may be felt in the liver. Treatment is the same as for intestinal coccidiosis.

Mucoid enteritis tends to affect younger rabbits and can be confused with intestinal coccidiosis due to the similarity of symptoms. Thus, the symptoms of mucoid enteritis include inactivity, anorexia, squinty eyes, and the ears tend to droop and lose their pinkish color. The infected animal often sits in a hunched position and may grind its teeth. Temperature is below normal and the animal may demonstrate a great thirst or refusal to drink. Constipation or, more commonly, diarrhea may be observed. In either case, the feces will have a clear, viscid appearance. The cause of mucoid enteritis is unknown and there is no reliably effective treatment.

Rabbits kept for periods of several days in laboratory housing may also develop an upper respiratory infection that is characterized by sneezing, loss of appetite, and nasal congestion. Animals with the common rabbit "cold" are not usually in danger of dying but are definitely compromised during both surgical and conditioning procedures. Even a mild respiratory infection can result in severe breathing difficulty during anesthesia or during the stress of restraint in an experimental session and can end in death. Thus, sneezing in a rabbit is cause for concern. The treatment consists of adding oxytetracycline HCl to the drinking water. Any of several commercially available veterinary compounds such as Medamycin soluble powder available from Medtech, Inc. is recommended. A one-quarter-teaspoon dose in the drinking water (1 pt) is sufficient. The dosage should be used every other day or for a week followed by a week of no dosage for more severe cases. Continued use will result in diarrhea as with any such medication. Again, hay supplementing the regular chow diet can control medication-induced diarrhea.

Eye problems may occur in animals prepared for NM conditioning as described later. Problems frequently arise within a day or two after suturing the NM. Too large or too small a loop in the suture may initially irritate the inner surface of the eyelids. The animal may compound the irritation by rubbing the area with a forepaw. Satisfactory results may be obtained by several daily applications of ophthalmic ointments containing sulfonamides or antibiotics such as sulfathiozole 5% or chlortetracycline HCl. In cases of severe irritation, where there is marked swelling of the eyelids and a watery or purulent discharge, the suture should be removed until the animal has fully recovered.

Another problem that may arise with an experimentally naive rabbit is that the animal, when first restrained, may struggle with sufficient force to fracture a vertebra. When returned to the home cage, the animal tends to lie on its side and drag its hindquarters when moving. Bladder and bowel control are often absent. Failure to observe a strong hind leg flexion in response to a tail or toe pinch is a good indicator of vertebral damage. Animals suffering from a broken back should be sacrificed with an overdose of a barbiturate as soon as possible. The probability that an animal may break its back during the first exposure to the restraint may be reduced considerably by placing the backplate of the restrainer on top of, rather than behind, the animal. This procedure prevents the animal from placing its hind legs in a position where forceful exertion is possible. Once the animal has adapted to the restraint, no special precautions are necessary.

Whereas the rabbit may be extensively cared for as an experimental subject, the experimenter must also be considered. In working for long periods with rabbits, the experimenter may develop or have an initial allergy to the rabbit. This allergy or sensitivity is generally due to the dander or skin dust from the rabbit and secondarily to the hair of the animal's coat. In mild cases, the symptoms are generally itching eyes and a runny nose with an occasional sneeze. More serious or severe cases produce nasal mucosal swelling, eye redness and extreme itching, often continuous sneezing, and sometimes a feeling of lightheadedness. In very severe cases, respiratory distress may result in addition to an exaggeration of the other symptoms. These symptoms can be a true allergic reaction or a less-severe reaction brought on by the stress of dealing with the animals in an experimental situation. For mild cases, a drug such as Chlor-Trimeton, an over-the-counter antihistamine, at a dose of 4–8 mg will abort or prevent the symptoms. More severe cases may require the experimenter to seek medical help, wear protective masks or hoods during contact with the animals, or change to another experimental subject. The chances of developing an allergic reaction to the rabbit with continued contact are fairly good and should be a sign for treatment when first noticed to avoid increasingly severe reactions.

BEHAVIORAL TECHNIQUES

The Paradigm

The Pavlovian conditioning paradigm has been detailed by various authors (e.g., Gormezano, 1966; Patterson, 1976; Thompson, Patterson, & Teyler, 1972). From the experimental viewpoint, it has several features that provide unique advantages for the analysis of the learning process as well as certain problems that are difficult to overcome in the experimental situation. Gormezano's (1966) classic description of the paradigm, and more recent theoretical article (Gormezano & Kehoe, 1975), present the features and controversial points clearly.

From the standpoint of techniques, the Pavlovian conditioning situation, as it has evolved in the tradition of American psychology, incorporates, in its simplest form, the presentation of two stimuli to the subject. The unconditioned stimulus (US) is a stimulus that has been shown by test to reliably produce a target response, the unconditioned response (UR), without prior training. Obviously, the target response is but one of a spectrum of responses produced and may be in either the visceral or musculoskeletal systems. The selection of a target response to any stimulus from among those produced by the US is generally based upon the ease of response measurement, theoretical factors, response reliability, and so forth. The other stimulus is termed the conditioned or conditioning stimulus (CS) and is selected in such a way that its presentation does not elicit the target response of the US. The response to the CS, or conditioned response (CR), is that response that develops under appropriate training conditions and is the indicator of learning. The UR and CR are historically considered to be in the same response system, the CR developing over training to resemble the UR, although differences in latency, amplitude, and time course often occur. Controversy currently surrounds the point of whether the CR and UR should necessarily be in the same response system, but, as Gormezano and Kehoe (1975) point out, this aspect is one of the hallmark features of classical conditioning. One of the commonly held beliefs about the selection of a CS is that it should produce no response in the response system being measured; that is, that the CS should be "neutral." This is not a necessity, especially when dealing with neurophysiological aspects of the paradigm, but the use of a CS that produces any response in the target system necessitates the careful delineation of nonassociative from associative responses through control groups (see Gormezano, 1966; Gormezano & Kehoe, 1975; Patterson, 1976). These and other aspects of the conditioning paradigm are also discussed elsewhere in the present volume.

The use of a CS and US in classical conditioning presents unique opportunities for stimulus and response control. The basic paradigm requires that the CS and US be presented independent of the animal's response to the stimuli.

Thus, the experimenter is in complete control of stimulus timing and hence of when the responses will be elicited. This situation allows for a great deal of predictability in data collection and in trial and session sequencing. However, the theoretical necessity of invariant stimulus presentation (except for test trials when the US is omitted) produces the corollary problem of obtaining sufficient control of the organism to be able to insure accurate stimulus delivery. Once such control is established, response measurement is generally greatly facilitated.

Restraint Techniques

The necessity of providing invariant stimulus presentation to the rabbit in the Pavlovian paradigm has resulted in the general use of animal restraint devices coupled with various stimulus presentation techniques. The basic restraint device has been described by Gormezano (1966). Basically, the restrainer is a Plexiglas box about 23 cm long, 10 cm wide, and 20 cm high. The box has a sloping front plate with a U-shaped slot about 7 cm wide and 17 cm deep through which the animal's head can protrude, and an adjustable stock that slips over the slot to keep the head in place. An adjustable padded clamp is used to pin the ears back to the stock to further immobilize the head. The top of the box is usually open with a rear plate that can be adjusted up to the animal's hindquarters to keep the body firmly restricted. Figure 1.1 shows such a restraint box. Some experimenters modify the box to include a sliding

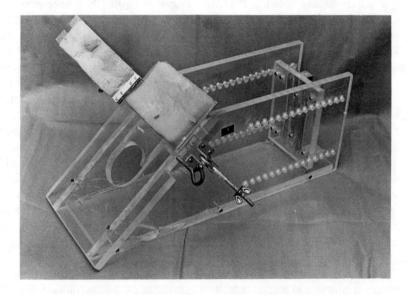

Fig. 1.1   A rabbit restraint box fashioned after the one described by Gormezano (1966).

Plexiglas plate that can be inserted into grooves to cover the top of the box, thus further restricting body movements.

The box described and shown has the advantages of being easily built, of holding the animal securely, of allowing access to the animal's head while holding the head practically still, and it is well tolerated by the animal. As noted earlier, a naive rabbit may occasionally struggle when being adapted to the restraint box and suffer a broken back. This problem can be alleviated somewhat by leaving the head stock and back plate somewhat looser than usual during adaptation, but an occasional broken back will occur despite the experimenter's best efforts. In the case of a broken back, the animal must be sacrificed as described previously.

The basic restraint system can be modified in various ways for various purposes. Frey, Englander, and Roman (1971) describe a restraint system in which the animal's head protrudes through the top of a completely enclosed box for their studies of eyelid conditioning. The major purpose of any restraint system, however, is to restrain the animal from gross movements, thus allowing both accurate stimulus placement and relatively invariant response recording both within and between training sessions. The basic restraint setup and most of the recording equipment described later can be obtained from the Waltke Scientific Instrument Co., 603 East University, Bloomington, Indiana 47401.

Conditioning Environments

Although the restraint devices described earlier provide adequate immobilization for the rabbit, it is necessary to further isolate the animal during conditioning sessions. An adequate environment for Pavlovian conditioning should isolate the animal from extraneous sources of stimulation. For the albino rabbit, uncontrolled sound is the extraneous variable most likely to interfere with the conditioning process, although changes in illumination and odors may also prove disruptive. Performance level may also be affected by the temperature level and relative humidity in the conditioning environment. The influence of these environmental variables may be eliminated or significantly reduced through the use of a well-designed experimental chamber located in an air-conditioned room.

Various devices are available for use as isolation and environmental chambers. The choice of which will be used must be made upon economic, experimental, and spatial considerations. The most economical chamber that provides sufficient isolation is simply a deactivated refrigerator shell. Discarded refrigerators are available free from appliance stores and can easily be stripped of motor, compressor, nonfunctional wires, etc., and the necessary wires, lights, and speakers put into the refrigerator compartment. The enclosure must also be ventilated to maintain temperature and air supply. Although providing good isolation for the usual study, refrigerator shells are bulky, often nonuniform in size, and do require considerable work to convert. They do, however, provide good electrical as well as sound isolation due to the metal box and insulation.

A second type of isolation chamber can be constructed from fireproof file cabinets. The usual commercial fireproof file cabinet is configured 2, 3, or 4 drawers per cabinet, each isolated by surrounding walls of fire retardant material. Legal-size drawers are best used due to space needs. Such enclosures are economical of space but are considerably more expensive than converted refrigerators. File cabinets also require considerable work to convert to suitable chambers. Besides ventilation, which must be brought in through baffles to retard sound transmission, wires must be led through the drawer front, preferably via through-the-wall connectors to minimize sound transmission that would occur if holes were simply put through the drawer. The floor of the drawer should either be epoxy coated or a removable bottom pan put in to facilitate cleaning of the inevitable urine secreted during the conditioning sessions. Stimulus panels must be constructed and mounted, usually on the front wall of the drawer, and guides put on the drawer bottom to accept the restraint box in a standard position relative to the stimuli. The advantage of file cabinet enclosures is mainly a space savings, because squads of 12 subjects can easily be run simultaneously in a small room. However, file drawers may not be sufficiently large to house associated amplification equipment if neurophysiological studies are to be run, and they may not provide sufficient electrical isolation.

A third enclosure type is the commercially available enclosure. Such enclosures are available from several equipment suppliers in various grades. These enclosures have the advantage of providing good isolation, needing little modification, and being available in various configurations. Thus, enclosures are available that provide almost complete sound attenuation, complete electrical isolation, and through-the-wall attachments for all stimulus and response signals. Of course, these enclosures are also fairly expensive, making them an unfeasible choice for some investigators.

If the enclosures are to be utilized for both behavioral and neurophysiological studies, the experimenter should consider additional factors. Neural recording necessitates the use of chambers with good electrical isolation as well as sound and temperature control. In addition, it is often necessary to put preamplifiers near the animal and to have easy and unimpeded access to the subject's head for adjusting electrodes or head plugs. For this reason, enclosures larger than file drawers may be necessary for such studies, and it is often best to sacrifice the space convenience here and utilize refrigerator shells, commercial enclosures, or specially built enclosures. Such enclosures, if specially constructed from refrigerators or designed after commercial units, should have wire mesh screen in the walls and door beneath sound-deadening insulation to isolate the enclosure electrically. It may be necessary to put two separate layers of copper mesh screen around the enclosure to achieve sufficient isolation. Refrigerator shells have the advantage of the metal cabinet that provides a degree of electrical isolation itself. Proper ground straps are necessary for such enclosures, ensuring that all connections are firm on the cable running directly to earth ground.

Thus, the choice of experimental enclosure will be determined by cost factors, space limitations, and experimental use. File drawers, the most advantageous spacially, are the least suited to neurophysiological studies. Refrigerator shells are the most economical, but bulky, and may provide nonuniform interiors. Commercial units can be ordered in many configurations but are expensive. The compromise of building enclosures to specification is also expensive but may be the only way to achieve certain combinations of size, and of electrical and stimulus isolation characteristics desired. Figure 1.2 shows a restrained rabbit in a refrigerator enclosure with recording gear (described later) attached.

Stimulus Presentation

One of the most important features of the Pavlovian conditioning paradigm is the control provided the experimenter over the delivery of stimuli to the organism. This feature has the advantage of allowing both CS and US to be pre-

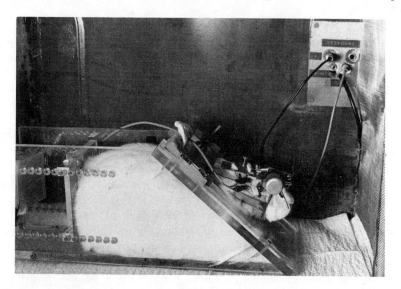

Fig. 1.2   A restrained rabbit prepared for NM conditioning inside a converted refrigerator shell. Note the rabbit's headgear and the copper mesh screening lining the inside of the shell.

sented at the predetermined times in precise relationships independent of the animal's response. However, this requirement also means that strenuous efforts must be made to ensure that the stimuli are presented in such a way that the animal's activity cannot alter the stimulus receipt, and that the stimuli are uniform both from subject to subject and from session to session for each subject. If these requirements are not met, the paradigm can become confused with instrumental paradigms in which the subject's responses do influence stimulus receipt or determine stimulus delivery, or dilute one of the major experimental advantages of Pavlovian conditioning; the ability to measure response characteristics accurately, which presupposes invariant stimulus receipt by the organism.

General Considerations.   As noted, the Pavlovian conditioning paradigm presupposes that the animal's response does not affect delivery or receipt of either the constant CS or US. This characteristic leads to the necessity for adequate isolation from other animals and sources of interfering stimuli. If interfering sounds reach the animal, a tone CS may not be invariant from trial to trial for the animal. Auditory stimuli will also interfere with performance of a response to a visual stimulus in the rabbit. In addition, variations in stimulus intensities over trials can give inaccurate measures of response characteristics developing over trials. Thus, in each of the experimental enclosures, care must be taken to ensure stimulus isolation and invariant delivery to all subjects.

Auditory Stimuli.   The most common CS for the rabbit is the auditory stimulus. The rabbit, especially the albino, is a highly auditorially oriented animal. In most enclosures, the tone, click, or other auditory stimulus is presented through a speaker mounted above or in front of the restrained subject. If the Gormezano restraint box is used, the ears are clamped back at a slant and turned so that the auditory meati are exposed, thus ensuring good auditory reception. In other types of restrainers when auditory stimuli are used, the orientation of the ear pinnae should be checked carefully and positioned systematically. The position of the animal in the chamber is also critical. When tone level is calibrated, the experimenter will notice changes of several decibels from one area of the chamber to another by moving the db meter around the chamber. This is caused, except in the most carefully designed chambers, by cancellations and augmentations of the wavefronts reflecting off the box walls. Thus, the calibration should be done so as to define a position in the chamber where the desired auditory level is present, and the guides for the restraint box adjusted such that the rabbit's ears are always positioned at that spot. Changes of a few centimeters can often make a difference of several db in sound pressure levels. Thus, when using auditory stimuli, close attention must be given to uniform subject placement within the auditory field.

Tone stimuli are generally delivered via good quality speakers and generated by standard tone generators and amplifiers. Often a second speaker is placed in the enclosure to deliver a constant white masking noise throughout the experimental session to further insure a lack of outside interference. Tone frequencies can range from 800 to 5000 Hz. Sound pressure levels at the rabbit's ear can range from lows of 25 db referenced to .0002 dynes/cm², to levels of 90–100 db or more. If white noise background is used, it is often set at a level of about 55–60 db and the tone level set at 72–75 db. Such parameters have been found to provide good stimulus discriminability. Kettner, Shannon, Nguyen, and Thompson (1980) have reported a study of signal detection in classical conditioning using a white noise CS showing thresholds to be very stable within animals across sessions, but variable between animals. Click stimuli, broken tones, and other auditory stimuli have also been successfully utilized as the CS. Thus, whereas the auditory stimulus is most often used as the CS in rabbit Pavlovian conditioning, it must be used with care, carefully calibrated and invariant, and the animal placed in the auditory field precisely to insure invariant stimulus delivery.

Visual Stimuli.   Whereas the rabbit, especially the albino, is heavily dependent on the auditory sense, visual stimuli are also successfully used as the CS. In most experimental chambers, there will be a houselight providing some, usually fairly dim, chamber illumination. Because the albino rabbit has unpigmented eyes, it has poor visual discrimination but senses illumination changes well. Thus, dark–light, light–dark, and lesser changes in illumination levels can all be used as effective stimuli (e.g., Powell, Schneiderman, Elster, & Jacobson, 1971). As with the auditory stimulus, care must be taken to insure uniform illumination levels either by placing the stimulus source directly in front of the restrained subject, or by providing a uniform reflecting surface for a light source mounted elsewhere in the enclosure. Many enclosures include a stimulus panel directly in front of the animal, a convenient arrangement almost necessary if file cabinet drawers are used. Illumination can be provided adequately by 12 or 24 v.d.c. bulbs, and effective stimulus panels include such a bulb behind a milk glass diffusing plate to provide uniform illumination over a wider area. Typical background illumination is about .15 ml as measured by a Macbeth illuminometer and Powell et al. (1971) report successful conditioning to a CS changing from .13 ml to .34 ml. Illumination changes in this range produce little or no alpha response blink in the rabbit.

Whereas auditory and visual stimuli are by far the most commonly utilized CSs in the rabbit preparation, other stimuli can be used. Gormezano (1966) reports using vibrotactile stimuli as the CS, whereas several investigators have used intracranial stimulation (e.g., Martin, Land, & Thompson, 1980; Mis, Gormezano, & Harvey, 1979; Moore, Marchant, Norman, & Kwaterski, 1973, Patterson, 1970). Thus, most stimuli, if sufficient control can be maintained over stimulus delivery, can serve as the CS. For further discussions of the theoretical determinants of a CS and US, see Gormezano (1966) and Gantt (1968).

Electrical Stimuli. The use of electric shock as an aversive US is widespread in Pavlovian conditioning with the rabbit. Shock stimulation has certain advantages in that it is easily administered, readily calibrated, and elicits generally well-defined responses. It has the disadvantage of producing a large stimulus artifact if neural recordings are being made. However, as noted later, such artifacts can be either minimized or ignored under certain conditions.

In the rabbit preparation, shock has been utilized primarily as an aversive stimulus to elicit target responses of the eyeball and eyelids. In this regard, its use has become fairly standard for many investigators using the preparation. The shock stimulus is most easily administered through Clay–Adams (or equivalent) 9 mm stainless steel wound clips that are clipped into the skin at the desired position around the eye (Gormezano, 1966). The area into which the clips are to be put should first be shaved closely and, for optimal contact, depilated with a cream depilatory. The clips may then be left in the skin for several days without danger of infection or discomfort. Frey and Gavin (1975) utilized suture wire looped into the skin and twisted as electrodes for shock delivery. Such wires sutured into the skin are perhaps less likely to be pulled out, but the ease of placing wound clips makes suturing unnecessary. VanDercar, Swadlow, Elster, and Schneiderman (1969) described a method for delivering shock to the eyelids through stainless steel tailor hooks mounted on piano wire springs. The hooks served the purpose of shock electrodes as well as retracting the external eyelids (see section on Recording Techniques).

The use of clip or wire electrodes allows positioning of the shock at various locations relative to the eye. Most studies have placed the shock electrodes about 2 cm caudal to the eye and about 1.5 cm apart. Some experimenters prefer to place one electrode above and one below the eye, analogous to shock delivery through the tailor hooks. Salafia, Daston, Bartosiak, Hurley, and Martino (1974) found conditioning performance to be an indirect function of distance of shock delivery from the eye, and Kettlewell and Papsdorf (1971) found that alteration of the afferent activity from the shock by anesthetizing the eye or placing the shock at the ear tip resulted in poor or no conditioned responding. Thus, it is important for optimal conditioning of the constellation of eye responses that the electrodes be placed as to direct the shock to the eye, and to adopt a standard elecrode placement to avoid response variability.

Shock stimuli are routinely constant current, in the range of 1–4 ma. The usual stimulus is a 60 Hz sine wave and its duration is optimal in the range of

50–100 msec. Shorter durations require excessively large current and longer may cause undue struggling in the animal. Masterson (1981) has recently provided an excellent analysis of peripheral shock, its generation, delivery, and uses. Several excellent shock generator schematics are included in this article. In addition, many excellent commercial shock sources are available that provide excellent control over all shock parameters.

Air Stimuli. An air-puff stimulus has been a favorite US in many Pavlovian conditioning studies of the eye-blink response. Utilized in the rabbit preparation, the air puff to the eye is a mildly aversive stimulus that produces a well-defined response complex. Unlike the shock stimulus, however, the action of the closing eyelids or nictitating membrane (NM) can, if not carefully controlled, alter the properties of the stimulus, thus changing the conditioning situation. Thus the air-puff US must be used with care. Also unlike the electrical stimulus, the puff causes no artifact to interfere with neural recording.

The air-puff stimulus is best delivered to the back half of the eyeball with the external eyelids held open by means of retractors. The movements of the NM are generally not so great as to cover the back portion of the eyeball, thus the problem of stimulus alteration can be kept to a minimum. The puff should be carefully calibrated and an adequate pressure at the point of delivery to the eye will be between 270–350 gm/cm^2 with a duration of 100 msec. It is important to note that the air puff, unlike shock stimuli, has a latency between the opening of the delivery valve and delivery at the eye. This delay may be between 15 and 45 msec depending on the length of the delivery tubing. It is necessary to carefully measure this delay and calibrate US onset time on the response recording apparatus accordingly.

Water Stimuli. Shock and air-puff stimuli are aversive stimuli that are used in the rabbit to produce target responses in the eye region, and elsewhere. Water, on the other hand, has been utilized as an appetitive stimulus to produce a target response of jaw movement associated with ingestion (Smith, DiLollo, & Gormezano, 1966). The use of water as a US in the Pavlovian paradigm necessitates a deprivation procedure for the subject that is not necessary with the aversive stimuli. As with the other stimulus modalities, it is very important to insure that the water is delivered directly to the oral cavity so that the subject's responses have no bearing on stimulus delivery or receipt.

The rabbit's mouth is constructed well for the delivery of an aqueous stimulus. There is a gap between the incisor and molar teeth through which liquid can be squirted even when the mouth is shut. Smith et al. (1966) devised a method by which a cannula is placed in the animal's cheek and a small tube inserted for water delivery. Basically, a hole is punched in the depilated cheek of the anesthetized animal with a leather punch. A cannula made from a 1-inch length of PE–240 polyethylene tubing flared at one end with a 5/16 inch polyethylene washer on it is inserted from the inside of the cheek out. A second washer is put over the outer end of the tube and the tube heat flared. This cannula is easily installed and remains in place for weeks without apparent discomfort to the animal. Water is delivered by slipping into the cannula a blunted 16-gauge hypodermic needle that is attached to the delivery tube. Studies by Swadlow, Hosking, and Schneiderman (1971) report a second method in which a U-shaped hypodermic needle is clipped into the animal's cheek by a wound clip and inserted into the corner of the mouth to deliver the liquid. Although somewhat easier, this method is more prone to loss of the stimulus.

Early studies with the water reinforcer (e.g., Coleman, Patterson, & Gormezano, 1966; Smith et al., 1966) found that a deprivation regime of 2 hr water access per day for 6 days prior to conditioning served adequately. Swadlow et al. (1971) deprived the rabbits completely for 7 days prior to conditioning. However, the latter regime was prior to conditioning a lever-lick response and was therefore necessarily more severe. In any case, a deprivation regime for use with a water US must be tailored to the amount of water consumed during conditioning and be adequate to fulfill the animal's basic needs. Generally, rabbits of 2–3 kg can survive well on 100 cc of water/day and remain in a state of mild deprivation.

As a stimulus, a 1-cc squirt of water delivered over 200–500 msec to the deprived animal serves well. Early studies (e.g., Coleman et al., 1966) found only small effects of utilizing a saccharine-flavored solution over the plain-water US. It has since been found that US magnitude has a much more pronounced effect than sweetness of the solution (e.g., Sheafor & Gormezano, 1972). Thus, when using a water US, the magnitude of US delivered per trial is a critical factor. In this regard, it is important to insure a reliable flow of water in the delivery system. Gormezano has developed a pressurized system that injects water at a constant rate independent of the amount of liquid in the system. Whereas such a system is very precise and necessary for exacting studies of US parameters, a gravity flow system that insures a constant water level over trials is adequate for many purposes. Thus, the water stimulus is quite effective in the water-deprived rabbit for eliciting swallowing jaw movements.

Response Recording

The Pavlovian conditioning situation provides an unparalleled advantage over many other learning situations in the area of response quantification. Due to the precise control over stimulus delivery afforded by the situation, the experimenter is able to select one or more target responses for examination and for use as indicators of the effects of stimulus presentation. The specification of the target response is determined by the choice of US, as the response must be reliably elicited by the US. Also, the conditioned response that appears is in the same response system and similar to the UR (see Gormezano & Kehoe, 1975). These constraints are an integral part of the Pavlovian conditioning paradigm and also afford it a great elegance in stimulus–response definition.

In developing the rabbit preparation for Pavlovian conditioning, Gormezano (1966) attempted to find a response system or systems that would enhance the elegance of the procedural characteristics of the Pavlovian paradigm. Responses with great variability, frequent random or ongoing baseline rates, or those that would be difficult to measure accurately would not allow the power of the paradigm to be fully utilized. Such responses would preclude accurate measures of latency, amplitude, fine alterations in rate, and other properties. In the initial paper introducing the rabbit preparation, Schneiderman et al. (1962) described Pavlovian conditioning of the rabbit eyelid response. In the next two papers conditioning of the NM (Gormezano et al., 1962) and eyeball retraction (Deaux & Gormezano, 1963) responses were described. All three responses are part of the response complex elicited by an air puff to the cornea or a shock to the orbital region. They each have the advantages of being easily measured, having low spontaneous rates, having short onset latencies, and being little affected by stimuli such as tones and lights. Thus, the responses of the eyeball and surrounding structures seemed ideal as target responses for Pavlovian conditioning. Obviously these are not the only responses elicited in the rabbit by infraorbital shock or air puff. A variety of autonomic responses such as heart rate alterations, vascular responses, and others are elicited. Other skeletal responses such as head movements also occur. However, the eye-related responses are both pronounced and accessible. More recently, the jaw-movement response to water in the mouth has been developed in the rabbit, some work has been done with leg muscle tension, and heart rate has been extensively measured. The present section describes the common responses of the rabbit used in Pavlovian studies and their measurement.

Nictitating Membrane Response.   The most widely used target response in Pavlovian conditioning of the rabbit is the nictitating membrane (NM) response. The NM is a sheet of conjunctiva and cartilage located behind the inner canthus of the eye. When the eyeball is stimulatd, the NM sweeps laterally across the cornea, usually covering ½ to ¾ of the exposed surface. Gormezano (1966) has fully described the basic NM recording apparatus and NM characteristics; thus we give only a brief account here. It is now known (Cegavske et al., 1976) that the NM movement is secondary to eyeball retraction. Thus, the action of the retractor bulbi muscle controlled by cranial nerve VI, the abducens, along with small contributions from some of the other extraocular muscles, pulls the eyeball into the socket, displacing the NM out over the corneal surface. Retraction of the NM is largely passive, but may have some active component through action of the oculomotor nerve on striate muscle fibers in the NM. Thus, the rabbit NM activity contrasts with that of the cat, in which retraction is controlled by smooth muscle activated by the superior cervical ganglion. It is now also clear that the neural activity of the abducens nerve in the rabbit originates in both the abducens nucleus and the accessory abducens (Gray, McMaster, Harvey, & Gormezano, 1981).

The NM is readily accessible and can be extended by light pressure on the eyeball. With the rabbit restrained in the box previously described, the membrane can be easily made to appear by holding the external lids apart and blowing on or touching the cornea.

Recording the movements of the NM is also readily accomplished. The most often used method entails suturing a small loop of 6–0 monofilament nylon suture into the outer edge of the membrane. This is easily accomplished when the rabbit is restrained, although care must be taken not to tie the suture tight or rip the membrane. The suture must be placed about .5 mm back from the membrane edge to insure sufficient rigidity for recording. As detailed previously, a well-placed suture produces no irritation, but occasionally eye irritation will result and appropriate steps must be taken to ease the irritation. To record NM movements, the external eyelids are commonly retracted with tailor hooks fastened to the ends of the velcro straps. The hooks are inserted under the lids and the straps passed around the head and fastened together (see Fig. 1.3). Some experimenters forego the external lid retraction and record adequate NM movements with freely moving external lids. For direct recording, a small hook can then be inserted into the suture loop, the hook being attached by a fine thread to the arm of the recording device. The transducing apparatus may take several forms. Most commonly used until very recently was a minitorque potentiometer supplied by Conrac Corporation. The potentiometer had a very low loading and was light and durable. However, the company has ceased production except on special order and cost is prohibitive ($600–$700 each). A wire arm coupled to the potentiometer shaft provided the lever for the thread and was counterbalanced. The potentiometer is then mounted on a headgear that fits over the animal's muzzle and through a ring slipped over the ears prior to restraint. The headgear can also be mounted on a bolt that is placed surgically on the animal's skull, thus providing an even more stable mounting. Such a bolt is easily placed if electrodes are being implanted in the brain prior to conditioning. Mounting the transducer on the head provides for optimal response recording because head movements also move the transducer, thus such movements do not interfere with NM records. Movements of the NM are translated into resistance changes by the potentiometer and are easily recorded on polygraphs, oscilloscopes, or digitized by computers for analysis.

With the declining availability of potentiometers, other transducers were developed. Gormezano originally designed a small bakelite box that houses a small light source and photosensitive diode separated by a flag on the axle attached to the NM. Movements of the NM rotate the wire axle causing the flag to allow more or less light into the diode. The diode output is easily recorded as voltage changes on standard recording devices. More recently, Gormezano has utilized a light source separated from a phototransistor by one stable and one movable Polaroid filter. As the movable filter is rotated by the axle attached to the NM, its axis of transmission aligns more or less with the fixed filter, allowing more or less light to pass. The phototransistor signals are then recorded. This apparatus provides a more linear signal than the flag and both are lighter than the potentiometer.

Other methods for NM recording have been described. Especially noteworthy is one by VanDercar et al. (1969). A wheat grain bulb and a cadmium sulfide photocell are mounted side by side but shielded from each other in a small aluminum tube. The tube is positioned in front of the eye so that the light shines through a hole in the tube onto the cornea. Light is reflected from the cornea back to the photocell and the amount modulated by NM move-

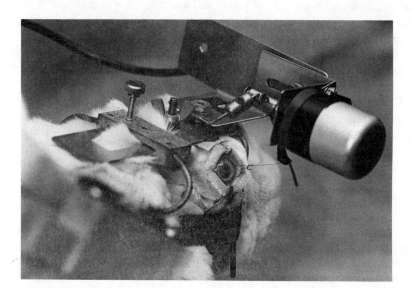

Fig. 1.3   Close-up of rabbit with headgear and minitorque potentiometer. A thread on the counterbalanced arm attached to the potentiometer has a hook at one end to allow attachment to the NM suture. Tailor hooks fastened to Velcro straps are used to retract the eyelids.

ments. This has the advantage of not loading the NM. However, with care, the direct methods described do not load the NM significantly.

The NM response itself is of short latency to the shock or air US, having a 20–25 msec onset latency. The peak latency and amplitude are determined largely by stimulus intensity and change with conditioning (e.g., Smith, Coleman, & Gormezano, 1969). The membrane cannot be held extended by the rabbit and has a very low (less than 1 movement/min) spontaneous rate. The response itself has a sharp onset, thus response onset latency and other response characteristics are easily determined. With the increasing use of computers to analyze responses, it is feasible to measure response onset and peak latencies, speed, amplitude, and other response dynamics accurately.

Eyelid Response.   First measured in the original studies (Scheneiderman et al., 1962), the eyelid response is the second most widely used measure in Pavlovian conditioning in the rabbit. Eyelid movements are controlled by the facial nerve (cranial nerve VII) as is readily demonstrated by nerve section. The first studies demonstrated that the eyelid and NM responses showed very similar characteristics during learning. A more recent study by McCormick, Lavond, and Thompson (1982) has confirmed those characteristics. The eyelid response was measured by methods similar to the NM measurement, except that the lids were not held open and a velcro tab was attached to the upper lid. A second tab was meshed with the first and a thread attached to the potentiometer axle from the second tab (Gormezano, 1966). As with the NM recording, care must be taken to insure that the mechanical coupling between animal and transducer is unimpeded by hair or other factors and is straight. The use of NM suture or velcro applied to the lid ensures a measure of repeat reliability for both responses of the placement of the measuring devices over sessions. Frey et al. (1971) have described their eyelid recording procedures in detail, and they are almost identical with those described here.

Eyeball Retraction.   The third response of the constellation originally reported was eyeball retraction (Deaux & Gormezano, 1963). This response showed features during conditioning that were very similar to the NM and eyelid responses. Because eyeball retraction is the source of NM movement, the retraction should be a more direct measure of the muscle activity. The actual movements were recorded in much the same way as the NM, except that a small polyethylene loop was mounted on a balanced lever and placed against the corneal surface. Eyeball retractions were then transduced through the lever and a thread to the potentiometer. Other methods, such as contact lenses on the cornea, can also be used. In measuring retraction, the external lids and the NM must be held back to allow unimpeded recording.

A variant of eyeball retraction and eyelid movement recording is corneoretinal recording (VanDercar et al., 1969). Here, electrodes on either side of the eyeball record differences in the potential from cornea to the back of the eyeball. This can be done by placing small stainless steel electrodes under the top and bottom lids. The potential recorded by the electrodes alters as the ball moves and can be measured by standard instruments.

Of the three responses, the NM response appears to be the easiest to use and the best suited to analysis. With the demonstration of the linkage between eyeball retraction (the hardest to measure) and NM movements, it is possible to closely link the NM to muscle and motor nerve activity. The eyelid movements are also simple to measure but are slightly more spontaneously active and the motor control more complex, making that response system less desirable for neural analysis.

Jaw Movements.   The jaw-movement response has been developed as an appetitive response (Smith et al., 1966), in contrast to the eye constellation of responses described earlier. The rabbit exhibits a typical sinusoidal jaw movement as it ingests water. The movement is measured by attaching a wire through a wound clip attached under the chin. The wire leads to a potentiometer or phototransister device mounted on the rabbit's head in much the same way as that described for NM recording. Jaw movements are then translated to voltage changes and recorded. Here, a transducer mounted on a head bolt can provide a sufficiently stable recording platform to accurately record jaw movements as the rabbit hops down a runway. The jaw-movement response, unlike the NM response, generally consists of several cycles of movement as the animal swallows.

Heart Rate.   The heart rate (HR) response is unlike the previously described responses in that it is an autonomically controlled response. It has been utilized in several conditioning studies (e.g., Powell & Milligan, 1975; Swadlow et al., 1971) quite successfully. Heart rate in the rabbit is easily recorded, the usual procedure being to insert stainless steel safety pins in the skin in the area of the left haunch and right front leg. Alligator clip leads can easily be attached to the pins, which remain in the subject for days with no apparent irritation. Powell and Lipkin (1975) have shown an early occurring deceleration of HR during conditioning, followed by an acceleration later in training. The characteristics of the HR response make it somewhat more difficult to quantify than skeletal responses, because it is more labile and is recorded against an ongoing and fluctuating baseline. However, the HR response is a useful measure of the rabbit's autonomic system response pattern.

Other Response Systems.   The responses outlined earlier are the most studied in the rabbit during Pavlovian conditioning. However, other systems have been used and may offer advantages for certain situations. Powell and Lipkin (1975) describe measuring head turning and leg flexion to foot shock in the rabbit. Swadlow (1970) reports a procedure for conditioning a lever-lick in the restrained rabbit. Breathing rates can be measured by either bellows around the chest or a thermocouple placed in front of the nose (see VanDercar et al., 1969). Various EMG recordings are possible and may be particularly useful for recording from skeletal muscle groups in the tightly restrained animal. Thus, besides the well-explored and documented systems, many other responses can be accurately measured if the situation warrants.

NEUROPHYSIOLOGICAL TECHNIQUES

During the first 10 years of work with the rabbit in Pavlovian conditioning, from the early 1960s to the early 1970s, a great deal of information was gathered on the characteristics of the behavioral aspects of the NM, eyelid, and jaw-movement responses. This massive amount of parametric data and the general characteristics of the rabbit as a behavioral subject in Pavlovian conditioning set the stage for the beginning of neurophysiological studies with the preparation.

As noted by Thompson (Thompson, Berger, Cegavske, Patterson, Roemer, Teyler, & Young, 1976), during the preparation of an *Annual Review* chapter on the neurophysiology of learning (Thomspon et al., 1972), the authors identified a need for a standardized preparation in which to study the neurophysiology of Pavlovian conditioning. In identifying the primary characteristics of such a preparation, the rabbit NM response system emerged as an almost ideal candidate. The characteristics of the system included such features as single-session conditioning requiring a significant number of trials, lack of alpha responses to the CS, lack of sensitization or pseudoconditioning, and well-characterized parametric features of the response and response development. In addition, the rabbit was a relatively inexpensive subject, readily available and easily restrained. By the time the Thompson et al. (1972) article appeared, work was already underway in Thompson's lab beginning the task of assessing the neurophysiological correlates of Pavlovian NM conditioning (e.g., Thompson, Cegavske, & Patterson, 1973). This work has been very productive, leading from identification of the abducens nucleus as the motor nucleus controlling NM movement via eyeball retraction, to the unusual role of the hippocampus in Pavlovian conditioning (see Thompson et al., 1976), to the recent findings of cerebellar involvement in the development of the CR (see Thompson's chapter, this volume). This section of the chapter is devoted to presenting the neurophysiological techniques useful in working with the rabbit and, in particular, with those techniques for recording the rabbit's neural activity during learning. Portions of the anesthesia and stereotaxic sections are excerpted from an article by the first author that appeared in the Kopf Carrier, October, 1977. These are excerpted by kind permission of Kopf Instruments, as are Fig. 1.4–6. The original article is available from the first author or David Kopf Instruments, 7324 Elmo Street, Tujunga, California 91042.

Anesthesia

Although the use of barbiturates as a general anesthetic for rabbits can often be troublesome, sodium pentobarbital (Nembutal) is perhaps the most commonly employed anesthetic agent for rabbits. The drug is easily administered intravenously through the medial or marginal ear vein via a 23-gauge butterfly infusion set. Initially, the tube and needle should be filled with normal saline, inserted into the vein, and taped in place prior to anesthetic injection. The vein cannulation is most easily accomplished with the animal in a restraining box, and the vein can be more easily seen by shaving and wetting the skin over the vein, then tapping the vein gently to produce dilation. The usual method of aspiration to determine if the needle is in the vein often does not result in blood being drawn back into the tube or syringe because the vein wall frequently blocks the needle lumen. It is thus best to inject very small amounts of saline once the needle is thought to be in the vein lumen. If a bleb does not appear, more saline can be injected to be certain a good placement has been made. The Nembutal can then be injected from a second syringe followed by more saline to flush the anesthetic into the vein.

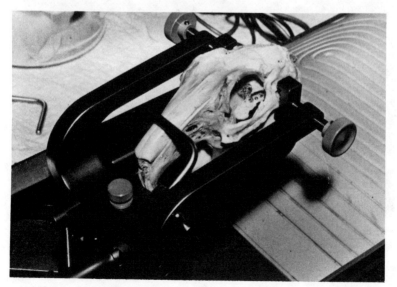

Fig. 1.4 A rabbit skull correctly placed in a Kopf rabbit stereotaxic headholder. Note the position of the zygoma clamps on the temporal process of the zygomatic arch.

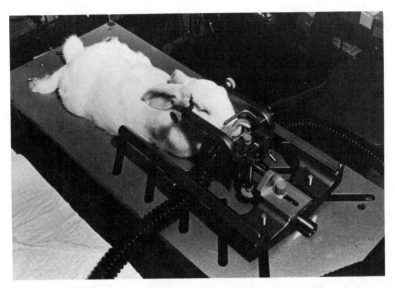

Fig. 1.5 A rabbit in a Kopf rabbit stereotaxic headholder fitted with the gas delivery mask described by Patterson and Gormezano (1978).

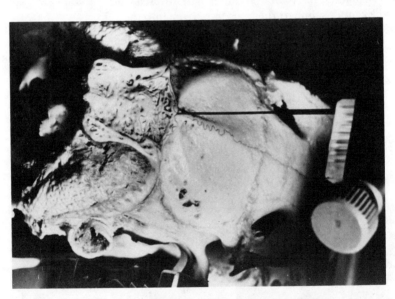

Fig. 1.6 Close-up of a rabbit skull with a needle electrode positioned on the lambda bony landmark. Note the bregma landmark at the coronal and longitudinal suture crossing just behind the orbits and the slight offset of the coronal sutures at the midline.

For most 2–2.5kg animals, 1 cc (50 mg/cc) of Nembutal given over 30–40 seconds and flushed in with saline is sufficient to produce anesthesia. The animal will become limp immediately after the initial injection but continue to become more deeply anesthetized for several minutes. If the initial dose is insufficient to produce surgical anesthesia in about 5 minutes, an additional .5 cc of anesthetic can be given. Care must be taken, however, as the rabbit has a small safety margin with pentobarbital and can be overdosed with the addition of very small amounts of anesthesia above those necessary for surgery. The absence of either a moderate leg flexion to hard toe pinch or eye blink to corneal touch is a danger sign, and the animal will stop breathing if a bit too much pentobarbital is given. Breathing can be maintained under such circumstances by grasping the animal's chest just behind the front legs with thumb and forefinger and squeezing. Each squeeze will usually produce reflex breathing that can often save the subject.

Once a suitable anesthetic level is reached and surgery begun, it is necessary to give small additional doses of anesthesia every 30–45 minutes to maintain surgical levels as the drug is short acting in the rabbit. For this reason, it is advisable to leave the cannula taped in the vein for the duration of surgery, flushing occasionally with saline to prevent clogging. Recovery from pentobarbital is uneventful, and the animal is usually mobile within an hour after the last dose. Interperitoneal pentobarbital injection is not recommended due to the extreme variability in effectiveness of the anesthetic when given by this route.

The preferred anesthetic agent for rabbits is the gas, halothane. Because halothane is a much safer drug for the animal than pentobarbital, the disadvantage of using halothane is that it requires expensive equipment and a special vaporizer for its use. The equipment is available from most medical equipment supply houses. As with many inhalation anesthetics, halothane should only be used in well-ventilated rooms or with closed-delivery systems due to the possible deleterious effects with long-term exposure in humans.

Anesthesia induction can be carried out with the rabbit restrained in a box or wrapped in a towel by placing a small animal nose cone over the nose and mouth. With a 5% halothane concentration delivered with .8 liters of oxygen per minute, induction takes 10–15 minutes. After this brief induction time, recovery to the stage of struggling takes about 3–5 minutes, so the animal must quickly be placed in the surgical apparatus and anesthesia resumed. A special gas delivery mask that fits over the tooth bar of the Kopf headholder can be used to deliver anesthesia when stereotaxic surgery is to be performed (Patterson & Gormezano, 1978). Once the animal is in place, the halothane concentration can be reduced to 1.5–2% for the duration of the surgery. We have had almost no fatalities with halothane, and the animal does not have respiratory distress such as that often seen with pentobarbital.

If a more excitable nervous system is desired for such projects as brain mapping, etc., alpha chlorolose can be used in the rabbit. Gormezano (personal communication) has recently found that a dose of 85–90 mg/kg body weight of chlorolose dissolved in propylene glycol and injected I.V. as described earlier produces good surgical anesthesia. For animals below 2 kg, the lower dose is indicated, whereas above 2 kg the 90 mg/kg is often required. As with pentobarbital, the rabbit has a small safety margin for alpha chlorolose and care must be taken to avoid overdose. The induction time for alpha chlorolose is about 20–30 minutes after I.V. injection, and the first signs of induction include a pronounced horizontal nystagmus. As with Nembutal, the cannula should be left in place and flushed before and after anesthetic administration. To prepare the anesthesia, it is best to mix a 5% solution by putting 1.0 gram of chlorolose powder into 20 cc of propylene glycol heated to 40°C. The powder is not sufficiently soluble in cool glycol and, even at 40°C, stirring for about 30 minutes is necessary to dissolve the powder. If the glycol is heated to over 40°C, some of the alpha chlorolose will be changed to beta chlorolose, a less effective anesthetic. Once in solution, the mixture can be held at body temperature for administration and will keep in a water bath for several hours.

Following induction, chlorolose anesthesia is prolonged, one dose sufficient for 2–3 hours. Small supplementary doses can be given through the ear vein cannula. Recovery is risky although we have let several animals recover with no apparent ill effects such as kidney damage. However, chlorolose is not recommended for procedures in which recovery is necessary.

When an even more active brain is necessary and no recovery is desired, chlorolose and urethane can be combined. A dose of 40 mg/kg chlorolose and .75 grams/kg urethane I.V. may be used. The chlorolose is mixed as before, and the urethane mixed in distilled water. The animal's response will vary somewhat to this combination, but the effect is long lasting and produces an active nervous system. Kidney damage and edema of the lungs are side effects of the urethane, thus recovery is not to be expected.

Of the anesthesia methods described here, sodium pentobarbital will be the drug of choice for most investigators due to its low cost and ease of delivery, and the fact that no equipment other than needle and syringe are needed for its use. It has been our experience that some variability in tolerance to pentobarbital will be seen between strains, and that some dose adjustment may be necessary before a low loss rate is achieved. However, once the experimenter has had some experience with his particular strain, he should find almost no loss due to anesthesia if it is given I.V. and sufficient care is taken to monitor the animal's level during induction. However, if funds are available, the gas anesthesia is safer and requires less care during surgery than pentobarbital provided a good delivery system is used.

Stereotaxic and Surgical Procedures

Many of the commonly used neurophysiological procedures require stereotaxic surgery of some sort. Acute and chronic electrode placement as well as lesion production necessitate accurate electrode localizing procedures. The rabbit presents particular problems with stereotaxic surgery due to the head and ear configurations. Lacking the easily accessible and conveniently placed external auditory meati of the rat or cat, the rabbit must be placed in the stereotaxic device and oriented to the frame using external landmarks. The most commonly used stereotaxic device is that made by David Kopf Instruments and is what is described here. A stereotaxic device using a mouth clamp and having a built-in anesthesia mask has been described by Cegavske and Biela (1980) but is only available on special order.

Once a suitable level of anesthesia is induced, the rabbit may be placed in the stereotaxic instrument. For initial placement in the headholder, the animal should be grasped by the back of the head with one hand while the other hand opens the lower jaw and positions the upper teeth over the tooth bar. Care should be taken not to get the tongue caught in the tooth bar as this restricts free breathing. The nose clamp should then be brought down over the nose and tightened lightly. Once the teeth are in place, the zygoma clamps may be positioned. The temporal process of the rabbit's zygomatic arch extends about two-thirds of the way from the eye to the ear at a level just below the eye. The clamps should be positioned vertically over these processes and tightened lightly. The head should then be checked visually to see that it is about level from side to side and that it is straight in the holder. If a gross tilt to one side is noted, the clamps can be loosened and the head straightened. If any deviation from alignment from front to back is seen, the skin on the side too far back can be slipped forward under the zygoma clamp to make the nose slide to the opposite side. If this does not correct a less than perfect alignment, reset the clamps. When it appears that the head is straight in both dimensions (front-to-back and side-to-side), the clamps should be tightened until they are snug. Figures 1.4 and 1.5 show a rabbit skull correctly placed in a Kopf stereotaxic instrument and a rabbit in the instrument equipped with gas delivery system.

If the animal is under pentobarbital anesthesia, this is the most crucial part of the operation because the clamp pressure frequently causes the animal to stop breathing. Typically, a slightly too heavily anesthetized animal will exhale and remain in forced exhalation until the heart stops if the chest is not squeezed. Often one or two reflex-produced inhalations will be enough to restart normal breathing. If prolonged respiratory difficulty is seen, a leather thong or light wire tied around the chest with a reasonable pressure will cause continued respiration and save the animal. If breathing cannot be restarted within 20 seconds, the clamps should be released and the animal allowed to rest for a few minutes before another attempt is made to put it into the headholder. The problem of respiratory distress while putting animals anesthetized with halothane into the clamps does not occur. Obviously, if the animal begins to struggle while the clamps are being tightened, it should be released and more anesthesia administered. Once the animal is in place and the clamps positioned properly, the screws should be tightened until firm when turned, both screws being advanced about equally. Care should be taken not to tighten the clamps too tightly as this will break the temporal zygomatic process and perhaps the underlying manibular condyles. It is usually necessary to retighten the clamps a turn or two after 30–45 minutes as the tissue fluids are forced from the tissues under the pressure of the clamps.

Once the animal's head is firmly secured in the headholder, the top of the head should be shaved if this has not been done already and a 5–7 cm incision made along the midline starting between the eyes and extending back to the point where the skull slopes sharply down. Hemostats clamped midway along the skin edges open the wound for easy visualization and scraping of the tissue away from the skull. The periosteum should be separated away from the bone until most of the top of the skull is clear. In smaller rabbits, the zygoma clamps may interfere with obtaining sufficient lateral clearing of the skull, and, in this case, the head may have to be repositioned with the clamps set somewhat lower.

Once bared, the skull usually has several areas of bleeding that can be stopped with bone wax. The skin and muscle edges may also need some mild cautery to stop oozing of blood, although often a small covering of cotton or gelfoam will suffice. The bleeding must be completely stopped in order that the skull landmarks can be pinpointed and, if electrodes or cannulae are to be chronically implanted, so that the dental cement will adhere to the bone.

Due to the fact that positioning of the head in the headholder is variable during initial placement, the head must be leveled within the stereotaxic frame using skull bony landmarks. Most current rabbit atlases are constructed with the skull positioned such that the two main skull landmarks, bregma and lambda, are set with lambda 1.5 mm below bregma. In order to visualize these marks, the skull should be cleaned with normal saline or with a dilute hydrogen peroxide solution. The cleaning usually leaves the skull sutures clearly visible as red or brown lines across the field. Bregma, the crossing of the coronal and longitudinal sutures, is often difficult to place precisely due to the failure of the two halves of the coronal suture to meet at the midline. In this case, a felt tip pen should be used to make a mark midway between the two halves of the coronal sutures for future reference. Lambda, the crossing of the occipital and longitudinal sutures, is also sometimes hard to accurately place for similar reasons and because it is on the steep down slope at the back of the skull. A mark at the best guess for lambda is also indicated in such cases (see Fig. 1.6). Once the two suture landmarks have been defined, the head must be positioned level from side to side and with lambda 1.5 mm below bregma. A blunt needle is best used for this purpose as a sharp needle is more apt to penetrate the skull without being noticed. The needle is put in an electrode carrier and moved to touch bregma. With the needletip resting on bregma, the dorso-ventral reading is taken from the carrier. The needle is then moved to lambda where a second reading is taken. Care must be taken to accurately position the needle for the lambda reading because the slope of the skull can cause the needle to slip down as it is lowered, causing large errors. If the bregma–lambda difference is 1.5 mm, the horizontal plane is correct in the anterior–posterior dimension. Corrections are made by tilting the headholder up or down.

The alignment of the longitudinal suture should also be checked as the needle is moved from front to back. To adjust the alignment in this plane, the zygoma clamps must be loosened and the skin pulled through under one or the other clamp to force the nose to the appropriate side. In some cases, the animal will have to be repositioned completely. Obviously, the sagittal plane is the hardest to straighten because there is no adjustment in the headholder that allows the holder to pivot from side to side. Thus, if the adjustment is necessary, it should be made before further attempts to level the bregma-lambda axis.

Once the skull has been positioned correctly in the sagittal plane and the bregma–lamda difference correctly set, side-to-side variations in the horizontal plane should be checked. For this, the needle should be taken 5 mm to each side of bregma and vertical readings taken. If the difference between the sides is more than .1 mm, the holder should be rotated about its central axis to assure a level horizontal placement.

These corrections for head placement can be somewhat time consuming, especially for the inexperienced investigator. Obviously, they are crucial in achieving accurate electrode or cannula placement and, therefore, must be done with care. David Kopf Instruments has introduced a rabbit alignment tool, modified after the planilabe designed by Crawford, Kennedy, and Lipton (1977), to assist in positioning the rabbit's head correctly. The device attaches to an electrode carrier and consists of a fixed tip, which is centered over bregma, and a movable tip, 1.5 mm lower than the fixed tip, which is moved in the anterior–posterior dimension until it is centered over lambda. In addition, two other tips are spaced 5 mm on either side of the bregma point to check for side-to-side variations in the horizontal plane. The use of such a device reduces stereotaxic error considerably.

Electrode Implants

Chronic electrodes may be fashioned from insulated stainless steel insect pins (size 00). The pins should be dipped in an insulating compound such as

Insl-X or Epoxylite and baked at a temperature of at least 90°C, for a minimum of 20 minutes between dips. Although individual pins may be dipped by hand, it is easier to insert the blunt ends of the pins in a cork and dip the pins with the aid of a slow motor to insure that the pins are drawn out of the insulation at a slow and steady rate. The number of dips required for adequate insulation will vary from 6–15 with the thickness of the insulating compound. However, the use of too thick a compound frequently leads to bubbling of the insulation along the shaft of the pin. If bubbling does occur, the electrodes should be discarded and the compound thinned with the appropriate solvent before attempting to insulate a new set of pins. Visual inspection of the electrodes under a light microscope should reveal which electrodes should be culled due to uneven insulation or cracks. Any anomalies in the remaining electrodes can be detected at a later stage. Under high magnification, the insulation at the tip can be scraped off with a sharp scalpel blade. For recording multiple unit activity ("hash") or for a moderate spread of stimulation, a 50–100 micron tip should be sufficient. From this point on, the electrode should be handled carefully as the scraping process stresses the tip and even a minor impact may be sufficient to bend or break it. Care should also be taken when the connecting wire is soldered to the shaft of the electrode as the heat may cause the insulation to break down. This problem may be avoided by using a soldering acid flux thus reducing the amount of heating time required for a good solder joint. Several rinses in alcohol and distilled water should remove any foreign particles or flux that may be adhering to the shaft or tip of the electrode. Once the electrode is in its finished form, with the tip scraped and connecting wire attached, the electrical resistance at the tip and along the insulated shaft should be checked. For this, one side of an ohmeter should be attached to a small loop of wire that is dipped in a soapy solution. The other side of the meter is attached to the connecting wire of the electrode and the resistance at the tip and along the shaft checked by passing the electrode through the soap bubble in the wire loop. The resistance at the tip should be about 10–30 kilohms, and generally not more than 50 kilohms, whereas near infinite resistance should be observed along the insulated shaft. After the electrode has been checked and found to be good, it should be thoroughly rinsed in alcohol and distilled water to remove any soap film.

Because chronic electrode implants must be cemented in place, a fairly large area of the skull should be exposed. Moreover, the skull surface should be dry and clean if the dental cement is to adhere well. Cotton sponges along the skin edges should stop oozing of blood onto the skull, whereas bone wax will stop any bleeding from the skull itself. The skull may be bleached by cleaning it with a dilute hydrogen peroxide solution or by swabbing it with Caulk cavity primer. Although the primer is designed to make the dental cement adhere well, four holes should be drilled part way through the skull with a dental burr and anchoring screws inserted. Two stainless steel 2–56 × ⅛″ screws should go approximately 3 mm on either side of the longitudinal suture and 3 mm anterior to bregma. The other two screws should be placed approximately 7 mm posterior to bregma and 5 mm to either side of the longitudinal suture. A fifth hole should be drilled over the nasal sinus for an indifferent or ground screw to which a connecting wire has been attached. Stereotaxic zero coordinates for the electrode are established by carefully positioning the electrode at bregma and taking the three readings from the electrode carrier. The electrode is then moved to the desired location and a felt tip pen is used to mark the spot where the hole should be drilled. Once the hole is drilled, the electrode should be moved to the proper horizontal coordinates and lowered slightly into the hole to be sure of adequate clearance around the electrode. The electrode is then moved safely away while a 22-gauge needle is used to remove any bone chips from the hole and to pierce the dura. Piercing the dura before lowering the electrode is critical, especially for small-tipped electrodes, as penetrating the dura with the electrode may distort the electrode tip, and the pressure of the electrode on the dura may depress the underlying brain before penetration occurs. Once a good electrode placement has been achieved, the hole surrounding the electrode is sealed with bone wax to prevent leakage of cerebrospinal fluid and to protect the brain from contact with the dental cement. The first layer of dental cement should cover as much of the exposed skull as possible as well as the ground and anchor screws. The electrode and a good part of the connecting wire should also be sealed in dental cement and the cement allowed to harden before attempting to free the electrode from the electrode carrier. Once the carrier is removed, the connecting wires from the ground screw and electrode may be inserted into a plastic plug assembly for connection to the recording apparatus. The portion of the insect pin above the solder joint may then be cut and the plug assembly and connecting wires sealed in place. At this point, denture material rather than dental cement may be used, as a strong bond with the skull surface is provided by the foundation of dental cement. Care should be taken that all conducting materials such as the protruding end of the insect pin are adequately insulated with a layer of the denture material. Mounting nuts and bolts for recording devices may be embedded in the denture material and sealed in place. Furacin, or some other topical antibiotic, should be sprinkled into the wound before closing. The wound may be closed with either 2–0 silk suture or with stainless steel wound clips.

The preceding description is for chronically implanted multiple-unit electrodes. Single-unit electrodes are generally used acutely, following similar stereotaxic procedures. Recently, Thompson has described a microdrive that is chronically mounted on the rabbit's head and allows multiple penetrations with a multiple-unit electrode in the awake, restrained animal (see the

Thompson chapter in this volume). Other details of single and multiple-unit electrode recording are available in Thompson and Patterson (1973), which contains several chapters on electrodes and recording techniques.

Besides the implantation of chronic or acute electrodes, stereotaxic surgery is generally required for the production of brain lesions in the rabbit. Generally similar techniques are used except that, for small cortical or subcortical lesions, the electrode is lowered and a current (e.g., 20 ma) is passed for several seconds through the electrode. Large aspiration lesions are made following cutting away a portion of the skull to visualize the area to be destroyed, and the cavity is packed with an absorbable hemostat such as Gelfoam after hemostasis is achieved. Care must be taken to avoid packing too tightly and to be sure bleeding has stopped so that swelling and pressure will not cause death as the animal recovers from anesthesia. Often animals that have had lesions need special attention during recovery, such as in neodecortication (e.g., Oakley & Russell, 1972).

Perfusion

Perfusion and removal of the brain is required in order to histologically verify the placement of lesions and electrode or cannula implants. The general procedure consists of flushing the blood vessels in the brain with normal saline followed by 10% formalin. Once the brain is removed, it is usually best to let it soak in 10% formalin for several days before attempting to section it.

Rabbits are easily perfused either intracardially or through the carotid arteries. If an intracardial perfusion is to be performed, the animal is deeply anesthetized, the chest is shaved, and an incision is made just below the tip of the sternum. The rib cage is then raised and the chest cavity opened by gripping the tip of the sternum with a pair of hemostats while a pair of large scissors are used to cut the ribs free from the left side of the sternum. Horizontal incisions across the upper and lower portions of the rib cage will allow it to be reflected and clamped out of the way. The pericardial membrane is dissected away from the heart, and a blunt 19-gauge needle is inserted into the left ventricle. The other end of the needle leads to a tube of either a 50 cc syringe filled with saline or a container of saline suspended above the animal. The right auricle is cut and either gravity or the plunger of the syringe forces the saline through the system. Two hundred cc of saline followed by 200 cc of formalin is usually sufficient to perfuse even a large rabbit.

For a carotid perfusion, the animal is deeply anesthetized, the neck area is shaved and a 5 cm incision is made over the trachea. The carotid arteries and vagus nerves may be seen on either side of the trachea. It is sometimes necessary to manipulate the wound in order to see the arteries clearly. A 3 cm length of each artery should be dissected away from the surrounding tissue and vagus nerve. This may be accomplished by carefully penetrating the connective tissue between the artery and the vagus nerve with the closed tips of a blunt pair of hemostats and then spreading the hemostats open. Several attempts are often necessary in order to expose a sufficient length of the artery. Once the artery has been so exposed, a length of cotton thread is slipped around the artery and tied in a very loose overhand knot. After both arteries have been exposed, a moistened tongue depressor should be slipped under the arteries in order to provide stability and the lower ends of the arteries should be clamped. Each artery is then cannulated with the needle of a 23-gauge butterfly infusion set and the knotted thread tightened around the artery and needle. One hundred cc of saline is forced into each artery simultaneously and at equal rates using either two large syringes or gravity. This is followed by 100 cc of 10% formalin flushed into each artery. The head is then severed from the body and the skin and flesh cut away from the skull. Bone cutters and rongeurs are used to cut the skull from the brain, with special care being necessary around the area of the cerebellum to avoid damage to the various cerebellar lobes. After removal, the brain is usually placed in a 10% formalin solution (or other solution if other than routine sectioning is to be done) for several days before sectioning.

The rabbit brain has not received the same amount of study as has the rat or cat brains. Therefore, stereotaxic atlases of the rabbit brain are not as plentiful or complete as those for the rat or cat. Following is a list of several atlases commonly used in rabbit brain area identification.

McBride, R. L., & Klemm, W. R. (1969). Stereotaxic atlas of rabbit brain based on the rapid method of photography of frozen, unstained sections. *Communications in Behavioral Biology, 2,* 179–215.

Monnier, M., & Gangloff, H. (1961). *Rabbit brain research* (Vol. I.) *Atlas for stereotaxic brain research on the conscious rabbit.* Amsterdam: Elsevier.

Sawyer, C. H., Everett, J. W., & Green, J. D. (1954). The rabbit diencephalon in stereotaxic coordinates. *Journal of Comparative Neurology, 101,* 801–824.

Urban, I., & Richard, P. (1972). *A stereotaxic atlas of the New Zealand rabbit's brain.* Springfield, IL: Thomas.

Neural Recording

Recording of neural activity from the rabbit following chronic electrode implants is readily accomplished. Even in the free-moving animal, such records can be extremely stable (Gabriel, 1974). In the work that has been done on recording neural activity during NM conditioning, the recording has been accomplished using tone and light as a CS and air puff as a US. As previously noted, such stimuli produced no artifacts to interfere with the neural signals. Brakel, Babb, Mahnke, and Verzeano (1971) have described an amplifier with the initial stage of amplification mounted on the rabbit's head that minimizes movement and 60-Hz interference. However, when shock is used as a US, the proximity of the shock delivery to the brain electrode may cause problems in such an amplifier. Sufficient current apparently passes from the electrode through the FET stage or first amplifier stage back to the head ground to partially polarize the system. Thus, the neural signal, in addition to showing blocking artifacts with the shock delivery, often decreases in amplitude over trials. It is necesasry, if this occurs with eye shock, to utilize an amplifier with different input characteristics, such as a Grass P-15 preamplifier or to fully disconnect the amplifier with relays as the shock is delivered. Delivery of the shock through a grid to the animal's feet can, however, be utilized successfully with an FET amplifier at levels (e.g., 1.5 ma) commonly used (Gabriel, Saltwick, & Miller, 1976).

In most neural recording studies with the rabbit, neural signals are fed to a computer either on-line or off-line from a taped recording and analyzed as desired. Several such systems are available and have been described (e.g., Roemer, Cegavske, Thompson, & Patterson, 1975; Scandrett & Gormezano, 1980).

ACKNOWLEDGMENTS

Preparation of this chapter was supported in part by Grants 81-08-023 from the American Osteopathic Association and 14545 from the National Institute of Neurological and Communicative Disorders and Stroke to the first author.

REFERENCES

Brakel, S., Babb, T., Mahnke, J., & Verzeano, M. (1971). A compact amplifier for extracellular recording. *Physiology and Behavior, 6,* 731–733.

Cegavske, C. F., & Biela, J. (1980). A rabbit headholder for stereotaxic use with gaseous anesthetics. *Brain Research Bulletin, 5,* 619–623.

Cegavske, C. F., Thompson, R. F., Patterson, M. M., & Gormezano, I.(1976). Mechanisms of efferent neuronal control of the reflex nictitating membrane response in rabbit *(Oryctolagus cuniculus). Journal of Comparative and Physiological Psychology, 90,* 411–423.

Coleman, S. R., Patterson, M. M., & Gormezano, I. (1966). Conditioned jaw movement in the rabbit: Deprivation procedure and saccharin concentration. *Psychonomic Science, 6,* 39–40.

Crawford, I. L., Kennedy, J. I., & Lipton, J. M. (1977). A simple "planilabe" for rapid establishment of the stereotaxic horizontal zero plane in rabbits. *Brain Research Bulletin, 2,* 397–398.

Deaux, E. B., & Gormezano, I. (1963). Eyeball retraction: Classical conditioning and extinction in the albino rabbit. *Science, 141,* 630–631.

Frey, P. W., Englander, S., & Roman, A. (1971). Interstimulus interval analysis of sequential CS compounds in rabbit eyelid conditioning. *Journal of Comparative and Physiological Psychology, 77,* 439–446.

Frey, P. W., & Gavin, W. (1975). Overnight incubation of a partially conditioned eyeblink response in rabbits. *Animal Learning & Behavior, 3,* 114–118.

Gabriel, M. (1974). A system for multiple-unit recording during avoidance behavior of the rabbit. *Physiology and Behavior, 12,* 145–148.

Gabriel, M., Miller, J. D., & Saltwick, S. E. (1976). Multiple-unit activity of the rabbit medial geniculate nucleus in conditioning, extinction and reversal. *Physiological Psychology, 4,* 124–134.

Gantt, W. H. (1968). The distinction between the conditional and the unconditional reflex. *Conditional Reflex, 3,* 1–3.

Gormezano, I (1966). Classical conditioning. In J. B. Sidowski (Ed.), *Experimental methods and instrumentation in psychology.* New York: McGraw-Hill.

Gormezano, I., & Kehoe, E. J. (1975). Classical conditioning: Some methodological-conceptual issues. In W. K. Estes (Ed.), *Handbook of learning and cognitive processes* (Vol. 2), *Conditioning and behavior theory.* Hillsdale, NJ: Lawrence Erlbaum Associates.

Gormezano, I., Schneiderman, N., Deaux, E., & Fuentes, I. (1962). Nictitating membrane: Classical conditioning and extinction in the albino rabbit. *Science, 138,* 33–34.

Gray, T. S., McMaster, S. E., Harvey, J. A., & Gormezano, I. (1981). Localization of retractor bulbi motoneurons in the rabbit. *Brain Research, 226,* 93–106.

Kettlewell, N. M., & Papsdorf, J. D. (1971). A role for cutaneous afferents in classical conditioning in rabbits. *Journal of Comparative and Physiological Psychology, 75,* 239–247.

Kettner, R. E., Shannon, R. V., Nguyen, T. M., & Thompson, R. F. (1980). Simultaneous behavioral and neural (cochlear nucleus) measurement during signal detection in the rabbit. *Perception & Psychophysics, 28,* 504–513.

Martin, G. K., Land, T., & Thompson, R. F. (1980). Classical conditioning of the rabbit *(Oryctolagus cuniculus)* nictitating membrane response, with electrical brain stimulation as the unconditioned stimulus. *Journal of Comparative and Physiological Psychology, 94,* 216–226.

Masterson, F. A. (1981). Grid and peripheral shock stimulation. In M. M. Patterson & R. P. Kesner (Eds.), *Electrical stimulation research techniques.* New York: Academic Press.

McCormick, D. A., Lavond, D. G., & Thompson, R. F. (1982). Concomitant classical conditioning of the rabbit nictitating membrane and eyelid responses: Correlations and implications. *Physiology & Behavior, 28,* 769–775.

Mis, F. W., Gormezano, I., & Harvey, J. A. (1979). Stimulation of abducens nucleus supports classical conditioning of the nictitating membrane response. *Science, 206,* 473–475.

Moore, J. W., Marchant, H. G., III, Norman, J. B., & Kwaterski, S. E. (1973). Electrical brain stimulation as a Pavlovian conditioned inhibitor. *Physiology and Behavior, 10,* 581–587.

Oakley, D. A., & Russell, I. S. (1972). Neocortical lesions and Pavlovian conditioning. *Physiology and Behavior, 8,* 915–926.

Patterson, M. M. (1970). Classical conditioning of the rabbit's *(Oryctolagus cuniculus)* nictitating membrane response with fluctuating ISI and intracranial CS. *Journal of Comparative and Physiological Psychology, 72,* 193–202.

Patterson, M. M. (1976). Mechanisms of classical conditioning and fixation in spinal mammals. In A. H. Riesen & R. F. Thompson (Eds.), *Advances in psychobiology* (Vol. 3). New York: Wiley.

Patterson, M. M., & Gormezano, I. (1978). A mask for rabbit stereotaxic gas anesthesia. *Behavior Research Methods & Instrumentation, 10,* 41–42.

Powell, D. A., & Lipkin, M. (1975). Heart rate changes accompanying differential classical conditioning of somatic response systems in the rabbit. *Bulletin of the Psychonomic Society, 5,* 28–30.

Powell, D. A., & Milligan, W. L. (1975). Effects of partial and continuous reinforcement of conditioned heart rate and corneoretinal potential responses in the rabbit *(Oryctolagus cuniculus). The Psychological Record, 25,* 419–426.

Powell, D. A., Schneiderman, N., Elster, A. J., & Jacobson, A. (1971). Differential classical conditioning in rabbits *(Oryctolagus cuniculus)* to tones and changes in illumination. *Journal of Comparative and Physiological Psychology, 76,* 267–274.

Roemer, R. A., Cegavske, C. F., Thompson, R. F., & Patterson, M. M. (1975). An acquisition and analysis system for on-line experiments on the neurophysiology of learning. *Behavior Research Methods & Instrumentation, 7,* 157–161.

Rubin, H. B., & Brown, H. J. (1969). The rabbit as a subject in behavioral research. *Journal of the Experimental Analysis of Behavior, 12,* 663–667.

Salafia, W. R., Daston, A. P., Bartosiak, R. S., Hurley, J. & Martino, L. J. (1974). Classical nictitating membrane conditioning in the rabbit *(Oryctolagus cuniculus)* as a function of unconditioned stimulus locus. *Journal of Comparative and Physiological Psychology, 86,* 628–636.

Scandrett, J., & Gormezano, I. (1980). Microprocessor control and A/D data acquisition in classical conditioning. *Behavior Research Methods & Instrumentation, 12,* 120–125.

Schneiderman, N., Fuentes, I., & Gormezano, I. (1962). Acquisition and extinction of the classically conditioned eyelid response in the albino rabbit. *Science, 136,* 650–652.

Sheafor, P. J., & Gormezano, I. (1972). Conditioning the rabbit's *(Oryctolagus cuniculus)* jaw-movement response: US magnitude effects on URs, CRs, and pseudo-CRs. *Journal of Comparative and Physiological Psychology, 81,* 449–456.

Smith, M. C., Coleman, S. R., & Gormezano, I. (1969). Classical conditioning of the rabbit's nictitating membrane response at backward, simultaneous, and forward CS–US intervals. *Journal of Comparative and Physiological Psychology, 69,* 226–231.

Smith, M. C., DiLollo, V., & Gormezano, I. (1966). Conditioned jaw movement in the rabbit. *Journal of Comparative and Physiological Psychology, 62,* 479–483.

Swadlow, H. A. (1970). Operant conditioning of the restrained rabbit. *Physiology and Behavior, 5,* 629–630.

Swadlow, H. A., Hosking, K. E., & Schneiderman, N. (1971). Differential heart rate conditioning and lever lift suppression in restrained rabbits. *Physiology and Behavior, 7,* 257–260.

Thompson, R. F., Berger, T. W., Cegavske, C. F., Patterson, M. M., Roemer, R. A., Teyler, T. J., & Young, R. A. (1976). The search for the engram. *American Psychologist, 31,* 209–227.

Thompson, R. F., Cegavske, C., & Patterson, M. M. (1973). *Efferent control of the classically conditioned nictitating membrane response in the rabbit.* Paper presented at the meeting of the Psychonomic Society, St. Louis, November.

Thompson, R. F., & Patterson, M. M. (Eds.) (1973). *Bioelectric recording techniques* (Part A) *Cellular processes and brain potentials.* New York: Academic Press.

Thompson, R. F., Patterson, M. M., & Teyler, T. J. (1972). The neurophysiology of learning. *Annual Review of Psychology, 23,* 73–104.

VanDercar, D. H., Swadlow, H. A., Elster, A., & Schneiderman, N. (1969). Nictitating membrane and corneo–retinal transducers for conditioning in rabbits. *American Psychologist, 24,* 262–264.

2 Neurobiological Bases of Conditioned Bradycardia in Rabbits

Neil Schneiderman, Philip M. McCabe,
James R. Haselton, Howard H. Ellenberger,
Theodore W. Jarrell, and Christopher G. Gentile
University of Miami

Neuroscientists have been working for many years to comprehend the mechanisms by which the nervous system stores and retrieves information. Although considerable progress has been made in some areas, many fundamental questions remain unsolved. One reason for the general lack of progress is that relatively few experimental response systems have been developed in adequate detail. The few model biological systems that have been proposed to study the neuronal correlates of learning have generated exciting new findings. But even these systems have been either fairly restrictive in the questions they can ask or are still in an early stage of development.

Kandel and Spencer (1968) listed several criteria that they felt were important in the construction of a model biological system to study the neuronal correlates of learning. Of these, two criteria appear to be particularly important. The first is that the anatomical details of the pathways activated by the conditioned and unconditioned stimuli must be specific. The second is that neuronal activity must be directly related to a significant behavior. Cohen (1974) has suggested two additional criteria that are useful in the development of the model system. The first is that the system must be compatible with the demands of cellular neurophysiological experiments. The second is that the system should permit the study of a broad range of questions regarding the mechanisms of information storage and retrieval.

The experiments described in the present chapter represent important steps in the construction of a mammalian model system that is suitable for studying the neuronal correlates of learning. This system involves the Pavlovian conditioning of bradycardia (heart rate slowing) in rabbits. First, our approach of starting at the periphery and working back into the CNS should ultimately allow us to specify the pathways mediating the unconditioned and conditioned stimuli (USs and CSs) and mediating the unconditioned and conditioned responses (URs and CRs). Second, stimulation of the baroreceptors in conjunction with stimulation, lesion neuroanatomical labeling, and extracellular unit recording techniques has allowed us to specify the role played by individual cardiovascular interneurons that are considerably removed from the periphery.

Our studies should also be of considerable value in the development of model systems that are also suitable for studying the integration of cardiovascular changes other than learning mediated by the CNS. At least some of the cardiovascular adjustments mediated by the CNS arise in response to environmental events. The specific CNS mechanisms and pathways that mediate cardiovascular adjustments in the face of various environmental stressors is relatively poorly understood, although the neural mechanisms underlying defensive reactions, baroreceptor attenuation, and changes in the regional distribution of the blood flow have begun to be studied. Possible CNS mechanisms by which intermittent behavioral stressors can lead to long-term changes in cardiovascular performance, and even the development of pathology, are also poorly understood. The possibility that some of these adjustments may be learned needs further exploration. The model biological system that is presently being constructed offers one possibility for systematically studying the CNS mechanisms underlying learned as well as unlearned cardiovascular adjustments.

Our research bears some resemblance to other research that is attempting to describe the neuronal mechanisms by which mammals store and retrieve information in order to adjust to their environments. In contrast to some of these programs, however, our basic strategy is neither to focus upon isolating a specific engram independent of its response system nor upon attempting to discover the basic mechanisms underlying memory retrieval. Instead, an assumption underlying our research is that pathways involved in learning can be profitably studied in conjunction with behavioral responses. Whereas it is likely that learned changes such as concepts can be acquired independent of motor systems, some learning occurs that is specifically tied to response system characteristics. In some of our early work, reviewed by Schneiderman (1972), we were struck by the finding that in the same conditioning situation, an animal might evince bradycardia CRs on every trial after less than 10 CS–US pairings; whereas, a nictitating membrane response might show no evidence of conditioning for more than 20 CS–US pairings and then reveal a gradual increase in percentage CRs during the next couple of dozen trials. The use of appropriate control procedures indicated that both the heart rate and nictitating membrane CRs reflected conditioning. Based upon these and other differences in response system characteristics, we came to the conclusion that it would be profitable to study the neuronal correlates of conditioning in terms of specific response systems. Cardiovascular responses were chosen because they seemed intrinsically interesting and important, they had been studied in some detail, and their study was compatible with the demands of cellular neurophysiological investigation.

The model biological system that we have constructed to study the neuronal bases of cardiovascular conditioning should ultimately allow us to achieve the following long-term goals:

1. To describe the neuronal circuits in the CNS that control cardiodecelerative responses.

2. To determine the extent to which *bradycardia* CRs and URs are mediated by the same central efferent pathways.

3. To determine the extent to which CR and UR pathways share sites where input from other neuronal systems can influence the terminal behavioral response.

In order to develop a comprehensive model biological system our research has had to develop from several approaches. First, a preparation had to be developed for studying conditioning that is compatible with the demands of cellular neurophysiology. Second, intracranial electrical stimulation and electrolytic lesions were used as preliminary tools for studying the CNS organization of cardiovascular responses. Third, extracellular single-unit recording techniques were used to identify the cells of origin of the cardiac vagus nerve, and to study functional relationships involving cardiovascular related interneurons in the brain. Fourth, histological techniques were used to identify the CNS pathways underlying cardiovascular activity. The remainder of this chapter is concerned with the developments that have occurred using each of the several approaches.

THE BASIC CONDITIONING PREPARATION

The classical conditioning paradigm offers several advantages for studying the neuronal correlates of learning. First, the important stimulus and response events can be carefully specified. Second, appropriate control procedures are available, which permit the learned response to be distinguished from other types of URs. Third, in conjunction with extinction procedures, the classical conditioning paradigm is suitable for studying long-term information storage. Fourth, the stimulus parameters (e.g., CS–US interval) in the experiment can be adjusted to insure that the learned response reflects neuronal rather than hormonal changes (e.g., Cohen, 1969; Cohen & Pitts, 1968). Fifth, the conditioning procedure is convenient for using restrained subjects when acute extracellular recordings are being made.

Most of the conditioning experiments in the present chapter examined cardiodeceleration as the CR. This particular response system offers several advantages for studying the neuronal correlates of learning. First, cardiodeceleration in the rabbit offers an easily recorded, quantifiable response. Second, the behavioral response has previously been the subject of considerable study, so that much is known about the selection of appropriate conditioning parameter values. Third, the CR develops quickly so that it is possible to record acutely from a single unit during the habituation, conditioning, and extinction of the heart rate response. Fourth, it should be possible to couple the motor outflow from the CNS with the behavioral CR, because the neuronal outflow is mediated solely by the vagus nerves.

In our initial experiments examining heart rate (HR) changes during classical conditioning in rabbits, a tone CS was paired with peripheral shock as the US (Schneiderman, Smith, Smith, & Gormezano, 1966; Schneiderman, VanDercar, Yehle, Manning, Golden, & Schneiderman, 1969; Yehle, Dauth, & Schneiderman, 1967). These experiments indicated that: (1) the original response (OR) to the CS was cardiodecelerative, (2) this response habituated within a few trials, (3) the CR also consisted of bradycardia, (4) it developed within 10 pairings of the CS and US, and (5) it was not confounded by nonassociative responses. Separate CS-alone and US-alone as well as CS and US mixed groups were used to control for nonassociative responses.

The experiments by Schneiderman et al. (1969) and Yehle et al. (1967) examined changes in blood pressure as well as HR during conditioning. In general we found that with a high US intensity both the bradycardia CR and UR were related to induced elevations in blood pressure. In contrast, at a lower US intensity only the HR UR appeared to be a reflexive response to an increase in systemic arterial pressure, whereas the bradycardia CR occurred in the absence of primary blood pressure changes. Administration of selective autonomic blocking agents provided support for the view that, at a relatively low (3.0 mA) US intensity of peripheral electric shock, the bradycardia UR was a reflexive response to the blood pressure increase, whereas the HR CR was not. With the exception of the Yehle et al. experiment, all our conditioning experiments employing electric shock as the US have used a relatively low-current intensity.

In addition to the experiments just described, we conducted other behavioral conditioning experiments in which a tone or light CS was paired with peripheral electric shock as the US. Most of these studies used a differential conditioning procedure. In some of these experiments, within-subject comparisons were made comparing the HR CR with other measures such as nictitating membrane and breathing-rate responses. Some of these studies manipulated stimulation parameters such as the CS–US interval and delay-versus trace-conditioning procedures. The major relevance of these experiments (summarized by Schneiderman, 1970, 1973) for the study of the neuronal correlates of cardiovascular conditioning is that they helped to establish suitable parameter values for conditioning HR.

Electrical Stimulation of Brain as US

In another series of experiments we used electrical stimulation of the hypothalamus or septal region as the US during classical conditioning. The major purpose of these experiments was to develop a preparation for helping to study the manner in which different brain locations play a role in the elaboration of various heart rate and blood pressure responses. In our initial classical conditioning experiments using high-frequency (100 pulses per sec), short pulse-train duration (1.0 sec) stimulation of a large number of septal region and hypothalamic sites as the US, we elicited CRs and URs similar to those obtained using a peripheral electric shock US (e.g., VanDercar, Elster, & Schneiderman, 1970). The URs invariably consisted of vasopressor responses and reflexive bradycardia, and the CR consisted of bradycardia mediated by the vagus nerves (e.g., Fredericks, Moore, Metcalf, Schwaber, & Schneiderman, 1974).

We have also used lower frequency (25 pulses per sec), longer pulse-train duration (10 sec) intracranial stimulation as the US. Whereas stimulation at these parameter values most often elicits a vasopressor response and tachycardia from medial hypothalamic locations, the same stimulation values elicit vasodepressor responses from lateral hypothalamic electrode sites (Sampson, Wallach, Schneiderman, & Francis, 1977). Using tone as the CS and 25 pulse per sec, 10-sec train-duration stimulation of the posterior lateral hypothalamus as the US, Brickman and Schneiderman (1977) observed URs consisting of a vasodepressor response and a biphasic HR response as the UR and a vasodepressor response unaccompanied by systematic changes in heart rate as the CR.

Recent work in our laboratory has further examined the medio-lateral functional organization of the hypothalamus to electrical stimulation (Gellman, Schneiderman, Wallach, & LeBlanc, 1981). In conscious rabbits, stimulation of the lateral hypothalamus produced quiet inactivity with bradycardia and a slight depressor response. Stimulation of the medial hypothalamus elicited aggressive behavior, circling movements, and a pressor response, whereas stimulation of an intermediate zone elicited immobility except for orienting-like movements of the head, bradycardia, and a pressor response.

Although peripheral electric shock has been used as the US in several experiments investigating the neuronal correlates of learning, the intracranial stimulation procedures also provide important tools for this research. Both the CRs induced by peripheral electric shock and by short pulse-train intracranial stimulation consist of bradycardia unaccompanied by changes in blood pressure, but the URs evoked by the intracranial US are more reliable than those elicited by peripheral shock. First, the UR to peripheral shock tends to habituate within and across sessions, whereas the UR to intracranial stimulation does not. Second, the UR to intracranaial stimulation of short pulse-train duration invariably consists of a vasopressor response accompanied by bradycardia, whereas bradycardia, tachycardia, or biphasic responses occur in different animals following peripheral shock. These findings suggest that short pulse-train intracranial stimulation of a US may be quite valuable when comparisons are desired between HR CRs and URs. The use of intracranial electrical stimulation as the US is also of considerable value because it permits more than one cardiovascular response pattern to be studied under controlled conditions.

Conditioning Studies Using Intracranial Stimulation as US

Several investigators have demonstrated that various circulatory changes could be conditioned using electrical stimulation of the brain as the US. Magnitskii (1953) used electrical stimulation of the posterior hypothalamus in rabbits and observed conditioned increases in blood pressure. Lico and associates (Lico, Hoffman, & Covian, 1968) produced conditioned and unconditioned decreases in blood pressure following septal stimulation in anesthetized rabbits.

These results are consistent with functional neuroanatomical studies by Hess (1957) and by Ban (1966). According to Ban, for example, the septal region and parts of the lateral hypothalamus mediate parasympathetic activity, whereas the ventromedial hypothalamus is a sympathetic region. In addition, the anterior and posterior hypothalamus contain neuronal mechanisms involved in the regulation of baroreceptor reflexes (Gimpl, Brickman, Kaufman, & Schneiderman, 1976). Thus, a series of studies in our laboratory using intracranial electrical stimulation sought to clarify the relationship between cardiovascular CRs and URs and related learned circulatory adjustments to the known facts of cardiovascular integration.

Prior to using brain stimulation as a US in conditioning paradigms, we noted that by merely adjusting current intensity of hypothalamic stimulation, the direction of HR responses and somatic activity could be divided into two distinct classes. One class consisted of an increase in HR accompanied by overt movement and the other class was characterized by HR deceleration unaccompanied by movement. These findings led us to investigate the relationship between somatic activity and the topography of HR URs and CRs (Elster, VanDercar, & Schneiderman, 1970).

Elster et al. (1970) utilized a differential conditioning paradigm in loosely restrained rabbits. The US consisted of short pulse-train stimulation of the midbrain central gray, subthalamus, or various regions of the hypothalamus.

One CS (designated CS +) was immediately followed by the US, whereas another CS (designated CS −) was never followed by the US. When the animal learned to respond to the CS+ but produced little or no response to the CS −, differentiation was considered to have occurred.

Differential conditioning was induced by all USs. However, a greater differential conditioning was induced by diencephalic stimulation than by midbrain stimulation. For diencephalic stimulation, there was a particularly strong positive relationship between diffuse movement and cardioaccelerative CRs and URs.

Cardiodecelerative CRs were observed when US stimulation elicited bradycardia and an absence of movement. These stimulation sites were primarily in the lateral hypothalamus and subthalamic region. Conversely, cardioaccelerative CRs occurred in instances where US stimulation elicited tachycardia accompanied by diffuse somatic activity. Therefore, this study implies that cardiac-somatic coupling occurs when short pulse-train electrical stimulation of the diencephalon is used as the US. Several investigators (e.g., Eliasson, Lindgren, & Uvnas, 1952; Hess, 1957; Kaada, 1960) have emphasized that the hypothalamus and other limbic system structures are involved in the concomitant regulation of somatic and cardiovascular changes. The nature of cardiac-somatic coupling has also been examined with regard to exercise (e.g., Rushmer, 1962; Rushmer & Smith, 1959) and conditioning (e.g., Obrist, 1965; Obrist & Webb, 1967).

In our next study, we examined both HR and blood pressure changes during differential conditioning induced by US stimulation of the hypothalamus or septal region (VanDercar et al., 1970). In an attempt to examine HR conditioning in the absence of somatic activity, the US intensity was kept below the threshold for eliciting gross motor activity.

It was found that HR could be differentially conditioned, but no conditioned blood pressure changes were observed. The HR URs and CRs both consisted of bradycardia, and the blood pressure URs were pressor responses. The latency of onset to response following UR stimulation was shorter for the blood pressure elevation than that for the HR deceleration, suggesting that the unconditioned bradycardia was reflexive in nature. Stimulation in either the hypothalamus or septal region produced similar URs and CRs; however, greater stimulation current intensities were required in the septal region to produce responses comparable in size to those produced by hypothalamic stimulation.

Because, in our experiments, we have elicited a similar UR constellation following stimulation at sites throughout the hypothalamus and septal region, we were concerned that our results might be due to some nonspecific, aversive effect such as the stimulation of pain fibers associated with cerebral vessels. In addition, we were interested in the general relationship between motivation and cardiovascular responses. Consequently, an experiment was conducted to examine cardiovascular classical conditioning using appetitive or aversive hypothalamic stimulation as the US (Sideroff, Elster, & Schneiderman, 1972).

Rabbits were implanted with stimulating electrodes in either the lateral or ventromedial hypothalamus. Upon recovery, each animal was tested to determine if it would bar-press to receive stimulation and later tested in a shuttle box preference situation. Following these initial tests, each animal received differential conditioning in which the US consisted of medial or lateral hypothalamic stimulation.

It was found that rabbits having access to lateral hypothalmic stimulation bar-pressed to receive stimulation and made approach responses in the shuttle box. In contrast, animals with access to medial hypothalamic stimulation did not bar-press for stimulation and made escape responses in the shuttlebox. As in previous studies, the cardiovascular URs consisted of a pressor response and bradycardia, whereas the CRs consisted only of bradycardia. Therefore, although medial and lateral hypothalamic stimulation had very different motivational properties, both provided effective USs for eliciting HR CRs. Thus, the directionality and topography of cardiovascular changes are not necessarily influenced directly by whether a US is appetitive or aversive.

The possibility that the HR UR in the VanDercar et al. (1970) experiment was a reflexive response to an increase in blood pressure is of interest, because the HR CR, which also consisted of bradycardia, occurred in the absence of a blood pressure CR. Therefore, this suggests that the HR CR was not a reflexive response to a change in blood pressure. Consequently, it seemed likely that the CR and UR might be controlled by different CNS mechanisms. In order to examine this possibility, we conducted a series of studies in which cardiovascular CRs and/or URs were selectively abolished by various pharmacological blocking agents.

Peripheral vasoconstriction, which is mediated by alpha adrenergic innervation of the arterioles, was abolished by administration of phentolamine. In contrast, the sympathetic innervation of the heart is primarily beta-adrenergic. Therefore, the beta-adrenergic blocking agent, propranolol, was used to antagonize the sympathetic innervation of the heart. Because the parasympathetic (vagal) innervation of the heart is cholinergic, atropine was used to block vagal influences on the heart. Both atropine sulfate and the peripherally acting form of atropine, atropine methyl nitrate, were used in these experiments to assess central versus peripheral effects of cholinergic blockade (Carlton, 1962; Downs, Cardozo, Schneiderman, Yehle, VanDercar, & Zwilling, 1972; Giarman & Pepeu, 1964).

The initial pharmacological study examined the effects of autonomic blocking agents on cardiovascular URs elicited by intracranial stimulation (Powell, Goldberg, Dauth, Schneiderman, & Schneiderman, 1972). Unanesthetized rabbits received high-frequency, short (1.0-second) pulse-train stimulation of the septal region or hypothalamus at current intensities not producing obvious gross movement.

Intracranial stimulation elicited an increase in arterial pressure accompanied by bradycardia. Both of these parameters showed a dose-dependent attenuation following systemic injection of phentolamine. Because phentolamine blocks the innervation of the arterioles rather than the heart, the results suggested that the bradycardia was a reflexive response to the increase in blood pressure. Propranolol injection augmented the reflexive bradycardia, whereas atropine administration converted the HR decrease to a reliable acceleration. These results suggest that the HR UR to intracranial stimulation is determined by antagonistic action of both sympathetic and parasympathetic influences, and that the parasympathetic activity is prepotent.

The physiological bases of HR URs and CRs in unanesthetized animals were assessed in two experiments utilizing autonomic blocking agents (Fredricks et al., 1974). As in the Powell et al. (1972) study, the US consisted of high-frequency, short pulse-train stimulation of the hypothalamus or septal region.

In the initial experiment, differential conditioning was established first, followed by administration of phentolamine, propranolol, atropine sulfate, or atropine methyl nitrate. Because we were interested in comparing the effects of pharmacological blockade on URs and CRs, each session included US-alone as well as CS + and CS − trials. The major finding of this experiment was that phentolamine severely attenuated the HR UR but had little effect on the HR CR. Because the baselines were similar on the CS + trials and on those using the US-alone, the attenuation of the HR UR cannot be attributed to a change in the HR baseline. The results suggested that whereas the HR UR to short pulse-train stimulation is a reflexive deceleration to a sympathetically induced change in blood presure, the HR CR is not. In addition, both HR URs and CRs were unaffected by administration of propranolol but abolished by injection of atropine. This indicated that the autonomic mediation of the bradycardia responses consisted of an increase in vagal tone.

In the second experiment of this study, we differentially conditioned rabbits injected with either saline or phentolamine. The phentolamine-injected rabbits never exhibited HR or blood pressure URs but nevertheless developed decelerative HR CRs. This suggested that the development of bradycardia CRs was not dependent on baroreceptor feedback to the CNS following US stimulation.

In summary, the UR following intracranial electrical stimulation of the hypothalamus or septal region consisted of a bradycardia that was reflexive to a sympathetically induced increase in arterial blood pressure. On the other hand, the CR consisted of a primary bradycardia unaccompanied by a blood pressure change. Both the HR URs and CRs were abolished by administration of atropine, which indicated that an increase in vagal tone was responsible for the UR and CR bradycardia. The development of bradycardia CRs was not dependent on baroreceptor feedback following US stimulation because rabbits exhibited bradycardia CRs after blood pressure and HR URs had been abolished by phentolamine. In addition, the directionality and topography of the UR and CR cardiovascular changes were not influenced by whether the US was appetitive or aversive. Finally, cardiac-somatic coupling occurred when high-current intensity, short pulse-duration electrical stimulation of the diencephalon was used as the US. This provided HR accelerations accompanied by diffuse somatic activity and HR decelerations in the absence of movement.

THE ROLE OF THE TELENCEPHALON
IN CONDITIONING

Several experiments have examined the effects of lesions upon cardiovascular conditioning in species other than the rabbit. These studies suggested that instrumental conditioning of cardiovascular responses in rats may require an intact cortex (Dicara, Braun, & Pappas, 1970), and that the integration of cardiovascular changes during classical conditioning in monkeys involves structures as far rostral as the hypothalamus (Smith, Devito, & Astley, 1982). In addition, work by Cohen (Cohen, 1975; Cohen & Goff, 1978; Cohen & MacDonald, 1976; Cohen & Schnall, 1970; Durkovic & Cohen, 1969) on pigeons has suggested that, in conjunction with other methods (e.g., histology, electrical stimulation of the brain, extracellular recording), lesion techniques can provide an important tool for studying the cardiovascular pathways involved in learned cardiovascular adjustments.

Lesion experiments in the rabbit have suggested the importance of the limbic structures in conditioned bradycardia. Buchanan and Powell (1982) explored the effects of cingulate cortex damage and found that: (1) medial lesions abolished conditioned bradycardia, (2) anterior lesions attenuated the CR but facilitated the OR, (3) posterior lesions enhanced the CR. They further substantiated the role of the anterior cingulate cortex in the HR modulation by demonstrating that large bradycardia responses could be elicited by low-current electrical stimulation of this area. The stimulation-induced bradycardia was shown to be abolished by atropine methyl nitrate. However, they found that respiratory changes were elicited at all sites that they stimulated, even in the absence of any detectable HR change. These investigators did not, however, utilize artificial ventilation or neuromuscular blockade, so that it is uncertain if the changes in HR are secondary to respiratory changes.

It is noteworthy that the cingulate cortex was shown to be a cardiodecelerative area by Buchanan and Powell (1982). Domesick (1969, 1970, 1972) demonstrated that the cingulate cortex and medial thalamus are reciprocally interconnected. Furthermore, West, Jackson, and Benjamin (1979) reported that the medial thalamus shares reciprocal interconnection with the amygdala, which in turn projects to the medullary nuclei known to mediate bradycardia responses (Schwaber, Kapp, & Higgins, 1980; Schwaber, Kapp, Higgins, & Rapp, 1982).

In an effort to clarify the role of the septal-hippocampal complex in HR conditioning, Powell and Buchanan (1980) assessed the effects of dorsal hippocampal lesions on HR conditioning. They demonstrated that this treatment augmented the magnitude of the CR but did not alter shock thresholds or the HR UR. Buchanan and Powell (1980) subsequently examined the effects of hippocampectomy on the acquisition and reversal of conditioned HR, in a discrimination paradigm. The lesions included all the dorsal hippocampus in all animals and substantial damage to the posteriorventral hippocampus in several animals. In both hippocampal-lesioned and cortical-(control) lesioned animals, the CR was attenuated during both acquisition and reversal. Buchanan and Powell (1982) sought to clarify the role of the dorsal hippocampus as compared to the overlying cortex. This study utilized more optimal stimulus parameters than their previous study. However, they again found that damage of the cingulate cortex, overlying the dorsal hippocampus, could account for the impairment of the CR. Apparently dorsal hippocampus lesions alone could not account for any of the response decrement, as the effect of combined lesions was not significantly different from cingulate cortex lesions.

Hernandez and Powell (1981) utilized assays of forebrain norepinephrine(NE) and serotonin(5-HT) to elucidate the mechanisms by which septal lesions affect HR conditioning. During the first acquisition session, septal lesions increased the magnitude of the CR whereas during the second session, the HR response reversed into a cardioacceleration. Forebrain NE levels were depleted by approximately 30% but this change appeared to be related to lesion-induced changes in the CR. In unlesioned animals, however, the concentrations of NE and 5-HT were correlated with the magnitude of the CR. These findings led Powell, Milligan, and Mull (1982) to examine the effects of more discrete septal lesions on the HR CR and the HR UR to unsignaled shock. Lateral septal lesions intensified the CR but did not alter the UR. Medial septal lesions had no affect on the CR. Therefore the findings of the previous study (Hernandez & Powell, 1981) were probably attributable to the lateral extent of the septal area, although no amine assays were conducted in the present study to substantiate this conclusion.

Kapp and his colleagues (Kapp, Frysinger, Gallagher, & Haselton, 1979) examined the effects of amygdala central nucleus (ACE) lesions on the acquisition of conditioned bradycardia in a Pavlovian conditioning paradigm. Rabbits were presented with the CS-alone during 15 consecutive trials, and then with the CS paired with US (2mA periorbital shock) during conditioning trials. Baseline HR and HR OR data were determined from the CS-alone trials. Furthermore, as a control for nonassociative responding to the CS and US, additional rabbits were exposed to a pseudoconditioning sequence that consisted of unpaired trials of CS-alone and US-alone in a randomized order.

The results from this experiment suggested that: (1) the OR (bradycardia) habituated over the successive CS-alone trials, but ACE lesions had no effect on the OR or its habituation; (2) ACE lesions had no effect on baseline HR; (3) the CR consisted of a bradycardia that was clearly distinguishable from nonassociative responses; (4) ACE lesions markedly attenuated the CR; (5) the UR (tachycardia) habituated, to some extent, over trials; and (6) ACE lesions attenuated the habituation of the UR. As with all lesion studies, the interpretation of these results is complicated by the possibility that damage sustained by fibers of passage may have contributed to these results.

A recent study in our laboratory (Gentile, Jarrell, Teich, McCabe, & Schneiderman, 1985) examined the role of ACE in the *retention* of differentially conditioned bradycardia. Electrodes were implanted bilaterally in ACE or in control sites just dorsal and rostral to ACE. Two days following surgery, animals were subjected to differential conditioning in which one tone (CS +) was paired with periorbital shock and a second tone (CS –) was presented alone. Each animal received one conditioning session per day until evidence of differential HR responses were obtained. Bilateral electrolytic lesions were then made. Thirty minutes after lesioning, animals received an additional conditioning session.

Both control and ACE groups demonstrated differential HR responses prior to lesioning. In the control group, lesions had no effect on HR responses or bradycardia response magnitude. However, the ACE lesion group failed to demonstrate differential HR responses after lesioning. Furthermore, bradycardia conditioned response magnitude was greatly attenuated. In both groups, lesions had no effect on the HR orienting response, unconditioned response, or baseline. These findings suggest that ACE also plays a role in the retention of differential Pavlovian conditioning of bradycardia in rabbits. Bilateral ACE lesions abolished differential HR responses and profoundly attenuated bradycardia response magnitude.

Other work in Kapp's laboratory (Applegate, Frysinger, Kapp, & Gallagher, 1982) has implicated the ACE in the conditioned HR response. Utilizing multiple recording within ACE during their conditioning paradigm (e.g., Kapp et al., 1979), they found a rapid development of short-latency increases in the multiple unit activity of ACE in response to a tone CS. At two placements within ACE the changes in unit activity were significantly correlated with the magnitude of the CR across trials.

As a step toward clarifying the role of ACE per se as opposed to fibers of passage, and to further elucidate ACE mechanisms involved in conditioned bradycardia, Gallagher, Kapp, Frysinger, and Rapp (1980) utilized adrenergic manipulation of ACE during another set of experiments. In an earlier experiment, Gallagher, Kapp, Musty, and Driscoll (1977) had demonstrated that adrenergic blockade within the amygdala impaired retention of aversive conditioning in rats. Taking her lead from this and other neurochemical studies, Gallagher et al. (1980) compared animals with intracerebral injections of equivalent doses of: (1) the beta-antagonist dl-propranolol, (2) the weaker beta-antagonist d-propranolol, (3) the combination of beta-antagonist dl-propranolol and beta-agonist l-isoproterenol, and (4) the vehicle alone.

The results suggested that (1) the cardiodecelerative CR was clearly distinguishable from nonassociative responses; (2) administration of dl-propanolol into ACE impaired conditioning, but not baseline HR or the HR OR; (3) the weaker dextro-isomer of propranolol was ineffective, indicating stereospecificity of the effect of dl-propranaolol; (4) B-agonist administration partially attenuated the effects of dl-propranolol; and (5) the effects of dl-propranolol were either ineffective or substantially reduced in areas surrounding ACE. Baseline HR and OR data essentailly duplicated that of their previous lesion study. The fact that B-blockade did not alter baseline HR or OR suggested that the impaired conditioning that resulted from dl-propranolol probably did not result from gross changes in sensory processing. Collectively the data, from the previous lesion study and the present pharmacological manipulation experiment, strongly suggest that the ACE, and in particular the B-adrenergic mechanisms within ACE, play a substantial role in the classical conditioning of bradycardia in rabbits.

Further research sought to explore still other neurochemical mechanisms within ACE. An early study by Gallagher and Kapp (1978) found that opiate manipulations of the amygdala, in rats, altered retention of aversive conditioning. Other laboratories had demonstrated that opiates are highly concentrated within ACE (Elde, Hokfelt, Johansson, & Terenius, 1976; Gors, Pradelles, Humbert, Dray, Le Gal LaSalle, & Ben–Ari, 1978; Sar, Stumpf, Miller, Chang, & Cuatrecasas, 1979; Simantov, Kuhar, Uhl, & Snyder, 1977). Therefore, Gallagher and colleagues (Gallagher, Kapp, McNall, & Pascoe, 1981) compared the effects of central administration of: (1) the opiate agonist levorphanol, (2) the inactive isomer of levorphanol, dextrophan, (3) combined agonist and antagonist, levorphanol and naloxone, respectively, and (4) vehicle alone. As previously, injections were located in, and adjacent to, ACE. Pseudoconditioning groups were also used as controls for nonassociative responding.

It was shown that: (1) levorphanol decreased the magnitude of the CR, (2) naloxone increased the magnitude of the CR, (3) dextrophan did not significantly alter the CR, and (4) combined administration of levorphanol and naloxone produced no significant alteration of the CR, as might be expected because these two agents are thought to act competitively at the opiate receptor. The fact that naloxone increased the magnitude of the CR is noteworthy. As Gallagher points out, this result may well reflect the effect of blocking endogenous opioid peptides within ACE. Whereas opiates may mediate analgesic effects in some situations, Rodgers (1978) reported the intraamygdala manipulation of opiates did not alter shock sensitivity. Therefore, it is doubtful that the results of Gallagher et al. (1981) can be attributed to a diminished sensitivity to the US, although these investigators did not test this possibility.

In a more recent experiment, Gallagher, Kapp, and Pascoe (1982) assessed the effects of enkephalin analogue administration into ACE on the acquisition of conditioned HR responses. Using a paradigm similar to those previously described (e.g., Gallagher et al., 1981), these authors demonstrated that the injection of D–ALA^2, MET^5-enkephalinamide(DALA) into ACE significantly attenuated the aquisition of conditioned bradycardia. In contrast, injection of D–ALA^2, D–LEU^5-enkephalin(DADL) did not reduce aquisition significantly from vehicle-injected animals. Because DALA possesses greater affinity for the MU-opiate receptor and DADL favors the delta-opiate receptor, it was suggested that MU receptor activity plays some role in the conditioning process.

In summary, studies by Powell, Kapp, Gallagher, and colleagues have described the role of several forebrain regions in conditioned bradycardia. Medial and anterior lesions of the cingulate cortex abolished conditioned bradycardia, whereas posterior lesions of the same structure enhanced the CR. Electrical stimulation of the anterior cingulate cortex elicited a large bradycardia that was mediated through the vagus nerve suggesting that the cingulate cortex is part of a conditioned bradycardia pathway. The dorsal hippocampus and septal regions have also been shown to be involved in HR conditioning, although the role of these structures is not presently clear. Lesions of the ACE abolished the bradycardia CR but not the UR to periorbital shock. In addition, changes in single-unit activity of ACE neurons was correlated with the onset and the magnitude of the CR. It has also been demonstrated that beta-adrenergic and opiate mechanisms in the ACE play an important role in conditioned bradycardia.

ELECTROPHYSIOLOGICAL AND NEUROANATOMICAL STUDIES: TRACING CENTRAL BRADYCARDIA PATHWAYS

During the past several years we have been interested in tracing central bradycardia pathways. As mentioned previously, the cingulate gyrus and the ACE appear to be involved in short-latency conditioned bradycardia. Work in our laboratory has electrophysiologically traced an oligosynaptic brady-cardia pathway that courses from the ACE through the lateral hypothal-amus, lateral zona incerta, and parabrachial nuclues of the pons before reaching the vagal cells of origin in the dorsal vagal nucleus and the nucleus ambiguus. We have also presented neuroanatomical evidence that monosyn-aptic connections exist between ACE and the dorsal medulla. Because it has been demonstrated that destruction of ACE eliminates conditioned brady-cardia but does not disrupt the unconditioned bradycardia (Kapp et al., 1979), it seems likely that the amygdala-vagal pathway that we have de-scribed is the CR pathway.

In order to trace the central bradycardia pathways we have used the approach of first defining the motor outflow and then working our way back into the CNS. During an initial study using this tack, Schwaber and Schneiderman (1975) determined that the extracellular single neuron record-ings could be obtained from the cells of origin of vagal preganglionic cardio-inhibitory motoneurons in dorsal vagal nucleus (DVN) of rabbits. Prior to this study the electrophysiological identification of these neurons within the CNS had been intractible in all species. In this study, which was conducted upon conscious animals, the vagal preganglionic cardiomotor neurons were identified using: (1) antidromic activation induced by electrical stimulation of the cervical vagus nerve, (2) synaptic activation induced by stimulation of aortic nerve (AN), (3) systematic variation of the neuron's firing rate with spontaneous or elicited changes in heart rate, and (4) postexperimental con-firmation that the recorded cell was in the region of DVN producing the lowest threshold ($< 30 \mu A$) for bradycardia during stimulation experiments. Stimulation of aortic nerve was used to establish that the motoneuron was barosensory related, because in rabbit AN appears to be devoid of chemo-receptor input and has been shown to be primarily barosensory (Chalmers, Korner, & White, 1967; Douglas, Ritchie, & Schaumann, 1956; Gernandt, 1946; Schmidt, 1932).

Jordan, Khalid, Schneiderman, and Spyer (1982) replicated the findings of Schwaber and Schneiderman (1975) by recording from preganglionic vagal cardiomotor neurons in DVN of urethane anesthetized rabbits. In addition, recordings were also made from preganglionic vagal cardioinhibitory neu-rons in nucleus ambiguus (NA). The activity of the medullary neurons was re-corded via multibarreled micropipettes, in which one barrel was filled with DL-homocysteic acid. Of 82 neurons located in DVN that had axons in the B fiber range (i.e., 4–14.5m/sec), 22 were excited by electrical stimulation of AN (latencey to onset: 6–25msec; mean: 13 msec). Of these, 15 had resting activity; the other 7 fired in response to the iontophoresis of DL-homocysteic acid. All 22 neurons showed an expiratory rhythm, firing primarily during the period of phrenic silence. Each neuron's discharge in response to DL-homocysteic acid consistently elicited a small bradycardia response. This effect was not seen in response to a current control. In addition to these DVN neurons, 14 others with identical properites were found in NA. The properties of the cardioinhibitory motoneurons recorded from DVN and NA of rabbits were essentially the same as those recorded from the NA of cats (McAllen & Spyer, 1976, 1978).

Experiments in which the cervical vagus nerve has been dipped in HRP have indicated to us that the distribution of vagal preganglionic cell bodies in NA is far sparser than in DVN for rabbits (Ellenberger, Haselton, Liskowsky, & Schneiderman, 1982). In addition, bradycardia responses are easily elicited by low-intensity ($<30\mu A$) stimulation in DVN but not in NA. However, when: (1) recording microelectrodes are inserted into the region of NA where vagal preganglionic cell bodies have been located using HRP, (2) a unit is identified as a vagal preganglionic cardioinhibitory neuron using our usual criteria, and (3) electrical stimulation is transmitted through the electrode previously used for recording, bradycardia can be elicited at current intensities of less than $10\mu A$.

Injection of horseradish peroxidase (HRP) into the dorsal medulla including DVN (Wallach, Ellenberger, Liskowsky, Hamilton, & Schneiderman, 1979) produced pronounced retrograde cell body labeling in the ACE as well as in the lateral hypothalamus. Other investigations (Schwaber, Kapp, & Higgins, 1980; Schwaber, Kapp, Higgins, & Rapp, 1982) have reported similar findings. Furthermore, Kapp (Kapp, Gallagher, Underwood, McNall, & Whitehorn, 1982) showed that electrical stimulation of ACE produced marked bradycardia that was either abolished or markedly attenuated by intravenous injections of atropine methylnitrate. The bradycardia was shown not to be an artifact of respiratory changes or gross motor activity, as it persisted after artificial ventilation and immobilization with Flaxedil. Therefore, the bradycardia produced by ACE stimulation is vagally mediated, as one would expect in light of its monosynaptic projections to NTS and DVN.

Interestingly, we have also found that train stimulation of the ACE in lightly anesthetized rabbits elicits bradycardia and a depressor response. This suggested to us that the bradycardia elicited by stimulation of the hypothalamus might be attributable to fibers of passage originating in the amygdala central nucleus. Consequently, we lesioned the central nucleus unilaterally and then stimulated the ipsilateral and contralateral hypothalamus 30 min or 10–14 days after the lesion (Gellman et al., 1981). We found that stimulation of the lateral hypothalamus only failed to elicit bradycardia responses when the stimulation was presented ipsilateral to the lesion site 10–14 days postlesion. Because fibers in the hypothalamus would be expected to be degenerated by 10 days after destruction of their cell bodies in the amygdala, the results of the Gellman et al. study suggest that the bradycardia elicited by stimulation of the lateral hypothalamus is due to fibers originating in the amygdala ACE.

In a study in our laboratory examining the lateral hypothalamus as a mediator of bradycardia, Wallach et al. (1979) found that: (1) train microstimulation of the lateral hypothalamus elicited primary bradycardia, which was abolished by bilateral vagotomy, and (2) single-pulse stimulation of the lateral hypothalamus activated vagal preganglionic cardiomotor neurons in DVN at a mean latency of 10 msec.

In the Wallach et al. (1979) experiment, unilateral injections of HRP were made into the dorsal medulla. Retrograde cell body labeling was found in the regions of the lateral hypothalamus where bradycardia is elicited by train stimulation and where vagal cardioinhibitory motoneurons can be activated by single-pulse stimulation. Because single-pulse stimulation in the lateral hypothalamus activated units oligo rather than monosynaptically, we concluded that the functional connections between the lateral hypothalamus and dorsal medulla (i.e., NTS and DVN) established in our electrophysiological experiments may be parallel but are not identical with the anatomical connections found in our HRP experiments.

In further exploring more caudal aspects of the diencephalon of rabbits for cardiovascular responsiveness, we found that train microstimulation (100 Hz) of the lateral zona incerta of the subthalamus produced pronounced bradycardia (94 beat/min drop from an average baseline of 250 beats/min), which in turn slightly decreased blood pressure (Mean: −6 mmHg) (Kaufman, Hamilton, Wallach, Petrick, & Schneiderman, 1979). These changes were prevented by bilateral vagotomy. Stimulation of the medial zona incerta produced a pronounced pressor response.

Stimulation of bradycardia-producing sites in the lateral zona incerta activated cardiovascular-related interneurons (neurons activated by aortic nerve stimulation, but not antidromically activated by vagus nerve stimulation) in NTS and DVN, and cardioinhibitory motoneurons in DVN. Although mean onset latency of these medullary neurons to lateral zona incerta stimulation was relatively short (6 msec), these stimuli did not follow repeated stimuli faithfully. Therefore, the connection between the lateral zona incerta and the dorsal medulla is probably not monosynaptic. However, a short train of pulses (100 msec, 100Hz) elicited greater firing rates than single pulses did. Therefore, it is possible that some connections between lateral zona incerta and the dorsal medulla may be monosynaptic but may require a high degree of temporal summation.

Another structure that showed retrograde cell body labeling in the Wallach et al. experiment after injection of HRP into the dorsal medulla was the parabrachial nucleus (PBN) of the pons. The PBN had previously been implicated in the regulation of autonomic activity (e.g., Wang & Ranson, 1939), respiration (e.g., Bertrand & Hugelin, 1971), defense reactions (Coote, Hilton, & Zbrozyna, 1973), and adrenocorticotropin release (Ward, Grizzle, & Grann, 1976), but its role in the mediation of bradycardia was unknown.

We therefore set out to study the role of PBN in the mediation of bradycardia and in the reception of barosensory information (Hamilton, Ellenberger, Liskowsky, & Schneiderman, 1981). Train stimulation of either medial or lateral PBN produced primary bradycardia (mean peak change: − 74 beats/min) associated with a pressor response (mean peak change: 14 mmHg) of longer latency. Section of the cervical vagus nerve indicated that the rate and blood pressure responses to train stimulation did not vary systematically as a function of respiratory pattern; paralyzing animals with decamethonium hydrochloride and artificially ventilating them also did not qualitatively influence the cardiovascular responses to stimulation. Single-pulse stimulation of PBN in conjunction with extracellular single-neuron recording established that PBN projects to the commissural region of NTS at a latency of about 4 msec where synapse is made with neurons receiving barosensory input.

In addition to establishing the existence of descending functional projections from PBN to NTS, injections of HRP into PBN revealed direct anatomical projections from regions of the forebrain previously implicated in the mediation of bradycardia. These included the ACE, lateral preoptic region, medial forebrain bundle, bed nucleus of stria terminalis, anterior, and lateral hypothalamus and lateral zona incerta. The correspondences between these HRP findings and the results of our previous functional studies implicating the ACE, lateral hypothalamus, and lateral zona incerta in the mediation of bradycardia is quite striking. Important correspondence also exists between the results of injecting HRP into the PBN in our study and into the dorsal medulla as reported by Schwaber et al. (1980).

An interesting aspect of the studies in which HRP was injected into the dorsal medulla was that extensive retrograde cell body labeling was found in the paraventricular nucleus of the hypothalamus (Schwaber et al., 1980; Wallach et al., 1979). The paraventricular nucleus is located rather medially in the hypothalamus, and in preliminary experiments we have found that stimulation of this structure produces tachycardia and a pressor response. Moreover, single-pulse stimulation of aortic nerve suppresses the firing rate of neurons in the paraventricular nucleus. These findings taken together suggest that stimulation of the paraventricular nucleus may suppress the firing rate of neurons in NTS and/or DVN that are normally activated by barosensory stimulation.

Jordan, Khalid, Schneiderman, and Spyer (1979) reported on a preliminary experiment in which stimulation of the ventromedial hypothalamus in rabbits and the hypothalamic defense area in cats suppressed the firing rate of cardioinhibitory vagal motoneurons. By constructing peri-stimulus time histograms of vagal unit activity during hypothalamic stimulation, an inhibitory influence was revealed that had an onset latency of approximately 10 msec and a duration of 200 msec. Furthermore, the excitatory response of vagal neurons to aortic nerve stimulation (a 500 Hz train of 3 pulses) was suppressed by a conditioning stimulus delivered to the hypothalamus 20–150 msec earlier. We tested whether the suppression could be explained as a consequence of an enhanced inspiratory drive. Because the inhibition of vagal activity during inspiration was previously found to be blocked by iontophoretically applied atropine (Garcia, Jordan, & Spyer, 1979), we investigated its effect on the inhibitory influence of hypothalamic stimulation. Although in our work acetylcholine applied iontophoretically inhibited vagal discharge (neurons were firing in response to DL-homocysteic acid) and this was antagonized by atropine, atropine had no effect on hypothalamically evoked inhibition. The suppression of the baroreceptor input to these neurons seen during hypothalamic stimulation was also unaffected.

Our data suggest that vagal cardiomotor preganglionic neurons are under at least two distinct inhibitory controls. There is an inhibitory input to vagal motoneurons from the hypothalamus that is independent of inspiratory-mediated inhibition. Where hypothalamic stimulation evokes an enhanced inspiratory drive, it is likely that both inhibitory processes contribute to the suppression of the cardiac component of the baroreceptor reflex.

As previously mentioned, we have observed that single-pulse stimulation of PBN can activate barosensory-sensitive neurons in NTS and cardioinhibitory vagal preganglionic neurons in DVN (Liskowsky, Ellenberger, Haselton, Schneiderman, & Hamilton, 1981). However, because: (1) extensive attempts to backfire barosensory-sensitive neurons in PBN by stimulating NTS or DVN were unsuccessful, (2) latencies and other characteristics of NTS and DVN neuronal responses to PBN stimulation suggested the presence of an oligosynaptic pathway, and (3) relatively sparse labeling was seen in PBN after injection of HRP into the NTS/DVN complex, attempts were made to identify alternate putative synapses in the central bradycardia pathway between PBN and cardioinhibitiry motor neurons.

Anterograde and retrograde labeling using HRP conjugated with wheat germ agglutinin revealed the presence of direct projections from PBN to NTS and from PBN to NA synapsed in either the A5 region or nucleus reticularis gigantocellularis. Direct projections were traced from NA to DVN, and reciprocal connections were observed between NTS and NA.

Extensive exploration of the caudal pons and rostral medulla indicated that train stimulation (100 μA) of the A5 region and ventral nucleus retiscularis gigantocellularis elicited bradycardia responses that were similar to those elicited by stimulating PBN. These responses were eliminated by bilateral vagotomy but not by artificial ventilation in decamethonium paralyzed animals. Bradycardia responses were also elicited at lower current intensities ($< 30 \mu$A) by stimulating NTS, DVN, and NA. The results suggest that the bradycardia pathway(s) descending through PBN may have their outflow from DVN with intermediate synapse in NTS, and from NA either without intervening synapse or with intervening synapse in the A5 region of the ventral nucleus reticularis gigantocellularis.

Liskowsky et al. (1981) also found that electrical stimulation of the principle nucleus of V elicited bradycardia responses. The form and characteristics of these bradycardia responses were similar to the trigeminal depressor response described by Kumada, Reis, Terui, and Dampney (1979). Injection of HRP into the principle nucleus of V showed that the descending trigeminal depressor response pathway is anatomically distinct from the descending bradycardia pathway that passes through PBN. In view of the neuroanatomical projections to NA observed by Liskowsky et al., we have conducted a detailed electrophysiological analysis of the vagal preganglionic cardiomotor neurons in NA.

The results of our work using electrical stimulation and extracellular single-neuron recording techniques in rabbits may be briefly summarized as follows. First, we have established that cardioinhibitory vagal preganglionic motoneurons are located in DVN and NA. Second, we have described a putative polysynaptic central pathway that mediates bradycardia, which extends from ACE to vagal cardioinhibitory motoneurons in the medulla and appears to include in its trajectory the lateral hypothalamus, lateral zona incerta, and PBN. Third, we have documented a functional connection between the ventromedial hypothalamus and DVN, which is capable of surpressing the spontaneous firing rate of vagal cardiomotor neurons as well as the cardiac component of the baroreceptor reflex. Although our electrophysiological data indicate that the descending CNS pathway(s) mediating bradycardia are polysynaptic, they seem to parallel closely monosynaptic connections that we have seen using HRP histochemistry.

Conceptual Framework

The evidence from the preceding studies suggests that an oligosynaptic CNS bradycardia pathway courses through the cingulate cortex, ACE, lateral preoptic area, lateral hypothalamus, lateral zona incerta, and PBN before reaching the cardiomotor cell bodies of the vagus in DVN and NA. As noted previously, Kapp and associates (Kapp et al., 1979) have demonstrated that ACE lesions abolish the HR CR but leaves the UR intact. A recent study in our laboratory (Jarrell, McCabe, Teich, Gentile, VanDercar, & Schneiderman, in press) examined the effect of lateral zona incerta (LZI) lesions on the HR CR, UR, and orienting response. Briefly, electrodes were implanted bilaterally in LZI or in control sites just dorsal or ventral to LZI. Two days following surgery, animals were subjected to Pavlovian conditioning in which a tone was paired with periorbital shock (3 mA; .5 sec) or to pseudoconditioning in which tones and shocks were unpaired. After bradycardia conditioning was established, bilateral electrolytic lesions were produced by passing anodal DC current (0.2–0.4 mA) for 30 sec. Thirty minutes later, animals were subjected to a post-lesion conditioning or pseudoconditioning session. Lesions had no effect on the HR orienting response, UR, baseline, or lack of response to pseudoconditioning. Bilateral LZI lesions abolished the HR CR. However, HR CRs were unaffected in the control lesion group including two animals with unilateral LZI damage.

In order to determine whether LZI selectively mediates the HR CR or a more general learning process, a second experiment was conducted that examined the effect of LZI lesions on another CR, the classically conditioned corneo-retinal potential response (CRP). Bilateral electrode implantations were made in LZI or control sites. Beginning two days later, animals received one conditioning session per day until CRP CRs were seen on 65% of the trials during a session. Once CRP criterion was met, bilateral electrolytic lesions were made. Bilateral LZI lesions abolished the HR CR without affecting CRP CRs.

In summary, bilateral LZI lesions abolished the classically conditioned bradycardia response but not other HR responses (e.g. OR and UR). Furthermore, LZI lesions had no effect on the CRP CR supporting the hypothesis that LZI is part of an efferent pathway that selectively mediates the HR CR in rabbits.

It seems reasonable to suggest that this CR pathway runs separate from, but possibly parallel to, the UR pathway. In the conditioning paradigm in which periorbital shock serves as the US, the afferent US pathway projects via the trigeminal nerve and trigeminal nuclei. Liskowsky et al. (1981), using electrical stimulation and HRP injections, suggested that a bradycardia pathway courses through the principle trigeminal nucleus and that this pathway is anatomically distinct from the amygdalo-vagal pathway. Previous work by Kumada, Dampney, and Reis (1975, 1977) has shown that trigeminal nerve stimulation or stimulation of trigeminal sensory nuclei elicits bradycardia that is in part mediated through the vagus nerve. Thus, it seems feasible that this trigeminal-cardiovascular pathway could serve as the US/UR pathway during Pavlovian conditioning of HR using periorbital shock as the US.

The notion of parallel circuits has been presented before. Moore (personal communication) has proposed a model utilizing parallel pathways to describe the conditioned nictitating membrane response. The model assumes that associative learning occurs as a result of converging input from CS + and a collateral branch of an afferent unit in the UR circuit. The learning is mediated by a premotor element. This element can be suppressed by a conditioned inhibitor(CS –), thereby suppressing the CR but not the UR. Conversely, the premotor element can be pre and/or postsynaptically facilitated to amplify the flow of information from the CS + to motorneurons, thereby generating the CR.

In Moore's model, the anatomical convergence of the CS, CR, US/UR pathways is essential. The pathways involved in the HR conditioning paradigm seem to meet this criterion. Because the CS in our paradigm was a tone, the CS pathway would involve the CNS auditory system, which originates in the hair cells of the inner ear and projects to the dorsal cochlear nucleus, superior olivary nucleus, inferior colliculus, and medial geniculate nucleus before ascending to the auditory cortex. A recent study in our laboratory (Jarrell, Gentile, McCabe & Schneiderman, in press) examined the role of the medial geniculate nucleus (MGN) in differentially conditioned bradycardia. Injections of horseradish peroxidase into the ACE produced cell body and fiber labeling at the ventral and medial borders of MGN. The role of this region in the mediation of differential conditioning of HR decelerations and CRP responses was then examined. Bilateral electrolytic lesions were made in the medial portion of MGN or in control sites dorsal or rostral to MGN. Ten days following surgery, lesioned animals and unoperated control animals were subjected to 7 days (1 session/day) of differential conditioning consisting of trials in which one tone (CS +) was paired with periorbital shock and a second tone (CS −) was presented alone. The 7 acquisition days were followed by 2 days of extinction in which both tones were presented alone.

Each group demonstrated bradycardia responses to both the CS + and CS − . In the control-lesion and unoperated groups, the CS + consistently elicited larger bradycardia responses than the CS − . However, animals with bilateral MGN lesions did not demonstrate differential bradycardia responses. Bradycardia conditioned response magnitude was not significantly different among the three groups. Evidence of CRP differential conditioning was present in each group. These findings suggest that a region just medial to MGN or fibers passing through this region selectively mediate HR differential conditioning in rabbits. The fact that bradycardia responses are still present after lesions at the medial border of MGN suggests that other auditory regions may also be involved in the mediation of the bradycardia conditioned response.

The amygdala-vagal pathway(CR), the trigeminal-cardiovascular pathway(US/UR), and the auditory pathway(CS) all seem to converge in the caudal pons/rostral medulla. It is tempting to speculate that the association between CRs and URs could occur at this location. Indirect support for this notion comes from studies by Thompson (McCormick, Lavond, Clark, Kettner, Rising, & Thompson, 1981; McCormick, Lavond, Clark, & Thompson, 1981), and Moore (Desmond & Moore, 1982), who have implicated regions of the ipsilateral rostral reticular formation and deep cerebellar nuclei as essential substrates for Pavlovian conditioning of the nictitating membrane response.

Of course, much work is necessary to determine the precise pathways in the caudal pons/rostral medulla that may be involved in HR conditioning. In addition, the mechanisms of interactions between these pathways must be explored before any comprehensive model of associative conditioning of bradycardia in the rabbit can be proposed.

REFERENCES

Applegate, C. D., Frysinger, R. C., Kapp, B. S., & Gallagher, M. (1982). Multiple unit activity recorded from amygdala central nucleus during Pavlovian heart rate conditioning in rabbit. *Brain Research, 238,* 457–462.

Ban, T. (1966). The septo-preoptico-hypothalamic system and its autonomic function. In T. Tokizane & J. P. Schade (Eds.), *Progress in brain research: Correlative neurosciences. Part A. Fundamental mechanisms.* Amsterdam: Elsevier.

Bertrand, F., & Hugelin, A. (1971). Respiratory synchronizing function of nucleus parabrachialis medialis: Pneumotaxic mechanisms. *Journal of Neurophysiology, 34,* 189–207.

Brickman, A., & Schneiderman, N. (1977). Classically conditioned blood pressure decreases induced by electrical stimulation of posterior hypothalamus in rabbits. *Psychophysiology, 14,* 287–292.

Buchanan, S. L., & Powell, D. A. (1980). Divergencies in Pavlovian conditioned heart rate and eyeblink responses produced by hippocampectomy in the rabbit. *Behavioral and Neural Biology, 30,* 20–38.

Buchanan, S. L., & Powell, D.A (1982). Cingulate cortex: Its role in Pavlovian conditioning. *Journal of Comparative and Physiological Psychology, 96,* 755–774.

Carlton, P. L. (1962). Some behavioral effects of atropine and methylatropine. *Psychological Research, 10,* 579–582.

Chalmers, J. P., Korner, P. I., & White, S. W. (1967). The relative roles of the aortic and carotid sinus nerves in the rabbit in the control of respiration and circulation during arterial hypoxia and hypercapnia. *Journal of Physiology (London), 188,* 435–450.

Cohen, D. H. (1969). Development of a vertebrate experimental model for cellular neurophysiologic studies of learning. *Conditioned Reflexes, 4,* 61–80.

Cohen, D. H. (1974). The neural pathways and informational flow mediating a conditoned autonomic response. In L. V. DiCara (Ed.), *Limbic and autonomic nervous systems research.* New York: Plenum Press.

Cohen, D. J. (1975). Involvement of avian amygdalar homolog (archistriatum posterior and medial) in defensively conditioned heart-rate change. *Journal of Comparative Neurology, 160,*(1), 13–35.

Cohen, D. H., & Goff, D. M. (1978). Effect of avian basal forebrain lesions, including septum, on heart rate conditioning. *Brain Research Bulletin, 3,* 311–318.

Cohen, D. H., & MacDonald, R. L. (1976). Involvement of the avian hypothalamus in defensively conditioned heart rate change. *Journal of Comparative Neurology, 167,* 465–480.

Cohen, D. H., & Pitts, L. H. (1968). Vagal and sympathetic components of conditioned cardioacceleration in the pigeon. *Brain Research, 9,* 15–31.

Cohen, D. H., & Schnall, A. M. (1970). Medullary cells of origin of vagal cardioinhibitory fibers in the pigeon. II. Electrical stimulation of the dorsal motor nucleus. *Journal of Comparative Neurology, 140,* 321–342.

Coote, J. H., Hilton, S. M., & Zbrozyna, A. W. (1973). The ponto-medullary area integrating the defense reaction in the cat and its influence on muscle blood flow. *Journal of Physiology (London), 229,* 257–274.

Desmond, J. E., & Moore, J. W. (1982). A brain-stem region essential for the classically conditioned but not unconditioned nictitating-membrane response. *Physiology and Behavior, 28*(6), 1029–1033.

DiCara, L. V., Braun, J. J., & Pappas, B. A. (1970). Classical conditioning and instrumental learning of cardiac and gastrointestinal responses following removal of neocortex in the rat. *Journal of Comparative Physiological Psychology, 73,* 208–216.

Domesick, V. B. (1969). Projections from the cingulate cortex in the rat. *Brain Research, 12,* 296–320.

Domesick, V. B. (1970). The fasciculus cinguli in the rat. *Brain Research, 20,* 19–32.

Domesick, V. B. (1972). Thalamic relationships of the medial cortex in the rat. *Brain, Behavior Evaluation, 6,* 457–483.

Douglas, W., Ritchie, J., & Schaumann, W. (1956). Depressor reflexes from medullated and non-medullated fibers in the rabbit's aortic nerve. *Journal of Physiology, 132,* 187–188.

Downs, D., Cardozo, C., Schneiderman, N., Yehle, A. L., VanDercar, D. H., & Zwilling, G. (1972). Central effects of atropine upon aversive classical conditioning in rabbits. *Psychopharmacologia, 23,* 319–333.

Durkovic, R. G., & Cohen, D. H. (1969). Effect of rostral midbrain lesions on conditioning of heart and respiratory rate responses in the pigeon. *Journal of Comparative Physiology and Psychology, 68,* 184–192.

Elde, R., Hokfelt, T., Johansson, & C. Terenius (1976). Immunohistological studies using antibodies to leucine-enkephalin: Initial observations on the nervous system of the rat. *Neuroscience, 1,* 349–351.

Eliasson, S., Lingren, P., & Uvnas, B. (1952). Representation in the hypothalamus and the motor cortex in the dog of the sympathetic vasodilator outflow to the skeletal muscle. *Acta Physiologie Scandinavia, 27,* 18–37.

Ellenberger, H. H., Haselton, J. R., Liskowsky, D. R., & Schneiderman, N. (1982). Localization of cardioinhibitory motor neurons in the medulla of the rabbit. *Federation Proceedings Abstracts, 41,* 1517.

Elster, A., VanDercar, D. H., & Schneiderman, N. (1970). Classical conditioning of heart rate discriminations using subcortical electrical stimulation as conditioned and unconditioned stimuli. *Physiology & Behavior, 5,* 503–508.

Fredericks, A., Moore, J. W., Metcalf, F. U., Schwaber, J. S., & Schneiderman, N. (1974). Selective autonomic blockade of conditioned and unconditioned heart rate changes in rabbits. *Pharmacology, Biochemistry, & Behavior, 2,* 493–501.

Gallagher, M., & Kapp, B. S. (1978). Manipulation of opiate activity in the amygdala alters memory process. *Life Sciences, 23,* 1973–1978.

Gallagher, M. B., Kapp, S., Frysinger, C., & Rapp, R. (1980). Beta-adrenergic manipulation in amygdala central n. alters rabbit heart rate conditioning. *Pharmacology, Biochemistry, & Behavior, 12,* 419–426.

Gallagher, M., Kapp, B. S., McNall, C. L., & Pascoe, J. P. (1981). Opiate effects in the amygdala central nucleus on heart rate conditioning in rabbits. *Pharmacology, Biochemistry, and Behavior, 14,* 497–505.

Gallagher, M., Kapp, B. S., Musty, R. E., & Driscoll, P. A. (1977). Memory formation: Evidence for a specific neurochemical system in the amygdala. *Science,* 423–425.

Gallagher, M., Kapp, B. S., & Pascoe, J. P. (1982). Enkephalin analogue effects in the amygdala central nucleus on conditioned heart rate. *Pharmacology, Biochemistry, and Behavior, 17*(2), 217–222.

Garcia, M., Jordan, D., Spyer, K. M. (1979). Studies of the properties of cardiac vagal neurones. *Neuroscience Letters Supplement, 1,* 516.

Gellman, M., Schneiderman, N., Wallach, J., & LeBlanc, W. (1981). Cardiovascular responses elicited by hypothalamic stimulation in rabbits reveal a medio-lateral organization. *Journal of the Autonomic Nervous System, 4,* 301–317.

Gentile, C. G., Jarrell, T. W., Teich, A. H., McCabe, P. M., & Schneiderman, N. (1985). Amygdala central nucleus as mediator of differential Pavlovian conditioning of bradycardia in rabbits. *Neuroscience Abstracts, 11,* 1111.

Gernandt, B. E. (1946). A study of the respiratory reflexes elicited from the aortic and carotid bodies. *Acta Physiologica Scandinavica, 11,* Supplement 35.

Giarman, H. J., & Pepeu, G. (1964). The influence of centrally acting cholinolytic drugs on brain acetylcholine levels. *British Journal of Pharmacology, 23,* 123–130.

Gimpl, M. P., Brickman, A. L., Kaufman, M. P., & Schneiderman, N. (1976). Temporal relationships during barosensory attenuation in the conscious rabbit. *American Journal of Physiology, 230,* 1480–1486.

Gors, C., Pradelles, P., Humbert, J., Dray, F., Le Gal La Salle, G., & Ben–Ari, Y. (1978). Regional distribution of met-enkephalin within the amygdaloid complex and bed nucleus of the stria terminalis. *Neuroscience Letters, 10,* 193–196.

Hamilton, R. B., Ellenberger, H., Liskowsky, D., & Schneiderman, N. (1981). Parabrachial area as mediator of bradycardia in rabbits. *Journal of the Autonomic Nervous System, 4,* 261–281.

Hernandez, L. L., & Powell, D. A. (1981). Forebrain norepinephrine and serotonin concentrations and Pavlovian conditioning in septal damaged and normal rabbits. *Brain Research Bulletin, 6,* 479–486.

Hess, W. (1957). *Functional organization of the diencephalon.* New York: Grune & Stratton.

Jarrell, T. W., McCabe, P. M., Teich, A. H., Gentile, C. G., VanDercar, D. H., & Schneiderman, N. (in press). Lateral subthalamic area as mediator of classically conditioned bradycardia in rabbits. *Behavioral Neuroscience.*

Jarrell, T. W., Gentile, C. G., McCabe, P. M., & Schneiderman, N. (in press). The medial geniculate nucleus as mediator of differential Pavlovian conditioning of bradycardia in rabbits. *Brain Research.*

Jordan, D., Khalid, M., Schneiderman, N., & Spyer, K. M. (1979). The inhibitory control of vagal cardiomotor neurons. *Journal of Physiology (London), 296,* 20–21.

Jordan, D., Khalid, M. E. M., Schneiderman, N., & Spyer, K. M. (1982). Localization and properties of ganglionic cardiomotor neurons in rabbits. *Pflugers Archiv, 395,* 244–250.

Kaada, B. R. (1960). Cingulate, posterior orbital, anterior insular, and temporal pole cortex. In J. Field, H. W. Magoun, & V. E. Hall (Eds.), *Handbook of physiology,* (Vol. II). Baltimore: Williams & Wilkins.

Kandel, E. R., & Spencer, W. A. (1968). Cellular neurophysiolgoical approaches to learning. *Physiological Review, 48,* 65–134.

Kapp, B. S., Frysinger, R. C., Gallagher, M., & Haselton, J. R. (1979). Amygdala central nucleus lesions: Effect on heart rate conditioning in the rabbit. *Physiology and Behavior, 23,* 1109–1117.

Kapp, B. S., Gallagher, M., Underwood, M. D., McNall, C. C., & Whitehorn, D. (1982). Cardiovascular responses elicited by electrical stimulation of the amlygdala central nucleus in the rabbit. *Brain Research, 234,* 251–262.

Kaufman, M. P., Hamilton, R. B., Wallach, J. H., Petrik, G. K., & Schneiderman, N. (1979). Lateral subthalamic area as mediator of bradycardia responses in rabbits. *American Journal of Physiology, 236,* H471–H479.

Kumada, M., Dampney, R. A. L., & Reis, D. J. (1975). The trigeminal depressor response: A cardiovascular reflex originating from the trigeminal system. *Brain Research, 92,* 485–489.

Kumada, M., Dampney, R. A. L., & Reis, D. J. (1977). The trigeminal depressor response: A novel vasodepressor response originating from the trigeminal system. *Brain Research, 119,* 305–326.

Kumada, M., Reis, D. J., Terui, N., & Dampney, R. A. L. (1979). The trigeminal depressor response and its role in the control of cardiovascular functions. In C. Mc C.Brooks, K. Koizumi, & A. Sato (Eds.), *Integrative functions of the autonomic nervous system.* Tokyo: University of Tokyo Press.

Lico, M. C., Hoffman, A., & Covian, M. R. (1968). Autonomic conditioning in the anesthetized rabbit. *Physiology and Behavior, 3,* 673–675.

Liskowsky, D. R., Ellenberger, H. H., Haselton, J. R., & Schneiderman, N. (1981). Descending bradycardia pathway(s) from parabrachial nucleus in rabbits. *Neuroscience Abstracts, 7,* 824.

Magnitskii, A. M. (1953). Attempt to apply the "dominant" concept to the analyses of blood pressure changes in hypertension, "Problemly eksperimental 'noi gipert. onicheskoi bolezni," *Trudy Akad. Med. Nauk. 3:22.* Cited by E. Simonson & J. Brojek, Russian research on arterial hypertension. *Annuals of Internal Medicine,* 129–193.

McAllen, R. M., & Spyer, K. M. (1976). The location of cardiac pre-ganglionic motoneurones in the medulla of the cat. *Journal of Physiology (London), 258,* 187–204.

McAllen, R. M., & Spyer, K. M. (1978). Two types of vagal preganglionic motoneurones projecting to the heart and lungs. *Journal of Physiology (London), 282,* 353–364.

McCormick, D. A., Lavond, D. G., Clark, G. A., & Thompson, R. F. (1981). Ipsilateral cerebellar lesions abolish a simple learned response. *Bulletin of the Psychonomic Society, 18*(2), 69.

McCormick, D. A., Lavond, D. G., Clark, G. A., Kettner, R. E., Rising, C. E., & Thompson, R. F. (1981). The engram found questionable: Role of the cerebellum in classical-conditioning of nictitating membrane and eyelid responses. *Bulletin of the Psychonomic Society, 18*(3), 103–105.

Obrist, P. A. (1965). Heart rate during conditioning in dogs: Relationship to respiration and gross bodily movements. *Proceedings of 73rd Annual Convention of the American Psychological Association,* 165–166.

Obrist, P. A. (1981). *Cardiovascular psychophysiology: A perspective.* New York: Plenum Press.

Obrist, P. A., & Webb, R. A. (1967). Heart rate during conditioning in dogs: Relationship to somatic-motor activity. *Psychophysiology, 4,* 7–34.

Powell, D. A., & Buchanan, S. L. (1980). Autonomic-somatic relationships in the rabbit (*Oryctolagus Cuniculus*): Effects of hippocampal lesions. *Physiological Psychology, 8,* 455–462.

Powell, D. A., Goldberg, S. R., Dauth, G. W., Schneiderman, E., & Schneiderman, N. (1972). Adrenergic and cholinergic blockade of cardiovascular responses to subcortical electrical stimulation in unanesthetized rabbits. *Physiology and Behavior, 8,* 927–935.

Rushmer, R. F. (1962). Effects of nerve stimulation and hormones on the heart: The role of the heart in general circulatory regulation. In W. F. Hamilton (Ed.), *Handbook of physiology: Circulation.* (2nd ed., Sec. 2, Vol. 1, pp. 533–550). Washington: American Physiology Society.

Rushmer, R. F., & Smith, O. A. (1959). Cardiac control. *Physiological Review, 39,* 41–68.

Rodgers, R. J. (1978). Influence of intra-amygdaloid opiate injection on shock thresholds, tail flick latencies, and open field behavior in rats. *Brain Research, 153,* 211–216.

Sampson, L. D., Wallach, J., Schneiderman, N., & Francis, J. S. (1977). Differential cardiovascular changes as a function of stimulation electrode site in rabbit hypothalamus. *Physiology and Behavior, 19,* 111–120.

Sar, M., Stumpf, W. E., Miller, R. G., Chang, K. G., & Cuatrecasas, P. (1979). Immunohistochemical localiation of enkephalin in rat brain and spinal cord. *Journal of Comparative Neurology, 182,* 17–38.

Schmidt, C. F. (1932). Carotid sinus reflexes to the respiratory center. *American Journal of Physiology, 102,* 94–118.

Schneiderman, N. (1970). Determinants of heart-rate conditioning. In J. Reynierse (Ed.), *Current issues in animal learning* (pp. 85–115). University of Nebraska Press.

Schneiderman, N. (1972). Response system divergences in aversive classical conditioning. In A. H. Black & W. F. Prokasy (Eds.), *Classical conditioning*. New York:Appleton–Crofts.

Schneiderman, N. (1973). *Classical (Pavlovian) conditioning*. Morristown, NJ: General Learning Press.

Schneiderman, N., Smith, M. C., Smith, A. C., & Gormezano, I. (1966). Heart-rate classical conditioning in rabbits. *Psychonomic Science, 6,* 241–242.

Schneiderman, N., VanDercar, D. H., Yehle, A. L., Manning, A. A., Golden, T., & Schneiderman, E. (1969). Vagal compensatory adjustment: Relationship to heart-rate classical conditioning in rabbits. *Journal of Comparative and Physiological Psychology, 68,* 176–183.

Schwaber, J. S., Kapp, B. S., & Higgins, G. (1980). The origin and extent of direct amygdala projections to the region of the dorsal motor nucleus of the vagus and the nucleus of the solitary tract. *Neuroscience Letters, 20,* 15–20.

Schwaber, J. S., Kapp, B. S., Higgins, G. A., & Rapp, P. R. (1982). Amygdaloid and basal forebrain direct connections with the nucleus of the solitary tract and the dorsal motor nucleus. *Journal of Neurosciences, 2,*(11), 1414–1438.

Schwaber, J., & Schneiderman, N. (1975). Aortic nerve activated cardioinhibitory neurons and interneurons. *American Journal of Physiology, 229,* 783–789.

Sideroff, S., Elster, A. J., & Schneiderman, N. (1972). Cardiovascular conditioning in rabbits using appetitive or aversive hypothalamus stimulation as the US. *Journal of Comparative and Physiological Psychology, 81,* 501–508.

Simantov, R., Kuhar, M. J., Uhl, G. R., & Snyder, S. H. (1977). Opioid peptide enkephalin: Immunohistochemical mapping in rat central nervous system. *Proceedings of the National Academy of Science (USA), 74,* 2167–2171.

Smith, O. A., Devito, J. L., & Astley, C. H. (1982). The hypothalamus in emotional behavior and associated cardiovascular correlates. In A. R. Morrison & P. L. Strick (Eds.), *Changing concepts of the nervous system* (pp. 569–584). New York: Academic Press.

VanDercar, D. H., Elster, A. J., & Schneiderman, N. (1970). Heart-rate conditioning in rabbits to hypothalamic or septal US stimulation. *Journal of Comparative and Physiological Psychology, 72,* 145–152.

Wallach, J. H., Ellenberger, H. H., Schneiderman, N., Liskowsky, D. R., Hamilton, R. B., & Gellman, M. D. (1979). Preoptic-anterior hypothalamic area as a mediator of bradycardia responses in rabbits. *Society for Neuroscience Abstracts, 5,* 52.

Wang, S. C., & Ranson, S. W. (1939). Autonomic responses to electrical stimulation of the lower brainstem. *Journal of Comparative Neurology, 71,* 437–455.

Ward, D. G., Grizzle, W. E., & Grann, D. S. (1976). Inhibitory and faciliatory areas of the rostral pons mediating ACTH release in the cat. *Endocrinology, 99,* 1220–1228.

West, C. H. K., Jackson, J. C., & Benjamin, R. M. (1979). An autoradiographic study of subcortical forebrain projections from mediodorsal and adjacent midline thalamic nuclei in the rabbit. *Neuroscience, 4,* 1977–1978.

Yehle, A., Dauth, G., & Schneiderman, N. (1967). Correlates of heart rate conditioning in curarized rabbits. *Journal of Comparative and Physiological Psychology, 64,* 98–104.

3 Identification of the Substrates of the Unconditioned Response in the Classically Conditioned, Rabbit, Nictitating-Membrane Preparation

Craig F. Cegavske
Theresa A. Harrison
Yasuhiro Torigoe
Department of Psychology and Center for Neurobehavioral Sciences
State University of New York

INTRODUCTION

This book is devoted to describing how one mammalian brain, that of the rabbit, functions during the environmental pressures that cause associative learning to occur. This chapter describes the reflex system that mediates closure of the nictitating membrane (NM) when a potentially noxious stimulus impinges on the eye region of the face in that species. It is this reflex that has been used in behavioral studies as the unconditioned response (UCR) system for a variety of training procedures, notably classical conditioning.

Describing the anatomy and physiology of this reflex pathway was adopted as the research approach necessary to lay the foundation for a causal analysis of the neural substrates of learning underlying classical conditioning in the rabbit NM preparation. The emphasis of the last statement is on causal

---

C. F. Cegavske's current address is 3747 Farnham Place, Riverside, CA 92503.

T. A. Harrison's current address is Department of Anatomy, Emory University, Atlanta, Georgia 30322.

Y. Torigoe's current address is Department of Anatomy, California College of Medicine, University of California at Irvine, Irvine, CA 92717.

analysis of substrates: That is, there is a distinction between neural correlates of learning and neural substrates of learning that has major implications for research into mechanisms of learning.

Substrates vs. Correlates

The rationale for the approach to be described here relies on an understanding of both the conceptual distinction between correlates and substrates, and the experimental procedures necessary for distinguishing between them within the nervous system. At this writing, no one can point to a group of brain structures and say, "in a particular environmental situation (e.g., a training procedure), these structures are necessary and sufficient to cause the organism to change its behavior from A to B." Even farther removed is the ability to say, "the cellular and subcellular mechanisms of associative learning are. . . ." The identification of such a group of structures has been elusive because the complexity (i.e., the number of interacting parts) of the mammalian brain has made it impossible to determine which groups of neurons in the central nervous system (CNS) are causally involved in the particular behavioral change being studied. Without knowledge of the appropriate brain structures to study, it is not possible to study underlying cellular mechanisms and, at the same time, be sure they are causally involved in the behavior of interest. It is easy to find some change in the brain that is correlated with a learned change of behavior. Indeed, there is a voluminous literature of structural changes, chemical changes, evoked potential changes, and cellular-activity changes that occur during one training procedure or another. It is not so easy to identify a specific structure as being a substrate of the behavior, or to specify just how such changes participate in producing the learned change of behavior.

From the conceptual standpoint, the nervous system processes information about many things simultaneously during a training procedure. These include body functions that have nothing to do with the learned behavior being studied, functions that are involved in the learning process (e.g., sensory, motor, motivational) but that are not directly involved in the association of information itself, and the actual associations of information that allow the conditioned response (CR) to develop. If the neural tissue containing the latter mechanism is the object of search, one can ignore the first of these types of information processing. The second, however, cannot be disposed of so easily because it involves two classes of information that must be distinguished: Information that is in the direct line of transmission to, or from, the cells responsible for making the association (cells that are therefore necessary for the association and resultant behavior to occur), and corollary information that is being sent to other brain structures that have no direct involvement with the association. Clearly, neural structures mediating the former would be classified as a substrate of the learned behavior. Structures mediating the latter would not, even though their activity might be highly correlated with the learned behavior. The distinction between the two classes of information cannot be made a priori. It can only be made from a framework that causally links the learned behavior to the appropriate antecedent neural events.

From the experimental standpoint, the solution to the problem of distinguishing substrates from correlates is obvious, and has been employed in some "model system" and "simple system" approaches. That is, the anatomical circuitry that mediates the learned behavior must be identified. The parts that are involved only in the transmission of information are identified and functionally separated from the parts that are actually involved in the processing of the information that leads to the learned behavioral response. Without knowing the neural circuitry involved, it is impossible to know whether changes seen in the nervous system result from the causative processes producing the behavioral change, or are simply a result of other corollary processes. Once the brain structures that do the processing are identified, it will be possible to study changes within those structures to determine the cellular mechanisms involved in the associational process while being sure that the proper brain structures are being studied.

Thus, before a fine-grained analysis of cellular mechanisms can occur, the anatomical circuitry must be identified. In mammals this may appear to be impossible because of the complexity of the brain. It is perhaps for this reason that very little work has been done to differentiate substrates of mammalian behaviors from correlates of those behaviors, even though it would seem that the best place to study the mammalian brain is in the mammalian brain itself. Instead, many interesting and valuable "model systems" have been developed using reduced (e.g., spinal cat) or invertebrate (e.g., *Aplysia*) preparations. An extremely important feature of these preparations is their relatively simple underlying anatomical circuitry. It limits the number of structures that must be investigated when looking for mechanisms responsible for the changes in behavior. Through the investigation of such systems it may well be possible to discover synaptic mechanisms and cellular interactions that prove to be the same as those operating in the mammalian brain. In fact, knowledge of such mechanisms could speed the discovery of similar mechanisms in the mammalian brain (it is easier to find something if you know what you are looking for). However, if the focus of interest is on how learning occurs in the mammalian brain, these "simple" and "model" systems have a significant drawback. They cannot provide an adequate solution by themselves because they do not have the same neural systems (e.g., thalamus, cortex, limbic, basal ganglia) interacting with each other as does the intact mammalian brain.

"Simple" and "model" systems preparations may provide invaluable information about the component parts of neurobiological systems that could be applicable to many species. To use an analogy to emphasize this point, a computer and a transistor radio might be built from identical semiconductor junctions (transistors). Understanding semiconductor junctions and their interactions would be essential for understanding how each system worked. However, each electronic system would have to be investigated in its own right to discover how the components were logically organized to form two different types of functional (logical) systems. Similarly, until a number of nervous systems in different species have been investigated (from their intact behaviors through the anatomical, physiological, and chemical substrates of those behaviors) it will not be possible to determine if the same mechanisms are at work in each. For the moment, one must be content with studying various nervous systems in their own right. Not until the substrates underlying a specific type of behavioral plasticity (training procedure) have been demonstrated in at least two types of organisms will it be possible to make meaningful comparisons of mechanisms. Because, at the present time, there are no a priori grounds for determining what kinds of mechanisms will be generalizable, nor the organizational level(s) at which they will be found, the neural substrates of a particular mammalian behavior can best be studied within the context of the systems in the brain of that mammal.

The Rabbit Nictitating Membrane Preparation

Analysis of the classically conditioned rabbit NM preparation was undertaken with the hope of reproducing, in the mammalian brain, the success of the circuit-analysis approach used in "simple-system" preparations. The essence of the circuit-analysis approach is to functionally identify the neural elements that constitute a necessary and sufficient system within which the learned change in behavior can develop. The interacting parts of this system can then be studied in terms of cellular and subcellular mechanisms involved in producing the learned change in behavior. In addition, the circuit can then be studied within the context of the whole brain, that is, in terms of the influences exerted upon it from external (to the circuit) modulating or controlling systems. Describing the circuit, however, is in itself an experimental process of many steps. In the rabbit NM preparation, a complete description of the NM reflex arc, i.e., the unconditioned response (UCR) pathway, is the first step in this analysis.

Generating a Space-Time Map of the UCR Pathway

Because the UCR is elicited on every trial, the UCR pathway is always functioning during the training procedures used for classical conditioning. In the

NM preparation, the UCR and the CR are both extensions of the NM. It is the onset latency of NM extension relative to the conditioning stimulus (CS) that distinguishes between the two responses. If extension begins after the CS, but prior to the UCS, the response is defined as a CR. Both the UCR and the CR are mediated by the same motor system (see the following). Logically then, the neural changes underlying the CR either develop within the confines of the UCR pathway or they do not. If they do not, neural information reflecting these changes must enter the UCR pathway somewhere. It is unlikely that the CR is developed within the UCR pathway (Torigoe, Owen, & Cegavske, 1983), therefore, it is of major importance to locate where CR information enters this pathway. Systematically tracing the connections from other brain structures into the UCR pathway should then set the stage for meaningful experiments about the participation of these structures in the conditioning phenomenon.

In order to identify the point (or points) where CR information enters the UCR pathway, it will be useful to develop a "space-time map" of the functioning UCR circuit. *Space* refers to the anatomical location of structures, or parts of structures, which are elements of the pathway. *Time* refers to when, in relation to the externally measured stimulus and behavioral events, information about these events is being processed through each of the component structures. It is necessary to characterize the neural information processing going on within the UCR pathway during unconditioned behavior if a change in the processing is to be detected when the conditioned response develops.

THE UNCONDITIONED RESPONSE PATHWAY

Because anatomical identification of the elements of the UCR pathway is the first and fundamental step in the strategy outlined previously, a large part of the research underway in our laboratory has been directed toward this aspect of the circuit analysis. In the following discussion the anatomical pathway, and the temporal characteristics of physiological activity through the pathway, will be considered to the extent that they are known. Our plan has been to characterize the UCR pathway in four stages: First, anatomically identify the effectors of NM behavior and the set of projection neurons (composed of sensory, internuncial, and motor components) that mediate the UCR; second, characterize the activity of cells within this set during the UCR to determine the time course of activity through the CNS; third, make discrete lesions (or knife cuts) through the axons of the projection neurons of the pathway to demonstrate behavioral disruption of the response; and fourth, determine synaptic interactions in the local circuitry at each relay point to determine the function of local circuit neurons, if any, that may be critical elements in the functional pathway.

Stage 1

Stage 1 involves the spatial localization of effectors and projection neurons that are involved in mediating the UCR. These are considered in four categories: (a) the effectors, (b) the motoneurons, (c) the internuncials, and (d) the sensory neurons.

The Effectors.   The nictitating membrane (NM) of the rabbit is a triangular piece of cartilage covered with epithelial tissue. In its normal resting position in the nasal canthus of the eye, only a small edge of the membrane epithelium is usually visible. Movement of the NM occurs as part of defensive reflexes of the eye. Stimulation of the cornea, or the eye region of the face, produces a reflex response involving three individually identifiable components: (a) withdrawal of the eyeball into the socket, (b) extension of the NM across all or part of the cornea, and (c) eyelid closure. In classical-conditioning training procedures utilizing this defensive reflex, the eyelids often are artificially held open so that extension of the NM can be measured without impediment. Extension of the NM, not eyelid closure or eyeball retraction, typically is measured as the unconditioned and conditioned responses.

Although recent research has cleared up much of the controversy generated by earlier reports, the peripheral effectors and mechanisms responsible for movement of the NM have not been completely specified as yet. The major questions usually asked about peripheral mechanisms of NM extension are presented here, along with the accumulated evidence and the conclusions that can be drawn.

1. Is the extension of the NM an independent event produced by the muscle attached to the NM, or is it a secondary event resulting as a consequence of eyeball withdrawal? The latter has been found to be true. The only muscle fibers directly inserting on the NM (see Fig. 3.1A) are part of the nasal branch of the levator palpebrae superioris (LPS) muscle of the eyelid (Harrison & Cegavske, 1981; Prince, 1964). These muscle fibers, when activated, have been shown to cause only NM retraction (Harrison & Cegavske, 1981). For NM extension to occur, withdrawal of the intact globe into the orbit is essential. If the eyeball is deflated, so that withdrawal does not produce compression and displacement of the orbital contents, the NM will not extend (Cegavske, Thompson, Patterson, & Gormezano, 1976).

2. What is the effector for eyeball withdrawal? It has been well established that the primary effector for this movement is the retractor bulbi (RB) muscle, which pulls the globe into the orbit (see Fig. 3.1B). Severing the attachments of the other extraocular muscles to the globe, leaving only the RB intact, does not alter the NM extension response (Bertheir & Moore, 1980; Mis, 1977). Electrical stimulation of the peripheral sixth nerve, which inner-

vates the RB and the lateral rectus muscle, produces only eyeball withdrawal and NM extension (Cegavske et al., 1976). It has been reported that lesioning the ipsilateral sixth nerve roots at the base of the brain eliminates eyeball withdrawal and NM extension to corneal stimulation (Cegavske et al., 1976), or at least dramatically reduces it (Berthier & Moore, 1980).

3. Is the retractor bulbi muscle the only effector contributing to NM extension? If the stimulus causing NM extension is only mildly noxious (e.g., an air puff), the answer to this quesiton seems to be yes. In terms of producing a normal, full, NM response, the RB is both necessary and sufficient for the response whereas the other extraocular muscles are not. The RB is necessary because lesions of the abducens nerve, which contains most of the innervation to the RB, eliminates normal NM extension to an air puff stimulus (Cegavske et al., 1976) and markedly reduces it when the stimulus is purposely made strong enough to produce a "maximal" response (Berthier & Moore, 1980). The reduced-amplitude retraction that remains in the latter case is presumably produced by the other extraocular muscles, that have their innervation still intact. The RB is sufficient to cause full NM responses after all the other extrocular muscles have been cut (Mis, 1977). These studies also demonstrate that the other extraocular muscles are neither necessary (Mis, 1977) nor sufficient (Berthier & Moore, 1980; Cegavske et al., 1976) to produce a full NM response. This interpretation of RB function is consistent with findings in the cat where it has been reported that only the part of the RB innervated by the accessory abducens nucleus is responsible for eyeball retraction. The two other sources of innervation to the RB (from the abducens and oculomotor nuclei) probably act in coordinated eye movements, not in retraction (Baker, McCrea, & Spencer, 1980). It would seem that the RB is primarily an effector for eyeball retraction and secondarily involved in coordinated eye movements whereas the other extraocular muscles are able to effect partial retraction of the eyeball only under the most severe conditions. It should be noted, however, that the other extraocular muscles (Lorente de No, 1933) and the motoneurons innervating at least some of them (Harrison, Cegavske, & Thompson, 1978) are active during eyeball retraction, probably to shorten these muscles as the globe retracts, allowing control over coordinated movements to be maintained (Harrison et al., 1978).

4. What role does the muscle attached to the NM play in the control of NM movement? This muscle, just described as part of the nasal branch of the LPS, plays a role in retraction (reopening) of the NM. Retraction, in this case, refers to pulling the NM into the nasal canthus of the eye. As part of the LPS muscle that maintains eyelid elevation, this muscle would be expected to relax when the eyelids close, and contract when the eyelids reopen. Normally, eyelid closure occurs simultaneously with NM extension, and eyelid reopening with NM retraction. Thus, at the periphery, eyelid and NM move-

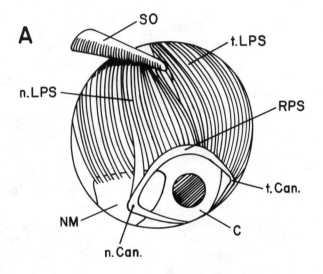

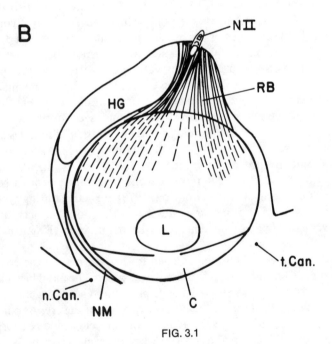

FIG. 3.1

ments appear not to be completely independent. Empirically, electrical stimulation of the ipsilateral oculomotor nerve, which innervates the LPS, results in a pulling of the NM toward the nasal corner of the eye (Cegavske et al., 1976), as does direct electrical stimulation of the muscle fibers inserting on the NM (Harrison & Cegavske, 1981). However, return of the NM to its resting position in the nasal canthus is in part passive, depending on the return of the withdrawn eyeball and the displaced Harder's gland to their normal resting positions. Whether the active retraction occurs as part of normal NM behavior has yet to be determined.

In summary, the picture of peripheral mechanisms of NM movement has become clearer as a result of recent investigations. The accumulated evidence now indicates that NM movement is primarily controlled by two muscles: the retractor bulbi (RB) muscle, which indirectly causes NM extension; and the nasal branch of the levator palpebrae superioris muscle (LPS), which can produce NM retraction. (The exceptions to this statement are, first, that slight NM movements of up to about a millimeter can be mechanically caused by connective tissue from the eyelids when the latter move [Cegavske et al., 1976], and, second, that the extraocular muscles [other than the RB] may cause partial NM closure when the cornea is subjected to a stimulus of tissue-damaging intensity [Berthier & Moore, 1980].) Nictitating membrane extension is a secondary effect of the contracting RB muscle. The primary effect of RB contraction is to pull the eyeball into the socket. Withdrawal of the eyeball displaces the less compressible contents of the orbit, including the

---

FIG. 3.1 *(Opposite page)* Diagrams of the left eye of the rabbit illustrating the muscles that cause nictitating membrane (NM) movement. A) The position of the levator palpebrae superioris (LPS) muscle in relation to the NM in its normal resting position with the upper eyelid open. Note that it is part of the nasal LPS that inserts on the NM, and that its physical position allows it to retract the NM only (Redrawn from Harrison & Cegavske, 1981). B) A horizontal view (from a dorsal perspective) through the center of the eye showing the relative positions of the NM, the retractor bulbi (RB) muscle, and the Harder's gland (HG). (The dorsal part of the lateral rectus muscle would be just below the plane of section and the ventral part of the medial rectus just above it.) The optic nerve and the origin of the RB have been drawn slightly more ventral than normal (i.e., they normally reach the bone slightly above the plane of section shown) for illustrative purposes. The RB muscle appears to be divided into four major slips. The positions of the ventral two (under the globe) are shown with dashed lines. Contraction of this muscle pulls the eye into the socket compressing HG that in turn forces the NM to extend over the cornea. The approximate locations of the nasal and temporal canthi are shown (i.e., where they would be) although the eyelids, conjunctiva, and skin have not been included in the drawings. Abbreviations: C = cornea; HG = Harder's gland; L = lens; NM = nictitating membrane; NII = optic nerve; n.Can. = nasal canthus; n.LPS = nasal levator palpebrae superioris muscle; RB = retractor bulbi muscle; RPS = rima palpebrae superioris; SO = superior oblique muscle; t.Can. = temporal canthus; t.LPS = temporal levator palpebrae superioris muscle.

Harder's gland that attaches to the cartilage of the nictitating membrane. As the Harder's gland is compressed by the retracted eyeball, it pushes the NM out from the nasal canthus across the cornea toward the temporal canthus. Return of the eyeball to its resting position returns the Harder's gland to its usual place and the NM retracts back into the nasal canthus. NM retraction may be directly assisted by the nasal branch of the LPS muscle, which is presumably contracting as the eyelids reopen following the eyeball withdrawal — NM extension — eyelid closure response.

Several questions remain unanswered about these peripheral mechanisms. First, of what significance is the activation of the extraocular muscles during eyeball retraction? What roles does active retraction of the NM by the LPS play in normal NM movement control? Finally, at a more general level, what degree of independence exists between the systems responsible for eyelid movement and those for NM movement, and at what levels do interactions occur? These questions will be most effectively answered through investigations of central mechanisms of NM-movement control and their relationship to underlying mechanisms of ocular-motor coordination.

The Motoneurons.   The first step in determining how the CNS might produce NM behavior is to determine the central locus of motor control of the muscles involved. Because of their established roles in NM movement control, the RB and LPS muscles have been focused on. Extension of the NM, produced by the RB muscle, is the parameter that defines both UCR and CR behaviors. Retraction of the NM by the LPS also is a component of the complete behavioral response, and has potential significance particularly in relation to mechanisms involved in extinction and differential conditioning. The motor end of the UCR pathway thus could be defined by locating the motoneurons in the brain stem innervating these two muscles, and determining the course of their axons through the brain and cranial nerves. This has been accomplished by means of retrograde transport of horseradish peroxidase (HRP) from the peripheral muscles.

Recent results of injections of HRP into the RB muscle have been reported for the cat (Glendenning, Hutson, & Masterton, 1979; Grant, Gueritaud, Horcholle-Bossavit, & Tyc-Dumont, 1979; Guegan, Gueritaud, & Horcholle-Bossavit, 1978l;Spencer, Baker, & McCrea, 1980) and the rabbit (Berthier & Moore, 1980; Disterhoft & Shipley, 1980; Gray, McMaster, Harvey, & Gormezano, 1981; Harrison, Torigoe, & Cegavske, 1983). These studies have reported one (Grant et al., 1979; Guegan et al., 1978), two (Berthier & Moore, 1980; Glendenning et al., 1979; Gray et al., 1981), or three (Harrison et al., 1983; Spencer et al., 1980) groups of motoneurons innervating this muscle. All reports agree that the accessory abducens nucleus provides the primary innervation to the muscle. Disagreement rises over whether other brain-stem nuclei also innervate it. We believe (Harrison et al., 1983) along with Spencer et al. (1980) that the RB is innervated by cells in the accessory abducens, the abducens, and the oculomotor nuclei. Some of the other studies also reported occasional transport of HRP to all three cell groups but the investigators believed this was caused by occasional leakage of HRP outside the desired injection site. The discrepancies probably are due to the different sensitivities of the various HRP procedures used. Additional evidence supporting the three-group results comes from electrophysiological work in the cat demonstrating that motoneurons in the oculomotor (Meredith, McClung, & Goldberg, 1981) and the abducens (Crandall, Wilson, & Goldberg, 1977) nuclei cause contractions in the RB muscle.

The results from our HRP work tracing the innervation of the RB muscle in the rabbit are summarized here (Harrison et al., 1983). All of the motoneurons in the accessory abducens nucleus were densely labeled following HRP injections into the RB muscle. The pathways of the axons from the accessory abducens and abducens nuclei are drawn in Fig 3.2. Axons leaving the accessory abducens traveled dorsally, almost directly toward the abducens nucleus. Tracing the course of individual axons demonstrated that they turned ventrally either below the abducens nucleus, or within the lower portion of that nucleus, and joined fibers from the abducens nucleus that emerge from the brain stem as the abducens nerve.

In the abducens nucleus, a sub-population of motoneurons was labeled by HRP injections into the RB muscle (Fig. 3.2). These cells were less densely labeled with the HRP reaction product and were smaller in size than the accessory abducens motoneurons.

Figure 3.3 shows the extent of the labeling seen in the oculomotor nucleus after RB injections of HRP. These cells also were not as densely labeled as those in the accessory abducens nucleus. They were a subgroup of the motoneurons comprising the medial and inferior rectus muscle groups (Akagi, 1978; Harrison et al., 1983), and their axons could be traced within the ipsilateral oculomotor nerve.

The outcome of these experiments indicates that three distinct groups of motoneurons innervate the RB muscle: the group making up the accessory abducens nucleus, a subgroup of cells within the group innervating the lateral rectus muscle (in the abducens nucleus), and a subgroup of cells within the group innervating the medial and inferior rectus muscles (in the oculomotor nucleus). Anatomically these three groups, taken together, contain the final common pathway for eyeball withdrawal and consequent NM extension. Whether or not all three are involved in producing the NM response remains to be conclusively demonstrated. However, it is argued later that the accessory abducens motoneurons are the motoneurons primarily, if not solely, responsible for this response when the animal is intact and normally responding to an air puff.

We now switch to the motor output that can cause retraction of the NM

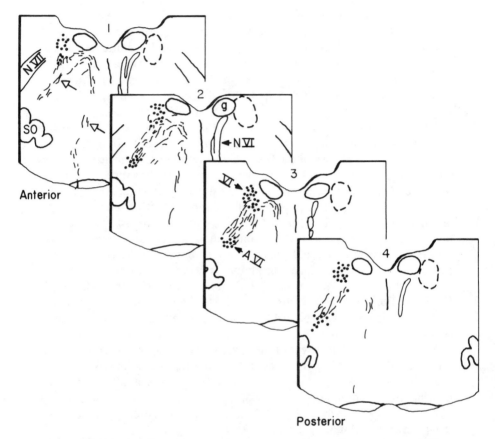

FIG. 3.2 Coronal-plane sections showing two of the three groups (see Fig. 3.3 for the third) of motoneurons (dots) innervating the retractor bulbi muscle, and the course of their axons (fine lines, identified by open arrows in section 1) through the brain stem. The cells in the abducens and accessory abducens nuclei, and their axons, were labeled after HRP was applied to the proximal end of the cut sixth nerve that had innervated the retractor bulbi muscle of the left eye. The composite drawings were each made by superimposing data from six 40-micron sections. The left side of each drawing shows labeled structures while the right side shows the morphological position of the structures. Abbreviations: AVI = accessory abducens nucleus: NVI = abducens nerve; NVII = facial nerve; Open arrows = labeled axons in abducens nerve; SO = superior olive; VI = abducens nucleus. (Modified from Harrison, Torigoe, & Cegavske, 1983)

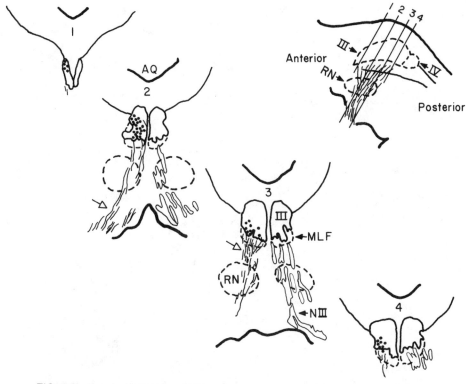

FIG. 3.3   Drawings of the oculomotor nucleus showing one of the three groups of motoneurons (dots) that innervate the retractor bulbi muscle (see Fig. 3.2 for the other two groups). These drawings were made using individual 40-micron sections from the same animal described in Fig. 3.2. The sagittal-plane drawing, in the upper right corner of the figure, shows the plane of the coronal sections through the midbrain. Abbreviations: AQ = cerebral aqueduct; MLF = medial longitudinal fasciculus; NIII = oculomotor nerve; Open arrows = labeled axons of the oculomotor nerve; RN = red nucleus; III = oculomotor nucleus; IV = trochlear nucleus. (Modified from Harrison, Torigoe, & Cegavske, 1983)

after it has been extended. The motoneurons responsible (Fig. 3.4) send their axons to the nasal branch of the LPS muscle, and were found contralateral to the injected muscle in the oculomotor nucleus (Akagi, 1978; Harrison et al., 1983). The majority of these cells formed a crescent shaped group that extended from the dorsal part of the oculomotor nucleus (start with section 2 in Fig. 3.4) caudally around the lateral aspect of the nucleus. The group then turned medially at the boundary of the trochlear nucleus. It continued its turn around the caudal part of the oculomotor nucleus until it extended rostrally, for a short distance, along the ventromedial edge of the nucleus.

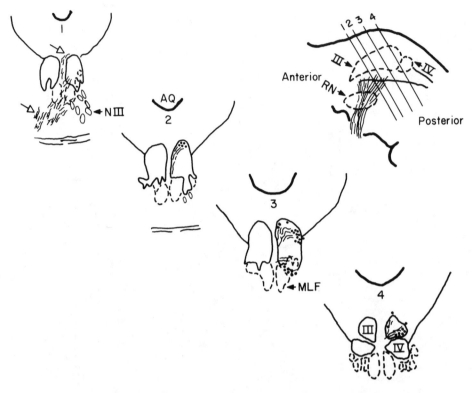

FIG. 3.4   Drawings of the oculomotor nucleus showing the neurons that innervate the part of the left nasal levator palpebrae superioris (n.LPS) muscle that is attached to the nictitating membrane. The contralateral motoneurons (dots) and their axons (fine lines, identified by the open arrows in section 1) were labeled after HRP injection into the n.LPS muscle. These drawings were made from individual 40-micron sections. The sagittal-plane drawing in the upper right corner of the figure, shows the locations of the coronal-plane sections through the midbrain. Abbreviations: AQ = cerebral aqueduct; MLF = medial longitudinal fasciculus; NIII = oculomotor nerve; Open arrows = labeled axons of the oculomotor nerve; RN = red nucleus; III = oculomotor nucleus; IV = trochlear nucleus. (Modified from Harrison, Torigoe, & Cegavske, 1983)

The axons of these cells could be traced coursing through the oculomotor nucleus to the midline and into the rostral portion of the nucleus ipsilateral to the injected muscle. They turned ventrally at the midline, or in the ipsilateral nucleus, and joined fibers of the ipsilateral third nerve (section 1 in Fig. 3.4). This positioning of LPS motoneurons, relative to other motoneuron groups in the oculmotor nucleus, is different from the situation in the cat and monkey where a medial LPS motoneuron group is found (Akagi, 1978; Tarlov & Tarlov, 1971; Warwick, 1953).

The Internuncials.   So far the motor components of the UCR pathway have been discussed. The afferents to the motoneurons are considered now. One set of these afferents could come from the trigeminal system and provide a single-neuron connection between the sensory and motor systems.

To test this single-internuncial hypothesis, HRP was injected into the abducens nucleus (Torigoe, Harrison, & Cegavske, 1983) and the accessory abducens nucleus (Torigoe, Owen & Cegavske, 1983). Afferents to the motoneurons in the oculomotor complex that project to the RB have not been studied yet. Results from the abducens study indicate that there are no trigeminal neurons, within the terminal fields of corneal afferents, that project directly into this nucleus. With small injections of HRP that were almost completely within the abducus nucleus, there were very few labeled cells in the trigeminal complex. This labeling was interpreted as being a result of HRP uptake by axons of passage that were damaged during the injection process (Torigoe, Harrison & Cegavske, 1983).

There are two additional bits of evidence supporting the nonexistence of a direct trigeminal-abducens connection. The first is a report that the dendrites of the cat abducens nucleus rarely extend outside of the cellular boundary of the nucleus (Highstein, Karabelas, Baker, & McCrea, 1982). If the dendrites are similar in the rabbit, our HRP injections should have covered all afferents. The second is a report, also using the cat, of intracellular recordings in the abducens nucleus where weak, long latency EPSPs (suggesting more than two synapses) were found after trigeminal nerve stimulation but rarely after stimulation of the cornea (Baker et al., 1980). If the connections are similar in the rabbit, there are two or more neurons interposed between the trigeminal and abducens nuclei. We concluded that the evidence does not support the kind of trigeminal-abducens connection necessary to mediate a robust nictitating membrane response (Torigoe, Harrison, & Cegavska, 1983).

The accessory abducens experiments did provide evidence of a single internuncial connecting the oralis and principalis division of the trigeminal complex with the accessory abducens nucleus (Fig. 3.5). When HRP injections were made small so that the injection site was almost contained within the boundaries of the nucleus, a few labeled cells were found in the trigeminal nuclei. However, when larger injections were made, that extended beyond the morphological boundaries of the nucleus (the dendrites of accessory abducens motoneurons extend outside the morphological boundary of the nucleus in the cat [Spencer et al., 1980]), transport was always found within the trigeminal nucleus.

Other direct evidence supporting the notion that these cells mediate the UCR includes responses of disynaptic latency being found in the accessory abducens nucleus of the cat (Baker et al., 1980) and the abducens nerve of the rabbit (Berthier & Moore, 1983) after activation of the trigeminal nerve. In

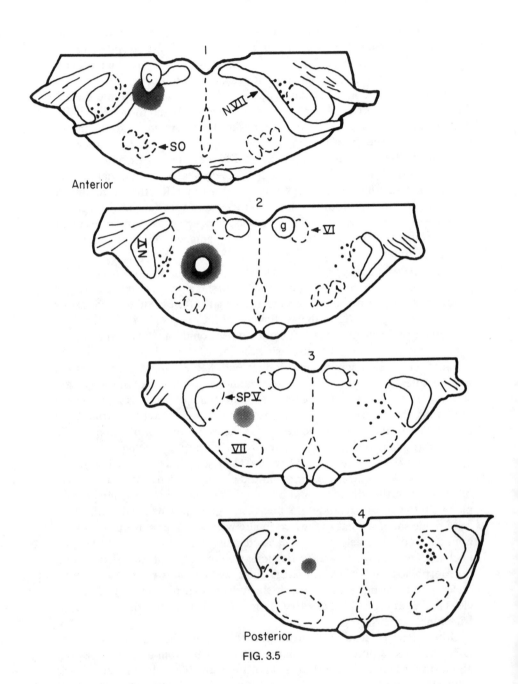

Anterior

Posterior

FIG. 3.5

addition, indirect evidence also supports the idea. The dendrites of the accessory abducens nucleus of the cat extend toward the spinal trigeminal nucelus (Spencer et al., 1980) as would be expected if the dendrites received an input from neurons in the latter structure (Ariens Kappers, 1917). Again this presupposes a similarity between the cat and the rabbit.

The Sensory Neurons. The next step was to determine what part of the trigeminal system relays sensory information from a UCS to the internuncials. Typically either an air puff or an electric shock to the eye-region of the face is used as the UCS for behavioral conditioning of the NM. The air puff is directed at the cornea, but the area of stimulation also includes the upper and lower eyelids because of the air-stream "fringe." When electric shock is used, it usually is administered to the skin around the eye so that current may spread to the cornea. In both conditions, parts of the ophthalmic and maxillary subdivisions of the trigeminal system are activated.

There is a potential problem for tracing the sensory input into the CNS that arises from the different ways electric-shock and air-puff stimuli activate the nervous system. Besides providing activation of tactile sensory units in the cornea and surrounding tissue, as an air puff does, electric shock may activate other structures as well. Such structures could include axons from motoneurons traveling to the muscles of the face (and could thus antidromically affect the CNS through collaterals), and sensory afferents from proprioceptors that would not be stimulated by a tactile stimulus. Electric shock is clearly a very effective behavioral UCS. However, it is not clear what effect this "nonphysiological" input might have on information processing in the CNS. The emphasis of our research program is on determining how the nervous sytem functions under normal conditions; therefore, the potential problem(s) created by electrical stimulation are being set aside here because

---

FIG. 3.5 *(Opposite page)* Composite drawings of coronal-plane sections through the abducens and accessory abducens nucleus showing neurons (dots) in the trigeminal complex that project to the left accessory abducens nucleus. The internuncials of the UCR pathway are probably in the part of the ipsilateral trigeminal nucleus shown in sections 1 and 2. Note that contralateral trigeminal neurons also project to the accessory abducens nucleus, suggesting a pathway for the reflex from the contralateral eye. Each of the drawings was made by superimposing data from three adjacent brain sections. The animals in this study had cannulas chronically implanted into the accessory abducens nucleus at least a week before an injection cannula was inserted to the bottom of these cannulas for administration of HRP. The black area in the injection site is the dark core of the site, whereas the gray represents the area of HRP diffusion. The right side of each section is slightly more posterior than the left due to the plane of section. Abbreviations: C = hole made by the implanted cannula; g = genu of the facial nerve; NV = trigeminal nerve; NVII = facial nerve; SO = superior olive; SPV = spinal trigeminal nucleus; VI = abducens nucleus; VII = facial nucleus. (Modified from Torigoe, Owen, & Cegavske, 1983)

the "nonphysiological" part of the sensory input is not necessary for conditioning to occur—a tactile stimulus to the cornea (e.g., an air puff) is sufficient.

The strategy used to identify the neurons that mediate UCS information has been to first localize the projections from the cornea to the trigeminal nuclei (spinal and principal) in the brain stem, then to determine the projections of the ophthalmic and maxillary areas of the face into the same nuclei. The result will be the characterization of the maximum set of neurons (from ophthalmic and maxillary areas) that could mediate UCS information as well as the most likely subset (from the cornea).

The projection from the cornea into the CNS have been demonstrated in the rabbit by using the HRP technique (Torigoe & Cegavske, 1983). From the cornea, the sensory neurons travel into the CNS, creating terminal fields along the whole extent of the sensory trigeminal nuclei—from the anterior part of the principal trigeminal nucleus to the posterior part of the spinal trigeminal nucleus between C2 and C3 (Fig. 3.6A).

In the principal trigeminal nucleus, the labeling showed most projections to be in the ventral half with a few in the dorsal half of the nucleus. The projections into the dorsal part were in two groups, one just lateral to the motor trigeminal nucleus and the other in the area of the nucleus adjacent to the dorsal side of the facial nerve. In the spinal trigeminal nucleus the terminal fields were primarily found in the ventral-most aspect with some spreading within the nucleus depending on the anterior-posterior location. In addition, in some areas, the terminal fields extended ventrally from the nucleus into regions of the reticular formation and the dorsal part of the facial nucleus, and dorso-medially into the nucleus of the solitary tract.

The projections from part of the ophthalmic area of the face also have been demonstrated in the rabbit by the HRP technique (Wenokor, Torigoe, & Cegavske, 1983). In this study, the supraorbital nerve was cut and the prox-

---

FIG. 3.6 *(Opposite page)* Drawings of individual coronal sections through the trigeminal complex showing the projections of primary sensory neurons into the brain stem. A) Sections showing labeled ipsilateral axons (lines) and terminal fields (dots) after application of HRP to the cornea of the left eye (Modified from Torigoe & Cegavske, 1983). B) Similar sections after encapsulation of the supraorbital part of the trigeminal nerve. Note that these projection areas largely overlap those from the cornea and are bigger (Modified from Wenokor, Torigoe, & Cegavske, 1983). Also, note that the area above the facial nerve (NVII) that contains sensory projections in this figure is the same area that contains the afferents to the accessory abducens shown in Fig. 3.5. Abbreviations: MV = motor trigeminal nucleus; NV = trigeminal nerve (tract); NVI = abducens nerve; NVII = facial nerve; PV = principal trigeminal nucelus; SO = superior olive; SPV = spinal trigeminal nucleus; STN = solitary tract nucleus; VI = abducens nucleus; VII = facial nucleus.

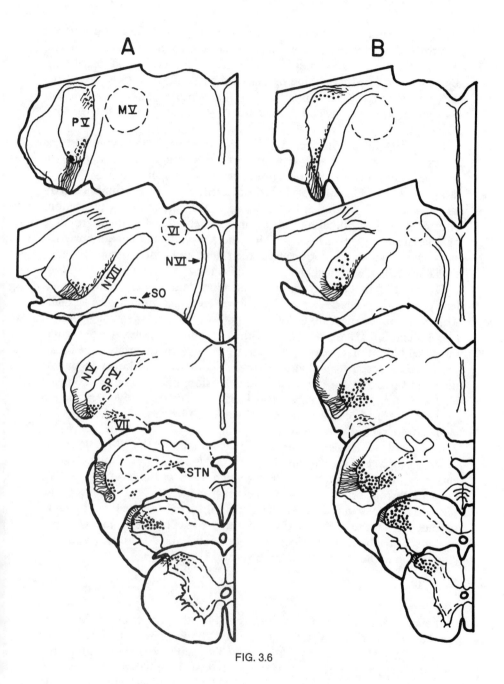

FIG. 3.6

imal end encapsulated in an HRP filled tube. The projecions passed from the supraorbital nerve into the ophthalmic branch of the trigeminal nerve, through the trigeminal ganglion, and then into the trigeminal nuclei (Fig. 3.6B). They created larger and denser terminal fields than those seen from the cornea (compare A and B in Fig. 3.6). These projections overlap the corneal projections and extend further dorsally within the spinal trigeminal nucleus.

The central projections from the maxillary part of the face have yet to be reported in the rabbit. However, the afferent projections we found in the trigeminal complex from the ophthalmic region are similar to those in the cat (Marfurt, 1979). This suggests that the afferent projections from the maxillary area also may be similar in the two species. In the cat, these projections into the spinal trigeminal nucleus lie immediately dorsal to those from the ophthalmic area (Marfurt, 1979). The general agreement between our HRP work and previous work, done with the rabbit and other species (see e.g., Darian-Smith, 1966), further supports this idea.

The question that aries from these trigeminal data is where, within the extensive terminal fields of primariy sensory afferents, is synaptic contact made with the secondary neurons of the UCR pathway? The answer is suggested in Fig. 3.5 and 3.6. There is an area of the trigeminal complex where the terminal fields of primary sensory neurons from the cornea overlap the cells that project to the accessory abducens nucleus. This area covers the caudal part of the principal and rostral part of the oralis divisions of the complex. Comparing the portion of this area above the facial nerve (NVII) in Fig. 3.5 and 3.6 reveals the overlap clearly. Additional work will be necessary, however, to demonstrate synaptic connectivity.

Other evidence also exists supporting the notion that the NM reflex arc is through this area of the trigeminal complex. It is a well known clinical observation in man that lesions of the trigeminal tract at the level of the obex (which interrupt primary sensory fibers that project to levels below the lesion) do not block the corneal reflex but do block pain and temperature sensations. Even more compelling is the finding that cutting this tract at a level just caudal to the facial nucleus does not abolish the NM reflex to corneal stimulation in the rabbit (Berthier & Moore, 1983).

Stage 2

This stage involves the time course of activity in the projection neurons during their mediation of the UCR. Anatomical findings by themselves cannot be taken as conclusive proof that the UCR actually is mediated by the pathway they suggest. It is still necessary to demonstrate that the pathway is physiologically active during mediation of the UCR (and the time course of the activity), and that disruption of the pathway by cutting it at any of its axonal projections (stage 3) will eliminate the UCR.

On the motor side, Cegavske et al. (1976) reported that electrical stimulation of the abducens nerve caused eyeball withdrawal after a mean latency of 12.1 msec (SD = .32 msec) and NM extension after a mean latency of 16.1 msec (SD = .74 msec). The consistent 4–5 msec difference in latency was due to "mechanical" activation of the NM by the Harder's gland as the eyeball retracted into the socket. Presumably the eyeball has to move a certain distance before there is enough pressure exerted on the Harder's gland to cause it to force the NM over the cornea. It also was reported by Cegavske et al. (1976) that the NM could be retracted (after being experimentally held extended) by electrical stimulation of the oculomotor nerve. The mean latency of this response was 10.4 msec (SD = 1.74 msec).

On the sensory side, there is evidence that it may take as little as 3 msec for activation of cells in the spinal trigeminal nucleus, pars oralis, after electrical stimulation of the rabbit cornea (Dolinsky, Daly, & Cegavske, unpublished observation). Berthier and Moore (1983) have reported a latency of 2.6 msec in the trigeminal nerve (at its point of entrance to the brain stem) after electrical stimulation of the paraorbital area. If a synaptic delay of 0.4 msec is added to this figure, one gets the 3.0 msec figure of the former observation. Berthier and Moore (1983) also reported that the central delay, between a trigeminal-nerve afferent volley and an abducens-nerve efferent volley, is 1.3 msec. They interpreted this delay as reflecting a disynaptic pathway through the brain stem. This interpretation is consistent with our anatomical findings reviewed previously.

If the latencies are added (2.6 msec afferent, 1.3 msec central delay, and 16.1 msec efferent) a reflex time of 20.0 msec is obtained. This latency seems a bit short, especially if an air-puff UCS is used, and probably is close to a minimum obtainable from the reflex arc. There are at least two sources of error that should be considered when evaluating these latency data. The first of these involves the effects of anesthesia on the nervous system. All latencies that involve synaptic delays may be effected. A strong reflex arc, such as the one that causes NM extension, may be driven by electrical stimulation while the animal is anesthetized without interference from possible modulatory influences. However, when the animal is undrugged and behaving normally, such influences may cause an increase in latency of the reflex arc (at least to weak stimuli). The variability in the latency of the NM response at the beginning of conditioning sessions testifies to this point. The second source of error is from the transducer used to measure NM movements. It can introduce a delay while the inertia of the moving parts is being overcome. To the extent that a precise time course through the UCR pathway is required in the normally behaving animal, additional research will still be required in this stage.

Stage 3

Stage 3 involves disrupting the UCR pathway at major points of projection and testing the behavioral NM response to insure that the projection neurons suggested by anatomical work are essential for the response.

On the motor side of the UCR pathway, Cegavske et al. (1976) reported that lesions of the abducens nerve completely eliminated the UCR to air-puff stimulation. Berthier and Moore (1980) cut the sixth nerve and found only a 50% reduction in NM-response size to a mechanical stimulation of the cornea that was intentionally made strong enough to produce a maximum response. We interpret these data to mean that the RB is the normal effector for NM extension but that the other extraocular muscles can be recruited to produce the response under extreme conditions. It should be added that a part of the Berthier and Moore (1980) study strongly supports other findings indicating that the accessory abducens nucleus produces the only motor output that causes eyeball retraction (and NM extension) under normal conditions. Even under the extreme stimulus conditions of their study no NM extension was caused by the motoneurons in the oculomotor nucleus that innervate part of the RB muscle. With the sixth nerve lesioned and all the extraocular muscles detached except the RB, this group of motoneurons projecting to the RB through the third nerve was the only motor system left intact, and it produced no reflexive eyeball retraction.

On the sensory side, no direct test of the NM response has been made after lesioning the primary sensory projections from the cornea. However,, in a series of denervation experiments in the rabbit by Zander and Weddell (1951), a clear demonstration of the intervation mediating the corneal eyeblink was shown. Sectioning of the ciliary nerve, the trigeminal ganglion and the area around the cornea prevented the reflex. Interestingly, sectioning of the orbital nerve, a distal extension of a branch of the maxillary nerve, had no effect on the reflex.

No lesions through the internuncial part of the UCR pathway have been reported yet.

Stage 4

Stage 4 deals with the local circuit connections of the UCR pathway. The other three criteria dealt with characterizing the location of projection neurons and the conduction time involved in different parts of the pathway during the reflex response. Now that all of the projection neurons have been tentatively identified, more refined anatomical techniques (e.g., intracellular HRP, double labeling, transsynaptic transport, and EM) can be brought to bear to demonstrate synaptic connectivity and thereby demonstrate the presence or absence of local circuit neurons. This will be the final step in characterizing the anatomical components of the UCR pathway.

SUMMARY AND CONCLUSIONS

At the present time, the space-time map of the UCR pathway is still incomplete. The status of the four research stages, that will be required to complete it, can be summarized as follows. Stage 1 (the anatomical identification of the effectors for NM behavior and the projection neurons mediating the UCR) has been completed (see Fig. 3.7). Nictitating membrane extension is produced by the RB muscle pulling the eyeball into the orbit that compresses the Harder's gland and forces the NM to extend over the cornea. Under nor-

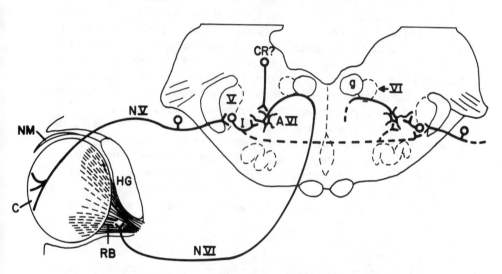

FIG. 3.7   Summary diagram of the unconditioned response pathway showing an afferent neuron from the cornea synapsing on or internuncial neuron which synapses, in turn, on a motoneuron in the accessory abducens nucleus that projects to the retractor bulbi muscle. The contralateral connection (shown with dashed lines) is taken from Baker et al. (1980) and is spectulative with regard to its being a collateral of the internuncial, its synaptic connections, and its pathway to the other side. It was included in the figure because some such pathway exists to mediate the contralateral UCR (see text). Abbreviations: AVI = acessory abducens nucleus; C = cornea; CR? = undetermined afferent that mediates conditioned response information to the accessory abducens nucleus; g = genu of the facial nerve; HG = Harder's gland; I = internuncial; NM = nictitating membrane; NV = trigeminal nerve; NVI = abducens nerve; RB = retractor bulbi muscle; V = part of the principal and part of the spinal trigeminal nucleus (see text); VI = abducens nucleus.

mal conditions (when the animal is intact, stimulation is not tissue damaging, and stimulation activates only cutaneous sensory receptors) the data show compellingly that the contraction of the RB muscle and subsequent NM extension is exclusively caused by motoneurons in the accessory abducens nucleus that project their axons to the muscle through the sixth cranial nerve. Consequently, the UCR and the CR must both be mediated by motoneurons in the accessory abducens nucleus.

Because the accessory abducens motoneurons are responsible for NM extension, the afferents to these neurons must include a group of cells that transmits UCR information. A candidate group has been found in the principal and oralis divisions of the trigeminal complex (I in Fig. 3.7). These cells are overlapped by terminal fields of primary sensory neurons from the cornea.

The nasal part of the levator palpebrae superioris muscle is the only muscle directly attached to the NM and it is capable of causing active NM reopening. Passive reopening also may occur as the eyeball returns to its resting position after being retracted. The nasal-LPS muscle has the capability of modulating NM extension and therefore the "shape" of the NM response although this has yet to be demonstrated experimentally. The motoneurons controlling the nasal-LPS muscle are located in the oculomotor nucleus contralateral to the muscle and send their axons through the third cranial nerve.

Stage 2 (characterization of the activity of the projection neurons that mediate the UCR to determine the time course of activity through the CNS) has been completed for acute preparations, but not for the normally behaving, drug-free, animal. In acute preparations it takes about 3 msec for sensory information from the cornea to fire the internuncials, another approximately 0.9 msec for the information to be transmitted to and through the accessory abducens nucleus to where the sixth nerve emerges from the brain stem, another 12 msec for the neural information to initiate muscle contraction and subsequent eyeball withdrawal, and finally, 4 msec for the NM to start extending. The latency in the motor system will probably be found to be reasonably accurate (depending on transducer accuracy), but that of the sensory system may reflect the conduction velocity of the fastest fibers in the nerve that may not be the mediators of UCS information. Data from chronically implanted electrodes among the accessory abducens and the internuncial neurons of drug-free animals, being behaviorally tested with air-puff stimuli, will be necessary to get an accurate measure of the time course of activity (and the locus of its variability) through the pathway.

Stage 3 (demonstrate disruption of the behavioral UCR by cutting the pathway at each projection neuron) has been partly completed. The abducens nerve has been cut with a resultant loss of the UCR to air-puff stimulation and a marked reduction in the response to extreme stimulation. This has been interpreted to mean that the abducens nerve contains all the motor output under conditions of mild or moderate tactile stimulation, but that the other extraocular muscles can be recruited (through the third and fourth cranial nerves) under conditioning of extreme stimulation to produce a partial NM extension. On the sensory side, the NM response has not been tested after lesioning the ophthalmic part of the trigeminal nerve. However, it is suggestive that the corneal reflex is abolished after such a lesion in the cat. The internuncials have not been lesioned yet.

Stage 4 (determine synaptic interactions in the local circuitry at each relay point to identify and determine the function of local circuit neurons that may be critical elements in the functional pathway) has not been approached yet.

Once the four stages are completed, the UCR pathway will be characterized adequately in a space-time format to allow the statement (mentioned previously) to be useful, i.e., the CR is either developed within the confines of the UCR pathway or connected into it at some point(s). Electrophysiological recordings made in structures directly projecting to the UCR pathway will then be able to distinguish between these two possibilities by determining which structure(s), if any, transmit(s) CR information into the pathway. Because UCRs have been reported to be bilateral, and CRs largely unilateral (Disterhoft, Kwan, & Lo, 1977), it is unlikely (although certainly not impossible) that CRs are connected through the internuncials to the accessory abducens nucleus. Consequently, some other afferent to the accessory abducens nucleus will probably be found to mediate CR information (the "CR?" neuron in Fig. 3.7).

In conclusion, although there are still holes in the space-time map of the UCR pathway, it would seem that they can be filled in a straight-forward fashion. There are no apparent technological, methodological, or theoretical obstacles. This means that the rabbit brain itself may be amenable to analysis in a space-time format that will allow substrates of classical conditioning to be distinguished from structures and functions that are correlated, but not in a causative way, with the behavior being studied. The underlying foundation of this approach to neural substrates is the neuroanatomy of the system being studied. Anatomy first—not necessarily in the sense of chronological research projects, but before conclusive statements can be made about the locations of the substrates of the behavior. Knowledge of the locations of the substrates is necessary to allow meaningful experiments to be performed on the microanatomy, the physiology and the neurochemistry of the system. The rabbit NM preparation seems ideally suited for the study of the biological mechanisms of mammalian associative learning because of the abundance of well documented research on its behavior, and the eventual ability of researchers to study the actual substrates of the behavior at the neuroanatomical, neurophysiological, and neurochemical levels.

ACKNOWLEDGEMENTS

The research presented here was supported in part by grants from the SUNY/ Research Foundation, University Awards Program; and by NIMH grants MH-29865 and MH-32154.

REFERENCES

Akagi, Y. (1978). The localization of the motor neurons innervating the extraocular muscles in the oculomotor nuclei of the cat and rabbit, using horseradish peroxidase. *Journal of Comparative Neurology, 181,* 745–762.

Ariens Kappers, C. U. (1917). Further contributions on neurobiotaxis. *Journal of Comparative Neurology, 27,* 261–298.

Baker, R., McCrea, R. A., & Spencer, R. F. (1980). Synaptic organization of cat accessory abducens nucleus. *Journal of Neurophysiology, 43,* 771–791.

Berthier, N.E., & Moore, J.W. (1980). Role of extraocular muscles in the rabbit (*Oryctolagus cuniculus*) nictitating membrane response. *Physiology & Behavior, 24,* 931–937.

Berthier, N. E., & Moore, J. W. (1983). The nictitating membrane response: an electrophysiological study of the abducens nerve and nucleus and the accessory abducens nucleus in rabbit. *Brain Research, 258,* 201–210.

Cegavske, C. F., Thompson, R. F., Patterson, M. M., & Gormezano, I. (1976). Mechanisms of efferent neuronal control of the reflex nictitating membrane response in rabbit, (*Oryctolagus cuniculus*). *Journal of Comparative and Physiological Psychology, 90,* 411–423.

Crandall, W. F., Jr., Wilson, J. S., & Goldberg, S. J. (1977). Branching axons to "functionally independent" muscles in the cat oculomotor system. *Society for Neuroscience Abstracts, 3,* 153.

Darian-Smith, I. (1966). Neural mechanisms of facial sensation. *International Review of Neurobiology, 9,* 301–395.

Disterhoft, J. F., Kwan, H. H., & Lo, W. D. (1977). Nictitating membrane conditioning to tone in the immobilized albino rabbit. *Brain Research, 137,* 127–143.

Disterhoft, J. F., & Shipley, M. T. (1980). Accessory abducens nucleus innervation of rabbit retractor bulbi motoneurons localized with HRP retrograde transport. *Society for Neuroscience Abstracts, 6,* 478.

Glendenning, K. K., Hutson, K. A., & Masterton, R. B. (1979). Accessory nucleus of the abducens nerve in cat. *Anatomical Record, 193,* 550.

Grant, K., Gueritaud, J. P., Horcholle-Bossavit, G., & Tyc-Dumont, S. (1979). Anatomical and electrophysiological identification of motoneurones supplying the cat retractor bulbi muscle. *Experimental Brain Research, 34,* 541–550.

Gray, T. S., McMaster, S. E., Harvey, J. A., & Gormezano, I. (1981). Localization of retractor bulbi motoneurons in the rabbit. *Brain Research, 226,* 93–106.

Guegan, M., Gueritaud, J. -P., & Horcholle-Bossavit, G. (1978). Localisation des motoneurones du muscle retractor bulbi par transport retrograde de peroxydase exogene chez le Chat. *C. R. Acad. Sc. Paris, 286,* 1355–1357.

Harrison, T. A., & Cegavske, C. F. (1981). Role of the levator palpebrae superioris (LPS) muscle in effecting nictitating membrane movement in the rabbit. *Physiology & Behavior, 26,* 159–162.

Harrison, T. A., Cegavske, C. F., & Thompson, R. F. (1978). Neural activity recorded in the abducens and oculomotor nuclei during nictitating membrane conditioning in the rabbit. *Society for Neuroscience Abstract, 4,* 259.

Harrison, T. A., Torigoe, Y., & Cegavske, C. F. (1983). Organization of the cranial nerve nuclei innervating the eye muscles in the rabbit: A study using the HRP tracer technique. Unpublished manuscript.

Highstein, S. M., Karabelas, A., Baker, R., & McCrea, R. A. (1982). Comparison of the morphology of physiologically identified abducens motor and internuclear neurons in the cat: a light microscopic study employing the intracellular injection of horseradish peroxidase. *Journal of Comparative Neurology, 208,* 369–381.

Lorente de No, R. (1933). The interaction of the corneal reflex and vestibular nystagmus. *American Journal of Physiology, 103,* 704–711.

Marfurt, C. F. (1979). Somatotopic organization of trigeminal sensory nuclei. *Society for Neuroscience Abstracts, 5,* 710.

Meredith, M. A., McClung, J. R., & Goldberg, S. J. (1981). Retractor bulbi muscle responses to oculomotor nerve and nucleus stimulation in the cat. *Brain Research, 211,* 427–432.

Mis, F. W. (1977). A midbrain-brain stem circuit for conditioned inhibition of the nictitating membrane response in the rabbit (*Oryctolagus cuniculus*). *Journal of Comparative and Physiological Psychology, 91,* 975–988.

Prince, J. H. (Ed.). (1964). *The rabbit in eye research.* Springfield, IL: Charles C. Thomas.

Spencer, R. F., Baker, R., & McCrea, R. A. (1980). Localization and morphology of cat retractor bulbi motoneurons. *Journal of Neurophysiology, 43,* 754–770.

Tarlov, E., & Tarlov, S. R. (1971). The representation of extraocular muscles in the oculomotor nuclei: Experimental studies in the cat. *Brain Research, 34,* 37–52.

Torigoe, Y., & Cegavske, C. F. (1983). Projections of corneal afferents into the trigeminal nuclei of the rabbit as demonstrated by HRP. Unpublished manuscript.

Torigoe, Y., Harrison, T. A., & Cegavske, C. F. (1983). Afferents to the abducens nucleus of the rabbit as demonstrated by transport of HRP. Unpublished manuscript.

Torigoe, Y., Owen, J., & Cegavske, C. F. (1983). Afferents to the accessory abducens nucleus of the rabbit as demonstrated by transport of HRP. Unpublished manuscript.

Warwick, R. (1953). Representation of the extra-ocular muscles in the oculomotor nuclei of the monkey. *Journal of Comparative Neurology, 98,* 449–503.

Wenokor, W., Torigoe, Y., & Cegavske, C. F. (1983). Projections of the supraorbital nerve into the trigeminal nuceli of the rabbit as demonstrated by transport of HRP. Unpublished manuscript.

Zander, E., & Weddell, G. (1951). Observations on the innervation of the cornea. *Journal of Anatomy, 85,* 68–99.

Analyses of the Auditory Input and Motor Output Pathways in Rabbit Nictitating Membrane Conditioning

4

John F. Disterhoft
Kevin J. Quinn
Craig Weiss
Department of Cell Biology and Anatomy
Northwestern University Medical School

The rabbit nictitating membrane conditioning preparation, initially developed by Gormezano (33), offers several advantages as a mammalian system in which to analyze the neurophysiological substrates of learning (21,81). With appropriate parameters, conditioning occurs within one session even when the animal's head is firmly fixed in a manner appropriate for single-neuron recording (21). This allows single neurons to be followed during the acquisition of the conditioned response (49). Because the rabbit's head is fixed, auditory conditioned stimulus (CS) control comparable to that commonly used in neurophysiological studies of the auditory system in acute, anesthetized preparations may be used during training (48,49). The major behavior monitored is nictitating membrane extension. Primary motor output elements have been specified as axons traveling in the abducens nerve (16).

We have concentrated our studies of rabbit nictitating membrane conditioning on the auditory CS input and, recently, the motor output pathways. We have utilized a variety of neurophysiological, neuroanatomical, lesion, and stimulation techniques in these studies. The goal of our experiments is to help delineate the nictitating membrane reflex arc from CS input to conditioned response (CR) output. Both hippocampal and cerebellar neurons, which Thompson and his colleagues have demonstrated to play important roles in NM conditioning (5,6,7,83), certainly are known to be central interneurons in the arc. These, and other integrative regions, may be systematically related to the auditory CS and trigeminal US (14) afferent and NM output pathways with the approach we have utilized. This fact, and the progress we and others have made in delineating the pathway, makes the rabbit NM conditioning paradigm a powerful one in which to pursue the neurophysiological and neuroanatomical substrates of learning in mammalian brain.

THE AUDITORY PATHWAY

Cochlear Nucleus

The rabbit auditory pathway has not been extensively studied. Most auditory neurophysiology and neuroanatomy has been done on the cat. But we wish to design and interpret studies to detect possible changes in rabbit auditory system processing of the tone auditory CS as it becomes significant during the learning process. A series of very elegant anatomical and physiological correlative studies have been done on cat cochlear nucleus (CN) that have allowed detailed structure–function relations to be worked out in this nuclear region (44,45,65). Because the cochlear nucleus is the first central region that processes the tone CS in the NM reflex arc, it seemed a logical place to begin work on the auditory pathway. The large body of information on cat cochlear nucleus would be useful for this purpose. So we did comparative anatomical and physiological analyses of rabbit and cat cochlear nuclei.

The rabbit cochlear nucleus may be seen to be cytoarchitectonically organized into anteroventral (AVCN), posteroventral (PVCN) and dorsal cochlear nuclei (DCN) in Nissl stained sections (23). It looks quite similar to that of cat (72), except that DCN is somewhat more prominent (73). We were particularly interested in doing an analysis of Golgi-impregnated material to gain a close-up view of the elements from which our single-unit potentials arise in neurophysiological recording studies. Rabbit cochlear nucleus was seen to be organized similarly to cat CN at the level of neuronal morphology as well, using the atlas of Brawer, Morest, and Kane (11) as our basis for comparison. In fact, we saw almost all the same cell types, distributed in the same manner, as were found in the cat.

For example, a prominent cell type in AVCN was the "bushy" cell, having a spherical soma and one or more main dendritic branches with small, short branches at its end. Figure 4.1 shows examples of various types of bushy cells with one or two main dendritic branches.

Another good example is the fusiform cell of DCN. These cells appear to be the organizing elements of this subregion. They form a distinct row of cells between the more superficial molecular layer and the deeper polymorphic layers. The other cell types appear to be arrayed in relation to them. Figure 4.2 shows two examples of fusiform cells. Notice that the apical dendrites bore many spines and were well branched. Some of them also exhibited

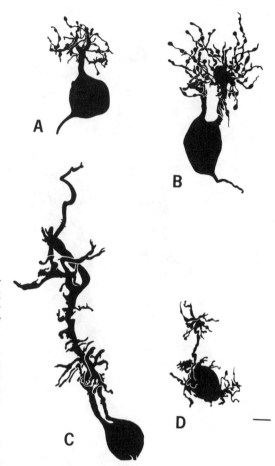

FIG. 4.1 Typical sample of bushy cells from AVCN. A. Bushy cell with one main dendrite. B. Bushy cell with two main dendrites of equal length. C. Bushy cell with two main dendrites, one much larger than the other. D. Bushy cell similar to the "adendritic" bushy cell of Brawer et al. (11), although it does have a small main dendrite. Golgi–Kopsch impregnations from four rabbits. A. Horizontal section; B, C, and D, transverse sections. 100X oil, N.A. 1.30, calibration 10 μm.

broad, flat processes that extended perpendicular to the main dendritic branches within the many fine axons that run parallel to the pial surface (left cell in Fig. 4.2).

Our overall conclusion on the basis of Nissl and Golgi data was that rabbit cochlear nucleus has a similar neuronal morphology to that of other mammalian species that have been well studied. In particular, rabbit and cat cochlear nuclei are very similar. Perry and Webster (73) reached the same conclusion in their anatomical studies of rabbit cochlear nucleus.

A single-unit recording study of cochlear nucleus in the unanesthetized, paralyzed rabbit was also done (41). Most of the 76 neurons were recorded from DCN. We used the classification schemes of both Evans and Nelson (28) and of Pfeiffer (74). These schemes characterize units in terms of relative amounts of excitation and inhibition in their tuning curves and of post-stimulus histogram shape, respectively. Figure 4.3 shows examples of the

FIG. 4.2   Two fusiform cells from DCN. The apical dendrites of the cell on the left are characterized by broad, flat dendritic processes extending perpendicular to the radically oriented dendrites. Golgi-Kopsch impregnations from two rabbits, transverse sections, dorsal to the top. 100X oil, N.A. 1.30, calibration 10 μm.

types of histogram shapes we recorded in DCN and illustrates well the relative complexity of DCN response types. Notice the large change in response shape shown in Fig. 4.3,C when the stimulus frequency was changed slightly.

In general, we found that DCN neurons in the unanesthetized rabbit responded to pure tones like those that had been described in the decerebrate (28,87) and awake (84) cat. Perry and Webster (73) did a more thorough survey of the ventral cochlear nucleus in their single-unit recording studies than we did. They classified their units according to Pfeiffer's (74) categories. They found "primary-like", "chopper" and "onset" units in ventral cochlear nucleus. In DCN, response types were more variable and there was more inhibition. They found, as we did, that "buildup", "pauser" and "chopper" patterns predominated. Perry and Webster also reported that the three subdivisions of rabbit cochlear nucleus were tonotopically organized in a dorsal (high frequency) to ventral (low frequency) direction.

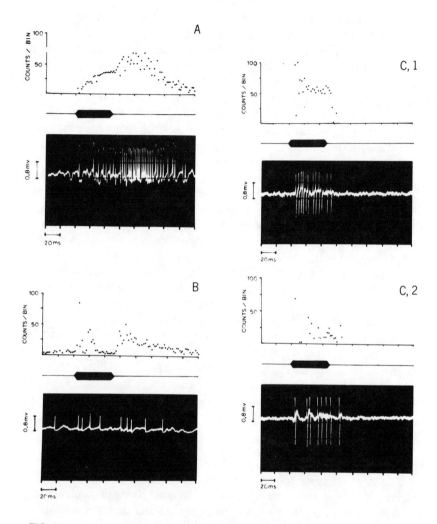

FIG. 4.3 Responses shown by three DCN neurons. Each histogram represents 125 repetitions. The time of arrival of the 50–ms tone burst at the rabbit's ear is represented below the histogram. The oscilloscope tracings show one of the trials averaged in the histogram. A - buildup response pattern. The characteristic frequency (CF) tone: 7.2 kHz, 20 dB above CF threshold. Note that the excitation lasts at least 100 ms after tone termination. B - complex response pattern composed of an "on" component followed by suppression and off excitation. CF tone: 8.6 kHz, 30 dB above threshold. C - change in response pattern at different segments of the neuron's excitatory response area. 1: A primary-like response is seen to a CF tone, 16.5 kHz, 30 DB above threshold. 2: a pauser response is seen to a 14-kHz tone, 45 dB above CF threshold.

Thus, both our anatomical and physiological data and that of Perry and Webster (73) agree that rabbit cochlear nucleus is quite similar to those of other mammalian species that have been studied, especially the cat. We've not yet done the most exciting part of this analysis; that is, to determine how these neurons behave during NM conditioning. However, Kettner and Thompson (43) have shown that multiple units in AVCN do not show behaviorally relevant alterations in firing pattern when rabbits are performing NM conditioning in a signal detection mode. It would appear premature to conclude from these data alone that no cochlear nucleus neurons change during NM conditioning because AVCN seems to be the cochlear nucleus subregion least likely to mediate auditory system plasticity. DCN is a much more likely candidate as it is a more complex region both anatomically and physiologically (23,41,73). Recordings from DCN have not been reported. However, Thompson and his colleagues (83) have reported that multiple and single units in central nucleus of inferior colliculus respond identically on detection and nondetection trials in their signal detection task. We have recorded single units in central nucleus of inferior colliculus during the process of NM conditioning and have found no reliable differences in responsivity to the tone CS (during the first 100 msec after tone onset) on trials from the periods before and after learning (Weiss and Disterhoft, unpublished observations). Because DCN fusiform cells project heavily to central nucleus of inferior colliculus (79), it would be expected that if this important class of DCN neurons were showing response plasticity during or after NM conditioning, this alteration would be reflected in inferior colliculus. Thus, although the evidence is indirect, the data do suggest that DCN fusiforms neurons, at least, do not alter their response to a tone CS during conditioning.

Auditory Cortex

When we began our single-unit studies of rabbit auditory cortex during NM conditioning, we again found a paucity of normative data against which to analyze possible changes during learning. In fact, no single-neuron analysis of rabbit auditory cortex had yet been reported and that was our first task (48).

In the course of these studies we took advantage of the fact that our rabbits had their heads fixed to develop a closed-sound system for the rabbit. The sound was transduced by an enclosed, dynamic earphone and led out through a stainless steel tube. The tube passed through a silastic earmold that was made to fit the external auditory meatus snugly and terminated near the tympanic membrane. The sound delivery tube had a sound measuring probe tube, attached to a condensor microphone, concentric within it. This arrangement allowed us to deliver and monitor acoustic stimuli under a level of control similar to that used in acute auditory neurophysiological experiments

(18). Similar systems were used by Martin et al. (54) and Perry and Webster (73), attesting to the utility of the conscious, head-fixed rabbit for auditory as well as conditioning research.

We examined the responses of 140 single neurons in 18 young adult, male rabbits (48). Auditory responsive cortex was found to lie behind the rhinal sulcus, from its midpoint to its inferior border. A variety of tuning curves and response types were found. Figure 4.4 shows examples of the post-stimulus time (PST) histogram response patterns found in 12 neurons stimulated at their best frequency. We found in auditory cortex, as we had in DCN, that a change in stimulus frequency or intensity often altered the response pattern of a neuron. Another point particularly relevant to the possible role of auditory cortex neural plasticity in NM conditioning was the tendency of some neurons to show "spontaneous" changes in response over time. These changes included increases or decreases in response size to a constant auditory stimulus, as well as changes in selected portions of the PST histograms.

The conclusions regarding our rabbit auditory cortex single-neuron normative data were surprisingly similar to those we had about cochlear nucleus. That is, the characteristics we described were very similar to those that had been described previously for auditory cortex in other species, especially the cat and monkey (1,12,29,31). This was true in regard to tuning curve shape, PST response type, spontaneous rate, and latency. Response variability had also been reported in other species, especially in the conscious state (31,59,62).

Our survey of auditory cortex neurons in the conscious rabbit led us to anticipate that we would discover neurons there that would change their processing of the tone CS during NM conditioning. The spontaneously variable neurons described earlier, for example, appeared to be affected by non-acoustic factors such as alertness or attention. Previous multiple-unit studies of auditory cortex in other species had shown systematic modification in multiple-unit activity that was correlated with auditory learning (13,22,26, 37,70,71). It was interesting that almost all the reported changes in the literature were increases in stimulus-evoked activity. On the other hand, single-unit studies in previously trained animals had shown that auditory cortex neurons changed, but that these modifications varied from cell to cell, in relation to variables such as attention, task performance, and task complexity (3,4,39,40,47,61,62,75,76,86). And our single-unit studies of auditory cortex in the naive rabbit had shown heterogeneity in a variety of response parameters (see Fig. 4.4, for example) as well as the response variability shown by some cells.

Our experiments were designed to examine the responses of single auditory cortex neurons in the learning context. They were an attempt to relate the auditory cortex multiple-unit studies that had been done during the learning process to those single-unit studies done in previously trained animals.

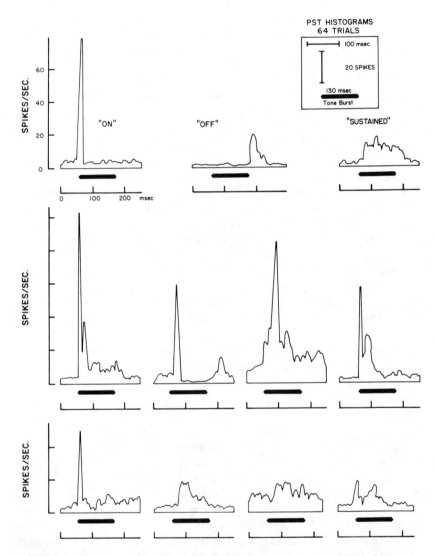

FIG. 4.4 Response patterns of 11 different auditory cortex neurons evoked by tone bursts (130 msec, presented 1/sec) at the neuron's CF. Some responses can be described as "on", "off", and "sustained" activity. Other histogram configurations attest to the variety of combinations of excitation and inhibition that are characteristic of auditory cortex neurons.

Our procedures were straightforward. We isolated neurons in rabbit auditory cortex and determined their best or characteristic frequency (46). We then used the best frequency tone as the CS in the NM conditioning or pseudoconditioning session that followed. The speed of learning varied among the rabbits. This variation was taken into account in constructing CS evoked PST histograms for evaluating changes that may have occurred during learning. The response of neurons to the CS tone when the rabbit was behaviorally naive (Initial Trials), when he was just learning the NM conditioned response (Transitional Trials), and when the CR was learned (Trained Trials) and well established (Overtrained Trials) were compared.

Neurons in the conditioned animals were more than twice as likely to show CS evoked response changes as were the pseudoconditioned control rabbits (51% vs. 19%). These changes were evident in both the early (0–60 msec) and late (60–250 msec) portions of the CS–US interval. Response changes were equally likely to be increases or decreases in response amplitude. Response pattern tended to remain relatively constant but in some neurons subcomponents of the response were seen to change independently of each other. Figure 4.5 shows two examples of increased CS evoked responses between Initial and Trained Trials. In Figure 4.5B, the statistically significant increase was restricted to the later portion of the CS–US interval.

Two other aspects of our data should be mentioned. First, response alterations were not evident until the CR was established (Trained Trials). They were not evident during the Transition Trials in our sample. Secondly, in our sample of 36 neurons in rabbit auditory association cortex, the location of those cells, which changed during training, was coextensive with those that remained constant. Figure 4.6 illustrates this fact and demonstrates where our cells were recorded.

These data clearly demonstrate that auditory cortex cells change the manner in which they process a CS tone as that tone becomes significant during learning. But it should be noted that almost half the neurons we sampled did not change during learning. This would suggest that response plasticity is mediated by a subset of auditory cortex neurons.

Response change, when analyzed at the single-neuron level, was equally likely to be manifested as an increase or as a decrease in CS-evoked response amplitude with variable response patterns. In this sense, our data suggested that previous multiple-unit studies (13,22,26,37,71) may have over estimated the homogeneity of response changes in auditory cortex. These studies had generally reported increases in a rather standard PST histogram characterized by an excitatory peak response at stimulus onset followed by a sustained response throughout the CS. The heterogeneous response changes we found were much more similar to the single-unit data gathered from trained animals in nonlearning contexts (3,4,39,47,61,62,76,86). The significance of this het-

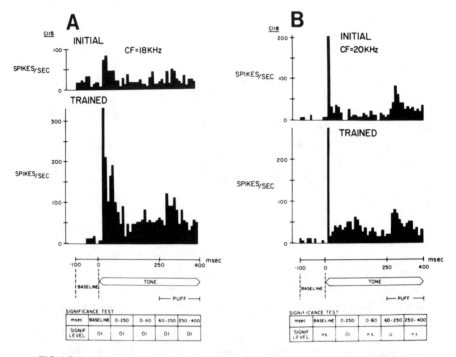

FIG 4.5   Auditory cortex neural activity occurring during "Initial" Trials (rabbit behaviorally naive) is shown for comparison with that occuring during "Trained" Trials (CR
has been learned). Each histogram consists of firing rate summed over 20 trials. The stimulus configuration and statistical changes in neural activity occurring during various
components are illustrated. The CF of each unit is indicated. A: Generalized increase in
CS-evoked firing rate with training. Note the accompanying decrease in spontaneous firing rate. B: Increase in CS-evoked activity selective to the late (60–250 ms) portion of the
CS–US interval.

erogeneity is its strong suggestion that auditory learning during NM conditioning is not a mere "enhancement" phenomenon at the level of auditory
cortex. Rather, it most likely involves complex alterations of cortical circuitry utilizing both excitatory and inhibitory components.

Response changes were not evident during Transition Trials, when the rabbits were acquiring the response, but rather were expressed when the CR was
established during Trained Trials. This would suggest that auditory cortex is
not required for NM conditioned response acquisition, at least when a single
tone CS is used. This is not surprising, because decorticate rabbits can acquire this NM response (27,64,68,69). But these data do indicate that, even if
auditory cortex is not essential, it changes when the tone signaled NM response is learned in the intact animal. Because it becomes active at the point
when the motor CR has been acquired, it may well be integrating or storing

auditory information that had been held elsewhere in the brain during early stages of learning.

One obvious candidate for an early storage site would be hippocampus, which Berger and Thompson have shown to change very early in NM conditioning (5,6,7) well before auditory cortex. Mishkin has delineated a possible memory circuit for visual learning in the monkey that involves the demonstrated reciprocal connections between the limbic system and sensory cortices via the insular cortex (63). Such a circuit is likely to be at least one of those involved in storing information in rabbit auditory cortex during NM conditioning. Posterior thalamus, which has been shown to change very early during auditory learning in the rat (22,26) and which projects to auditory association cortex (20,85), is another site that may well project preprocessed auditory information to cortex for storage. The interesting possible relations between these forebrain, and other lower brain regions during NM conditioning remain to be worked through.

OUTPUT MOTONEURONS

Nictitating membrane extension in the rabbit occurs primarily as a result of contraction of the retractor bulbi muscle, which pulls the eyeball into the orbit and forces the NM out and across the cornea from the medial side in a passive fashion (14). Cegavske and Thompson showed that fibers in the VIth

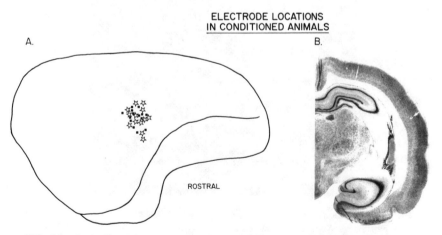

FIG. 4.6 A: Auditory cortex electrode locations in conditioned animals are shown on the lateral surface of the right cerebral hemisphere. Stars indicate neurons that showed significant changes in firing rate with learning. Dots mark the location of neurons that did not change. B: Coronal section of a rabbit's right hemisphere. An electrode lesion, located deep in the granular layer (IV), is indicated by an arrow.

cranial nerve, the abducens, controlled NM extension. They also found that multiple units in the principal abducens nucleus (Abd) fired with a very high correlation to conditioned and unconditioned NM extension (15).

Abd is associated with control of the lateral rectus muscle as well as the retractor bulbi. So we injected horseradish peroxidase into retractor bulbi to determine if there was a subregion associated wth each muscle. We found retrogradely labeled motoneurons in Abd and also accessory abducens (Acc Abd) nuclei after such injections (Fig. 4.7; 25). This observation was made by several other laboratories at about this time (9,14,35). Physiological and anatomical studies on control of the retractor bulbi muscle in the cat concluded that the major control of the retractor bulbi was from Acc Abd (2,34,42,80).

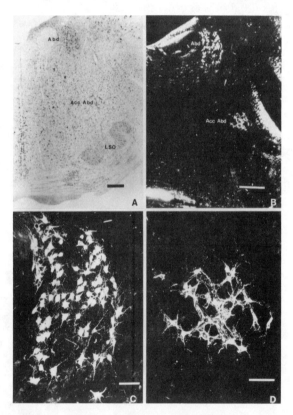

FIG. 4.7   Location of principal and accessory abducens nuclei in coronal section of rabbit brainstem. A. Abducens nucleus (Abd), Accessory Abducens nucleus (Acc Abd), and Lateral Superior Olive (LSO) are indicated. Fascicles of nerve VI may be seen exiting toward the base of the brainstem. Bar = 0.5mm. B. Polarized light (PL) photomicrograph at same level as 3A. HRP was injected into the Retractor Bulbi muscles (RB). Cells in Acc Abd are heavily labeled. Bar = 0.5 mm. C. Higher power, PL view of Abd shown in 3B. Bar = 0.1 mm. D. Higher power, PL view of Acc Abd shown in 3B. Bar = 0.1 mm.

The Abd motoneurons projecting to retractor bulbi, and those from the oculomotor nucleus, were thought to allow the lateral and medial slips of retractor bulbi to aid the lateral and medial recti in patterned eye movements (2,17,58,80).

We concluded from anatomical experiments that Acc Abd was primarily responsible for controlling retractor bulbi contraction in rabbit as it was in cat (25). Berthier and Moore (9) and Cegavske (14) reached the same conclusion as we had on the basis of their anatomical work. Gray et al. (35,36), however, reported that Abd controlled both retractor bulbi and lateral rectus in rabbit. In fact, they found that 72% of Abd motoneurons projected to retractor bulbi. The multiple-unit recording data of Cegavske and Thompson (15) also suggested strongly that Abd controlled NM extension. This type of species difference between cat and rabbit, i.e., that Abd was more prominently involved in controlling retractor bulbi, seemed quite possible. The rabbit (prey) does not exhibit the same range of patterned eye movements as does the cat (predator), minimizing the need for fine control of lateral rectus. So we decided to examine the relative roles of Abd and Acc Abd in control of NM extension in further recording, stimulation, and lesion experiments that we have been doing recently. These experiments are not fully complete but their results are quite relevant to the theme of this book. So we describe them in preliminary fashion here. [Experiments complete at publication (24)].

We incorporated a technical modification into our experimental preparation for these experiments. Both principal, and especially accessory, abducens nuclei are relatively small nuclear regions that lie 15–20 mm below the dural surface. So we have done all of our experiments with physiological guidance from antidromic field potentials evoked by chronically implanted VIth nerve-stimulating electrodes. This approach takes a bit longer than merely using stereotaxic coordinates but gives us considerably more confidence about the placement of our lesions, recording sites, and injections.

NM extension is an indirect consequence of eyeball retraction in the rabbit (16). We wished to measure the behavioral response directly to be able to more accurately relate unit activity with size and pattern of muscular response and to evaluate lesion effects precisely. So we designed a method for doing accurate, repeatable measurements of eyeball retraction in the rabbit (78). A film strip on which a light intensity grating has been exposed is attached to a contact lens. The lens is placed on the cornea and the intensity grating is placed between an infrared LED and photodiode. The contact lens—film strip moves freely when the eyeball is retracted and the photodiode gives a linear output with eyeball movement. Not surprisingly, eyeball retraction measured with our device can be classically conditioned in the same fashion as NM extension. This behavioral finding was shown originally by Gormezano (19). We have not used this device in all our experiments, so for consistency we discuss NM extension and not eyeball retraction. The differences between the two behavioral measures are not crucial for our discussion here.

Accessory Abducens

Well-isolated single neurons have been recorded within the Acc Abd field potential region in the conditioned and unconditioned rabbit (24). Neurons in Acc Abd nucleus have essentially no background firing rate. Single-unit activity is seen *only* during spontaneous or elicited NM sweeps. Single- and multiple-unit activity in Acc Abd always shows vigorous driving to corneal and periorbital somatosensory stimulation. All cells we have recorded show an increase in firing associated with the beginning of the NM sweep, with some variation in response pattern during the remainder of the sweep. Figure 4.8 shows an example of three such cells. They all fire just at or before the onset of the NM sweep. The "burst" (Fig. 4.8A) cell fires early in NM extension, the "tonic" (Fig. 4.8B) cell shows a faithful representation of the NM extension pattern in its PST histogram, and the "burst-tonic" (Fig. 4.8C) cell fires a

ACCESSORY ABDUCENS UNITS

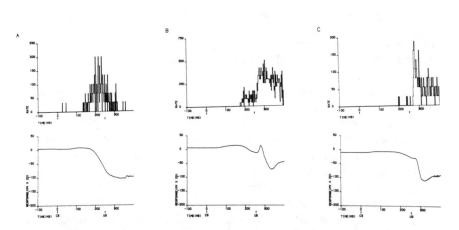

FIG. 4.8   Behavioral and accessory abducens region cellular responses during paired presentation of tone and airpuff. In A, B, and C top trace is PST histogram of single-unit activity, bottom trace is averaged NM sweep (NM extension is downward deflection). Data collected during paired tone-air puff conditioning trials. A. "Burst" cell: Onset of unit activity clearly precedes onset of NM sweep, unit firing decreases back to 0 spontaneous rate while NM still sweeps across eye. B. "Tonic" cell: Unit firing increases with onset of NM sweep and remains at high rate for duration of behavioral response. C. "Burst-tonic" cell: Unit firing increases with onset of behavioral response but then falls to a lower stable rate for duration of behavioral response. Note complete absence of spontaneous activity in the three cells.

burst early in NM extension with further spikes during the maintained extension.

We have recorded some cells during the acquisition of the NM response. In these cases, the trial on which unit activity first appeared before US onset (in the CR period) was the first trial on which a CR appeared behaviorally. We are seeking more examples of this phenomenon.

Microstimulation within accessory abducens elicits NM sweeps at currents as low as $10\mu a$.

Our single-unit observations in the conscious rabbit expand upon those of Berthier and Moore in the anesthetized rabbit (9) and on the observations that have been made in anesthetized cat (2). The heavy corneal trigeminal input exists in both species. Our demonstration that single Acc Abd neurons are highly correlated with body unconditioned and conditioned NM extensions was anticipated on the basis of the anatomically demonstrated connections between Acc Abd motoneurons and the retractor bulbi muscles discussed earlier.

Electrolytic lesions that destroyed all or most of Acc Abd immediately reduced the size of conditioned and unconditioned NM extensions (or eyeball retractions) in 8 of 10 cases (24). However, the responses generally returned to, or exceeded, prelesion amplitudes within 3 days (see Fig. 4.9A). In the three cases with the largest postlesion reduction, the response never returned to their prelesion sizes (see Fig. 4.9B).

We plan to do more Acc Abd lesion experiments to confirm our result and to get a better estimate of the amount of the permanent reduction. A problem in evaluating the completeness of the amount of Acc Abd electrolytic lesions is the difficulty specifying the location of the nucleus within the reticular formation of Nissl stained material. It is at least possible, but highly unlikely, that we have failed to destroy some Acc Abd in those lesions that we very conservatively judged to be complete. In our remaining lesion experiments, we will inject HRP into the retractor bulbi muscle as a final step following behavioral testing to insure that no Acc Abd neurons remain after the lesion. It should also be noted that Berthier and Moore (8) showed that the extraocular muscles can mediate a NM response that is only reduced 50% from normal after VIth nerve section and that Lorente de No (51) showed that retractor bulbi *and* the other six extraocular muscles responded to corneal stimulation in rabbit. So we shall detach the recti and oblique extraocular muscles from the the eyeball to get a more accurate estimate of reduction in retractor bulbi contraction strength. In the one experiment in which we have detached the extraocular muscles, other than retractor bulbi, and then done an accessory abducens lesion, the eye retraction response was eliminated and did not return.

Our lesion data are in the direction that we predicted on the basis of the anatomical data, but the effects are not as large as we expected. We must repeat

A

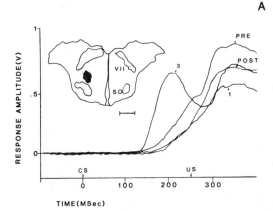

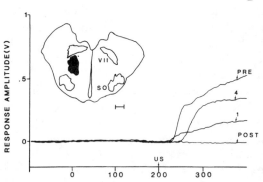

FIG. 4.9   Accessory Abducens lesion effects on eyeball retraction response. (A.) A lesion largely confined to Acc Abd caused an immediate reduction in conditioned and unconditioned response amplitude (Pre vs. Post). The postlesion effect on the conditioned response had disappeared by 3 days after the lesion, although in this case the unconditioned response remained reduced. (B.) A large lesion caused a large postlesion unconditioned response reduction that was still reduced 4 days after the lesion. The CS in A was white noise, the US in A & B was periorbital air puff. The eyeball retraction responses are 15(A) and 10(B) trial averages. The insets show outline drawing of section through Acc Abd with largest lesion (VII facial nerve; SO—Superior Olivary complex).

our observation of the apparently large contribution of the other extraocular muscles to eye retraction and insure lesion completeness in our remaining experiments. It is important to stress, though, that the lesion data do not negate accessory abducens involvement in conditioned and unconditioned nictitating membrane extension. Our single-unit recording data and that of Berthier and Moore (9) plus the anatomically demonstrated efferents of accessory abducens to retractor bulbi (8,14,24,36) prove that accessory abducens motoneurons are one mediator of NM extension in rabbit.

We do have multiple-unit recording data from principal abducens nucleus that is in agreement with that of Cegavske and Thompson (15), i.e., Abd multiple-unit firing is highly correlated with NM extension. We also have found that microstimulation in Abd with current as low as 20 μa is sufficient to elicit eyeball retraction. The recording data, with our Acc Abd lesion data, have led us to conclude that Abd nucleus can serve as one of the final output pathways for eyeball retraction in the rabbit by its control of lateral rectus and/or retractor bulbi. This, of course, is in agreement with Cegavske and Thompson (15,16).

The relative importance of oculomotor neurons in eyeball retraction is not clear. Lorente de No (51) showed by direct observation that the recti and obliques, in addition to retractor bulbi, contract after corneal stimulation. Oculomotor multiple units fire in correlation with NM extension (38). Oculomotor neurons send axons to the retractor bulbi muscles in cat (58,80). But Berthier and Moore (8) showed that section of the VIth nerve and the extraocular muscles other than retractor bulbi eliminated NM extension in rabbit. Because the oculomotor fibers to retractor bulbi would have been intact in their experiments, their data suggest a minimal role for oculomotor nucleus in retractor bulbi control. But they do offer strong support for oculomotor neuronal involvement in the normal rabbit eyeball retraction because contraction of the recti and obliques can cause a substantial NM extension.

The results of our Acc Abd lesion experiments raise two new possibilities concerning control of NM extension at the motor end. First, Abd and the oculomotor nuclei remain intact immediately after Acc Abd destruction, but they do not mediate conditioned or unconditioned NM extension. This suggests that their premotor influence may be temporarily inactivated. A disruption in this premotor area activity by the lesioning current could certainly cause the large postlesion reponse reduction we have observed. Thus, an important eyeball retraction premotor region could lie in reticular formation surrounding Acc Abd or at least interacts significantly with it. A second possibility is that the return of the response to prelesion levels reflects a mechanism of postlesion plasticity by which Abd and/or oculomotor nucleus take over function that was mediated in or around Acc Abd before the lesion. These two possibilities remain to be tested.

Our current working hypothesis is that three separate motoneuron pools exist for controlling eyeball retraction—the principal and accessory abducens nuclei and the oculomotor nucleus. Each of these pools may be sufficient but not necessary output pathways through which conditioned and unconditioned eyeball retraction may occur. The fact that there are apparently three pools of final output motoneurons controlling NM extension offers a unique experimental advantage for the next stage in retrogradely tracing the NM reflex arc. At some point, there should be a common premotor area that controls the three output regions, because all are highly correlated with NM extension (15,38,77). This common premotor interneuron should not be too many synapses upstream from the output motoneurons, given their close correlation. Behavioral evidence has also shown that conditioned eyeblink, controlled by the facial nucleus, is highly correlated with conditioned NM extension (57). This is understandable, because eyeblink and NM extension are parts of the same defensive reflex in the rabbit's natural behavioral repertoire. The facial nucleus motoneurons that control orbicularis oculi are in the dorsomedial portion of the facial nucleus (25). These facial motoneurons should also be under control of the premotor elements that govern Acc Abd, Abd, and oculomotor neurons in conditioned NM extension (57).

An obvious strategy for localizing such a common premotor neuron efferent pool is to inject retrograde tracers into Acc Abd, Abd, the oculomotor nucleus, and the orbicularis oculi portion of the facial nucleus. Common premotor regions should become evident. Single-unit recording may then be done in candidate premotor regions to determine their relative importance for NM conditioned and unconditioned responses. We have begun to implement this approach by determining the afferents to Abd with retrograde tracing after small injections of wheat germ agglutinin-conjugated horseradish peroxidase (WGA–HRP) (32).

All our injections have been placed in Abd under physiological control. We first thoroughly mapped the location of Abd by recording antidromic field potentials through tungsten microelectrodes. We then substituted a glass micropipette that permitted physiological recording and placed the pipette in the center of abducens nucleus using stereotaxic coordinates confirmed by recording the antidromic field potentials. Injections were made under pressure.

Thus far, we have made injections of 1–2% WGA–HRP into Abd in nine rabbits. After 48 hours, the rabbits were perfused and the brains processed with the tetramethylbenzidine reaction procedure of Mesulam (60). Five of the injections have been less than 10 nl in volume. In these cases, the injection sites have been largely confined to Abd.

The regions that consistently have shown retrogradely labeled cells after WGA–HRP injections confined to the Abd are the vestibular complex, nucleus prepositus hypoglossi, the reticular formation near Abd both rostral and caudal, and the oculomotor complex. Labeling in the vestibular complex, reticular formation, and prepositus hypoglossi is bilateral. The oculomotor labeling is contralateral. Some other, less prominent and thus far less consistent, sources of afferent projections are being examined in further experiments.

Our results are in agreement with the afferents that have been reported for cat Abd (10,30,53). We have not yet been able to do systematic single-neuron recording in any of these premotor regions during NM conditioning. Clearly, any region which projects to Acc Abd, as well as Abd, will be of particular interest. Thompson and his colleagues have recently demonstrated that cerebellar lesions selectively affect conditioned, and not unconditioned, NM extension (50,55,56). The critical lesion locus is apparently in the cerebellar hemisphere and dentate/interpositus nuclei. It will be interesting to determine how the cerebellum interacts with the premotor areas we have been discussing. It is obligatory that cerebellum control these brainstem premotor regions fairly directly if, as has been hypothesized, the engram for NM conditioning is located there (55,56). The precise pathways by which this cerebellar control is expressed remain to be delineated.

Comments

The studies that we have done thus far on rabbit nictitating membrane conditioning, as well as the extensive behavioral, physiological, and anatomical work reviewed in the other chapters of this volume, are convincing evidence of the utility of the rabbit NM preparation as a model system with which to make concrete progress in analyzing the mechanisms of learning in mammalian brain.

We have made observations that are relevant to the rabbit NM preparation, but also to the use of the rabbit in other kinds of neurobiological research. In recent years, the rabbit has not been the species of choice in anatomical and physiological work. But our detailed neuroanatomical and neurophysiological analyses of the rabbit cochlear nucleus and auditory cortex have shown these regions to be very similar in rabbit and the species that had previously been extensively studied (23,41,48). These similarities were true even at the cellular level, both anatomically and physiologically. The restrained rabbit is an extremely tractable subject for single-neuron studies in a behavioral, or nonbehavioral, context (48,49). This tractability has the added advantage of facilitating stimulus application and control (48) and behavioral measurement (78). The rabbit's brain is large enough to make electrode placement feasible—a particularly important advantage for work in the brainstem—and the cortex is lissencephalic, facilitating electrode track reconstruction. Finally, rabbits are less expensive to purchase and maintain than cats, dogs, or primates. All these advantages make the rabbit NM paradigm attractive and suggest adapting the rabbit in other experimental contexts, as well.

Our experiments, and those that other groups have been doing, on rabbit NM conditioning have sensitized us to the elegant complexity of the neuroanatomical and neurophysiological substrate that must underly this apparently simple Pavlovian conditioning paradigm. Even though the conditioning can be mediated at the brainstem level (27,64,66,67,68,69), auditory cortex (49) and hippocampal (5,6,7) neurons clearly change and are involved in laying down the memory trace in the intact brain. At cochlear nucleus, the central region where the auditory CS is initially processed, and at the final output regions for CR expression, information relevant to the NM conditioned reflex arc flows in multiple pathways. It is likely that an engram underlying NM conditioning lies in hippocampus (82) and in cerebellum (55,56,83). But the parallel loops and reciprocal connections in the brain areas through which information relevant to NM conditioning flows (52) offer several other candidate loci for plastic change. A systematic anatomical and physiological analysis at the single-neuron level will allow a determination of whether the engram for NM conditioning is located in one locus, in several loci, or as a distributed network within the forebrain, brainstem, and cerebellum.

ACKNOWLEDGMENTS

The participation of Dr. Geoffrey Hui, Dr. Nina Kraus, and Dr. Michael Shipley in portions of the research summarized here was very much appreciated.

This work was supported by NIH Grants 5 RO1 NS12317, NS17489, SO7 RR05370, and NIMH Grant T32-MH16097.

REFERENCES

1. Abeles, M., & Goldstein, M. H., Jr. (1972). Responses of single units in primary auditory cortex of the cat to tones and to tone pairs. *Brain Research, 42,* 337–352.
2. Baker, R., McCrea, R. A., & Spencer, R. F. (1980). Synaptic organization of cat accessory abducens nucleus. *Journal of Neurophysiology, 43,* 771–791.
3. Beaton, R., & Miller, J. M. (1975). Single cell activity in the auditory cortex of unanesthetized, behaving monkey: Correlation with stimulus controlled behavior. *Brain Research, 100,* 543–562.
4. Benson, D. A., & Heinz, R. D. (1978). Single unit activity in the auditory cortex of monkeys selectively attending left vs. right ear stimulation. *Brain Research, 159,* 307–320.
5. Berger, T. W., Alger, B., & Thompson, R. F. (1976). Neuronal substrates of classical conditioning in the hippocampus. *Science, 192,* 482–485.
6. Berger, T. W., & Thompson, R. F. (1978a). Identification of pyramidal cells as the critical elements in hippocampal neuronal plasticity during learning. *Proceedings of the National Academy of Sciences, 75,* 1572–1576.
7. Berger, T. W., & Thompson, R. F. (1978b). Neuronal plasticity in the limbic system during classical conditioning of the rabbit nictitating membrane response, I. The hippocampus. *Brain Research, 145,* 323–346.
8. Berthier, N. E., & Moore, J. W. (1980). Role of extraocular muscles in the rabbit (*Oryctolagus cuniculus*) nictitating membrane response. *Physiology and Behavior, 24,* 931–937.
9. Berthier, N. E., & Moore, J. W. (1983). The nictitating membrane response: An electrophysiological study of the abducens nerve and nucleus and the accessory abducens nucleus in rabbit. *Brain Research, 258,* 201–210.
10. Bienfang, D. C. (1978). The course of direct projections from the abducens nucleus to the contralateral medial rectus subdivision of the oculomotor nucleus in the cat. *Brain Research, 145,* 277–289.
11. Brawer, J. R., Morest, D. K., & Kane, E. C. (1974). The neuronal architecture of the cochlear nucleus of the cat. *Journal of Comparative Neurology, 155,* 251–300.
12. Brugge, J. F., & Merzenich, M. M. (1973). Patterns of activity of single neurons in auditory cortex in monkey. In A. R. Moller (Ed.), *Basic Mechanisms of Hearing,* (pp. 745–772). New York: Academic Press.
13. Buchwald, J. S., Halas, E. S., & Schramm, S. (1966). Changes in cortical and subcortical unit activity during behavioral conditioning. *Physiology and Behavior, 1,* 11–22.

14. Cegavske, C. F., Harrison, T. A., & Torigoe, Y. (In preparation). *Identification of the substrates of the unconditioned response in the classically conditioned, rabbit, nictitating membrane preparation.*

15. Cegavske, C. F., Patterson, M. M., & Thompson, R. F. (1979). Neuronal unit activity in the abducens nucleus during classical conditioning of the nictitating membrane response in the rabbit (*Oryctolagus cuniculus*). *Journal of Comparative and Physiological Psychology, 93,* 595–609.

16. Cegavske, C. F., Thomson, R. F., Patterson, M. M., & Gormezano, I. (1976). Mechanisms of efferent neuronal control of the reflex nictitating membrane response in rabbit (*Oryctolagus cuniculus*). *Journal of Comparative and Physiological Psychology, 90,* 411–423.

17. Crandall, W. F., Goldberg, S. J., Wilson, J. S., & McClung, J. R. (1981). Muscle units divided among retractor bulbi muscle slips and between the lateral rectus and retractor bulbi muscles in cat. *Experimental Neurology, 71,* 251–260.

18. Dallos, P. (1973). *The auditory periphery: biophysics and physiology.* New York: Academic Press.

19. Deaux, E. B., & Gormezano, I. (1963). Eyeball retraction: Classical conditioning and extinction in the albino rabbit. *Science, 141,* 630–631.

20. Diamond, I. T. (1978). The auditory cortex. In R. Naunton & G. Fernandez (Eds.), *Evoked electrical activity in the auditory nervous system,* (pp. 463–486). New York: Acadaemic Press.

21. Disterhoft, J. F., Kwan, H. H., & Lo, W. D. (1977). Nictitating membrane conditioning to tone in the immobilized albino rabbit. *Brain Research, 137,* 127–143.

22. Disterhoft, J. F., & Olds, J. (1972). Differential development of conditioned unit changes in thalamus and cortex of rat. *Journal of Neurophysiology, 35,* 665–679.

23. Disterhoft, J. F., Perkins, R. E., & Evans, S. (1980). The neuronal morphology of the rabbit cochlear nucleus. *Journal of Comparative Neurology, 192,* 687–702.

24. Disterhoft, J. F., Quinn, K. J., Weiss, C., & Shipley, M. T. (1985). Accessory abducens nucleus and conditioned eye retraction nictitating membrane extension in rabbit. *Journal of Neuroscience, 5,* 941–950.

25. Disterhoft, J. F., & Shipley, M. T. (1980). Accessory abducens nucleus innervation of rabbit retractor bulbi motorneurons localized with HRP retrograde transport. *Society for Neuroscience Abstracts, 6,* 478.

26. Disterhoft, J. F., & Stuart, D. K. (1976). The trial sequence of changed unit activity in auditory system of alert rat during conditioned response acquisition and extinction. *Journal of Neurophysiology, 39,* 266–281.

27. Enser, L. D. (1976). *A study of classical nictitating membrane conditioning in neodecoricate, hemidecorticate and thalamic rabbits.* Unpublished doctoral dissertation, University of Iowa, Iowa City.

28. Evans, E. F., & Nelson, P. G. (1973). The responses of single neurones in the cochlear nucleus of the cat as a function of their location and anesthetic state. *Experimental Brain Research, 17,* 402–427.

29. Evans, E. F., & Whitfield, I. C. (1964). Classification of unit responses in the auditory cortex of the unanesthetized and unrestrained cat. *Journal of Physiology (Lond.), 171,* 476–493.

30. Gacek, R. R. (1979). Location of abducens afferent neurons in the cat. *Experimental Neurology, 64,* 342–353.

31. Goldstein, M. H., Jr., & Abeles, M. (1975). Single unit activity of the auditory cortex. In W. E. Keidel & W. D. Neff (Eds.), *Handbook of sensory physiology of the auditory system* (Vol. V/2, pp. 199–218). Berlin: Springer-Verlag.

32. Gonatas, N. K., Harper, C., Mizutani, T., & Gonatas, J. (1979). Superior sensitivity of conjugates of horseradish peroxidase with wheat germ agglutinin for studies of retrograde axonal transport. *Journal of Histochemistry and Cytochemistry, 27,* 728–734.

33. Gormezano, I., Schneiderman, N., Deaux, E. G. & Fuentes, I. (1962). Nictitating membrane: Classical conditioning and extinction in the albino rabbit. *Science, 138,* 33–34.

34. Grant, L., Gueritaud, J. P., Horcholle-Bossavit, G., & Tyc–Dumont, S. (1979). Anatomical and electrophysiological identification of motoneurons supplying the cat retractor bulbi muscle. *Experimental Brain Research, 34,* 541–550.

35. Gray, T. S., McMaster, S. E., Harvey, J. A., & Gormezano, I. (1980). Localization of the motoneurons which innervate the retractor bulbi muscle in the rabbit. *Society for Neuroscience Abstracts, 6,* 16.

36. Gray, T. S., McMaster, S. E., Harvey, J. A., & Gormezano, I. (1981). Localization of retractor bulbi motoneurons in the rabbit. *Brain Research, 226,* 93–106.

37. Halas, E. S., Beardsley, J. V., & Sandlie, M. E. (1970). Conditioned neuronal responses of various levels in conditioning paradigms. *Electroencephalography and Clinical Neurophysiology, 28,* 468–477.

38. Harrison, T. A., Cegavske, C. F., & Thompson, R. F. (1978). Neuronal activity recorded in the abducens and oculomotor nuclei during nictitating membrane conditioning in the rabbit. *Society for Neuroscience Abstracts, 4,* 259.

39. Hocherman, S., Benson, D. A., Goldstein, M. H., Jr., Heffner, H. E., & Heinz, R. D. (1976). Evoked unit activity in auditory cortex of monkeys performing a selective attention task. *Brain Research, 177,* 51–68.

40. Hubel, D. M., Henson, C. O., Rupert, A., & Galambos, R. (1959). "Attention" units in the auditory cortex. *Science, 129,* 1979–1980.

41. Hui, G. S., & Disterhoft, J. F. (1980). Cochlear nucleus unit responses to pure tones in conscious rabbit. *Experimental Neurology, 69,* 576–588.

42. Hutson, K. A., Glendenning, K. K., & Masterson, R. B. (1979). Accessory abducens nucleus and its relationship to the accessory facial and posterior trigeminal nuclei in cat. *Journal of Comparative Neurology, 188,* 1–16.

43. Kettner, R. E., & Thompson, R. F. (1982). Auditory signal detection and decision processes in the nervous system. *Journal of Comparative and Physiological Psychology, 96,* 328–331.

44. Kiang, N. Y.-S (1975). Stimulus representation in the discharge patterns of auditory neurons. In D. B. Tower (Ed.), *The nervous system* (Vol. 3, pp. 81–96). New York: Raven Press.

45. Kiang, N. Y.-S., Morest, D. K., Godfrey, D. A., Guinan, J. J., Jr., & Kane, E. C. (1973). Stimulus coding at caudal levels of the cat's auditory nervous system. I. Response characteristics of single units. In A Moller (Ed.), *Basic mechanisms in hearing,* (pp. 445–478). New York: Academic Press.

46. Kiang, N. Y.-S., Watanabe, T., Thomas, E. C., & Clark, L. F. (1965). *Discharge patterns of single fibers in the cat's auditory nerve.* Cambridge: M.I.T. Press.

47. Kitzes, L. M., Farley, G. R., & Starr, A. (1978). Modulation of auditory cortex unit activity during the performance of a conditioned response. *Experimental Neurology, 62,* 678–697.

48. Kraus, N., & Disterhoft, J. F. (1981). Location of rabbit auditory cortex and description of single unit activity. *Brain Research, 214,* 275–286.

49. Kraus, N., & Disterhoft, J. F. (1982). Response plasticity of single neurons in rabbit auditory association cortex during tone-signalled learning. *Brain Research, 246,* 205–215.

50. Lincoln, J. S., McCormick, D. A., & Thompson, R. F. (1982). Ipsilateral cerebellar lesions prevent learning of the classically conditioned nictitating membrane/eyelid response. *Brain Research, 242,* 190–193.

51. Lorente de No, R. (1933). The interaction of the corneal reflex and vestibular nystagmus. *American Journal of Physiology, 103,* 704–711.

52. Lorente de No, R. (1933). Vestibulo — ocular reflex arc. *Archives of Neurology and Psychiatry, 30,* 245–329.

53. Maciewicz, R. J., Eagen, L., Kaneko, C. R. S., & Highstein, S. M. (1977). Vestibular and

medullary brainstem afferents to the abducens nucleus in the cat. *Brain Research, 123,* 229–240.

54. Martin, G. K., Lonsbury–Martin, B. L., & Kimm, J. (1980). A rabbit preparation for neurobehavioral auditory research. *Hearing Research, 2,* 65–78.

55. McCormick, D. A., Clark, G. A., Lavond, D. G., & Thompson, R. F. (1982). Initial localization of the memory trace for a basic form of learning. *Proceedings National Academy of Science, 79,* 2731–2735.

56. McCormick, D. A., Lavond, D. G., Clark, G. A., Kettner, R. E., Rising, C. E., Thompson, R. F. (1981). The engram found? Role of the cerebellum in classical conditioning of nictitating membrane and eyelid responses. *Bulletin of the Psychonomic Society, 18.*

57. McCormick, D. A., Lavond, D. G., & Thompson, R. F. (1982). Concomitant classical conditioning of the rabbit nictitating membrane and eyelid responses: Correlations and implications. *Physiology and Behavior, 28,* 769–775.

58. Meredith, M. A., McClung, J. R., & Goldberg, S. J. (1981). Retractor bulbi muscle responses to oculomotor nerve and nucleus stimulation in the cat. *Brain Research, 211,* 427–432.

59. Merzenich, M. M., & Brugge, J. F. (1973). Variation of excitability of neurons in primary auditory cortex in the unanesthetized macaque monkey: Effects of sleep and body movement. *Journal of the Acoustical Society of America, 53,* 1.

60. Mesulam, M. M. (1978). A tetramethyl benzidine method for the light microscope tracing of neural connections with horseradish peroxidase (HRP) neurohistochemistry. In *Neuroanatomical Techniques,* Soc. for Neuroscience Short Course.

61. Miller, J. M., Beaton, R. D., O'Connor, T., & Pfingst, B. E. (1974). Response pattern complexity of auditory cells in the cortex of unanesthetized monkeys. *Brain Research, 69,* 101–113.

62. Miller, J. M., Sutton, D., Pfingst, B., Ryan, A., Beaton, R., & Gourevitch, G. (1972). Single cell activity in auditory cortex of rhesus monkey, behavioral dependency. *Science, 177,* 449–451.

63. Mishkin, M. (1982). A memory system in the monkey. *Royal Society of London Philosophical Transactions, 298,* 85–96.

64. Moore, J. W., Yeo, C. H., Oakley, D. A., & Russell, I. S. (1980).Conditioned inhibition of the nictitating membrane response in neodecorticate rabbits. *Behavioral Brain Research, 1,* 397–410.

65. Morest, D. K., Kiang, N. Y.-S., Kane, E. C., Guinan, J. J., Jr., & Godfrey, D. A. (1973). Stimulus coding at caudal levels of the cat's auditory nervous system. II. Patterns of synaptic organization. In A. Moller (Ed.), *Basic mechanisms in hearing.* (pp. 479–504). New York: Academic Press.

66. Norman, R. J., Buchwald, J. S., & Villablanca, J. R. (1977). Classical conditioning with auditory discrimination of the eye blink in decerebrate cat. *Science, 196,* 551–553.

67. Norman, R. J., Villablanca, J. R., Brown, K. A., Schwafel, J. A., & Buchwald, J. S. (1974). Classical eyeblink conditioning in the bilaterally hemispherectomized cat. *Experimental Neurology, 44,* 363–380.

68. Oakley, D. A., & Russell, I. S. (1972). Neocortical lesions and Pavlovian conditioning. *Physiology and Behavior, 8,* 915–926.

69. Oakley, D. A., & Russell, I. S. (1976). Subcortical nature of Pavlovian differentiation in the rabbit. *Physiology and Behavior, 17,* 947–954.

70. Olds, J., Disterhoft, J. F., Segal, M., Kornblith, C. L., & Hirsh, R. (1972). Learning centers of rat brain mapped by measuring latencies of conditioned unit responses. *Journal of Neurophysiology, 35,* 202–219.

71. Oleson, T. D., Ashe, J. H., & Weinberger, N. M. (1975). Modification of auditory and somatosensory system activity during pupillary conditioning in the paralyzed cat. *Journal of*

Neurophysiology, 38, 1114–1139.

72. Osen, K. K., (1969). Cytoarchitecture of the cochlear nuclei in the cat. *Journal of Comparative Neurology, 136,* 453–484.

73. Perry, D. R., & Webster, W. R. (1981). Neuronal organization of the rabbit cochlear nucleus: Some anatomical and electrophysiological observations. *Journal of Comparative Neurology, 197,* 623–638.

74. Pfeiffer, R. R. (1966). Classification of response patterns of spike discharges for units in the cochlear nucleus: Tone-burst stimulation. *Experimental Brain Research, 1,* 220–235.

75. Pfingst, B. E., & O'Connor, T. A. (1981). Classification of neurons in auditory cortex of monkeys performing a simple auditory task. *Journal of Neurophysiology, 45,* 16–34.

76. Pfingst, B. E., O'Connor, T. A., & Miller, J. M. (1977). Response plasticity of neurons in auditory cortex of the rhesus monkey. *Experimental Brain Research, 29,* 393–404.

77. Quinn, K. J., Disterhoft, J. F., & Weiss, C. (1982). Accessory abducens single unit activity during NM conditioning in the rabbit. *Society for Neuroscience Abstracts, 8,* 314.

78. Quinn, K. J., Kennedy, P. R., Weiss, C., & Disterhoft, J. F. (1984). Eyeball retraction latency in conscious rabbit measured with a new photodiode technique. *Journal of Neuroscience Methods, 10,* 29–39.

79. Roth, G. L., Aitkin, L. M., Andersen, R. A., & Merzenich, M. M. (1978). Some features of the spatial organization of the central nucleus of the inferior colliculus of the cat. *Journal of Comparative Neurology, 182,* 661–680.

80. Spencer, R., Baker, R., & McCrea, R. A. (1980). Localization and morphology of cat retractor bulbi motoneurons. *Journal of Neurophysiology, 43,* 754–770.

81. Thompson, R. F. (1976). The search for the engram. *American Psychologist, 31,* 209–227.

82. Thompson, R. F. (1980). The search for the engram, II. In D. McFadden (Ed.), *Neural mechanisms of behavior* (pp. 172–222). New York: Springer-Verlag.

83. Thompson, R. F., McCormick, D. A., Lavond, D. G., Clark, G. A., Kettner, R. E., and Mauk, M. D. (1983). The engram found? Initial localization of the memory trace for a basic form of associative learning. In *Progress in Psychobiology and Physiological Psychology,* (Vol 10, pp. 167–196). New York: Academic Press.

84. Webster, W. R. (1977). Chopper units recorded in the cochlear nucleus of the awake cat. *Neuroscience Letters, 7,* 261–265.

85. Winer, J. A., Diamond, I. T., & Raczkowski, D. (1977). Subdivisions of the auditory cortex of the cat: The retrograde transport of horseradish peroxidase to the medial geniculate body and posterior thalamic nuclei. *Journal of Comparative Neurology, 176,* 387–418.

86. Woody, C. D., Knispel, J. D., Crow, T. J., & Black-Cleworth, P. A. (1976). Activity and excitability to electrical current of cortical auditory receptive neurons of awake cats as affected by stimulus association. *Journal of Neurophysiology, 39,* 1045–1061.

87. Young, E. D., & Brownell, W. E. (1976). Responses to tones and noise of single cells in dorsal cochlear nucleus of unanesthetized cats. *Journal of Neurophysiology, 39,* 282–300.

5 Neural and Behavioral Mechanism Involved in Learning to Ignore Irrelevant Stimuli

Paul R. Solomon
Bronfman Science Center
Williams College

INTRODUCTION

Most investigations of the learning process involve what has come to be known as excitatory conditioning. At the simplest level, this refers to the association of a previously unimportant event (e.g., the conditioned stimulus, CS) with an event that has significance to the organism (e.g., the unconditioned stimulus, UCS). Once this occurs, the previously unimportant event also takes on significance. The significance of the CS can be measured in a number of ways, but in the classical conditioning paradigm the primary measure is the emergence of the conditioned response.

The processes that govern excitatory conditioning are both complicated and important. Nevertheless, as many of the chapters in this volume indicate, researchers have made considerable progress toward understanding these phenomena at both the behavioral and neural levels. There is, however, another approach to the conditioning process that has steadily gained attention over the past decade. This approach asks the question, how do organisms learn to ignore stimuli that do not signal an important event (see Konorski, 1948; Pavlov, 1927). Although this process is only beginning to receive the attention that excitatory conditioning has, it seems to be an equally important question. Indeed, just as organisms must learn to attend and respond to important aspects of their environment, they also must learn to ignore the irrelevant aspects.

In this chapter I review some of the work aimed at understanding the behavioral and neural mechanisms involved in learning to ignore irrelevant stimuli. Most of this work has been performed using the rabbit's classically conditioned nictitating membrane response (NMR), although we have carried out parallel studies in the two-way avoidance task in the rat. In performing some of these studies we have also gained insight into the neural processes governing acquisition of the conditioned response and, where appropriate, I discuss these findings.

LEARNING TO IGNORE IRRELEVANT STIMULI – BEHAVIORAL PARADIGMS

Although there are a number of paradigms that may require an animal to learn to ignore an irrelevant stimulus (see Mackintosh, 1975 for a review), two paradigms that seem to offer the most direct approach are latent inhibition and blocking.

In the latent inhibition paradigm, the organism learns to ignore a stimulus that predicts no change in the occurrence of a motivationally significant event (e.g., a reinforcer or a UCS). In blocking, the organism learns a slightly more complex relationship: that even though a stimulus predicts the occurrence of a motivationally significant event, it can be ignored because it is redundant; that is, it gives no information beyond what other stimuli already present predict.

Latent Inhibition

Lubow and Moore (1959) coined the term latent inhibition (LI) to refer to the finding that a series of nonreinforced preexposures to a to-be-continued stimulus retards conditioning to that stimulus when it is subsequently paired with a UCS or reinforcing event. There are a number of theoretical interpretations of latent inhibition (see Ludow, Schnur, & Rifkin, 1976; Mackintosh, 1975; Moore & Stickney, 1980; Rescorla & Wagner, 1972; Wagner, 1979; Weiss & Brown, 1974), but most share the view that the retardation of conditioning following preexposure is due to the preexposed stimulus losing salience via an habituation-like process whereby the organism learns to ignore the irrelevant stimulus. As Mackintosh has put it, the animal learns that the preexposed stimulus is irrelevant, thus when the stimulus is rendered important by being paired with a UCS, the animal must first overcome the attentional bias before conditioning can occur (see Moore, 1978). Experimental investigations of latent inhibition in a variety of preparations are consistent with this view (e.g., GSR, Maltzman, Raskin, & Wolff, 1979; rabbit NMR, Reiss & Wagner, 1972; CER, Rescorla, 1971; Solomon, Brennan, & Moore, 1974; two-way avoidance, Solomon, Kiney, & Scott, 1978).

Retardation of conditioning following stimulus preexposure is generally taken as evidence that the preexposed stimulus has become a latent inhibitor.

The retardation of conditioning alone, however, is not sufficient to conclude that this is the case.

Learning theorists now distinguish between two tyes of inhibitors—latent and conditioned. Although the procedures used to produce these forms of inhibition are quite different, both have the effect of producing a retardation of the acquisition of the conditioned response. This retardation is, however, brought about by two different processes. Whereas a latent inhibitor is produced by preexposing a stimulus, a conditioned inhibitor is produced by presenting a stimulus that uniquely predicts the *nonoccurrence* of the UCS.

There are a number of ways to produce a conditioned inhibitor, but the procedure originally described by Pavlov (1927) seems to be the most efficacious in the rabbit (Marchant, Mis, & Moore, 1971). In this procedure, the animal is first taught to discriminate between CS_A that is always followed by the UCS and a compound consisting of CS_A and a second stimulus, CS_B, which is never followed by the UCS. In this way the animal gradually forms the appropriate discrimination: responding to CS_A but not to the compound consisting of $CS_A + CS_B$. Because CS_B uniquely predicts the nonoccurrence of the UCS, it is the conditioned inhibitor.

It is important to note that in the conditioned inhibition paradigm the animal cannot ignore CS_B even though, like a latent inhibitor, it is not followed by the UCS. If the animal did this, the $CS_A/CS_A + CS_B$ discrimination would be impossible. It appears then, that the processes by which stimuli are endowed with conditioned or latent inhibitory properties are quite different. One requires that the animal learn to ignore a stimulus whereas the other requires that the animal attend to a stimulus (CS_B) that predicts nonreinforcement, and to withhold responding to a previously reinforced stimulus (CS_A) in its presence.

Like a latent inhibitor, when a conditioned inhibitor is presented alone and reinforced in a retardation test, the emergence of the CR is retarded. Thus the finding of retardation of conditioning is not sufficient to conclude latent inhibition. To draw this conclusion the results of a second test, the summation test, are necessary. In a summation test, the inhibitor (either latent or conditioned) is presented in compound with an excitatory CS: a CS previously paired with the UCS. If the inhibitor is of the latent type we would expect it to have no effect on the excitatory CS; that is, the animal should emit CRs. This is because the animal has learned to ignore the latent inhibitor. If, however, the stimulus is a conditioned inhibitor, we would expect it to inhibit responding to the excitatory CS.

Blocking

Most of our studies investigating how animals learn to ignore irrelevant stimuli have used the latent inhibition paradigm. We and others, however,

TABLE 5.1
Possible Interpretations of Experiments That Employ Both Summation
and Retardation Tests

Procedures to Produce Behavioral Affect	Summation	Retardation	Conclusions
Conditioned excitation CS_{B+}	no $CS_C < CS_{BC}$	no $CS_B > CS_{B \, naive}$	This is brought about by pairing a CS with a UCS. This leads to an excitatory summation effect because both CS_B and CS_C are excitatory. It also leads to faster conditioning for the experimental animal than a naive control in retardation testing because CS_B has received prior pairings with the UCS.
Latent inhibition CS_{B-}	no $CS_C = CS_{BC}$	yes $CS_B < CS_{B \, naive}$	This is produced by presenting a CS (CS_B) alone. The preexposed CS is thought to lose salience through a habituation-like process. Thus in summation testing it does not detract from the ability of an excitatory CS to elicit a CR. Specifically, because CS_B is turned out, the compound of $CS_B + CS_C$ is functionally identical to CS_C alone. When the preexposed CS is paired with the UCS during retardation testing, acquisition of the CR is retarded relative to controls who do not receive CS preexposures.
Conditioned inhibition CS_{A+} CS_{AB-}	yes $CS_C > CS_{BC}$	yes $CS_B < CS_{B \, naive}$	A stimulus that is explicitly unpaired with reinforcement (CS_B) in the presence of an excitatory stimulus (CS_A) becomes capable of reducing some ongoing behavior that is attributed to excitation; hence an inhibitory summation effect. In addition, since CS_B predicts the nonoccurrence of the UCS, experimental animals show retarded conditioning relative to naive controls when CS_B is subsequently paired with the UCS.

(see Mackintosh, 1973, 1975) have also begun to use a second paradigm that we believe involves a similar process. This paradigm, first developed by Kamin (1968), is called blocking.

The typical blocking paradigm in the rabbit NMR preparation consists of a two group design (Cf. Marchant & Moore, 1973; Table 5.2). In Stage 1 the experimental group is presented with CS_A paired with a UCS until the conditioned response is well established. Animals in the control condition simply sit in the apparatus for a corresponding amount of time with no CS or UCS presentations. In Stage 2, both groups are conditioned to a compound CS consisting of CS_A plus a second CS, CS_B. After both groups show a high level of conditioning to the compound, the test phase is introduced. During testing, all animals are presented with nonreinforced presentations of CS_A interspersed with nonreinforced CS_B presentations. In general, animals in the control condition give CRs to both CS_A and CS_B, whereas animals in the blocking groups respond only to the CS_A (e.g., Marchant & Moore, 1973). Although Kamin (1968) initially suggested that prior conditioning to the CS_A caused the animal not to notice CS_B when it was presented in compound with CS_A, subsequent accounts of the phenomena (Kamin, 1969; Mackintosh, 1973, 1975) suggest that the animal does initially attend to the redundant CS but does not condition to it because this stimulus provides no new information regarding the UCS. Like LI, blocking appears to involve a process in which the animal learns to ignore an irrelevant stimulus.

BEHAVIORAL STUDIES OF LATENT INHIBITION

The general procedures that we used to classically condition the rabbit's NMR are those described by Gormezano (1966). Each rabbit is restrained in a Plexiglas holder with an adjustable plate and ear clamp holding the head and a second plate placed over the animal's back to restrict body movement. Animals are run in individual sound attenuated and ventilated chambers. A

TABLE 5.2
Blocking Paradigm

	Stage 1	Stage 2	Stage 3 (test)
Experimental	CS_{A+}	CS_{AB+}	CS_{A-} CS_{B-}
Control	Apparatus	CS_{AB+}	CS_{A-}
	SIT		CS_{B-}

Note: + refers to CS plus UCS
− refers to CS alone.

panel in front of each animal contains lights and speakers that can serve as visual and auditory CSs. The UCS is typically a 2mA ac shock of 50 msec duration applied to the right (recorded) eye via 9 mm stainless steel wound clips.

Most of our sessions last for 50 minutes with each rabbit receiving 100 trials at a constant 30 sec intertrial interval. We typically use a 450 msec CS–UCS interval with the UCS overlapping the last 50 msec of the CS. Recording of the CR and UCR is accomplished by a rotary transducer mounted atop the animal's head and attached to a suture in the rabbit's NM. The potentiometer provides a dc signal that is recorded on a polygraph. We define a CR as an extension of the NM (usually less than 1 mm) that produces a 1 mm pen deflection during the CS–UCS interval. The presentation of all stimuli is controlled on line by a KIM 1 microprocessor (Solomon & Babcock, 1979).

The first of our investigations of LI in the rabbit were designed to see if stimulus preexposure in our preparation would produce a latent inhibitor. To accomplish this we used both the retardation and summation tests.

In our first experiment (Solomon, Brennan, & Moore, 1974), we preexposed separate groups of rabbits to either a 75 or a 95 dB tone. Two additional groups of rabbits simply sat in the apparatus for a corresponding amount of time. Following 450 tone preexposures (or 4 1/2 days of sitting in the apparatus), we paired the CS with a shock UCS in a retardation test. Animals in the 75 dB group and one of the sit control groups were conditioned to a 75 dB tone whereas animals in the 95 dB group and the remaining control group were conditioned to the 95 dB tone.

Figure 5.1 shows the result of this experiment. A clear retardation of conditioning (i.e., latent inhibition effect) can be seen in the 75 dB condition with preexposed animals giving significantly fewer CRs than their nonpreexposed counterparts. Examination of the 95 dB animals reveals two noteworthy effects. First, these animals conditioned faster than the 75 dB group. This is to be expected because more salient CSs generally lead to faster rates of conditioning (see Gormezano & Moore, 1969). But more important from our point of view was the finding that the LI effect was greatly attenuated in this group. If we assume that LI involves learning to ignore the preexposed stimulus, it follows that it should be more difficult to learn to ignore a more intense CS during stimulus preexposure. Thus, when the 95 dB CS is subsequently paired with the UCS, conditioning is not as retarded (but see Lubow et al., 1976, for an alternative view).

Our next experiment (Solomon et al., 1974, Experiment 2) involved a summation test. In this study rabbits were first given 5 days of conditioning to a light CS. This stimulus was later used as the excitatory CS during summation test. Next, the rabbits were assigned to one of the same four groups as in Experiment 1. After 4 1/2 days of preexposure to either a 75 or 95 dB tone (or a corresponding time sitting in the apparatus), each animal received 25 light alone presentations interspersed with 25 presentations of a compound consisting of the light plus the preexposed tone. None of these CSs was followed by a UCS. The summation test continued on the following day, but this time each animal received 50 presentations of each stimulus. As Fig. 5.2 indicates, there was no indication of a summation effect in either of the preexposed groups. Although there was a slight tendency for the tone to inhibit responding to the light in the preexposed animals in the 75 dB condition, this effect was not significantly different than that seen in the nonpreexposed controls. In the 95 dB group this trend reversed. Animals in the control group actually showed more of an inhibitory summation effect than the preexposed rabbits. Once again, this is consistent with the view that with stimulus preexposure, the animal learns to ignore the preexposed stimulus. Specifically, because the control group experienced the 95 dB tone for the first time during the summation test, it follows that the decreased responding to the light was due to the distracting effect of the tone (external inhibition, see Rescorla, 1967). Support for this view comes from the data for the 95 dB preexposed animals. The distracting effects of the tone in this case were significantly less. This would be expected if the animals had, at least in part, learned to ignore the tone during the stimulus preexposure phase.

The results of these studies on LI are consistent with the data from other studies of LI in the rabbit (Reiss & Wagner, 1972; Siegel, 1972; Solomon,

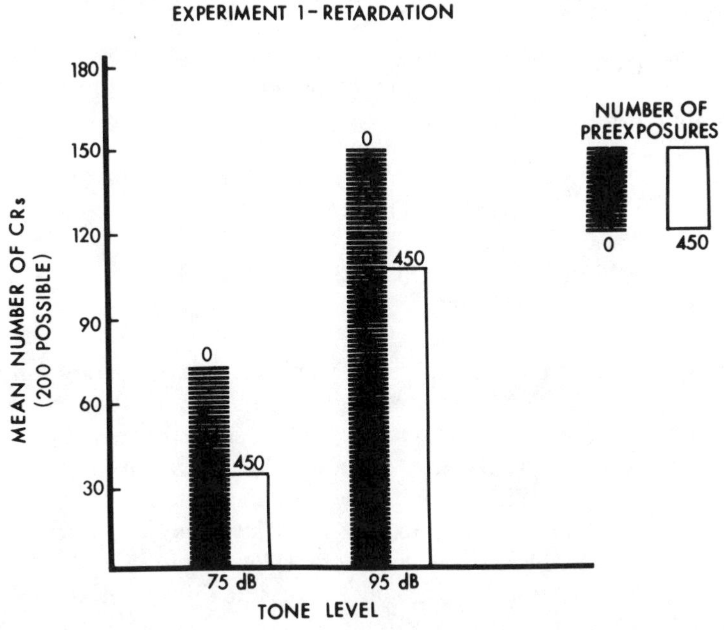

FIG. 5.1   Mean number of CRs (250 possible) as a function of CS intensity and number of preexposures. From Solomon, Lohr, and Moore (1974).

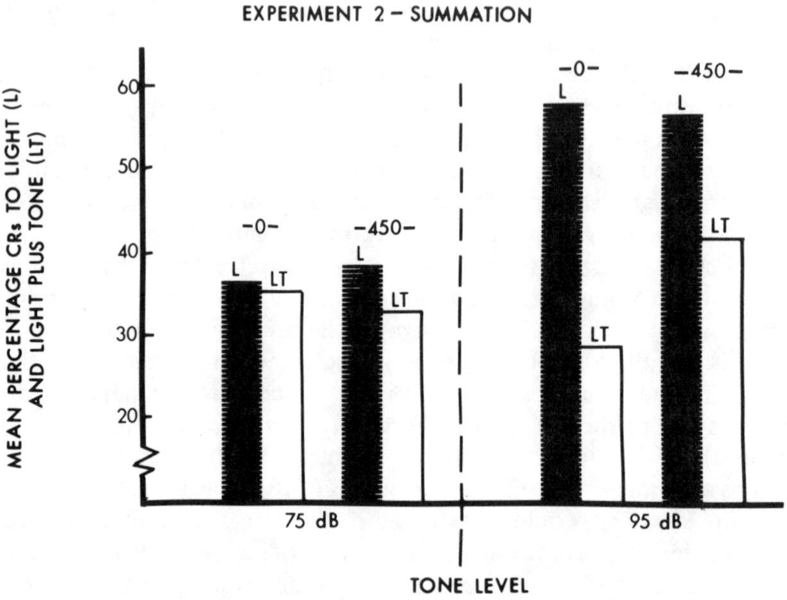

EXPERIMENT 2 – SUMMATION

FIG. 5.2   Mean percentage of CRs to light (L) and light plus tone (LT) as a function of stimulus intensity and number of preexposures. From Solomon, Lohr, and Moore (1974).

Lohr, & Moore, 1974) in indicating that animals learn to ignore the preexposed stimulus.

PHYSIOLOGICAL STUDIES

Hippocampal Lesions – Latent Inhibition, Blocking, and Conditioned Inhibition

When we began our studies, LI had already received considerable attention at the behavioral level, but work investigating physiological mechanisms of this behavior was sparse. A number of studies using other paradigms, however, had suggested that the hippocampus might be involved in inhibitory processes (Douglas, 1967; Kimble, 1968) or the coding of nonreinforced stimuli (Douglas, 1972). Thus our first study involved investigating the effects of hippocampal lesions on the LI process in rabbits.

In this study, we initially divided our rabbits into three surgical conditions: bilateral dorsal hippocampal ablations, lesions of the overlying cortex, or unoperated controls. Next, each surgical condition was subdivided into a sit control and a preexposed group. The final design consisted of 6 groups with 2 preexposure levels crossed with 3 surgical conditions. Animals in each of the 3 preexposure groups received 450 preexposures to the tone alone CS whereas the control animals simply sat in the apparatus for a corresponding amount of time. All animals then received 350 tone shock pairings in a retardation test. As we expected (see Fig. 5.3), normal (unoperated) animals showed a clear latent inhibition effect with preexposed rabbits giving significantly fewer CRs than sit controls. This was also the case for the rabbits with cortical lesions. In animals with hippocampal lesions, however, there was no latent inhibition effect. It seemed that hippocampal lesions had disrupted the rabbit's ability to learn to ignore the irrelevant stimulus. Before we could draw this conclusion, however, it was necessary to perform two additional tests.

Because the rate of conditioning is directly related to the intensity of the CS and the UCS, it is possible that the enhanced conditioning in the preexposed hippocampal animals was due to an increased sensitivity to one or both of these stimuli. Indeed, Jarrard (1973) had suggested that this was especially

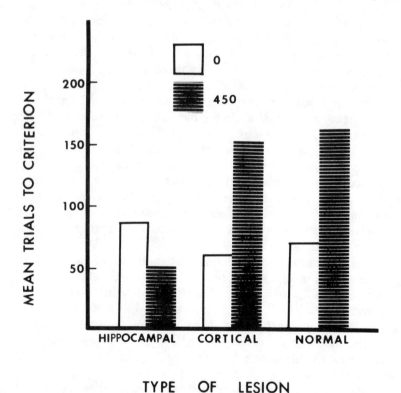

FIG. 5.3   Mean number of CRs (350 possible) as a function of lesion type and number of preexposures. From Solomon and Moore (1975).

possible in animals with hippocampal lesions. To test for the possibility that there was a change in CS sensitivity following hippocampal lesions we simply presented the CS (paired with the UCS) at successively softer dB levels until we reached a point where the animal gave CRs less than 50% of the time. Because these animals had all previously been trained to give CRs virtually 100% of the time, we reasoned that any decrement in responding was due to the inability to hear the tone. The results of the auditory sensitivity test were clear: There were no differences in tone sensitivity. In order to evaluate shock sensitivity we presented a low-level shock (.25 mA) and measured the amount of habituation, as indicated by the decrease in the UCR, over 40 trials. Once again, there were no differences among the six groups.

The finding that dorsal hippocampal ablations disrupt LI is not unique to the rabbit. In an earlier study, Ackil, Melgren, Halgren, and Frommer (1969) had reported similar findings in the rat using a two-way avoidance paradigm. Similarly, McFarland, Kostas, and Drew (1978) reported disruption of LI in a taste aversion paradigm in animals with hippocampal lesions.

To further test the view that the hippocampus is involved in learning to ignore irrelevant stimuli, we investigated the effects of hippocampal ablations in Kamin's two-stage blocking paradigm (Solomon, 1977, Experiment 1).

As in the hippocampal-LI study, rabbits received either bilateral aspiration lesions of the dorsal hippocampus or lesions of the overlying cortex. A third group served as unoperated controls. Next, half the rabbits in each surgical condition were assigned to the blocking group whereas the remaining half served as sit controls. Animals in the blocking groups received 100 conditioning trials per day to a tone CS until they emitted 90% or more CRs for 2 consecutive days. Animals in the control condition simply sat in the apparatus for a corresponding amount of time. During Stage 2, animals in both groups received 5 days of conditioning (100 trials per day) to a compound consisting of the tone from Stage 1 plus a light. On the day following the completion of Stage 2, testing began and continued for 2 days. Each day consisted of 50 light (nonreinforced) and 50 tone (nonreinforced) presentations in an unsystematic order.

As I indicated earlier, the predominant interpretation of the blocking paradigm is that the animal does initially attend to the redundant CS, the light, but does not condition to it because it provides no new information regarding the occurrence of the UCS. Thus the paradigm is similar to LI in that the animal must learn to ignore the irrelevant stimulus. We reasoned that if a tuning out process similar to the one in LI is operating, then hippocampal lesions should disrupt the blocking effect. Our findings were consistent with this view.

The data from this experiment are best expressed in terms of a suppression ratio in which the number of CRs emitted to light during testing is divided by the total number of CRs (L/L + T). A score below .5 indicates fewer responses to light than tone (i.e., blocking). Figure 5.4 shows the results of this study. Animals in the unoperated and cortical control groups showed a robust blocking effect with rabbits in the blocking groups responding much less frequently to light than tone (low suppression ratios) during testing. Animals in the control conditions showed about the same number of responses to each stimulus. There was no evidence of a blocking effect in animals with hippocampal lesions. Rabbits in both the control and blocking groups responded at about the same levels to the tone and light. Studies by Rickert, Bennett, Lane and French (1978) and Rickert, Lorden, Dawson, Smyly, and Callahan (1979) have found a similar disruption of blocking. It is also interesting that Schmajuk, Spear, and Isaacson (1983) have reported that hippocompectomized rats do not show overshadowing.

It appears then that the data from the blocking experiment further support the argument that the hippocampus is involved in learning to ignore irrelevant stimuli. These data also suggest that an irrelevant stimulus is not necessarily the same as a nonreinforced stimulus. In the blocking paradigm, even though the light is followed by the UCS, it is an irrelevant or redundant stimulus. It does not uniquely predict any change in the occurrence of the UCS and thus, like a preexposed stimulus in LI, it can be ignored.

To further pursue the idea that whether or not a stimulus is relevant is not necessarily related to whether or not it is followed by a reinforcing event, we examined the effects of hippocampal ablations on conditioned inhibition in

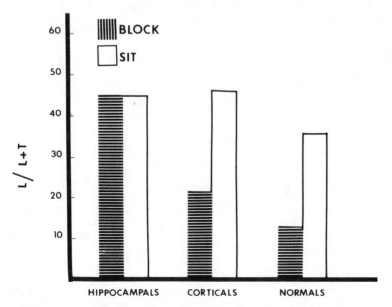

FIG. 5.4 Mean number of CRs to light divided by responses to light and tone for hippocampals, corticals, and normals. From Solomon (1977).

the rabbit. Recall that CI involves discriminating between CS_A (reinforced) and a second stimulus comprised of CS_A plus CS_B (nonreinforced). In our experiment (Solomon, 1977, Experiment II), three groups of animals, those with hippocampal or cortical ablations, and unoperated controls, were trained to discriminate between a light (reinforced) and a light plus tone compound (unreinforced). Although this is a difficult discrimination for the rabbit (see Marchant et al., 1972; Marchant & Moore, 1974), animals in all three groups reached satisfactory discrimination levels at the end of 15 days (100 trials per day, Fig. 5.5). Next, all animals underwent retardation testing that consisted of pairing the tone with a UCS until the CR was well established. Once again there were no differences among the three groups (Fig. 5.5). Taken together, these two pieces of information indicate that the hippocampus is not essential for conditioned inhibition of the rabbit's NMR.

Although a number of theoretical accounts of hippocampal function have stated that the hippocampus plays a direct role in Pavlovian conditioned (e.g., Kimble, 1968) or internal (e.g., Douglas, 1967) inhibition, we believe that our study was the first attempt to test this idea in a Pavlovian CI para-

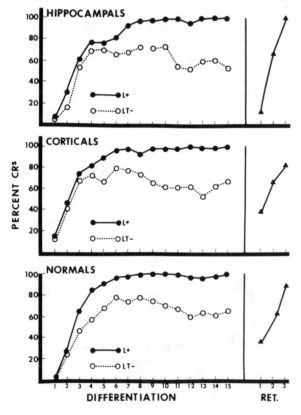

FIG. 5.5 Left Panels: Mean percentage conditioned responding to the light (CS +) and the light plus tone (CS −) for hippocampals, corticals, and normals over the 15 days of differentiation. Right Panels: Mean percentage conditioned responding to the tone for hippocampals, corticals, and normals over the 3 days of retardation (RET) testing. From Solomon (1977).

digm (see also Micco & Schwartz, 1971). Despite the apparent conflict between our data and previous theoretical accounts, the results were not surprising from our perspective. Specifically, even though CS_B was never followed by the UCS, it was a relevant stimulus and could not be ignored because it was the only stimulus that uniquely predicted the nonoccurrence of the UCS.

The data from the CI study combined with the results of the LI and blocking studies appear to support the notion that the hippocampus is part of a neural system involved in learning to ignore irrelevant stimuli. With this in mind, we have turned our attention to (1) electrophysiological studies designed to trace the flow of information through the hippocampus, and (2) studies designed to delineate other neuroanatomical and neurochemical aspects of the system. We have also further investigated the role of the hippocampus in acquisition of the rabbit's conditioned NMR.

Electrophysiological Studies in Hippocampus-Latent Inhibition and Related Paradigms

To my knowledge, the only electrophysiological investigation of LI was performed by Best and Best (1976). In their study, Best and Best presented rats with 15-20 preexposures to a tone. They then recorded single-unit activity from hippocampus when the tone was paired with a foot shock. They reported an increase in the rate of firing of hippocampal cells during the tone for nonpreexposed animals and a slight decrease for preexposed rats. It is difficult to specify precisely what these changes in firing rate signify, but they do, as the authors point out, indicate that the hippocampus is influenced by the salience of a stimulus and thus may be involved in determining the importance of that stimulus. Although the Best and Best study is the only study to date that directly addresses latent inhibition, a number of investigators have looked at hippocampal correlates of CS-alone presentations or unpaired presentations of the CS and UCS.

Vinogradova and her co-workers (see Vinogradova & Brazhnik, 1978, for a review) have recorded single-unit activity in the hippocampus of the unrestrained rabbit during presentations of a variety of sensory stimuli. In area CA3 of the intact hippocampus, they found either a prolonged increase in firing rate (outlasting the stimulus by 3-5 msec or more) or a shorter duration decrease following sensory stimulation. But perhaps more importantly from our point of view is their finding that repeated presentations of the same stimulus produced a gradual and complete habituation of the neuronal response within 8-30 presentations. Based on these and related findings, Vinogradova has raised the possibility that the hippocampus may be involved in determining the importance of a sensory stimulus.

More recently, Vinogradova and Brazhnik (1978) have examined the effects of deafferenting the hippocampus on single-unit activity following sensory stimulation. In these studies, they reported that lesions of the perforant path eliminate the habituation of the neuronal response.

The finding that the perforant path is important in hippocampal responses to repeated sensory stimuli is in agreement with a study that we have recently completed (Weisz, Clark, Yang, Thompson, Solomon, & Berger, 1982). In this study, we recorded from identified single granule cells in the dentate gyrus during both paired and unpaired presentations of the CS and UCS. During paired training, the granule cells exhibited a short-latency increase in firing rate to the tone. These responses often took the form of rhythmical bursting activity in the theta range. During unpaired presentations of the CS and UCS, the dominant response of the dentate granule cells to the CS was a decrease in firing. Thus, whereas cells in areas CA1 and CA3 of hippocampus are time locked to conditioned NM behavior (Thompson, Berger, Berry, Hoehler, Kettner, & Weisz, 1980), the cells in the dentate area appear to be more concerned with registering the stimuli. Moreover they respond differently to pairing of the CS and UCS versus separate presentations of each stimulus.

In a related study, Weisz et al. (1982) recorded monosynaptic field potentials from the dentate gyrus in response to perforant path stimulation during NM conditioning. In agreement with the single-cell work, they found that granule cell excitability to the CS was higher in the paired conditioning group than in the unpaired group. It is important to note that a decrease in excitability was seen following tone presentations in the unpaired group.

A study reported by Lynch, Rose, and Gall (1978) in which they recorded dentate single-cell activity during a discrimination paradigm in the rat has produced results compatible with our single-cell work in the rabbit. Lynch et al. found a prolonged burst of firing in association with the tone that predicted reward, and an initial burst followed by a rapid return to baseline levels after the nonrewarded tone.

Work performed by Winson and his co-workers has also suggested that the perforant path-granule cell synapse may be an important "neuronal gate" for processing stimuli. Winson and Abzug (1977, 1978) found that field potentials in the dentate gyrus produced by perforant path stimulation could be altered depending on the behavioral state of the animal. In a subsequent study, Winson reported that restimulation of the medial raphe, which projects to the dentate gyrus, facilitating neuronal transmission at the perforant path-granule cell synapse whereas lesions in the same area had the opposite effect (see Winson, 1980). It is noteworthy that we have found that medial raphe lesions (Solomon, Nichols, Kiernan, Kamer, & Kaplan, 1980) as well as PCPA administration (Solomon, Kiney, & Scott, 1978) disrupt latent inhibition.

Although each of these lines of research suggests that the perforant path-granule cell synapse might be important in coding the importance of a stimulus, it is premature to suggest that they might be instrumental in the latent inhibition process. Unpaired presentations and discrimination paradigms may tap different behavioral processes than CS-alone presentations (see Moore, 1974; Rescorla, 1971). It will ultimately be necessary to examine granule cell activity during both stimulus preexposure and subsequent conditioning.

The Hippocampus and Acquisition of the Conditioned NMR

In addition to providing information regarding the role of the hipocampus in ignoring irrelevant stimuli, our work, along with that of others, has indicated that hippocampal lesions do not appear to affect acquisition of the conditioned NMR in a delay conditioning paradigm (Powell & Buchanan, 1980; Schmaltz & Theios, 1972; Solomon, 1977; Solomon & Moore, 1975; see Figs. 5.6 and 5.7). It is now well established, however, that the cells in the hippocampus increase their firing rate during acquisition of the NMR (see Berger & Weisz, this volume; Thompson et al., 1980 for reviews). Specifically both

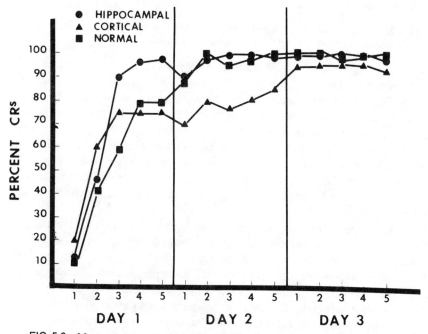

FIG. 5.6   Mean percentag conditioned responding to a 76 dB, 1200 Hz tone CS and a .2 mA infraorbital shock UCS for hippocampals, corticals, and normals.

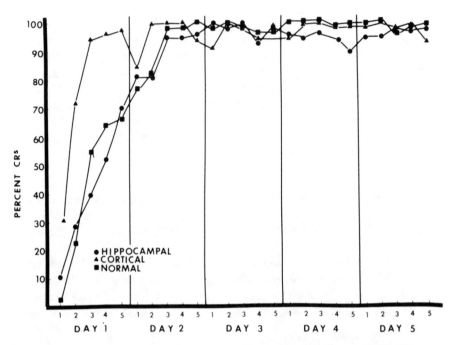

FIG. 5.7   Mean percentage conditioned responding to a light (6v) plus tone (76 dB, 1200 Hz) compound CS for hippocampals, corticals, and normals.

multiple (Berger, Alger, & Thompson, 1976; Berger & Thompson, 1978a) and single- (Berger & Thompson, 1978b) unit activity in the pyramidal cell layer of the dorsal hippocampus increases during the first few pairings of the CS and UCS. This increased neural activity precedes the behavioral response by 35–40 msec and forms a temporal model of the NMR.

These data indicate that even though the hippocampus is not essential for acquisition of the NMR in the delay conditioning paradigm, the structure is contributing to the process in the intact animal. This raises the important question of whether there are *any* acquisition paradigms in which the intact hippocampus is necessary.

We have recently begun to address this issue by examining the effects of bilateral dorsal hippocampal ablations on trace conditioning (Weisz, Solomon, & Thompson, 1980). In this paradigm, the tone remains on for 250 msec and is immediately followed by a 500 msec period in which no stimuli are present. A 100 msec air-puff UCS is then presented. The results of the study indicate that control animals acquire the CR in an average of 4 days (118 CS–UCS pairings per day). They appear to acquire the response much in the same way as animals acquire the CR in a delay paradigm: Initially CRs occur near the UCS onset, but as conditioning progresses the CRs move forward in the interval and continue to blend with the UCS. This finding is in general agreement with other studies of trace conditioning in the rabbit (e.g., Schneiderman, 1966). The behavior of rabbits with hippocampal lesions is markedly different. Throughout the 8 day period that we have run them, they do not acquire what is referred to an adaptive CR; that is, a CR that blends into the UCR (Boneau, 1958; Ebel & Prokasy, 1963). Hippocampal rabbits do occasionally emit short latency responses at the tone onset (600–700 msec prior to air-puff onset) that last for about 100 msec. These responses are often present early in training and are invariant in terms of latency and typography. To this extent, they may be examples of sensitization or pseudoconditioning. It is noteworthy that when we switch rabbits with hippocampal lesions to a standard delay paradigm (250 msec ISI), they readily acquire the CR.

The deficit in trace conditioning is consistent with the electrophysiological recordings from hippocampus during NMR conditioning. It is also consistent with recent views suggesting that hippocampus is important in coding of temporal relationships among stimuli and responses (see Berger, Clark, & Thompson, 1980; Moore, 1979; Moore & Solomon, 1980; Solomon, 1979, 1980; Thompson et al., 1980). Indeed, several researchers have suggested that learned time discriminations are an important factor in classical conditioning (Boneau, 1958; Ebel & Prokasy, 1963). Specifically, the time discrimination hypothesis postulates that the CR must overlap the UCS for reinforcement to occur, and that an important aspect of learning in this paradigm is timing the response. Nevertheless, a number of questions still remain regarding the trace paradigm and hippocampal lesions. First, will hippocampal lesions also disrupt long delay conditioning? A second question is whether hippocampal lesions disrupt only acquisition of the trace paradigm or also affect retention. Yet another question is whether the early responses detected in hippocampal animals are due to sensitization or pseudoconditioning.

In a related study, we have examined multiple-unit activity in area CA-1 of hippocampus during acquisition of the trace conditioned response. Three groups of animals were tested: Animals conditioned in the same trace paradigm used in the lesion study (Group T-500), animals that received explicitly unpaired presentations of the CS (tone) and UCS (air puff; Group UP) and animals that underwent conditioning with a 2,000 msec trace interval between CS offset and UCS onset (Group T-2000). Previous work has shown that this interval does not support behavioral conditioning (Hinson & Siegel, 1980).

Animals in the T-500 group acquired the behavioral CR within an average of 500 trials. Early in training, and well before any CRs had occurred, there was a substantial increase in hippocampal neuronal activity that began during the CS and persisted through the trace interval (Fig. 5.8). There was also an increase in the UCS period. Here, the neuronal activity both preceded the

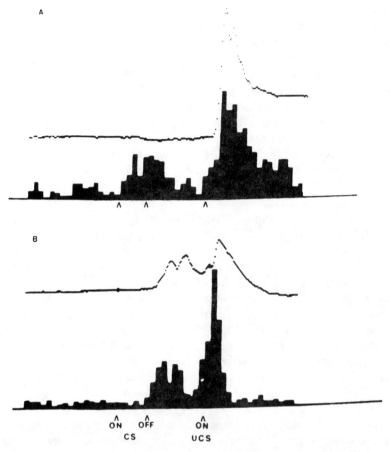

FIG. 5.8 (A) Average nictitating membrane response (NM; upper trace) and hippo-campal unit poststimulus histogram (Hipp; lower trace) for the first block of 8 trials on Day 2 of conditioning before the conditioned NMR develops. Data is from an individual subject. Time bins are 9 msec (B) NM and hippocampal units for the same animal during the first block of Day 10 after the rabbit has learned the conditioned NMR.

behavioral response and formed a temporal model of its amplitude-time course (see Berger & Thompson, 1978a). Later in conditioning, as CRs emerged, there was no longer neuronal bursting throughout the CS + Trace period. Rather, the activity shifted to later in the trace interval and formed a model of the amplitude-time course of the behavioral CR. Activity in the UCS period was similar to that seen earlier in conditioning. Animals in Groups UP and T-2000 showed no behavioral conditioning and no increased neuronal activity. The failure to find increased activity in Group T-2000 may be particularly interesting because it indicates that only CS–UCS pairings in intervals that support conditioning produce this increased neuronal response.

We are as yet uncertain as to the significance of the increased firing early in trace period early in conditioning. It is, however, tempting to speculate that this neuronal activity is somehow related to mediating the time between CS offset and UCS onset.

Based on these data and the data on the role of the hippocampus in LI and blocking, we have argued that although the hippocampus is not essential for simple forms of conditioning such as delay conditioning, it is essential for paradigms that require the coding of more complex temporal relationships (see Hoehler & Thompson, 1980; Solomon, 1979, 1980).

These findings are also reminiscent of the "Principle of Compensation" put forth by J. Hughlings Jackson (Croonian Lectures, 1884). According to Jackson, the higher levels of the nervous system represent and rerepresent all "lower" nervous centers. In terms of the conditioning process, it is possible that relatively simple processes, such as delay conditioning, are represented at several levels of the nervous system. This redundancy may explain why even though the hippocampus is involved in delay conditioning, its removal does not affect the acquisition process. This, of course, suggests that "lower" brain centers can mediate this process and there is now evidence that the brainstem and cerebellum may be capable of governing acquisition of the conditioned NMR in a delay paradigm (McCormick, Lavond, Clark, Kettner, Rising, Thompson, 1981; Mis, Gormezano, & Harvey, 1979; Moore, Desmond, & Berthier, 1982; Norman, Buchwald, & Villablanca, 1977). In learned behaviors involving more complex temporal relationships, such as LI, blocking, and acquisition in a trace paradigm, "higher" neural representation is necessary. The data suggest that the limbic system, and the hippocampus in particular is critical. Discrimination learning also seems to be represented in higher neural centers. Although complete decortication does not affect acquisition of the conditioned NMR (Oakley & Russell, 1972) or retention (Oakley & Russell, 1977), it does affect discrimination learning (Oakley & Russell, 1975). Gabriel has also demonstrated the importance of the cingulate cortex in discrimination learning in rabbits during a wheel-turning avoidance paradigm (see Gabriel, Foster, Orona, Saltwick, & Stanton, 1980 for a review).

PHARMACOLOGICAL AND NEUROCHEMICAL STUDIES — LATENT INHIBITION, BLOCKING, AND NMR ACQUISITION

Nauta (1958) in his elegant description of the "Limbic-Midbrain System" suggested that this system may be important in governing reactions to sensory stimuli. Since that time considerable effort has been directed toward elucidating these pathways (Swanson, 1978; Swanson & Cowan, 1977; Swanson & Cowan, 1979) and especially in tracing the neurochemical systems that form the limbic and midbrain connections (see Crow, 1977 for a review). There is now substantial data to indicate dopaminergic (see Moore & Bloom, 1978, for a review), serotonergic (Azmita & Segal, 1978), and noradrenergic (see Moore & Bloom, 1979, for a review) mesolimbic projections. Moreover, many of the newly identified neural peptides may be important in mediating transmission through these systems (e.g., substance P. Malthe-Sorenssen, Cheney, & Costa, 1978, B-endorphin, Moroni, Cheney, & Costa, 1977). As Nauta (1958) has put it there are "substantial escape pathways from this [limbic system] circuitous neural apparatus."

Although the neuroanatomy and neurochemistry of the limbic midbrain system are now beginning to be well understood, the relationship of this system to specific behaviors remains obscure. Nevertheless, a good deal of research suggests that this system plays a central role in processes that come under the general heading of attention (e.g., Crowne & Ratcliff, 1975; Douglas & Pribram, 1966; Lindsley & Wilson, 1975; Pribram & McGuinness, 1975).

The data indicating that many neural transmitters and neural modulators conduct information in the mesolimbic system make it unlikely that only one of them is involved in a behavior as complex as learning to ignore irrelevant stimuli. Rather, an interaction of several systems appears to be a more likely candidate (see Kokkinidis & Anisman, 1980, for a review). In support of this view, research indicates that changing the level of one transmitter in the brain has substantial effects on others (e.g., Antelman & Caggiula, 1977; Trulson & Jacobs, 1979).

The Cholinergic System — LI and NMR Acquisition

Our first studies (Moore, Goodell, & Solomon, 1976) sought to examine the effects of disruption of the cholinergic system on both LI and acquisition of the rabbit's conditioned NMR. Our choice of the cholinergic system was based on existing behavioral and neurochemical data. Carlton (1968, 1969) had reviewed a substantial body of literature and concluded that the cholinergic system was involved in habituation and inhibition. A similar conclusion had been reached by Douglas (1972). There were also a number of studies indicating that disruption of the cholinergic system produced effects on learning similar to those found following hippocampal lesions (see Issacson, 1974, for a review).

We were also influenced by Shute and Lewis (1967) (also see Lewis and Shute, 1967) who identified a cholinergic projection that originated in the substantia nigra and projected to the septo-hippocampal complex. This pathway, which they referred to as the ventral tegmental path, however, now appears to be dopaminergic rather than cholinergic (see Kuhar, 1976).

In our study, we gave rabbits daily injections of scopolamine hydrobromide (1.5 mg/kg), scopolamine methylbromide (1.5 mg/kg), or saline.

Half the rabbits received 450 preexposures to a tone, whereas the remaining half served as sit controls. All animals were then given tone-eye-shock pairings until they reached a criterion of 5 consecutive CRs.

Our results indicated a strong LI effect in all three conditions suggesting that the cholinergic blockade did not affect the LI process (Fig. 5.9). As Fig. 5.9 indicates, however, scopolamine hydrobromide disrupted acquisition of the conditioned response. Subsequent tests for CS and UCS sensitivity indicated that although scopolamine hydrobromide had no effect on shock sensitivity, it did decrease the sensitivity of the auditory system. This does not seem surprising in view of the evidence indicating a cholinergic component to the olivo-cochlear bundle (Jasser & Guth, 1973).

In an attempt to determine if the decreased sensitivity to the tone CS was responsible for the scopolamine-induced disruption of conditioning, and to again examine the effects of scopolamine on LI, we repeated the experiment using a light CS. The results of the experiment were virtually identical to the first study: latent inhibition in all three drug conditions and a strong disruption of conditioning in the scopolamine hydrobromide animals. But in this experiment there was no difference in sensitivity to the light CS among the

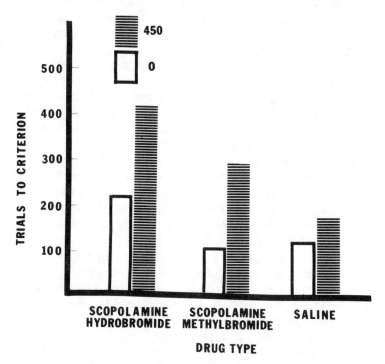

FIG. 5.9   Mean number of trials to reach a criterion of 4 CRs in any block of 5 trials as a function of drug type and number of preexposures (o versus 450).

three groups. It appears that disruption of the cholinergic system does not affect LI and that the scopolamine-induced disruption of conditioning was not due to changes in light sensitivity.

Our data indicating that the cholinergic system is important in rabbit NMR conditioning are consistent with other data in the rabbit (Downs, Cardoza, Schneiderman, Yehle, Van Decar, & Zwilling, 1972; Harvey & Gormezano, 1981) as well as data from other paradigms and preparations that indicate cholinergic involvement in certain types of learning and memory (see Carlton, 1968, 1969; Deutsch, 1971, Karezmar, 1978, for reviews). Moreover, several converging lines of research now suggest that the disruptive effects of anticholinergics on NMR conditioning may be due to their effect on the septo-hippocampal complex. This becomes a particularly attractive hypothesis in view of both the electrophysiological evidence pertaining to septal and hippocampal activity during NMR conditioning, and the anatomical evidence indicating a cholinergic pathway in the rabbit originating in the medial septum and projecting to the hippocampus (Bland, Kostopeulos, & Phillips, 1974; Dudar, 1975; Smith, 1974).

Berry and Thompson (1978) reported that the rate of NMR conditioning can be predicted by examining hippocampal EEG patterns immediately prior to CS–UCS pairings. Rabbits that displayed high levels of activity in the low-frequency range (2–8Hz) conditioned significantly faster than animals that had a preponderance of activity in the high-frequency range (8–22 Hz; also see Gabriel & Saltwick, 1980). Interestingly, systemic administration of scopolamine disrupts hippocampal RSA in the rabbit (Stumpf, Petsche, & Gogolak, 1962). A study by Solomon & Gottfried (1981) also suggests septo-hippocampal cholinergic involvement in NMR conditioning. In this study, we examined the effects of microinjecting scopolamine (1 μl bilaterally, 20 $\mu g/\mu l$) directly into the medial septal nucleus. We found that these injections retarded acquistion of the CR to a light CS and eye shock UCS (Fig. 5.10), while having no effect on sensitivity to either stimulus. Powell, Buchanan, and Hernandez (1980) have reported similar results for cardiac conditioning in the rabbit. Although it will be important to determine if these microinjections disrupt hippocampal RSA, studies in the rat indicate that this does appear to be the case (cf. Bennett, 1975).

Several investigators have suggested that these findings, when coupled with data indicating that hippocampal lesions do not disrupt delay conditioning, indicate that manipulations that produce certain patterns of activity in the hippocampus may be more detrimental to delay conditioning than removing the structure (see Berry & Thompson, 1979). Consistent with this view are the data indicating that: (1) hippocampal theta disrupting medial septal lesions (Berry & Thompson, 1979), (2) seizure-producing intrahippocampal penicillin injections (Thompson et al., 1980), and (3) seizure-producing posttrial hippocampal stimulation (Salafia, Romano, Tynan, &

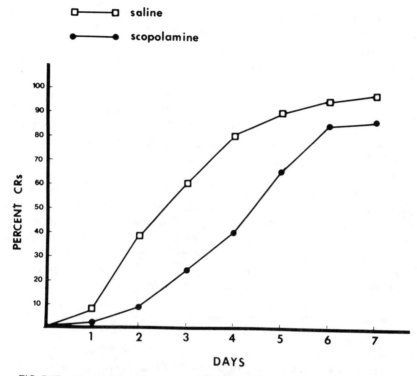

FIG. 5.10   Mean percentage of conditioned responses for animals in Groups Septal Saline and Septal Scopolamine over the 7 days of training. From Solomon and Gottfried (1981).

Host, 1977) all retard NMR conditioning. Whether small medial septal lesions, systemic scopolamine administration, posttrial hippocampal stimulation, hippocampal penicillin injections, and scopolamine applied to the medial septal nucleus each effects the hippocampus in a similar way is an open question. But it is important to note that all these manipulations have similar effects on acquisition of the conditioned NMR. They delay the onset of conditioning, but once CRs begin to occur the rate of acquisition is similar to that of controls. Moreover, all animals eventually reach asymptotic levels of conditioning. These data would appear to fit nicely into Prokasy's (1972) two-stage model of conditioning.

In a recently completed study, we (Solomon, Solomon, Vander Schaaf, & Perry, 1983) have attempted to directly test the notion that altered activity in the hippocampus is more detrimental to conditioning than removing the structure. Because systemic administration of scopolamine in the rabbit both alters hippocampal neuronal activity by blocking hippocampal theta and retards acquisition of the NMR, this manipulation provides a useful tool for investigating the relationship between altered neuronal activity in the hippocampus and retarded acquisition of the conditioned NMR. Specifically, if the retarded conditioning following systemic administration of scopolamine is due to altered neuronal activity in the hippocampus, there should be no such alteration of conditioning in scopolamine treated rabbits with hippocampal ablations. This is exactly the effect we found.

In this study, animals with hippocampal ablations, cortical ablations, or unoperated controls were given either scopolamine or saline. They were then conditioned to a light CS and an eyeshock UCS in a delay conditioning paradigm. The data from this study were consistent with earlier reports in indicating that: (1) dorsal hippocampal ablations do not affect conditioning of the conditioned NMR, and (2) systemic administration of scopolamine retards acquisition of the CR in normal animals and those with cortical lesions. The most interesting finding of the study, however, was that scopolamine did not affect conditioning in rabbits with hippocampal ablations (Fig. 5.11). These results suggest that certain patterns of neuronal activity in hippocampus are more detrimental to conditioning than ablating the structure. One important question that this raises is how does this altered activity in hippocampus affect other brain structures to disrupt conditioning.

The Serotonergic System and Latent Inhibition

There is substantial evidence for a mesolimbic serotonergic system. Specifically anatomical, (Bobillier, Petitjean, Salvert, Ligier, & Seguin, 1975), and

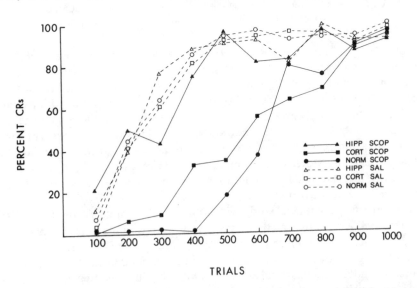

FIG. 5.11 Mean percentage of CR's over 10 days of training for animals in each of the six experimental conditions. From Solomon et al. (1983).

histochemical (Geyer, Puerto, Dawsey, Knapp, Ballard, & Mandell, 1976; Jacobs, Wise, & Taylor, 1974; Lorens & Guldberg, 1974) studies indicate a serotonergic pathway originating in the medial raphe nucleus and projecting to the septohippocampal complex. There is also research to suggest that the serotonergic system may be important in behaviors that require learning to ignore an irrelevant stimulus. For example, spontaneous alternation in a Y maze, a task that like LI may require the animal to learn to ignore irrelevant cues, is disrupted following depletion of serotonin by either parachlorophenylalanine (PCPA; Swonger & Rech, 1972) or medial raphe lesions (Geyer, Puerto, Menkes, Segal, & Mandell, 1976). Similarly, reversal but not acquisition of a discrimination in a T maze is disrupted following medial raphe lesions (Asin, Wirtschafter, & Kent, 1979). It is also interesting that like LI, spontaneous alternation is disrupted following hippocampal or septal lesions (see Douglas, 1975). Based on these data we decided to investigate the role of the serotonergic system in LI.

The studies examining the role of the serotonergic system in LI were performed in both the rabbit and the rat. We did this for two reasons. First, to see if we could obtain similar findings using different species and paradigms (a similar approach has been advocated by Thompson et al., 1980, in studying acquisition of the conditioned NMR) and secondly, to begin to develop the LI paradigm in the rat. This seemed particularly important in view of the abundant data regarding the nature of the mesolimbic pathways in this animal.

The procedures used to produce LI in the rabbit were like those of the previous studies. The experiments performed in the rat used a two-way avoidance procedure. In these experiments, rats were placed in a two-way avoidance chamber and given 5 minutes of free exploration. Next, rats in the preexposure conditions were given 30 five-second presentations of an 80 dB tone. Animals in the control group were allowed to explore the apparatus for an equivalent amount of time (15 minutes). Testing was the same for all animals and consisted of acquisition of the conditioned avoidance response (CAR). Each trial was signaled by the onset of the tone followed 5 seconds later by the onset of a .5 mA foot shock. We define an avoidance response as a crossing into the opposite compartment during the tone and before the shock presentation. We typically use two measures of performance: trials to criterion and total conditioned avoidance responses (CARs).

Our initial investigations involved parallel studies in the rat and rabbit on the effects of PCPA on LI. In the rat study (Solomon, Kiney, & Scott, 1978), animals were given a single injection of PCPA (400 mg/kg) or the vehicle control 3 days prior to testing for LI. On the day of testing, rats were assigned to either the preexposed or control condition. As Fig. 5.12 indicates, both the number of trials to criterion and total number of CARs indicate a strong LI effect in the control group with animals in the preexposure condition taking

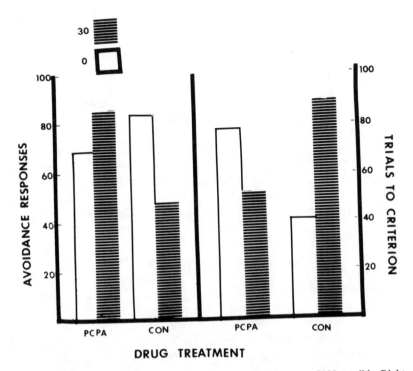

FIG. 5.12   Left Panel: Mean number of Avoidance Respnses out of 100 possible. Right Panel: Mean number of trials to reach a criterion of 4 avoidance responses in any block of 5 trials for animals in each of the four treatment conditions. From Solomon, Kiney, and Scott (1978).

more trials to reach criterion and giving fewer total CARs than their non-preexposed counterparts. In the PCPA animals, however, this pattern was reversed, albeit, not significantly. Subsequent tests for tone and shock sensitivity revealed no differences among the four groups.

Although this experiment was consistent with several others (e.g., Ackil et al., 1969; Weiss, Friedman & McGregor, 1974) in revealing a retardation of conditioning in control animals following tone preexposures in a two-way avoidance task, it was necessary to perform a summation test before we could reach the conclusion that the tone had become a latent inhibitor. Table 5.3 shows the procedure used to conduct this test and Table 5.4 depicts the results. The results of this procedure were consistent with the results in the rabbit NMR preparation in indicating that stimulus preexposure produces a latent inhibitor as demonstrated by the summation and retardation tests (Solomon et al., 1978, Experiment 2).

The results from the rabbit portion of the PCPA study also suggest that the drug disrupts the LI process (see Moore, 1978). It is also noteworthy that, as

TABLE 5.3
Procedures Used for Summation Test

	Stage 1	Stage 2	Stage 3
PCPA	L + (8/10 criterion)	T – (30)	L– (50) LT– (50)
CON	L + (8/10 criterion)	15 Min Free Exploration	L– (50) LT– (50)

TABLE 5.4
Mean Number of Responses to Light (±SEM; 50
Possible) and Light Plus Tone (50 Possible)
During Summation Test

Group	Stimulus	
	L	LT
CON	20.4 ± 5.4	18.9 ± 5.9
PCPA	26.1 ± 6.2	24.0 ± 5.9

in the rat avoidance task, PCPA does not seem to affect acquisition of the rabbit's NMR.

The PCPA study suggested serotonergic involvement in LI but gave no indication of which serotonergic system or systems were involved. It is now well documented that there are two major ascending serotonergic pathways: the mesolimbic serotonergic system that originates in the medial raphe nucleus and projects to the septo-hippocampal complex and the mesostriatal serotonergic projection that has its cell bodies in the dorsal raphe nucleus and projects to the striatum (Azmita & Segal, 1978; Conrad, Leonard & Pfaff, 1974; Jacobs et al., 1974; Moore, 1975). Although the PCPA data, coupled with the findings that both hippocampal and septal lesions (Weiss & Brown, 1974) disrupt LI, implicate the mesolimbic system in latent inhibition, because PCPA depletes whole brain serotonin (Tenen, 1967) it is impossible to determine if this is the case based on our data.

Several investigations have reported that lesions of the dorsal raphe selectively deplete striatal serotonin, whereas lesions of the medial raphe deplete septo-hippocampal serotonin (Geyer et al., 1976; Lorens & Guldberg, 1974). Based on these findings, we decided to evaluate the role of the mesostriatal and mesolimbic serotonergic systems by placing discrete lesions in either the dorsal or medial raphe and examining the effects on both LI and septo-hippocampal serotonin levels (Solomon et al., 1980).

Rats received lesions of the dorsal raphe, medial raphe, or served as unoperated controls. Each group was further subdivided into preexposed and control conditions. As in the PCPA study, rats in the preexposed conditions received 30 preexposures to a tone that was later used as the CS in the two-way avoidance task. Rats in the control condition simply sat in the apparatus for 15 minutes. Next, all animals acquired the CAR. Figure 5.13 shows the results of this portion of the study. A clear LI effect is present in the unoperated control animals and in animals with dorsal raphe lesions. There was no LI effect in rats with medial raphe lesions. All animals were then tested for both tone and shock sensitivity. This seemed particularly important in this case because there is a controversy as to whether serotonin depletion affects shock sensitivity with some studies suggesting that it produces heightened shock sensitivity (Harvey & Yunger, 1973; Tenen, 1967) whereas others have reported no change (Harvey, Schlosberg, & Yunger, 1974; Hole, Fuxe, & Jonsson, 1976; Srebro & Lorens, 1975). The data from our study indicated that, at least for the parameters we used, neither dorsal nor medial ra-

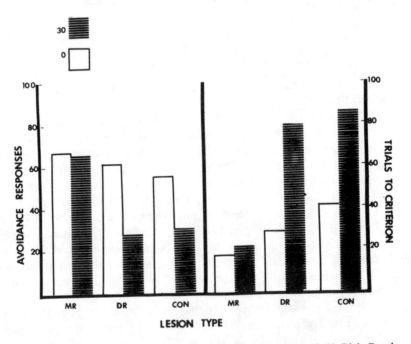

FIG. 5.13   Left Panel: Mean number of Avoidance Responses out of 100. Right Panel: Mean number of trials to reach a criterion of four conditioned avoidance responses in any block of five trials for animals in the six treatment conditions (MR = medial raphe, DR = dorsal raphe, CON = control). From Solomon, Nichols, Kiernan, Kramer, and Kaplan (1980).

phe lesions altered tone or shock sensitivity. There was also no difference in tone sensitivity.

Following behavioral testing, half the animals in each of the six conditions were assayed for serotonin in the septohippocampal complex using a modification of the spectrofluorometric procedure initially outlined by Barchas, Erdelyi, and Angwin (1972). In accordance with the results of previous studies (Jacobs et al., 1974; Lorens & Guldberg, 1974), we found a depletion of septo-hippocampal serotonin following medial but not dorsal raphe lesions (see Table 5.5).

The data from these studies are consistent with the work on hippocampal and septal lesions on LI indicating the importance of the mesolimbic system, and in particular the mesolimbic serotonergic system in LI. It is also interesting that one major projection of the serotonergic medial raphe fibers is to the dentate gyrus (Azmita & Segal, 1978). This fits in nicely with the electrophysiological evidence reviewed earlier suggesting a pivotal role for the dentate gyrus in learning to ignore irrelevant stimuli.

Catecholaminergic Systems — Latent Inhibition and Blocking

As indicated earlier, learning to ignore irrelevant stimuli, like most complex behaviors, is likely to be governed by a complex interaction of many neurotransmitters and neuromodulators. Consistent with this view, a number of investigators have pointed out the interrelationship between the brain catecholamines (especially dopamine) and serotonin (see Antelman & Caggiula, 1977, for a review). For example, Goetz and Klawans (1974) found that 5-hydroxytryptophan inhibited apomorphine induced stereotypy. Similarly, raphe lesions facilitate apomorphine-induced locomotor activity (Grabowska, 1974). A study by Trulson and Jacobs (1979) that reported that chronic but not acute administration of d-amphetamine decreased both serotonin and 5-hydroxyindolacetic acid is also consistent with this view.

These data suggest that increases in catecholamine levels may have the same effect as decreases in serotonin levels. As an initial test of this idea, we examined the effects of chronic amphetamine administration on LI. Our selection of amphetamine was based on its widespread effects on the catecholamines and on data indicating that it decreased serotonin levels in the brain (Trulson & Jacobs, 1979). We were also influenced by data indicating that chronic amphetamine administration in humans mimics certain behavior disorders (e.g., Angrist, Sathananthan, Wilk, & Gershon, 1974) and that these disorders are often associated with an inability to ignore irrelevant aspects of the environment (e.g., Chapman & Chapman, 1973; Joseph, Frith, & Waddington, 1979; Neale & Cromwell, 1977; Shakow, 1977).

TABLE 5.5
Mean (±SE) Septohippocampal 5-HT Concentrations
(in ng/g) After Selective Midbrain Raphe Lesions

Group	n	5-HT	% Control
Control	8	230 ± 16	–
Dorsal raphe	7	231 ± 12	101
Medial raphe	10	82 ± 15	36[a]

Note: 5-HT = serotonin.
[a]$p < .001$, differences between the medial raphe and control and between medial raphe and dorsal raphe groups.

In our first study (Solomon, Crider, Winkelman, Turi, Kamer, & Kaplan, 1981), we examined the effects of chronic amphetamine administration on LI in the rat in the two-way shuttle box procedure. We initially assigned rats to one of three treatment groups: 4mg/kg d-amphetamine, 1 mg/kg d-amphetamine, or saline control. Animals were given a daily injection of the drug or saline for 5 consecutive days and then assigned to either the 0 or 30 preexposure condition. The results of the study (see Fig. 5.14) indicated that only the high dose of amphetamine disrupted LI.

A related study extended our findings on LI to the blocking paradigm (Crider, Solomon, & McMahon, 1982). In this study we found that chronic administration (5 consecutive days) of 4 mg/kg of d-amphetamine disrupted the blocking of a light by a tone in the two-way avoidance paradigm. Lorden, Rickert, Lawson, and Pettymounter (1980) have shown that the norepinephrine system is also important in blocking in a CER task in the rat.

Although d-amphetamine has a number of effects (see Groves & Rebec, 1976; Rebec & Babshore, 1982; Segal & Janowsky, 1978), our working hypothesis has been that the drug's disruptive effects on LI are due to its actions on the mesolimbic dopaminergic systems. This would be consistent with our previous work on neural mechanisms of LI and would also be consistent with the view that increasing DA levels in this system is similar in effect to depleting serotonin. Partialing out the effects of d-amphetamine has proven to be a very difficutl task (see Kokkinidis & Anisman, 1980). To begin to test the idea that the effects we were observing on LI were due to the drug's action on the DA system, we decided to see if low doses of the drug, not sufficient themselves to disrupt LI, would act synergistically with DA supersensitivity to disrupt LI (Solomon et al., 1981). Similar strategies have been productive in attempting to partial out the contribution of DA and NA system in d-amphetamine induced stereotypy (e.g., Klawans, Nausieda, & Weiner, 1980).

To induce DA supersensitivity, we gave rats 21 daily injections of haloperidol (0.5 mg/kg) followed by a 7 day drug free period. One group of control animals received the same daily regimen of saline. To control for the sedating effects of haloperidol, a third group received 21 injections of sodium pentobarbital (50 mg/kg). Animals in each group were then assigned to a 0 or 30 preexposure condition. Prior to being tested in the LI paradigm, all animals received a single dose of 1 mg/kg of d-amphetamine, a dose in itself not sufficient to disrupt LI. The results showed a standard LI effect in normal and sodium pentobarbital animals with preexposed animals taking longer to condition than their nonpreexposed counterparts. Animals pretreated with haloperidol, however, had a disruption of LI (Fig. 5.15).

A second group of similarly treated rats was used to check for DA receptor supersensitivity in the mesolimbic system. A number of studies had shown that systemic administration of haloperidol produced DA receptor supersensitivity in the striatum (see Muller & Seeman, 1980; Snyder & Creese, 1980 for reviews), but there was little evidence to suggest the involvement of the mesolimbic DA system. Therefore, we measured 3H-dopamine receptor binding in the nucleus accumbens of the septum using a modification of the procedures initially described by Hitri, Weiner, Borison, Diamond, Naus-

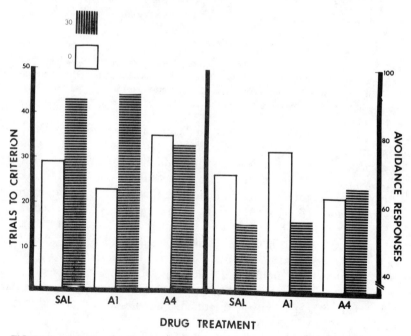

FIG. 5.14 Left Panel: Mean number of trials to reach a criterion of four conditioned avoidance responses in any block of five trials for animals in each of the six treatment conditions. Right Panel: Mean number of conditioned avoidance responses in 100 trials (SAL = Saline, Al = 1 mg/Kg d-amphetamine, A4 = 4 mg/Kg d-amphetamine). From Solomon, Crider, Winkelman, Turi, Kamer, and Kaplan (1981).

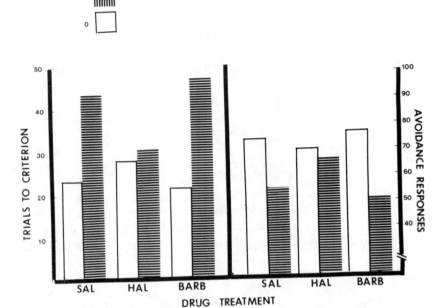

FIG. 5.15   Left Panel: Mean number of Avoidance Responses out of 100. Right Panel: Mean number of trials to reach a criterion of four conditioned avoidance responses in any block of five trials for animals in the six treatment conditions (SAL = Saline, HAL = Haloperidol, BARB = Sodium pentobarbital). From Solomon et al. (1981).

ieda, and Klawans (1978). The results indicated a 50% increase in DA binding in animals treated with haloperidol relative to saline controls but no change in binding in animals treated with sodium pentobarbital (see Kamer, Turi, Solomon, & Kaplan, 1981; Solomon et al., 1981). We do not know whether this increase indicates an increased number of receptors or an increase of the DA affinity at the existing sites. Nevertheless, the data do show DA supersensitivity in the mesolimbic system and in this respect they are in agreement with behavioral (Davis, Hollister, & Fritz, 1978) and neurochemical (Muller & Seeman, 1977) studies. These data also suggest that the disruption of LI following d-amphetamine administration is due to the drug's effects on the DA system (although effects on the noradrenergic systems cannot be ruled out), and that the mesolimbic dopamineregic system may be critical.

A recently completed study by Blockel, Solomon, and Crider (1982) has extended these findings to the blocking paradigm. In this study, DA supersensative rats failed to show the blocking effect.

Our most recent study is an attempt to further evaluate the role of the mesolimbic DA system in LI. In this study (Solomon & Staton, 1982), we implanted bilateral cannulae in either the nucleus accumbens septi (NA) or the caudate putamen (CPU, see Staton & Solomon, 1979). The animals were given a 2-week recovery period and then given 5 daily microinjections (1 μl bilaterally, 20 μg/μl) of either *d*-amphetamine or saline. Animals were then assigned to either the preexposed or control conditions. The final design, then, consisted of three main treatment conditions and eight groups: two cannula placements (NA or CPU), crossed with two drug treatments (saline or *d*-amphetamine), crossed with two preexposure levels (0 vs. 30).

The results of the study (Fig. 5.16) indicated that animals given saline in either the NA or CPU showed the LI effect. Animals that received *d*-amphetamine in the CPU also showed the LI effect. However, animals that received *d*-amphetamine in the NA behaved much in the same way as animals that received systemic *d*-amphetamine—they showed a disruption of LI.

Taken together with the results of the mesolimbic supersensitivity study, these data suggest that the disruptive effects of *d*-amphetamine on the rat's ability to learn to ignore an irrelevant stimulus are likely to be due to the drug's effects in the mesolimbic DA system. It is premature, however, to rule out possible contributions of the NE system. A review by Kokkinidis and Anisman (1980) suggests that attentional processes may be mediated by an interaction of the DA and NE systems. Specifically, they suggest that attentional processes may be disrupted by a hyperdopaminergic system coupled

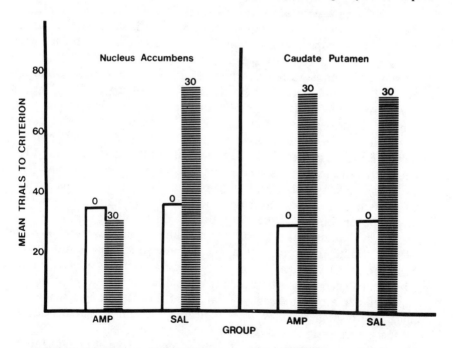

FIG. 5.16   Mean number of trials to reach a criterion of eight avoidance responses in any block of 10 trials for animals in the eight treatment conditions (AMP = Amphetamine, SAL = Saline). From Solomon and Staton, 1982.

with a depletion of NE (also see Antelman & Caggiula, 1977, who suggested a more general view of this idea). In support of this, Mason and Lin (1980) have reported that NE-depleting 6-OHDA lesions disrupt LI in an operant discrimination paradigm in the rat. These studies coupled with our work would seem to reinforce the idea that behaviors as complex as learning to ignore irrelevant stimuli are governed by an interaction of several transmitter systems.

SUMMARY AND CONCLUSIONS

This chapter has been concerned with the neural and behavioral mechanisms by which animals learn to ignore irrelevant aspects of their environment. To study this problem, we have used the latent inhibition and blocking tasks in the rabbit NMR, and to a lesser extent the rat two-way avoidance paradigms. From the behavioral point of view, it appears that LI and blocking tap related processes. Both tasks require that the animal learn that a stimulus is irrelevant in that it does not make any unique prediction about the occurrence of a motivationally significant event. Once this occurs, the adaptive response is for the animal to learn to ignore that stimulus.

Our work on the physiological mechanisms suggests that the mesolimbic system is important in this "tuning out" process. We have found that hippocampal lesions disrupt LI and blocking, and others have found similar results following septal lesions. We have also found that depletion of both whole brain serotonin and serotonin depletion limited to the mesolimbic system disrupts LI. Other studies have indicated that an increase in catecholaminergic activity disrupts LI and blocking. To this end, chronic, high doses of *d*-amphetamine disrupt both LI and blocking. Subsequent studies suggested that the disruptive effects of *d*-amphetamine were most likely due to the drug's effects on the mesolimbic DA system. Specifically, we found that: (1) low doses of the drug that were not in and of themselves sufficient to disrupt LI combined with DA receptor supersensitivity in the nucleus accumbens to disrupt LI, and (2) microinjections of *d*-amphetamine into the nucleus accumbens but not the caudate putamen disrupted the LI.

Although all these data suggest that the animal's ability to learn to ignore irrelevant stimuli is governed by a complex interaction of the mesolimbic neural transmitter systems, they do not suggest a mechanism by which this might occur. There is, however, electrophysiological data suggesting perforant path-dentate synapses may be important. This fits nicely with the anatomical and histochemical evidence indicating mesolimbic adrenergic and serotonergic projections to this area.

In addition to more extensive electrophysiological studies designed to investigate the perforant path-dentate synapse, subsequent research is likely to focus on further delineation of the systems that might interact in the control of LI and blocking. Some of this research may ultimately aid in the understanding of certain human disorders. For example, the inability to learn to ignore or to filter out irrelevant stimuli has been hypothesized to be a factor in disorders of human memory (e.g., Butters & Cermack, 1975; Weiskrantz & Warrington, 1975) as well as certain psychopathological states (see Crider, 1979).

A final concern of this chapter has been to discuss the role of the hippocampus in acquisition of the rabbit's conditioned NMR. The emerging picture based on our data and the data of others is that: (1) even though the hippocampus is not essential in the delay paradigm in which the CS and UCS occur contiguosly in time, it does play a modulatory role, and (2) the hippocampus may be essential in tasks such as trace conditioning in which the CS and UCS are separated in time (see Moore & Solomon, in press).

ACKNOWLEDGMENTS

Parts of the research described in this chapter were supported by NIMH grant MH33381, NSF grant BNS 77-14871, and a Faculty Research grant from Williams College. Some of the research was conducted while the author was a visiting research fellow in R. F. Thompson's laboratory at the University of California-Irvine and supported by a fellowship from NIMH (MH-8105A). Preparation of the manuscript was supported by a fellowship by the National Science Foundation (SPI-7914900).

REFERENCES

Ackil, J. R., Melgren, R. L., Halgren, C., & Frommer, S. P. (1969). Effects of CS preexposure on avoidance learning in rats with hippocampal lesions. *Journal of Comparative and Physiological Psychology, 69,* 739–747.

Angrist, B., Sathananthan, G., Wilk, S., & Gershon, S. (1974). Amphetamine psychosis: Behavioral and biochemical aspects. *Journal of Psychiatric Research, 11,* 13–23.

Antelman, S. M., & Caggiula, A. R. (1977). Norepinephrine-dopamine interactions and behavior. *Science, 195,* 646–650.

Asin, K. E., Wirtschafter, D., & Kent, E. W. (1979). Discrimination learning and reversal following electrolytic median raphe lesions. *Society for Neuroscience Abstracts, 5,* 269.

Azmita, E. C., & Segal, M. (1978). An autoradiographic analysis of the ascending projections of the dorsal and median raphe nuclei in the rat. *Journal of Comparative Neurology, 179,* 641–668.

Barchas, J., Erdelyi, E., & Angwin, P. (1972). Simultaneous determination of indole – and catecholamines in tissue using a weak lotion – exchange resin. *Analytical Biochemistry, 50,* 1–17.

Bennett, T. L. (1975). The electrical activity of the hippocampus and processes of attention. In R. L. Isaacson & K. H. Pribram (Eds.), *The hippocampus,* (Vol. II). New York: Plenum.

Berger, T. W., Alger, B. E., & Thompson, R. F. (1976). Neuronal substrates of classical conditioning in the hipocampus. *Science, 192,* 483–485.

Berger, T. W., Clark, G. A., & Thompson, R. F. (1980). Learning-dependent neuronal responses recorded from limbic system brain structures during classical conditioning. *Physiological Psychology, 8,* 155–167.

Berger, T. W., & Thompson, R. F. (1978a). Neuronal plasticity in the limbic system during classical conditioning of the rabbit's nictitating membrane response: 1. The hippocampus. *Brain Research, 145,* 323–336.

Berger, T. W., & Thompson, R. F. (1978b). Identification of pyramidal cells as the critical elements in hippocampal neuronal plasticity during learning. *Proceedings of the National Academy of Sciences, 75,* 1572–1576.

Berry, S. D., & Thompson, R. F. (1978). Prediction of learning rate from hippocampal EEG. *Science, 200,* 1298–1300.

Berry, S. D., & Thompson, R. F. (1979). Medial septal lesions retard classical conditioning of the nictitating membrane response of rabbits. *Science, 205,* 209–210.

Best, M. R., & Best, P. J. (1976). The effects of state of consciousness on latent inhibition in hippocampal unit activity in the rat during conditioning. *Experimental Neurology, 51,* 564–573.

Bland, B. H., Kostopeulos, G. K., & Phillips, J. W. (1974). Acetylcholine sensitivity in hippocampal formation neurons. *Canadian Journal of Physiology and Pharmacology, 52,* 966–971.

Blockel, L. M., Solomon, P. R., & Crider, A. (1982, April). *Disruption of blocking with dopaminergic receptor supersensativity.* Paper presented at Eastern Psychological Association, Baltimore, MD.

Bobillier, P. F., Petitjean, D., Salvert, M., Ligier, M., & Seguin, S. (1975). Different projections of the nucleus raphe dorsalis and nucleus raphe centralis as revealed by autoradiography. *Brain Research, 85,* 205–210.

Boneau, C. A. (1958). The interstimulus interval and the latency of the conditioned eyelid response. *Journal of Experimental Psychology, 56,* 464–472.

Butters, N., & Cermak, L. (1975). Some analysis of amnesic syndromes in brain-damaged patients. In R. L. Isaacson & K. H. Pribram (Eds.), *The hippocampus,* (Vol. II). New York: Plenum.

Carlton, P. L. (1968). Brain acetylcholine and habituation. *Progress in Brain Research, 28,* 48–60.

Carlton, P. L. (1969). Brain acetylcholine and inhibition. In J. Tapp (Ed.), *Reinforcement: Current theory and research.* New York: Academic Press.

Chapman, L. J., & Chapman, J. P. (1973). *Disordered thought in schizophrenia.* Englewood Cliffs, NJ: Prentice-Hall.

Conrad, C. A., Leonard, C. M., & Pfaff, A. W. (1974). Connections of the median and dorsal raphe nuclei in the rat: An autoradiographic study. *Journal of Comparative Neurology, 156,* 179–205.

Crider, A. (1979). *Schizophrenia: A biopsychological perspective.* Hillsdale, NJ: Lawrence Erlbaum Associates.

Crider, A., Solomon, P. R., & McMahon, M. (1982). Disruption of selective attention in the rat following chronic *d*-amphetamine administration: Possible relationship to schizophrenic attention disorder. *Biological Psychiatry, 17,* 351–361.

Crow, T. J. (1977). Neurotransmitter-related pathways: The structure and function of central monoamine neurones. In A. N. Davison (Ed.), *Biochemical correlates of brain structure and function.* New York: Academic Press.

Crowne, D. P., & Ratcliff, D. D. (1975). Some characteristics and functional relationships of the electrical activity of the primate hippocampus and hypothesis of hippocampal function. In R. L. Isaacson & K. H. Pribram (Eds.), *The hippocampus* (Vol. II). New York: Plenum.

Davis, K. L., Hollister, L. E., & Fritz, W. C. (1978). Induction of dopaminergic mesolimbic receptor supersensitivity by haloperidol. *Life Sciences, 23,* 1543–1548.

Deutsch, J. A. (1971). The cholinergic synapse and the site of memory. *Science, 174,* 788-794.

Douglas, R. J. (1967). The hippocampus and behavior. *Psychological Bulletin, 67,* 416-442.

Douglas, R. J. (1972). Pavlovian conditioning and the brain. In R. A. Boakes & M. S. Halliday (Eds.), *Inhibition and learning.* New York: Academic Press.

Douglas, R. J. (1975). The development of hippocampal function: Implications and theory and for therapy. In R. L. Isaacson & K. H. Pribram (Eds.), *The hippocampus* (Vol. II). New York: Plenum.

Douglas, R. J., & Pribram, K. H. (1966). Learning and limbic lesions. *Neuropsychologia, 4,* 197-220.

Downs, D., Cardoza, C., Schneiderman, N., Yehle, A. L., VanDercar, D. H., & Zwilling, G. (1972). Central effects of atropine upon aversive classical conditioning in rabbits. *Psychopharmacologia, 23,* 319-333.

Dudar, J. D. (1975). The effect of septal nuclei stimulation on the release of acetylcholine from rabbit hippocampus. *Brain Research, 83,* 123-133.

Ebel, H. C., & Prokasy, W. F. (1963). Classical eyelid conditioning as a function of sustained and shifted interstimulus intervals. *Journal of Experimental Psychology, 65,* 52-58.

Gabriel, M., Foster, K., Orona, E., Saltwick, S. E., & Stanton, M. (1980). Neuronal activity of cingulate cortex, anteroventral thalamus, and hippocampal formaton in discriminative conditioning: Encoding and extraction of the significance of conditional stimuli. *Progress in Psychobiology and Physiological Psychology, 9,* 125-231.

Gabriel, M., & Saltwick, S. E. (1980). Rhythemic, theta-like unit activity of the hippocampal formation during acquisition and performance of avoidance behavior in rabbits. *Physiology and Behavior, 24,* 303-312.

Geyer, M. A., Puerto, A., Dawsey, W. J., Knapp, S., Bullard, W. P., Mandell, A. J. (1976). Histologic and enzymatic studies of the mesolimbic and mesostriatal serotonergic pathways. *Brain Research, 106,* 257-270.

Geyer, M. A., Puerto, A., Menkes, D. B., Segal, D. S., & Mandell, A. J. (1976). Behavioral studies following lesions of the mesolimbic and mesostriatal serotonergic pathways. *Brain Research, 106,* 257-270.

Gormezano, I. (1966). Classical conditioning. In J. B. Sidowski (Ed.), *Experimental methods and instrumentation in psychology.* New York: McGraw-Hill.

Gormezano, I., & Moore, J. W. (1969). Classical conditioning. In M. H. Marx (Ed.), *Learning: Processes.* Toronto: Codieu-MacMillan.

Grabowska, M. (1974). Influence of midbrain raphe lesion on some pharmacological and biochemical effects of apomorphine in rats. *Psychopharmacologia* (Berl.), *39,* 315-322.

Groves, P. M., & Rebec, G. V. (1976). Biochemistry and behavior: Some central actions of amphetamine and antipsychotic drugs. *Annual Review of Psychology, 27,* 91.

Harvey, J. A., & Gormezano, I. (1981). Effects of haloperidol and pimozide on classical conditioning of the rabbit nictitating membrane response. *Journal of Pharmacology and Experimental Therapeutics, 218,* 712-719.

Harvey, J. A., & Gormezano, I. (1982). Drug effects on classical conditioning of the rabbit nictitating membrane response. *Society for Neuroscience Abstract, 7,* 359.

Harvey, J. A., Schlosberg, A. J., & Yunger, L. M. (1974). Effects of p-chlorophenylalanine and brain lesions on pain sensitivity and morphine analgesia in the rat. *Advances in Biochemical Psychopharmacology, 10,* 233-245.

Harvey, J. A., & Yunger, L. M. (1973). Relationship between telencephalic content of serotonin and pain sensitivity. In J. Barchas & E. Usdin (Eds.), *Serotonin and behavior.* New York: Academic Press.

Hinson, R. E., & Siegel, S. E. (1980). Trace conditioning as an inhibitory procedure. *Animal Learning and Behavior, 8,* 60-66.

Hitri, A., Weiner, W. J., Borison, R. L., Diamond, B. I., Nausieda, P. A., & Klawans, H. L.

(1978). Dopamine binding following prolonged haloperidol pretreatment. *Annals of Neurology, 3*, 134–140.

Hoehler, F. K., & Thompson, R. F. (1980). Effect of interstimulus interval (CS–UCS) on hippocampal unit activity during classical conditioning of the nictitating membrane response of the rabbit (*Oroctolagus cuniculus*). *Journal of Comparative and Physiological Psychology, 94*, 201–215.

Hole, K., Fuxe, K., & Jonsson, G. (1976). Behavioral effects of 5-dihydroxytryptamine lesions of the ascending 5-hydroxytryptamine pathways. *Brain Research, 107*, 385–399.

Isaacson, R. L. (1974). *The limbic system*. New York: Plenum.

Jacobs, B. L., Wise, W. D., & Taylor, R. M. (1974). Differential behavioral and neurochemical effects following lesions of the dorsal or median raphe nuclei in rats. *Brain Research, 79*, 353–361.

Jarrard, L. E. (1973). The hippocampus and motivation. *Psychological Bulletin, 79*, 1–12.

Jasser, A., & Guth, P. S. (1973). The synthesis of acetylcholine by the olivocochlear bundle. *Journal of Neurochemistry, 20*, 45–54.

Joseph, M. H., Frith, C. D., & Waddington, D. L. (1979). Dopaminergic mechanisms and cognitive deficit in schizophrenia. *Psychopharmacology, 63*, 273–280.

Kamer, R. S., Turi, A. R., Solomon, P. R., & Kaplan, L. J. (1981). Increased mesolimbic dopamine binding following chronic haloperidol treatment. *Psychopharmacologia, 72*, 261–263.

Kamin, L. J. (1968). "Attention-like" processes in classical conditioning. In M. R. Jones (Ed.), *Miami symposium on the prediction of behavior*. Miami: University of Miami Press.

Kamin, L. J. (1969). Predictability, surprise, attention and conditioning. In B. A. Campbell & R. M. Church (Eds.), *Punishment and aversive behavior*. New York: Appleton-Century-Crofts.

Karezmar, A. G. (1978). Exploitable aspects of central functions, particularly with respect to the EEG, motor, analgesic, and neonatal functions. In D. J. Jenden (Ed.), *Cholinergic mechanisms and psychopharmacology*. New York: Plenum.

Kimble, D. P. (1968). Hippocampus and internal inhibition. *Psychological Bulletin, 76*, 285–295.

Klawans, H. L., Nausieda, P. A., & Weiner, W. (1980). The effect of lithium on haloperidol-induced supersensitivity to *d*-amphetamine and apomorphine. In W. E. Frann, R. C. Smith, J. M. Davis, & E. M. Domino, (Eds.), *Tradive dyskinesia*. Jamaica, NY: Spectrum.

Kokkinidis, L., & Anisman, H. (1980). Amphetamine models of paranoid schizophrenia: An overview and elaboration of animal experimentation. *Psychological Bulletin, 88*, 551–579.

Konorski, J. (1948). *Conditioned reflexes and neuron organization*. Cambridge: Cambridge University Press.

Kuhar, M. J. (1978). The anatomy of cholinergic neurons. In A. M. Goldberg & I. Hanin (Eds.), *Biology of cholinergic function*. New York: Raven Press.

Lewis, P. R., & Shute, C. C. D. (1967). The cholinergic limbic system: Projections to the hippocampal formation, medial fornix, nuclei of the ascending cholinergic reticular system, and the subfornical organ and supraoptic crest. *Brain, 40*, 521–540.

Lindsley, D. B., & Wilson, C. L. (1975). Brain stem-hypothalamic systems influencing hippocampal activity and behavior. In R. L. Isaacson & K. H. Pribram (Eds.), *The hippocampus, Volume II: Neurophysiology and behavior*. New York: Plenum.

Lorden, J. F., Rickert, E. J., Lawson, R., & Pettymounter, M. A. (1980). Forebrain norepinephrine and the selective processing of information. *Brain Research, 190*, 569–573.

Lorens, G. A., & Guldberg, H. C. (1974). Regional 5-hydroxytryptamine following selective midbrain raphe lesions in the rat. *Brain Research, 78*, 45–56.

Lubow, R. E., & Moore, A. U. (1959). Latent inhibition: The effect of non-reinforced preexposure to the conditioned stimulus. *Journal of Comparative and Physiological Psychology, 52*, 415–419.

Lubow, R. E., Schnur, P., & Rifkin, B. (1976). Latent inhibition and conditioned attention theory. *Journal of Experimental Psychology: Animal Behavior Processes, 2,* 163–174.

Lynch, G., Rose, G., & Gall, C. (1978). Anatomical and functional aspects of the septo-hippocampal projections. In *Functions of the septo-hippocampal system,* Ciba Foundation Symposium 58. New York: Elsevier/North-Holland.

Mackintosh, N. J. (1973). Stimulus selection: Learning to ignore stimuli that predict no change in reinforcement. In R. A. Hinde & J. Stevenson-Hinde (Eds.), *Constraints on learning.* New York: Academic Press.

Mackintosh, N. J. (1975). A theory of attention: Variations in the associability of stimuli with re-inforcement. *Psychological Review, 82,* 276–298.

Malthe-Sorenssen, D., Cheney, D. L., & Costa, E. (1978). Modulation of acetylcholine metabo-lism in the hippocampal cholinergic pathway by intraseptally injected substance P. *Journal of Pharmacology and Experimental Therapeutics, 206,* 21–28.

Maltzman, I., Raskin, D. C., & Wolff, C. (1979). Latent inhibition of the GSR conditioned to words. *Physiological Psychology, 7,* 193–203.

Marchant, H. G., Mis, F. W., & Moore, J. W. (1972). Conditioned inhibition of the rabbit's nictitating membrane response. *Journal of Experimental Psychology, 95,* 408–411.

Marchant, H. G., & Moore, J. W. (1973). Blocking on the rabbit's conditioned nictitating mem-brane response in Kamin's two-stage paradigm. *Journal of Experimental Psychology, 101,* 155–158.

Marchant, H. G., & Moore, J. W. (1974). Below-zero conditioned inhibition of the rabbit's nictitating membrane response. *Journal of Experimental Psychology, 102,* 350–357.

Mason, S. T., & Lin, D. (1980). Dorsal noradrenergic bundle and selective attention in the rat. *Journal of Comparative and Physiological Psychology, 94,* 819–832.

McCormick, D. A., Lavond, D. G., Clark, G. A., Kettner, R. E. Rising, C. E., Thompson, R. F. (1981). The engram found? Role of cerebellum in classical conditioning of the nictitating membrane and eyelid response. *Bulletin of the Psychonomic Society, 18,* 103–105.

McFarland, D. J., Kostas, J., & Drew, W. G. (1978). Dorsal hippocampal lesions: Effects of preconditioning CS exposure on flavor aversion. *Behavioral Biology, 22,* 398–404.

Micco, D. J., & Schwartz, M. (1971). Effects of hippocampal lesions upon the development of Pavlovian internal inhibition. *Journal of Comparative and Physiological Psychology, 3,* 371–377.

Mis, F. W., Gormezano, I., & Harvey, J. A. (1979). Stimulation of abducens nucleus supports classical conditioning of the nictitating membrane response. *Science, 206,* 473–475.

Moore, J. W. (1974). *Contextual constraints on Pavlovian inhibitory control.* Paper presented at the annual meeting of the American Psychological Association, New Orleans.

Moore, J. W. (1979). Brain processes and conditioning. In A. Dickinson & R. A. Boakes (Eds.), *Associative mechanisms in conditioning.* Hillsdale, NJ: Lawrence Erlbaum Associates.

Moore, J. W., Desmond, J. E., & Berthier, N. E. (1982). The metencephalic basis of the condi-tioned nictitating membrane response. In C. D. Woody (Ed.), *Conditioning: Representation of involved neural function.* New York: Plenum.

Moore, J. W., Goodell, N. A., & Solomon, P. R. (1976). Central cholinergic blockade by sco-polamine and habituation, classical conditioning, and latent inhibition of the rabbit's nicti-tating membrane response. *Physiological Psychology, 4,* 395–399.

Moore, J. W., & Solomon, P. R. (Eds.) (1980, June). The role of the hippocampus in learning and memory. *Physiological Psychology,* (Special Edition).

Moore, J. W., & Solomon, P. R. (in press). Forebrain-brain stem interaction: Conditioning and the hippocampus. In N. Butters & L. R. Squire (Eds.), *The neuropsychology of memory.* New York: Guilford.

Moore, J. W., & Stickney, K. J. (1980). Formation of attentional-associative networks in real time: Role of the hippocampus and implications for conditioning. *Physiological Psychology, 8,* 207–217.

Moore, R. Y. (1975). Monoamine neurons innervating the hippocampal formation and septum: Organization and response to injury. In R. L. Isaacson & K. H. Pribram (Eds.), *The hippocampus.* New York: Plenum.

Moore, R. Y. (1978). Catecholamine innervation of the basal forebrain. *Journal of Comparative Neurology, 177,* 665–684.

Moore, R. Y., & Bloom, F. E. (1978). Central catecholamine neuron systems: Anatomy and physiology of the dopamine systems. *Annual Review of Neuroscience, 2,* 129–170.

Moore, R. Y., & Bloom, F. E. (1979). Central catecholamine neuron systems: Anatomy and physiology of the norepinephrine and epinephrine systems. *Annual Review of Neuroscience, 2,* 113–168.

Moroni, F., Cheney, D. L., & Costa, E. (1977). Inhibition of acetylcholine turnover in rat hippocampus by intraseptal injections of endorphins and morphine. *Archives of Pharmacology, 299,* 149–153.

Muller, P., & Seeman, P. (1977). Brain neurotransmitter receptors after long-term haloperidol: Dopamine, acetylcholine, serotonin, α-noradrenergic, and Naloxone receptors. *Life Sciences, 21,* 1751–1758.

Muller, P., & Seeman, P. (1980). Effects of long-term neuroleptic treatment of neurotransmitter receptors: Relation to tardive dyskinesia. In W. E. Fann, R. C. Smith, J. M. Davis, & E. F. Domino (Eds.), *Tardive dyskinesia.* Jamaica, NY: Spectrum.

Nauta, W. J. H. (1958). Hippocampal projections and related neural pathways of the midbrain in the cat. *Brain, 81,* 319–340.

Neale, J. M., & Cromwell, R. L. (1977). Attention and schizophrenia. In B. A. Maher (Ed.), *Progress in experimental personality research* (Vol. 5). New York: Academic Press.

Oakley, D. A., & Russell, I. S. (1972). Neocortical lesions and Pavlovian conditioning. *Physiology and Behavior, 8,* 915–926.

Oakley, D. A., & Russell, I. S. (1975). Role of cortex in Pavlovian discrimination learning. *Physiology and Behavior, 15,* 315–321.

Oakley, D. A., & Russell, I. S. (1977). Subcortical storage of Pavlovian conditioning in the rabbit. *Physiology and Behavior, 18,* 931–937.

Pavlov, I. P. (1927). *Conditioned reflexes.* London: Oxford University Press.

Powell, D. A., & Buchanan, S. (1980). Autonomic-somatic relationships in the rabbit (*Oryctolagus cuniculus*): Effects of hippocampal lesions. *Physiological Psychology, 8,* 455–462.

Powell, D. A., Buchanan, S., & Hernandez, L. (1980). Central scopolamine administration differentially affects the cardiac component of the orienting reflex and Pavlovian conditioning. *Society for Neuroscience Abstracts, 6,* 168.

Pribram, K. H., & McGuinness, D. (1975). Arousal, activation, and effort in the control of attention. *Psychological Review, 82,* 116–149.

Prokasy, W. F. (1972). Developments with the two-phase model applied to human eyelid conditioning. In A. H. Black & W. F. Prokasy (Eds.), *Classical conditioning II.* New York: Appleton–Century–Crofts.

Rebec, G. V., & Babshore, T. R. (1982). Comments on "Amphetamine models of paranoid schizophrenia": A precautionary note. *Psychological Bulletin, 92,* 403–409.

Reiss, S., & Wagner, A. R. (1972). CS habituation produces a "latent inhibition effect" but no active conditioned inhibition. *Learning and Motivation, 3,* 237–245.

Rescorla, R. A. (1967). Pavlovian conditioning and its proper control procedures. *Psychological Review, 74,* 71–80.

Rescorla, R. A. (1971). Variation in the effectiveness of reinforcement and nonreinforcement following prior inhibitory conditioning. *Learning and Motivation, 2,* 113–123.

Rescorla, R. A., & Wagner, A. R. (1972). A theory of Pavlovian conditioning: Variations in the effectiveness of reinforcement and nonreinforcement. In A. H. Black & W. F. Prokasy (Eds.),

Classical conditioning II: Current theory and research. New York: Appleton–Century-Crofts.

Rickert, E. J., Bennett, T. L., Lane, P., & French, J. (1978). Hippocampectomy and attenuation of blocking. *Behavioral Biology, 22,* 147–160.

Rickert, E. J., Lorden, J. F., Dawson, R., Smyly, E., & Callahan, M. F. (1979). Stimulus processing and stimulus selection in rats with hippocampal lesions. *Behavioral and Neural Biology, 27,* 454–465.

Salafia, W. R., Romano, A. G., Tynan, T. T., & Host, K. C. (1977). Disruption of rabbit (*Oryctolagus cuniculus*) nictitating membrane conditioning by post-trial electrical stimulation of hippocampus. *Physiology and Behavior, 18,* 207–212.

Schmaltz, L. W., & Theios, J. (1972). Acquisition and extinction of a classically conditioned response in hippocampectomized rabbits (*Oryctolagus cuniculus*). *Journal of Comparative and Physiological Psychology, 79,* 328–333.

Schneiderman, N. (1966). Interstimulus interval function of the nictitating membrane respone of the rabbit under delay versus trace conditioning. *Journal of Comparative and Physiological Psychology, 62,* 397–402.

Segal, I. S., & Janowsky, D. S. (1978). Psychostimulant-induced behavioral effects: Possible models of schizophrenia. In M. A. Lipton, A. D., Mascio, & K. F. Killam (Eds.), *Psychopharmacology: A generation of progress.* New York: Raven Press.

Shakow, D. (1977). Segmental set: The adaptive process in schizophrenia. *American Psychologist, 32,* 129–139.

Shute, C. C. D., & Lewis, P. R. (1967). The ascending cholinergic reticular system: Neocortical, olfactory, and subcortical projections. *Brain, 40,* 497–519.

Siegel, S. (1972). Latent inhibition and eyelid conditioning. In A. H. Black & W. F. Prokasy (Eds.), *Classical conditioning II: Current theory and research.* New York: Appleton–Century–Crofts.

Smith, M. C. (1974). Acetylcholine release from the cholinergic septohippocampal pathway. *Life Sciences, 14,* 2159–2166.

Snyder, S. H., & Creese, I. (1980). Chronic neuroleptic treatment and dopamine receptor binding: Relevance to tardive dyskinesia. In W. E. Fann, R. C. Smith, J. M. Davis, & E. M. Domino (Eds.), *Tardive Dyskinesia.* Jamaica, NY: Spectrum.

Solomon, P. R. (1977). Role of the hippocampus in blocking and conditioned inhibition of the rabbit's nictitating membrane response. *Journal of Comparative and Physiological Psychology, 91,* 407–417.

Solomon, P. R. (1979). Temporal versus spatial information processing views of hippocampal function. *Psychological Bulletin, 86,* 1272–1279.

Solomon, P. R. (1980). A time and a place for everything? Temporal processing views of hippocampal function with special reference to attention. *Physiological Psychology, 8,* 254–261.

Solomon, P. R., & Babcock, B. A. (1979). KIM and the rabbit: The use of the KIM-1 microprocessor to control classical conditioning of the rabbit's nictitating membrane response. *Behavior Research Methods and Instrumentation, 11,* 67–70.

Solomon, P. R., Brennan, G., & Moore, J. W. (1974). Latent inhibition of the rabbit's nictitating membrane response as a function of CS intensity. *Bulletin of the Psychonomic Society, 4*(5A), 445–448.

Solomon, P. R., Crider, A. C., Winkelman, J. W., Turi, A., Kamer, R. S., & Kaplan, L. J. (1981). Disruption of latent inhibition following chronic *d*-amphetamine administration on prolonged haloperidol pretreatment: Relationship to schizophrenic attention disorder. *Biological Psychiatry, 16,* 519–537.

Solomon, P. R., & Gottfried, K. E. (1981). The septo-hippocampal cholinergic system and classical conditioning of the rabbit's nictitating membrane response. *Journal of Comparative and Physiological Psychology, 91,* 322–330.

Solomon, P. R., Kiney, C. A., & Scott, D. S. (1978). Disruption of latent inhibition following systemic administration of parachlorophenylalanine (PCPA). *Physiology and Behavior, 20,* 265–271.

Solomon, P. R., Lohr, A. C., & Moore, G. W. (1974). Latent inhibition of the rabbit's nictitating membrane response: Summation tests for active inhibition as a function of number of CS preexposures. *Bulletin of the Psychonomic Society, 4,* 557–559.

Solomon, P.R., & Moore, J. W. (1975). Latent inhibition and stimulus generalization of the classically conditioned nictitating membrane response in rabbits (*Oryctolagus cuniculus*) following dorsal hippocampal ablation. *Journal of Comparative and Physiological Psychology, 89,* 1192–1203.

Solomon, P. R., Nichols, G. L., Kiernan, J. M., Kamer, R. S., & Kaplan, L. J. (1980). Differential effects of lesions in medial and dorsal raphe of the rat: Latent inhibition and septohippocampal serotonin levels. *Journal of Comparative and Physiological Psychology, 94,* 145–154.

Solomon, P. R., Solomon, S. D., Vander Schaaf, E., & Perry, H. E. (1983). Altered activity in hippocampus is more detrimental to classical conditioning than removing the structure. *Science, 220,* 329–331.

Solomon, P. R., & Staton, D. M. (1982). Differential effects of microinjections of *d*-amphetamine into the nucleus accumbens or the caudate-putamen on the rat's ability to ignore an irrelevant stimulus. *Biological Psychiatry, 17,* 743–756.

Srebro, B., & Lorens, S. A. (1975). Behavioral effects of selective midbrain raphe lesions in the rat. *Brain Research, 89,* 303–325.

Staton, D. M., & Solomon, P. R. (1979). An easily mass produced cannula system for chemical stimulation of the brain. *Pharmacology, Biochemistry, and Behavior, 11,* 363–365.

Stumpf, C., Petsche, H., & Gogolak, G. (1962). The significance of the rabbit's septum as a relay station between the midbrain and the hippocampus II. The differential influence of drugs upon both cell firing pattern and the hippocampus theta activity. *Electroencephalography and Clinical Neurophysiology, 14,* 212–219.

Swanson, L. W. (1978). The anatomical organization of septo-hippocampal projections. In Ciba Foundation Symposium, *Functions of the septo-hippocampal system.* New York: Elsevier.

Swanson, L. W., & Cowan, W. M. (1977). An autoradiographic study of the organization of the efferent connections of the hippocampal formation in the rat. *Journal of Comparative Neurology, 172,* 49–84.

Swanson, L. W., & Cowan, W. M. (1979). The connections of the septal region in the rat. *Journal of Comparative Neurology, 186,* 621–656.

Swonger, A. K., & Rech, R. H. (1972). Serotonergic and cholinergic involvement in habituation of activity and spontaneous alternation of rats in a Y maze. *Journal of Comparative and Physiological Psychology, 81,* 509–522.

Tenen, S. S. (1967). The effects of p-chlorophenylalanine, a serotonin depletor, an avoidance acquisition, pain sensitivity and related behavior in the rat. *Psychopharmacologia, 10,* 204–219.

Thompson, R. F., Berger, T. W., Berry, S. D., Hoehler, F. K., Kettner, R. E., & Weisz, D. J. (1980). Hippocampal substrate of classical conditioning. *Physiological Psychology, 8,* 262–279.

Trulson, M. E., & Jacobs, B. L. (1979). Long-term amphetamine treatment decreases brain serotonin metabolism: Implications for theories of schizophrenia. *Science, 205,* 1295–1297.

Vinogradova, O. S., & Brazhnik, E. S. (1978). Neuronal aspects of septohippocampal relations. In Ciba Foundation Symposium 58, *Functions of the septo-hippocampal system.* New York: Elsevier.

Wagner, A. R. (1979). Habituation and memory. In A. Dickinson & R. A. Boakes (Eds.), *Mechanisms of learning and motivation*. Hillsdale, NJ: Lawrence Erlbaum Associates.

Warrington, E. K., & Weiskrantz, L. (1973). An analysis of short-term and long-term memory deficits in man. In J. A. Deutsch (Ed.), *The physiological basis of memory*. New York: Academic Press.

Weiss, K. R., & Brown, B. (1974). Latent inhibition: A review and new hypothesis. *Acta Neurobiologica Experimentalis, 34*, 301–316.

Weiss, K. R., Friedman, R., & McGregor, S. (1974). Effects of septal lesions on latent inhibition and habituation of the orienting response in rats. *Acta Neurobiologica Experimentalis, 34*, 491–504.

Weisz, D. W., Clark, G. A., Yang, B. Y., Thompson, R. F., Solomon, P. R., & Berger, T. W. (1982). Activity of dentate gyrus during NM conditioning in the rabbit. In C. D. Woody (Ed.), *Conditioning: Representation of involved neural function*. New York: Plenum.

Weisz, D. J., Solomon, P. R., & Thompson, R. F. (1980). The hippocampus appears necessary for trace conditioning. *Bulletin of the Psychonomic Society, 16* (Abstract).

Winson, J. (1980, June). Behaviorally dependent gating of neuronal transmission in the hippocampus. In J. W. Moore & P. R. Solomon (Eds.), The role of the hippocampus in learning and memory. *Physiological Psychology* (Special edition).

Winson, J., & Abzug, C. (1977). Gating of neuronal transmission in the hippocampus: Efficacy of transmission varies with behavioral state. *Science, 196*, 1223–1225.

Winson, J., & Abzug, L. (1978). Neuronal transmission through hippocampal pathways dependent on behavior. *Journal of Neurophysiology, 41*, 716–732.

6 "Selective Association" in Compound Stimulus Conditioning with the Rabbit

E. James Kehoe
University of New South Wales

Any organism in even the most sterile environment is faced with a continual and multifaceted stream of stimulus events. To discover the laws governing behavioral adjustments to the exigencies of an environment, Pavlov (1927, pp. 110–113) and subsequent investigators have used compounds of two separable stimuli (e.g., tone + light) as a laboratory model for the array of innocuous events that antedate a biologically significant stimulus (e.g., Hull, 1943; Kehoe & Gormezano, 1980; Razran, 1965, 1971; Wickens, 1954, 1959, 1965). One major result of research with compound stimuli has been the discovery that the level of response acquisition to a given conditioned stimulus (CS) depends not only on its own degree of contiguity with the unconditioned stimulus (US) but also on the intensive, associative, and temporal characteristics of other CSs in a compound (e.g., Kamin, 1968, 1969a, 1969b; Wagner, Logan, Haberlandt, & Price, 1968). At a descriptive level, it appears that the learning process is selective as to which components of a compound will gain associative strength and thus gain the capacity to evoke responding. The present chapter reviews the contribution to this research literature made by investigations with the rabbit nictitating membrane response (NMR) and eyeblink response (EBR) preparations.

The following discussion is in three parts. The first part defines more precisely the scope of the present review. The second part outlines the relevant theoretical approaches to compound stimulus conditioning. Finally, the third part describes the findings obtained with rabbit conditioning preparations and their implications for the major theoretical approaches.

PRELIMINARY CONSIDERATIONS

Interaction and Integration Laws

In any compound stimulus conditioning procedure, it is logically possible to observe both the interaction and integration of the component stimuli. An interaction may be said to occur whenever response acquisition to one stimulus in a compound is influenced by training in conjunction with the other component. There are two types of interactions: the negative type, in which response acquisition to a stimulus is impaired by training in a compound stimulus, and the positive type, in which response acquisition to the target stimulus is facilitated by compound stimulus training. The studies of negative interactions are of primary interest in the present review, whereas studies of positive interactions have been dealt with elsewhere (e.g., Gormezano & Kehoe, 1981; Kehoe, Feyer, & Moses, 1981). Whereas an interaction law describes the relation between the components of a compound, an integration law describes the relation between the compound and its components (Kehoe & Gormezano, 1980). The lawfulness of the relation between responding to the compound and to its components is the central focus of research concerned with delineating combination rules for compound stimuli. However, historic controversies originating in Gestalt psychology (cf. Hull, 1943; Razran, 1939, 1965, 1971; Rescorla, 1972a, 1973a) have directed research toward a determination of whether or not a compound stimulus fuses into a "configuration," i.e., an event that is functionally distinct from its components (Baker, 1968; Bellingham & Gillette, 1981; Gillette & Bellingham, 1982; Kehoe & Gormezano, 1980; Razran, 1971). Although the resolution of issues concerning integration will have profound implications for theories of stimulus interaction (Kehoe, 1982a), it is still possible to deal with stimulus interactions in relative isolation. However, assumptions regarding integration laws will be noted where relevant.

The Bisensory Compound

The most common type of compound used with rabbit preparations has consisted of diffuse bisensory stimuli, e.g., tone and light (e.g., Kehoe, Gibbs, Garcia, & Gormezano, 1979; Wagner et al., 1968). Bisensory compound stimuli have both the advantage and limitation of bypassing processes of interaction and integration that operate within a single sensory system, thus more clearly revealing later stages of interaction and integration. Furthermore, stimulus events from different sensory modalities are unequivocally "separable" in a physical sense; that is to say, the component stimuli can be presented in a completely independent manner, and their compounding involves simply presenting them at the same time (Blough, 1972; Kehoe &

Gormezano, 1980; Riley & Leith, 1976). Ultimately, any comprehensive set of laws describing interactions and integrations will have to encompass all types of compound stimuli, and a unified account will most likely include a number of mechanisms intervening between the impact of physical forces of the sensory receptors and the final behavioral output (e.g., Hebb, 1949; Konorski, 1967). Nevertheless, the use of relatively simple and highly distinctive stimuli in a compound provides an interesting test case for revealing interactive and integrative processes in conditioning. The very simplicity and distinctiveness of such stimuli would seem to be most conducive to the formation of completely independent associations. Thus, the interactions and integrations that have been observed are all the more fascinating in their implications for associative theory.

THEORY

The impairment of CR acquisition to an otherwise effective CS as a result of compound stimulus training has been seen as raising doubts concerning the sufficiency of CS–US contiguity as a determinant of associative learning (Gormezano & Kehoe, 1981; Kamin, 1968, 1969a, b; Wagner, 1969a). In more concrete terms, doubts about the sufficiency of CS–US contiguity concern whether the empirical laws of response acquisition obtained with relatively isolated CS–US pairings are sufficient to predict the rate and level of response acquisition to the individual components of a compound (Gormezano & Kehoe, 1981; Wickens, 1959, 1965). As a consequence of these doubts, there have been intensive and diverse theoretical developments, which have led to the emergence of four distinct types of theories regarding selective association phenomena. Specifically, the various theories can be classified according to whether they assume that (1) there is either a deficit in the acquisition of associative strength or a failure to transfer existing associative strength from the stimulus context of the compound to that of component testing; (2) the critical interaction between the CSs involves either a "perceptual/attentional" interaction between the CSs themselves prior to the US or an interaction based on the relative associative strengths of the CSs at the time of the US; and (3) "informative" relations between CSs in a compound can override the associative consequences of CS–US contiguity.

Selective Attention Hypotheses

Selective attention hypotheses are the oldest of the recognized accounts of selective association effects, having their origins in the study of human perception and later animal discrimination learning with complex cues (cf. Sutherland & Mackintosh, 1971, pp. 1–2). Selective attention hypotheses assume that, in addition to CS–US contiguity, an active orientation ('attention') to a CS is necessary for associative strength to be established. Moreover, in a situation involving many stimulus inputs, there will be a competition among concurrent stimuli for the attentional capacity of the animal, which is usually assumed to be limited and relatively fixed. Selective attention hypotheses assume that the degree of "attention" to a CS is positive function of both the physical intensity of the CS and the previous number of CS–US pairings. Moreover, if a sensory "analyzer" suitable for a given CS has already been activated, that CS will be more likely to hold the attention of the animal and thus gain access to the associative apparatus. In summary, there can be a deficit in acquisition of associative strength to a CS if it fails to compete successfully with other CSs for the attention of the animal prior to the occurrence of the US.

Associative Trade-off Hypotheses

The most well-developed accounts of selective association effects originated with Rescorla and Wagner's (1972) "modified continuity" theory (e.g., Frey & Sears, 1978; Sutton & Barto, 1981). According to Rescorla and Wagner, changes in the associative strength of a CS depend on the existing associative strength of concurrent stimuli, because there is a fixed amount of associative strength that can be supported by a US on a given trial. Consequently, the associative strength that accrues to one CS in a compound becomes unavailable to any other CSs in the compound. Thus, if all CSs start with no associative strength, the CS with the highest intrinsic learning rate, as determined by its intensity, will rapidly garner the largest portion of the available associative strength to the relative detriment of concurrent CSs. Among theoretical developments inspired by the Rescorla–Wagner model, a model proposed by Mackintosh (1975) represents a divergent strand. Mackintosh (1975) dispenses with the assumption that there is a direct competition between CSs for a fixed quantity of associative strength. Instead, Mackintosh (1975) argues that trade offs can be achieved via a more open-ended process, in which the CS with the greatest relative associative strength on a trial gains a proportional increment in its learning rate parameter, whereas all other CSs suffer a decrement in their respective learning rate parameters (cf. Moore & Stickney, 1980; Pearce & Hall, 1980). Thus, a weak CS, which starts training with a low learning rate, will show a progressive decline in learning rate as concurrent, stronger stimuli gain associative strength over trials. In summary, the Rescorla–Wagner model and its successors all assume that selective association effects represent an actual impairment in the acquisition of associative strength based on a trade off between CSs at the time of reinforcement.

Generalization Decrement Hypotheses

In contrast to the selective attention and associative trade-off models, generalization decrement hypotheses postulate that each stimulus in a compound has unhindered access to the associative apparatus, but that there is a failure for the associative strength acquired to a stimulus inside the context of a compound to transfer outside that context (e.g., Borgealt, Donahoe, & Weinstein, 1972; Hull, 1943; Wickens, 1959). At an operational level, advocates of generalization decrement hypotheses note that a test trial for a single stimulus constitutes a change in the total stimulating conditions from those prevailing during compound stimulus training. At a theoretical level, generalization decrement hypotheses presuppose that the same nominal CS produces different perceptual encodings depending on whether or not it is presented in the context of other stimuli. The earliest exposition of a transfer hypothesis may be found in Hull's (1943, 1945) hypothesis of "neural afferent interaction." Hull (1943, p. 355) assumes that the encoding of a relatively weak CS will be highly modified by the presence of a relatively strong CS whereas the encoding of the stronger CS will be hardly modified at all. In subsequent single-stimulus testing, responding to the weaker CS will suffer a massive generalization decrement, whereas responding to the stronger CS will undergo little, if any, generalization decrement. More recent generalization decrement hypotheses have tended to assume that compounded CSs are functionally united into a single "configure" and that responding to a component depends on its similarity to the configural stimulus (e.g., Baker, 1972; Gaioni, 1982; cf. Kehoe & Gormezano, 1980). Presumably, a weaker component will contribute less to the configure than a stronger component. Thus, on a test trial, the weaker component would effectively differ more from the compound configural stimulus than would the stronger component. Despite the variations among generalization decrement hypotheses, they all contend that there is a "perceptual" interaction between the CSs themselves and that impairments in response acquisition to a CS represent a failure in the transfer of associative strength from compound training to component testing.

Information Hypotheses

Whereas all other accounts of selective association effects assume that CS–US contiguity is necessary to response acquisition, the information hypotheses come the closest to dispensing with CS–US contiguity as a fundamental variable to association (Egger & Miller, 1962; Seligman, 1966). Instead, they stress the temporal and statistical correlations between stimuli as being fundamental to the establishment of associations. Information hypotheses originated from investigations conducted by Egger and Miller (1962). They found that, after a series of stimuli (CSA–CSB) had been consistently paired with a food US, CSB by itself had less secondary reinforcing power for bar-press responding than CSA by itself. Furthermore, responding produced by CSB did not exceed the responding produced by a control stimulus that had been explicitly unpaired with food. To account for their findings, Egger and Miller (1962) proposed their information hypothesis that stressed the primacy of CSA in signaling the impending US rather than the relative contiguity of CSB to the US. According to the information hypothesis, if CSA and CSB are equally reliable "predictors" of the US, then associative strength will accrue to the initial CSA and not to the later "redundant" CSB. To test their hypothesis, Egger and Miller (1962) made CSA an "unreliable predictor" of the US by interspersing presentations of CSA-alone among the CSA–CSB–US presentations, thus rendering CSB the more reliable predictor of the US. In agreement with expectations of the information hypothesis, CSB was found to have acquired secondary reinforcing values, even though its relation to the US in the serial compound was unchanged. Subsequent developments of information hypotheses have branched in two directions. One branch has been concerned with phenomena arising from the relative reliability of a CS in predicting the US (e.g., Wagner, 1969a). However, this subclass of information hypotheses has been largely superceded by the associative trade-off hypotheses (Rescorla, 1972b). The other branch has concerned selective association effects arising from serial stimuli. The more recent information hypotheses contend that CSB in a serial compound will lose its effectiveness in gaining access to the associative apparatus if its occurrence is well predicted by preceding events, namely CSA (Cantor & Wilson, 1981; cf. Pearce & Hall, 1980, p. 535). The more well-articulated information hypotheses tend to merge with the associative trade-off hypotheses insofar as they contend that compound conditioning can produce actual impairments in the acquisition of associative strength to a CS based on the consistency of statistical and temporal relations between the CSs with each other and the US.

EMPIRICAL REVIEW

The design for "selective association" experiments has usually entailed holding constant the training parameters of one target stimulus (CSX) while varying the parameters of another stimulus (CSA) in the compound. The level of responding to CSX is then observed on individual test trials and compared to the level of responding observed with a corresponding single-CS control (Wickens, 1965). Using this general tactic, it has been found possible to impair CR acquisition to an otherwise effective CSX through manipulations of (1) the intensity of CSA, i.e., "overshadowing," (2) the schedule of CS–US pairings of CSA, e.g., "blocking," and (c) the relative CS–US intervals of CSA and CSB, i.e., "serial stimulus selection" (Kehoe, 1979; Mackintosh, 1974, pp. 45–51). In addition to demonstrations of overshadowing, blocking, and serial stimulus selection, research with rabbit preparations has been directed towards the testing of specific deductions from the alternative accounts of selective association effects. By taking advantage of the well-defined effects of CS–US interval manipulations on the rate and level of CR acquisition (e.g., Gormezano, 1972; Kehoe, 1979; Smith, Coleman, & Gormezano, 1969), investigations with the rabbit preparations have been well suited for delineating the role of CS–US contiguity in compound conditioning. Thus, it has been possible to pit CS–US contiguity as a quantitative variable against the quantitative effects of selective association variables. As is shown later, the findings from rabbit compound conditioning studies indicate that: (a) the same effects of CS–US interval that govern CR acquisition in single CS procedures also operate without hinderance in compound stimulus procedures, but (2) nevertheless, additional processes are engaged in a compound training procedure that operate to reduce the level of responding to an individual component. Moreover, the available findings suggest that perceptual or attentional interactions between the CSs are likely candidates.

Overshadowing

"Overshadowing" is said to occur when the rate and level of CR acquisition to CSX is reduced through compound training with another relatively intense CSA that is demonstrably capable of producing rapid response acquisition (e.g., Kamin, 1969a; Mackintosh, 1976; Pavlov, 1927, p. 141). In many ways, overshadowing may be regarded as the prototypical selective association effect insofar as the animal shows differential CR acquisition to two stimuli that are equally well paired with the US. In the rabbit NMR preparation, a systematic demonstration of overshadowing has been conducted by Kehoe (1982a, Experiment 1). Specifically, a visual CS (a 20-Hz flashing of an 8-W flourescent houselight) was held constant, whereas the intensity of an auditory CS (a 1,000-Hz tone superimposed on 80-dB white noise) was varied over the values of 85, 89, and 93 dB. One group of animals was trained with a light plus tone compound at each level of the tone intensity. These three groups received 54 reinforced compound trials per day, which were interspersed with three unreinforced test trials each to the light and appropriate tone. The compound groups were designated LT85, LT89, and LT93, respectively. In addition to the compound stimulus groups, there were four single-CS control groups: One was trained with the light (Group L), and the other three were trained with 85-, 89-, and 93-dB tones (Groups T85, T89, and T93). For all groups, the CS–US interval was 400-msec.

In brief, the results showed that the light was overshadowed by the more intense tones. Figure 6.1 shows the mean percentage of CRs across three blocks of light test trials, where each block is comprised of six test trials administered across 2 successive days of training. In comparison with the CR acquisition curve of Group L, the compound groups trained with the 89- and 93-dB tones showed consistently lower levels of responding to the light. However, the compound group trained with the 85-dB tone showed levels of responding to the light that were as high as those of the control group. Although CR acquisition to the light was progressively impaired by increases in tone intensity, there was no apparent reciprocal effect of the light on responding to the tone. Specifically, the overall level of responding to the tone in the compound groups reached asymptotic levels of 90% CRs and did not

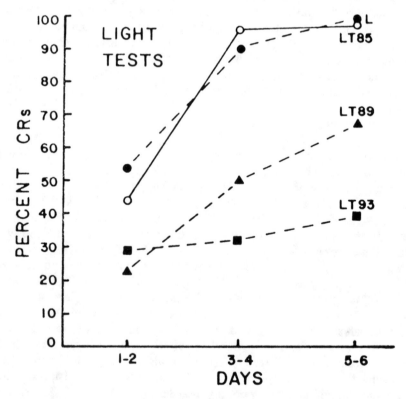

FIG. 6.1   Percentage CRs on light test trials plotted as a function of 2-day blocks. Separate acquisition curves are shown for four groups given reinforced training with light, light + 85-dB tone, light + 89-dB tone, and light + 93-dB tone, respectively (Kehoe, 1982a, Experiment 1).

differ systematically from the corresponding control groups trained with tone.

Reciprocal Overshadowing. As described earlier, Kehoe (1982a, Experiment 1) found that overshadowing was unidirectional or absent altogether. However, Mackintosh (1976) has contended that a mutual impairment in CR acquisition to both CSs can be obtained if both are relatively low in "salience." As an intervening variable, the "salience" of a CS is conventionally anchored, on the independent variable side, to its physical characteristics, e.g., intensity, and, on the dependent variable side, to the observed rate of response acquisition. As one means for lowering "salience," Kehoe (1982a, Experiment 2) reduced the overall rate of CR acquisition to both CSs by using a CS–US interval of 800 msec, which produces a modest but steady rate of CR acquisition in the rabbit NMR preparation (e.g., Kehoe, 1979; Smith et al., 1969). Moreover, in order to determine whether light could overshadow tone, Kehoe (1982a, Experiment 2) used one tone with an intensity of 73 dB.

In brief, Kehoe's (1982a, Experiment 2) contained three compound groups labeled LT73, LT85, and LT93, which received reinforced training with a light + tone compound, in which the tone intensities were 73, 85, and 93 dB, respectively. Moreover, there was a light control gorup, Group L, and three tone control groups, which were labeled T73, T85, and T93 according to the intensity of the tone. In all groups, the CS duration and CS–US interval were 800 msec. Figure 6.2 shows the mean terminal level of responding on light and tone test trials plotted as a function of the tone intensity during training. In brief, the results display clear evidence of reciprocal overshadowing in Groups LT85 and LT93. Specifically, examination of the left panel reveals that responding to the light in Groups LT85 and LT93 showed substantial impairments relative to the level of responding attained by the light control group. Likewise, examination of the right panel reveals that the terminal level of responding to the tone in Groups LT85 and LT93 fell substantially below that of their corresponding tone controls, Groups T85 and T93. Consequently, the present results supported Mackintosh's (1976) hypothesis that reciprocal overshadowing could be obtained when the salience, in the sense of the overall rate of CR acquisition, was lowered.

Although reciprocal overshadowing was evident in Groups LT85 and LT93, the performance of Group LT73 displayed what might be called "paradoxical overshadowing." As can be seen in Fig. 6.2, the performance of the control groups clearly reveals that the light was more salient than the 73-dB tone in so far as Group L (left panel) reached a higher level of CR acquisition than that of Group T73 (right panel). Accordingly, the light would be expected to overshadow the tone. However, the reverse occurred; CR acquisition to the light but not the tone showed substantial impairments. Specifically, the level of responding to the light in Group LT73 was substantially

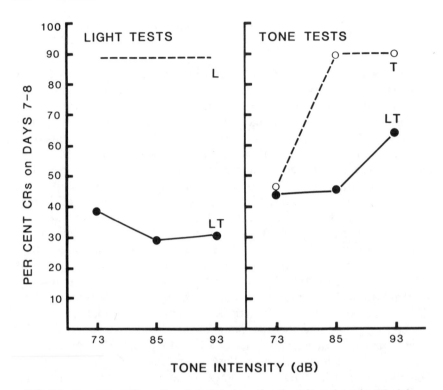

FIG. 6.2 Percentage CRs on Days 7–8 plotted as a function of tone intensity. The left panel shows the level of responding on light test trials. The upper line represents the level attained by a light group (L), and the lower curve represents the levels attained by the compound groups (LT). The right panel shows the level of responding on tone test trials for the tone (T) and compound (LT) groups (Kehoe, 1982a, Experiment 2).

lower than that of Group L, whereas the level of responding to tone was low in absolute terms but was no lower than that of Group T73. Subsequent experiments by Kehoe (1982a, Experiments 3 & 4) replicated this paradoxical overshadowing at the 800-msec CS–US but revealed reciprocal overshadowing when a 400-msec CS–US interval was used. If "salience" is to be anchored to the rate and level of CR acquisition produced by a stimulus when trained by itself, then Group LT73 would appear to be a case in which a less salient stimulus can unidirectionally overshadow a more salient stimulus.

Blocking and Relative Validity

Manipulations of the schedule of CS–US pairings for the components of a compound stimulus were first conducted by Wagner and his associates using a rabbit EBR preparation (Wagner, 1969a, b, c; Wagner et al., 1968). Specifically, the schedule of CS–US pairings for one stimulus, CSX, was fixed whereas the schedules for other stimuli (CSA1, CSA2, etc.) in the compound were manipulated by either (1) giving an A stimulus additional training by itself (Wagner, 1969b) or (2) varying the differential reinforcement of two compounds A1X and A2X (Wagner et al., 1968). In brief, it was found that, if the A stimuli were more frequently or more consistently paired with the US than the X stimulus, then subsequent test trials would yield a low level of responding to CSX. However, if the A stimuli were less frequently or less consistently paired with the US than was the X stimulus, then there would be a high level of responding to CSX on test trials. Thus, the level of CR acquisition to a component of the compound depended not only on its pairings with the US but also on the relative "validity" of the other components as signals for the US (Wagner, 1969a).

Similar findings were obtained in the NMR preparation by Marchant and Moore (1973) who duplicated portions of Kamin's (1968a, 1969a, b) pioneering studies of the "blocking" effect in the conditioned suppression paradigm. In all of Marchant and Moore's experiments, the main group (A–AX) received CSA–US pairings until the level of responding exceed 80% CRs. During the same stage, a second group (sit-AX) was exposed to handling and restraint in the experimental chambers but was not exposed to either the CS or US. Then, both groups received reinforced training with the AX compound. Finally, testing the CSX in extinction revealed a low level of responding in the A-AX group as compared to the sit-AX group. Because both groups had an equal number of AX training trials, the low level of responding to CSX in Group A-AX could not be attributed solely to a deleterious effect of compound training and/or generalization decrement arising from tests of CSX outside the stimulus context of the compound. Subsequently, this basic finding has been repeated in the NMR preparation (Kehoe, Schreurs, & Amodei, 1981, Experiment 2; Solomon, 1977) and in EBR preparations (Kinkaide, 1974; Maleske & Frey, 1979). In Marchant and Moore's (1973) experiments, they also demonstrated that the blocking effect depended on prior training with CSA, because training of CSA following AX compound training (AX-A) yielded a high level of responding to CSX during the final extinction testing. Furthermore, the impairment of CR acquisition to CSX depended on the compounding of CSA with CSX, because separate but successive training of CSA and CSX (A-X) yielded a high level of responding to CSX approaching that of a group that received only CSX–US training (sit-X).

Serial Stimulus Selection

One of the seminal findings in compound conditioning has been the observation that response acquisition to a CS relatively contiguous to the US may be impaired by a preceding stimulus that has a more remote temporal relation to the US (Egger & Miller, 1962; Wickens, 1959, 1965, 1973). Recently, Kehoe et al. (1979) conducted systematic demonstrations of the serial stimulus selection effect in the rabbit NMR preparation. In Kehoe et al. (1979, Experiment 1), the serial compound consisted of two components, namely CS1, which was a 400-msec, 1000-Hz tone, followed by CS2, which was a 400-msec, 20-Hz flashing houselight. The CS2–US interval was held constant at a value of 350 msec, while the CS1–US interval was manipulated across the values of 750, 1250, 1750, and 2750 msec, respectively. Thus, there were four groups, which were labeled T-O-L, T-.5-L, T-1-L, and T-2-L, which denote the CS1 (Tone), the duration of the 'trace' interval between CS1-offset and CS2-onset (0, .5, 1, and 2 sec), and the CS2 (Light). Training was conducted for 16 days, each day consisting of 60 CS1–CS2–US trials interspersed with two test trials each of CS1, CS2, and CS1–CS2.

Figure 6.3 depicts the mean percentage of CRs on CS1 and CS2 test trials across blocks of four test trials. Examination of the right panel of Fig. 6.3 reveals that, despite the constant 350-msec CS2–US interval, the rate of acquisition and terminal level of CRs to CS2 was an inverse function of the CS1–US/CS1–CS2 interval. In particular, Group T-O-L showed slow CR acquisition to an asymptote around 40% CRs. In a subsequent experiment, Kehoe et al. (1979, Experiment 2) replicated the low level of responding to

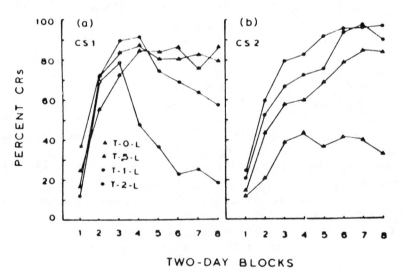

FIG. 6.3   Percentage CRs on CS1 and CS2 test trials plotted as a function of 2-day blocks. Groups T-O-L, T-.5-L, T-1-L, and T-2-L are labeled in terms of the tone (T) CS1, the trace interval (0, .5, 1, and 2 sec), and the light (L) CS2 (Kehoe, Gibbs, Garcia, & Gormezano, 1979).

CS2 in Group T-O-L and confirmed that it was significantly lower than the asymptote of 100% CRs obtained when the same CS was trained by itself at a 350-msec CS-US interval.

Examination of the left panel of Fig. 6.3 reveals that, despite the large differences in the CS1-US interval, the acquisition of CRs to CS1 was, at first, rapid and uniform across groups. All groups attained at least 80% CRs to CS1 before the groups trained under the longer CS1-US intervals, Groups T-1-L and T-2-L began to show declines in performance. Kehoe et al. (1979, Experiments 2 and 3) confirmed that the high levels of responding to CS1 in serial compounds represented a substantial augmentation over what could be obtained with the same CS trained by itself at the same long CS-US intervals.

The impairment in CR acquisition to CS2 would appear to be a particularly provocative challenge to the sufficiency of CS-US contiguity principles for at least two reasons. First, the variable of interest, namely CS-US interval, constitutes a manipulation along the dimensions most fundamental to any contiguity principle. Second, in overshadowing and blocking, an efficacious CS in terms of salience or prior training hinders CR acquisition to a comparatively inefficacious stimulus. However, serial stimulus selection entails a relatively inefficacious stimulus (CS1), in terms of its remote temporal relation to the US, impairing CR acquisition to a comparatively efficacious stimulus (CS2). Thus, serial stimulus selection is paradoxical from the perspectives of both contiguity principles and other selective association effects.

CS2-US Interval

The major alternative accounts of serial stimulus selection have been the information hypotheses (e.g., Cantor & Wilson, 1981; Egger & Miller, 1962) and the generalization decrement hypotheses (e.g., Borgealt et al., 1972; Hancock, 1982; Kehoe, 1979; Wickens, 1959, 1965, 1973). On the one hand, the information hypotheses imply that CS1's predictive value for CS2 or the US should render CS1 the prepotent stimulus in gaining access to the associative apparatus to the detriment of CS2, regardless of CS2's relative contiguity to the US. On the other hand, the generalization decrement hypotheses contend that, within the context of a compound, the particular encoding of a CS will have full access to the associative apparatus in accord with its individual conditioning parameters, especially its CS-US interval. In agreement with the generalization decrement hypotheses, there has been an accumulating body of evidence from rabbit conditioning studies that the degree of CS2-US contiguity determines the rate of CR acquisition to a serial compound and its components (Frey, Englander, & Roman, 1971; Kehoe, 1979, 1982b).

As examples of the profound effects of CS2-US contiguity on CR acquisition to a serial compound, Fig. 6.4 shows the acquisition curves to serial com-

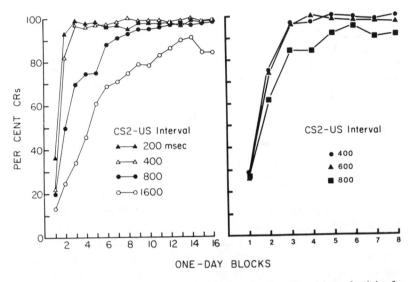

FIG. 6.4 Percentage CRs on compound trials plotted as function of days of training for each level of the CS2-US interval. The left panel shows the acquisition curves obtained with a tone–light sequential compound (Kehoe, 1979), and the right panel shows the acquisition curves obtained from a serial compound in which the tone overlapped the light (Kehoe, 1982b).

pounds obtained by Kehoe (1979, 1982b, Experiment 4). The left panel shows the CR acquisition curves obtained from compounds consisting of sequential presentations of a tone CS1 and light CS2, in which CS1's offset coincided with CS2's onset. The values of the CS2–US intervals were 200, 400, 800, and 1600 msec. Furthermore, the acquisition curve for each CS2–US interval represents the average of four groups, which differed in their respective CS1–CS2 intervals and thus their CS1–US intervals. Specifically, the CS1–CS2 intervals were 200, 400, 800, and 1600 msec. Inspection of the left panel reveals that the rate of CR acquisition to the serial compound was an inverse function of the CS2–US interval. The manipulation of the CS1–CS2 interval (and thus the CS1–US interval) had no systematic effect on responding to the serial compound at any level of the CS2–US interval.

The right panel of Fig. 6.4 shows CR acquisition curves obtained from a tone–light serial compound in which duration of CS1 was extended to overlap CS2 and coterminate with CS2 at the time of US onset. The overlapping compound was used in part to obviate the possibility that, in strictly sequential CS presentations, the interval between CS1-offset and the US may have determined the rate of CR acquisition to the compound. By using an overlapping compound, the interval between CS1-offset and the US was constant at a value of zero. The values of the CS2–US interval were 400, 600, and 800 msec, and the CS1–US interval was fixed at a value of 800 msec. Thus, the groups trained with the 400- and 600-msec CS2–US intervals were exposed to serial compounds, whereas the group trained with an 800-msec CS2–US interval was exposed to a simultaneous compound. As was seen in the strictly sequential compound, the rate of CR acquisition in the overlapping compound was inversely related to the CS2–US interval. The effect of the CS2–US interval in the overlapping compounds is particularly noteworthy, because CS1 was set at an intensity of 93 dB that was known to produce overshadowing of the light (Kehoe, 1982a). Thus, in the serial compounds, the CS2 was at a potential disadvantage in terms of both CS1's temporal primacy and CS1's relative salience.

Although the CS2–US interval determined the rate of CR acquisition to the compound, responding to CS2 outside the compound showed an impairment relative to corresponding single-stimulus control groups. Figure 6.5 shows the mean overall percentage of CRs on CS2 test trials as a function of the

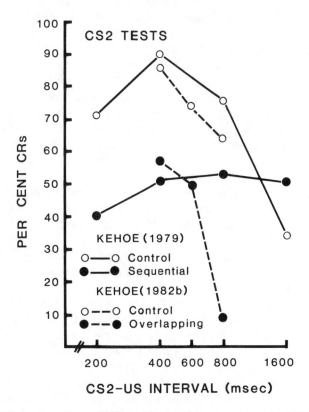

FIG. 6.5   Percentage CRs on CS2 test trials plotted as a function of the CS2–US interval. The upper two curves were obtained from single CS control conditions, and the lower two curves were obtained from sequential and serial overlapping compound conditions (Kehoe, 1979; 1982b).

CS2–US interval. Two pairs of curves are plotted. One pair depicts the overall performance obtained from sequential compound groups and their single-stimulus controls (Kehoe, 1979), and the other pair depicts the overall performance obtained from overlapping compounds and their single-stimulus controls (Kehoe, 1982b). Inspection of Fig. 6.5 reveals that the single-stimulus controls in both experiments generally showed a level of responding that decreased across CS2–US intervals. In contrast to the control groups, the compound groups showed a substantially lower level of responding to CS2, except at the 1600 msec CS2–US interval. In the sequential compound groups, the level of responding across CS2–US intervals was relatively constant, but, in the overlapping compound groups, the levels of responding to CS2 reflected the effects of the CS2–US interval during serial compound training.

The observation that responding on CS2 test trials in the overlapping compound groups was inversely related to the CS2–US interval indicates that CS2–US contiguity can partially counteract the effects of an overshadowing stimulus (Kehoe, 1982b). Specifically, the performance of the group trained with the 800-msec CS2–US interval may be taken as starting point, for it was trained with a simultaneous compound and would be subject only to overshadowing processes. In responding to CS2, the simultaneous compound group showed both the lowest absolute level of responding (mean = 9% CRs) and the largest difference from its single-stimulus control (difference = 55 percentage points). In contrast, the groups that received training with overlapping serial compounds were subject to any deleterious effects of CS1's primacy as well as overshadowing. Contrary to the expectations of an information hypothesis, the levels of responding in the serial overlapping compound groups (means = 50% and 57% CRs) were higher than that of the simultaneous compound group and were closer to those of their respective control groups (differences = 24 and 29 percentage points, respectively).

The finding that the CS2–US interval determines the rate of CR acquisition to a serial compound even when responding to CS2 outside the compound shows impairments, clearly contradicts information hypotheses, which minimize the role of CS–US contiguity (Egger & Miller, 1962; Seligman, 1966). The most recent version of the information hypothesis has attempted to explain the effects of CS–US interval manipulations in single-stimulus situations and the effects of CS1–CS2 interval manipulations in serial compound conditioning (Cantor, 1981; Cantor & Wilson, 1981). Nevertheless, this hypothesis still implies incorrectly that, if CS1 provides maximal information regarding the time of CS2's impending onset, the CS1–US interval ought to determine the rate of CR acquisition. In another attmept to save the information hypothesis, Seger and Scheuer (1977) argue that CS2 gains associative strength inside the compound because it provides temporal information about "when shock will occur" but only when CS2 is preceded by CS1. Although Seger and Scheuer's (1977) account uses the language of information hypotheses, it does not assume that a deficit occurs in the acquisition of associative strength to CS2 during serial compound training. Instead, their account proposes that there is a deficit in the transfer from serial compound training to the testing of CS2 outside the compound. In this respect, Seger and Scheuer's account converges with the generalization decrement accounts, which expect there to be a discrepancy between the efficacy of CS2–US contiguity inside a compound and the level of responding to CS2 outside the compound (cf. Hancock, 1982).

Evidence that substantial associative strength does accrue to CS2 inside a serial compound may be found in results that indicate that, even when the level of responding to CS2 outside a serial compound is low, the responding during CS2 inside the compound reaches levels comparable to those obtained when the same CS is trained by itself (Kehoe, 1979). To obtain an estimate of the associative strength of CS2 inside a sequential compound, Kehoe (1979) made measurements of responding during the segment of the serial compound filled by CS2. Figure 6.6 shows the mean likelihood of CR's being initiated during CS2 on a compound trial as a function of the CS2–US interval. An equivalent function is shown for the single-stimulus control groups based on corresponding CS2 test trials. Inspection of Fig. 6.6 reveals that the likelihood a CR during CS2 in both the serial compound groups and control groups showed similar concave functions across CS2–US intervals. Differences between the serial compound groups and the single-stimulus groups were statistically unreliable, which is in marked contrast to the low relative levels of responding to the same CS2 outside the serial compound, which were shown earlier in Fig. 6.5. This disparity between the apparent levels of responding to CS2 inside and outside the compound clearly agrees with the key deduction from generalization decrement hypotheses, namely that there is a deficit in transfer from compound training to component testing.

CS2 Intensity

The findings of Kehoe (1982b, Experiment 1) indicated that overshadowing of CR acquisition to CS2 in a serial compound can be attenuated by making CS2 more contiguous to the US than CS1. By the same token, the beneficial effects of increased CS2–US contiguity on the level of CR acquisition to CS2 were greater than any deleterious effects of CS1's temporal primacy. Nevertheless, CR acquisition to CS2 still showed substantial impairment. In order to determine whether it would be possible to combine the advantages of CS2–US contiguity and CS2 salience to further attenuate any effect of CS1's primacy and even perhaps overshadow CS1, Kehoe (1982b, Experiment 4) used light as CS1 and manipulated the intensity of tone as CS2 in a serial

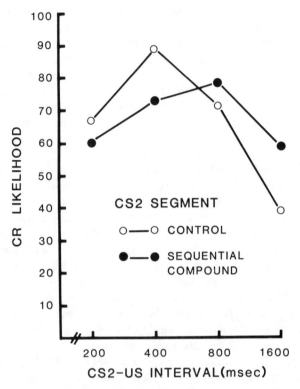

FIG. 6.6   CR likelihood during CS2 within a sequential compound for compound-trained groups and during CS2 on CS2 test trials for single-CS control groups plotted as a function of the CS2–US interval (Kehoe, 1979).

overlapping compound. There were three serial compound groups, in which CS1 was an 800 msec light, and CS2 was a 73-, 85-, or 93-dB 400-msec tone. The CS1–US interval was 800 msec, and the CS2–US interval was 400 msec. There were three corresponding tone control groups, which were trained with a 73-, 85-, or 93-dB tone at a CS–US interval of 400 msec. Finally, a light control group was trained with the light CS at a CS–US interval of 800 msec.

Figure 6.7 shows the mean percentage CRs on reinforced trials for all seven groups across days of training, each of which contained 104 reinforced trials. Inspection of the two panels in the figure shows that, in both serial compound and tone control groups, the rate of CR acquisition was positively related to CS2 (tone) intensity. Specifically, the 73d-dB tone CS2 produced slower CR acquisition than the 85- or 93-dB tones, which appeared to produce similar acquisition rates. Inspection of Group L's rate of CR acquisition under the 800-msec CS–US interval reveals that it fell below that of the serial compound groups. Consequently, CS2's intensity appears to determine the rate of CR acquisition in a compound much in the same way as does the CS2–US interval.

Figure 6.8 shows the level of responding to CS1 (light) and CS2 (tone) on test trials across blocks of six trials. With respect to CS1 (left panel), the serial compound groups and the light control group all showed similar rates of CR acquisition, reaching a terminal level around 70% CRs. Any apparent differences failed to attain statistical significance. Inspection of CS2 test trial data (right panel) reveals that responding in the serial compound groups and tone control groups was positively related to tone intensity, but responding to CS2 in the serial compound groups was nevertheless substantially lower than in the tone control groups. At this point, it should be noted that the 93-db tone CS2 was the same tone that had otherwise overshadowed the light which served as CS1 (cf. Kehoe, 1982a, 1982b, Experiment 1). Thus, the temporal primacy of CS1 in a serial compound gives it the ability to impair CR acquisition to a known overshadowing stimulus.

In summary, the responding of the animals was clearly sensitive to the intensity of CS2 as revealed by the positive effects of CS2 intensity on the level of responding to the compound and to CS2 on test trials. Nevertheless, even the most intense CS2 showed deficits in responding on test trials and, moreover, failed to overshadow CS1. Thus, the temporal primacy of CS1 clearly exerts a powerful effect on responding to CS2. Although information hy-

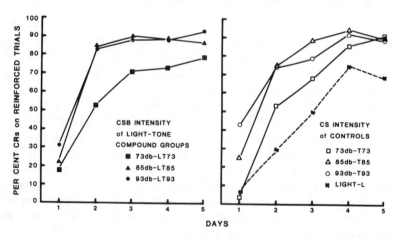

FIG. 6.7   Percentage CRs plotted as a function of 1-day blocks. The right panel depicts CR acquisition to a serial overlapping light–tone compound in which the tone CS2 (labeled here as CSB) was 73, 85, or 93 dB in intensity. The right panel depicts CR acquisition to single-stimulus control groups consisting Group L, which was trained with light at an 800-msec CS–US interval, and Groups T73, T85, and T93, which were trained with tones of 73, 85, and 93 dB at the CS–US interval of 400 msec (Kehoe, 1982b, Experiment 4).

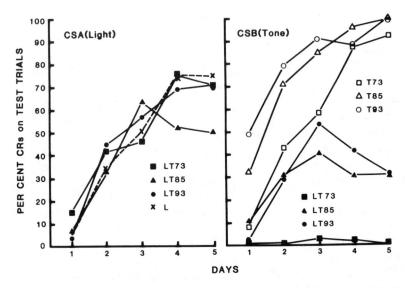

FIG. 6.8   Percentage CRs on test trials plotted as a function of 6-trial blocks. The left panel depicts CR acquisition to the light CS1 (labeled here as CSA) in the serial compound and light groups. The right panel depicts CR acquisition to the tone CS2 (labeled here as CSB) in the serial compound and tone control groups. Separate curves are shown for each level of the tone intensity (Kehoe, 1982b, Experiment 4).

potheses have clearly identified the temporal primacy of CS1 in a serial compound as having a deleterious effect on CR acquisition to CS2, a selective attention hypothesis would appear to offer a plausible alternative account of the present findings. Specifically, the onset of CS1 presumably engages the animal's attention, which the subsequent occurrence of even a highly salient stimulus has difficulty counteracting in the brief time available before the US. In contrast, the generalization decrement hypotheses face some difficulties in accounting for the findings of Kehoe (1982b, Experiment 4). On the one hand, the disparity between the positive effects of CS2 intensity inside the compound and the low level of responding to CS2 outside the compound is consistent with a deficit in transfer from compound training to component testing. On the other hand, the ability of the light CS1 to produce impairments in responding to the most salient CS2 exposes the chief weakness of generalization decrement hypotheses, namely the vague specification of the presumed stimulus encoding process. From the perspective of the generalization decrement hypotheses, there appears to be a profound asymmetry in the encoding process that depends on the temporal order of stimulus onset as well as the relative physical salience of the stimuli. One could postulate that the isolated portion of CS1 in a serial compound makes it effectively more salient than any succeeding stimuli, even one that is otherwise more salient, but this tactic risks converting a generalization decrement hypothesis into nothing more than an elaborate redescription of the known outcomes.

Blocking in Serial Compounds

The phenomenon of blocking has occupied a pivotal position in selective association research. Studies of blocking have provided some of the most compelling evidence for processes of competition between CSs for either attention (e.g., Sutherland & Mackintosh, 1971, pp. 114–118) or associative strength (e.g., Rescorla & Wagner, 1972). Conversely, generalization decrement hypotheses appear to face substantial difficulties in explaining the blocking effect. On a routine basis, investigations of blocking have shown that the impairment in response acquisition to the added-CS in a blocking group exceeds any detrimental effects of compound training, including any deficits in transfer from compound training to component testing (e.g., Kamin, 1969a; Marchant & Moore, 1973). Thus, the blocking procedure has appeared to be an ideal procedure for pitting competitive processes against CS-US contiguity processes. Consequently, Kehoe, Schreurs, and Amodei (1981) conducted three blocking experiments in which the relative and absolute contiguity of the added stimulus, CSX, was manipulated.

Kehoe et al.'s (1981) first experiment contained three groups that corresponded to Groups A-AX, sit-AX, and A-X of Marchant and Moore (1973). However, CSX was more contiguous to the US than CSA. Specifically, the CSX–US interval was 400 msec, which is a near optimal value for the NMR preparation, whereas the CSA–US interval was 800 msec, which yields a more modest rate of CR acquisition, although it does eventually produce asymptotic levels of performance near 100% CRs. Thus, CSX was functionally as well as procedurally more contiguous to the US than was CSA. The results of interspersed testing with CSX during the second stage of training revealed clear evidence of blocking: Group A-AX's mean level of responding to CSX (20% CRs) was low in absolute terms and was significantly lower than that of either Group sit-AX (45% CRs) or Group A-X (93% CRs). In a second experiment, Kehoe et al. (1981) compared blocking in serial and simultaneous compounds, which were created by manipulating the CSX–US interval to take on the values of either 400 or 800 msec, whereas the CSA–US interval was fixed at 800 msec. Test trials with CSX revealed that the magnitude of the blocking effect was about the same whether or not CSX was more contiguous to the US than CSA. Moreover, responding to CSX in the serial compound blocking group showed the lowest absolute performance level of any group. Thus, the greater CSX–US contiguity in the serial compound did not appear to be able to counteract the deleterious effects of CSA's prior training.

In Kehoe et al.'s (1981) first and second experiments, CSA overlapped CSX, which meant that some portions of CSA were as contiguous to the US as CSX. In order to remove any doubt that CSX's greater contiguity in the serial compound was only nominal and not effective, a third experiment was conducted in which CSA and CSX were presented in strict sequence. Specifically CSA's duration was shortened to 400-msec so that it occupied only the first half of the 800-msec CSA–US interval. The duration of the CSX and the CSX–US interval remained at 400-msec, making CSX more contiguous to the US than any portion of CSA. In addition to the standard A-AX and sit-AX conditions, a third group (X-AX) was added in which CSX received initial training at the 400-msec CSX–US interval. This latter group was included to determine whether symmetric blocking effects could be obtained among the components of a serial compound.

Figure 6.9 shows the percentage CRs on CSA and CSX trials across 2-day blocks of test trials. Inspection of the right panel reveals that prior training of CSA in the sequential compound produced partial blocking of CR acquisition to CSX. Specifically, Group A-AX showed a lower level of responding

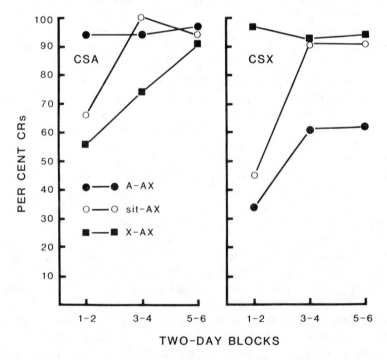

FIG. 6.9   Percentage CRs on CSA and CSX test trials plotted as a function of two-day blocks. Group A-AX received training with CSA (800-msec CS–US interval) prior to training with a CSA–CSX sequential compound Group X-AX received training with CSX (400-msec CS–US interval) prior to compound training. Group sit-AX received only restraint in the conditioning apparatus prior to compound training (Kehoe, Schreurs, & Amodei, 1981, Experiment 3).

to CSX than did Group sit-AX. Inspection of the left panel indicates that, at best, there was a transitory impairment in CR acquisition to CSA in Group X-AX. Although Group sit-AX showed CR acquisition to 100% CRs by the second block of serial compound training, Group X-AX's rate of CR acquisition to CSA was slower but nevertheless attained a level in excess of 90% CRs by the end of training. The apparent difference between Groups sit-AX and X-AX in the rate of CR acquisition to CSA failed to attain statistical significance. However, significant blocking of CR acquisition to CSA in a serial compound has been obtained by Gibbs (1979), who used a serial compound in which the added, 400-msec CSA was separated from the 400-msec CSX by a 1000 msec 'trace' interval.

The main finding that prior training with CSA blocks CR acquisition to CSX generally supports the proposition that competition for attention or associative strength can override the usual associative consequences of CS–US contiguity. However, the asymmetry in the level of blocking of CSA and CSX in the sequential compound supports selective attention hypotheses more strongly than the Rescorla–Wagner model. According to selective attention hypotheses (cf. Kehoe, 1979; Sutherland & Mackintosh, 1971), incoming stimuli are filtered according to both their previous training and temporal precedence. Thus, pretraining with CSA in a CSA–CSX serial compound would be expected to have a large deleterious effect on CR acquisition to CSX, as was seen in all three experiments of Kehoe et al. (1981). Conversely, even with pretraining, CSX would be expected to have difficulty in offsetting the temporal advantage of CSA in capturing the subject's attention on each trial. However, Gibb's (1979) results suggest that, if sufficient time is allowed to elapse after presentation of CSA, CSX will have a better chance of engaging the subject's attention.

The associative trade-off theories such as the Rescorla–Wagner model face some difficulty in accounting for the asymmetry in the magnitude of blocking effects in a sequential compound. The acquisition of CRs to CSA in Group X-AX of Kehoe et al. (1981, Experiment 3) could only be explained by arguing that the CRs to CSA did not represent direct CR acquisition to CSA through the CSA–US relation but, instead, resulted from second-order conditioning through the CSA–CSX pairings within the sequential compound. Although second-order conditioning is not a formal part of the Rescorla–Wagner model, there is nothing that would logically exclude its operation in connection with competition for associative strength (cf. Rescorla, 1972b, 1973b). In agreement with a second-order conditioning hypothesis, the 400-msec CSA–CSX interval used by Kehoe et al. (1981) has been found to be an optimal interval for second-order conditioning in the rabbit NMR preparation whereas the 1400-msec CSA–CSX interval used by Gibbs (1979) is less efficacious for second-order conditioning (Gormezano & Kehoe, 1981; Kehoe, Feyer, & Moses, 1981).

Unblocking

Although the associative trade-off theories of Rescorla and Wagner (1972) and Mackintosh (1975) parallel each other in many respects, one issue on which they diverge is that of "unblocking," which is the successful response acquisition to an added-CSX. According to the Rescorla–Wagner model, unblocking will occur only if the asymptotic associative strength is increased during compound training, thus making available additional associative strength to be divided between CSX and CSA. Conversely, any reduction in the asymptotic associative strength would not only insure blocking of CSX but lead to a decline in the associative strength of CSA. Whereas the Rescorla–Wagner model expects unblocking only if the reinforcement parameters are increased, Mackintosh's model would expect any change in the reinforcement parameters to produce unblocking by "surprising" the subject and thus promoting attention to new stimuli (cf. Kamin, 1969a; Mackintosh, 1975; Schreurs & Westbrook, 1982; Wagner, Mazur, Donegan, & Pfautz, 1980). Of course, a downward change in reinforcement parameters would be expected to yield unblocking only so long as the possible associative strength was not reduced to zero, which would prevent response acquisition to CSX even if the subject were attending to it.

Maleske and Frey (1979) have used a rabbit EBR preparation to assess theoretical expectations regarding unblocking. Specifically, they increased the CS–US interval from 500 msec to 1000 msec in conjunction with the transition from CSA training to AX compound training. The increase in the CS–US interval was intended to reduce the asymptotic level of associative strength and constitute a surprising event (cf. Schreurs & Westbrook, 1982). Final tests with CSX revealed no evidence of unblocking; that is to say, the mean level of responding to CSX in the A–AX group that received the shift in CS–US interval was low (36% CRs) and identical to that of an A–AX group that received a 1000 msec CS–US interval throughout training (36% CRs). In turn, the level of responding to CSX in both blocking groups was significantly lower than that of a sit-AX control (76% CRs).

The implications of Maleske and Frey's findings for the formulations under consideration are ambiguous. Specifically, it is debatable whether the increase in the CS–US interval actually lowered the maximal associative strength, because overall CR frequency did not decline following the shift. Consequently, defenders of the Rescorla–Wagner model could argue that the blocking of CR acquisition to CSX in the shifted condition agreed with the expectations of the model. As for Mackintosh's model, it is clear that the shift in CS–US interval had an effect on the animals, because CR latency increased dramatically following the shift in CS–US interval. Accordingly, the animals could be described as having "noticed" the shift and thus might have been expected to show some attention to the added stimulus with some consequent unblocking. However, defenders of an attentional hypothesis could perhaps take refuge in the absence of a change in overall CR frequency and argue that the shift was not sufficiently suprising to cause any alteration in the attention of the animal. In any case, Maleske and Frey's (1979) results revealed that not all changes in conditioning parameters, not even ones that produced clear behavioral alterations, will necessarily affect the degree of blocking.

In further research, Maleske and Frey (1979) obtained results that clearly cast doubt on the Rescorla–Wagner model. Specifically, Maleske and Frey attempted to produce unblocking by lowering the associative strength of the concurrent stimuli, thus making some associative strength available for the added-CSX. During the transition from A to AX training, a vibrotactile stimulus was inserted at the midpoint of the intertrial interval. This manipulation represented an attempt to alter the contextual stimuli and, through stimulus generalization decrement, to produce an aggregate of stimuli with a subasymptotic associative strength. (In this way, Maleske and Frey implicitly adopted a two-stage model of stimulus interaction, consisting of a contextual encoding/generalization decrement process combined with an associative trade-off process.) Following the transition to compound training, Maleske and Frey found some evidence of a context-dependent reduction in the total associative strength of the stimulus aggregrate, because responding to the compound accompanied by the vibrotactile stimulus showed a decrease, whereas responding to the compound in the unchanged, control condition showed an increase. However, contrary to the expectations of the Rescorla–Wagner model, testing with CSX yielded no evidence that the change in context attentuated the degree of blocking.

GENERAL DISCUSSION

Research with the rabbit NMR and EBR preparations has provided numerous insights into the interplay between associative processes based on CS–US contiguity and processes of stimulus interaction. The special contribution of the rabbit conditioned research arises from the well-defined effects of CS–US interval manipulations, which has made it possible to determine the precise, quantitative effects "CS–US contiguity" in compound stimulus conditioning procedures. Most notably, the data obtained from rabbit preparations suggest that CS–US contiguity plays a dominate role in determining CR acquisition to a compound and its components, even when there are substantial impairments in CR acquisition to one or both components. However, before attempting a resolution of the theoretical issues, it would be parochial to ignore the results obtained from other conditioning paradigms, particularly the conditioned suppression paradigm. Consequently, the following discussion will be divided into two parts, containing (1) a brief comparison of the major findings from rabbit NMR/EBR conditioning studies and rat conditioned suppression studies, and (2) a discussion of the implications of the major findings for the alternative theoretical positions.

Comparison with Conditioned Suppression

Overshadowing.   The degree of overshadowing observed in both rabbit and rat conditioning paradigms appears to vary with the overall rate of acquisition as well as the relative salience of the stimuli. In the rabbit NMR preparation, Kehoe (1982b) found that, when the overall conditioning rate was high, equally salient stimuli produced no overshadowing and stimuli of different salience produced unidirectional overshadowing of the weaker stimulus. However, when the overall rate of CR acquisition was lowered by increasing the CS–US interval, reciprocal overshadowing was observed. In the conditioned suppression procedures, Kamin (1969a, p. 56) found no overshadowing when the overall rate of acquisition was raised by increasing the shock intensity. However, under a lower shock intensity, Kamin (1969a, p.53) obtained unidirectional overshadowing with the same CSs. Similarly, Mackintosh (1976, Experiment 2) found no overshadowing between equally salient stimuli when their intensities were relatively high. When their intensities were lowered, reciprocal overshadowing was obtained. The only finding in the rabbit conditioning preparations that lack a close parallel in the conditioned suppression literature is Kehoe's (1982a, Experiment 2 & 3) finding of paradoxical overshadowing of a more salient CS by a weaker CS.

Serial Stimulus Selection and Blocking.   In addition to demonstrations of serial stimulus selection and blocking in both rabbit and rat conditioning paradigms, there is now converging evidence that substantial associative strength accrues to CS2 inside the context of a serial compound even when CS1 has received prior reinforced training. In rabbit NMR conditioning, Kehoe (1979) found high levels of responding during CS2 inside a serial compound, whereas the level of responding to CS2 on test trials outside the compound was low as compared to single-CS controls. Similarly, Seger and Scheuer (1977) found that, within a serial compound, CS2 produced more suppression than CS1. More recently, Gaioni (1982) examined blocking of CS2 in a serial compound and was able to detect that the addition of CS2 had a clear impact on response suppression inside the context of the serial compound. Gaioni first paired a 3-min CS1 with a shock US and then added a 30-sec CS2 just before the US to form a serial compound. Acquisition to CS2 as measured on test trials showed complete blocking. However, Gaioni examined the pattern of suppression inside the serial compound and found that suppression became localized to the CS2 segment. Moreover, Gaioni demonstrated that the suppression was specific to the CS2 by means of delaying the

presentation of CS2 on certain compound trials, which yielded a corresponding delay in the suppression of bar-press responding. In agreement with
Gaioni's findings, Kehoe et al. (1981) found that prior training of CS1 produced complete blocking of CS2 when responding was measured on test
trials. However, examinations of responding during the added-CS2 inside
the serial compound failed to reveal that CS2 had any impact on responding,
because CRs usually began during the first portion of the previously-trained
CS1, persisted into the portion occupied by CS2, and thus obscured the initiation of any further CRs.

Blocking and Overshadowing of CS1 in Serial Compounds.   The available data suggest that it is possible to impair response acquisition to CS1 in a
serial compound, but the results have been mixed. In serial compound conditioning of the rabbit NMR, minor impairments of CR acquisition to CS1
have been observed (Kehoe et al., 1979, Experiment 1) but have not been duplicated even when CS2 is a highly salient stimulus (Kehoe, 1982b, Experiment 3 & 4). By giving prior training with CS2, Kehoe et al. (1981, Experiment 3) found a transitory and nonsignificant impairment in CR acquisition
to CS1. However, when the CS1–CS2 interval was 1400 msec, Gibbs (1979)
was able to produce partial blocking of CR acquisition to CS1. In the conditioned suppression literature, Mackintosh and Reese (1979) found that serial
compound conditioning impaired CR acquisition to CS1. Moreover, Pearce,
Nicholas, and Dickinson (1981) produced partial blocking of CS1.

Unblocking.   The only area of apparent disagreement between findings
of the rabbit NMR/EBR conditioning and rat conditioned suppression research concerns unblocking. However, unblocking manipulations have received only limited investigation with rabbit preparations. Specifically,
Maleske and Frey (1979) failed to attenuate the blocking effect through either
increasing the CS–US interval or altering the contextual cues. In contrast, unblocking has been produced in the conditioned suppression procedures by
increasing shock intensity (Kamin, 1969a, p. 59), adding a second shock
(Dickinson, Hall, & Mackintosh, 1976; Kamin, 1969b), omitting a second
shock (Dickinson et al. 1976; Dickinson & Mackintosh, 1979), and post-
poning a second shock (Dickinson et al., 1976).

Theoretical Implications

Because there are substantial parallels between the results of studies with
rabbit NMR/EBR preparations and rat conditioned suppression procedures,
it would appear safe to discuss the general theoretical implications of the rabbit conditioning research. As may be already apparent, a theory of considerable scope will be needed to encompass the full set of findings concerning

negative interactions in compound conditioning. Among the available theoretical formulations, the hypotheses that presuppose a perceptual or attentional interaction between component stimuli appear to have gained substantial support from the most recent findings. Conversely, the information and associative trade-off hypotheses face challenges to their tenability as complete accounts of "selective association" effects. Because the available formulations are not mutually exclusive, the task at hand is one of weighing up the relative contribution played by the hypothesized processes rather than eliminating alternative hypotheses altogether.

Overshadowing. The degree of overshadowing between two simultaneous CSs has varied as a function their relative salience and overall level of acquisition from no overshadowing through unidirectional overshadowing to reciprocal overshadowing (Kehoe, 1982a). Overshadowing of any type is difficult for an information hypothesis to explain. To argue that one CS in a simultaneous compound is somehow "more predictive" of either the other CS or the US would turn an information hypothesis into an elaborate redescription of the known results. In contrast, the selective attention hypothesis (Sutherland & Mackintosh, 1971) and the Rescorla–Wagner model can readily explain overshadowing, but they tend to expect too much overshadowing. Because these accounts assume a strict trade off between the nominal CSs in their competition for attention or associative strength, they would expect some degree of reciprocal overshadowing to occur in all simultaneous compounds (Mackintosh, 1975, 1976). Thus, to account for instances of no overshadowing or unidirectional overshadowing, it would be necessary appeal to ceilings on response measurement or hypothetical third stimuli to defend the assumption of a zero-sum competitive process. Finally, the more open-ended trade-off hypotheses (e.g., Mackintosh, 1975) and generalization decrement hypotheses (e.g., Hull, 1943) can readily accommodate the full range of overshadowing results although at the cost of some indeterminancy in their predictions.

The paradoxical overshadowing of a light CS by a less salient 73-dB tone can be construed as support for generalization decrement hypotheses that postulate that a "configural" integration occurs betwen the components of a compound (Kehoe, 1982a). Under a configural hypothesis, the level of responding to the components would be attributed to stimulus generalization from the associative strength of the configural stimulus (Baker, 1972; Gillette & Bellingham, 1982; Kehoe & Gormezano, 1980; Rescorla, 1981, p. 69). In the case of unequal stimulus salience, responding to the more salient stimulus would presumably suffer some generalization decrement, but the less salient stimulus would suffer a greater generalization decrement vis a vis the configural stimulus. However, if the associative strength of the configural stimulus is relatively high, then even only a modest degree of generalization to a very weak stimulus would endow it with as much response strength as if it were trained by itself, thus yielding 'paradoxical' overshadowing.

Blocking.   The results of blocking studies have become more intriguing as they have accumulated. On the one hand, blocking has been considered a substantial stumbling block to generalization decrement accounts, because the routine control procedures demonstrate that the low level of responding to the added-CS cannot be attributed entirely to generalization decrement from compound training to component testing (Kehoe et al., 1981; Marchant & Moore, 1973). Although there is nothing in the rabbit blocking literature that directly supports a generalization decrement hypothesis, Gaioni's (1982) conditioned suppression results suggest that, inside the context of a serial compound, CS2 can acquire substantial associative strength even when CS1 has received prior training. Accordingly, the role that generalization decrement processes play in the blocking effect needs clarification in rabbit conditioning. If Gaioni's results can be confirmed, then a compelling theoretical question remains, namely, how does the pretraining of a CS lead to a greater alteration in the encoding of the added-CS?

No matter how large a role generalization decrement processes play in the blocking of CS2 in a serial compound, evidence that it is possible to partially block CR acquisition to CS1 in a serial compound (Gibbs, 1979) provides a challenge to generalization decrement hypotheses. Specifically, responding to the initial portion of CS1 is not subject to any generalization decrement during testing, because the stimulus context for CS1, namely the static apparatus stimuli, remain the same whether or not the CS2 subsequently occurs. Conversely, blocking of CS1 appears to support the selective attention, associative trade off, and information hypotheses. However, James and Wagner (1980) have recently offered a generalization decrement hypothesis suitable for explaining impairments in CR acquisition to CS1 in a serial compound. Following Hull's (1943) account of CR acquisition, James and Wagner contend that responding to the initial portion of CS1 depends on generalization of associative strength from the encoding of CS1 at the time of US occurrence (cf. Gormezano, 1972; Gormezano & Kehoe, 1981, p. 15). Consequently, the encoding of CS1 may be altered by the occurrence of CS2 just before US presentation, which would tend to reduce the generalization of associative strength from the point for reinforcement to the earlier portions of CS1. Because deficits in CR acquisition to CS1 in a serial compound have been small and unreliable in serial compound conditioning of the rabbit NMR (Kehoe et al., 1979; Kehoe, 1982b), CS2 appears to lack the intrinsic capacity to substantially alter the encoding of CS1. However, if pretraining does in fact endow a CS with additional capacity to alter the encoding of different stimuli, then it would be possible to explain the partial blocking of CS1 in a serial compound by a generalization decrement hypothesis. However, the extension of James and Wagner's (1980) hypothesis to blocking still leaves the mechanism of encoding unspecified.

Serial Stimulus Selection.   Generalization decrement hypotheses offer a straightforward account of the otherwise paradoxical results of serial compound manipulations. Because generalization decrement hypotheses assume that all stimuli in a compound have undiminished access to the associative apparatus, then it would be expected that the CS2–US interval and CS2 intensity would determine the rate of CR acquisition to a compound, provided that the conditioning parameters of CS1 are controlled (Frey et al., 1971; Kehoe 1979, 1982b). Likewise the ordered effects of the CS2–US interval and CS2 intensity on the level of responding to CS2 on test trials would presumably reflect the differences in CS2's associative strength gained inside the compound (Kehoe 1982b). Nevertheless, the relatively low level of responding on CS2 test trials would be expected, because of the disparity between the encoding of CS2 inside the context of the compound and the encoding of CS2 on test trials outside the compound. As explained in the previous paragraph, the lack of impairment in responding to CS1 in a serial compound would be expected, because the encoding of the initial portion of CS1 is only affected by static background stimuli, which are the same whether or not CS2 is subsequently presented.

As a plausible alternative to a generalization decrement hypothesis, a selective attention hypothesis would contend that the onset of CS1 would fully engage the subject's attention but, with the passage of time, attention to CS1 would wane (Kehoe, 1979). Accordingly, CR acquisition to CS2 would be most strongly hindered if CS2 were to have an onset simultaneous with CS1. However, if the CS2 onset were delayed, more attentional capacity would become available which CS2 could engage, enabling increased levels of CR acquisition to CS2. Moreover, because CS2 would take up unused attentional capacity, the temporal and intensive characteristics of CS2 would make a substantial contribution to overall CR acquisition, as was observed in the effects of the CS2–US interval and CS2 intensity on CR acquisition to the compound (Kehoe, 1979, 1982b). Although CS2 is able to take advantage of any currently unused attentional capacity, it does not appear to be well situated in a serial compound to detract from the previously established attention to CS1 even when CS2 is relatively salient (Kehoe, 1982b, Experiment 4). Thus, as has been observed, CR acquisition to CS1 would proceed independently of CS2 during training. Conversely, because CS2 is not able to divert attention fully on to itself, CR acquisition to CS2 would thus be impaired to some degree.

The associative trade-off hypotheses (e.g., Mackintosh, 1975; Pearce & Hall, 1980; Rescorla & Wagner, 1972) are difficult to extend to serial stimulus selection effects. Although these hypotheses have detailed trade-off processes that attenuate the associative effects of CS–US contiguity, they deal with "CS–US contiguity" in only a global fashion and do not address explicitly the effects that the degree of CS–US contiguity has on conditioning. However, these models do contain a growth parameter that is a function of CS intensity. To accommodate the precise effects of the CS1–US interval manipulations, it would be possible to assign growth parameters on the basis of the CS–US interval as well as CS intensity. Even using this tactic, the associative trade-off models would not be able to account for serial stimulus selection effects. Specifically, responding to CS1 in the serial compound is usually higher than responding to CS2. Accordingly, it would be necessary to find some basis for assigning a higher growth parameter to the longer CS1–US interval than to the shorter CS2–US interval. The most obvious source for independent estimates of growth parameters would be data collected from single-CS manipulations of the CS–US interval. However, in the rabbit NMR preparation, these data clearly demonstrate that shorter CS–US intervals produce higher rates of CR acquisition than longer CS–US intervals (Kehoe, 1979, 1982b; Smith et al., 1969). Accordingly, the single CS data would lead to the incorrect prediction that CS2 ought to impair CR acquisition to CS1 in a serial compound rather than vice versa.

Although Egger and Miller's (1962) information hypothesis was one of the earliest explanations of the serial stimulus selection effect, information hypotheses would appear to have great difficulty in encompassing the body of data concerning serial compound conditioning. Most notably, a simple information hypothesis would expect that the temporally predictive value of CS1 for the CS2 or the US in a serial compound to impair CR acquisition to CS2. Instead, Kehoe (1982b, Experiments 1 & 2) observed that there was a higher level of responding to CS2 after serial compound training than after simultaneous compound training, in which there was no temporal predictive relation between CS1 and CS2. Similarly, it would appear difficult for the information hypotheses to account for the observation that the CS2–US interval and CS2 intensity determined the overall level of CR acquisition to the compound, CS2, and even CS1.

Conclusions. The findings from compound conditioning in the rabbit NMR and EBR preparations indicate that processes of generalization decrement and/or selective attention play a greater role than previously thought (cf. Kamin, 1969a; Rescorla & Wagner, 1972). The feature that distinguishes the generalization decrement and selective attention hypotheses from the information and associative trade-off hypotheses is the temporal locus of the presumed critical interaction between the two CSs in a compound (James & Wagner, 1980; Mackintosh & Reese, 1979). In generalization decrement and selective attention hypotheses, the critical interaction between the CSs occurs while the stimuli are being processed prior to the onset of the US. Thus, associative strength will accrue to whichever stimulus encodings are present at the time of the US. However, in the associative trade-off hypotheses, the interaction between two CSs is based on their relative associative strengths at the time of the US occurrence. Prior to US occurrence, the functional representations of the concurrent CSs are assumed to be entirely independent. Recently, Mackintosh and Reese (1979) have proposed a similar distinction. Their evidence for a pre-US interaction, viz. competition for the animal's attention, involved demonstrations that an overshadowing effect can be obtained through a single pairing of a compound with the US (cf. James & Wagner, 1980). Because neither CS would possess any associative strength on the first trial, the observed overshadowing would have to arise from a direct interaction between the CSs and not on a trade off based on the accrued associative strengths of the CSs.

At present, several lines of research are opening, which may aid the further delineation of the processes governing negative interactions among the components of a compound stimulus. In the area of overshadowing, paradoxical overshadowing should be replicated, for it appears to support configural versions of generalization decrement hypotheses while challenging selective attention and associative trade-off hypotheses. One of the most promising avenues for theoretical development lies in the continued investigation of blocking in serial compounds. On the one hand, blocking CR acquisition to CS1 allows for the study of the interactive processes during actual compound conditioning free of deficits in transfer from compound training to CS testing. In particular, blocking of CS1 appears to favor selective attention and associative trade-off hypotheses (Kehoe et al., 1981), but a configural generalization decrement account can be constructed (James & Wagner, 1980). On the other hand, further examination of the pattern of responding to CS2 inside a compound and especially a duplication of Gaioni's (1981) findings would provide powerful evidence that impairments in CR acquisition to CS2 may be attributed to a generalization decrement from CS2's substantial associative strength inside the stimulus context of a compound.

ACKNOWLEDGMENTS

Portions of the research reported in this chapter were supported by grants from the Australian Research Grants Committee. Initial preparation of the manuscript was conducted during a Special Studies Project awarded by the University of New South Wales. The author thanks Professor I. Gormezano and his staff, who aided preparation of the manuscript.

REFERENCES

Baker, T. W. (1968). Properties of compound conditioned stimuli and their components. *Psychological Bulletin, 70,* 611–625.

Baker, T. W. (1972). Component dynamics within compound stimuli. In R. F. Thompson & J. F. Voss (Eds.), *Topics in learning and performance.* New York: Academic Press.

Bellingham, W. P., & Gillette, K. (1981). Spontaneous configuring to a tone–light compound using appetitive training. *Learning and Motivation, 12,* 416–428.

Blough, D. S. (1972). Recognition by the pigeon of stimuli varying in two dimensions. *Journal of the Experimental Analysis of Behavior, 18,* 345–367.

Borgealt, A. J., Donahoe, J. W., & Weinstein, A. (1972). Effects of delayed and trace components of a compound CS on conditioned suppression and heart rate. *Psychonomic Science, 26,* 13–15.

Cantor, M. B. (1981). Information theory: A solution to two big problems in the analysis of behavior. In P. Harzem & M. Zeiler (Eds.), *Advances in the analysis of behaviour. Vol. 2. Predictability, correlation, and contiguity.* New York: Wiley.

Cantor, M. B., & Wilson, J. F. (1981). Temporal uncertainty as an associative metric: operant simulations of Pavlovian conditioning. *Journal of Experimental Psychology: General, 110,* 232–268.

Dickinson, A., Hall, G., & Mackintosh, N. J. (1976). Surprise and the attenuation of blocking. *Journal of Experimental Psychology: Animal Behavior Processes, 2,* 313–322.

Dickinson, A., & Mackintosh, N. J. (1979). Reinforcer specificity in the enhancement of conditioning by posttrial surprise. *Journal of Experimental Psychology: Animal Behavior Processes, 5,* 162–177.

Egger, D. M., & Miller, N. E. (1962). Secondary reinforcement in rats as a function of information value and reliability of the stimulus. *Journal of Experimental Psychology, 64,* 97–104.

Frey, P. W., Englander, S., & Roman, A. (1971). Interstimulus interval analysis of sequential CS compounds in rabbit eyelid conditioning. *Journal of Comparative and Physiological Psychology, 77,* 439–446.

Frey, P. W., & Sears, R. J. (1978). Model of conditioning incorporating the Rescorla–Wagner associative axiom, a dynamic attention process, and a catastrophe rule. *Psychological Review, 85,* 321–340.

Gaioni, S. J. (1982). Blocking and nonsimultaneous compounds: Comparison of responding during compound conditioning and testing. *Pavlovian Journal of Biological Science, 17,* 16–29.

Gibbs, C. M. (1979). *Serial compound classical conditioning (CS1–CS2–UCS): Effects of CS2 intensity and pretraining on component acquisition.* Unpublished doctoral dissertation, The University of Iowa.

Gillette, K., & Bellingham, W. P. (1982). Loss of within-compound flavor associations: configural preconditioning. *Experimental Animal Behavior, 1,* 1–17.

Gormezano, I. (1972). Investigations of defense and reward conditioning in the rabbit. In A. H. Black & W. F. Prokasy (Eds.), *Classical conditioning II.* New York: Appleton-Century-Crofts.

Gormezano, I. (in press). Associative transfer in serial compound conditioning. In I. Gormezano, W. F. Prokasy, & R. F. Thompson (Eds.), *Classical conditioning.* Hillsdale, NJ: Lawrence Erlbaum Associates.

Gormezano, I., & Kehoe, E. J. (1981). Classical conditioning and the law of contiguity. In P. Harzem & M. D. Zeiler (Eds.), *Advances in analysis of behaviour. Vol. 2. Predictability, correlation, and contiguity.* New York: Wiley.

Hancock, R. A., Jr. (1982). Tests of the conditioned reinforcement value of sequential stimuli in pigeons. *Animal Learning and Behavior, 10,* 46-54.

Hebb, D. O. (1949). *The organization of behavior.* New York: Wiley.

Hull, C. L. (1943). *Principles of behavior.* New York: Appleton-Century-Crofts.

Hull, C. L. (1945). The discrimination of stimulus configurations and the hypothesis of neural afferent interactions. *Psychological Review, 52,* 133-139.

James, J. H., & Wagner, A. R. (1980). One-trial overshadowing: Evidence of distributive processing. *Journal of Experimental Psychology: Animal Behavior Processes, 6,* 188-205.

Kamin, L. J. (1968). Attention-like processes in classical conditioning. In M. R. Jones (Ed.), *Miami Symposium on the prediction of behavior, 1967: Aversive stimulation.* Coral Gables: University of Miami Press.

Kamin, L. J. (1969a). Selective association and conditioning. In N. J. Mackintosh & F. W. K. Honig (Eds.), *Fundamental issues in associative learning.* Halifax: Dalhousie University Press.

Kamin, L. J. (1969b). Predictability, surprise, attention, and conditioning. In B. A. Campbell & R. M. Church (Eds.), *Punishment and aversive behavior.* New York: Appleton-Century-Crofts.

Kehoe, E. J. (1979). The role of CS-US contiguity in classical conditioning of the rabbit's nictitating membrane response to serial stimuli. *Learning and Motivation, 10,* 23-38.

Kehoe, E. J. (1982a). Overshadowing and summation in compound stimulus conditioning of the rabbit's nictitating membrane response. *Journal of Experimental Psychology: Animal Behavior Processes, 8,* 313-328.

Kehoe, E. J. (1982b). *CS-US contiguity and CS intensity in conditioning of the rabbit's nictitating membrane response to serial and simultaneous compound stimuli.* Unpublished manuscript.

Kehoe, E. J., Feyer, A., & Moses, J. L. (1981). Second-order conditioning of the rabbit's nictitating membrane response as a function of the CS2-CS1 and CS1-US intervals. *Animal Learning and Behavior, 9,* 304-315.

Kehoe, E. J., Gibbs, C. M., Garcia, E., & Gormezano, I. (1979). Associative transfer and stimulus selection in classical conditioning of the rabbit's nictitating membrane response to serial compound CSs. *Journal of Experimental Psychology: Animal Behavior Processes, 5,* 1-18.

Kehoe, E. J., & Gormezano, I. (1980). Configuration and combination laws in conditioning with compound stimuli. *Psychological Bulletin, 87,* 351-378.

Kehoe, E. J., Schreurs, B. G., & Amodei, N. (1981). Blocking acquisition of the rabbit's nictitating membrane response to serial conditioned stimuli. *Learning and Motivation, 12,* 92-108.

Kinkaide, P. S. (1974). Stimulus selection in eyelid conditioning in the rabbit (Oryctolagus cuniculus). *Journal of Comparative and Physiological Psychology, 86,* 1132-1140.

Konorski, J. (1967). *Integrative activity of the brain.* Chicago: University of Chicago Press.

Mackintosh, N. J. (1974). *The psychology of animal learning.* New York: Academic Press.

Mackintosh, N. J. (1975). A theory of attention: Variation in the associability of stimuli with reinforcement. *Psychological Review, 82,* 276-298.

Mackintosh, N. J. (1976). Overshadowing and stimulus intensity. *Animal Learning and Behavior, 4,* 186-192.

Mackintosh, N. J., & Reese, B. (1979). One-trial overshadowing. *Quarterly Journal of Experimental Psychology, 31,* 519-526.

Maleske, R. T., & Frey, P. W. (1979). Blocking in eyelid conditioning: Effect of changing the CS-US and introducing an intertrial stimulus. *Animal Learning and Behavior, 7,* 452-456.

Marchant, H. G., III, & Moore, J. W. (1973). Blocking of the rabbit's conditioned nictitating membrane response in Kamin's two-stage paradigm. *Journal of Experimental Psychology, 101,* 155-158.

Moore, J. W., & Stickney, K. J. (1980). Formation of attentional-associative networks in real time: Role of the hippocampus and implications for conditioning. *Physiological Psychology, 8,* 207–217.

Pavlov, I. P. (1927). *Conditioned reflexes.* (Translated by G. V. Anrep.) London: Oxford University Press.

Pearce, J. M., & Hall, G. (1980). A model for Pavlovian learning: Variations in the effectiveness of conditioned but not of unconditioned stimuli. *Psychological Review, 87,* 532–552.

Pearce, J. M., Nicholas, D. J., & Dickinson, A. (1981). The potentiation effect during serial compound conditioning. *Quarterly Journal of Experimental Psychology, 33B,* 159–179.

Razran, G. (1939). Studies in configural conditioning: 1. Historic and preliminary experimentation. *Journal of General Psychology, 21,* 307–330.

Razran, G. (1965). Empirical codification and specific theoretical implications of compound-stimulus conditioning: Perception. In W. F. Prokasy (Ed.), *Classical conditioning.* New York: Appleton–Century–Crofts.

Razran, G. (1971). *Mind in evolution.* New York: Houghton–Mifflin.

Rescorla, R. A. (1972a). "Configural" conditioning in discrete-trial bar pressing. *Journal of Comparative and Physiological Psychology, 79,* 307–317.

Rescorla, R. A. (1972b). Informational variables in Pavlovian conditioning. In G. H. Bower (Ed.), *The psychology of learning and motivation* (Vol. 6). New York: Academic Press.

Rescorla, R. A. (1973a). Evidence for "unique stimulus" account of configural conditioning. *Journal of Comparative and Physiological Psychology, 85,* 331–338.

Rescorla, R. A. (1973b). Second-order conditioning: Implications for theories of learning. In F. J. McGuigan & D. Lumsden (Eds.), *Contemporary approaches to learning and conditioning.* New York: Winston.

Rescorla, R. A. (1981). Simultaneous associations. In P. Harzem & M. D. Zeiler (Eds.), *Advances in analysis of behaviour. Vol. 2. Predictability, correlation, and contiguity.* New York: Wiley.

Rescorla, R. A., & Wagner, A. R. (1972). A theory of Pavlovian conditioning: Variations in the effectiveness of reinforcement and nonreinforcement. In A. Black & W. F. Prokasy (Eds.), *Classical conditioning II.* New York: Appleton–Century–Crofts.

Riley, D. A., & Leith, C. R. (1976). Multidimensional psychophysics and selective attention in animals. *Psychological Bulletin, 83,* 138–160.

Schreurs, B. G., & Westbrook, R. F. (1982). The effects of changes in the CS–US interval during compound conditioning upon an otherwise blocked element. *Quarterly Journal of Experimental Psychology, 34B,* 19–30.

Seger, K. A., & Scheuer, C. (1977). The informational properties of S1, S2, and the S1-S2 sequence on conditioned suppression. *Animal Learning and Behavior, 5,* 39–41.

Seligman, M. E. P. (1966). CS redundancy and secondary punishment. *Journal of Experimental Psychology, 72,* 546–550.

Smith, M. C., Coleman, S. R., & Gormezano, I. (1969). Classical conditioning of the rabbit's nictitating membrane response at backward, simultaneous, and forward CS–US intervals. *Journal of Comparative and Physiological Psychology, 69,* 226–231.

Solomon, P. R. (1977). The role of the hippocampus in blocking and conditioned inhibition of the rabbit's nictitating membrane response. *Journal of Comparative and Physiological Psychology, 91,* 407–417.

Sutherland, N. S., & Mackintosh, N. J. (1971). *Mechanisms of animal discrimination learning.* New York: Academic Press.

Sutton, R. S., & Barto, A. G. (1981). Toward a modern theory of adaptive networks: Expectation and prediction. *Psychological Review, 88,* 135–170.

Wagner, A. R. (1969a). Incidental stimuli and discrimination learning. In R. M. Gilbert & N. S. Sutherland (Eds.), *Animal discrimination learning.* New York: Academic Press.

Wagner, A. R. (1969b). Stimulus selection and a "modified continuity theory". In G. Bower & J. T. Spence (Eds.), *The psychology of learning and motivation* (Vol. 3). New York: Academic Press.

Wagner, A. R. (1969c). Stimulus validity and stimulus selection in associative learning. In N. J. Mackintosh & W. K. Honig (Eds.), *Fundamental issues in associative learning.* Halifax: Dalhousie University Press.

Wagner, A. R., Logan, R. W., Haberlandt, K., & Price, T. (1968). Stimulus selection in animal discrimination learning. *Journal of Experimental Psychology, 76,* 171–180.

Wagner, A. R., Mazur, J. E., Donegan, N. H., & Pfautz, P. L. (1980). Evaluation of blocking and conditioned inhibition to a CS signalling a decrease in US intensity. *Journal of Experimental Psychology: Animal Behavior Processes, 6,* 376–385.

Wickens, D. D. (1954). Stimulus–response theory as applied to perception. In *Learning theory, personality theory, and clinical research: The Kentucky Symposium.* New York: Wiley.

Wickens, D. D. (1959). Conditioning to complex stimuli. *American Psychologist, 14,* 180–188.

Wickens, D. D. (1965). Compound conditioning in humans and cats. In W. F. Prokasy (Ed.), *Classical conditioning.* New York: Appleton–Century–Crofts.

Wickens, D. D. (1973). Classical conditioning, as it contributes to the analyses of some basic psychological processes. In F. J. McGuigan & D. B. Lumsden (Eds.), *Contemporary approaches to conditioning and learning.* New York: Winston.

7 Pavlovian Conditioning, Information Processing, and the Hippocampus

W. Ronald Salafia
Fairfield University

This chapter deals with the effects of a variety of behavioral and physiological manipulations on conditioning, latent inhibition, and single alternation learning. The research has been focused on two related issues, namely the apparent dichotomy between associative and representational memory systems and the role of the hippocampus in the functioning of these systems.

Before proceeding, some definitions are in order. First, an associative process refers to a situation in which a stimulus presented either through peripheral sensory channels or directly to the brain produces, through repeated exposure, measurable activity in another area of the brain not previously activated by that stimulus. This latter activity may be, but is not necessarily expressed as overt motor output. Thus, basic associative processes are akin to what others (e.g., Flaherty, Hamilton, Gandelman, & Spear, 1977) have referred to as "sensory recognition." Such processes would not require stored representation of stimuli that would permit their recall later when the stimuli are no longer being encountered.

For example, in Pavlovian nictitating membrane conditioning the rabbit may learn to make a conditioned NMR to a previously neutral tone but probably does not require a representation of that tone as a necessary condition for the occurrence of the response. On the other hand, neural activity generated by such associative processes, or the individual elements of such processes, may be represented in the brain in such manner that it can be employed for the subsequent performance of other behaviors. This is what is meant by a representational process. Latent inhibition and blocking are two well-known paradigms that probably require such representational processes.

The theme of the present chapter is that the basic associative process involved in the acquisition of conditioned responses is essentially a sensory recognition situation, with few, if any, representational elements required as fundamental aspects of the association. On the other hand, representations of separate stimulus and response elements or of the associative process itself, may be generated and stored elsewhere in different neural networks, ready to be retrieved as needed and to become part of subsequent, usually more complex situations. Although there are undoubtedly many such neural networks, the one to which most attention is devoted in this chapter is that which includes the hippocampus as a major component.

The associative versus representational distinction employed here is not meant as an exhaustive classification of memory systems. To the contrary, it is a convenient classification for present purposes and a useful first approximation around which the research to be presented may be organized. Similarly, the attribution of certain representational memory functions to the hippocampus implies neither that this is the only function of the hippocampus nor that the hippocampus is the only neural structure involved.

HIPPOCAMPUS AND BASIC ASSOCIATIVE PROCESSES

Until a few years ago, little was known about the role of the hippocampus in classical conditioning of the NMR other than that hippocampal lesioned animals displayed somewhat faster acquisition and poorer retention of extinction (Schmaltz & Theios, 1972). Because posttrial stimulation of various sites, including hippocampus, was a widely used tool for the investigation of memory processes (e.g., Kesner & Wilburn, 1974; McGaugh & Herz, 1972), we decided to investigate the effects of such stimulation on classical conditioning in the rabbit (Salafia, Chiaia, & Ramirez, 1979; Salafia, Romano, Tynan, & Host, 1977). We observed that both seizure producing and subseizure hippocampal stimulation produced disruption of NMR conditioning in comparison with unoperated and cortically stimulated control groups. The basic effect of posttrial hippocampal stimulation was the postponement of CR emergence, with stimulated groups often taking more than twice as many trials to begin conditioning. Once conditioning began, however, animals that received hippocampal stimulation displayed group acquisition curves the slopes of which were indistinguishable from those of the control groups.

In a more recent study Prokasy, Kesner, and Calder (1983) found that posttrial hippocampal stimulation could also produce facilitation of performance. Experiment 1 of this study, which was ostensibly designed as a replication of Salafia et al. (1979) found a small, although nonsignificant retardation effect. The most probable reason for the smaller retardation effect obtained by Prokasy, et al., was their use of a 450-msec delay between US offset and stimulation onset. In the Salafia, et al. study, stimulation onset coincided with both CS and US offset.

In Experiment 2, Prokasy et al. found that with massed trials hippocampal stimulation produced facilitation of performance. It is well known that massing of trials severely inhibits performance (e.g., Salafia, Terry, & Daston, 1975) so that the facilitation effect found by Prokasy et al. most probably reflected disruption of inhibition, rather than direct facilitation of conditioning. Support for this conclusion may be seen in the results of Prokasy et al. After 180 massed conditioning trials, unstimulated control animals reached a level of performance (about 35–40% CRs) that was exceeded after only 40 trials by the corresponding control group run in Experiment 1 at 20 trials per day. On the other hand, the massed trial/stimulated animals performed at an intermediate level, between the massed/unstimulated group and all other groups.

Regardless of interpretation, however, it has now been shown that hippocampal stimulation can, under appropriate circumstances, produce either retardation or facilitation of performance. Salafia et al. (1977, 1979) had suggested that posttrial hippocampal stimulation interfered with the establishment of memory for the CS–US association. Support for the hypothesis of hippocampal participation in the fundamental associative processes of NMR conditioning had been obtained by Berger, Alger, and Thompson (1976), Berger and Thompson (1977), and in several other studies by Thompson and his associates (see Thompson, Berger, Berry, & Hoehler, 1980; Thompson, Berger, Berry, Hoehler, Kettner, & Weisz, 1980; and Thompson, Berger, Cegavske, Patterson, Roemer, Teyler, & Young, 1976 for reviews). These researchers found that hippocampal multiple-unit discharges formed a virtually exact temporal representation of the behavioral CR but preceeded it by about 35 to 40 msec.

At the outset, then, there appears to be a major conflict. On the one hand hippocampal stimulation and electrophysiological activity point to a direct role in acquisition, but hippocampal lesions appear to have little effect on NMR conditioning. Schmaltz and Theios (1972) first demonstrated this lesion effect, or rather lack of effect and their results have been replicated in several laboratories (e.g., Salafia, Cardosi, Marini, Hogan, Olson, & Pollack, 1981; Solomon & Moore, 1975). Additionally, Lockhart and Moore (1975) have shown that large septal lesions do not produce impairment of conditioning, although certain related manipulations such as medial septal lesions (Berry & Thompson, 1979) and microinjection of scopolamine into medial septum (Solomon & Gottfried, 1981) have been found to retard conditioning. Even where some impairment has been shown, however, the animals eventually displayed high levels of conditioning. Thus, the presumption must be that the major aspects of the associative network involved in NMR acquisition do not require an intact hippocampus and probably reside in lower brain centers.

Support for this conclusion comes from several sources. In one series of experiments Oakley and Russell (1972, 1974, 1975, 1976, 1977) found that complete neodecortication produced retardation of the onset of conditioning but did not prevent NMR conditioning or discrimination learning. This general pattern of results is strikingly similar to that of our stimulation studies (Salafia et al., 1977, 1979) and the possibility that there are similar underlying mechanisms cannot be excluded.

The strongest support yet for a subcortical locus of the associative process has come from several recent investigations involving lesions and recording of activity in cerebellum and brain stem. McCormick, Lavond, Clark, Kettner, Rising, and Thompson (1981) found that lesions of the cerebellum ipsilateral to the conditioned membrane, in the area where neural-unit activity had been recorded during training, completely and permanently abolished CRs in previously well-trained animals although having no effect on URs. Additionally, they found that after the lesions, conditioning was easily established in the other nictitating membrane. These researchers concluded that an essential component of the neuronal plasticity that codes learning in the NMR preparation is localized in the cerebellum (McCormick, Clark, Lavond, & Thompson, 1982; Thompson, Berger, Berry, Clark, Kettner, Lavond, Mauk, McCormick, Solomon, & Weisz, 1982).

Another essential component may be a region of the dorsolateral pons, where lesions produced effects similar to those of McCormick et al. (Desmond, Berthier, & Moore, 1981; Desmond & Moore, 1982; Moore, Desmond, & Berthier, 1982); that is, lesions produced a reduction of CRs in some animals and virtual cessation in others. These studies point to the existence of a subcortical network (i.e., midbrain, brainstem, and cerebellum) as the locus of neuronal plasticity involved in NMR conditioning as well as a few related processes such as conditioned inhibition (Mis, 1977; Moore, Yeo, Oakley, & Russell, 1980).

Finally, evidence that high-level processing is not necessary for NMR conditioning may be inferred from several experiments involving the timing of conditioning events. Smith, Coleman, and Gormezano (1969) had established that rabbits do not condition at ISIs below 50 msec, while Salafia, Lambert, Host, Chiaia, and Ramirez (1980) using an ISI-transfer paradigm showed that acquisition usually began to occur, although weakly, at about 70 msec. However, a number of behavioral and physiological manipulations have been found to affect this minimum time. First, employing a gradual shift from a higher ISI, Salafia, Cardosi, and Salafia (1981) showed that conditioned NMRs could be maintained in some animals at 50 msec ISI. Additionally, Patterson (1970) was able to establish robust conditioned responses at an ISI of 50 msec using stimulation of the inferior colliculus as the CS, whereas Cevagske, Thompson, Patterson, and Gormezano (1976) and Moore and Desmond (1982) have shown that about 17 msec are required for the motor response. Doing a bit of mental arithmetic, it can be estimated that the central associative process may take as little as 20 msec or less, which does not permit much time for the participation of higher order representational processes.

Simply stated then, it appears that during and after acquisition, the CS–US association may be influenced by hippocampal stimulation, but that the neural substrate underlying the associative process does not require the hippocampus. Both the facilitation (Prokasy et al., 1983) and retardation (Salafia et al., 1977, 1979) effects are likely to have been indirect results of hippocampal stimulation. Consistent with this suggestion is a recent finding by Solomon, Schaaf, Perry, and Solomon (1982) that systemic scopolamine, which alters hippocampal neuronal activity, retards acquisition of the conditioned NMR in normal and cortical control animals but has no effect in hippocampal lesioned animals. This implies that altered hippocampal neuronal activity is more detrimental to acquisition than large ablations of the structure, a suggestion that might also explain why discrete medial septal lesions (Berry & Thompson, 1979) produce disruption whereas large, less discrete lesions (Lockhart & Moore, 1975) do not. Also, consistent with the projection notion is a recent finding (Salafia & Allan, 1982) that after terminal levels of conditioning have been established, hippocampal stimulation overlapping CS and US presentation can completely abolish CRs in some animals although having no effect on URs.

With regard to the hippocampal multiple-unit discharge (Berger et al., 1976, 1977) that was found to be correlated with the development and expression of behavioral CRs, the most likely alternative to a direct role in the associative process is that this unit activity is a sign that the association is being represented elsewhere in the brain. Much as the behavioral CR provides information to the experimenter that the association has taken place, the hippocampal discharge could be part of the brain's way of providing other centers with this information. Presumably, such a representation, although again, not necessary for the associative process, would be needed for the development of behaviors dependent on the information contained in the association, or for the modulation of the association by other areas, including the hippocampus itself.

LATENT INHIBITION: BEHAVIORAL MECHANISMS

Latent inhibition refers to the detrimental effect on subsequent conditioning, of preexposure to the to-be-CS. Because the latent inhibition (LI) paradigm appeared to be a situation requiring representational processes, we decided that it might be a promising task for the investigation of stimulation effects. The rationale was that LI is a task that involves the transfer of prior learning about the CS to the learning of a subsequent task involving that CS. As such, LI should be affected in systematic ways by various hippocampal manipulations.

Although the initial attempt to investigate LI employing the rabbit NMR preparation (Suboski, Di Lollo, & Gormezano, 1964) did not find the customary retardation of acquisition as a function of preexposure, perhaps because of too few trials, subsequent investigations using the rabbit nictitating membrane, eyelid, or pinna response have observed robust LI effects (Clarke & Hupka, 1974; Lubow, Markman, & Allen, 1968; Moore, Goodell, & Solomon, 1976; Prokasy, Spurr, & Goodell, 1978; Reiss & Wagner, 1972; Salafia & Allan, 1980, 1982; Siegel, 1969a, b, 1970; Siegel & Domjan, 1971; Solomon, Brennan, & Moore, 1974; Solomon, Lohr, & Moore, 1974; Solomon & Moore, 1975).

Attempts to explain the retardation of conditioning by CS preexposure have taken many forms. At various times response competition (Lubow & Moore, 1959), elicitation of alpha responses (Lubow, Markman, & Allen, 1968; Siegel & Domjan, 1971), Pavlovian conditioned inhibition (Reiss & Wagner, 1972; Rescorla, 1971; Solomon, Lohr, & Moore, 1974), and habituation (Carlton & Vogel, 1967; Sokolov, 1963) have been suggested as the underlying mechanisms. However, most suggestions have been systematically ruled out, often by those who first proposed them.

A behavioral explanation of LI, which relies heavily on attentional and conditioning mechanisms, has been proposed by Lubow and his associates (Lubow, Alek, & Arzy, 1975; Lubow, Schnur, & Rifkin, 1976; Lubow, Weiner, & Schnur, 1981). Their conditioned attention theory (CAT) assumes that attention is a response that is conditionable. With repeated CS presentation the attentional response inevitably declines. When a CS is paired with a US, as in the usual Pavlovian conditioning paradigm, the attentional response to the CS is initially increased by the presence of the US, leading to conditioned attention. In the LI paradigm, unreinforced CS preexposure leads to a decline of the attentional response and consequently to conditioned inattention. On the other hand, if, during preexposure the CS is followed by another stimulus, attention to the CS may be increased. In general, conditioned attention and inattention are construed to be responses that observe the general laws of Pavlovian conditioning.

Considerable support for CAT has been found, both in the older LI literature as well as in specific experiments designed to test its postulates (Lubow et al., 1981). The importance of CAT is that it provides a specific mechanism, namely Pavlovian conditioning, for the hypothetical attentional processes proposed by Mackintosh (1973), Weiss and Brown (1974), and others, to underlie the LI effect. The additional importance of CAT for the present purposes is that it provides a conception of LI processes that would require representational memory for CS information and therefore, suggests the likelihood of hippocampal involvement. It was this conception of LI that provided the rationale for our next series of experiments.

HIPPOCAMPUS AND LATENT INHIBITION

One notion that has dominated hippocampal theorizing for many years is that it plays a major role in behavioral inhibition (cf. e.g., Douglas, 1967, 1972; Kimble, 1968; McCleary, 1966). Douglas (1972) suggested that the hippocampus may be responsible for the regulation of attentional processes through modulation of midbrain arousal systems. In essence he proposed that the hippocampus performs its inhibitory function primarily by acting as a nonreinforcement register; that is, it is responsible for determining that a stimulus has been received and is *not* followed by reinforcement in which case it tunes out or gates out the stimulus.

This theory suggests a plausible physiological substrate for the conceptual mechanism of conditioned inattention. Ackil, Mellgren, Halgren, and Frommer (1969) found that hippocampectomized rats in comparison with cortical and unoperated controls failed to show LI in an active avoidance task. Solomon and Moore (1975) reported that whereas 450 preexposures of a tone that later became the CS in an NMR conditioning experiment resulted in retarded acquisition for normal and cortical control animals, rabbits with dorsal hippocampal lesions not only showed no deficit but a slight increment in acquisition rate. The increment suggests the possibility that in intact animals there can be some development of LI during acquisition, a possibility that has received experimental support (Hall & Pearce, 1979; Pearce & Hall, 1980).

Furthermore, Solomon (1977) found that dorsal hippocampal ablation eliminated blocking of a light stimulus in Kamin's (1969) blocking paradigm but did not affect the formation of Pavlovian conditioned inhibition (CI). Blocking, reduced to its essentials is a situation in which a second stimulus if compounded with an already conditioned stimulus, acquires little or no associative strength in spite of many pairings with the US. These results have often been taken as support for Douglas' theory in that the blocking paradigm is assumed to involve tuning-out processes similar to those involved in LI, whereas CI is thought to involve active withholding of responses rather than tuning out. Cast in the framework presented earlier, LI and blocking seem to require representational processes whereas CI may be the flip side of excitatory conditioning, requiring a similar neural substrate.

We have conducted two studies the results of which support and expand the view of substantive hippocampal involvement in the development and expression of LI (Salafia & Allan, 1980, 1982). The procedures were similar in both experiments and basically involved examining the effects of electrical stimulation of hippocampus during CS preexposure, during conditioning after preexposure, or during test trials after conditioning. Although a number of the preexposure and conditioning parameters differed in the two studies, the major difference was the intensity of the hippocampal stimulation.

In the first experiment Salafia and Allan (1980) stimulated the hippocampus at a fairly high intensity. The design and basic results are presented in Table 7.1. Groups 1 and 4 were placed in the experimental cubicles for an amount of time and under conditions equivalent to those of the other groups, the only difference being that this group received no preexposure of the to-be-CS and no brain stimulation. Groups 2, 3, and 5 were given tone preexposures, but in Group 3 each CS presentation was overlapped by electrical stimulation to the hippocampus. Stimulation parameters were 50 μA intensity, 2 msec pulse width, and 100 pulses per second (pps). For Groups 4 and 5, the CS on each paired trial was accompanied by hippocampal stimulation. In essence the design allowed us to determine if electrical stimulation of hippocampus would affect conditioning in the absence of preexposure, the development of LI, or the expression of LI.

Significant retardation in conditioning was found in Group 2, whereas both Groups 3 and 5 showed intermediate amounts of retardation indicating attenuation of LI for both groups. On the other hand, the effect of stimulation during conditioning, but without preexposure, was relatively small in comparison with its effects on LI. To summarize, the experiment showed that hippocampal stimulation attenuated both the development and the expression of LI. The implication is that hippocampal stimulation overlapping the CS affected processing of the CS more than it affected the associative process.

The second experiment (Salafia & Allan, 1982) was run in three phases the first two of which, preexposure and conditioning, were similar in design to

TABLE 7.1
Design and Results Expressed as the Mean Percentage of CRs
Made During Conditioning

Group	N	Preexposure	Conditioning	Mean % CRs
1	5	SIT	CS–US	71
2	5	CS	CS–US	39
3	6	CS/HS	CS–US	50
4	6	SIT	CS/HS–US	65
5	6	CS	CS/HS–US	57

TABLE 7.2
Design and Results Expressed as the Mean Percentage of CRs
Made During Conditioning

Group	N	Preexposure	Conditioning	Mean % CRs
1	5	SIT	CS–US	88
2	7	CS	CS–US	64
3	8	CS/HS	CS–US	51
4	3	CS/COS	CS–US	58

the previous experiment. Four groups were run including a SIT control group (Group 1) and a CS-preexposed group (Group 2). Animals in Group 3 received hippocampal stimulation and those in Group 4 received cortical stimulation overlapping the tone during preexposure. Stimulation parameters were 200 μsec pulses at a rate of 40 pps and an intensity of 30 μA.

The basic design and results of this phase of the study are presented in Table 7.2. Again a strong LI effect can be seen in all preexposed groups. However, the difference between the stimulated groups and the group receiving only CS preexposure was not statistically reliable, due apparently to the substantial degree of variability displayed by the stimulated animals.

High variability had been noted in previous hippocampal stimulation studies and attributed to the experimental designs and procedures. In Group 4 (cortical stimulation) this appeared to be random variation, whereas in Group 3 (hippocampal stimulation) there seemed to be a distinct performance dichotomy. Four animals showed no effect of the stimulation, performing at about the same level as Group 2, whereas the other four showed substantially greater retardation of conditioning, as though the very low-level hippocampal stimulation employed in this experiment had augmented the LI effect.

Having decided to investigate this differential performance further, one animal was chosen from Group 3 and presented with hippocampal stimulation at various levels, while we checked for effects on CRs. It was observed that a train of 100 μA, 2 msec pulses at 100 pps abolished CRs but had no apparent effect on URs. The remaining seven animals in Group 3 along with the animals from Group 4 were then subjected to a test that consisted of 20 extinction trials with hippocampal or cortical stimulation at this level (designated CS–S trials). Stimulation was turned off for the next 10 trials (CS-alone), on for another 10, and finally, off for the last 10. Four animals selected at random from Group 2 were also given 50 extinction trials for comparison.

The results of the test are depicted in Table 7.3 as six 10-trial blocks. The first block consisted of 10 CS–US trials to establish a baseline whereas the re-

TABLE 7.3
Mean Percentage of CRs per 10 Trial Block during the Test
for Stimulation Effects (TSE)

		Trial Block					
		1	2	3	4	5	6
Group		CS–US	CS–S	CS–S	CS–Alone	CS–S	CS–Alone
2		100	88	58	65	38	32
3 –	HS-1	98	0	0	93	0	63
	HS-2	100	95	98	92	88	70
4		92	40	37	73	37	53

maining five blocks were as indicated earlier. Of course, animals in Group 2, being unoperated, received no stimulation during any of these trials.

The results of the test phase were striking. Animals in Group 2 showed a typical extinction pattern with a progressively declining rate of conditioned responding. Those in Group 4 showed some lessening of conditioned responding during CS–S periods, but there was no clear pattern of stimulation effects and all animals in this group made some responses during these periods. The pattern for Group 3, on the other hand, was quite different, with three animals (designated HS-1) showing complete absence of CRs during the CS–S periods. Moreover, these animals showed no apparent carry-over effects of the CS–S trials. Thus, after 20 such trials they were still generating CRs at a rate of 93% when brain stimulation was absent. By the final block the rate was down to 63%, but this is in the same range of performance as Group 2 after only 10 CS-alone trials (58%). It appears, therefore, that the trials accompanied by hippocampal stimulation had little or no effect on performance during subsequent CS-alone trials, as if the tone was not being registered or processed on stimulation trials.

On the other hand, the remaining four animals (designated HS-2) responded at the highest rate of all during the CS–S trials but also showed little or no extinction during or as a result of these trials. Carrying the analysis one step further, we reevaluated the performance of Groups HS-1 and HS-2 in the prior conditioning phase and found that the four animals of Group HS-2, which showed augmented responding during the test, were the four that had shown augmentation of the LI effect. The performance of these animals in the conditioning phase ($\overline{X}$ = 37% CRs) was significantly lower than that of Group 2 ($\overline{X}$ = 64% CRs). On the other hand, the performance of Group HS-1 ($\overline{X}$ = 67% CRs) did not differ from that of Group 2.

It is still unclear why the stimulation, ostensibly presented in the same fashion, at the same time and to the same locus, should have had two different effects, but such outcomes are not that unusual in the stimulation literature (Prokasy et al, 1983; Salafia et al., 1979). Salafia and Allan (1982) suggested that the stimulation may have interacted with ongoing hippocampal activity, but further research will be required before a definitive answer can be found. Nevertheless, the overall pattern of results points consistently to a single conclusion, namely that hippocampal stimulation overlapping the CS affects primarily the processing of that CS.

HIPPOCAMPUS AND SINGLE ALTERNATION PATTERNING

The next series of studies was developed to examine representational processes more closely. The task of choice for this phase of the research was Pavlovian single alternation patterning. Operationally, the single alternation (SA) paradigm simply involves the alternate presentation of reinforced (R) and nonreinforced (N) trials. In Pavlovian conditioning, a temporal component may be added to the pattern by variation of the intervals between successive elements of the pattern. Thus for example, each N trial (CS-alone) might follow each R trial (CS-US) by a short temporal interval, whereas a much longer interval intervenes between each N trial and the next R trial. This sequence is referred to as the R-N pattern. The N-R pattern would have the same temporal arrangement of intervals, except that the short interval would intervene between the N and the R trials.

Leonard and Theios (1967) were unable to elicit simple SA-pattern learning with the rabbit NMR preparation using a 60 sec interval between each successive trial. However, the fact that some patterning was obtained by Holmes and Gormezano (1970) and Poulos, Sheafer, and Gormezano (1971) with the rabbit jaw-movement preparation, suggested to Hoehler and Leonard (1973) that the problem was not species specific. Hoehler and Leonard reexamined SA patterning with the NMR, using either an R-N pattern or an N-R pattern as defined earlier. With 10 sec (short) and 60 sec (long) intervals, they found that rabbits could discriminate the R-N, but not the N-R pattern. A pilot study was run in my laboratory and we obtained good performance using the R-N pattern with 3 sec and 30 sec intervals. Thus, an important variable for SA patterning using the rabbit NMR, appears to be that the interval between R and N trials be relatively short whereas that between successive pairs of trials be relatively long.

Reduced to its essentials, the PA task requires the processing of specific information over brief temporal intervals. Because the CS is identical for both R and N trials, the response on a given trial should be determined by the events of the previous trial (i.e., whether it was an R or N trial) and/or the length of the time interval since the last trial; that is, there must be some carry-over or representation of the prior events in order to perform properly.

Our first SA study (Salafia, Cardosi, Marini, Hogan, Olson, & Pollack, 1981) consisted of two experiments each of which involved two phases, namely conditioning followed by a shift to alternation testing. The rationale for the separate phases was that if all animals had already acquired the conditioned NMR prior to the introduction of alternation testing, the relevant variable in Phase 2 should be the temporal pattern of R and N trials. Also, the procedure ensured that all groups had successfully acquired the conditioned NMR to about the same level prior to the introduction of the alternation pattern.

In the conditioning phase, animals were divided into six groups. Three groups were conditioned at an ISI of 250 msec whereas the remaining three were conditioned at 1000 msec ISI. At each ISI, the three groups consisted of a dorsal hippocampal lesion group, a cortical lesion group, and an unoperated control group. All groups acquired the NMR at a rate appropriate to the ISI; that is, the groups run at 1000 msec took longer to condition and displayed greater variability than those at the 250-msec ISI.

The second phase of the experiment was the single alternation patterning test. Eight animals (two unoperated, two cortical, and four hippocampal) were run at each ISI during SA testing. Each SA set consisted of an R trial (CS–US) at an ISI of either 250 or 1000 msec, followed after a 3 sec interval (RNI) by an N trial (CS-alone). A 30 sec ITI intervened between each SA set.

The results of the SA patterning test for the 250- and 1000-msec ISI groups are depicted in Fig. 7.1 and 7.2, respectively. As expected, there was virtually complete overlap in the performance of the unoperated and cortical groups so that they were combined into a single control group at each ISI for comparison with the appropriate hippocampal group.

Although there appeared to be an overall SA patterning effect for both groups at the 250 msec ISI as indicated by the lower percentage of CRs on N trials, no statistically reliable difference or interaction could be found between the control and hippocampal animals. At 1000 msec ISI, however, there was a significant hippocampal deficit in SA patterning.

The pattern of alternation performance suggested several relationships. First, at 250 msec ISI it appeared that both groups displayed about the same moderate degree of SA patterning, i.e., that the hippocampal lesions did not produce impairment in SA performance (Fig. 7.1). However, there was some question as to whether the behavior really represented alternation learning, because the difference between R and N trials was so large initially and did not change much between the second and third block of trials. A portion of the difference in all groups could have been a function of other variables than the pattern of R and N trials, a point to which I return in Experiment 2.

The picture was somewhat different at 1000 msec ISI. By the third block, control animals were responding 90% of the time on R trials but only about 15% of the time on N trials. On the other hadn, the behavior of hippocampal

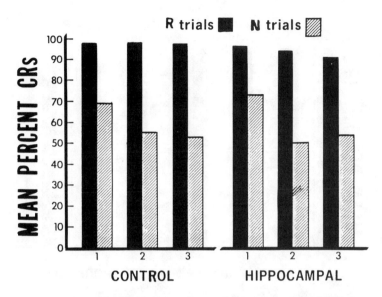

FIG. 7.1   Single alternation performance for control and hippocampal groups at 250 msec ISI (R = reinforced trials; N = nonreinforced trials). The control group included both cortical and unoperated animals.

animals was similar to the behavior of animals run at 250-msec ISI, i.e., at best a moderate degree of patterning behavior. If the previous suggestion is correct, the behavior of the hippocampal group may not actually indicate any substantive discrimination of the SA pattern. Even if that interpretation is incorrect, however, the results at 1000-msec ISI show that hippocampal lesions markedly retarded learning of the SA pattern at the longer ISI.

Several considerations pointed to the possibility that some of the apparent SA patterning in all groups might be due to variables other than the temporal pattern of R and N trials. First, during the SA phase, there was by definition, a 50% nonrandom reinforcement schedule. Second, Salafia, Mis, Terry, Bartosiak, and Daston (1973) have shown that other things being equal, reducing the ITI below about 15 seconds leads to substantial decrements in NMR conditioning. In the present case, the RNI was only 3 seconds. This combination of factors could have produced a tendency to respond less often on the second trial of the set, quite aside from the SA pattern itself. To test this possibility we ran a second experiment employing unoperated animals in what we termed a quasialternation (QA) control procedure.

The QA task had the same pattern of long and short intervals as the SA task in Experiment 1 and the same number of R and N trials. The only difference was that R and N trials were distributed randomly over the session with

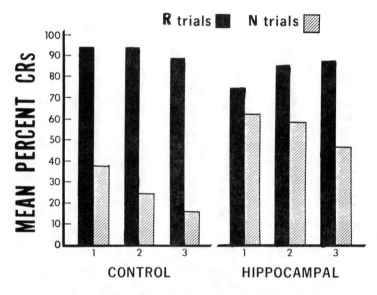

FIG. 7.2   Single alternation performance for control and hippocampal groups at 1000 msec ISI (R = reinforced trials; N = nonreinforced trials). The control group included both control and unoperated animals.

the single requirement that if the first trial of a QA set was an R trial, the second was N and vice versa.

We found that at both the 250-msec and the 1000-msec ISI, there were fewer responses on the second trial of the QA set (which would have been an N trial in SA learning) than on the first. At 250-msec ISI the mean number of CRs on the second trial of the QA set was 5% lower than that on the first trial, whereas at 1000 msec the difference was 16%. An additional factor played a role at 250 msec, namely, if the first trial of a set was an R trial, there was a stronger tendency for animals not to respond on the second trial, than if the first trial was an N trial. These QA results confirm that variables other than the temporal pattern of R and N trials are operative in SA pattern learning. Thus, they support the suggestion that the hippocampal deficit in Experiment 1 may be more substantial than it appears to be at first glance.

Further evidence of hippocampal involvement in SA learning has been provided recently by Hoehler and Thompson (1979), who monitored hippocampal multiple-unit activity during an SA task with the same interval between R-N trials and N-R trials. They found no evidence of behavioral discrimination, in agreement with Hoehler and Leonard (1973) but differential hippocampal multiple-unit activity during and preceeding CS presentation on the R and N trials.

Recently Couvillon and Bitterman (1981) argued that two major processes could account for alternation patterning. First, aftereffects of one trial could be *carried over* to the next trial without need for representational processes. Second, there could be a mnemonic representation of one trial upon which the animal relies for correct performance on the next. Couvillon and Bitterman use the term *reinstatement* in reference to this process.

Applying this distinction to our SA experiments, it seems probable that those aspects of performance of 250-msec ISI not accounted for by other processes may result from a carry-over effect.

This conclusion is supported by the finding that in the QA task, there were fewer CRs on N trials that followed R trials, even though there was no consistent R–N pattern throughout training. The consistent SA pattern should tend to amplify this effect. The absence of such an effect on the QA task at 1000 msec, as well as the extent of pattern discrimination in the SA task for control animals, suggests that at 1000 msec, performance resulted partly from the use of true representational memory. This would account for the magnitude of the hippocampal deficit at the longer ISI; that is, the lesions eliminated the representational process, while leaving lower level carry-over processes as well as the effect of the 50% schedule to account for the residue of apparent SA patterning.

Though these suggestions may appear speculative at this point, data from a recently completed experiment confirm that as the RNI is increased from 2.5 to 10 sec in intact animals, SA performance deteriorates at 250 msec ISI (carry-over no longer possible), but not at 1000 msec ISI (representation still available for processing). This latter result is encouraging, because it shows not only that the SA task may be a powerful tool for the study of representational processes in memory, but also that the task may permit the separate manipulation of different processes simply by altering temporal intervals.

CONCLUSIONS

The data presented here support the fundamental conclusion that although the hippocampus may ordinarily play a modulatory role in NMR acquisition processes, it is not necessary for those processes. On the other hand, an intact hippocampus appears to be a prerequisite to the development of LI, blocking, and SA patterning at long RNI's. The fact that hippocampal involvement or noninvolvement in SA patterning appears to be a function of two temporal intervals (RNI and ISI) is a particularly intriguing result, because it implies that the SA paradigm may be a useful tool in research on representational neural processes.

These data and conclusions can be accounted for within the framework of several recent theories of hippocampal functioning, such as the contextual-retrieval theory (Hirsh, 1974, 1980) or a working-memory theory (Olton, Becker, & Handelman, 1979, 1980). On the other hand, it is difficult to see how a spatial-information-processing theory (O'Keefe & Nadel, 1978, 1979) could accommodate a number of these results without substantial modification. In SA patterning, for example, the significant dimension appears to be temporal rather than spatial. In other instances, such as LI and blocking, explanation in terms of the processing of spatial information seem at best strained (Moore, 1979; Solomon, 1979).

Oakley (1983) has introduced an elaborate and useful classification of memory systems into which the present data can be accommodated. In Oakley's classification, event memory is at a low level, followed by several reference and working-memory systems. Varieties of reference memory include association, representational, and abstract memory, each of which may involve different procedures and learning/memory paradigms. Working memory, on the other hand, refers to a variety of short-term holding systems, each of which functions in conjunction with one or more of the reference systems.

The research surveyed in the present chapter could be integrated directly within the framework of Oakley's reference memory system. Alternatively, association memory might be considered as a separate system, perhaps a level above event memory but nevertheless separate from representational and abstract memory. The information content of event memory (e.g., CS-preexposure) and association memory (e.g., NMR conditioning) could be represented in one or more reference systems and from there be utilized as suggested previously in the performance of more complex tasks (e.g., LI or SA patterning), through the operation of one or more of the working-memory systems.

ACKNOWLEDGMENTS

I am grateful to Richard Hirsh, Ralph Miller, Fred Mis, David Oakley, and Norman Spear for their comments on an earlier version of this chapter.

REFERENCES

Ackil, J. E., Mellgren, R. L., Halgren, C., & Frommer, G. P. (1969). Effects of CS preexposure on avoidance learning in rats with hippocampal lesions. *Journal of Comparative and Physiological Psychology, 69,* 739–747.

Berger, T. W., Alger, B., & Thompson, R. F. (1976). Neuronal substrate of classical conditioning in the hippocampus. *Science, 192,* 483–485.

Berger, T. W., & Thompson, R. F. (1977). Limbic system interrelations: Functional division among hippocampal-septal connections. *Science, 197,* 587–589.

Berry, S. D., & Thompson, R. F. (1979). Medial septal lesions retard classical conditioning of the nictitating membrane response in rabbits. *Science, 205,* 209–211.

Carlton, P. L., & Vogel, J. R. (1967). Habituation and conditioning. *Journal of Comparative and Physiological Psychology, 63,* 348-351.

Cegavske, C. F., Thompson, R. F., Patterson, M. M., & Gormezano, I. (1976). Mechanisms of efferent neuronal control of the reflex nictitating membrane response in rabbit (*Oryctolagus cuniculus*). *Journal of Comparative and Physiological Psychology, 90,* 411-423.

Clarke, M. E., & Hupka, R. B. (1974). The effects of stimulus duration and frequency of daily preconditioning stimulus exposures on latent inhibition in Pavlovian conditioning of rabbit nictitating membrane response. *Bulletin of the Psychonomic Society, 4,* 225-228.

Couvillon, P. A., & Bitterman, M. E. (1981). Analysis of alternation patterning in goldfish. *Animal Learning and Behavior, 9,* 169-172.

Desmond, J. E., Berthier, N. E., & Moore, J. W. (1981). Brain stem elements essential for the classically conditioned nictitating membrane response of rabbit. *Society for Neuroscience Abstracts, 7,* 650.

Desmond, J. E., & Moore, J. W. (1982). A brain stem region essential for the classically conditioned but not unconditioned nictitating membrane response. *Physiology and Behavior, 28,* 1029-1033.

Douglas, R. J. (1967). The hippocampus and behavior. *Psychological Bulletin, 67,* 416-442.

Douglas, R. J. (1972). Pavlovian conditioning and the brain. In R. A. Boakes & M. S. Halliday (Eds.), *Inhibition and learning.* New York: Academic Press.

Flaherty, C. F., Hamilton, L. W., Gandelman, R. J., & Spear, N. E. (1977). *Learning and memory.* Chicago: Rand McNally.

Hall, G., & Pearce, J. M. (1979). Latent inhibition of a CS during CS-US pairings. *Journal of Experimental Psychology: Animal Behavior Processes, 5,* 31-42.

Hirsh, R. (1974). The hippocampus and contextual retrieval of information from memory: A theory. *Behavioral Biology, 12,* 421-444.

Hirsh, R. (1980). The hippocampus, conditional operations, and cognition. *Physiological Psychology, 8,* 175-182.

Hoehler, F. K., & Leonard, D. W. (1973). Classical nictitating membrane conditioning in the rabbit (*Oryctolagus cuniculus*): Single alternation with differential intertrial intervals. *Journal of Comparative and Physiological Psychology, 85,* 277-288.

Hoehler, F. K., & Thompson, R. F. (1979). The effect of temporal single alternation on learned increases in hippocampal unit activity in classical conditioning of the rabbit nictitating membrane response. *Physiological Psychology, 7,* 345-351.

Holmes, J. D., & Gormezano, I. (1970). Classical appetitive conditioning of the rabbit's jaw movement response under partial and continuous reinforcement schedules. *Learning and Motivation, 1,* 110-120.

Kamin, L. J. (1969). Predictability, surprise, attention, and conditioning. In B. Campbell & R. Church (Eds.), *Punishment and aversive behavior.* New York: Appleton-Century-Crofts.

Kesner, R. P., & Wilburn, M. W. (1974). A review of electrical stimulation of the brain in context of learning and retention. *Behavioral Biology, 10,* 259-293.

Kimble, D. P. (1968). Hippocampus and internal inhibition. *Psychological Bulletin, 70,* 285-295.

Leonard, D. W., & Theios, J. (1967). Classical eyelid conditioning in rabbits under prolonged single alternation conditions of reinforcement. *Journal of Comparative and Physiological Psychology, 64,* 273-276.

Lockhart, M., & Moore, J. W. (1975). Classical differential and operant conditioning in rabbits with septal lesions. *Journal of Comparative and Physiological Psychology, 88,* 147-154.

Lubow, R. E., Alek, M., & Arzy, J. (1975). Behavioral decrements following stimulus preexposure: Effects of number of preexposures, presence of a second stimulus, and interstimulus interval in children and adults. *Journal of Experimental Psychology: Animal Behavior Processes, 1,* 178-188.

Lubow, R. E., Markman, R. E., & Allen, J. (1968). Latent inhibition and classical conditioning of the rabbit pinna response. *Journal of Comparative and Physiological Psychology, 66,* 688–694.

Lubow, R. E., & Moore, A. N. (1959). Latent inhibition: The effect of nonreinforced preexposure to the conditioned stimulus. *Journal of Comparative and Physiological Psychology, 52,* 416–419.

Lubow, R. E., Schnur, P., & Rifkin, B. (1976). Latent inhibition and conditioned attention theory. *Journal of Experimental Psychology: Animal Behavior Processes, 2,* 163–174.

Lobow, R. E., Weiner, I., & Schnur, P. (1981). Conditioned attention theory. In G. H. Bower (Ed.), *The psychology of learning and motivation* (Vol. 15). New York: Academic Press.

Mackintosh, N. J. (1973). Stimulus selection: Learning to ignore stimuli that predict no change in reinforcement. In R. A. Hinde & J. Stevenson–Hinde (Eds.), *Constraints on learning.* London: Academic Press.

McCleary, R. A. (1966). Response-modulating functions of limbic system: Initiation and suppression. In E. Stellar & J. M. Sprague (Eds.), *Progress in physiological psychology* (Vol. 1). New York: Academic Press.

McCormick, D. A., Clark, G. A., Lavond, D. G., & Thompson, R. F. (1982). Initial localization of the memory trace for a basic form of learning. *Proceedings of the National Academy of Sciences, 79,* 2731–2735.

McCormick, D. A., Lavond, D. G., Clark, G. A., Kettner, R. E., Rising, C. E., & Thompson, R. F. (1981). The engram found? Role of the cerebellum in classical conditioning of nictitating membrane and eyelid responses. *Bulletin of the Psychonomic Society, 18,* 103–105.

McGaugh, J. L., & Herz, M. J. (1972). *Memory consolidation.* San Francisco: Albion.

Mis, F. W. (1977). A midbrain-brainstem circuit for conditioned inhibition of the nictitating membrane response in the rabbit (*Oryctolagus cuniculus*). *Journal of Comparative and Physiological Psychology, 91,* 975–988.

Moore, J. W. (1979). Information processing in space–time by the hippocampus. *Physiological Psychology, 7,* 224–232.

Moore, J. W., & Desmond, J. E. (1982). Latency of the nictitating membrane response to periocular electro-stimulation in unanesthetized rabbits. *Physiology and Behavior, 28,* 1041–1046.

Moore, J. W., Desmond, J. E., & Berthier, N. E. (1982). The metencephalic basis of the conditioned nictitating membrane response. In C. W. Woody (Ed.), *Conditioning: Representation of involved neural functions.* New York: Plenum.

Moore, J. W., Goodell, N. A., & Solomon, P. R. (1976). Central cholinergic blockade by scopolamine and habituation, classical conditioning, and latent inhibition of the rabbit's nictitating membrane response. *Physiological Psychology, 4,* 395–399.

Moore, J. W., Yeo, C. H., Oakley, D. A., & Russell, I. S. (1980). Conditioned inhibition of the nictitating membrane response in decorticate rabbits. *Behavioral Brain Research, 1,* 397–409.

Oakley, D. A. (1983). The varieties of memory: A phylogentic approach. In A. Mayes (Ed.), *Memory in animals and humans.* Wokingham: Van Nostrand Reinhold.

Oakley, D. A., & Russell, I. S. (1972). Neocortical lesions and Pavlovian conditioning. *Physiology and Behavior, 8,* 915–926.

Oakley, D. A., & Russell, I. S. (1974). Differential and reversal conditioning in partially neodecorticate rabbits. *Physiology and Behavior, 13,* 221–230.

Oakley, D. A., & Russell, I. S. (1975). Role of cortex in Pavlovian discrimination learning. *Physiology and Behavior, 15,* 315–321.

Oakley, D. A., & Russell, I. S. (1976). Subcortical nature of Pavlovian differentiation in the rabbit. *Physiology and Behavior, 17,* 947–954.

Oakley, D. A., & Russell, I. S. (1977). Subcortical storage of Pavlovian conditioning in the rabbit. *Physiology and Behavior, 18,* 931–937.

O'Keefe, J., & Nadel, L. (1978). *The hippocampus as a cognitive map.* London: Oxford University Press.

O'Keefe, J., & Nadel, L. (1979). Precis of O'Keefe & Nadel's the hippocampus as a cognitive map. *The Behavioral and Brain Sciences, 2,* 487–453.

Olton, D. S., Becker, J. T., & Handelmann, G. E. (1971). Hippocampus, space, and memory. *The Behavioral and Brain Sciences, 2,* 313–322.

Olton, D. S., Becker, J. T., & Handelmann, G. E. (1980). Hippocampal function: Working memory or cognitive mapping. *Physiological Psychology, 8,* 239–246.

Patterson, M. M. (1970). Classical conditioning of the rabbit's (*Oryctolagus cuniculus*) nictitating membrane response with fluctuating ISI and intracranial-CS. *Journal of Comparative and Physiological Psychology, 72,* 193–202.

Pearce, J. M., & Hall, G. (1980). A model for Pavlovian learning: Variations in the effectiveness of conditioned but not unconditioned stimuli. *Psychological Review, 87,* 532–552.

Poulos, C. X., Sheafer, P. J., & Gormezano, I. (1971). Classical appetitive conditioning of the rabbit's (Oryctolagus Cuniculus) jaw-movement response with a single alternation schedule. *Journal of Comparative and Physiological Psychology, 75,* 231–238.

Prokasy, W. F., Kesner, R. P., & Calder, L. D. (1983). Posttrial electrical stimulation of the dorsal hippocampus facilitates acquisition of the nictitating membrane response. *Behavioral Neuroscience, 97,* 890–896.

Prokasy, W. F., Spurr, C. W., & Goodell, N. A. (1978). Preexposure to explicitly unpaired conditioned and unconditioned stimuli retards conditioned response emergence. *Bulletin of the Psychonomic Society, 12,* 155–158.

Reiss, S., & Wagner, A. R. (1972). CS habituation produces a "Latent Inhibition Effect" but no active "Conditioned Inhibition." *Learning and Motivation, 3,* 237–245.

Rescorla, R. A. (1971). Summation and retardation tests of latent inhibition. *Journal of Comparative and Physiological Psychology, 75,* 77–81.

Salafia, W. R., & Allan, A. M. (1980). Attenuation of latent inhibition by electrical stimulation of hippocampus. *Physiology and Behavior, 24,* 1047–1051.

Salafia, W. R., & Allan, A. M. (1982). Augmentation of latent inhibition by electrical stimulation of hippocampus. *Physiology and Behavior, 29,* 1125–1130.

Salafia, W. R., Cardosi, K. M., Marini, D., Hogan, J. M., Olson, D. R., & Pollack, E. J. (1981). Disruption of single alternation learning in rabbits by hippocampal lesions. *Society for Neuroscience Abstracts, 7,* 237.

Salafia, W. R., Cardosi, K. M., & Salafia, A. B. (1981). *Nictitating membrane conditioning with gradual and abrupt shifts in ISI.* Paper presented at the annual meeting of the Psychonomic Society, Philadelphia.

Salafia, W. R., Chiaia, N. L., & Ramirez, J. J. (1979). Retardation of rabbit nictitating membrane conditioning by subseizure electrical stimulation of hippocampus. *Physiology and Behavior, 22,* 451–455.

Salafia, W. R., Lambert, R. W., Host, K. C., Chiaia, N. L., & Ramirez, J. J. (1980). Rabbit nictitating membrane conditioning: Lower limit of the effective interstimulus interval. *Animal Learning and Behavior, 8,* 85–91.

Salafia, W. R., Mis, F. W., Terry, W. S., Bartosiak, R. S., & Daston, A. P. (1973). Conditioning of the nictitating membrane response of the rabbit (*Oryctolagus cuniculus*) as a function of length and degree of variation of intertrial interval. *Animal Learning and Behavior, 1,* 109–115.

Salafia, W. R., Romano, A. G., Tynan, T., & Host, K. C. (1977). Disruption of rabbit nictitating membrane conditioning by posttrial electrical stimulation of hippocampus. *Physiology and Behavior, 18,* 207–212.

Salafia, W. R., Terry, W. S., & Daston, A. P. (1975). Conditioning of the rabbit nictitating membrane response as a function of trials per session, ISI, and ITI. *Bulletin of the Psychonomic Society, 6,* 505–508.

Schmaltz, L. W., & Theios, J. (1972). Acquisition and extinction of a classically conditioned response in hippocampectomized rabbits. *Journal of Comparative and Physiological Psychol-*

ogy, 79, 328-333.

Siegel, S. (1969a). Effects of CS habituation on eyelid conditioning. *Journal of Comparative and Physiological Psychology, 68,* 245-248.

Siegel, S. (1969b). Generalization of latent inhibition. *Journal of Comparative and Physiological Psychology, 69,* 157-159.

Siegel, S. (1970). Retention of latent inhibition. *Psychonomic Science, 20,* 161-162.

Siegel, S., & Domjan, M. (1971). Backward conditioning as an inhibitory procedure. *Learning and Motivation, 2,* 1-11.

Smith, M. C., Coleman, S. R., & Gormezano, I. (1969). Classical conditioning of the rabbit's nictitating membrane response at backward, simultaneous, and forward CS-US intervals. *Journal of Comparative and Physiological Psychology, 69,* 226-231.

Sokolov, E. N. (1963). *Perception and the conditioned reflex.* New York: Pergamon.

Solomon, P. R. (1977). Role of the hippocampus in blocking and conditioned inhibition of the rabbit's nictitating membrane response. *Journal of Comparative and Physiological Psychology, 91,* 407-417.

Solomon, P. R. (1979). Temporal versus spatial information processing theories of hippocampal function. *Psychological Bulletin, 86,* 1272-1279.

Solomon, P. R., Brennan, G., & Moore, J. W. (1974). Latent inhibition of the rabbit's nictitating membrane response as a function of CS intensity. *Bulletin of the Psychonomic Society, 4,* 445-448.

Solomon, P. R., & Gottfried, K. E. (1981). The septohippocampal cholinergic system and classical conditioning of the rabbit's nictitating membrane response, *Journal of Comparative and Physiological Psychology, 95,* 322-330.

Solomon, P. R., Lohr, A.C., & Moore, J. W. (1974). Latent inhibition of the rabbit's nictitating membrane response: Summation tests for active inhibition as a function of number of CS preexposures. *Bulletin of the Psychonomic Society, 4,* 557-559.

Solomon, P. R., & Moore, J. W. (1975). Latent inhibition and stimulus generalization of the classically conditioned nictitating membrane response in rabbits following dorsal hippocampal ablation. *Journal of Comparative and Physiological Psychology, 89,* 1192-1203.

Solomon, S. D., Schaaf, E. V., Perry, H., & Solomon, P. R. (1982). *Is a malfunctioning hippocampus more detrimental to conditioning than none at all?* Paper presented at the annual meeting of the Eastern Psychological Association, Baltimore.

Suboski, M. D., DiLollo, V., & Gormezano, I. (1964). Effects of unpaired preacquisition exposure of CS and UCS on classical conditioning of nictitating membrane response of the albino rabbit. *Psychological Reports, 15,* 571-576.

Thompson, R. F., Berger, T. W., Berry, S. D., Clark, G. A., Kettner, R. N., Lavond, D. G., Mauk, M. D., McCormick, D. A., Solomon, P. R., & Weisz, D. J. (1982). Neuronal substrates of learning and memory: Hippocampus and other structures. In C. W. Woody (Ed.), *Conditioning: Representation of involved neural functions.* New York: Plenum.

Thompson, R. F., Berger, T. W., Berry, S. D., & Hoehler, F. K. (1980). The search for the engram, II. In D. McFadden (Ed.), *Neural Mechanisms in Behavior: A Texas Symposium.* New York: Springer-Verlag.

Thompson, R. F., Berger, T. W., Berry, S. D., Hoehler, F. K., Kettner, R. E., & Weisz, D. J. (1980). Hippocampal substrate of classical conditioning. *Physiological Psychology, 8,* 262-279.

Thompson, R. F., Berger, T. W., Cegavske, C. F., Patterson, M. M., Roemer, R. A., Teyler, T. J., & Young, R. A. (1976). The search for the engram. *American Psychologist, 31,* 209-227.

Weiss, K. R., & Brown, B. L. (1974). Latent inhibition: A review and a new hypothesis. *Acta Neurobiologiae Experimentalis, 34,* 301-316.

Single Unit Analysis of Hippocampal Pyramidal and Granule Cells and Their Role in Classical Conditioning of the Rabbit Nictitating Membrane Response

8

Theodore W. Berger
University of Pittsburgh

Donald J. Weisz
Yale University

INTRODUCTION

In recent years, the rabbit nictitating (NM) membrane preparation has been used extensively to examine cellular activity in different brain regions during classical conditioning (Berger, Alger, & Thompson, 1976; Berger & Thompson, 1977, 1978a,b; Berry & Thompson, 1978; Cegavske, Patterson, & Thompson, 1979; Thompson, Berger, Berry, & Hoehler, 1980). In the early phases of adopting this preparation for use with electrophysiological techniques, we focused our analysis on the neural activity of limbic system structures, most notably that of the hippocampus. Primarily two reasons led us to do so. First, a well-known literature has established an important role for the hippocampus and related structures in human and animal memory function (Berger & Orr, 1982; Milner, 1966; O'Keefe & Nadel, 1978; Olton, Becker, & Handelmann, 1979; Squire, 1982; Squire & Zola–Morgan, 1982). Second, an abundance of information exists concerning anatomical and electrophysiological characteristics of hippocampal neurons (Anderson, 1959; Andersen, 1960a,b; Andersen, Eccles, & Løyning, 1964a,b; Blackstad, 1956; Lorente de No, 1934; MacVicar & Dudek, 1980; Nicholl & Alger, 1981; Raisman, Cowan, & Powell, 1965; Ramon y Cajal, 1911; Schwartzkroin, 1975; Spencer & Kandel, 1968; Swanson, Sawchenko, & Cowan, 1980; Swanson, Wyss,

& Cowan, 1978; Wong, Prince, & Basbaum, 1979). In particular, the connectional relations of the principal hippocampal cells to their major afferent and efferent brain structures have been well defined and well characterized (Hjorth-Simonsen & Jeune, 1972; Jacobs, Foote, & Bloom, 1978; Loy, Koziell, Lindsey, & Moore, 1980; Mosko, Lynch, & Cotman, 1973; Nauta, 1956; Raisman, Cowan, & Powell, 1966; Steward, 1976; Swanson & Cowan, 1977; Swanson, Wyss, & Cowan, 1980). Coupled with the organizational simplicity of the structure (Andersen, Bliss, & Skrede, 1971a), the latter information allows recording from identified anatomical cell types during conditioning with knowledge of the relative position of that cell type within the circuitry of the hippocampus as a whole. Because of these conditions, we felt there was a high probability: (1) that any changes in hippocampal cellular activity recorded during conditioning would be relevant to normal mnemonic processes; (2) that we would distinguish changes in cellular activity that are "local" to the hippocampus from those that are occurring in afferent regions and are merely reflected in hippocampal responsivity; (3) that if changes in cellular responses are occurring within the hippocampus, the antecedent neural activity necessary for the development of hippocampal cellular plasticity could be described accurately; and (4) that the effect of changes in hippocampal activity on efferent target neurons could be determined.

One of our first objectives was to determine whether any changes in hippocampal unit activity occurred during the course of NM conditioning. The most expedient method for answering this question was the use of multiple-unit recording techniques, which allow data from small populations of neurons to be gathered relatively quickly. If multiple-unit methods indicated that changes in activity specific to learning were occurring in the hippocampus, then those cellular changes would be subjected to a more intensive and time consuming single-unit analysis.

METHODS

All surgical procedures were carried out using halothane anesthesia. Animals were allowed at least 1 week of recovery before training began. Conditioning procedures utilized a 1K Hz (85 db SPL) tone followed 250 msec after its onset by a 100 msec airpuff. Tone and airpuff terminated simultaneously. The first and every ninth trial was a tone-alone trial. The inter-trial-interval varied from 50–70 sec, with an average of 60 sec; animals received a maximum of 135 trials per session. Control animals given unpaired training were presented with a pseudorandom sequence of tone-alone and airpuff-alone trials. The intertrial interval varied from 20–40 sec, with an average of 30 sec. A maximum of 240 trials was presented per session.

For multiple-unit recordings, insulated stainless steel electrodes with 5–10 μ tip diameters and 40–50 μ exposed shafts were permanently implanted in or near the pyramidal cell layers of the dorsal hippocampus. Precise location of recording sites was determined by monitoring unit discharge from the electrode during implantation. A lead from each electrode was connected to pins in a plastic headstage mounted to the animal's skull with screws and dental acrylic. Connectors (with first-stage FET's) fastened to the headstage during behavioral conditioning allowed recording from various hippocampal regions throughout learning. For single-unit recordings, a lightweight microdrive was implanted on the skull overlying the dorsal hippocampus. In addition, bipolar stimulation electrodes were implanted either in the fornix near the rostral pole of the hippocampus or in the angular bundle. Etched, insulated stainless steel electrodes used for single-unit recordings typically had tip diameters of 2–4 μ and impedances of 20–30 Mohms (tested at 135 Hz, in vitro). For single-unit recordings, electrodes were lowered into the hippocampus at the beginning of each training session and removed at the end of the session.

Action potentials detected from both types of electrodes were recorded directly onto one channel of an audio tape recorder. During analysis, spikes were converted to TTL level pulses using an amplitude discriminator, and pulses were collected using digital inputs of a computer.

Nictitating membrane movement was recorded using a nylon suture sewn into the membrane. The suture was connected to the wiper blade of a potentiometer attached to headgear worn by the animal during training. Thus, extension of the membrane over the corneal surface was transduced to a potential change in the potentiometer output. NM movement was monitored throughout the session on a polygraph but also modulated a carrier frequency (6750 Hz) for recording onto one channel of an audio tape recorder. During analysis, the carrier frequency was demodulated and the reproduced NM response collected through analog-to-digital converters of a computer.

A final channel of the tape recorder was used to record timing pulses indicating onsets of the trial, CS and UCS. Both unit and NM data were collected for 250 msec preceding CS onset for a measure of background spontaneous activity (PreCS period), for 250 msec between CS onset and UCS onset (CS period), and for 250 msec following UCS onset.

RESULTS

Multiple-Unit Recordings From the Hippocampus

As stated earlier, one of the initial reasons for recording from the hippocampus during NM conditioning was that previous work has shown bilateral hippocampectomy to result in a severe anterograde amnesia in humans (Milner, 1970) and, under certain conditions, profound learning disabilities in animals (Douglas, 1967; Kimble, 1968; O'Keefe & Nadel, 1978). Although this data indicated that the hippocampus participates in mnemonic processing, it does not indicate how hippocampal neurons are activated or respond under normal learning conditions. Our first studies, then, asked whether or not hippocampal-unit activity was altered by the conditioning process, that is, whether hippocampal activity changes as the animal changes its behavior. If so, we would also seek to determine whether the changes in cellular activity were related to associative aspects of the learning paradigm, as opposed to other nonassociative effects of conditioning such as changes in levels of motor responding or levels of arousal.

Results of multiple-unit recording from in and around the pyramidal cell layers of the hippocampus indicated that the answer to both these questions was affirmative (Berger, Alger, & Thompson, 1976). Increases in the number of action potentials recorded during both the UCS and CS periods of conditioning trials increased over training trials as the animal learned (see Fig. 8.1), though increases were both greater and occurred earlier during training in UCS period components of the conditioning trial (Berger & Thompson, 1978a). Opposite changes occurred during extinction. As animals' conditioned behavior extinguished, the number of action potentials occurring during tone-alone presentations decreased with repeated trials. Furthermore, decreases during the course of extinction occurred earliest in that segment of the trial where the UCS had occurred during conditioning (Berger & Thompson, 1982).

One of the distinct advantages of the NM preparation (particularly when airpuff is used as the UCS) is that the distribution of action potentials, as well as their number, can be measured within conditioning trials. Analysis of the distribution of hippocampal cell responses within trials revealed a striking correlation between the probability of cell response and the amplitude of the conditioned behavior (Fig. 8.2); that is, when the amplitude of the conditioned NM responses was greatest, the probability of hippocampal cell activation also was greatest; when the amplitude of the conditioned NM response was lowest, the probability of cell response was lowest. The result was a strong parallel between the pattern of hippocampal cell firing and the spatiotemporal parameters, or topography, of the learned NM response (Berger, Laham, & Thompson, 1980). Other behavioral responses besides the nictitating membrane are altered by conditioning, for example, heart rate (Powell, Lipkin, & Milligan, 1974; Schneiderman, 1972). The latter result is particularly important, then, because it indicates that changes in activity of hippocampal neurons are probably related to changes in the nictitating membrane response per se, as opposed to these other response systems.

Analysis of temporal relationships between neural discharges and conditioned NM behavior revealed that increases in hippocampal activity preceded conditioned behavioral NM responses both across and within training trials. Across trials, increases above background levels in hippocampal activity

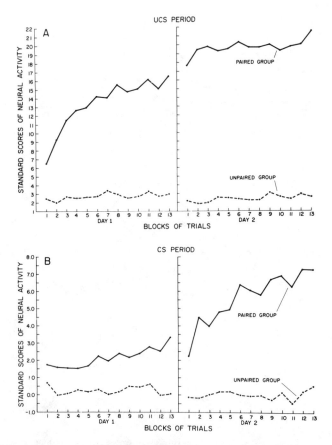

FIG. 8.1 Group curves of standard scores of hippocampal multiple-unit activity recorded throughout paired conditioning (solid lines) and unpaired (broken lines) training. A: standard scores of unit activity occurring in UCS period component of trials. B: standard scores of unit activity occurring in CS period component. Paired group N = 21; unpaired group N = 14.

were detectable, on the average, within the first block (of eight) conditioning trials. In contrast, conditioned NM responses were not evident until, on the average, seven or eight blocks of trials (Berger & Thompson, 1978a). Increases in hippocampal activity preceded behavioral NM responses within trials as well, by approximately 45 msec (Berger, Laham, & Thompson, 1980).

Hippocampal activity recorded from control animals given unpaired presentations of tones and airpuffs was not enhanced across training. A slight increase in the number of action potentials was recorded in response to UCS-alone trials, but this evoked response did not change with repeated stimulation; essentially no evoked response to tone presentations was recorded (Fig.

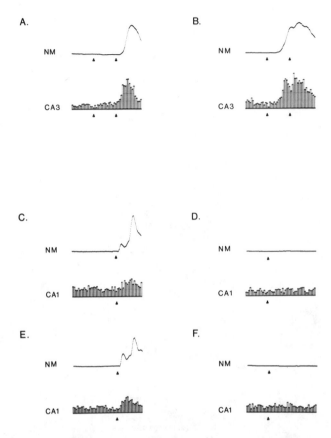

FIG. 8.2   Hippocampal multiple-unit responses recorded from one animal given paired training (A,B) and one animal given unpaired training (C-F). Upper trace shows averaged NM response for eight trials; lower trace shows cumulated peristimulus histogram for eight trials. Early cursor indicates tone onset; late cursor indicates airpuff onset. A and B show NM and unit responses from paired trials early on Day 1 and late on Day 2 of training, respectively. C and E show data from airpuff-alone trials early on Day 1 and late on Day 2, respectively. D and F show data from tone-alone trials early on Day 1 and late on Day 2, respectively.

8.2). The differences between hippocampal activity under the paired and unpaired conditions could be produced within the same animals as well. A separate group of rabbits given unpaired training followed by paired conditioning showed low levels of hippocampal responsiveness during control procedures followed by a substantial enhancement over spontaneous firing rates during conditioning (Fig. 8.3). In addition, increased discharge of hippocampal neurons was never seen during spontaneous NM movements, even when such movements occurred during the intertrial interval of well-trained animals (Berger & Thompson, 1978a). These results, and others (see Berger & Thompson, 1978a), clearly indicated that the changes in hippocampal cellular activity recorded during NM conditioning were related to the associative aspects of the learning paradigm, and were not simply a result of increased activation of the organism, or increased levels of motor responding.

In an additional series of studies designed to test the generality of the hippocampal phenomenon, it was found that the same types of unit changes are seen in recordings from cat hippocampus (Patterson, Berger, & Thomp-

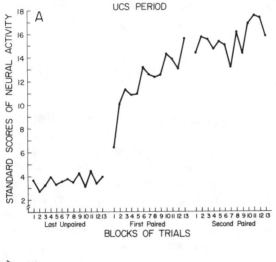

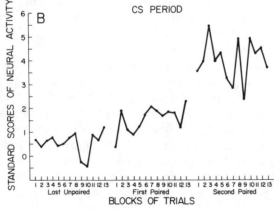

FIG. 8.3 Group curve of standard scores of multiple-unit activity from hippocampus of animals given successive phases of unpaired and paired training ($N = 5$).

son, 1979) and when light is used as a CS in rabbit NM conditioning (Coates & Thompson, 1978). Thus, the hippocampal neural plasticity described earlier is neither species- nor stimulus modality-dependent.

In total, multiple-unit studies revealed that behavioral NM conditioning is accompanied by a change in the activity of hippocampal neurons that is learning dependent. Hippocampal cellular activity is altered only by specific environmental conditions that also induce changes in behavior. In addition, changes in the activity of hippocampal neurons predict changes in learned behavior, both in terms of the time course of behavioral changes and in terms of learned response topography. The predictive relationship between hippocampal neural activity and learned NM behavior holds both during acquisition (see also Berry & Thompson, 1978; Berry, this volume) and extinction.

Multiple-Unit Recordings From Structures Afferent to the Hippocampus

A major issue in the field of learning-related cellular activity concerns localization (see Thompson, Berger, & Madden, 1983); that is, are the changes in hippocampal neural activity occurring within the hippocampus, or are they occurring in other structures afferent to the hippocampus? If the latter is true, hippocampal responsivity to conditioning stimuli may be altered as a result of learning, but only because input to the hippocampus also is altered. To partially address this issue, we recorded simultaneously from the hippocampus and medial septum during classical conditioning of the NM response, again using multiple-unit recording techniques. The medial septal nucleus has been shown to be the origin of a major cholinergic input to both the pyramidal and granule cell regions of the hippocampus (Ibata, Desireju, & Pappas, 1971; Meibach & Siegel, 1977; Mosko, Lynch, & Cotman, 1973; Raisman, 1966; Swanson & Cowan, 1979).

Results of this experiment revealed that medial septal cells exhibited responses during conditioning that were qualitatively different than simultaneously recorded hippocampal activity (Berger & Thomson, 1977, 1978b). Cells in the medial septum showed short-latency, phasic, excitatory responses to onsets of the CS and UCS (Fig. 8.4). Moreover, identical responses were seen during unpaired presentations of the tone and airpuff, and the magnitude of response seen under both paired and unpaired conditions decreased over the course of training. These results strongly suggested that the origin of the pyramidal cell response recorded during conditioning was not the medial septum. In addition, this experiment suggests that input from the medial septum may be transmitting information about the conditioning stimuli (e.g., occurrence and temporal relationship of the CS and UCS) that is essential for the

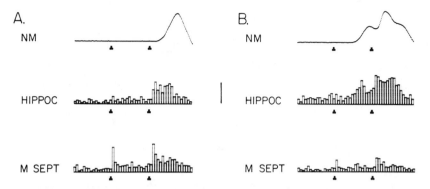

FIG. 8.4   Hippocampal and medial septal unit responses recorded simultaneously from a paired conditioning animal. Upper trace: average nictitating membrane response from one block of 8 trials. Middle trace: hippocampal unit peristimulus histogram for one block of eight trials. Lower trace: medial septal unit peristimulus histogram for one block of 8 trials. A: 1st block of paired conditioning trials, day 1. B: 13th block of paired trials, day 2. First cursor indicates tone onset; second cursor indicates airpuff onset.

development of the hippocampal pyramidal cell response (Berger & Thompson, 1978b). The latter suggestion is, in fact, supported by a recent experiment conducted by Berry and Thompson (1978; also see Berry, this volume) demonstrating that lesions of the medial septum disrupt the parallel between hippocampal cell discharges and the NM response and also retard the onset of behavioral conditioning.

The second major afferent to the hippocampus examined was the entorhinal cortex. Cells in layers II and III of entorhinal give rise to axons terminating on both hippocampal granule and pyramidal cells (Lorente de No, 1934; Hjorth–Simonsen & Jeune, 1972; Steward, 1976). Initial results of recording simultaneously from the dentate and entorhinal were difficult to interpret because the small size of granule cells makes their action potentials difficult to discriminate from nearby CA¾ pyramidal neurons (Berger & Thompson, 1978a). This necessitated a single-unit analysis of granule cell activity during NM conditioning, the results of which are described in a later section. Simultaneous recordings from hippocampal pyramidal zones and entorhinal, however, revealed some similarities and some differences between hippocampal and entorhinal activity during conditioning. Clark, Berger, and Thompson (1978) recorded multiple-unit activity in the entorhinal cortex and found that entorhinal cells exhibited conditioned increases in unit activity during NM conditioning that were of similar latency and topography to those seen in CA1 and CA3; however, the entorhinal increases were much smaller than those seen in the hippocampus. Of greater import was the finding that the conditioned increase in entorhinal activity peaked

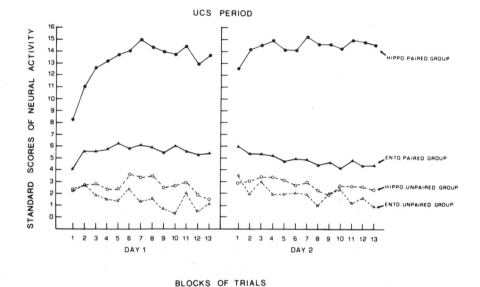

FIG. 8.5   Group curves of standard scores of simultaneously recorded hippocampal and entorhinal multiple-unit activity through training. Only scores for the UCS period trial component are shown.

very early in training, long before the conditioned hippocampal response reached asymptote (Fig. 8.5). Thus, the major changes in cellular activity of hippocampal neurons occur without associated changes in entorhinal activity, again suggesting that hippocampal neural plasticity described in earlier studies is local to the hippocampus. The final verdict regarding the roles of entorhinal cortex and medial septum in the formation of the conditioned pyramidal cell responses, however, must be preceded with studies utilizing single-unit recordings of antidromically identified cells that are shown to project to the hippocampus.

Results of Single-Unit Recording From the Hippocampus Proper

Although the results of the above analysis of the activity of hippocampal afferents during NM conditioning is still ongoing, these initial findings strongly suggest that the plasticity recorded from hippocampal neurons of Ammon's horn is generated or develops within the hippocampus itself. That these initial results were promising prompted us to examine hippocampal cellular activity during conditioning in greater detail. More precisely, we sought to determine whether the anatomical cell type exhibiting the changes in cellular activity described previously was one of the principal hippocampal neurons (e.g., a pyramidal neuron) or an interneuron of some kind. As pointed out earlier, one of the advantages of the hippocampal system is that such a question can be addressed experimentally rather easily. Neuroanatomical data indicates that only pyramidal neurons project an axon via the fornix (Ramon y Cajal, 1911; Lorente de No, 1934). After implanting bipolar stimulation electrodes in the fornix, we used chronic, single-unit recording techniques (see Methods) to monitor the activity of different subtypes of hippocampal neurons during conditioning of the NM response. Pyramidal neurons were the only cell type that could be conclusively identified (using fornix stimulation), and they were identified using the following criteria: (1) short latency to activation, (2) little or no variability in that latency, and (3) failure of antidromic activation due to collision. The collision test was performed on only a subset (25%) of the total neurons examined ($N = 178$) (Berger, Rinaldi, Weisz, & Thompson, 1983; Berger & Thompson, 1978c).

Cell Classification.   Of the total 178 neurons analyzed, 107 (60%) responded with an almost invariant latency (less than 0.1 msec variability) to fornix stimulation. Of those tested, spontaneous discharges of 18 cells were successfully collided using delayed fornix shock triggered by the occurrence of a spontaneous action potential. Thus, of 178 cells, 18 were conclusively identified as pyramidal neurons using the collision criterion. Pyramidal neurons identified by successful collision after fornix shock consistently shared a number of spontaneous discharge characteristics. All 18 cells had basal firing rates less than 10/sec, averaging 2.6/sec ($\pm$ 0.16 S.E.M.). All pyramidal cells (100%) also exhibited complex action potentials and all (100%) had action potential durations that exceeded 0.5 msec.

Another 46 units that were not tested for collision but did demonstrate constant latency responses to fornix shock also were classified as pyramidal neurons because they exhibited spontaneous firing characteristics identical to those cells that were collided. All of these 46 neurons had low basal firing rates (100% less than 10/sec; mean = 3.12/sec $\pm$ 0.20 S.E.M.) and action potential durations that exceeded 0.5 msec. In addition, all displayed at some time, complex action potentials. As a result, both groups of neurons: (1) those collided and (2) those not tested for collision but exhibiting the above spontaneous characteristics in combination with short-latency/low-variability responses to fornix stimulation, were classified as pyramidal neurons.

Unit Responses During Classical Conditioning.   Response patterns of pyramidal neurons during conditioning were highly consistent. The majority of pyramidal cells increased firing rates during conditioning trials. T-test comparisons of firing rates in PreCS versus CS and UCS trial periods showed that 83% (40/48) of all pyramidal neurons significantly increased firing rate within either the CS period or the UCS period. The majority of pyramidal cells also exhibited a pattern of firing within conditioning trials that correlated positively with the amplitude-time characteristics of the conditioned NM response (Fig. 8.6). The correlation ratio computed between the averaged unit histogram and the averaged NM response for each pyramidal cell was significant at the $p < .05$ level in 37/48 cases (77%). The activity of pyramidal cells during conditioning contrasts sharply with that seen for pyramidal cells recorded during unpaired training (Fig. 8.7). During unpaired training, no pyramidal neurons ($N = 16$) exhibited significantly increased discharge rates to tone-alone trials, and only three cells significantly increased firing during airpuff-alone presentations. For two of the three cells (18%) was the distribution of action potentials during airpuff-alone trials was significantly correlated with the topography of the reflex NM response. Thus, the activity of pyramidal neurons was changed as a result of classical conditioning in two respects. During conditioning trials, pyramidal cells both increased firing rate and displayed a pattern of firing that correlated with magnitude of the conditioned response.

The enhanced activity recorded from pyramidal cells of conditioned animals developed very early during the course of training and was seen in recordings on the first day of conditioning. Six identified pyramidal neurons were recorded from naive animals, and in five cases those neurons increased within-trial discharge rates as a result of conditioning. In initial conditioning trials, pyramidal cells exhibited only basal or slightly enhanced firing rates. Very rapidly, however, those rates increased. For example, rates of all five

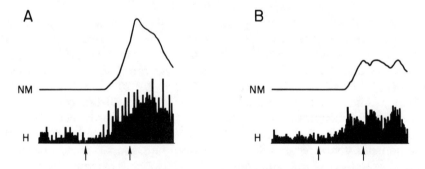

FIG. 8.6   Averaged NM responses and cumulated peristimulus histograms generated by single-unit recordings of two identified pyramidal neurons during paired conditioning. Early arrow indicates tone onset; late arrow indicates airpuff onset. Note that animal in A exhibits a monophasic conditioned NM response, which is accompanied by a unimodal unit histogram. Animal in B exhibits a triphasic conditioned NM response, which is accompanied by a trimodal unit histogram.

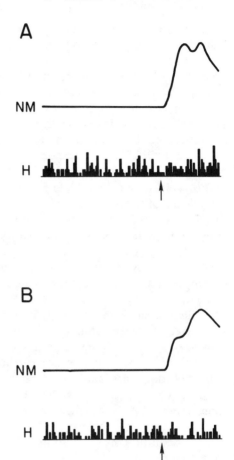

FIG. 8.7   Averaged NM responses and cumulated peristimulus histograms generated by single-unit recordings of two, identified pyramidal neurons during airpuff-alone presentations. Arrow indicates airpuff onset.

pyramidal cells had increased by several hundred percent (relative to PreCS rates) within the UCS period by trial 10. By the same number of trials, three cells also were showing enhanced activity in the CS period as well, though usually of smaller magnitude. In contrast to these rapid neuronal changes, no conditioned behavioral responses were seen in 4/6 animals while alterations in unit activity were occurring. Two pyramidal cells were recorded long enough for behavioral conditioning to occur. For those two neurons, changes in cellular activity occurred before the appearance of the first conditioned NM response. Pyramidal cell activity in both CS and UCS periods, then, increased rapidly as a function of exposure to conditioning trials and changed before any behavioral learning was evident.

In a previous analysis of multiple-unit hippocampal activity during NM conditioning, we used correlational techniques[1] to examine within-trial latency differences between the onset of increased hippocampal activity and onset of the conditioned NM response (Berger, Laham, & Thompson, 1980). Results showed that on the average, hippocampal activity began increasing approximately 45 msec before the onset of conditioned NM responding. We used the same correlational techniques in the present study to determine latency differences between the onset of increased pyramidal cell activity and onset of conditioned NM responding. Considerable differences among identified pyramidal cells were found. Although the majority of pyramidal cells (62%) increased firing rate before the onset of conditioned NM responding, a significant number of cells increased firing rate either coincidentally (22%) or after (16%) behavioral onset. In short, results indicated that a complete unit representation of the conditioned NM response is produced by the simultaneous activities of many pyramidal cells. Although some pyramidal neurons can exhibit an enhanced activity pattern that correlates highly with most phases of the NM response, many cells respond only during a portion of the NM response (Fig. 8.8).

In summary, the single-unit analysis demonstrated that pyramidal neurons are the cell type within Ammon's horn that exhibit the neural plasticity first documented with multiple-unit techniques. Because synaptic relations between pyramidal neurons and one of their principal intrinsic afferents— granule cells of the dentate gyrus—are well established, we were able to ask additional questions concerning the role of dentate granule cell activity in the responsiveness of pyramidal cells during NM conditioning.

Results of Single-Unit Recording From the Dentate Gyrus

Cell Classification.   The next step, then, was to determine if conditioned unit responses also could be observed in dentate granule cells that form the major link between the entorhinal cortex and areas CA3 and CA1 of hippocampus (Andersen, Bliss, & Skrede, 1971a; Lorente de No, 1934). In this experiment we recorded from single cells in the granule cell layer (Weisz, Clark, Yang, Solomon, Berger, & Thompson, 1980) of dentate gyrus during NM

---

[1]In brief, successive correlation coefficients were computed between the array of values representing the unit histogram and the array of values representing the NM response as the unit histogram array was shifted (in 3 msec increments) relative to the NM array. Both arrays were judged to be "in phase", or to have a zero delay, when the correlation coefficient value was maximized. The number of 3-msec "shifts" needed to produce the maximal coefficient value was used to determine the latency difference between onset of conditioned hippocampal response and onset of conditioned NM response (see Berger et al., 1980b).

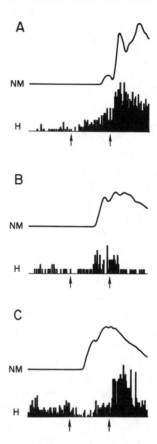

FIG. 8.8   Averaged NM responses and cumulated peristimulus histograms generated by single-unit recordings of three identified pyramidal neurons during paired conditioning. Note that activity of cell shown in A correlates with all features of the NM response, whereas activity of cells shown in B and C correlate with only certain phases of the conditioned response.

conditioning. Briefly single cells were isolated in the granule cell layer using both electrophysiological recordings and measurements of the distance of the electrode tip from the dura. Cells were characterized by spike morphology, spontaneous activity, and the ability of perforant path stimulation to drive the cell. Most of the cells that were isolated had the following characteristics: (1) the cell could be driven orthodromically by perforant path stimulation at a latency of 4–6 msec (the population spike had the same latency); (2) the unfiltered width of the spike was approximately .15–.3 msec at the base of the spike; (3) the cell sometimes fired in synchrony with "theta" rhythm (rhythmical slow wave activity (RSA) usually 4–8 Hz in our recordings); (4) the cell had a pretraining spontaneous firing rate of from 5.8/sec to 35.5/sec. Based on the work of Bland and others (Bland, Andersen, Granes, & Sveen, 1980), we felt that cells with these characteristics were granule cells.

Unit Reponses During Classical Conditioning.   Marked differences appeared between paired and unpaired cell responses within the first block of trials. The dominant response of 27 paired cells in 8 of 9 animals was an increased firing rate beginning in the CS period and continuing through the UCS period. Within a cell, the latency of the increased firing was stable and appeared to be locked to the tone. Between cells, the latency of the increased firing varied from 30–100 msec. In some cases the excitatory response was preceded by an inhibitory response to the CS. For approximately one-half of the cells the increased firing took the form of rhythmical bursting with an interburst interval of approximately 125 msec. Fig. 8.9 shows a cumulative peri-stimulus histogram for a granule cell on trials 10–18 on Day 1. The animal shows no sign of behavioral conditioning at this point; however there is a rhythmical burst beginning in the CS period and lasting throughout the trial. Fig. 8.9 shows the response from another granule cell from the same animal on trials 1–9 on Day 2. By Day 2 the animal had developed a well-conditioned NM response, but there was no obvious change in the granule cell firing pattern from the early Day 1 pattern. Overall, following the first 18 trials, there were no major changes in the cell response patterns (in either latency or amplitude) to the CS and UCS across cells within a given animal.

Results from unpaired control animals indicated that the increased firing exhibited by the paired animals was learning dependent. Figures 8.10A and 8.10B show representative poststimulus histograms for an unpaired cell during the first block of training on Day 1, and Fig. 8.10C and 8.10D depict histograms for the same cell on block 5 of Day 1. The dominant response to CS-alone and UCS-alone presentations was inhibition during the first block of unpaired training. Strong inhibition to the UCS remained throughout the first 2 days of unpaired training; however, in almost all cases inhibition to the CS decremented with further CS-alone presentations.

Thus, the learning-dependent plasticity observed in granule cells is characterized best by the contrasting cell responses in paired and unpaired animals. Granule cells increased their firing to paired CS–UCS presentations, whereas

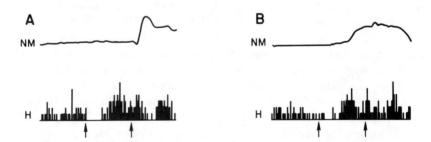

FIG. 8.9   Averaged NM responses and cumulated peristimulus histograms generated by single-unit recordings of an identified dentate granule cell during paired conditioning. Early arrow indicates tone onset; late arrow indicates airpuff onset. See text for explanation.

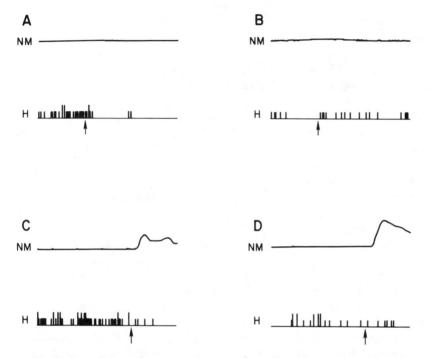

FIG. 8.10 Averaged NM responses and cumulated peristimulus histograms generated by single-unit recording of an identified dentate granule cell during unpaired training. See text for explanation.

unpaired cells inhibited to both stimuli initially and to the UCS throughout training.

CA3-Dentate Comparison. The response patterns observed in dentate during NM conditioning were qualitatively and quantitatively different from the responses of pyramidal cells in CA3 and CA1 of hippocampus. First, the granule cells responded at a fixed latency to the presentation of the CS throughout paired conditioning, whereas many pyramidal cells responses preceded the conditioned behavior by approximately 45 msec. As an animal acquired the conditioned NM response, the behavior and the responses of the pyramidal cell but not of the granule cells moved closer to the CS onset. Second, the patterns of conditioned unit responses were different for the two types of cells. The firing patterns of only pyramidal cells formed temporal models of the conditioned NM responses. Third, the conditioned pyramidal cell responses grew rapidly over the first 60–70 trials. In almost all animals, minimal changes were seen in granule cell responses after the first 18 trials of paired training. Fourth, granule cells responded with inhibition to both CS and UCS presentations in unpaired control animals, whereas pyramidal cells increased slightly their firing rates following UCS presentations and exhibited no change following CS presentations.

Facilitation of Entorhinal-to-Dentate Synaptic Transmission During NM Conditioning

The results from the single-cell study in dentate gyrus were supported by a study in which the dependent variable was the amplitude of dentate population spikes elicited during training (Weisz et al., 1980). The dentate population spike amplitude is considered to be representative of the number of granule cells activated (Andersen, Bliss, & Skrede, 1971b) and has been used to measure their excitability. For this work we implanted chronic bipolar stimulating electrodes in the perforant path and a chronic recording electrode slightly ventral to the granule cell layer in the dorsal blade of the dentate gyrus. During all CS presentations for paired and unpaired animals, a 0.1 msec electrical stimulus was administered to the perforant path so that a population spike of moderate size would be elicited. The electrical stimulus was presented 225 msec after CS onset, which in paired animals was 25 msec prior to delivery of the UCS. Also, potentials were elicited randomly between trials when no tone or airpuffs were present. The results are depicted in Fig. 8.11. Spikes elicited during tones (within-trial) were significantly smaller than between-trial potentials. In addition, spikes elicited from paired conditioning animals were reliably larger than spikes from unpaired controls. For the paired group there was a significant increase in the amplitudes of both within-trial and between-trial spikes; however, the increase occurred after animals had acquired conditioned NM responses. For the unpaired control animals the greatest inhibition to the tone occurred on the first block; however, slight inhibition to the tone remained throughout both days of unpaired training.

The population spike data generally are consistent with the single-cell results. Both approaches revealed that as early as the first block, there were differences between paired and unpaired animals in the excitability of granule cells. Both approaches also showed that the greatest inhibition to the tone in unpaired animals occurred on the first block of training. The one major difference in the two sets of findings is that the population potential study revealed increased cell excitability during the last half of Day 2 whereas the single-cell results failed to show this. One possible explanation is that more granule cells were recruited across training rather than any one cell gradually increasing its firing rate as the animal learned. More single cells need to be recorded early in training before conclusions can be made regarding this possibility.

The population potential results are consistent with the hypothesis that the conditioned granule cell response is generated locally. The input to the gran-

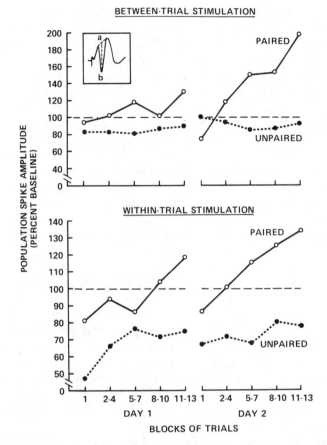

FIG. 8.11   Average amplitude of the dentate granule cell population spike plotted as a function of training trials. Baseline amplitude (100%) was determined by averaging the amplitudes of 16 population spikes elicited immediately prior to start of training on Day 1. Inset depicts the measurement used for amplitude determination. The distance from a to b was used as the spike amplitude.

ule cell was held constant across conditioning trials, but the amplitude of the population spike increased both in response to the CS and when elicited between trials. There are at least two explanations for these results. First, it is possible that the perforant path-granule cell synapses undergo long-term increases in synaptic efficacy as a result of the conditioning procedures. This effect would be very similar to the long-term potentiation or LTP effect obtained when trains of electrical stimuli are delivered to the perforant path. Alternatively, the conditioning procedures may alter the excitability of the granule cells by changing the tonic level of a major input to the dentate gyrus, e.g., the inputs from median raphe or from locus coeruleus. Winson (1980) has shown that amplitude of dentate population spikes covary in a systematic manner with behavioral state with the largest spikes elicited during slow wave sleep and the smallest during still alert states. The input from median raphe was found to be critical for the large amplitude spikes that are elicited during slow wave sleep. Thus it is possible that a tonic change in the median raphe input to the hippocampus as a result of NM conditioning could result in altered population spike amplitudes. Knowledge of the activities of the inputs to dentate gyrus will be necessary before these two hypotheses can be evaluated fully. In addition, the effect of NM conditioning on the amplitude of the dentate population EPSP and afferent fiber volley needs to be determined. If the conditioning procedures increase the amplitude of the EPSP without affecting the size of the fiber volley, then a strong argument could be made that the change in granule cell excitability is locally generated.

Results of Recordings From Hippocampal Efferent Targets

In addition to analyzing the nature of afferent input to the hippocampus, we are also engaged in recording from structures that are efferent to the hippocampus in order to determine the eventual target of information transmitted by the hippocampal system. The fact that pyramidal neurons were the cells exhibiting the learning-dependent pattern of activity strongly suggested that the major monosynaptic targets of the hippocampus should display similar discharge patterns. If not, then hippocampal output was being transformed in some manner, and the nature of that transformation might provide clues as to the behavioral consequence of hippocampal activation during NM conditioning.

The first efferent structure we recorded from was the lateral septum (Berger & Thompson, 1978b), which has been known for some time to receive monosynaptic input from hippocampus (Nauta, 1956; Raisman et al., 1966; Swanson & Cowan, 1977). The results of this analysis were very clear and showed that lateral septal neurons responded very similarly to hippocampal pyramidal neurons (Fig. 8.12). Lateral septal activity increased incrementally over the course of conditioning, exhibited a pattern of within-trial discharge that correlated strongly with the conditioned NM response and remained at low, unchanging levels during unpaired presentations of tone and airpuff. Thus, lateral septal neurons displayed all the major characteristics of hippocampal cellular responses during conditioning of the NM response.

A second major efferent target of the hippocampus is the subicular cortex, an adjoining allocortical brain region (Swanson & Cowan, 1977). Only in recent years has it become clear that the subiculum receives a much more prominent projection from hippocampus than the lateral septal area and in this sense becomes an important structure to examine in the course of our analy-

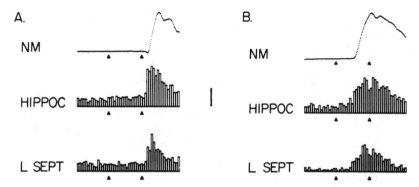

FIG. 8.12   Simultaneously recorded hippocampal and lateral septal unit responses from a paired conditioning animal. Upper trace: average nictitating membrane response for one block of eight trials. Middle trace: hippocampal unit peristimulus histogram for one block of 8 trials. Lower trace: lateral septal unit peristimulus histogram for one block of 8 trials. A: one block of paired conditioning trials early on Day 1. B: one block of conditioning trials late on Day 1. First cursor indicates tone onset. Second cursor indicates airpuff onset.

sis. We have recently described the anatomical organization of hippocampo-subicular projections in the rabbit (Berger, Swanson, Milner, Lynch, & Thompson, 1980) and are now ready to use that anatomical data to guide a single-unit analysis of orthodromically activated (by stimulating hippocampus) subicular neurons during NM conditioning. The latter experiment is currently in progress.

Behavioral Significance of Hippocampal Cellular Changes During NM Conditioning

The goal of examining activity of structures efferent to hippocampus is to track the learning-dependent hippocampal response to its ultimate target. Our working hypothesis is that the ultimate target is the abducens and/or accessory abducens nucleus and most likely all motoneurons controlling ocular movements. The rabbit response to corneal airpuffs is a complex of reflexes involving all of the ocular nuclei innervating striatal musculature (McCormick, Lavond, & Thompson, in preparation). In short, our working hypothesis is that hippocampal cellular responses during conditioning are causally related to learned behavior. But to this point our only data have been changes in cellular activity during conditioning that parallel changes in behavioral learning and a causal relationship between cellular events and behavioral events cannot be established solely by correlative data. This issue is particularly relevant to learning-induced changes in hippocampal activity during NM conditioning, because work by others and ourselves has shown that an intact hippocampus is not necessary for behavioral learning in the delay paradigm that we have used for most past studies (Berger & Orr, 1982, 1983; Schmaltz & Theios, 1972; Solomon & Moore, 1975). Yet our electrophysiological work has shown that robust changes in hippocampal activity are consistently induced by such a learning paradigm. There are a number of explanations for such a disparity, ranging from dismissing hippocampal cellular changes during NM conditioning as epiphenomenal, to defining a role for hippocampal activity in a motor feedback or "reafference" system (Moore, 1979), to suggesting that the hippocampus functions as one of a number of parallel circuits mediating conditioned behavior (Thompson, Berger, Berry, & Hochler, 1980).

We have persued an additional possibility, namely that although the mnemonic function performed by the hippocampus and surrounding structures is activated under all learning conditions, that function is necessary only for certain types of learned behavior. That the hippocampus is not necessary for all learned behaviors is consistent with data from both humans (Cohen & Corkin, 1981; Cohn & Squire, 1980; Sidman, Stoddard, & Mohr, 1968) and animals (Douglas, 1967; Kimble, 1968; O'Keefe & Nadel, 1978). For example, in many instances bilateral hippocampectomy does not affect discrimination learning but consistently has been reported to interfere with discrimination reversal (Hirsh, 1974); that is, animals with hippocampal lesions typically are capable of acquiring discriminative behavior to a CS+ and a CS− but are incapable of reversing their discriminative responding when the stimuli serving as CS+ and CS− are reversed. This selective effect of hippocampectomy has been observed under a variety of training conditions with the use of several different species (Kimble, 1968; see Mahut & Zola, 1973). We tested the hypothesis, then, that hippocampal damage would selectively prevent reversal learning of the NM response as well, and if so, suggest the functional significance of hippocampal cellular changes occurring during NM conditioning. For this experiment, rabbits were trained using a two-tone conditioning paradigm, one tone serving as the CS+ (always followed by the airpuff UCS), the other serving as the CS− (never followed by the airpuff). In addition the CS–UCS interval was expanded from the 250 msec used in past studies to 750 msec, so that an 850 msec duration CS (+ or −) was used. The CS+ and UCS still coterminated. Twelve blocks of 8 CS+ and 8 CS− trials were given each day. Animals were trained at the initial discrimination until reaching a behavioral criteria of >85% response rate to the CS+ and <15% response rate to the CS−. The tones serving as CS+ and CS− then were reversed, and animals were trained until reaching a criteria of >85% to the new CS+ and <50% to the new CS−, or until 8 weeks of training were completed.

Normal animals, animals with bilateral hippocampal lesions and animals with control, neocortical lesions all learned the initial discrimination at the same rate (see Fig. 8.13). During reversal, however, only animals with hippocampal lesions exhibited abnormal rates of learning, taking up to four

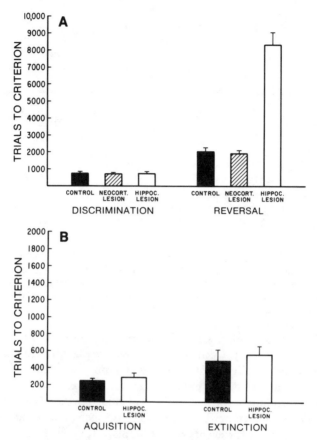

FIG. 8.13   A: Mean total trials required by operated control animals (solid bars), animals with neocortical lesions (striped bars), and animals with hippocampal lesions (open bars) to reach two-tone discrimination and reversal criteria. Error bars represent S.E.M.s. *B*: Mean total trials required by operated control animals (solid bars) and animals with hippocampal lesions (open bars) to reach one-tone delay and unpaired extinction criteria. Error bars represent S.E.M.s.

times as long to reach behavioral criterion. Animals with hippocampal damage failed at reversal by responding at high rates to both the CS + and the CS − ; that is, they learned to respond to the new CS + (the old CS −) but did not decrease responding to the new CS − (the old CS +), and so did not behaviorally differentiate between the CS + and CS − during reversal (Fig. 8.14). An additional study showed that the latter effect of hippocampectomy cannot be accounted for by increased resistance to extinction or "perseveration"; that is, hippocampectomized rabbits exhibit normal extinction of learned NM behavior (Berger & Orr, 1983).

A number of explanations could be offered as to the mnemonic process necessary for reversal learning and disrupted by hippocampal lesions (see

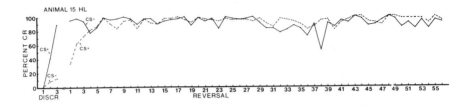

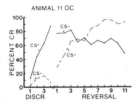

FIG. 8.14 Conditioned NM response rates during two-tone discrimination (Discr.) and reversal learning for one control (OC) animal and one hippocampal lesioned (HL) animal. For both animals, a 1K Hz tone served as the CS+ during discrimination training and the CS− during reversal training. All values represent CR rates for the last half of each training session.

Hirsh, 1974; Olton et al., 1979). Though we have not yet fully supported our position experimentally, we are intrigued by an explanation that is consistent with present interpretations of the human temporal lobe amnesic syndrome. To elaborate, early studies of patients after surgical removal of temporal lobe structures (including the hippocampus) concluded that the hippocampus was involved in global memory processes, because such patients could not form long-term memories for events that took place following the surgery (Penfield & Milner, 1958; Scoville & Milner, 1957). However, a long line of animal studies has failed to confirm a global role for the hippocampus in learning and memory processes. Some animal learning tasks (e.g., reversal learning, see Hirsh, 1974) are sensitive to hippocampal lesions whereas many others (e.g., delay classical conditioning, Schmaltz & Theios, 1972) are not. This apparent conflict has troubled hippocampal investigators for many years; however, recent findings regarding hippocampal function have reduced the apparent gap between the human and animal literatures. The memory deficits in humans do not appear to be global but rather are specific for some types of memories. For example, perceptual and perceptual-motor skills are learned by human amnesics even though they are not aware of their previous experiences with the task. H. M., who received a bilateral medial temporal lobectomy in the early 1950s, acquired mirror-reading skills although he failed to remember specific words that he had read (Cohen & Squire, 1980). He also showed improvement over successive sessions on the Tower of Hanoi perceptual-motor puzzle but failed to remember having worked on the puzzle previously (Cohen & Corkin, 1981). These findings have led to suggestions that there is more than one memory system, with the hippocampus and related structures involved in one but not in others. A recently developed theory of hippocampal function makes a distinction between memory for rules and procedures (procedural memory) in which the hippocampus is not involved, and memory for specific information (declarative or memory) that require an intact hippocampus (Squire & Zola–Morgan, 1982).

The declarative-procedural memory distinction may be extended to account for the effects reported here of hippocampal lesions on reversal learning of the rabbit NM response. As demonstrated in the second experiment, bilateral hippocampectomy does not disrupt NM learning in a one-tone, delay paradigm. This is consistent with the declarative-procedural distinction because an intact procedural memory is sufficient to learn the task. An example of the relevant rule-based memory might be, "when a tone occurs, extend nictitating membrane." No specific features of the stimulus (e.g., frequency) are relevant to controlling behavior, so the delarative memory component of the task is minimal. Although bilateral hippocampectomy does not affect delay conditioning, it does severely retard reversal learning of the NM response. This result also is consistent with the declarative-procedural memory notion to the extent that successful discrimination learning is dependent on hippocampal function until a temporal delay is introduced between presentation of the two stimuli to be discriminated (Sidman, Stoddard, & Moher, 1968). In the present experiment, CS+ and CS− presentations were separated by 20–40 sec (i.e., the intertrial interval) which is outside the range of temporal contiguity needed for successful discrimination learning in humans with temporal lobe damage (Sidman, Stoddard, & Moher, 1968). At first consideration, this interpretation would predict that animals in the present study would fail at both initial discrimination learning and reversal. However, successful discriminative responding is a function both of temporal factors that allow comparison of the CS+ and CS−, and the degree of disparity between the CS+ and CS−. In the present experiment the temporal delay between presentation of the CS+ and CS− represented by the intertrial interval was constant throughout discrimination and reversal training, but the degree of disparity between the CS+ and the CS− was not. During initial discrimination conditioning, the CS+ is distinguished from the CS− along two dimensions: frequency (Hz), and pairing with the UCS. In the transition from discrimination to reversal conditioning, however, only the frequency dimension is consistent in distinguishing the CS+ from the CS−. So although the need for simultaneous comparison of the CS+ and CS− (i.e., short intertrial interval) is minimized during initial discrimination learning when the CS+/CS− distinction is great, delayed comparison is particularly disruptive during reversal learning when the CS+/CS− distinction is significantly lessened. What we are suggesting is that even though lesioned animals have an impaired declarative memory, there are enough externally supplied distinctions or mnemonic "supports" during initial discrimination to allow for successful learning. That hippocampectomized animals in the present study fail to recognize the difference between the CS+ and CS− during reversal learning is supported by the fact that they respond at equal rates to both CS+ and CS−. Procedural memory is still intact in these animals, however, because during reversal they also are responding at high rates to both CS+ and CS−.

Recent reports from Thompson and co-workers (Lincoln, McCormick, & Thompson, 1982; McCormick, Clark, Lavond, & Thompson, 1982; see Thompson et al., this volume) have shown that the cerebellum is necessary for learning classically conditioned NM extension even in a one-tone, delay paradigm. We believe the cerebellar system is potentially the anatomical substrate for procedural memory (see Berger & Orr, 1983), and that output from the hippocampal system modifies cerebellar activity during learning paradigms that require declarative memory. We are currently engaged in neuro-anatomical investigations to define multisynaptic pathways capable of transmitting information from the hippocampus to the cerebellum (Bassett & Berger, 1981; Semple-Rowland, Bassett, & Berger, 1981). Although the parallel between our lesion findings and the human amnesic syndrome are obviously tentative, we are encouraged to more closely examine hippocampal neural activity during behaviors such as reversal learning that maximize the necessity of hippocampal function in learning. As a result, many of our present experiments are focusing on the nature of hippocampal cellular activity during discrimination reversal conditioning of the NM response (see Berger, 1982).

DISCUSSION

Experimental Strategies: The Search For Primary Sites of Learning-Induced Neural Plasticity

As has been recognized by other workers in this field, the localization of primary sites of learning-induced neural plasticity often is hindered by the fact that changes in cellular activity at one point in a multisynaptic pathway can induce changes in neurons postsynaptic to that site of change. Thus, many neurons in a given pathway may exhibit learning-related activity, but only in a trivial sense because their responses are secondary to primary changes occurring in an afferent brain region. Given the synaptic complexity of the mammalian brain, and in particular, the high degree of divergence that commonly occurs in successive stages of efferent projections, the localization problem is compounded in mammalian species. This has been one of the major justifications for use of invertebrate models of learning (Kandel, 1976), because the simplicity of invertebrate nervous systems places welcome constraints on the number of possible primary sites of neural plasticity. In a system with a small number of neurons, the localization problem can be solved in the straightforward manner of recording sequentially from all neurons in a multisynaptic circuit, from input to output. The first synaptic junction where presynaptic activity is constant and postsynaptic response is variable can be identified as a primary site of neural plasticity.

Employing the same strategy in a mammalian species is considerably more difficult because of the numbers of neurons involved and, as mentioned earlier, the divergence in projections exhibited by many CNS brain regions. We feel the rabbit nictitating membrane preparation significantly alleviates these problems, because the behavior the animal exhibits is only a simple, discrete response. The only motoneurons involved are those controlling the ocular muscles (Berthier & Moore, 1980; McCormick et al., in preparation) and the only motoneurons necessary to maintain NM behavior are those of the abducens and accessory abducens nucleus (Disterhoft, Shipley, & Kraus, 1982; Gray, McMaster, Harvey, & Gormezano, 1981; Powell, Berthier, & Moore, 1979). By using a preparation in which the behavior of the organism is simple, discrete, and highly stereotyped, it is hoped that the number of multisynaptic circuits activated in the brain during NM conditioning will be minimal. In this regard, although most reports to date using the rabbit NM preparation have stressed positive findings of unit changes or unit activation during conditioning, many areas of the brain have been found that are activated only minimally or not at all (e.g., mammillary nuclei, Berger & Thompson, 1978b; anterior dorsal, ventral, and medial thalamic nuclei, Berger, Clark, & Thompson, 1980; caudate n., Thompson, personal communication; anterior cingulate cortex, Hoehler & Thompson, personal communication). Not only should there be a minimum of circuits activated, but there should be less divergence in the transmission of information along circuits that are activated, because the number of ultimate motoneuronal targets are so few. With regard to this point, analysis of monosynaptic and disynaptic subcortical targets of the hippocampus has shown that only one target, the lateral septum, responds similarly to hippocampal pyramidal neurons during NM conditioning, whereas others (mammillary nuclei and anterior thalamic nuclei) do not. These notions are still assumptions, and their validity will certainly be tested in the next few years. If the assumptions are correct, however, the probability of localizing a primary site of neural plasticity essential for NM conditioning should be high, because only a small number of circuits will need to be subjected to study, and an input-output analysis of those circuits will be more tractable with limited divergence in the projection of learning-induced neural signals.

An additional advantage of the rabbit NM preparation is that although at least two response systems are conditioned during paired training (NM responses and cardiovascular responses), analysis of within-trial patterns and latencies of unit discharge provide a means for distinguishing different activated circuits mediating different conditioned reponses. For example, hippocampal pyramidal neurons respond with a pattern of discharge and a latency to excitation that correlate highly with parameters of conditioned NM behavior (Berger, Laham, & Thompson, 1980) but not conditioned heart-rate responses.

The Human Amnesic Syndrome: Hints For the Solution of the Localization Problem

One strategy for localizing primary sites in the mammalian brain is modeled after the approach used with invertebrate preparations; that is, recording from motoneurons or first-order sensory neurons and analyzing the activity of cell populations at successive stages along each pathway until a learning-dependent difference between input and output is found. This strategy is being used by several investigators, not only with the rabbit NM preparation but also with other vertebrate preparations (Cohen, 1974; Disterhoft et al., 1982; Woody, 1974). We chose a strategy that differs from that outlined earlier only in terms of where to begin the input–output analysis. At the time we began the present series of studies there was a considerable literature on the role of the hippocampus and surrounding temporal lobe areas in human memory (see Squire, 1982), and evidence from some animal conditioning studies that the activity of hippocampal neurons was modified durng learning (Olds, Disterhoft, Segal, Kornblith, & Hirsh, 1972; Segal, 1973). The work on human amnesia was particularly important because it meant that the localization problem in humans had at least been partially solved; that is, the surgically performed temporal lobectomies appeared, at the very least, to disrupt part of a major multisynaptic circuit essential for normal mnemonic processes and also strongly suggested that a primary site of learning-induced neural change is the hippocampus or one of its monosynaptic connections. We sought to take advantage of the degree of localization of memory function that these data provided by beginning our analysis with the hippocampus. Our rationale has been to initially see whether the hippocampal circuit was activated during NM conditioning, and if so, to begin the input–output analysis in search of the primary site of plasticity responsible for hippocampal cellular changes. By using the rabbit NM preparation, which we assume will limit the number of brain areas and circuits involved in learning, and beginning our analysis with the hippocampus, which appears to be at least one component in a circuit known to be essential for normal learning and memory, we hope to more rapidly identify a primary site of learning-induced neural plasticity in a mammalian species.

The studies we have reviewed here indicate that the hippocampal circuit is indeed preferentially activated during NM conditioning, and that hippocampal pyramidal neurons respond with a specific pattern of discharge only when the animal is being conditioned. The pattern of discharge is apparently coding specific parameters of the learned NM behavior. Analysis of hippocampal afferents to date has failed to find neural activity in any of three structures examined that can account for the neural plasticity seen in hippocampus. Our analysis is not complete, however, and we are continuing to screen other structures that are known to project to the hippocampus (e.g., locus coeruleus, raphe n., n. reuniens, and others).

Differences Between Hippocampal Pyramidal and Granule Cell Activity During NM Conditioning

The hippocampus has been the focus of considerable electrophysiological and anatomical analysis, largely because it is a simple cortical structure with a laminar arrangement of its neurons and neuronal processes that make it ideal for the study of synaptic transmission. The results of this past work have described the dentate mossy fiber-to-CA3/4 projection as one of the major components of the hippocampal tri-synaptic pathway. The tri-synaptic pathway begins with afferents from the entorhinal cortex terminating on the outer 2/3 of granule cell dendrites (Lorente de No, 1934). This entorhinal input is powerfully excitatory (Andersen, Holmquist, Voorhoeve, 1966a), and is glutaminergic in nature (Nadler et al., 1976). Granule cells, in turn, give rise to a mossy fiber system that synapses on proximal apical and basal dendrites of CA3 and CA4 pyramidal neurons (Gaarskjaer, 1978; Lynch et al., 1973). This projection also is powerfully excitatory (Alger & Teyler, 1976; Andersen, Bliss, & Skrede, 1971a). CA3 and 4 pyramidal neurons project to CA1 and 2 pyramids via a Schaffer collateral system that terminates onto apical and basal dendritic processes (Hjorth–Simonsen, 1973; Swanson et al., 1978), forming the final component of the tri-synaptic circuit. Electrical stimulation studies conducted in anesthetized animals (Andersen et al., 1966b, 1971b) awake, behaving animals (Winson & Abzug, 1978), and in vitro tissue slices (Skrede & Westgaard, 1971) have demonstrated that each of these synapses is not only excitatory but sufficiently powerful that activation of the perforant path can elicit disynaptically evoked responses in the CA3/4 area and even tri-synaptically evoked responses in the CA1/2 pyramidal zone. The organization and potency of this three-synapse chain has led to its characterization as the major input–output circuit of the hippocampal system (Andersen, Holmquist, & Voorhoeve, 1966b; Andersen, Bland, & Dudar, 1973).

Results from the studies presented here, however, are not consistent with such a characterization, at least with respect to the mossy fiber-to-CA3/4 projections. Single-unit responses of dentate granule cells during NM conditioning exhibit a high degree of homogeneity, and are strongly phase-locked to a theta rhythmicity. In contrast, hippocampal pyramidal neurons display a response pattern during conditioning that correlates with the form of the NM response. Although granule cells exhibit a similar discharge pattern even between animals, pyramidal neuron responses vary between animals to the extent that different animals display different forms of NM response (see Fig. 8.8). Even the time course of changes in pyramidal and granule cells across trials is different. Granule cell activity is altered very early during conditioning, as is pyramidal activity; but granule cell responses remain invariant from that point on, whereas pyramidal cell responsiveness continues to be gradually altered over successive training trials.

This disparity we have found between granule-pyramidal cell activity in the awake, behaving animal is supported by work of others as well (Rose & Lynch, personal communication; Segal, Disterhoft, & Olds, 1972). The disparity cannot be accounted for on the basis of the observations being made in the awake, unanesthetized animal, because Winson and Abzug (1979) have described a consistent perforant path-to-CA1, tri-synaptic activation in an unanesthetized, behaving preparation. The major difference in that electrical stimulation has been used in studies that have characterized the tri-synaptic circuit as the major hippocampal input–output pathway, whereas studies such as ours have used peripheral stimulation of the awake organism. The obvious conclusion is that the electrical stimulation studies have identified the *capacity* of the hippocampal system for tri-synaptic transmission, though under the behavioral conditions used by us, Segal et al. (1972), and Rose and Lynch, that capacity may not be utilized. Our work and the work of Segal et al. (1972), however, have shown a high degree of correspondence between the activities of CA3/4 pyramidal neurons and CA1/2 pyramidal neurons. During behavioral conditioning, then, the second and third components of the tri-synaptic circuit appear to be more tightly coupled than the first and second components. If in a variety of other behavioral situations the same lack of correspondence between dentate and CA3/4 activity is corroborated, our present conceptions of the nature of mossy fiber-to-CA3/4 synaptic transmission must be modified. It is possible, for example, that under normal, behavioral conditions dentate granule cell activity is not a potent, driving input to CA3/4 pyramids but instead serves as a more subtle, modulating input (see suggestions by Segal et al., 1972). On the other hand, granule cell input to CA3/4 may be very potent under awake, behaving conditions, but what we are describing as "disparities" between dentate input and CA3 output is a nonlinear transformation of dentate activity. The strong correspondence between CA3/4 and CA1/2 pyramidal responses may result from a qualitatively different synaptic organization that allows for linear transformations. These possibilities reflect issues and questions concerning signal processing in the CNS that we have yet to address but are of obvious importance in making judgments about the transmission of learning-dependent unit responses through the nervous system.

Behavioral Consequence of Hippocampal Cellular Activity During NM Conditioning

If we can interpret the effects of hippocampectomy in terms of a declarative or data-based memory function for hippocampus, it is not clear why such profound changes in hippocampal cellular activity occur during delay conditioning that does not require an intact hippocampus. One possibility is that the declarative process is operative under all learning conditions, but that only certain learning conditions require the results of that process for successful learning. An alternative possibility is that the declarative process, as indexed by the level of hippocampal activity during learning, is activated to differing degrees depending on task requirements. For example, one might expect hippocampal activity to be highly active during a reversal learning paradigm but not during a delay conditioning paradigm. The former possibility is consistent with the data reviewed here on unit recordings from the hippocampus durng NM conditioning, though a final evaluation must await the results of hippocampal recordings during reversal learning for comparison. Previous studies completed by Olds, Segal, and Disterhoft also have shown little substantive difference between levels of hippocampal activity during a one-tone task, a discrimination task, and a reversal task (Disterhoft & Segal, 1978; Segal & Olds, 1972). Deadwyler, West, and Lynch, (1979a,b) however, have shown that granule cell activity was unaltered during learning in a one-tone operant task, but that during discrimination and reversal tasks, granule cells exhibited differentially enhanced responses to the CS + . So it appears that support for both alternatives exist.

If hippocampal neurons are highly activated under all learning conditions but the mnemonic process represented by that activity is necessary for learning only certain types of tasks, (as appears to be true for NM conditioning), one implication is that structures efferent to the hippocampus are functioning in ways other than simply relaying hippocampal output, and thus, play an important role in the transmission of hippocampal information to ultimate motoneurons. Lesion data (e.g., Schmaltz & Theois, 1972) suggest that although during a delay paradigm hippocampal activity is highly responsive, that activity has little ultimate influence on motoneurons controlling NM behavior. One possibility, then, is that at some point in the multisynaptic projection of hippocampal activity to brain stem regions, hippocampal responses are "gated" out or inhibited from influencing the final common path. Such an hypothesis implies that we will detect a significant difference between the activities of structures efferent to the hippocampus under conditions of a delay paradigm compared to conditions of a reversal paradigm. In contrast, other nonlesion data suggest that hippocampal output does have an ultimate influence on reflex pathways mediating the NM response, even during a delay paradigm. For example subseizure electrical stimulation of the hippocampus and lesions of medial septum (that disrupt hippocampal activity) both delay the onset of conditioned NM responded (Berry & Thompson, 1978; Salafia, Chiaia, & Ramirez, 1979). A second hypothesis, then, is that a neural organization efferent to hippocampus functions in an "or-gate" capacity to allow hippocampal output or equivalent output from some other brain structure to influence the final common path. The latter possibility necessitates that the same neural function be mediated by two different brain structures, so that parallel circuits exist for mediating learned behavior. There are other possibilities as well, but the issues raised here indicate that a complete understanding of the role of the hippocampus in classical conditioning of the NM response must come from analyses that extend beyond the hippocampus and the limbic system.

ACKNOWLEDGMENTS

This work was supported by grants from The McKnight Foundation, NSF (BNS-8021395), and NIMH RCDA award (MH-00343) to T.W.B., and grants from NIMH (MH-36506 and MH-37545) to D.J.W.

REFERENCES

Alger, B. E., & Teyler, T. J. (1976). Long-term and short-term plasticity in the CA1, CA3, and dentate regions of the rat hippocampal slice. *Brain Research, 110,* 436–480.

Andersen, P. (1959). Interhippocampal impulses. I. Origin, course and distribution in cat, rabbit, and rat. *Acta Physiologica Scandinavica, 47,* 63–90.

Andersen, P. (1960). Interhippocampal impulses. II. Apical dendritic activation of CA1 neurons. *Acta Physiologica Scandinavica, 48,* 178–208.

Andersen, P. (1960). Interhippocampal impulses. III. Basal dendritic activation of CA3 neurons. *Acta Physiologica Scandinavica, 48,* 209–230.

Andersen, P., Bland, B. H., & Dudar, J. D. (1973). Organization of the hippocampal output. *Experimental Brain Research, 17,* 152–168.

Andersen, P., Bliss, T. V. P., & Skrede, K. K. (1971a). Lamellar organization of hippocampal excitatory pathways. *Experimental Brain Research, 13,* 222–238.

Andersen, P., Bliss, T. V. P., & Skrede, K. K. (1971b). Unit analysis of hippocampal population spikes. *Experimental Brain Research, 13,* 208–221.

Andersen, P., Eccles, J. C., & Løyning, Y. (1964a). Location of postsynaptic inhibitory synapses on hippocampal pyramids. *Journal of Neurophysiology, 27,* 592–607.

Andersen, P., Eccles, J. C., & Løyning, Y. (1964b). Pathway of postsynaptic inhibition in the hippocampus. *Journal of Neurophysiology, 27,* 608–619.

Andersen, P., Holmqvist, B., & Voorhoeve, P. E. (1966a). Entorhinal activation of dentate granule cells. *Acta Physiologica Scandinavica, 66,* 448–460.

Andersen, P., Holmqvist, B., & Voorhoeve, P. E. (1966b). Excitatory synapses on hippocampal apical dendrites activated by entorhinal stimulation. *Acta Physiologica Scandinavica, 66,* 461–472.

Bassett, J. L., & Berger, T. W. (1981). Non-thalamic efferent projections of the posterior cingulate gyrus in the rabbit. *Society for Neuroscience Abstracts, 7,* 885.

Berger, T. W. (1982). Hippocampal pyramidal cell activity during two-tone discrimination and reversal conditioning of the rabbit nictitating membrane response. *Society for Neuroscience Abstracts, 8,* 483.

Berger, T. W., Alger, B., & Thompson, R. F. (1976). Neuronal substrate of classical conditioning in the hippocampus. *Science, 192,* 483–485.

Berger, T. W., Clark, G. A., & Thompson, R. F. (1980). Neuronal activity recorded from limbic structures during conditioning. *Physiological Psychology, 8,* 155–167.

Berger, T. W., Laham, R. I., & Thompson, R. F. (1980). Hippocampal unit-behavior correlations during classical conditioning. *Brain Research, 193,* 229–248.

Berger, T. W., & Orr, W. B. (1982). Role of the hippocampus in reversal learning of the rabbit nictitating membrane response. In C. D. Woody (Ed.), *Conditioning: Representation of involved neural functions.* New York: Plenum Press.

Berger, T. W., & Orr, W. B. (1983). Hippocampectomy selectively disrupts discrimination reversal conditioning of the rabbit nictitating membrane response. *Behavioral Brain Research, 8,* 49–68.

Berger, T. W., Rinaldi, P., Weisz, D. J., & Thompson, R. F. (1983). Single-unit analysis of hippocampal cellular activity during classical conditioning of the rabbit nictitating membrane response. *Journal of Neurophysiology, 50,* 1197–1219.

Berger, T. W., Swanson, G. W., Milner, T. A., Lynch, G. S., & Thompson, R. F. (1980). Reciprocal anatomical connections between hippocampus and subiculum: Evidence for subicular innervation of regio superior. *Brain Research, 183,* 265–276.

Berger, T. W., & Thompson, R. F. (1977). Limbic system interrelations: Functional division among hippocampal-septal connections. *Science, 197,* 587–589.

Berger, T. W., & Thompson, R. F. (1978). Neuronal plasticity in the limbic system during classical conditioning of the rabbit nictitating membrane response. I. The hippocampus. *Brain Research, 145,* 323–346.

Berger, T. W., & Thompson, R. F. (1978b). Neuronal plasticity in the limbic system during classical conditioning of the rabbit nictitating membrane response. II. Septum and mammillary bodies. *Brain Research, 156,* 293–314.

Berger, T. W., & Thompson, R. F. (1978c). Identification of pyramidal cells as the critical elements in hippocampal neuronal plasticity during learning. *Proceedings of the National Academy of Sciences, 75,* 1572–1576.

Berger, T. W., & Thompson, R. F. (1982). Hippocampal cellular plasticity during extinction of classically conditioning nictitating membrane behavior. *Behavioural Brain Research, 4,* 63–76.

Berry, S. D., & Thompson, R. F. (1978). Prediction of learning rate from the hippocampal electroencephalogram. *Science, 200,* 1298–1300.

Berthier, N. E., & Moore, J. W. (1980). Role of extraocular muscles in the rabbit (Orycotolagus cuniculus) nictitating membrane response. *Physiology and Behavior, 24,* 931–937.

Blackstad, T. W. (1956). Commissural connections of the hippocampal region in the rat, with special reference to their mode of termination. *Journal of Comparative Neurology, 105,* 417–537.

Bland, B. H., Andersen, P., Ganes, T., & Sveen, O. (1980). Automated analysis of rhythmicity of physiologically identified hippocampal formation neurons. *Experimental Brain Research, 38,* 205–219.

Cegavske, C. F., Patterson, M. M., & Thompson, R. F. (1979). Neuronal unit activity in the abducens nucleus during classical conditioning of the nictitating membrane response in the rabbit. *Journal of Comparative and Physiological Psychology, 93,* 595–609.

Clark, G. A., Berger, T. W., & Thompson, R. F. (1978). Role of entorhinal cortex during classical conditioning: Evidence for entorhinal-dentate facilitation. *Society for Neuroscience Abstracts, 4,* 217.

Coates, S. R., & Thompson, R. F. (1978). Comparing neuronal plasticity in the hippocampus during classical conditioning of the rabbit nictitating membrane response to light and tone. *Society for Neuroscience Abstracts, 4,* 256.

Cohen, D. H. (1974). The neural pathways and informational flow mediating a conditioned autonomic response. In L. DiCara (Ed.), *Limbic and autonomic nervous system research.* New York: Plenum Press.

Cohen, N. J., & Corkin, S. (1981). The amnesic patient: Learning and retention of a cognitive skill. *Society for Neuroscience Abstracts, 7,* 235.

Cohen, N. J., & Squire, L. R. (1980). Preserved learning and retention of pattern analyzing skill in amnesia: Dissociation of knowing how and knowing that. *Science, 210,* 207–209.

Deadwyler, S. A., West, M., & Lynch, G. (1979a). Synaptically identified hippocampal slow potentials during behavior. *Brain Research, 161,* 211–225.

Deadwyler, S. A., West, M., & Lynch, G. (1979b). Activity of dentate granule cells during learning: Differentiation of perforant path input. *Brain Research, 169,* 29–43.

Disterhoft, J. F., & Segal, M. (1978). Neuron activity in rat hippocampus and motor cortex during discrimination reversal. *Brain Research Bulletin, 3,* 583–588.

Disterhoft, J. F., Shipley, M. T., & Kraus, N. (1982). Analyzing the rabbit NM conditioned reflex arc. In C. D. Woody (Ed.), *Conditioning: Representation of involved neural function.* New York: Plenum.

Douglas, R. J. (1967). The hippocampus and behavior. *Psychological Bulletin, 67,* 416–442.

Gaarskjaer, F. B. (1978). Organization of the mossy fiber system of the rat studied in extended hippocampi. II. Experimented analysis of fiber distribution with silver impregnation methods. *Journal of Comparative Neurology, 178,* 73–88.

Gray, T. S., McMaster, S. E., Harvey, J. A., & Gormezano, I. (1981). Localization of retractor bulbi motoneurons in the rabbit. *Brain Research, 226,* 93–106.

Hirsh, R. (1974). The hippocampus and contextual retrieval of information from memory: A theory. *Behavioral Biology, 12,* 421–444.

Hjorth-Simonsen, A. (1973). Some intrinsic connections of the hippocampus in the rat: An experimental analysis. *Journal of Comparative Neurology, 147,* 145–162.

Hjorth-Simonsen, A., & Jeune, B. (1972). Origin and termination of the hippocampal perforant path in the rat studied by silver impregnation. *Journal of Comparative Neurology, 144,* 215–232.

Ibata, Y., Desiraju, T., & Pappas, G. D. (1971). Light and electron microscopic study of the projection of the medial septal nucleus to the hippocampus of the cat. *Experimental Neurology, 33,* 103–122.

Jacobs, B. L., Foote, S. L., & Bloom, F. E. (1978). Differential projection of neurons within the dorsal raphe nucleus of the rat: A horseradish peroxidase (HRP) study. *Brain and Research, 147,* 149–153.

Kandel, E. R. (1976). *Cellular basis of behavior.* San Francisco: Freeman.

Kimble, D. P. (1968). Hippocampus and internal inhibition. *Psychological Bulletin, 70,* 285–295.

Lincoln, J. S., McCormick, D. A., & Thompson, R. F. (1982). Ipsilateral cerebellar lesions prevent learning of the classically conditioned nictitating membrane/eyelid response. *Brain Research, 242,* 190–193.

Lorente de No, R. (1934). Studies on the structure of the cerebral cortex. II. Continuation of the study of the ammonic system. *Journal of Psychological Neurology, 46,* 113–177.

Loy, R., Koziell, D. A., Lindsey, J. D., & Moore, R. Y. (1980). Noradrenergic innervation of the adult rat hippocampal formation. *Journal of Comparative Neurology, 189,* 699-710.

Lynch, G., Smith, R. L., & Mensah, P., Cotman, C. (1973). Tracing the dentate gyrus mossy fiber system with horseradish peroxidase histochemistry. *Experimental Neurology, 40,* 516-524.

MacVicar, B. A., & Dudek, F. E. (1980). Dye-coupling between CA3 pyramidal cells in slices of rat hippocampus. *Brain Research, 196,* 494-497.

McCormick, D. A., Clark, G. A., Levond, D. G., & Thompson, R. F (1982). Initial localization of the memory trace for a basic form of learning. *Proceedings of the National Academy of Sciences (Wash.), 79,* 2731-2742.

McCormick, D. A., Lavond, D. G., & Thompson, R. F. (in preparation). *Concomitant classical conditioning of the rabbit nictitating membrane and eyelid response: Correlations and implications.*

Mahut, H., & Zola, S. M. (1973). A non-modality specific impairment in spatial learning after fornix lesions in monkeys. *Neuropsychologia, 11,* 255-269.

Meibach, R. C., & Siegel, A. (1977). Thalamic projections of the hippocampal formation: Evidence for an alternate pathway involving the internal capsule. *Brain Research, 134,* 1-12.

Milner, B. (1966). Amnesia following operation on the temporal lobes. In C. W. M. Whitly & O. L. Zangwill (Eds.), *Amnesia.* London: Butterworths, Ch. 5.

Milner, B. (1970). Memory and the medial temporal regions of the brain. In K. H. Pribram & D. E. Broadhert (Eds.), *Biology of memory.* New York: Academic Press.

Moore, J. W. (1979). Brain processes and conditioning. In A. Dickinson & R. A. Boakes (Eds.), *Mechanisms of learning and motivation: A memorial volume to Jerzy Konorski.* Hillsdale, NJ: Lawrence Erlbaum Associates.

Mosko, S., Lynch, G., & Cotman, C. W. (1973). The distribution of septal projections to the hippocampus of the rat. *Journal of Comparative Neurology, 152,* 163-174.

Nadler, V. J., Vaca, K. W., White, W. F., Lynch, G. S., & Cotman, C. W. (1976). Aspartate and glutamate as possible transmitters of excitatory hippocampal afferents. *Nature, 260,* 538-540.

Nauta, W. J. H. (1956). An experimental study of the fornix system in the rat. *Journal of Comparative Neurology, 104,* 247-272.

Nicoll, R. A., & Alger, B. E. (1981). Synaptic activation may activate a calcium-dependent potassium conductance in hippocampal pyramidal cells. *Science, 212,* 957-959.

O'Keefe, J., & Nadel, L. (1978). *The Hippocampus as a Cognitive Map.* Oxford University Press.

Olds, J., Disterhoft, J. F., Segal, M., Kornblith, C. L., & Hirsh, R. (1972). Learning centers of rat brain mapped by measuring latencies of conditioned unit responses. *Journal of Neurophysiology, 35,* 202-219.

Patterson, M. M., Berger, T. W., & Thompson, R. F. (1979). Hippocampal neuronal plasticity recorded from cat during classical conditioning. *Brain Research, 163,* 339-343.

Penfield, W., & Milner, B. (1958). Memory deficit produced by bilateral lesions in the hippocampal zone. *American Medical Association Archives of Neurology and Psychiatry, 79,* 475-497.

Powell, G. M., Berthier, N. E., & Moore, J. W. (1979). Efferent neuronal control of the nictitating membrane response in rabbit (Oryctolagus cuniculus): A reexamination. *Physiology and Behavior, 23,* 299-308.

Powell, D. A., Lipkin, M., & Milligan, W. L. (1974). Concomitant changes in classically conditioned heart rate and corneoretinal potential discrimination in the rabbit (Oryctolagus cuniculus). *Learning and Motivation, 5,* 532-547.

Raisman, G. (1966). The connexions of the septum. *Brain, 89,* 317-348.

Raisman, G., Cowan, W. M., & Powell, T. P. S. (1965). The extrinsic afferent, commissural and association fibres of the hippocampus. *Brain, 88,* 963-995.

Raisman, G., Cowan, W. M., & Powell, T. P. S. (1966). An experimental analysis of the efferent projection of the hippocampus. *Brain, 89,* 83–108.

Ramon y Cajal, S. (1911). *Histologie du systeme nerveux de l'homme et des vertebres.* Paris, Maloine.

Salafia, W. R., Chiaia, N. L. & Ramirez, J. J. (1979). Retardation of rabbit nictitating membrane conditioning by subseizure electrical stimulation of hippocampus. *Physiology and Behavior, 22,* 451–455.

Schmaltz, L. W., & Theios, J. (1972). Acquisition and extinction of a classically conditioned response in hippocampectomized rabbits (Oryctolagus cunniculus). *Journal of Comparative and Physiological Psychology, 79,* 328–333.

Schneiderman, N. (1972). Response system divergencies in aversive classical conditioning. In A. H. Black & W. H. Prokasy (Eds.), *Classical conditioning II: Current theory and research* (pp. 341–376). New York: Appleton–Century–Crofts.

Schwartzkroin, P. A. (1975). Characteristics of CA1 neurons recorded intracellularly in the hippocampal in vitro slice preparation. *Brain Research, 85,* 523–436.

Scoville, W. B., & Milner, B. (1957). Loss of recent memory after bilateral hippocampal lesions. *Journal of Neurology & Neurosurgical Psychiatry, 20,* 11–21.

Segal, M. (1973). Flow of conditioned responses in limbic telencephalic system of the rat. *Journal of Neurophysiology, 36,* 840–845.

Segal, M., Disterhoft, J. F., & Olds, J. (1972). Hippocampal unit activity during classical aversive and appetitive conditioning. *Science, 175,* 792–794.

Segal, M., & Olds, J. (1972). Behavior of units in hippocampal circuit of the rat during learning. *Journal of Neurophysiology, 35,* 680–690.

Semple-Rowland, S. L., Bassett, J. L., & Berger, T. W. (1981). Subicular projections to retrosplenial cortex in the rabbit. *Society for Neuroscience Abstracts, 7,* 886.

Sidman, M., Stoddard, L. T., & Mohr, J. P. (1968). Some additional quantitative observations of immediate memory in a patient with bilateral hippocampal lesions. *Neuropsychologia, 6,* 245–254.

Skrede, K., & Westgaard, R. H. (1971). The transverse hippocampal slice: A well-defined cortical structure maintained in vitro. *Brain Research, 35,* 589–593.

Solomon, P. R., & Moore, J. W. (1975). Latent inhibition and stimulus generalization of the classically conditioned nictitating membrane response in rabbits (Oryctolagus cuniculus) following dorsal hippocampal ablation. *Journal of Comparative and Physiological Psychology, 89,* 1192–1203.

Spencer, W. A., & Kandel, E. R. (1968). Cellular and integrative properties of the hippocampal pyramidal cell and the comparative electrophysiology of cortical neurons. *Journal of International Neuroscience, 6,* 266.

Squire, L. R. (1982). The neuropsychology of human memory. *Annual Review of Neuroscience, 5,* 241–273.

Squire, L. R., & Zola-Morgan, S. (1982). The neurology of memory: The case for correspondence between the findings for man and non-human primate. In J. A. Deutsch (Ed.), *The physiological basis of memory* (2nd ed.). New York: Academic Press.

Steward, O. (1976). Topographic organization of the projections from the entorhinal area to the hippocampal formation of the rat. *Journal of Comparative Neurology, 167,* 285–314.

Swanson, L. W., & Cowan, W. M. (1977). An autoradiographic study of the organization of the efferent connections of the hippocampal formation in the rat. *Journal of Comparative Neurology, 172,* 49–84.

Swanson, L. W., & Cowan, W. M. (1979). Connections of the septal region in the rat. *Journal of Comparative Neurology, 186,* 621–655.

Swanson, L. W., Wyss, J. M., & Cowan, W. M. (1978). An autoradiographic study of the organization of intrahippocampal association pathways in the rat. *Journal of Comparative Neurology, 181,* 681–716.

Thompson, R. F., Berger, T. W., Berry, S. D., & Hoehler, F. K. (1980). The search for the engram. II. In D. McFadden (Ed.), *Neural mechanisms in behavior: A Texas symposium.* New York: Springer-Verlag.

Thompson, R. F., Berger, T. W., & Madden, J. (1983). Cellular processes of learning and memory in the mammalian CNS. In W. M. Cowan, Z. W. Hall, & E. R. Kandel (Eds.), *Annual review of neurosciences* (pp. 447–491). Palo Alto, CA: Annual Reviews, 6.

Weisz, D. J., Clark, G. A., Yang, B. Y., Solomon, P. R., Berger, T. W., & Thompson, R. F. (1980). Dentate single unit and field potential activity during NM conditioning in rabbit. *Society for Neuroscience Abstracts, 44,* 937–950.

Winson, J. (1980). Influence of raphe nuclei on neuronal transmission from perforant pathway through dentate gyrus. *Journal of Neurophysiology, 44,* 937–950.

Winson, J., & Abzug, C. (1978). Neuronal transmission through hippocampal pathways dependent on behavior. *Journal of Neurophysiology, 41,* 716–732.

Wong, R. K. S., Prince, D. A., & Basbaum, A. T. (1979). Intradendritic recordings from hippocampal neurons. *Proceedings of the National Academy of Science, USA, 76,* 986–990.

Woody, C. D. (1974). Aspects of the electrophysiology of cortical processes related to the development and performance of learned motor responses. *The Physiologist, 17,* 49–69.

9 Neural Correlates of Acquisition Rate

Stephen D. Berry
Miami University

Donald J. Weisz
Yale University

Laura A. Mamounas
Stanford University

NEURAL CORRELATES OF ACQUISITION RATE

A number of correlational studies have implicated the hippocampus and related structures in classical conditioning of the nictitating membrane (NM) response in rabbits (for a review, see Thompson, Berger, Berry, & Hoehler, 1980). In their summary, Thompson et al. conclude:

> In the learning paradigm we employ, *the growth of the hippocampal unit response is completely predictive of subsequent behavioral learning.* If the hippocampal response does not develop, the animal will not learn. If it develops rapidly, the animal will learn rapidly. If it develops slowly, the animal will learn slowly. Further, the temporal form of the hippocampal response predicts the temporal form of the behavioral response. (p. 212)

One test of this hypothesized hippocampal involvement in classical NM conditioning would be to assess the behavioral effects of disruption of hippocampal activity. Although hippocampal lesions have little effect upon initial acquisition (Schmaltz & Theios, 1972), Salafia and his colleagues (Salafia & Allan, 1980; Salafia, Romano, Tynan, & Host, 1977) have demonstrated severe disruption of NM conditioning after direct electrical stimulation of the hippocampus. Other treatments that affect hippocampal activity, such as septal lesions (Powell, Milligan, & Buchanan, 1976) and anticholinergic drugs (Moore, Goodell, & Solomon, 1976; Powell, 1979; Solomon & Gottfried, 1981), have been shown to retard acquisition of the NM response. Unfortunately, neural recordings have not typically been performed during or after such disruptive treatments, so the precise impact of, for example, septal lesions or anticholinergic drugs on hippocampal activity in the learning situation is not known. Rather than assuming that such treatments alter the hippocampus-learning relationships described by Thompson et al. (1980), it is important to conduct experiments that measure *both* neural and behavioral effects of manipulations that retard conditioning. This chapter is a summary of some experiments of that nature. Specifically, we tested correlations between neural activity and behavioral learning in (1) intact, undrugged animals displaying variations in conditioning rate, (2) animals with disruptive medial septal lesions, and (3) animals treated with Δ^9-THC, a psychoactive component of marijuana with demonstrated effects on hippocampal activity (Cosroe, Jones, & Laird, 1976; Segal, 1978). In all experiments, recordings were taken of CA1 hippocampal EEG and multiple-unit activity as well as behavior.

EXPERIMENT 1

An aspect of conditioning that has important implications for behavioral and psychobiological studies of learning is the occurrence of individual differences in acquisition rate. In the absence of specific manipulations, substantial variations in learning rate can be observed, even in well-controlled classical conditioning paradigms such as the rabbit nictitating membrane response. Such variations are especially important to hypotheses on the neural substrates of conditioning because differences in behavioral acquisition should correlate highly with variations in relevant neural processes. This experiment demonstrates a significant relationship between learning rate and several indices of hippocampal electrical activity, most notably the hippocampal EEG.

Methods

The standard NM conditioning procedure developed by Gormezano (1966) was used. Animals were given 13 blocks of trials, with each block consisting of eight paired (tone-air puff) trials and one test trial (tone-alone). The conditioned stimulus (CS) was a 1-KHz, 85-dB, 350-msec tone. The unconditioned stimulus (UCS), a 210-g/cm² corneal air puff, was given 250 msec after tone onset. The mean intertrial interval was 60 sec, varying between 50 and 70 sec.

Control animals received explicitly unpaired tone and air puff presentations with a 30-sec mean intertrial interval.

Under halothane anesthesia, 16 subjects were implanted with chronic, stainless steel multiple-unit electrodes in area CA1 of the dorsal hippocampus. After a 1-week recovery period, the rabbits were given one session of adaptation to the conditioning apparatus, followed by up to 4 days of paired training. Unit spike discharges (from small clusters of neurons) and slow waves were recorded on magnetic tape for off-line analysis on a PDP-12 computer. Two-minute samples of spontaneous EEG and unit activity were recorded before and after each training session. The analysis of unit activity changes during trials consisted of converting spikes larger than a preset discriminator level into standard pulses. The data collection program counted the number of unit discharges in each 3-msec time bin throughout the trial. Data collection began 250 msec prior to CS onset (PreCS period or baseline), continued through 250 msec of the CS period (tone on), and ended with a 250-msec sample after UCS onset (UCS period). Thus, each trial yielded 750 msec of data, which were accumulated across eight trials to produce peristimulus time histograms of multiple-unit activity. These data were converted into standard scores for the CS and UCS periods for each block of trials. Each score consisted of the mean change in unit counts ($\overline{CS}$ or $\overline{UCS}$ minus $\overline{PreCS}$ baseline) divided by the standard deviation of the PreCS activity.

Analysis of slow wave frequencies used a zero crossing program that measured the period between successive positive-going baseline crossings in the EEG, converted this to frequency, and accumulated the number of waves in each frequency during a 2-minute sample. The records were band-pass filtered from 0.1-22 Hz for this analysis. The NM extension response was measured with a transducer conducted to a nylon loop in the nictitating membrane. The output was recorded on magnetic tape with the neuronal records of each trial. In analysis, the NM activity was digitized at 3-msec intervals and stored as an average response along with the eight trial averages of unit activity. Subjects were trained to a criterion of eight conditioned responses (CRs) in nine consecutive trials, or for a maximum of four training sessions. A CR was defined as ½ mm of NM extension prior to UCS onset or, on test trials, within 500 msec of CS onset.

Results and Discussion

An analysis of hippocampal EEG frequencies indicated that a 2-minute baseline sample of spontaneous EEG, recorded prior to the start of training, predicted the subsequent rate of NM conditioning. Observing a systematic difference in the shape of frequency histograms between fast- and slow-learning rabbits, we correlated the number of trials to reach asymptotic criterion (TTC) with the amount of activity in frequencies from 2 to 22 Hz. Negative correlations between TTC and 2–8 Hz activity ($r = -.66$, $df = 14$, $p < .01$) indicated that those frequencies predicted faster acquisition rates, whereas higher frequencies (8–22 Hz) predicted slower learning ($r = .64$, $df = 14$, $p < .01$). An index of the overall distribution of EEG frequencies (the proportion of high to low frequencies: 8–22/2–8) was significantly correlated with TTC ($r = .72$, $df = 14$, $p < .01$), as illustrated in the scatterplot in Fig. 9.1.

There is a strong similarity between the change in type (sign) of correlation at or near 8 Hz in our study and the discovery of pharmacologically distinct systems controlling hippocampal EEG frequencies in rats and rabbits. Vanderwolf and his colleagues (Vanderwolf, Kramis, & Robinson, 1978) have shown that activity below 7 Hz can be blocked by atropine but not urethane, whereas activity from 7 to 12 Hz is unaffected by atropine but blocked by

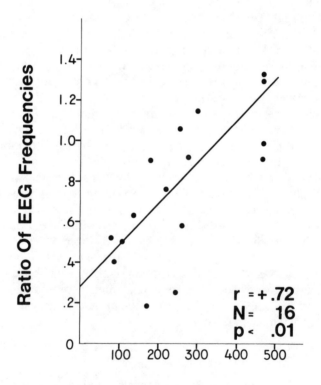

Trials To Criterion

FIG. 9.1   Scatterplot illustrating the correlation between trials to criterion and a ratio of slow-wave frequencies, consisting of the amount of 8–22 Hz activity divided by the 2–8 Hz activity. Slow-wave samples were recorded prior to the start of training. (Redrawn from Berry & Thompson, 1978.)

PRETRAINING

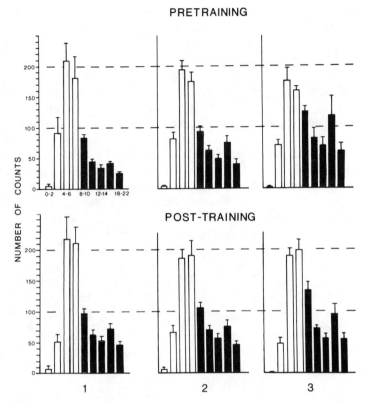

POST-TRAINING

FIG. 9.2 Frequency histograms of 2 minute slow-wave samples, showing the amount of activity in the 2–22 Hz range. Top shows means of pretraining samples for: (1) animals reaching criterion on Day 2, (2) criterion on Days 2 or 3, and (3) Day 4 or criterion not reached. Bottom shows postcriterion samples for the same three groups. Note that the posttraining samples are more similar than the pretraining. (Redrawn from Berry, 1982.)

urethane. Their interpretation specified movement-related hippocampal functions that we have not assessed, but our results support some distinction between hippocampal EEG frequencies on behavioral grounds — operation of the atropine-sensitive system correlates with rapid behavioral acquisition, whereas the presence of frequencies not blocked by atropine (8–22 Hz) predicts slower learning. Figure 9.2 shows the averaged frequency histograms for fast (<120 TTC), medium (120–240 TTC), and slow learners (>240 TTC). Note the clear differences in frequency composition in averaged histograms across the top row. The bottom row shows the mean histograms for the same three groups derived from a 2-minute sample taken at the end of each subject's criterion training session. Note that the differences between these groups are not as strong as above, a fact borne out by the lack of correlation between the postcriterion frequency index and TTC ($r = .01$). Analy-

sis of pretraining to posttraining change in EEG frequencies indicated that
fast- and slow-learning subjects showed opposite shifts across training. Figure 9.3 shows the "difference histograms" derived by subtracting the pretraining EEG sample from the postcriterion frequency histogram. On the left
are differences in total 2–8 and 8–22 Hz activity for the three learning-rate
groups. Note the opposite changes in groups 1 versus 3. On the right the
pre–post changes are shown for each frequency, again illustrating the qualitative difference in the type of shift seen between groups. In order to assess
these shifts on an individual basis, we computed the pre–post difference in
EEG frequency index for each animal and correlated it with TTC. Figure 9.4
is a scatterplot showing the strength of the EEG shift-TTC relationship
($r = .86$, $df = 14$, $p < .01$). It is important to note that unpaired control
subjects ($N = 4$) showed no consistent shift across two sessions, and that
several of the medium-learning-rate trained subjects showed no shift. The occurrence of such a range of EEG shifts across training may help interpret dis-
crepant findings by others on hippocampal EEG changes during learning.
For example, studies of hippocampal EEG changes during operant conditioning of cats have yielded both increases (Adey, 1966) and decreases
(Coleman & Lindsley, 1977; Grastyan, Lissak, Madarasz, & Donhoffer,
1959) in low frequencies ("theta") across training. If their results were re-

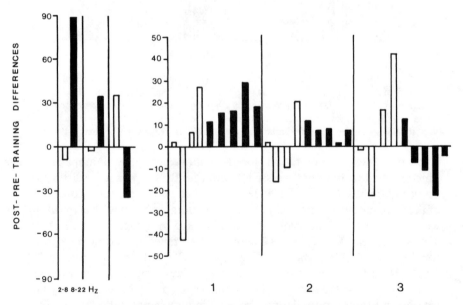

FIG. 9.3   Difference histograms illustrating (left) mean changes across training of the
total 2–8 Hz activity and the 8–22 total for three groups defined in Fig. 9.2. At right,
changes in individual frequency categories are shown for each group. Note the opposite
direction of change in Group 3 relative to 1 and 2. (Redrawn from Berry, 1982.)

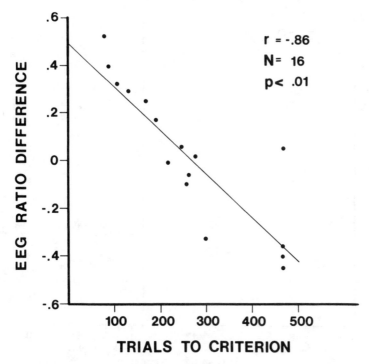

FIG. 9.4   Scatterplot showing the correlation between changes in the frequency ratio across training and trials to criterion. (Redrawn from Berry, 1982).

examined in light of potential learning-rate differences and possible over-training effects, our finding that direction of EEG shift correlates with learning *rate*, not learning per se, could explain the contradiction in their findings.

The examination of multiple-unit activity in the context of the learning rate of individual subjects indicated that the EEG predictors of behavioral learning also predicted the growth of unit activity in the hippocampus. Figure 9.5 illustrates the differences in multiple-unit standard scores for the three groups on the last day of training. The scores are for the last 125 msec of the CS period (left) and the first 125 msec of the UCS period, times during which conditioned responses were most likely. It is interesting to note that some animals not displaying a great increase in standard scores across training still performed at postcriterion levels behaviorally, that is, the Day 2 and 3 criterion groups were performing learned behaviors even though their standard scores were significantly lower than those of faster learning animals. These data reflect the differences seen throughout training in the responsiveness of hippocampal cells to the conditioning stimuli, differences that were predicted, along with learning rate, by the state of hippocampal EEG prior to the start of training. Because standard scores reflect mean activity change di-

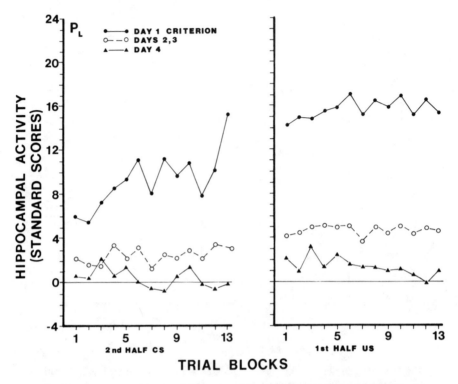

FIG. 9.5   Standard scores of multiple-unit activity recorded from the same electrode as the slow waves on the final day of training. Each score reflects the mean change in amount of unit activity for one trial block during the second half of the tone period or the first half of the air puff. The mean increase (or decrease) from baseline was divided by the standard deviation of the baseline. Thus, low scores could reflect either (1) less mean increase or (2) higher baseline variation. Subjects in all three groups had learned by this day. (Redrawn from Berry, 1982.)

vided by baseline variability, these lowered standard scores during training could be due to either a lack of responsiveness or an increase in variability of hippocampal cells (both have been observed). The fast learning group had the greatest mean percent increase in multiple-unit firing, accompanied by the lowest mean standard deviation in the baseline period. This was reversed in the slowest group, with the median group falling between. Thus, the differences in unit activity between groups reflected a combination of factors affecting responsiveness and variability.

In examining the way in which EEG frequencies relate to unit activity, we found a relationship between the EEG frequency index and the PreCS standard deviation. Although not significant ($r = .274$, $df = 13$), this statistic suggests a positive relationship between EEG frequencies and variability of baseline unit activity. This variability (as reflected in baseline S.D.) also correlated with the percent increase in unit activity during both the tone ($r = -.379$) and air puff periods ($r = -.394$). Finally, the magnitude of unit response to the tone CS was a highly significant negative correlate of trials to criterion ($r = -.668$, $df = 13$, $p < .01$). Thus, the mechanism by which hippocampal EEG predicts learning rate may be that it corresponds to: (1) greater variability in the background rate of unit activity that, in turn, predicts (2) reduced responsiveness to the conditioning stimuli, leading to (3) slower acquisition.

EXPERIMENT 2

Another approach to clarifying the nature of the hippocampus-learning relationships found in Experiment 1 is to manipulate hippocampal activity and observe any related behavioral effects. Because the hippocampal EEG is predictively related to learning rate, this experiment assessed the behavioral and neural effects of small medial lesions of the medial septal nucleus that are known to disrupt normal hippocampal EEG frequencies (for reviews, see CIBA Symposium, 1978; DeFrance, 1976).

Methods

The subjects were seven New Zealand White rabbits treated as in Experiment 1, with the exception that they received small, electrolytic lesions of the medial septal nucleus during the surgical implantation of the hippocampal recording electrodes. Lesion current was 0.8–1.0 ma for 8–10 sec, through a stainless steel electrode insulated except for 0.2 mm at the tip. Controls were seven of the subjects from Experiment 1 that were being trained at the same time as animals in the lesion group.

Results and Discussion

Medial septal nucleus (MSN) lesions were intentionally small (see Fig. 9.6) to insure that hippocampal output through the lateral septum was anatomically intact. Although low EEG frequencies were still present after these lesions, the MSN and control groups differed significantly on the EEG frequency index that predicted learning rate in Experiment 1 [$t(11) = 2.42$, $p < .05$]. As expected, MSN lesions reduced overall levels of 2–8 Hz activity and increased higher frequencies. This effect is illustrated in Fig. 9.7, which also indicates that the lesion-EEG effect persisted in posttraining EEG samples.

The behavioral effect of these lesions (see Fig. 9.8) was a delay in the appearance of conditioned responses followed by relatively normal rates of

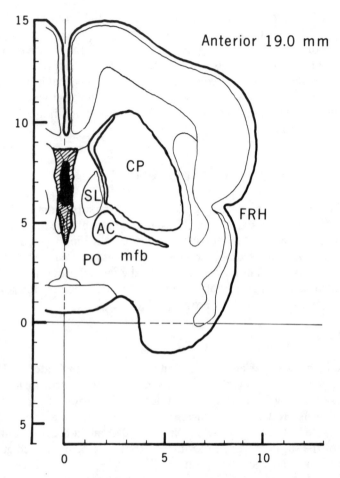

FIG. 9.6 Coronal plate of rabbit brain illustrating the maximal (cross-hatched) and minimal (black) extent of lesions in animals in the medial septal lesion group. (Redrawn from Berry & Thompson, 1979.)

acquisition—a type of behavioral deficit seen in NM conditioning following electrical disruption of the hippocampus (Salafia & Allan, 1980), cholinergic blockade of the septum (Solomon & Gottfried, 1981), or systemic drug treatments that probably disrupt hippocampal EEG (Moore et al., 1976; Powell, 1979). Other experiments on the effects of septal lesions on NM conditioning provide mixed results. Lockhart and Moore (1975) found no effect on behavioral acquisition (but poorer discrimination performance), whereas Powell et al. (1976) found both acquisition and discrimination to be impaired. A third study (Maser, Dienst, & O'Neal, 1974) reported enhanced acquisition following septal damage, although they trained the outer eyelid and used a much longer ISI. All of those studies involved massive septal ablations that damaged the lateral septal nuclei as well as the MSN, a treatment that interrupts most, if not all, of the subcortical hippocampal output (Swanson & Cowan, 1979). Thus, the impact of abnormal hippocampal activity upon diencephalic and brainstem mechanisms would be reduced.

MSN lesions also appeared to attenuate the responsiveness of hippocampal multiple-unit activity, as reflected by lower standard scores than seen

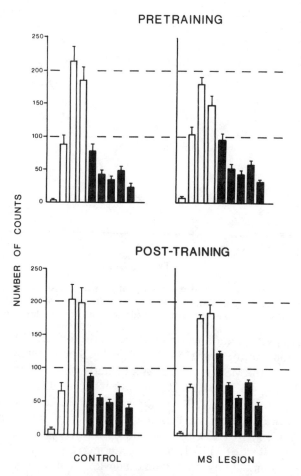

FIG. 9.7   Pretraining averaged EEG histograms for subjects in the control (left) and medial septal lesion groups (right). Note the relative decrease in low frequencies in the lesion group. The EEG index ratio (8–22 Hz/2–8 Hz) differed significantly between these groups [t (11) = 2.42, $p < .05$]. (Redrawn from Berry, 1982.)

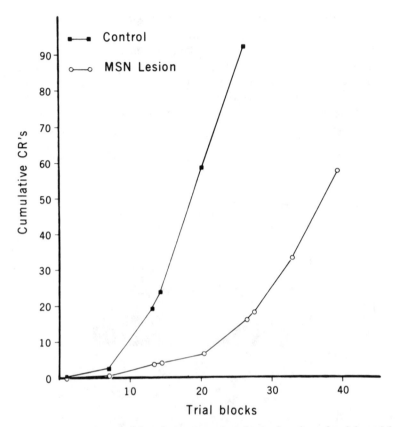

FIG. 9.8   Cumulative conditioned responses plotted as a function of training trial blocks for both control and medial septal lesion groups. The lesion group displayed a relatively later onset of conditioned responding. (Redrawn from Berry & Thompson, 1979.)

in controls. Analyses of variance on standard score data for the last 125 msec of the CS period and the first 125 msec of the UCS period showed that, on Day 1 of training, the MSN group had significantly smaller hippocampal responses [$F\,(1, 9) = 13.12, p < .01$] to the CS but did not differ from controls in responses to the UCS [$F\,(1, 9) = 2.98$, n.s.]. On the last day of training, however, significant differences between groups were observed in response to both CS [$F\,(1, 9) = 11.20, p < .01$] and UCS [$F\,(1, 9) = 8.73, p < .05$]. One interesting effect of MSN lesions was an increase in variability of the baseline rate of unit activity. The standard deviation of the prestimulus period was almost twice (185%) that of the control group. Higher variability was also seen in slow-learning animals in Experiment 1, suggesting that variability of background firing rate may be a factor in the slowing of the learning process.

EXPERIMENT 3

Drug manipulations can also be used to disrupt hippocampal activity without direct damage to the septo-hippocampal system. Therefore, the EEG-behavior relationships seen in Experiments 1 and 2 were examined further in a pharmacological study in which delta-9-tetrahydrocannabinol (THC), which has been shown to alter hippocampal EEG and unit activity patterns (Cosroe et al., 1976; Segal, 1978), was administered prior to the training sessions.

Methods

Training was conducted as in Experiments 1 and 2, with the exception that subjects received intravenous injections of either control vehicle (poly vinyl pyrrolidone, PVP, and saline), 0.5 mg/kg THC, or 1.0 mg/kg THC. Injections were given 10 min prior to the start of training.

Results and Discussion

Figure 9.9 shows the shifts in various EEG frequency categories 10 min after administration of either PVP, 0.5 mg/kg THC, or 1.0 mg/kg THC. In a dose-dependent manner, THC administration caused a decrease in 4–8 Hz EEG activity. These decreases were even more pronounced at 60 min postinjection (see Fig. 9.10). For statistical purposes, the following frequency categories were analyzed: 0–4 Hz, 4–8 Hz, 8–12 Hz, and 12–18 Hz. Significant drug effects were obtained for the 0–4 and 4–8 Hz categories during both the 10- and 60-minute postinjection EEG samples. Analyses of variance showed differences in 0–4 Hz at 10 minutes [F (2, 16) = 4.23, $p < .05$] and 60 minutes [F (2, 16) = 6.18, $p < .05$]. EEG from 4–8 Hz also differed at 10 [F (2, 16) = 9.14, $p < .05$] and 60 minutes [F (2, 16) = 6.72, $p < .05$]. Newman–Keuls tests revealed significant differences between the 1.0 mg/kg THC group and the PVP controls for 0–4 Hz and 4–8 Hz categories in both 10- and 60-minute samples. The 0–4 and 4–8 Hz frequencies in the 0.5 mg/kg THC group were significantly different from controls in the 60-minute sample. In general, THC increased 0–4 Hz and decreased 4–8 Hz activity. These effects were dose dependent; that is, the higher THC dose produced greater effects.

In this experiment, behavioral training began immediately after the 10-minute postinjection EEG sample. Figure 9.11 depicts the percentage conditioned responses (CRs) for trial blocks on the first 2 days of training. As can be seen, there was a dose-dependent effect of THC on CRs as measured by the number of trials necessary to reach a criterion of eight CRs in nine con-

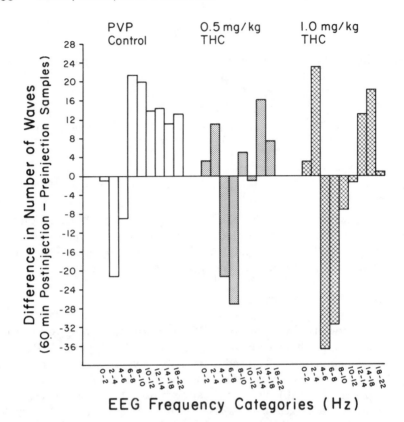

FIG. 9.9   Difference histogram (predrug histogram subtracted from 10-minute post-injection histogram). This measure was calculated for each subject, then averaged within dosage group: control, 0.5 mg/kg THC, 1.0 mg/kg THC. Note the drug-produced decrease in low frequencies.

secutive trials ($\overline{X}_{PVP}$ = 157 trials; $\overline{X}_{0.5THC}$ = 270.1 trials; $\overline{X}_{1.0THC}$ = 327.2 trials). Newman–Keuls tests of the significant group effect [F (2, 17) = 4.34, $p < .05$] indicated that only animals in the highest THC dose group differed from controls.

Correlation coefficients were calculated using the trials to criterion for each animal as one variable and the shifts in EEG frequencies as the other. There was a significant positive correlation between trials to criterion and shifts of 0–4 Hz activity from predrug values to 60 minutes postdrug (r = .52, df = 17, $p < .05$). Animals with higher postdrug activity in the 0–4 Hz range took longer to learn. Significant negative correlations were found between trials to criterion and shifts in 4–8 Hz EEG at 10 minutes (r = −.58, df = 17, $p < .05$) and at 60 minutes (r = −.60, df = 17, $p < .05$); that is, animals that had greater 4–8 Hz activity postinjection took fewer trials to learn. These results, especially those for the 4–8 Hz frequency category, are consistent with the findings of Experiments 1 and 2 in that EEG activity in this range correlates with faster NM acquisition.

GENERAL DISCUSSION

The major findings in these experiments emphasize the strong relationship between several parameters of hippocampal activity and classical NM conditioning in rabbits. In the intact, undrugged animal, the distribution of frequencies in the hippocampal EEG prior to the start of training predicts not only the responsiveness of hippocampal multiple-unit activity to the conditioning stimuli but also the behavioral rate of acquisition. Changes in these EEG frequencies across training are also highly related to learning, but the strongest correlations are with learning *rate,* not learning per se. Fast- and

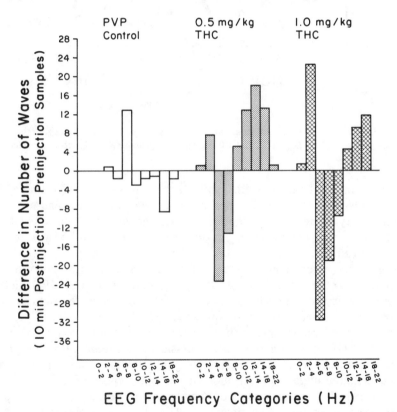

FIG. 9.10 Difference histogram of EEG samples recorded predrug and 60 minutes postinjection for control, 0.5 mg/kg THC, and 1.0 mg/kg THC groups.

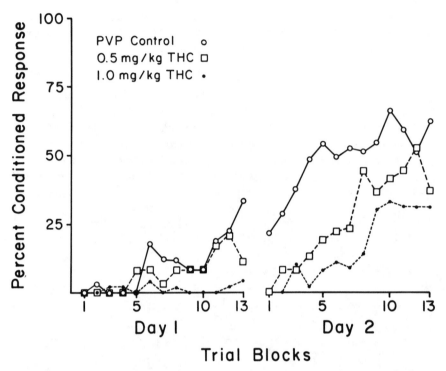

FIG. 9.11   Graph of percent conditioned responses on Days 1 and 2 of paired training for control, 0.5 mg/kg THC, and 1.0 mg/kg THC groups. Note the dose-dependent treatment effect on behavior.

slow-learning animals show EEG shifts in the opposite direction although all eventually learn the task. Disruptions of hippocampal EEG and multiple-unit activity by medial septal lesions or treatment with THC appear to retard, but not prevent, conditioning. A comparison of lesion and THC effects is shown in Fig. 9.12, indicating the similarity of behavioral disruption produced by these treatments. This type of learning impairment is similar to that reported by others (Salafia et al., 1977; Solomon & Gottfried, 1981) in that there is a delay in the appearance of conditioned responses, followed by a relatively normal increase to asymptotic levels. This form of disruption suggests a role for the hippocampus in the early stages of learning, termed phase 1 in Prokasy's (1972) two-phase model of classical conditioning. It is during this phase that attentional and/or motivational variables are presumed to have their maximal impact on learning. The altered hippocampal EEG and reduced neuronal responsiveness of slow-learning, medial-septal-lesioned or THC-treated animals (Experiments 1, 2, & 3, respectively) suggests that unimpaired hippocampal function may be essential for normal acquisition rates, but that disruption does not prevent learning. Furthermore, our data strongly suggest that hippocampal EEG activity reflects the operation of nonassociative variables because EEG recorded *prior* to the start of training predicts subsequent conditioned unit responses and behavioral learning rates.

We are now taking a first step in evaluating the hypothesis that these hippocampal parameters reflect motivational variables by recording hippocampal activity during an appetitive classical conditioning task – jaw movements conditioned by classical conditioning with tone-saccharin pairing (see Gormezano, 1972). Preliminary results indicate that the hippocampus responds differently to such training than it does in NM conditioning. Figure 9.13 illustrates the relationship between behavior (jaw movement – lower trace) and integrated multiple-unit activity from the hippocampus (upper trace). In the top row are two trials illustrating the behavioral and unit responses in relation to the tone onset and injection of saccharin. Although both stimuli occurred in each photo, the cursor has been moved to show tone

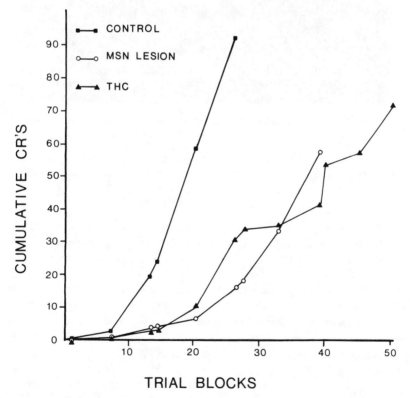

FIG. 9.12   Graph of cumulative conditioned responses across trial blocks for control, medial septal lesion, and 1.0 mg/kg THC groups. Note the similarity in behavioral impairment seen in the lesion and drug groups.

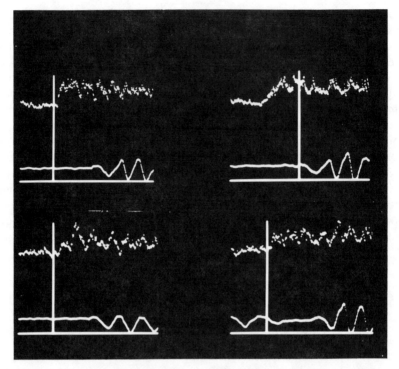

FIG. 9.13   Individual trial histograms of hippocampal activity and behavior in an appetitive jaw movement conditioning paradigm. Cursors in the upper traces indicate tone onset (left) and onset of saccharin injection (right). Unit activity was integrated with a 10-msec time constant. Note the short latency of unit responses to the tone. Bottom: single trial histograms showing behavioral and neural responses on a test trial consisting of tone-alone (left) and on a trial preceded by spontaneous jaw movement. Note that spontaneous movements are not accompanied by increased hippocampal-unit activity.

onset point (left) and saccharin injection (right) for each trial. The latency of hippocampal response to tone onset is markedly different from that reported for NM conditioning (Berger & Thompson, 1978). The bottom row of Fig. 9.13 illustrates behavioral and hippocampal responses on a test (tone-alone) trial (left), and a trial in which jaw movement was occurring prior to tone onset (right; demonstrating that spontaneous jaw movements are not accompanied by an increase in hippocampal-unit activity). In each of the integrated multiple-unit histograms of Fig. 9.13, the response is rhythmic — preceding and roughly correlating with the rhythmicity of the behavioral response. Although this pattern is different from that seen in NM conditioning, the strength of correspondence between behavior and hippocampal activity is similar.

The similarities between jaw movement and NM conditioning suggest that each is a viable behavioral preparation for examining brain-behavior relationships in learning. The differences suggest that new information can be obtained by examining hippocampus-behavior relations in an appetitive task that offers the same precision in measuring behavioral and neural responses that has yielded so much information in studies of NM conditioning.

ACKNOWLEDGMENTS

This research was supported in part by grants from NIH (MH36379) and the Miami University Faculty Research Committee (to S.D.B.), postdoctoral fellowship 5 F32 MH05052 (to S.D.B.), and grants to Richard F. Thompson from NSF (BMS 7500453), NIH (NS12268 and MH26530), and the McKnight Foundation. The authors wish to thank Dr. Thompson for his support and guidance in the experiments reported here. Some of these data have been published elsewhere (Berry & Thompson, 1978, 1979; Mamounas, Weisz, Berry, & Thompson, 1979).

REFERENCES

Adey, W. R. (1966). Neurophysiological correlates of information transaction and storage in brain tissue. In E. Stellar & J. M. Sprague (Eds.), *Progress in physiological psychology* (Vol. 1). New York: Academic Press.

Berger, T. W., & Thompson, R. F. (1978). Neuronal plasticity in the limbic system during classical conditioning of the rabbit nictitating membrane response. I. The hippocampus. *Brain Research, 145,* 323–346.

Berry, S. D. (1982). Septo-hippocampal activity and learning rate. In C. D. Woody (Ed.), *Conditioning: Representation of involved neural functions* (pp. 417–431). New York: Plenum Press.

Berry, S. D., & Thompson, R. F. (1978). Prediction of learning rate from the hippocampal electroencephalogram. *Science, 200,* 1298–1300.

Berry, S. D., & Thompson, R. F. (1979). Medial septal lesions retard classical conditioning of the nictitating membrane response in rabbits. *Science, 205,* 209–211.

CIBA Symposium 58. (1978). *Functions of the septo-hippocampal system.* New York: Elsevier.

Coleman, J. R., & Lindsley, D. B. (1977). Behavioral and hippocampal electrical changes during operant learning in cats and effects of stimulating two hypothalamic-hippocampal systems. *EEG Clinical Neurophysiology.*

Cosroe, P., Jones, B., & Laird, H. (1976). EEG and behavioral effects of Δ^9 tetrahydrocannabinol in combination with stimulant drugs in rabbits. *Psychopharmacology, 50,* 47–52.

DeFrance, J. F. (1976). *The septal nuclei.* New York: Plenum.

Gormezano, I. (1966). Classical conditioning. In J. B. Sidowski (Ed.), *Experimental methods and instrumentation in psychology.* New York: McGraw-Hill.

Gormezano, I. (1972). Investigations of defense and reward conditioning in the rabbit. In A. H. Black & W. F. Prokasy (Eds.), *Classical conditioning II: Current research and theory.* New York: Appleton–Century–Crofts.

Grastyan, E., Lissak, K., Madarasz, L., & Donhoffer, H. (1959). Hippocampal electrical activity during the development of conditioned reflexes. *EEG Clinical Neurophysiology, 11,* 409–430.

Lockhart, M., & Moore, J. W. (1975). Classical differential and operant conditioning in rabbits

(*Oryctolagus cuniculus*) with septal lesions. *Journal of Comparative and Physiological Psychology, 88,* 147–154.

Mamounas, L. A., Weisz, D. J., Berry, S. D., & Thompson, R. F. (1979). Disruption of rabbit hippocampal activity and conditioned behavior following administration of delta-9-THC. *Neuroscience Abstracts, 5,* 319.

Maser, J. D., Dienst, F. T., & O'Neal, E. C. (1974). The acquisition of a Pavlovian conditioned response in septally damaged rabbits: Role of a competing response. *Physiological Psychology, 2,* 133–136.

Moore, J. W., Goodell, N. A., & Solomon, P. R. (1976). Central cholinergic blockade by scopolamine and habituation, classical conditioning, and latent inhibition of the rabbit's nictitating membrane response. *Physiological Psychology, 4,* 395–399.

Powell, D. A. (1979). Peripheral and central muscarinic cholinergic blockade: Effects on Pavlovian conditioning. *Bulletin of the Psychonomic Society, 14,* 161–164.

Powell, D. A., Milligan, W. L., & Buchanan, S. L. (1976). Orienting and classical conditioning in the rabbit (*Oryctolagus cuniculus*): Effects of septal lesions. *Physiology and Behavior, 17,* 955–962.

Prokasy, W. F. (1972). Developments with the two-phase model applied to human eyelid conditioning. In A. H. Black & W. F. Prokasy (Eds.), *Classical conditioning. Vol. II. Current research and theory.* New York: Appleton–Century–Crofts.

Salafia, W. R., & Allan. A. M. (1980). Conditioning and latent inhibition with electrical stimulation of hippocampus. *Physiological Psychology, 8,* 247–253.

Salafia, W. R., Romano, A. G., Tynan, T., & Host, K. C. (1977). Disruption of rabbit (*Oryctolagus cuniculus*) nictitating membrane conditioning by posttrial electrical stimulation of hippocampus. *Physiology and Behavior, 18,* 207–212.

Schmaltz, L. W., & Theios, J. (1972). Acquisition and extinction of a classically conditioned response in hippocampectomized rabbits (*Oryctolagus cuniculus*). *Journal of Comparative and Physiological Psychology, 79,* 328–333.

Segal, M. (1978). The effects of SP-111, a water-soluble THC derivative, on neuronal activity in the rat brain. *Brain Research, 139,* 263–275.

Solomon, P. R., & Gottfried, K. E. (1981). The septo-hippocampal cholinergic system and classical conditioning of the rabbit's nictitating membrane response. *Journal of Comparative and Physiological Psychology, 95,* 322–330.

Swanson, L., & Cowan, W. M. (1979). The connections of the septal region in the rat. *Journal of Comparative Neurology, 186,* 621–656.

Thompson, R. F., Berger, T. W., Berry, S. D., & Hoehler, F. K. (1980). The search for the Engram, II. In D. McFadden (Ed.), *Neural mechanisms of behavior.* New York: Springer-Verlag.

Vanderwolf, C. H., Kramis, R., & Robinson, T. E. (1978). Hippocampal electrical activity during waking behavior and sleep: Analyses using centrally acting drugs. In CIBA Foundation Symposium 58, *Functions of the septo-hippocampal system.* New York: Elsevier.

10 Brain Stem Control of the Nictitating Membrane Response

N. E. Berthier
J. E. Desmond
J. W. Moore
University of Massachusetts

Any detailed understanding of the neural mechanisms underlying the conditioned nictitating membrane (NM) response begins with a characterization of the basic reflex pathway of the UR. Given this foundation one can attempt to link motoneurons to neural systems that subserve the CR. This chapter reviews research on the anatomy and physiology of brain stem systems implicated in the conditioned and unconditioned NM responses. In addition to the reflex pathway of the UR, we consider the evidence that two distinct anatomical entities are essential for the NM CR. One is the supratrigeminal reticular formation and the other is a circuit beginning in the cerebellum that includes red nucleus as an intermediary.

BRAIN STEM CONTROL OF THE UR

This section discusses peripheral control and central motoneurons participating in NM responses.

Peripheral Control of NM Extension.   NM extension in mammals seems to be the passive result of globe retraction. Motais (1885, cited by Bach–y–Rita, 1971) suggested that the NM extension is the result of the retracting globe forcing orbital fatty tissue and the Hardarian gland against the medial edge of the NM, thereby pushing the NM so as to protect and lubricate the corneal surface.

There are two ways the globe can be retracted and the NM extended. The most important is through the action of the retractor bulbi muscle. This muscle attaches to the medial surface of the globe, envelopes the optic nerve, and attaches to the skull near the optic foramen. Shortening of the muscle pulls the globe into the socket and causes NM extension. Cegavske, Thompson, Patterson, and Gormezano (1976) studied NM movement to stimulation of various cranial nerves and reported that stimulation of the abducens nerve elicited a NM extension (16 ms latency), that stimulation of the oculomotor nerve elicited NM retraction (10 ms latency), and that stimulation of the facial and trochlear nerves had no effect on NM position. Multiple-unit activity of the abducens nucleus paralleled NM extension. Cegavske et al. (1976) concluded that the abducens nerve controls NM extension by activating the retractor bulbi muscle, and that the oculomotor nerve controls NM retracton by activating a small muscle that inserts onto the dorsal surface of the NM.

There appears to be a second mechanism for generating NM extension. Powell, Berthier, and Moore (1979) showed that lesions of the abducens nucleus failed to abolish the NM extension, and Berthier and Moore (1980) showed that peripheral abducens nerve sections only reduced maximal extension of the NM by 50%. Harvey, Marek, Johannsen, McMaster, Land, and Gormezano (1983) confirmed that abducens nerve transection does not abolish NM extension. Evidently, the retractor bulbi muscle is not necessary for NM extension. One possibility is that the other extraocular muscles (the lateral, medial, superior, and inferior recti and the superior and inferior obliques) co-contract and pull the globe into the socket to produce NM extension. This hypothesis seems plausible because Bach–y–Rita, Collins, and Tengroth (1969) demonstrated that succinylcholine induces an endopthalmus of 2 mm in the cat. Because succinylcholine causes contraction of the recti and oblique muscles but not the retractor bulbi, this result shows that co-contraction of the six extraocular muscles can elicit globe retraction and hence NM extension.

The possibility that all the extraocular muscles normally participate in defensive globe retraction and the NM extension is supported by four investigations: (1) Using electrical stimulation of the trigeminal nerve in the orbit, Lorente de No (1932) elicited contraction of the recti and oblique as well as the retractor bulbi muscles; (2) in the cat, Baldissera and Broggi (1968) showed that both the lateral rectus and the retractor bulbi muscles contract to electrical stimulation of the trigeminal nerve; (3) Berthier and Moore (1980) demonstrated that globe retraction could only be abolished when abducens nerve cuts were combined with cuts of the oblique and recti muscles; (4) Disterhoft and Weiss (in press) showed that cuts of the recti and oblique extraocular muscles alter the topography of globe retraction, slowing its speed and reducing its maximum amplitude.

On the other hand, Harvey et al. (1983) suggested that the recti and oblique muscles do not participate in globe retraction and the NM extension. They found that lesions of the facial nerve but not cuts of extraocular muscles abolished NM extension when the abducens nerve was already sectioned. Recently, we have redone our abducens nerve cut experiment in light of Harvey et al.'s (1983) results (Berthier, 1984). Using six animals, we were able to observe a 3-5 mm extension of the NM after the abducens nerve had been severed peripherally. Severing the facial nerve before or after abducens nerve section had no discernable effect on NM extension. NM extension was only abolished after abducens and facial nerve cuts and extraocular muscle disinsertion. We conclude that these results, when considered together with those of Lorente de No (1932), Baldissera and Broggi (1968), Berthier and Moore (1980, and Disterhoft and Weiss (in press), provide overwhelming evidence that the extraocular muscles participate in globe retraction and NM extension. The actual contribution of the extraocular muscles to globe retraction may normally be minor because even with an extremely sensitive recording device, Disterhoft and Weiss were able to observe only slight reductions of globe retraction amplitude after cuts of oblique and recti muscles.

Location of the Motoneurons Controlling NM Extension.   Early studies using Wallerian degeneration methods concluded that the motoneurons supplying the retractor bulbi muscle lie in the accessory abducens nucleus (AAN) (Prezuiso, 1924; Van Gehuchten, 1903), and some textbooks accept this early finding (Arians-Kappers, Huber, & Crosby, 1967; Kuhlenbeck, 1975). Kuhlenbeck (1975) argues particularly strongly for this idea, noting that animals that do not possess AAN do not have a retractor bulbi muscle. The AAN is located approximately 2 mm ventrolateral to the abducens nucleus, lying in reticular formation dorsal to the superior olive (Berthier & Moore, 1980; Gray, McMaster, Harvey, & Gormezano, 1981).

Recent evidence suggests that the distribution of retractor bulbi motoneurons and the path of their axons is complex and may be different for different species. One group of investigators (Grant, Gueritaud, Horcholle-Bossavit, & Tyc-Dumont, 1979; Guegan, Gueritaud, & Horcholle-Bossavit, 1978) contend that retractor bulbi motoneurons in the cat are located solely in AAN. These investigators found that injection of any of the retractor bulbi muscle slips with horeseradish peroxidase (HRP) resulted in labeled cells only in ANN. Grant et al. (1979) recorded an antidromic response in the abducens nucleus to stimulation of the retractor bulbi branch of the abducens nerve, but when these units were intracellularly labeled it was discovered that their somata lay in AAN. Evidently the recorded responses from the abducens nucleus were fiber responses, as AAN axons pass through or immediately ventral to this structure. On the other hand, Spencer (1978), Spencer, Baker, and McCrea (1980), in the cat, and Berthier and Moore (1980), Cegavske, Harrison, and Torigoe (this volume), Disterhoft, Quinn, and Weiss (this volume), and Gray et al. (1981), in the rabbit, report labeled cells in the abducens, accessory abducens, and in some cases the oculomotor nuclei after HRP injections into the retractor bulbi muscle. It seems reasonable to conclude that some small number of retactor bulbi motoneurons lie in the abducens and oculomotor nuclei.

Neurophysiology of Retractor Bulbi Motoneurons.   Our working hypothesis is that there are two population retractor bulbi motoneurons: One population is involved with defensive globe retraction and the other is involved with guided eye movements. Dusser de Barenne and de Kleyn (1928) demonstrated in the rabbit that caloric nystagmus is present after transection of the recti and oblique extraocular muscles, a result that suggests that the slips of the retractor bulbi act like the recti during nystagmus. Enucleation, followed by attachment of the medial and lateral slips of the retractor bulbi to strain gauges, showed that the medial and lateral retractor slips rhythmically contract to caloric stimulation. Oculomotor nerve cuts abolished nystagmatic activity of the medial but not the lateral retractor slips. In contrast, abducens nerve cuts did not affect nystagmus but did abolish simultaneous contraction of the retractor slips to nociceptive stimulation. Electrical stimulation of the oculomotor or abducens nerves elicited contraction of the retractor bulbi muscle. Dusser de Barenne and de Kleyn (1928) concluded that the retractor bulbi is innervated by both the oculomotor and abducens nerves and that the abducens nerve controls defensive retraction of the globe, whereas the oculomotor and abducens nerves control the retractor bulbi during nystagmus.

Additional evidence suggests that the retractor bulbi motoneurons of the oculomotor, trochlear, and abducens nuclei are concerned with guided eye movement, whereas those of AAN are concerned with defensive globe retraction. Retractor bulbi motoneurons of the abducens and AAN have different anatomy and physiology. Spencer, Baker, and McCrea (1980) showed that in comparison with smaller oculomotor and abducens motoneurons labeled by HRP injections of the retractor bulbi muscle, AAN motoneurons have large somatal diameter (30 to 72 microns), large dendritic trees, and low synaptic densities (.88 to 1.83 synapses per 100 microns^2). The dendritic arbors of AAN motoneurons extend only slightly in the rostrocaudal field and show an extension of the dorsoventral and medial lateral axes. One dendritic branch is typically oriented towards pars oralis of the spinal trigeminal nucleus, a region implicated in the UR (e.g., Durand, Gogan, Gueritaud, Horcholle-Bossavit, & Tyc-Dumont, 1983; Schreurs, 1984).

Baker, McCrea, and Spencer (1980) showed that cells of the accessory, but not of the principal abducens or oculomotor nuceli, showed large amplitude, short latency EPSPs to ipsilateral corneal electrical stimulation (2 to 2.8 ms latency). Cells of the oculomotor and abducens nuclei showed small EPSPs to trigeminal stimulation (3 to 5.2 ms latency). Congruent with Baker et al. (1980) are the results of Berthier and Moore (1983). Recording extracellularly from chloralose anesthetized rabbits, AAN cells responded to periorbital shock whereas cells of the abducens nucleus did not. Retractor bulbi motoneurons of AAN evidently have a lower threshold to orbital stimulation than motoneurons of the abducens nucleus.

Grant and Horcholle–Bossavit (1983) recently studied the response of accessory abducens retractor bulbi motoneurons to trigeminal stimulaton in an intracellular study of ketamine anesthetized cats. These differed from the other oculomotoneurons in excitability: Retractor bulbi motoneurons were normally silent, difficult to discharge with intracellularly applied depolarizing current, and fired only phasically during a prolonged step of depolarizing current. Electrical stimulation of the long ciliary nerves (corneal afferents), the supraorbital nerve, and the facial vibrissae resulted in EPSPs in retractor bulbi motoneurons (about 1.5 to 3 ms latency) of sufficient strength to elicit a burst of action potentials. Stimulation of the long ciliary nerves gave the strongest response in retractor bulbi motoneurons with a burst of up to 5 spikes. The spike burst was often followed by a prolonged (15–20 ms) and large (10–15mV) hyperpolarization. Grant and Horcholle–Bossavit (1983) suggest that the postburst hyperpolarization allows for rapid retraction of the nictitating membrane.

Two groups have recorded extracellulary from retractor bulbi motoneurons of AAN of rabbit and found that their results parallel the data from the cat. Berthier and Moore (1983) recorded from chloralose anesthetized rabbits and found that single accessory abducens cells produced spike trains of about 4 ms latency to periorbital electrical stimulation. Berthier and Moore (1983) found that AAN cells were very homogeneous; 32 of 35 cells responded between 3.7 and 5 ms latency. No differences were discerned between cells on the basis of sensory threshold, latency of first spike, or duration of firing. Maximal stimulation resulted in a burst of firing about 17 ms in duration and composed of about 4 spikes. They found that the delay between the afferent and efferent nerve vollies was 1.3 ms, a delay they suggested was disynaptic. The reflex required only the rostral trigeminal areas because knife cuts isolating caudal trigeminal nuclei at the level of the obex were ineffective in disrupting the reflex. Disterhoft et al. (this volume) recorded from the awake animal and were able to classify accessory abducens units into three types: burst, tonic, and burst-tonic; none showed spontaneous firing unaccompanied by globe retraction and NM extension.

The Supratrigeminal Region (SR)

Investigations of the role of the brain stem in the conditioned NM response led to the discovery that unilateral destruction of a discrete region of the dorsolateral pons (DLP) eliminated previously acquired CRs to both light and tone CSs (Desmond, Berthier, & Moore, 1981; Desmond & Moore, 1982;

Moore, Desmond, & Berthier, 1982). Using the criterion of 0.5 mm of membrane extension to define a CR, we observed 0% CRs in some animals over 5 days of postsurgical testing. This result is striking in light of results from previous experiments in which CRs persisted following extirpation of the neocortex (e.g., Moore, Yeo, Oakley, & Russell, 1980; Oakley & Russell, 1977) or hippocampus (Solomon, 1977; Solomon & Moore, 1975).

DLP lesions not only disrupted retention of previously learned responses but also prevented acquistion of CRs when lesions were made prior to training. In both cases disruption was evident only for the eye ipsilateral to the lesion. Switching the US to the contralateral eye resulted in normal CRs from this eye, implying that the ability to attend to the CS was not impaired; the ipsilateral eye, however, remined disrupted. Contralateral CRs appeared almost immediately (transfer of training effect), suggesting that the disruption of the ipsilateral eye did not preclude convergence of CS and US information on the contralateral side. URs for both eyes appeared normal, suggesting that motor deficits were not produced by the lesions. Sensory deficits could not account for the disruption because CR-impairment was observed for CSs of different sensory modalities.

The disruptive lesions were predominately localized in a zone 1.5–4.2 mm rostral to the level of the abducens nerve (N. VI). However, some lesions extended either more rostral or more caudal to this zone (as far as 6.2 mm rostral to N. VI, at the level of the trochlear nucleus, and as far caudal as 0.7 mm rostral to N. VI, at the level of the caudal pole of the motor trigeminal nucleus). The volume of the lesions producing disruption ranged from 3.6–34.3 cubic mm, with a mean of 14.8 cubic mm. All disrupted animals showed tissue damage in the brachium conjunctivum (BC), parabrachial cell groups, and the supratrigeminal region (SR). The latter region roughly corresponds to the vaguely delimited supratrigeminal nucleus described by others (Astrom, 1953; Lorente de No, 1922; Mizuno, 1970) and is considered part of the trigeminal nuclear complex (Torvik, 1956). For our purposes, it is defined as the reticular formation dorsal and dorsolateral to the motor trigeminal nucleus and corresponds to the dorsolateral portions of region h of Meessen and Olszewsky (1949).

Our attention was focused on the SR because multiple-unit recordings in this region revealed a conditioned increase in activity that developed and extinguished concurrently with the acquisition and extinction of the behavioral CR (Desmond et al., 1981; Desmond and Moore, 1983; Moore et al., 1982). The conditioned activity was observed using both light and tone CSs. The onset of the conditioned unit activity preceded the onset of the CR by a mean of 43 ms. Some of the animals received pseudoconditioning training (explicitly unpaired presentations of CSs and USs) prior to paired presentations of CS and US. Unit activity did not exhibit changes to CS presentations under this control procedure, indicating that the increase in activity observed under paired CS–US training was an associative learning phenomenon.

In an attempt to investigate whether bilateral representation of conditioning exists, some animals were initially trained on the eye contralateral to the electrode. We found that conditioned unit activity occurred when CRs contralateral to the electrode were made, but that the magnitude was somewhat less pronounced than that observed for ipsilateral CRs. This pattern of activity may represent a physiological substrate for the transfer of training effect described earlier.

Also relevant was the observation that trains of electrical stimulation, administered through the recording electrode, elicited an ipsilateral NM response and eyeblink in a number of cases. Most of the effective sites were in SR, and many of these required as little as 30 μA of current to elicit the response. Estimations of current spread suggest that motoneurons in AAN were not directly stimulated. Thus, projections from SR to AAN could account for the results.

Anatomical support for such projections was supplied by experiments in which crystalline HRP was implanted into the accessory abducens region (Desmond, Rosenfield, and Moore, 1983). The abducens nucleus proper was not included in the implant site. We found a large number of retrogradely labeled neurons in SR, approximately 20 μm in somatal diameter (long axis), along with a dense network of fibers and apparent terminals surrounding the motor trigeminal nucelus. The density of fibers and the number of labeled SR neurons decreased precipitously at the rostral termination of the motor trigeminal nucleus.

The labeled neurons in our study were distributed bilaterally in the SR with an ipsilateral predominance. In addition, HRP administered to the dorsolateral pons (including SR) revealed labeled cells in the contralateral SR, along with decussating fibers coursing just ventral to the periventricular gray. Commissural fibers associated with SR have been reported by others (Mizuno, 1970; Smith, 1975). The pattern of interconnectivity suggested by these results is consistent with the transfer of training described earlier.

Although the stimulation data coupled with the HRP results suggest possible projections from SR to AAN, caution in this interpretation should be exercised for the following reasons: (1) the stimulating electrodes could have excited fibers of passage from some other brain region en route to AAN; (2) labeling of SR neurons could have resulted from interruption of projections of these neurons to regions of the brain other than AAN. With regard to this point it is relevant to note that in cases in which HRP was administered to regions of the parvocellular reticular formation caudal to the region surrounding AAN, labeling was observed in fibers and terminals around the motor trigeminal nucleus, but not in SR neurons. This suggests that SR cells may terminate only in more rostral regions of the parvocellular reticular formation and that our accessory abducens implants (Desmond et al., 1983) did not interrupt more caudal-bound projections; (3) even if one assumes that a population of SR neurons projects monosynaptically to AAN and that stimulation of these cells produces a NM response, one cannot infer that these neurons are the same neurons responsible for the conditioned unit activity recorded in the SR. A more rigorous demonstration of this equivalence would involve the isolation of a single SR unit with CR-associated firing properties, followed by the observation of antidromic activation of this unit to stimulation of AAN.

As reviewed in the next section, a circuit involving nucleus interpositus of the cerebellum (IP) and red nucleus (RN) appears to be essential for NM/ eyelid conditioning in the rabbit. In apparent contradiction, Norman, Buchwald, and Villablanca (1977) reported that rostropontine and mesencephalic transections of the brain stem of cats did not prevent the acquisition of eyelid CRs to an auditory CS. At least five of these animals were transected at the level of the inferior colliculus — clearly caudal to RN. These transections isolated RN from the facial nerve motoneurons controlling the eyelid response and interrupted connections of IP in BC. Given the close correlation between the NM response and the eyeblink in rabbit, in terms of both rate of conditioning ($r = .97$) and shifts in onset latencey ($r = .99$) (McCormick, Lavond, and Thompson, 1982), the results of Norman et al. (1977) imply the existence of a circuit sufficient for CRs confined to more caudal regions of the brain stem, perhaps at the level of the trigeminal and abducens nerves. Although a locus of NM conditioning in close proximity to the motor trigeminal nucleus may seem unlikely because relevant motoneurons are associated with N. VI., the motor trigeminal nucleus the and AAN differentiate from a common nuclear mass in the developing rabbit (Kimmel, 1940).

Cerebellum and Red Nucleus (RN)

Despite the negative evidence from the Normal et al. (1977) study regarding the contribution of RN to conditioned eyelid responding in the cat, the evidence from lesion studies involving rabbits speaks overwhelmingly for an essential contribution of this structure (Haley, Lavond, & Thompson, 1983; Rosenfield, Dovydaitis, & Moore, 1984; Rosenfield & Moore, 1983). McCormick, Lavond, Clark, Kettner, Rising, and Thomspon (1981) were the first to report that the cerebellum is essential for NM/eyelid conditioning. Since then, an elegant series of studies from this group of investigators has delineated some of the subdivisions of cerebellum most intimately involved in this behavior and some of their physiological and pharmacological properties (see e.g., McCormick & Thompson, 1983, for an overview). To summarize only the lesion data, destruction confined largely to ipsilateral IP prevents learning or retention by the ipsilateral eye, a result also reported by Yeo, Hardiman, Glickstein, and Steele–Russell (1982). This nucleus connects with contralateral RN via BC. Therefore, the finding by McCormick, Guyer, and Thompson (1982) that destruction of BC also causes disruption of ipsilateral lesions of IP pointed toward RN as a possible link in the circuit controlling the CR. Desmond et al. (1983) showed that HRP implanted into the accessory abducens region labels neurons of contralateral RN, thus supporting the link hypothesis. Thus, control of the CR seems to involve a circuit that begins in the ipsilateral cerebellum, projecting from IP neurons and synapsing on contralateral RN neurons. Some of these project to accessory abducens (and probably other) motoneurons mediating the CR. Axons of this projection would be contained within that portion of the rubrospinal tract that terminates within the brain, the so called rubrobulbar tract (see Mizuno, Mochizuki, Akimoto, Matsushima, & Nakamura, 1973).

The precise location and trajectory of the rubrobulbar tract between RN and AAN was recently determined by Rosenfield et al. (1984). Unilateral implantation of HRP into RN produced orthograde transport and detectable labeling of the rubrobulbar tract as it crosses the midline in the ventral tegmental bundle and assumes a ventrolateral position at the level of the trigeminal nerve and caudally. With this information it became possible to determine the phi correlation between disrupted conditioned responding produced by brain stem lesions with the various links in the circuit involving RN. Histological material from 70 animals was examined, of which 28 came from animals with disrupted conditioned responding from one or both eyes. All but one of these disrupted cases involved significant damage to BC, RN, or the rubrobulbar tract. The lesion in the exceptional case was largely confined to SR. Unaccountably, one of the 42 nondisrupted cases involved significant destruction of the rubrobulbar tract. The resulting phi coefficient of .94 ($p < .001$) indicates that, barring the two exceptional cases, brain stem lesions that disrupted conditioning were significantly related to destruction of one or more links in the circuit involving RN; lesions that did not involve this circuit failed to disrupt conditioning.

The anatomical relationship between RN and SR is fundamental to formulating hypotheses about their respective roles in generating the CR. Our HRP studies to date have failed to indicate direct connections between neurons of RN and SR (Desmond et al., 1983; Rosenfield et al., 1984). The rubrobulbar tract described by Rosenfield et al. (1983) assumes a position at the level of the trigeminal nerve ventral to SR, and the two structures do not overlap. Therefore, neurons of both RN (contralaterally) and SR (bilaterally) appear to terminate in the accessory abducens region without interacting enroute. It therefore appears unlikely that SR's role in generating the CR is one of linking motor commands for the CR from RN.

Another possibility we have considered is that SR is a link in a more direct circuit from IP to AAN motoneurons, i.e., one not involving RN as an intermediary. Although no such pathway has been described in modern neuroanatomical literature, a number of cases of retrograde labeling in IP following HRP implantation in DLP were reported by Desmond et al. (1983). Given the evidence from Rosenfield et al. (1984) regarding the location of the rubrobulbar tract and the likelihood of fiber uptake in the earlier study, the evidence for a link from IP to SR is highly suspect. Furthermore, the one case from the Desmond et al. (1983) study where HRP implantation appeared to be confined to SR (Animal 20) showed no labeling of neurons within IP or other cerebellar nuclei.

What then are the respective contributions of RN and SR to the CR? For the present it appears as though there may be two parallel systems involved in generating the CR, one relatively local system involving SR and a more wide ranging system involving cerebellum and RN, among other possible components. Both systems appear to be essential: One may prime motoneuron pools whereas the other dictates the actual form or topography of the CR. It is premature to speculate further in the absence of single-unit recording data from relevant brain regions, concurrently with conditioned responding, supplemented by further delineation of anatomical relationships among essential components.

REFERENCES

Arians-Kappers, C. U., Huber, G. C., & Crosby, E. C. (1967). *The comparative anatomy of the nervous system of vertebrates including man* (Vol. 1). New York: Hafner.

Astrom, K. E. (1953). On the central course of afferent fibres in the trigeminal facial, glossopharyngeal, and vagal nerves and their nuclei in the mouse. *Acta Physiologica Scandinavia, 29,* 209-320.

Bach-y-Rita, P. (1971). Neurophysiology of eye movements: In P. Bach-y-Riga & C. Collins (Eds.), *Symposium on the control of eye movements.* New York: Academic Press.

Bach-y-Rita, P., Collins, C. C., & Tengroth, B. M. (1969). Influence of extraocular muscle cocontraction on globe length. *American Journal Opthalmology, 66,* 906-909.

Baker, R., McCrea, R. A., & Spencer, R. F. (1980). Synaptic organizations of the cat accessory abducens nucleus. *Journal of Neurophysiology, 43,* 771-791.

Baldissera, F., & Broggi, G. (1968). Analysis of a trigemino-abducens reflex in the cat. *Brain Research, 7,* 313-316.

Berthier, N. E. (1984). The role of the extraocular muscles in the rabbit nictitating membrane response: a reexamination. *Behavioural Brain Research, 14,* 81-84.

Berthier, N. E., & Moore, J. W. (1980). Role of extraocular muscles in the rabbit (*Oryctolagus cuniculus*) nictitating membrane response. *Physiology & Behavior, 24,* 931-937.

Berthier, N. E., & Moore, J. W. (1983). The nictitating membrane response: An electrophysiological study of the abducens nerve and nucleus and the accessory abducens nucleus in rabbit. *Brain Research, 253,* 201-210.

Cegavske, C. F., Thompson, R. F., Patterson, M. M., & Gormezano, I. (1976). Mechanisms of efferent cntrol of the nictitating membrane response in rabbit (*Oryctolagus cuniculus*). *Jour-*

nal of Comparative and Physiological Psychology, 90, 411-423.

Desmond, J. E., Berthier, N. E., & Moore, J. W. (1981). Brain stem elements essential for the classically conditioned nictitating membrane response of rabbit. Society for Neuroscience Abstracts, 7, 650.

Desmond, J. E., & Moore, J. W. (1982). A brain stem region essential for the classically conditioned but not unconditioned nictitating membrane response. Physiology & Behavior, 28, 1029-1033.

Desmond, J. E., & Moore, J. W. (1983). A supratrigeminal region implicated in the classically conditioned nictitating membrane response. Brain Research Bulletin, 10, 765-773.

Desmond, J. E., Rosenfield, M. E., & Moore, J. W. (1983). An HRP study of the brainstem afferents to the accessory abducens region and dorsolateral pons in rabbit: Implications for the conditioned nictitating membrane response. Brain Research Bulletin, 10, 747-763.

Disterhoft, J. F., & Weiss, C. (in press). Motorneuronal control of eye retraction/nictitating membrane extension in rabbit. In D. L. Alkon & C. D. Woody (Eds.), Neural mechanisms of conditioning. New York: Plenum.

Durand, J., Gogan, P., Gueritaud, J. P., Horcholle-Bossavit, & Tyc-Dumont, S. (1983). Morphological and electrophysiological properties of trigeminal neurons projecting to the accessory abducens nucleus of the cat. Experimental Brain Research, 53, 118-128.

Dusser de Barenne, J. G., & de Kleyn, A. (1928). Uber vestibularen Nystagmus nach Exstirpation von allen sechs Augenmuskeln beim Kaninchen; Beitrag zur Wirkung und Innervation des Musculus retractor bulbi. Pflugers Archiv. European Journal of Physiology, 221, 1-14.

Grant, K., Gueritaud, J., Horcholle-Bossavit, G., & Tyc-Dumont, S. (1979). Anatomical and physiological identification of motoneurons supplying cat retractor bulbi muscle. Experimental Brain Research, 34, 249-274.

Grant, K., & Horcholle-Bossavit, G. (1983). Convergence of trigeminal afferents on retractor bulbi motoneurones in the anaesthetized cat. Journal of Physiology (London), 339, 41-60.

Gray, T. S., McMaster, S. E., Harvey, J. A., & Gormezano, I. (1981). Localization of retractor bulbi motoneurons in the rabbit. Brain Research, 226, 93-106.

Guegan, M., Gueritaud, J., & Horcholle-Bossavit, G. (1978). Localization of motoneurons of bulbi retractor muscle by retrograde transport of exogene horseradish peroxidase in the cat. Comptes Rendus (D), 286, 1355-1358.

Haley, D. A., Lavond, D. G., & Thompson, R. F. (1983). Effects of contralateral red nucleus lesions on retention of the classically conditioned nictitating membrane response/eyelid response. Society for Neuroscience Abstracts, 9, 643.

Harvey, J. W., Marek, G. J., Johannsen, A. M., McMaster, S. E., Land, T., & Gormezano, I. (1983). Role of the accessory abducens nucleus in the nictitating membrane response of the rabbit. Society for Neuroscience Abstracts, 9, 330.

Kimmel, D. L. (1940). Differentiation of the bulbar motor nuclei and the coincident development of associated root fibers in the rabbit. Journal of Comparative Neurology, 72, 83-148.

Kuhlenbeck, H. (1975). The central nervous system of vertebrates: Spinal cord and deuterencephalon. Basal: Karger.

Lorente de No., R. (1932). The interaction of the corneal reflex and vestibular nystagmus. American Journal of Physiology, 103, 704-711.

McCormick, D. A., Guyer, P. E., & Thompson, R. F. (1982). Superior cerebellar peduncle lesions selectively abolish the ipsilateral classically conditioned nictitating membrane/eyelid response of the rabbit. Brain Research, 224, 347-350.

McCormick, D. A., Lavond, D. G., & Thompson, R. F. (1982). Concomitant classical conditioning of the rabbit nictitating membrane and eyelid responses: Correlations and implications. Physiology & Behavior, 28, 769-775.

McCormick, D. A., Lavond, D. g., Clark, G. A., Kettner, R. E., Rising, C. E., & Thompson, R. F. (1981). The engram found? Role of the cerebellum in classical conditioning of nictitating membrane and eyelid responses. Bulletin of the Psychonomic Society, 18, 103-105.

McCormick, D. A., & Thompson, R. F. (1983). Cerebellum: Essential involvement in the classically conditioned eyelid response. *Science, 223,* 296–299.

Meessen, H., & Olszewsky, J. (1949). *A cytoarchitectonic atlas of the rhombencephalon of the rabbit.* Basel: Karger.

Mizuno, N. (1970). Projection fibers from the main sensory trigeminal nucleus and the supratrigeminal region. *Journal of Comparative Neurology, 139,* 457–472.

Mizuno, N., Mochizuki, K., Akimoto, C., Matsushima, R., & Nakamura, Y. (1973). Rubrobulbar projections in the rabbit. A light and electron microscopic study. *Journal of Comparative Neurology, 147,* 267–280.

Moore, J. W., Desmond, J. E., & Berthier, N. E. (1982). The metencephalic basis of the conditioned nictitating membrane response: In C. H. Woody (Ed.), *Conditioning: Representation of involved neural function.* New York: Plenum.

Moore, J. W., Yeo, C. H., Oakley, D. A., & Russell, I. S. (1980). Conditioned inhibition of the nictitating membrane response in neodecorticate rabbits. *Behavioural Brain Research, 1,* 397–410.

Norman, R. F., Buchwald, J. S., & Villablanca, J. R. (1977). Classical conditioning with auditory discrimination of the eye blink in decerebrate cats. *Science, 196,* 551–553.

Oakley, D. A., & Russell, I. S. (1977). Subcortical storage of Pavlovian conditioning in the rabbit. *Physiology & Behavior, 18,* 931–937.

Powell, G. M., Berthier, N. E., & Moore, J. W. (1979). Efferent neuronal control of the nictitating membrane response in rabbit. *(Oryctolagus cuniculus):* A reexamination. *Physiology & Behavior, 23,* 299–308.

Prezuiso, L. (1924). Sul nucleo accessorio del neuvo abducente in aluine uccelli e mamiferi, *Nuovo Ercolani,* 161–217.

Rosenfield, M. E., Dovydaitis, A., & Moore, J. W. (1985). Brachium conjunctivum and rubrobulbar tract: Brain stem projections of red nucleus essential for the conditioned nictitating membrane response. *Physiology & Behavior, 34,* 751–759.

Rosenfield, M. E., & Moore, J. W. (1983). Red nucleus lesions disrupt the classically conditioned nictitating membrane response in rabbits. *Behavioural Brain Research, 10,* 393–398.

Schreurs, B. G. (1984). Computer control of electrical brain stimulation in the rabbit. *Kopf Carrier, 11,* 1–3.

Smith, R. L. (1975). Axonal projections and connections of the principal sensory trigeminal nucleus in the monkey. *Journal of Comparative Neurology, 148,* 423–446.

Solomon, P. R. (1977). Role of the hippocampus in blocking and conditioned inhibition of the rabbit's nictitating membrane response. *Journal of Comparative and Physiological Psychology, 91,* 407–417.

Solomon, P. R., & Moore, J. W. (1975). Latent inhibition and stimulus generalization of the classically conditioned nictitating membrane response in rabbits *(Oryctolagus cuniculus)* following dorsal hippocampal ablation. *Journal of Comparative and Physiological Psychology, 89,* 1192–1203.

Spencer, R. (1978). Identification and localization of motoneurons innervating the cat retractor bulbi muscle. *Society for Neuroscience Abstracts, 4,* 168.

Spencer, R., Baker, R., & McCrea, R. A. (1980). Localization and morphology of cat retractor bulbi motoneurons. *Journal of Neurophysiology, 43,* 754–770.

Torvik, A. (1956). Afferent connections to the sensory trigeminal nuclei, the nucleus of the solitary tract and adjacent structures. *Journal of Comparative Neurology, 106,* 51–132.

Van Gehuchten, A. (1903). Degeneration Wallerienne indirecte des nerfs moteurs, nerf oculomotor externe. *Nevrake, Lourian, 5,* 278–287.

Yeo, C. H., Hardiman, M. J., Glickstein, M., & Steele-Russell, I. (1982). Lesions of cerebellar nuclei abolish the classically conditioned nictitating membrane response. *Society for Neuroscience Abstracts, 8,* 22.

11 A Perspective on the Acquisition of Skeletal Responses Employing the Pavlovian Paradigm

William F. Prokasy
University of Illinois-Urbana-Champaign

INTRODUCTION

The purpose of this chapter is to offer a perspective on processes observed during the course of the acquisition of skeletal responses with the Pavlovian method. The words were chosen deliberately. It is not a chapter devoted to a perspective on or a theory of Pavlovian conditioning. As I've observed elsewhere (Prokasy, 1965, p. 208), Pavlovian, or classical, conditioning as a label has been used in many ways: as virtually synonymous with a unit of behavior; as a representation of a general process of learning; as one form of learning with properties unique to the method; as a measure of associative strength; and as a set of experimental operations.

It is this last view, that Pavlovian operations constitute a method of inquiry designed to answer explicit questions not about Pavlovian conditioning, but about the processes of the organism to which the experimental operations are applied, that is assumed here. However, any set of laboratory operations is designed, deliberately or not, to amplify some properties of the organism and to attenuate others. Pavlovian operations would not very likely be employed to examine foraging behavior or the shaping of a highly skilled, complex, response pattern. Similarly, they are not likely to be used in examining the processes by which humans generate sentences.

Pavlovian operations can be, and are, employed to ask questions about associating, or relating, environmental stimuli. It is a method that, because of the typical features of the response systems selected, can be employed to examine questions about associative networks that have been raised since the time of Aristotle. The experimental paradigm is one in which, typically, the response options are highly limited, the signal-to-noise ratio of both the conditioned stimulus (CS) and the unconditioned stimulus (US) is high, and the effector systems of both the conditioned response (CR) and the unconditioned response (UR) are the same. That the paradigm has these characteristics does not mean that there is a learning, or associative, or memorial, process uniquely aligned with the operations. Rather it is a highly defined situation that permits us to assess inferred processes, processes that we presume to be particularly amplified by the method. It is not, therefore, so much a method that assists us in developing a theory of behavior so much as it is one that allows us to increase our understanding of the processes that yield the behavior.

This book, and this chapter, focus on the rabbit preparation. As observed by Thompson, Berger, Cegavske, Patterson, Rosemer, Teyler, and Young (1976), the use of the Pavlovian method with rabbits as subjects constitutes a model preparation. Developed by Gormezano and his colleagues (e.g., Gormezano, 1972) the preparation has since been employed in an extensive array of behavioral, psychophysiological, neurophysiological, and psychopharmacological investigations as the existence of this book attests. Although a thorough understanding of a single preparation risks the evolution of theory that is unique both to preparation and to species, it does have the virtue when contrasted with comparable research in other species of permitting an assessment of what is general and what is specific.

There are three sections to this chapter. The first summarizes the steps through which the organism goes in the acquisition of a conditioned skeletal response. The second section is devoted to the process of analysis through which the experimental data are interpreted. This takes the form of a descriptive model, the two-phase model, which has been useful in understanding more precisely the effects of various experimental manipulations. The final section describes some selected research from a number of laboratories in an effort to provide a sampling of what we have learned about the processes operative during the acquisition of a conditioned nictitating membrane response.

ACQUISITION STAGES

The changes that take place from the initiation of training through the stabilization of a response pattern with continued exposure to CS-US pairing are not viewed as changes ascribable simply to a modification in the strength of an inferred association. Four categories, or stages, of changes have been described in past research (Prokasy & Williams, 1979): contingency detection, response category selection, change and stabilization of relative response frequency, and topographical and latency refinement. These stages or categories are not to be interpreted as falling in a lock-step sequence. Rather they more likely represent an overlapping flow of change or transformation in which change categorized in one stage may well interact with that in another.

Contingency Detection

The Pavlovian paradigm contains many environmental contingencies (Prokasy, 1965, pp. 209–212): temporal distribution of trials, temporal distribution of interstimulus intervals, reinforcement schedules and redundancies, intensive and qualitative stimulus characteristics and their relationships, and, specifically, the (usually) two stimuli chosen to comprise the CS–US pairing. Contingency detection, therefore, includes more than the detection of a CS–US pairing. It constitutes learning about the environment, or, in other words, the organization of information that defines context. This is analogous to a more generalized version of the neuronal model of a stimulus developed by Sokolov (1963, pp. 286–294).

The environmental context can be seen at three levels. There is, first, the general experimental situation that would include the characteristics of the experimental chamber, any devices that restrain the organism, and any devices that are manipulable. Although this aspect of the context remains constant throughout training, experimental subjects do absorb information from it. As subjects organize information relating to the demand characteristics of the manipulated stimulus contingencies, they incorporate information about the larger context even though it may have little to do with the information necessary and sufficient to learn the target response. For example, research in observing responses (e.g., Prokasy, 1956; Wyckoff, 1952) illustrates clearly that organisms acquire contextual information that is wholly uncorrelated with experimenter-selected rewards and punishments.

The second contextual level is the set of contingencies generated with the presentation of the CS and US. As observed earlier, presenting a pair of stimuli implies many contingencies or redundancies and it is clear that the organism does learn about them during the course of training. For example, Prokasy (1965, pp. 211–212) has summarized research that shows that human subjects acquire information about both the average amount of time elapsing between trials and the characteristics of the trial distribution that determine the average time elapsing between trials. In other research it has been demonstrated that subjects respond to redundancies in reinforcement schedules (e.g., Prokasy, Carlton, & Higgins, 1967; Prokasy, Higgins, & Carlton, 1968). Similarly, the marked shifts in response latencies associated with within-subject changes in interstimulus interval reflect knowledge of elapsed time between CS and US onsets (e.g., Ebel & Prokasy, 1963). The point is that subjects not only acquire this information but that it, in turn, influences the acquisition and stabilization of responding. The information contained only in the CS–US pairing is insufficient to understand the processes that result in CR acquisition.

The third context level is the contingency of most interest in conducting the experiment: the CS–US pairing or correlation. The two stimuli typically have high signal-to-noise ratios; that is to say that they occur in close temporal proximity and are usually well above sensory thresholds in a larger context with few other discrete external events. The consequence should be clear: The CS–US contingency is one that is detected quite rapidly, substantially before there is any evidence of skeletal conditioned responses. Organizing information about the larger context very likely takes place over many trials and isn't necessarily complete even with extended training (i.e., there may be contingencies in the environment about which the subject learns nothing). Evidence for the clear temporal disparity between when pairing of the CS and US is learned and when skeletal responses first emerge comes from both psychophysiological and neurophysiological research. For example, Schneiderman and his colleagues have shown that differential heart-rate conditioning occurs in rabbits within very few trials even at interstimulus intervals too long to permit acquisition of the nictitating membrane response (Prokasy, 1965; Schneiderman, 1972). In addition, Thompson and his colleagues (Thompson et al., 1976) have demonstrated enhanced multiple-unit activity in dorsal hippocampus in eight or fewer trials in the model rabbit preparation even though the conditioned nictitating membrance response does not usually emerge for 20 or more trials.

It is important to make the distinction between the contingency detection associated with CS–US pairing and the emergence, indeed, the selection, of a CR. This is not a new distinction but it typically has not been incorporated in theories designed to account for the acquisition of a CR within the Pavlovian paradigm. The distinction is analogous to that between knowledge and performance commonly made in contemporary theoretical treatments of human memory. It serves to emphasize the awkwardness of employing a CR measure as an index of associative strength in other than an entirely circular manner. In particular such measures cannot be employed as anything more than a limited index of the strength of the memory representation of the CS–US contingency.

Response Category Selection

Once a distinction between contingency detection and response emergence is made, a second stage, called *response category selection* mentioned earlier above,is implied. A partial index of this stage (though it may overlap with other stages) is the number of trials or the amount of time elapsing between contingency detection and response emergence. Earlier theorists (e.g., Hull, 1943; Spence, 1956) can account for this discrepancy in the way they accounted for the lapse of trials between the onset of training and the emergence of the first CR. Subthreshold increments in response strength were assumed to occur with each CS–US pairing and CRs would not be observed until response threshold is exceeded. Implied in such an interpretation, as well as in more recent treatments (e.g., Estes, 1973; Rescorla and Wagner, 1972; Wagner, 1978) is a stimulus substitution interpretation of response category selection. The words "stimulus substitution" are used here to mean *only* that the same category of response that occurs to the US is acquired to the CS. No assumptions are made about the mechanism through which the response is acquired. Thus, once the UR is selected, the response category is selected and acquisition amounts to increasing the likelihood that the occurrence of the CS will result in the emission of a UR that, when occurring in the presence of a CS, defines the CR. Variations in response topography are possible through differences in local and immediate context, but CR category selection routinely has been assumed to be a passive, and automatic, consequence of UR selection.

It is entirely possible that for some species, or for some responses in some species, stimulus substitution provides a sufficient account of response selection. It is unlikely, however, to provide a general account for the selection and acquisition of skeletal CR's with the Pavlovian paradigm. This judgment derives from an array of data beginning with Pavlov and affirmed by others because what is learned to the CS is not necessarily an observed part of the UR and what occurs in the way of UR classes does not necessarily become acquired to the CS. An obvious example of the latter is the startle reflex. An alternative is that there exists an active response category selection during Pavlovian conditioning. Selection is determined at least in part by the information available to the subject concerning the nature and locus of the US, the relationship of the US to other stimulus events, situational constraints, and predisposing tendencies based upon evolutionary and behavioral history. The emphasis is upon characteristics of the US, not upon the nature of the UR. Thus, the organism is not a passive emitter to the CS of whatever response is elicited by the US.

The possibility of active involvement of the subject in CR selection i.e., of selection based upon characteristics of the US, has not been explored systematically with the Pavlovian paradigm. A likely reason for this is that experimenters historically have restrained experimental subjects, thus eliminating some response alternatives, have selected those preparations in which there is a close similarity between CR and UR, and have selected measures to reflect the similarity. Such selective judgments on the part of the experimenter have helped foster various forms of stimulus substitution theories and, as well, have made us less sensitive than we should be to the manifold changes that do take place during Pavlovian conditioning. Active response selection, in my judgment, is one of those changes.

Changes in Relative CR Frequency

The third acquisition stage refers to the changes in and eventual stabilization of relative response frequency. For reasons described later other response attributes are treated separately as a fourth stage. Changes in relative response frequency are governed by two contexts: global and local. The global context includes what has been described earlier as two levels of context, basically supratrial information about the environment including the redundancies in the schedule of CS–US presentations. This information, together with evolutionary and behavioral history, not only contributes to response selection but also regulates the parameters that determine rates of change and limits of performance. Thus, US intensity does set an upper bound for relative response frequency, this similar in some ways to what Rescorla and Wagner (1972, p. 75–77) mean by an associative limit being determined by what the US will support.

The local context is that set of information available with each trial-by-trial outcome. As Bush and Mosteller (1955) observed, the Pavlovian situation is one in which the results of a trial can be categorized as a combined experimenter–subject event. For example, when the CS occurs the US may or may not be presented and the CR may or may not occur. The four possible trial-outcome combinations will determine, together with the global parameters, whether or not there is an increase or a decrease in relative response frequency and whether or not there are differential rates of change in either or both the increases and decreases in relative frequency. This is not to say that all trial-outcome information is detected by the organism or, if detected, has a differential effect. Rather, it is to make clear that there are trial-by-trial influences on responding the parameters of which may be set during the initial organization of information or development of a neuronal model. Trial-by-trial outcomes can influence subsequent behavior in one or two ways: either by transformation of traces on and after a trial that makes unnecessary any subsequent knowledge of what happened on the most recent trial or by transformation that takes place when, for example, the next CS occurs and there is a recall of past trial outcomes. Because it is abundantly clear both in human (e.g., Prokasy et al., 1967, 1968) and rabbit (e.g., Hoehler & Thompson, 1979) research that subjects can remember and use information at least from the immediately preceding trial, allowance must be made for a transformation of relative response frequency based upon memory for at least the most recent trial outcome. Whether or not this is predominantly how the transformation takes place is unknown.

Regardless of the contextual elements that control changes in response frequency, there are three ways in which a response can fail to occur. The first is that a response chain is not initiated. Whatever events are required to result in activation of an effector system are not present in their entirety. The second is that an effector system is initiated but that intervening events prevent the system from exhibiting its overt response form. This may be either through response suppression or response competition. The third is that the response chain is initiated but is not completed within the typical recording span. Thus, with the nictitating membrane preparation an interstimulus interval of 100 msec may be too short a time in which to observe responses if there are no test trials to permit observations beyond the 100 msec interval.

There are currently no data that permit determination of whether changes in relative response frequency are attributable to reductions in the length of a response chain or to increases in the likelihood with which a response chain is initiated. We do know, however, that some independent variable manipulations result in differential terminal response frequencies simply because the response chain, though initiated, is not completed during the defined recording window at some independent variable levels. A case in point is the finding (Prokasy, 1965) that a substantial part of the asymptotic performance differences between short and long intertrial intervals in human conditioning is attributable either to longer response chains or to delays in initiating a response chain at the shorter intertrial interval.

Though what happens during changes in response frequency remains to be identified, it is clear that failure to complete an uninterrupted response chain during the recording window does not account for all failures to respond. For example, with interstimulus intervals sufficiently long to include CR latencies, asymptotic latency distributions are complete (Schneiderman & Gormezano, 1964; Smith, Coleman, & Gormezano, 1969) even though response likelihood is less than 1.0. Thus, there are occasions on which, even with an easily detected signal, no response chain is initiated, or, if initiated, is disrupted via alternative events. The failure of responses to occur in a context in which the CS–US contingency is clearly learned and the CS easily detected is not understood.

Response Shaping

The fourth acquisition stage, response refinement, is distinguished from relative response frequency simply because there is clear evidence of change in topography and latency beyond the number of trials required for response frequency to stabilize. This stage can occur simultaneously with, and extend beyond, the third stage. It has been argued (Prokasy, 1965, pp. 215–222) that response shaping occurs during the conditioning of skeletal responses. Response latency and topography were interpreted to be shaped by the relationship of response attributes to the US. This idea has been extended and enriched through the careful analyses of Martin and Levey (1969) of human conditioning performance. Other investigators, notably Gormezano and his colleagues, have reported topographical and latency changes in the rabbit nictitating membrane preparations (e.g., Gormezano, 1972, pp. 165–169).

Latency and topographical changes appear to be finely tuned to the relationship of CR and US, suggesting that there is a feedback system that permits information about the relationship between the two events to be incorporated in subsequent response patterns. Again, whether this is a transformation that occurs during or immediately following a trial outcome or is one that occurs upon presentation of the subsequent CS, with corresponding recall of the last trial's output, is unknown. The major point is that a skeletal response acquired with Pavlovian operations exhibits many of the characteristics of a motor skill in relying upon some form of feedback. Nowhere is this more clearly demonstrated than in research (Prokasy, 1965, p. 221) that shows that, even though response frequency has stabilized, the rate of change in response topography changes in an orderly fashion across the last 15,000 trials in a human eyeblink-conditioning situation involving nearly 27,000 trials.

Though it appears that topograpy is shaped through feedback based upon the relationship of CR form to US, research in human conditioning suggests that topography also varies as a function of pretraining experience and the characteristics of independent variables that have little apparent relationship to trial-by-trial shaping. For example, Grant and his colleagues (Grant, 1972, pp. 47–58) have demonstrated that there are consistent individual differences in topography, these differences at least in part a function of differences in the perceived meaning of the stimuli. In addition, Grant argued that some subjects could be viewed as selecting from preformed responses whereas others went through a process of topography development, this, too, being a function of situational constraints and choice of independent variable levels. Thus, it is likely that response form is shaped not only by local contingencies such as the relationship between CR and US but is also determined by past experience and choice of experimental parameters.

THE TWO-PHASE MODEL

In the development and understanding of a model preparation much is learned about laboratory controls, brain structure, anatomy and physiology, and the effects of various experimental manipulations. It is equally important to understand the fine-grain texture of the data. More will be said about this later, but suffice it at this point merely to note that the purpose of this section is to describe the two-phase model that does account in detail for the changes in relative response frequency that take place during Pavlovian conditioning with the rabbit as a subject. To understand and use the model, however, requires as well that we understand some of its constraints, some strategies for analytic purposes, and the extent to which the model does describe data. Each is considered in turn.

The Model

Prokasy and Harsanyi (1968) introduced a two-phase model of a simple Pavlovian conditioning of skeletal reflexes. It is a two-phase model in that there is assumed a kind of discontinuity in performance. During Phase 1, response likelihood, P_i, on trial i, remains constant at some a priori base level, P_o. During Phase 2 response likelihood changes. The changes are described by linear operators each associated with a distinct trial outcome. Consider the case in which there is a pairing of a single CS with a single US, but in which the US does not always occur. This typifies an intermittent reinforcement schedule. The equations[1] would be:

(1) $P_i = P_o, 1 \leq i \leq K$
(2) $P_i = P_{i-1} + \theta_1(\lambda_1 - P_{i-1}); i > K;$ given $\underline{CR},US$ on Trial i.
(3) $P_i = P_{i-1} + \theta_2(\lambda_2 - P_{i-1}); i > K;$ given $\overline{CR},US$ on Trial i.
(4) $P_i = P_{i-1} + \theta_3(\lambda_3 - P_{i-1}); i > K;$ given $\underline{CR},\overline{US}$ on Trial i.
(5) $P_i = P_{i-1} + \theta_4(\lambda_4 - P_{i-1}); i > K;$ given $\overline{CR},\overline{US}$ on Trial i.

where K is the trial of transition between Phase 1 and Phase 2, the θ's are rate parameters, and the λ's are operator limits. Note that the Phase 2 equations, (2) through (5), provide a distinct pair of parameters for each trial outcome. These equations were employed by Bush and Mosteller (1955) in defining combinations of experimenter-defined and subject-defined events for any particular trial. The operators are the same as those employed, for example, by Hull (1943, 1952), Estes (1950), Spence (1956), and Rescorla and Wagner (1972).

Though it is beyond the scope of this chapter, the system easily is extended to discrimination learning by introducing additional operators for the nonreinforced CS. Such an extension, of course, would require making assumptions about similarity of stimuli, how the stimuli come to be "seen" as distinct, and how the organism attends to stimuli, issues that already have been treated within the context of formal models, (e.g., Bush & Mosteller, 1953; Estes, 1955).

---

[1]In the four operators it is be noted that the subscripts refer to different kinds of trials depending upon the trial outcome. For example, subscript 2 refers to the operator for trials on which there was no CR but on which the US did occur. The subscripts are used throughout this chapter in the same manner, each one referring to a different operator as defined by the trial events specified in equations 2 through 5.

Constraints

The two-phase model is an "output" model. To the extent that it provides a detailed description of the fine-grain structure of the data it is a description of the results of an experiment. Nonetheless, although it is a descriptive model both theoretical and experimental assumptions are made in its application. Some of them merit note.

The model is not associated with any particular theory of the system that yields observed behavior, but it is not, and cannot be, theory independent. It is entirely possible that other descriptive models would do as well as the two-phase model but that the underlying structure would vary considerably. However, different underlying structures reflect, at least to some degree, different theoretical pedilections and can influence, therefore, the evolution of theoretical understanding.

As noted earlier, for example, the two-phase model is similar in structure to the formal representation of the theories of Hull (1943, 1952), Spence (1956), Estes (1950), and Rescorla and Wagner (1972). Although these theories vary substantially in assumed mechanisms, they have in common several characteristics. One is that the transformation of P_{i-1} to P_i is governed by the fixed parameters of linear operators and the events that occur on Trial i-1. The parameters are either given prior to the experiment or set early in training. For example, P_o is assumed to be fixed no later than the onset of training trials. Similarly, the parameters of the Phase 2 linear operators are assumed to be fixed by the end of Phase 1. Thus, what operates on the transformation are whatever processes maintain the operator parameters and the impact of immediate events. This implies that the subject need not have memory for specific events in past trials other than for those of Trial i-1, a characteristic of the aforementioned theories.

Another characteristic implicitly follows: The independence-of-path assumption. How P_{i-1} came to be its particular value is immaterial. Its transformation into P_i is wholly independent of the sequence of events up to Trial i-1.

Finally, there are constraints imposed by the model on when mechanisms can influence P_i. Although no assumptions are made explicitly about the nature of the mechanisms that operate during changes in P_i, whatever changes take place must occur within the time bounded by Trial i-1 and Trial i. Though only at the descriptive level, the model includes this assumption in common with the previously cited theories.

There are experimental as well as theoretical constraints implicit in the model. The model is designed to apply to some experimenter operations, and is not appropriate for others. For example, it does not allow for the fact that redundancies in reinforcement schedules have an influence on performance. Thus, in humans a double alternation reinforcement pattern in human eyeblink conditioning results in some subjects responding to pattern and some responding as though there were no pattern (Prokasy, Carlton, & Higgins, 1967). Another example of redundancy, which the model is not designed to address, is the influence of within-schedule variations in intertrial intervals (Prokasy, 1965). Thus, the model is not a complete model for all experimental manipulations within Pavlovian conditioning. Though it can be expanded in application with additional assumptions, it is designed only for situations in which the effective redundancies are in the specific stimulus events, the interstimulus interval, and the pairing arrangement among stimuli.

The point to noting the constraints is to emphasize the fact that a descriptive model is not a neutral model. There are assumptions, some more explicit than others, in its application. Its value rests in the extent to which it describes the data and to which it provides a basis for asking better questions.

In the first section of this chapter four acquisition stages were summarized. Two of these can be associated with Phase 1 of the model and two with Phase 2. Establishing an associative network and selecting a response are what happen during Phase 1. The change to Phase 2 is accompanied by transformations in response likelihood. The parameter K, then, is an index of the number of trials required to complete the first two acquisition stages. Phase 2 can be identified with increases or decreases in response probability, or the third acquisition stage. During Phase 2 the fourth acquisition stage, the shaping of response form and latency, also occurs but the model does not address those measures.

Analytic Strategy

A successful output model, that is, one that describes or summarizes the texture of the data of interest, can be used in two ways. It can be used to assess whether or not a particular theoretical proposition can stand the test of data. This is determined by whether or not the parameters of the model associated with a particular theoretical construct modify as predicted from a theory. Second, the model can be used to determine the locus of independent variable effects. This is accomplished not by contrasting overall mean performances of an experimental and a control group but by identifying through parameter estimation just what properties of the data are different in the contrasted treatments.

In either instance it is necessary to estimate parameters separately for each subject. The particular technique employed in past research is described elsewhere (Prokasy, 1973; Prokasy & Gormezano, 1979) and need not be detailed here. The essential point is that the data protocol from an experiment, a matrix of 1's and 0's (i.e., CRs and failures to make CRs) with subjects defining one dimension and trials the other, is used with hill-climbing techniques to obtain estimates of parameters for each subject. Hill-climbing techniques permit estimation of best fit parameters under the assumption that the model being employed is correct (i.e., actually does describe the texture of the data). The result is a second two-way matrix, this defined by subjects and the parameter estimates for each subject. If the model adequately describes the data, then the second two-way matrix is a summary of the data. This summary is in the form of estimates of the parameters in equations (1) through (5), which constitute derived dependent variables.

An example of the two-way matrix of derived dependent variables (i.e., estimates of parameters) is provided in Table 11.1 These are the individual-subject best fit parameter estimates from an experiment that contrasted avoidance and classical conditioning of leg flexion with dogs serving as subjects (Prokasy, 1974). Note that an (arbitrary) letter is assigned to subjects depending upon how many parameters are needed to describe any individual subject's data. The letters assigned to the following classes of results:

A: $\theta_1 = \theta_2; \lambda = \lambda_2$
B: $\theta_1 = \theta_2; \lambda_1 = \lambda_2$
C: $\theta_1 = \theta_2; \lambda_1 \neq \lambda_2$
D: $\theta_1 \neq \theta_2; \lambda_1 \neq \lambda_2$

Two operators are required for sets B, C, and D, whereas only one operator is required for set A. The subscript "1" refers to CR trials, whereas the subscript "2" refers to non-CR trials.

These dependent variables, as estimates of parameters in an output model, differ sharply in meaning from those typically employed in the Pavlovian situation. Usually measures such as the average response probability in arbitrarily-sized blocks of trials or the average number of trials required before a response criterion is met are reported in the literature. Based on these measures conclusions are drawn that assume that the group performance functions represent what individuals are doing and, moreover, that all individuals are performing with the same operations (e.g., that equations (1) and (2) are necessary and sufficient to describe the data of each and every subject).

There are two kinds of individual differences with the current strategy. The first is commonly assumed: There are individual differences in the values obtained as estimates of the various parameters. P_o, θ_1, K, etc. will vary across subjects. The kind of variability obtained is illustrated in Table 11.1. However, obtaining these estimates on a subject-by-subject basis acknowledges that arbitrarily selected characteristics of group data are not necessarily representative of what is happening. There is no reason, for example, to assume that comparing the block of Trials 6 to 10 across treatments is to compare numbers meaningfully. A simple illustration of this are the large individual differences in the parameter K. Selecting such a block of trials means that it is possible for some subjects to be in Phase 1 and for others to be in Phase 2. If the model is a satisfactory data descriptor, a proper comparison would be of the estimates of K. It is easily seen, for example, that if one treatment group

TABLE 11.1
Best fit Parameters for Individual Subjects in Groups P (Pavlovian Conditioning)
and A (Avoidance Conditioning)[a]

Group	S	K	θ_1	λ_1	θ_2	λ_2	Assumption[b]
	1	34	.114	.818	.114	.087	C
	2	110	.164	.699	.164	.203	C
	3	54	.222	.931	.221	.158	C
	4	2	.146	.783	.146	.037	C
	5	10	.205	.807	.205	.066	C
	6	59	.121	.809	.121	.023	C
P	7	2	.189	.973	.189	.113	C
	8	117	.246	.797	.246	.172	C
	9	1	.211	.985	.211	.049	C
	10	145	.136	.764	.136	.075	C
	11	91	.112	.720	.112	.071	C
	12	15	.160	.875	.108	.040	D
	13	2	.691	.390	.126	.022	D
	14	2	.099	.873	.071	.029	D
	1	2	.015	.991	.015	.991	A
	2	20	.011	.977	.011	.977	A
	3	2	.033	.983	.033	.983	A
	4	16	.009	1.000	.030	1.000	B
	5	10	.000	.904	.078	.904	B
	6	125	.132	.949	.132	.201	C
	7	127	.095	.991	.095	.195	C
	8	1	.174	.973	.174	.049	C
A	9	1	.159	.943	.159	.091	C
	10	80	.093	.991	.093	.070	C
	11	165	.109	.978	.109	.031	C
	12	31	.058	.984	.058	.020	C
	13	1	.105	.887	.076	.013	D
	14	36	.123	.980	.059	.049	D

[a]Adapted from Table 1 of Prokasy (1974).
[b]There are four assumptions categories, each designated by a letter. These categories are described in the text. Note that when S required a common θ or λ, the same value is entered under θ_1, and θ_2 or λ_1, and λ_2.

averages both a large K and large θ's the group curve might not differ from that of a group that had, on an average, a smaller K and smaller θ's. One value of the two-phase model, and of the particular assessment strategy, is that these individual differences are employed to advantage in understanding the data.

The second kind of individual differences has to do with the number of operators that may be required to describe each subject's data. Table 11.1 illustrates these differences in that category A requires one operator whereas the rest require two. Hill-climbing techniques need not presuppose, for example, that in an intermittent reinforcement situation all four operators (equations (2) through (4)) are needed to describe the data of all subjects. Thus, the approach is to ask, for each subject, how many operators are sufficient to account for the data. One of the striking facts of our past research is that one, two, three, or four operators may be needed to describe the intermittent reinforcement data of any given subject. Although all subjects may exhibit a general increase in response likelihood, they go about it in very different ways even within a common treatment. Averaging data across these subjects obscures qualitatively different individual functions.

The approach, then, is one in which parameters are estimated separately for each subject, the parameter estimates are used as dependent variables, and in which individual differences in the functioning rules of behavior change are recognized. This particular approach permits one to ask two questions more precisely than is otherwise possible.

What Information is in the Data?   By selecting those parameters that produce a best fit to the data and by selecting the minimum number of operators required to describe the data the object is to extract information with minimal redundancy. It is also to extract as much information as possible in a form that is theoretically, or practically, useful. For example, plotting data in the form of typical learning curves produces information but also obscures information. Estimating parameters for a model that is known to be descriptive of the preparation under investigation escapes that problem while paying heed to individual differences not as variability around a common function but as a reality that itself is subject to analysis.

What Affect did the Independent Variable Have?   In some sense this question is addressed in most experiments. However, for the most part one is left with fragmentary information. Drawing on a historical example, considerable research was devoted to determining how an increase in drive (e.g., operationally an increase in US intensity) would affect performance. This question derived from then current theories such as those of Hull or Spence. To test the theory, however, required making a set of additional assumptions about parameters. Parameters other than those of direct interest were assumed to be constant across treatments, the experiment was conducted, and some general data (is average performance greater in one treatment than another?) were obtained. Whether or not the data conformed to the assumptions required to make the contrast was not assessed as a rule. That the results could be misleading is addressed in an earlier paper (Prokasy, 1967).

The strategy advocated here answers the question differently. It makes no assumptions about which parameters will or won't be affected but lets the resulting parameter estimates identify where an experimental manipulation has its effects. In short, the process permits summarizing what an independent variable does. If overall performance is higher, is it because K is shorter, θ is greater, λ is greater or because, in a control comparison, a decrementing operator characterizes the performance of some subjects? In addition to being a better descriptor of independent variable influence, the approach permits one to test theoretical assumptions to the effect that selected parameters are constant across treatments.

Is the Model Descriptive?

The strategy discussed earlier is predicted on the idea that the two-phase model does, in fact, provide a good description of data generated in experiments concerned with the acquisition of skeletal responses with the Pavlovian method. The evidence to date is consistent with that assumption. There are three ways to demonstrate it: contrast with other descriptive models, internal consistency, and value in answering both theoretical and empirical questions. The last of the three is addressed in the next section of this chapter.

Prokasy (1972, p. 125–142) contrasted an early version of the two-phase model with two other descriptive models. One was a simple linear operator assumed to operate from the first trial. This is, in effect, equation (2) and the test asks whether or not that equation is sufficient or if Phase 1 is required. The clear answer is that Phase 1 is necessary: Generally subjects have a number of initial trials over which there is no change in response likelihood that means, in turn, that the linear operator cannot be applied beginning with Trial 1. The parameter K is routinely greater than one. This means that any theory that predicts increases in response strength from the outset in training is either wrong or must postulate that these increases are occurring before it has reached an accumulative strength to be reflected in responding. The latter assumption was built into earlier theories of Hull and Spence and is implicitly made by Rescorla and Wagner (1972). It is clear, in any event, that it cannot be assumed that a simple linear operator is descriptive of the observed data.

The second contrast was with a finite integer model (Theios, 1968). It was possible to interpret changes in response likelihood during Pavlovian conditioning to reflect a finite set of changes from one state to another. Subjects might, for example, begin at a low response level of .03, jump after a set number of trials to .25, and then to .65, and finally to .96. That would be a four-state model with three transitions. Tests showed (employing human subjects) that once the best fit parameters were obtained, tests of stationarity failed (Prokasy, 1972, pp. 138–142); that is, subjects are required to have a constant response rate within each state. It was demonstrated that, after optimizing parameter estimates, the requirement was not met. The finite integer model is specifically contraindicated as an adequate descriptor of conditioning data.

The third model against which comparisons might be made is the catastrophe model (Frey & Sears, 1978). Detailed comparisons have not been made, so it is not possible to conclude that it cannot work as well as the two-phase model. On the other hand, detailed tests of fit of the catastrophe model to conditioning data have not been made. The consequence is that it is available as a possible alternative but that rigorous goodness-of-fit tests are unavailable.

In contrast, detailed goodness-of-fit tests have been made for the two-phase model. The process is outlined here but it, and many of the tests, are published in Prokasy (1972, 1973). A standard procedure is to generate, with each set of parameters, 25 Monte Carlo data sets. If the two-phase model does describe the empirical data well, then each Monte Carlo data set can be considered to be a random sample from a population of data sets defined by the best-fit parameters. In that case, the empirical data set would be one more such sample. The Monte Carlo sets were combined in a way that permitted calculation of a variety of statistics: For example, what is the mean response probability over the last 25 trials of the experiment? The mean of the empirical data set is contrasted with the counterpart estimate from the Monte Carlo sets: Can the empirically obtained statistic be interpreted as falling in an acceptable confidence interval defined by the standard error of estimate in the Monte Carlo sets? An example of goodness-of-the-fit, drawn from past research (Prokasy, 1973) is provided in Table 11.2.

The data come from a study conducted by Theios and Brelsford (1966) in which 100 rabbit subjects received 150 paired CS–US trials. Table 11.2, redone from Table 11.3 in Prokasy (1973), provides mean response likelihood in blocks of 10 trials. The expected response likelihood are based on estimates of parameters and the standard errors of expectation are based upon 25-Monte Carlo simulations generated from the estimated parameters. Across the 15 trial blocks only twice is there a significant departure from expectation (i.e., greater than two standard errors). Note that the standard errors of expectation are quite small and that, therefore, small absolute differences in likelihood can result in significant differences from expectation.

Similar contrasts have been made with sequential data and a variety of other statistics (e.g., mean expectation of the first CR) and the consistent re-

TABLE 11.2

Response Likelihood, Expected Response Likelihood, and Standard Error
of Response Likelihood in Blocks of 10 Trials[a]

Trial block	1	2	3	4	5
Obtained	.0693	.2050[b]	.3139	.4436	.5297
Expected	.0735	.1827	.3132	.4335	.5210
Standard error	.0053	.0081	.0088	.0076	.0080
Trial block	6	7	8	9	10
Obtained	.6257	.6802	.7465	.7723	.8010
Expected	.6076	.6858	.7742	.7686	.7908
Standard error	.0098	.0110	.0123	.0065	.0103
Trial block	11	12	13	14	15
Obtained	.8485[b]	.8871	.9030	.9030	.9079
Expected	.8253	.8717	.8998	.9112	.9053
Standard error	.0096	.0083	.0091	.0068	.0081

[a]Adapted from Table 3 in Prokasy (1973) from the data of Theios and Brelsford (1966).
[b]Departs from expectation by more than 2 SE.

sult is that the two-phase model does a creditable job in describing the data. Adopting a .05 rejection region, approximately 10% of all comparisons depart significantly from expectation, roughly twice as many as would be expected by chance. Given the sensitivity of the hill-climbing techniques to perturbations in the data that can be caused by any number of extraneous factors, the overall fit is quite good and is numerically quite precise.

THEORETICAL DEVELOPMENTS

The existence of a descriptive model of changes in response likelihood provides a more powerful basis for inference than is otherwise possible and is particularly valuable in the use of an experimental model preparation. Whether theory is at a sophisticated formal level such as that represented by Rescorla and Wagner (1972) or at a schematic, more heuristic level such as that represented by the four acquisition stages described at the beginning of this chapter, development of theory is limited by the degree to which the fine-grain structure of the data is understood. It is entirely possible for a theoretical proposition to be confirmed when tests are based on common aggregate statistics but fail upon closer examination of the data texture. A descriptive model permits closer examination and, in turn, permits better assessment of

TABLE 11.3
Best Fit Parameter Estimates for Latent Inhibition Study[a]

Group	Po	Median K	Assumption[b]	n	Means θ_1	λ_1	θ_2	λ_2
-S	.020	71.0	A	7	.461	.368	.461	.368
			C	8	.401	.676	.401	.301
			D	2	.159	.952	.652	.462
			NR	3				
-L	.016	27.5	A	7	.197	.863	.197	.863
			C	10	.231	.923	.231	.370
			D	1	.137	.972	.580	.616
			NR	2				
SS	.018	264.5	A	5	.809	.360	.809	.360
			C	5	.443	.657	.443	.213
			NR	9				
SL	.012	33.2	A	9	.265	.925	.265	.925
			C	9	.367	.897	.367	.444
			D	1	.116	.942	.061	.123
			NR	1				
LS	.015	288.5	A	3	.180	.681	.180	.681
			C	4	.572	.588	.572	.203
			D	1	.602	.726	.240	.198
			NR	10				
LL	.020	45.0	A	12	.304	.926	.304	.926
			C	6	.317	.866	.317	.457
			D	1	.284	.933	.161	.130
			NR	1				

[a]Adapted from Table 1 of Spurr (1979, p. 24).
[b]NR refers to subjects failing to respond beyond base level. See text for meaning of A, C, and D assumption categories.

theory as well as more refined theory development. In this section the model is employed in two ways. First, it is used to make a closer examination of the validity of selected theoretical propositions and, second, it is used to make the case that the first two stages of acquisition not only exist but are aligned with Phase 1 of the model.

The Model in Assessment

Three long-standing theoretical propositions are examined: subthreshold response strength, latent inhibition, and inhibition generated via nonreinforced trials.

Latent Inhibition.   The retardation of acquisition following repeated exposures to a nonreinforced CS was observed initially by Konorski and Szwejkowska (1952). Lubow and Moore (1959) labeled the phenomenon *latent inhibition* and since then there has been an extensive amount of related research. Although there have been several different interpretations of latent inhibition, the one that has currency is that unreinforced preexposures to the CS results in reduced attention (e.g., Lubow, 1965) or in reduced cue salience (e.g., Mackintosh, 1973; Reiss & Wagner, 1972; Rescorla, 1971; Solomon, Brennan, and Moore, 1974).

If latent inhibition is best understood as an attention deficit or a learned irrelevance of stimuli, then it is reasonable to expect subsequent acquisition to reflect retardation in rather specific ways with respect to the two-phase model. Latent inhibition should be primarily, if not exclusively, a Phase 1 effect. A preexposed stimulus when subsequently paired with a US might be more difficult for the subject to associate with the US because it is not a salient stimulus. This would extend the duration of Phase 1. Similarly, once a sufficient associative network is established, and a response selected, there is no reason to expect prior exposure to have any further effects. Specifically, responding during Phase 2 reasonably can be expected to be the same whether or not there is unreinforced stimulus preexposure.

Spurr (1979), in a dissertation designed to examine a conditioning interpretation of latent inhibition, evaluated with the two-phase model where latent inhibition training had its effect in subsequent acquisition training. Because the experiment and its results will be of value later, it is worth the time to describe the study. Six groups of rabbit subjects were employed in a 3 × 2 factorial design. The experiment was conducted in three parts. All subjects, first, were given an initial adaptation session to the experimental chamber. The second part constituted latent inhibition procedures and the third part involved conditioning procedures. Both of these parts were conducted within a single experimental session.

During latent inhibition exposures there were three treatments: tone absent (-), a soft tone (S), or a loud tone (L). The first of the three treatments was, in effect, further habituation to the apparatus. The second two were composed of 100 presentations each of, respectively, a 70-dB (A) and a 90dB (A) 1200 Hz tone against a 60-dB (A) white noise background. During conditioning there were two treatments. Each of the three latent inhibition treatment groups was subdivided into two groups. One of each pair received 300 CS-US paired trials with, respectively, tone S or tone L serving as the CS. The US for all subjects was a 3.5 mA infraorbital shock of 50 msec duration. The interstimulus interval was 350 msec, tone duration was 400 msec, and the intertrial interval was 25 sec. Further details are provided in Spurr (1979).

The data of interest are presented in Table 11.3. These are the averages of the best fit parameter estimates across different assumption sets within groups and across all groups. The only effects specifically associated with latent inhibition training were in the estimates of K. Groups SS and LS both had significantly greater values of K than did Group -S. Groups SL and LL both had greater values of K, but only the contrast between Groups LL and -L was statistically significant.

Spurr, then, found that latent inhibition training produced an extension of Phase 1 but had no effect on Phase 2 parameter estimates. This result does not, of course, differentiate between attention and cue salience theories of latent inhibition, but it does confirm in detail precisely the locus of its effect. The result is also consistent with the proposition that Phases 1 and 2 can be interpreted as quite distinct segments of acquisition. That a single parameter in the model absorbs all the variance attributable to latent inhibition is itself a striking result.

Response Strength.   In one form or another for over 40 years formal theories have postulated the existence of an associative connection the strength of which modifies from trial to trial with reinforcement (increment in strength) or nonreinforcement (decrement in strength). The associative strength could be between stimulus elements or between a stimulus element and a response. Although the function was not necessarily specified, a monotonic relationship between associative strength and observed response strength was assumed. Thus, an index of observed response strength was interpreted to be monotonically related to a theoretical index of associative strength.

One of the problems recognized by many investigators was that the range over which theoretical associative strength could vary might be larger than the range over which observed response strength could vary. Thus, a zero likelihood of response did not mean zero associative strength. Incrementing and decrementing of associative strength could occur even though its absolute level were insufficient to exceed a minimal response threshold.

Given this interpretation, the initially slow changes in response likelihood observed in skeletal conditioning experiments were thought to have resulted from the number of trials required to bring an increasing associative strength up to a level which could be observed in the response domain. It is this proposition that is to be examined. The two-phase model operationally defines a span of trials over which base-level responding occurs, the number of trials being defined by the parameter K. The proposition can be expressed in a single question: Is it plausible to interpret the orderly changes in response likelihood observed after Trial K (i.e., in Phase 2) as reflecting changes in associative strength that are continuous from pre-Trial K increments?

Based upon an examination of parameter estimates, the conclusion is that the proposition is not plausible. To begin with, the values of θ routinely obtained from the human eyeblink and the rabbit nictitating membrane preparations are high, averaging .1 and more. Changes in response likelihood are occurring at a rate that, given the size of K, means that if there are subresponse-threshold changes in associative strength, and if these are monotonically related to response strength, then only a small portion of the change in associative strength can be mapped onto observed response strength.

Consider the example in Table 11.3. Of particular interest are the values of K and the values of θ. Given a mean value of K as high as 288 and mean values θ_1 and θ_2 well in excess of .1 it is implausible to conclude that post-Trial-K changes in P_i reflect a continuous change in associative strength which begins with the first few trials. This is because, with the parameter values exhibited in Table 11.3, subjects would move from P_o to a initial performance limit within fewer than 10 trials. If associative strength increases as a growth function and maps monotonically onto response strength, then there has to be massive change in associative strength before the average of K trials. The changes observed following Trial K would constitute only a trivial portion of the total change in response strength. This result does not make the initial proposition wrong, but it does mean, if the proposition is true, either that some unusual mapping functions must be assumed or that changes in response strength are at best a modest index of changes in theoretical associative strength.

However, there are further complications. It has been observed in a number of experiments that an independent variable manipulation has increased the value of K but has left untouched the parameters of the Phase 2 equations. Table 11.3 is again relevant. Spurr's results (Table 11.3) show that use of a low CS intensity increased the value of K markedly (i.e., extended the duration of Phase 1) but, if anything, also increased the value of θ. If there were changes in theoretical associative strength below the observable response domain, an increase in the value of K necessarily would result in a decrease in the value of θ unless further assumptions were made about initial associative strength levels or mapping rules. It is to be noted, too, that we do not routinely obtain significant within-treatment correlations of θ and K, a further indication that there is no direct linkage between the duration of Phase 1 (number of subresponse-threshold associative strength trials) and changes in response strength during Phase 2.

Although the proposition with which this section began is not a plausible one, it is not to be concluded that changes in an associative network are not taking place during Phase 1. Rather, it means that what takes place there doesn't have any necessary relationship to increases in performance, or to Phase 2. Equations that link Phases 1 and 2 through the assumption of a continuous change in associative strength with a common set of equations fail in these circumstances. These results lend credence to the view that Phases 1 and 2 are functionally distinct and should be treated as such. More about this is said later.

Inhibition. It has long been assumed either that response strength decreased with the omission or that inhibition was generated with each US omission (e.g., Hull, 1943; Rescorla & Wagner, 1972; Spence, 1956). This assumption helped, among other things, to account for the fact that response levels are lower with intermittent reinforcement training than with continuous reinforcement training and to account for the reduction in response strength associated with extinction trials. It plays a particularly important role in the Rescorla–Wagner theory as it applies to such phenomena as blocking and compound stimulus training.

At a very general level, the assumption works. The question, however, is whether or not it will stand scrutiny when examined carefully. Research reported by Prokasy and Gormezano (1979) and Prokasy and Williams (1979) suggests that, at best, the assumption cannot be made generally.

If, during intermittent reinforcement schedule training, omission of the US results in a decrement in response likelihood, then it follows that there must be a distinct operator associated with US-omission trials. Specifically, either equations (4) and (5) or a single equation representing both must emerge in the search for parameters. The latter is tantamount to saying that $\theta_3 = \theta_4$ and $\lambda_3 = \lambda_4$.

Prokasy and Williams (1979) found limited support for the assumption with the human eyelid reflex preparation. The experiment was one in which four groups of subjects received, respectively, reinforcement schedules of 100, 75, 50, and 25%. Each group received a total of 240 trials (combined CS and CS–US trials) at an interstimulus interval of 500 msec and an average intertrial interval of 9 sec. The mean best fit parameter estimates are provided in Table 11.4. The letters beside subsets of subjects within each group reflect the following categories:

A: $\lambda_1 = \lambda_2 = \lambda_3 = \lambda_4$
B: $\lambda_1 = \lambda_2 \neq \lambda_3 = \lambda_4$
C: $\lambda_1 = \lambda_3 \neq \lambda_2 = \lambda_4$
D: $\lambda_1 \neq \lambda_2 \neq \lambda_3 \neq \lambda_4$

The value of θ was assumed to be the same for all operators for a given subject, an assumption based on the fact that detecting overall differences in θ is not likely when the mean estimated values are well in excess of .1. It also reduces estimation costs substantially and permits focusing on operator limits, the parameter of most interest in Phase 2. The decremental effect of the intermittent reinforcement schedule is attributable to three effects: an increase in the duration of Phase 1; the approximately half the subjects who required equations (4) or (5) in describing their data; and a decrease in the limit of the CR, US operator. The increase in the duration of Phase 1 is consistent with the assumption. While the half of the subjects requiring a US-omission

TABLE 11.4
Mean Parameter Estimates for Assumption Categories Within Groups

Percent Reinforcement			Assumption	n	λ_1	λ_2	λ_3	λ_4
100	P_0 =	.102	A	17	.844	.844	.844	.844
	K =	16.9	C	8	.825	.329	.825	.329
	θ =	.391						
75	P_0 =	.142	A	10	.687	.687	.687	.687
	K =	36.8	B	6	.748	.748	.339	.339
	θ =	.482	C	5	.782	.162	.782	.162
			D	4	.661	.384	.296	.344
50	P_0 =	.200	A	8	.709	.709	.709	.709
	K =	47.4	B	10	.747	.747	.236	.236
	θ =	.389	C	3	.513	.278	.513	.278
			D	4	.725	.681	.232	.091
25[a]	P_0 =	.112	A	16	.281	.281	.281	.281
	K =	75.0	B	3	.740	.740	.287	.287
	θ =	.521	C	3	.639	.294	.639	.294
			D	1	.404	.000	.000	.732

[a]Data of three subjects were excluded because K exceeded 200, thus making Phase 2 parameter estimates unreliable.

decremental operator are performing as mandated by the inhibition assumption, the other half are not. It is, of course, possible that the analytic techniques were not powerful enough to detect on an individual subject basis what did exist in the way of small decrements following US omission for some subjects. It is no less possible that US omission made no difference for those subjects in that experimental context. The reduced operator limit does not follow from the inhibition assumption, hence is not easily reconciled with the theory.

A different picture emerges with the rabbit nictitating membrane preparation. Prokasy and Gormezano (1979) found virtually no evidence to support the inhibition assumption. In this experiment, 50 and 100% reinforcement schedules were contrasted in both the aversive nictitating membrane preparation and the appetitive jaw-movement preparation in rabbits. Table 11.5 summarizes the mean parameter estimates for each group. The letters beside each subset of subjects have the same meaning as those described earlier in the human intermittent reinforcement preparation. Phase 1 duration was greater with the intermittent reinforcement schedule, but, save for a few subjects, neither US-omission operator was required to account for the data. The Phase 2 parameters for a 50% reinforcement schedule were, for all prac-

TABLE 11.5
Mean Parameter Estimates for Each Assumption Category Across Aversive and Appetitive Treatments[a]

Treatment 4	Assumption	N	K^b	θ^2	λ_1	λ_2	λ_3	λ_4
AV 100	A	9	7.5	.209	.965	.965	.965	.965
	C	10	7.5	.209	.965	.162	.965	.162
AV 50	A	2	53.9	.175	.975	.975	.975	.975
	C	17	53.9	.175	.953	.123	.953	.123
	D	3	53.9	.175	.960	.420	.930	.063
AP 100	A	16	34.6	.317	.787	.787	.787	.787
	C	16	34.6	.317	.839	.283	.839	.283
AP 50	A	13	41.1	.317	.775	.775	.775	.775
	C	18	41.1	.317	.827	.118	.827	.118
	D	3	41.1	.317	.840	.480	.610	.000

[a]Adapted from Prokasy & Gormezano (1979).
[b]These values were pooled across all subjects within each treatment and hence are listed as the same for each assumption category within that treatment.

tical purposes, the same as those for the 100% reinforcement schedule. Thus, for the rabbit preparation reduced performance associated with intermittent reinforcement resulted primarily from an extended duration of Phase 1, a result that is discussed later.

The difficulty these results pose for theoretical purposes is not minor. On the one hand there exists an assumption that US omission has a decremental effect on performance. It has yielded not simply an account of known laboratory phenomena but when extended to more complex Pavlovian arrangements has been used to predict interesting and at times counterintuitive results (e.g., Wagner and Rescorla, 1972). On the other hand the very theoretical basis on which the predictions are made, at least for the rabbit preparation, is demonstrably wrong.

It is possible that theories of the role of inhibition involving multiple stimuli, compounding, and the like must be treated as a class distinct from that required to account for acquisition with a single CS; that is, the introduction of multiple stimuli, and the contrasts made with them, may generate the decremental effects of inhibition. Simple acquisition with a single CS might involve a simpler structure, one in which the effects of US omission during intermittent reinforcement training have more to do with the associative network developed during Phase 1 than with local trial-by-trial effects during Phase 2. Although the partitioning between single stimuli and multiple stimuli offers a resolution for the theoretical problems, it is post hoc, without theoretical rationale, and, hence, is not entirely satisfactory.

Stages of Learning

A guiding heuristic for acquisition in the rabbit preparation was described in the first part of this chapter. Four acquisition stages were considered, and it was suggested that the first two, contingency detection and response selection, take place during Phase 1. The purpose of this section is to show that Phase 1 is more than a convenient mathematical representation; that, in fact, it is separable from Phase 2 in the functioning of the organism and is associated with contingency detection. Response selection is not addressed but is assumed to occupy a constant portion of the duration of Phase 1.

Two of the results discussed earlier are fully consistent with a sharp partitioning between the two phases. One is the difficulty that an alternative explanation (subresponse-threshold increments in associative strength) has in accounting for the extended initial period during which there are no changes in response likelihood. The other is the sharp distinction implied when latent inhibition training affects only the duration of Phase 1 but has no effect on parameters in Phase 2.

However, the case is much stronger, particularly when interpreted from the framework of the four learning stages. If it is true that contingency detection occurs early in training and, once a response is selected, has little to do with performance beyond its role in setting Phase 2 parameter values, then it should be possible to extend Phase 1 by introducing either degraded information or information negatively correlated with a subsequent CS–US pairing. The first example of this is an intermittent reinforcement schedule. In both human and rabbit preparations (see Tables 11.4 and 11.5) Phase 1 was extended with the degraded schedule. The increased duration of Phase 1 was negatively correlated with reinforcement ratio in the human preparation. This result is not a strong one in and of itself because the increase in Phase 1 duration can be interpreted to follow strictly from a difference in the number of paired trials received by the organism.

A clearer demonstration is provided with Prokasy, Spurr, and Goodell (1978). The purpose of the experiment was to determine whether or not brief exposures to a negatively correlated sequence of CS and US would differentially affect subsequent acquisition performance, that is, if the two stimuli were presented in an explicitly unpaired fashion such that the occurrence of one assured that the other would not take place for a minimum period of time, would there be a retardation in the rate at which CRs first manifest themselves in a subsequent training session?

A total of seven groups of subjects was employed in a two-session experiment. The first session was a preexposure session whereas the second was a standard training session with a 250 msec CS–US interval and an average intertrial interval of 50 sec. The seven groups differed only in the treatment received during the preexposure session. Group 1 received 15 CS–US trials; Group 2 received 15 US–CS trials; Group 3 received 15 explicitly unpaired presentations each of the CS and US; Group 4 received 15 CS presentations; Group 5 received 15 US presentations; Group 6 received no stimuli while in the experimental chamber; and Group 7 was not given a preexposure session. The critical comparison was between Groups 3 and 6. The remaining groups were designed to contrast with Group 6 to control for possible effects of various preexposure experiences. A limited number of preexposure trials was employed in part because there is evidence that subjects learn contingencies rapidly (e.g., Prokasy, 1965; Thompson et al., 1976) and in part to minimize the likelihood of the development of latent inhibition.

The data are summarized in Table 11.6. The only statistically significant result occurred precisely where it was expected: the estimates of the parameter K are significantly greater in Group 3 than in Group 6, thus indicating that explicitly unpaired presentations of the CS and US extended the duration of Phase 1. There were no significant effects in Phase 2 parameters, and the performance of none of the control groups differed from that of Group 3. In view of the fact that preexposure to the negatively correlated CS and US was limited to a number of trials less than that required typically to effect re-

TABLE 11.6
Mean Parameter Estimates and Terminal Response Probability[a]

Group	K^b	Assumption	n	θ_1	λ_1	θ_2	λ_2
1	25.20	A	8	.339	.877	.339	.877
		C	6	.600	.928	.600	.448
2	28.75	A	8	.298	.909	.298	.909
		C	7	.408	.880	.408	.449
3	48.29	A	7	.203	.843	.208	.843
		C	7	.532	.866	.532	.408
		D	1	1.000	.848	.263	.034
4	27.20	A	10	.229	.890	.229	.890
		C	5	.458	.926	.458	.353
5	37.25	A	12	.324	.859	.324	.859
		C	3	.509	.795	.509	.291
6	32.30	A	14	.321	.873	.321	.873
		C	2	.450	.826	.450	.503
7	30.80	A	12	.309	.878	.309	.878
		C	2	.222	.882	.222	.438
		D	1	.778	.942	.390	.088

[a]Adapted from Prokasy et al. (1978).
[b]Averaged across all assumptions within each group.

sponse selection but yet was long enough to encompass the time during which contingencies between CS and US can be detected, it is reasonable to conclude that the negative continency preexposure made it more difficult for the organism to detect and store the subsequent reliable CS–US pairing arrangement.

Supportive, but less direct because the assessment was not formal, are the data of Salafia, Romano, Tynan, and Host (1977). These investigators, using the rabbit preparation, administered posttrial electrical stimulation of dorsal hippocampus following each paired trial during aquisition. The animals receiving brain stimulation exhibited retarded acquisition. However, when the acquisition curves were superimposed beginning from when changes in response likelihood were first observed, the difference in learning rate disappeared. Brain stimulation apparently extended the number of trials required before responses occurred, but once CRs did emerge there was little or no additional effect on performance. The current interpretation is that brain stimulation disrupted contingency detection or response selection but, once these stages were completed, did not affect performance even though hippocampal stimulation was continued throughout training.

The evidence so far, then, strongly supports the proposition that there is a distinct Phase 1 and that experimental manipulations that alter the rate at which contingency detection takes place do not necessarily have an influence during Phase 2. Although it is attractive to make the inference that contingency detection can be delayed and manipulated in a way that affects exclusively Phase 1 duration, it would be even more attractive to find relatively independent verification of Phase 1. Two studies provide independent evidence for a distinct Phase 1.

Berry and Thompson (1979) examined the effects of small medial septal lesions on acquisition in the rabbit preparation. The lesions retarded acquisition. However, these investigators analyzed the data in a way that permitted a separation of Phase 1 and Phase 2. The difference in acquisition rates was attributable, in the medial septal subjects, to an extended number of trials required before CRs first occurred. Once CRs emerged, the acquisition functions were the same for both groups. This case is interesting because lesions had differential effects exclusively associated with Phase 1.

A more interesting result was obtained by Berry and Thompson (1978) and by Thompson, Berry, Rinaldo, and Berger (1979). Berry and Thompson, using the rabbit preparation, calculated the ratio of percentage of 8- to 22-Hz EEG activity to percentage of 2- to 8-Hz activity just prior to administering conditioning trials. This ratio was correlated .72 (across subjects) with the number of trials required to reach an asymptotic learning criterion. Thus, as the relative amount of theta activity (2- to 8-Hz) increased, the number of trials taken to reach a learning criterion decreased.

The related result obtained by Thompson et al. (1979) is more useful for present purposes. These investigators calculated the amount of *change* in low-to-high EEG ratio across conditioning trials and obtained a correlation of − .93 between the amount of change and the number of trials required to reach the fifth CR. This means that the greater the relative *decrease* in proportion of theta activity, the fewer the trials required to reach the fifth CR. As Thompson et al. conclude, the two results indicate that fast learners shift to a desynchronized EEG as they learn while slow learners exhibit a desynchronized EEG initially and then move slowly toward a greater percentage of theta.

The high negative correlation (− .93) between EEG change and number of trials to reach the fifth CR is particularly striking because unpublished calculations of correlations[2] between estimates of K and the number of trials required to reach the fifth CR are at least .97. For all practical purposes this means that a neurophysiological measure (change in EEG across trials) and a behavioral measure (number of trials to reach the fifth CR) are nearly perfectly correlated with a single parameter, K, of a mathematical model that describes the behavioral information. Essentially the three measures are indexing the same thing: the differentiation of Phase 1 from Phase 2.

Combined across the several cited experiments the data strongly support the proposition that the two-phase model not only is descriptive in detail of data protocols obtained from the rabbit nictitating membrane preparation but is also identifying separable phases in learning.

SUMMARY COMMENTS

This chapter outlines four stages through which organisms go in the acquisition of a classically conditioned skeletal reflex: contingency detection, response selection, changes in response frequency, and response shaping. A two-phase model of response output was described. In particular, it was shown how such a model, being a precise descriptor of the data, can be employed to evaluate the adequacy of theories, or hypotheses, designed to account for performance in conditioning.

The model was used in two ways. First, it was employed to assess three long-standing propositions about acquisition. The view that conditioned responses emerge in training as a continuation of subthreshold increments in response strength was found to be less tenable than the proposition that there are at least two phases during acquisition the first of which has little to do with increments in response strength.

It was also shown that to account for the decremental effects of intermittent reinforcement schedules by assuming trial-by-trial decremental effects associated with each US omission is inadequate. Because these assumed decremental effects are employed to account for a variety of phenomena in conditioning (e.g., compounding effects, blocking) it is evident that explanations of these phenomena require substantial modification.

Finally, it was shown that latent inhibition has a one-parameter effect on performance: It retards the appearance of conditioned responses but has no

---

[2]Charles Spurr calculated across many treatment groups in several experiments the trial on which the first, second, third, fourth, etc. response occurred. Maximum correlations routinely were obtained with the trial on which either the fourth or fifth CR occurred. That the correlations were so high (e.g., 95 and above) means that either of these indices can serve as an estimate of K.

discernable effect on the rate of acquisition once they do appear. This result is consistent both with attention and cue salience theories of latent inhibition and is locatable quite precisely in the structure of data.

The second way in which the model was employed, in conjunction with neurophysiological data, was to identify quite clearly that there are at least two phases during acquisition. In the first phase contingency detection and response selection occur. The parameters of performance in the second phase (i.e., during changes in response likelihood and in response topography) are frequently independent of the parameter that defines the duration of the first phase. The important consequence of this is that the parameters that characterize performance in the second phase tell us nothing about the development of an associative network during the first phase. We therefore cannot employ the usual acquisition data as a basis to make inferences about the rate at which contingency detection, or an associative network, develops.

ACKNOWLEDGMENT

The writing of this chapter was supported in part by a research grant from the Public Health Service (MH-31606).

REFERENCES

Berry S. D., & Thompson, R. F. (1978). Prediction of learning rate from the hippocampal electroencephalogram. *Science, 200,* 1298-1300.

Berry, S. D., & Thompson, R. F. (1979). Medial septal lesions retard classical conditioning of the nictitating membrane response in rabbits. *Science, 205,* 209-211.

Bush, R. R., & Mosteller, F. (1955). *Stochastic models for learning.* New York: Wiley.

Ebel, H. C., & Prokasy, W. F. (1963). Classical eyelid conditioning as a function of sustained and shifted interstimulus interval. *Journal of Experimental Psychology, 65,* 52-58.

Estes, W. K. (1950). Toward a statistical theory of learning. *Psychological Review, 57,* 94-107.

Estes, W. K. (1955). Statistical theory of distributional phenomena in learning. *Psychological Review, 62,* 369-377.

Estes, W. K. (1973). Memory and conditioning. In F. J. McGuigan & D. Barry Lumsden (Eds.), *Contemporary approaches to conditioning and learning.* Washington, DC: V. H. Winston.

Frey, P. W., & Sears, R. J. (1978). Model of conditioning incorporating the Rescorla-Wagner associative axiom, a dynamic attention process, and a catastrophe rule. *Psychological Review, 85,* 321-340.

Gormezano, I. (1972). Investigations of defense and reward conditioning in the rabbit. In A. H. Black & W. F. Prokasy (Eds.), *Classical conditioning II.* New York: Appleton-Century-Crofts.

Grant, D. A. (1972). A preliminary model for processing information conveyed by verbal conditioned stimuli in classical conditioning. In A. H. Black & W. F. Prokasy (Eds.), *Classical conditioning II.* New York: Appleton-Century-Crofts.

Hoehler, F. K., & Thompson, R. F. (1979). The effect of temporal alternation of learned increases in hippocampal unit activity in classical conditioning of the rabbit nictitating membrane response. *Physiological Psychology, 7,* 345-351.

Hull, C. L. (1943). *Principles of behavior*. New York: Appleton–Century–Crofts.

Hull, C. L. (1952). *A behavior system*. New Haven: Yale University Press.

Konorski, J., & Szwejkowska, G. (1952). Chronic extinction and restoration of conditioned reflexes, IV: The dependence of the course of extinction and restoration of conditioned reflexes on the "history" of the conditioned stimulus (The principle of the primacy of first training). *Acta Biologiae Experimentalis, 16*, 95–113.

Lubow, R. E., & Moore, A. U. (1979). Latent inhibition: The effect of nonreinforced preexposure to the conditioned stimulus. *Journal of Comparative and Physiological Psychology: Animal Behavior Processes, 2*, 163–174.

Martin, I., & Levey, A. B. (1969). *The genesis of the classical conditioned response*. New York: Pergamon Press.

Mackintosh, N. J. (1973). Stimulus selection: Learning to ignore stimuli that predict no change in reinforcement. In R. A. Hinde & J. Stevenson-Hinde (Eds.), *Constraints on learning*. New York: Academic Press.

Prokasy, W. F. (1956). The acquisition of observing responses in the absence of differential external reinforcement. *Journal of Comparative and Physiological Psychology, 49*, 131–134.

Prokasy, W. F. (1965). Classical eyelid conditioning: Experimenter operations, task demands, and response shaping. In W. F. Prokasy (Ed.), *Classical conditioning: A symposium*. New York: Appleton–Century–Crofts.

Prokasy, W. F. (1967). Unconditioned stimulus intensity and asymptotic performance eyelid conditioning. *Psychonomic Science, 8*, 149–150.

Prokasy, W. F. (1972). Developments with the two-phase model of classical conditioning. In A. H. Black & W. F. Prokasy (Eds.), *Classical conditioning II*. New York: Appleton–Century–Crofts.

Prokasy, W. F. (1973). A two-operator model account of aversive classical condition performance in humans and rabbits. *Learning and Motivation, 4*, 247–258.

Prokasy, W. F. (1974). Discriminated avoidance vs. classical conditioning: A two-phase model analysis. *Animal Learning and Behavior, 2*, 257–261.

Prokasy, W. F., Carlton, R. S., & Higgins, J. D. (1967). Effects of nonrandom intermittent reinfocement schedules in human eyelid conditioning. *Journal of Experimental Psychology, 74*, 282–288.

Prokasy, W. F., & Gormezano, I. (1979). The effect of US omission in classical aversive appetitive conditioning of rabbits. *Animal Learning & Behavior, 7*, 80–88/.

Prokasy, W. F., & Harsanyi, M. A. (1968). Two-phase model for human classical conditioning. *Journal of Experimental Psychology, 78*, 359–368.

Prokasy, W. F., Higgins, J. D., & Carlton, R. A. (1968). Sequential effects in differential human eyelid conditioning. *Psychonomic Science, 12*, 58.

Prokasy, W. F., Spurr, C. W., & Goodell, N. A. (1978). Preexposure to explicitly unpaired conditioned and unconditioned stimuli retards conditioned response emergence. *Bulletin of the Psychonomic Society, 12*, 155–158.

Prokasy, W. F., & Williams, W. C. (1979). Information processing and the decremental effect intermittent reinforcement schedules in human conditioning. *Bulletin of Psychonomic Society*.

Reiss, S., & Wagner, A. R. (1972). CS habituation produces a "latent inhibition effect" but no active conditioned inhibition. *Learning and Motivation, 3*, 237–245.

Rescorla, R. A. (1971). Summation and retardation tests of latent inhibition. *Journal of Comparative and Physiological Psychology, 75*, 77–81.

Rescorla, R. A., & Wagner, A. R. (1972). A theory of Pavlovian conditioning: Variations in the effectiveness of reinforcement and nonreinforcement. In A. H. Black & W. F. Prokasy (Eds.), *Classical conditioning II*. New York: Appleton–Century–Crofts.

Salafia, W. F., Romano, A. G., Tynan, T., & Host, K. C. (1977). Disruption of rabbit (Oryctologus cuniculus) nictitating membrane conditioning by post trial electrical stimulation of hippocampus. *Physiology & Behavior, 18,* 207–212.

Schneiderman, N. (1972). Response system divergences in aversive classical conditioning. In A. H. Black & W. F. Prokasy (Eds.), *Classical conditioning II.* New York: Appleton-Century-Crofts.

Schneiderman, N., & Gormezano, I. (1964). Conditioning of the nictitating membrane of the rabbit as a function of CS–UCS interval. *Journal of Comparative and Physiological Psychology, 57,* 188–195.

Smith, M. C., Coleman, S. R., & Gormezano, I. (1969). Classical conditioning of the rabbit's nictitating membrane response at backward, simultaneous, and forward CS–US intervals. *Journal of Comparative and Physiological Psychology, 69,* 226–231.

Sokolov, Y. N. (1964). *Perception and the conditioned reflex.* New York: Pergamon Press.

Solomon, P. R., Brennan, G., & Moore, J. W. (1974). Latent inhibition of the rabbit's nictitating membrane as a function of CS intensity. *Bulletin of the Psychonomic Society, 4,* 557–559.

Spence, K. W. (1956). *Behavior theory and conditioning.* New Haven: Yale University Press.

Spurr, C. W. (1979). *Preexposure stimulus intensity and the latent inhibition effect: A test of conditioning interpretation of latent inhibition with rabbits.* Unpublished Ph.D. Dissertation, University of Utah.

Theios, J. (1968). Finite integer models for learning in individual subjects. *Psychological Review, 75,* 292–307.

Theios, J., & Brelsford, J. W. (1966). A Markov model for classical conditioning: Application to eyeblink conditioning in rabbits. *Psychological Review, 73,* 393–408.

Thompson, R. F., Berger, T. W., Cegavske, C. F., Patterson, M. M., Rosemer, R. A., Teyler, T. J., & Young, R. A. (1976). The search for the engram. *American Psychologist, 31,* 209–227.

Thompson, R. F., Berry, S. D., Rinaldi, P. C., & Berger, T. W. (1979). Habituation and the orienting reflex: The dual process revisited. In H. D. Kimmel, E. H. Van Olst, & J. F. Orlebeke (Eds.), *The orienting response in humans.* Hillsdale, NJ: Lawrence Erlbaum Associates.

Wagner, A.R., & Rescorla, R. A. (1972). Inhibition in Pavlovian conditioning: An application of a theory. In R. A. Boakes & M. S. Halliday (Eds.), *Inhibition and learning.* New York: Academic Press.

Wagner, A. R., Rudy, J. W., & Whitlow, J. W. (1973). Rehearsal in animal conditioning. *Journal of Experimental Psychology, 97,* 407–426.

Wyckoff, L. B. (1952). The role of observing responses in discrimination learning: Part I. *Psychological Review, 59,* 431–442.

12 Appetitive-Aversive Interactions in Rabbit Conditioning Preparations

Michael J. Scavio, Jr.
California State University, Fullerton

This chapter presents the current results and implications of a research program investigating the bilateral transfer of training effects between the appetitive jaw-movement response (JMR) and aversive nictitating membrane response (NMR) conditioning paradigms for the rabbit. Specifically, the research has concentrated on how the CS and US used in appetitive conditioning influence subsequent NM CR acquisition and how the CS and US used in aversive conditioning contribute to later JM CR acquisition. The transfer outcomes are being pursued to elucidate the mediational effects of classical conditioning. In this regard, several theorists (e.g., Dickinson & Pearce, 1977; Hull, 1943; Trapold & Overmier, 1972) have postulated that the operations for classical conditioning produce the mediators for instrumental performance. However, researchers have disagreed as to how the mediational process is accomplished. Therefore, the present outcomes are relevant for evaluating the competing theoretical explanations for the Pavlovian mediation of instrumental performance. The following treatment begins with a consideration of Pavlovian mediational positions along with a summary of the traditional research methods for theory assessment. Next, the findings for the appetitive-aversive interactions with the rabbit classical conditioning paradigms are presented. The chapter concludes with an analysis of the presumed mechanisms of Pavlovian mediation based upon the current results.

INCEPTION AND DEVELOPMENT OF PAVLOVIAN
MEDIATIONAL THEORIES

The major premise of all Pavlovian mediational theories is that the goal-directed nature of instrumental performance is due to the intercession of classical conditioning operations. The first Pavlovian mediational account was developed by Hull (1929, 1930, 1931, 1934) who attempted to explain the purposive and adaptive character of instrumental behavior with deterministic principles. Basically, he tried to clarify how distal stimuli (i.e., reinforcers) controlled antecedant instrumental behaviors. In approaching this problem, Hull recognized that any instrumental conditioning situation also contains the operations for classical conditioning. In this regard, forward pairings of environmental or internal stimuli (CSs) with the reinforcer (US) fulfill the requirements for classical conditioning. As a result, situational CRs should be elicited concomitant with the occurrence of the instrumental behavior. Hull's solution to the purposive nature of instrumental responding was to assume that the situational CRs serve as the mediators.

Hull's major construct for mediation was the r_g–s_g mechanism. This construct represents the classical conditioning of an anticipatory goal response which serves to mediate instrumental appetitive behavior in the following manner. Fractional aspects (r_g) of the consummatory goal response (R_g) elicited by the reinforcer first become classically conditioned to drive stimuli serving as a CS complex. The stimulus consequence (s_g) of the r_g then becomes associated to the instrumental response through contiguity. Therefore, a mediational chain (i.e., drive stimuli → r_g → s_g → instrumental response) serves to direct the organism to goal objects.

Following its introduction, three different versions of the Pavlovian mediational model have been proposed. In the first approach, theorists (Amsel, 1958, 1962, 1967; Hull, 1943, 1951, 1952; Mowrer, 1947; Sheffield, 1966; Spence, 1956) have maintained that the conditioning of a *peripheral CR* serves as the basis for mediation. The peripheral (i.e., overt) CR has been assumed to regulate instrumental performance via secondary drive (e.g., Mowrer, 1947), secondary reinforcement (e.g., Hull, 1943), or incentive motivation (e.g., Spence, 1956). Theorists (Dickinson & Pearce, 1977; Konorski, 1967; Miller, 1963; Rescorla & Solomon, 1967), supporting the second approach, have relied upon the conditioning of *opponent-process* motivational states as the source of mediation. Opponent-process theorists have deviated from the peripheral CR accounts by assuming that the mediators of instrumental performance reside within the motivational structures of the brain. In the final theoretical version of Pavlovian mediation, researchers (Ghiselli & Fowler, 1976; Trapold & Overmier, 1972) have maintained that direct *associations* between situational CSs and the instrumental response account for the purposive nature of instrumental behavior. Therefore, the associative position denies that the acquisition of a peripheral or central CR is necessary for the mediation of instrumental behavior.

Peripheral CR Theories of Mediation

Peripheral CR theorists have claimed that the occurrence of conditioned activity in skeletal or autonomic structures produces the mediational influences for instrumental behavior. For example, Hull (1943, p. 100) identified the ability of a stimulus to mediate behavior in reward situations by its potential for eliciting a consummatory CR (r_g). According to Hull, the occurrence of the r_g produces a partial reduction of the drive state. Therefore, concurrent instrumental behaviors are secondarily reinforced by the drive reduction provided by r_g. Moreover, when Hull (1952) amended his theory to account for reward magnitude effects on instrumental appetitive performance (Crespi, 1944), the r_g-s_g mechanism assumed greater importance because it was used to determine the value of the incentive motivational influences upon behavior.

Mowrer (1947) forcefully brought Pavlovian mediational principles into the explanation of instrumental aversive behavior. Expanding upon distinctions drawn earlier by Schlosberg (1937) and Skinner (1938), Mowrer treated classical conditioning as necessary for the acquisition of emotional responses that are formed in the autonomic nervous system through CS–US contiguity. He also regarded instrumental conditioning as necessary for the acquisition of skeletal responses that are reinforced through drive reduction. In the course of instrumental aversive conditioning, Mowrer considered that an automatic fear CR must be acquired before the instrumental response can be established. The initial formation of the fear CR is necessary because it serves as the secondary motivator for instrumental aversive performance. Moreover, the termination of fear functions as the secondary reinforcer strengthening the intrumental aversive behavior.

Brief mention may be made of the other theorists who have contributed to the peripheral CR account of Pavlovian mediation. In addition to Hull (1952), Spence (1956) relied upon the r_g-s_g mechanism to explain incentive effects upon behavior. Later, Amsel (1958, 1962, 1967) introduced the concept of conditioned frustration (i.e., r_f-s_f mechanism) to account for the extinction of previously rewarded responses. According to Amsel, if the occurrence of r_g is not followed by reward, then a primary emotional reaction of frustration (R_f) is elicited. Moreover, frustration has a detachable component (r_f that can be classically conditioned to environmental stimuli. Additionally, r_f has a stimulus consequence (s_f) that evokes bodily reactions that compete with the execution of the instrumental response. Finally, Sheffield (1966) proposed a consummatory response theory of reinforcement to explain the ability of rewards to control behavior. In Sheffield's theory, the elicitation of conditioned consummatory responses produces positive emotional excitation, which augments the vigor of co-occurring instrumental activity.

Empirical Evaluation of Peripheral CR Theories

A popular means for studying the involvement of peripheral CRs in the mediation of instrumental behavior has been the concomitant recording technique. The tactic of the concomitant recording approach is to establish the temporal relationship between situational CRs and instrumental behaviors. If Pavlovian mediation is accomplished through motivational influences (e.g., Mowrer, 1947; Spence, 1956), then peripheral CRs should be observed before the formation of instrumental responses. On the other hand, if reinforcement is the basis for mediation (e.g., Hull, 1943; Sheffield, 1966), then situational CRs should be elicited after the initiation of instrumental responding.

Historically, the use of concomitant recordings can be traced to a series of investigations by Miller and Konorski (1928) with a detailed summary of their research given by Konorski (1967, Chapter 8). In general, Miller and Konorski found that the instrumental response for food usually occurred before the appearance of a situational salivary CR. Since the work of Miller and Konorski, several experiments utilizing concomitant measures have been completed. In instrumental appetitive situations, researchers (e.g., Ellison & Konorski, 1964, 1966; Kintsch & Witte, 1962; Lewis & Kent, 1961; Shapiro, 1962; Williams, 1965) have continued to rely upon the measurement of salivary CRs to indicate the presence of the mediational process. In instrumental aversive situations, investigators (e.g., Bersch, Notterman, & Schoenfield, 1956; Black, 1959; Carlson, 1960; Gantt & Dykman, 1957; Soltysik & Kowalska, 1960) have monitored heart-rate CRs to index mediational influences.

Reviews of concomitant measurement studies have been completed (e.g., Gormezano & Moore, 1969; Rescorla & Solomon, 1967; Scavio, 1972). These summaries indicate for both instrumental appetitive and aversive conditioning that no reliable relationship exists between the occurrences of peripheral CRs and instrumental responses. For example, on schedule controlled behavior, Williams (1965) found no consistent relationship for dogs regarding the onsets of salivary CRs and bar-press responses for food. In avoidance conditioning, Soltysik and Kowalska (1960) also observed for dogs differential onsets of heart-rate CRs and bar-press responses. Moreover, the inherent correlational nature of the data complicate the interpretation of concomitant recording studies. In this regard, no assurance can be given that the CR chosen for recording actually reflects the mediational process. In spite of the difficulties involved in the evaluation of concomitant measurement studies, Rescorla and Solomon (1967) have concluded that the inconsistent relationship between situational CRs and instrumental responding disqualifies peripheral mechanisms as the basis for Pavlovian mediation.

Opponent-Process Theories of Mediation

Following the decline of peripheral CR theories, several researchers have adopted a proposal for Pavlovian mediation that assumes the involvement of opponent-process motivational systems within the brain. The opponent-process formulation (cf. Dickinson & Pearce, 1977) may be briefly summarized. First, the hedonic properties of rewards activate the appetitive motivational system when a deprivation condition is present. Likewise, the hedonic properties of punishers excite the aversive motivational system. Secondly, CSs paired with rewards become elicitors of activity in the appetitive motivational system, and CSs paired with punishers become elicitors of activity in the aversive motivational system. Thirdly, the conditioned activity in the appetitive system strengthens instrumental behaviors for rewards, and conditioned activity in the aversive system augments instrumental behaviors removing noxious events. Finally, the appetitive and aversive systems are considered to have mutually inhibitory influences. Thus, the excitation of one system reduces the reactivity of the other system. Consequently, appetitive stimuli (CSs and USs) should inhibit instrumental behaviors controlled by aversive reinforcers, and aversive stimuli (CSs and USs) should retard instrumental behaviors for rewards. Therefore, when appetitive and aversive stimuli are simultaneously presented, the final quality and intensity of the motivation for behavior is determined by the algebraic summation of the strengths of the opposing motivational systems.

Mowrer (1960) provided the transition between peripheral CR and opponent-process theories of mediation. Mowrer (1960) replaced his original position (Mowrer, 1947) with a view that all mediational effects are the result of changes in fear states. In instrumental aversive situations, a CS paired with a noxious reinforcer elicits an increase in fear. However, if the noxious reinforcer fails to occur, then the CS will come to elicit a decrease in fear (i.e., "relief"). In instrumental appetitive situations, the presence of a drive condition is necessarily fear arousing. Therefore, if a CS is paired with reward, a conditioned decrease in fear (i.e., "hope") occurs. However, if the CS is terminated and the drive state has not been reduced, then an increase in fear (i.e., "disappointment") is conditioned. In summary, conditioned fear and disappointment inhibit instrumental performance through secondary punishment. Hope and relief facilitate instrumental performance through secondary reinforcement.

Miller (1963) revised Mowrer's (1960) proposal in terms of hypothetical cortical mechanisms to produce the first opponent-process theory of Pavlovian mediation. Miller considered that the central nervous system contains "go" motivational units that are activated whenever the organism experiences a drive-reducing event. The effect of go activity is to increase the vigor of instrumental behaviors. When go activity becomes classically conditioned to neutral stimuli in contiguity with the occurrence of drive reduction, instrumental behaviors preceding the reduction of drive are potentiated. Miller also considered that the central nervous system contains "stop" motivational units that are activated whenever the organism is exposed to drive-inducing events (i.e., the onset of either a deprivation condition or a painful stimulus). Stop activity inhibits the occurrence of instrumental behaviors. Consequently, when stop activity becomes classically conditioned to neutral stimuli in contiguity with the occurrence of drive-inducing events, instrumental behaviors leading to the induction of drive are blocked.

Miller also added the important assumption that go and stop activities are mutually incompatible. Therefore, if an attempt is made to elicit simultaneously go and stop activity, then reciprocal inhibition should reduce the strength of both. Consequently, the stronger of the two types of activity remains to control instrumental performance. For example, in the conditioned suppression paradigm (Estes & Skinner, 1941), the presentation of a CS that had been previously paired with shock retards the occurrence of instrumental responding for reward. In this situation, the stop motivational system appears to dominate over the go motivational system that then brings about a reduction in instrumental performance.

Following Miller's (1963) introduction, several other theorists (e.g., Dickinson & Pearce, 1977; Gray, 1975; Konorski, 1967; Rescorla & Solomon, 1967; Solomon & Corbit, 1974) have contributed to the opponent-process model of mediation. Although some modifications have been made in Miller's original formulation, the essential premise has been retained that hedonically opposite motivational states compete for the control over behavior. Moreover, Solomon and Corbit (1975) have extended the opponent-process model to explain drug addiction and risk-taking behavior.

Associative Theories of Mediation

Trapold and Overmier (1972) have presented an outline for an associative view of mediation that is based upon the assumption that the cue properties of CSs directly control instrumental behaviors. According to Trapold and Overmier's (1972) account, pairings of situational CSs with reinforcers allow the CSs to acquire a mediational connection promoting the occurrence of the instrumental response. On the other hand, unpaired presentations of situational CSs with reinforcers permit the formation of a mediator blocking the occurrence of the instrumental response.

Following Trapold and Overmier's statement, Ghiselli and Fowler (1976) have tried to establish more precise principles for the associative view of mediation. Ghiselli and Fowler hypothesized that CSs paired with reinforcers should acquire a general predictive value for reinforcement delivery. Likewise, CSs given in an unpaired manner with reinforcers should come to have a general predictive value for the absence of reinforcement. Moreover, the signaling properties of CSs, and not their hedonic values, are assumed to determine mediation. Therefore, a CS previously paired with any type of reinforcer should have positive transfer effects upon the acquisition of instrumental appetitive or aversive behavior as long as the CS continues to signal reinforcement delivery. In contrast, a CS previously given in an unpaired manner with any type of reinforcer should have negative transfer effects upon the acquisition of instrumental behavior reinforced by either appetitive or aversive events.

Empirical Evaluation of Opponent-Process and Associative Theories

The opponent-process and associative views of Pavlovian mediation have been investigated through the use of classical-instrumental transfer designs. In the prototypic transfer task (e.g., Estes & Skinner, 1941), separate stages of classical and instrumental conditioning are conducted. Then, in the test stage, the CS that had been established during classical conditioning is presented during the resumption of instrumental training. The usual result is that the rate of instrumental responding is changed following CS presentation. Therefore, the sensitivity of instrumental responding to the presence of the CS is assumed to indicate the involvement of Pavlovian mediational effects. Because the classical and instrumental conditioning stages may be either appetitive or aversive, a four-fold combination of classical aversive-instrumental transfer experiments is produced (i.e., classical appetitive-instrumental appetitive; classical appetitive-instrumental aversive; classical aversive-instrumental appetitive; and classical aversive-instrumental aversive).

Opponent-process and associative theories of Pavlovian mediation make different predictions regarding outcomes in the test stage of classical aversive-instrumental appetitive and classical appetitive-instrumental aversive transfer experiments. In these situations, the CS and the instrumental behavior have received training with hedonically opposite reinforcers. According to the opponent process theory (e.g., Dickinson & Pearce, 1977), presentations of a CS, that had been paired with an US whose hedonic value contrasts with the instrumental reinforcer's, should produce disruption of instrumental performance in the test stage. However, the associative view (e.g., Ghiselli & Fowler, 1976; Trapold & Overmier, 1972) would expect that the presentation of a CS, previously paired with any type of affective US, should augment reinforced instrumental responding in the first stage.

The outcomes of classical-instrumental transfer experiments have been reviewed (e.g., Dickinson & Pearce, 1977; Rescorla & Solomon, 1967). Evidence from the conditioned suppression paradigm (e.g., Estes & Skinner, 1941; Kamin, 1965) supports the opponent-process contention that aversive CSs should retard instrumental appetitive performance. However, appetitive CSs have been found to have both incremental (e.g., Bacon & Bindra, 1967; O'Neill & Biederman, 1974; Overmier & Payne, 1971) and decremental (e.g., Goodkin, 1976; Mellgren, Hunsicker, & Dyck, 1975) influences upon instrumental aversive behavior. Consequently, the inconsistent outcomes from classical appetitive-instrumental aversive transfer experiments do not offer firm support to either the opponent process or associative positions for Pavlovian mediation.

Several researchers (e.g., Gormezano & Kehoe, 1975; Scavio, 1972; Traplod & Overmier, 1972) have cited possible confounding factors that might limit the value of classical-instrumental transfer designs in testing Pavlovian mediational theories. A major problem with classical-instrumental transfer designs is the possibility that response system interactions, and not Pavlovian mediational effects, are responsible for the changes in instrumental behavior in the test stage. Response system interactions refer to the carry-over to the test stage of instrumental behaviors adventitiously acquired during the "classical conditioning" stage of training. The potential for response system interactions is especially acute in classical appetitive-instrumental aversive transfer experiments. In these situations, researchers (e.g., Goodkin, 1976; Mellgren et al., 1975; O'Neill & Biederman, 1974) have required an approach response so that the rewarding US can be paired with the CS during the classical conditioning stage. Consequently, the approach response may be elicited by the CS when it is later presented in the test stage. If the skeletal behavior evoked by the CS is compatible with the target instrumental response, then the CS would appear to enhance performance in the test stage. However, if the skeletal behavior evoked by the CS is incompatible with the target instrumental response, then the CS would seem to interfere with performance in the test stage. Because response system interactions may be an important consideration in all types of classical-instrumental transfer tasks, the true mediational effects of CSs must still be corroborated.

TESTING PAVLOVIAN MEDIATIONAL THEORIES BY CLASSICAL-CLASSICAL TRANSFER DESIGNS

Another strategy for assessing Pavlovian mediational theories is to employ classical-classical transfer designs. The basic arrangement for the classical-classical transfer task involves two successive stages of classical conditioning that utilize the same CS (e.g., Konorski & Szwejkowska, 1956; Scavio, 1974).

The transfer effects of the CS upon second stage conditioning are used to infer the nature of Pavlovian mediation. The simple design of the classical-classical transfer task allows the isolation of mediational effects to a single CS. Moreover, possible response system interactions, confounding the expression of Pavlovian mediational effects, can be evaluated by concomitantly recording the CR established in the first stage during the acquisition of the second stage CR and then applying the appropriate statistical tests.

As in the case of analogous classical-instrumental transfer experiments, the opponent-process and associative accounts of Pavlovian mediation make different predictions for classical-classical transfer studies involving successive stages of appetitive and aversive conditioning (i.e., classical appetitive-classical aversive transfer; classical aversive-classical appetitive transfer). Opponent-process theorists expect that reciprocal inhibition would disrupt the acquisition of the second stage CR if the affective quality of the US is changed between training stages. However, associative theorists predict that CS–US pairings in the first stage of training establish the CS as a general predictor for reinforcement. Therefore, the use of the CS in second stage conditioning should accelerate CR acquisition independently of the hedonic value of the US. In the following sections, a summary is given of the work investigating appetitive-aversive interactions revealed by classical-classical transfer experiments using the JMR and NMR paradigms.

Effects of an Aversive CS upon Appetitive Conditioning

In the initial experiment (Scavio, 1974), the effects of prior aversive NMR conditioning upon appetitive JMR conditioning with the same CS were assessed. Three groups of 12 rabbits each were respectively exposed in Stage 1 to 100, 200, and 400 tone-CS and paraorbital shock-US pairings for NMR conditioning in a single daily session. Two sets of control groups were also included in Stage 1. Three groups, each having 12 rabbits, represented one control set. These groups respectively received 100, 200, and 400 presentations of the tone and shock given in an explicitly unpaired manner (Rescorla, 1967) in a single daily session. Three other groups of 12 rabbits each, serving as the second control set, were respectively confined in the conditioning apparatus without tone and shock deliveries for the time periods required to give 100, 200, and 400 tone-shock pairings. In Stage 2, all 9 groups received 5 consecutive daily sessions of JMR conditioning with each session having 30 pairings of the tone-CS with an orally injected water-US. In order to allow for JMR conditioning, all rabbits were placed on a water deprivation schedule before the beginning of the experiment.

In Stage 1, the groups receiving tone-shock pairings showed overall NM CR percentages directly ordered to the training levels. For the groups given unpaired presentations, no NMR pseudoconditioning was observed. Finally, for the groups having no training, a negligible number of NMRs were found at times corresponding to the delivery of the tone on paired trials.

Figure 12.1 presents the transfer effects of the prior Stage 1 manipulations upon JMR conditioning to the tone in Stage 2. The JM CR percentages for the groups receiving 100, 200, and 400 tone-shock pairings in Stage 1 (i.e., Groups P-100, P-200, and P-400) were inferior to those obtained for groups having unpaired (i.e., Groups U-100, U-200, and U-400) and no (i.e., Groups N-100, N-200, and N-400) tone and shock deliveries in Stage 1. Therefore, the previous pairings of the tone and shock produced negative transfer effects upon subsequent JMR conditioning utilizing pairings of the tone with water. Furthermore, Fig. 12.1 indicates that no substantial differences occurred in the second stage performances of Groups P-100, P-200, and P-400. Thus, the inhibitory effects produced by Stage 1 were apparently maximized within 100 tone-shock pairings.

Groups P-100, P-200, and P-400 continued to have their NM CR performances monitored during JMR conditioning in Stage 2. Figure 12.2 presents the NM CR and JM CR percentages collapsed for Groups P-100, P-200, and P-400 on each training day in Stage 2. It is clear from the figure that NM CR performance declined as JM CR performance improved.

The concomitant recording of NM CRs and JM CRs in Stage 2 made possible a determination of whether the negative transfer effects of prior tone-

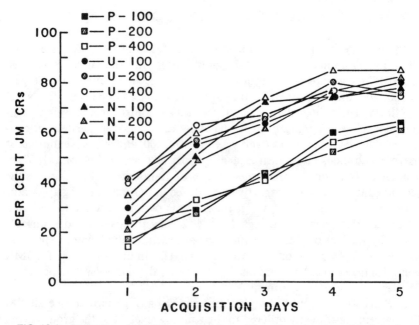

FIG. 12.1   Percentage of JM CRs over the 5 days of Stage 2 as a function of the Stage 1 training conditions (Scavio, 1974).

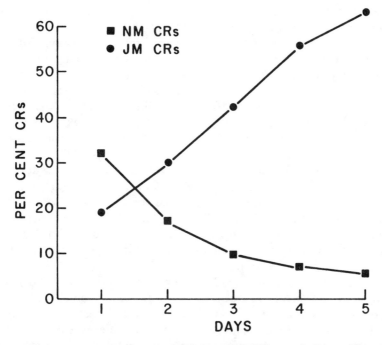

FIG. 12.2   Concomitant percentages of NM CRs and JM CRs over the 5 days of Stage 2 for Groups receiving NMR conditioning in Stage 1 (Scavio, 1974).

shock pairings upon second stage conditioning were due to motor incompatibility between the NMR and JMR. If the rabbit could not concurrently perform both the NM CR and the JM CR on the same presentation of the CS, then JM CR acquisition would have been delayed until sufficient extinction of the NM CR occurred. Whether motor incompatibility existed between the NMR and JMR was determined by the chi-square statistic used as a test of independence (Parzen, 1960). On each training day in Stage 2, the statistical test indicated that the JM CR occurrence was not influenced by the presence of the NM CR. Therefore, motor antagonisms between the NMR and JMR cannot account for the negative transfer effects found in the first experiment.

Effects of an Appetitive CS upon Aversive Conditioning

The previous experiment revealed that a CS previously paired with shock disrupted subsequent appetitive JMR conditioning. A second experiment (Scavio & Gormezano, 1980) determined whether a CS previously paired with water could influence aversive NMR conditioning. The experiment required 4 groups each having 12 rabbits. The groups were placed on a water deprivation schedule before the start of Stage 1. In Stage 1, which lasted 5 consecutive days, Group P was given daily 30 tone-CS and water-US pairings for JMR conditioning. Group U received daily 30 presentations each of the tone and water given in an explicitly unpaired manner. Finally, Groups N and NN, in lieu of tone and water deliveries, were confined daily in the conditioning apparatus for times corresponding to the length of a training session given to Groups P and U. In Stage 2, Groups P, U, and N received 80 tone-shock pairings daily for 4 days of NMR conditioning. Group NN, in Stage 2, continued with apparatus confinement free of tone and shock presentations. Each confinement period lasted the length of a training session given to Groups P, U, and N.

In Stage 1, Group P displayed substantial JM CR acquisition. Moreover, Group U showed a moderate level of JM pseudo CRs elicited by the unpaired tone. (As the work of Sheafor, 1975, and Sheafor and Gormezano, 1972, indicates, the susceptibility of the JMR to pseudoconditioning is a reliable outcome). Finally, in Stage 1, Groups N and NN maintained very low JMR base levels found during observation intervals given at times corresponding to the delivery of the tone for Group P.

The transfer effects of the prior Stage 1 manipulations upon NMR conditioning to the tone in Stage 2 are depicted in Fig. 12.3. As compared to Group N, Group P showed accelerated NM CR acquisition whereas Group U had retarded NM CR acquisition. Therefore, prior tone-water pairings (Group P) produced a positive transfer effects upon NMR conditioning; however, prior unpaired tone and water deliveries (Group U) yielded a negative transfer effect upon NMR conditioning. Figure 12.3 also illustrates that Group NN maintained a low NMR base level on observation intervals corresponding to the deliveries of the tone-CS for Groups P, U, and N. The steady base level means that no changes occurred in the reactivity of the NMR that might have influenced the transfer outcomes. Finally, the possibility was evaluated that the positive transfer effects for Group P might have resulted from the "accidental" conditioning of the NMR on the tone-water pairings of Stage 1. However, recordings of the NMR on five tone-alone presentations given after the last tone-water pairing in the first stage revealed no surreptitious NM CR acquisition.

Evaluation of Appetitive-Aversive Interactions for CSs

The previous experiments have uncovered asymmetrical appetitive-aversive interactions for CSs. Thus, prior tone-shock pairings for NMR conditioning retarded subsequent JMR conditioning on tone-water pairings. In contrast, prior tone-water pairings for JMR conditioning facilitated later NMR conditioning on tone-shock pairings. These results cannot be incorporated easily within either the opponent-process or associative accounts of Pavlovian mediation because both predict symmetrical transfer effects. However, the

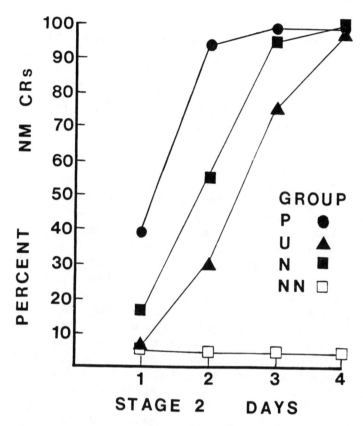

FIG. 12.3   Percentage of NM CRs over the 4 days of Stage 2 as a function of the Stage 1 training conditions (Scavio & Gormezano, 1980).

asymmetrical appetitive-aversive interactions might be understood by first noting that the transfer effects of the aversive CS upon appetitive conditioning were consistent with the opponent-process theory and that the transfer effects of the appetitive CS upon aversive conditioning were in agreement with the associative theory. Thus appetitive and aversive CSs may possess different mediational effects. The basis for the divergent transfer effects might be due to the lack of reciprocal inhibition between aversive and appetitive stimuli as proposed in the opponent-process theory. As suggested by the data, an aversive CS can disrupt appetitive conditioning, but an appetitive CS may not be able to return inhibition to aversive conditioning. Therefore, the associative properties of an appetitive CS may remain to influence aversive conditioning.

The asymmetrical transfer effects for CSs are important in elucidating the relationship between appetitive and aversive stimuli. The firm establishment that inhibition proceeds only from aversive to appetitive stimuli would force a major reconsideration of Pavlovian mediational theories. Therefore, the following experiment was conducted to ascertain whether asymmetrical appetitive-aversive interactions are seen with hedonically antipodal USs.

The Effects of Pairing Hedonically Opposite USs upon Appetitive and Aversive Conditioning

A determination (Scavio, Marshall, & Gormezano, in preparation) was made whether the asymmetrical appetitive-aversive interactions, observed with CSs, also extends to USs. Thus, another transfer study was conducted that used 4 groups, each having 24 rabbits. In Stage 1, which lasted 5 daily sessions, Group S–W received on each day 30 forward shock-water pairings. Group W–S was given daily 30 forward water-shock pairings. Group U was also administered shock and water with each event given 30 times daily in an unpaired manner. Finally, Group N was housed in the conditioning apparatus without shock and water for daily periods corresponding to the length of the training sessions used for the other groups. In Stage 2, also lasting 5 days, each of the 4 groups was divided into 2 squads of 12 rabbits each. The first 12 rabbits for Groups S–W, W–S, U, and N received daily 30 tone-shock pairings for NMR conditioning. The second 12 rabbits for Groups S–W, W–S, U, and N were given daily 30 tone-water pairings for JMR conditioning.

The results for Stage 1 revealed that Group S–W showed substantial JM CR acquisition to shock on its pairings with water. Also, pseudoconditioning of the JMR was evident for Group U on the unpaired deliveries of shock. Group W–S displayed considerable NM CR acquisition to water on its pairings with shock. Moreover, a relatively small amount of NMR pseudoconditioning was found for Group U on the unpaired presentations of water. The ability of USs to function as CSs for JMR and NMR conditioning is reminiscent of Erofeeva's (1916) early data showing the conditioning of a dog's salivary reaction to shock. Because pseudoconditioning of the JMR is known to occur to a tone (Sheafor, 1975; Sheafor & Gormezano, 1972), the observation of JM pseudo CRs on unpaired shock presentations was not surprising. However, the modest number of NM pseudo CRs on unpaired water presentations was unexpected because the NMR does not exhibit any pseudoconditioning to a tone (e.g., Gormezano, Schneiderman, Deaux, & Fuentes, 1962). Perhaps the greater biological significance of water over tone is important in the surfacing of NMR pseudoconditioning. Finally, Group N displayed low JMR and NMR base levels in observation intervals corresponding to the deliveries of shock and water for Group U.

The transfer effects of Stage 1 upon NMR and JMR conditioning in Stage 2 are illustrated by Fig. 12.4. The left panel of the figure shows how the rabbit

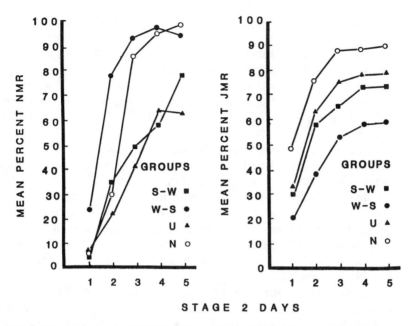

FIG. 12.4   Percentages of NM CRs (left panel) and JM CRs (right panel) over the 5 days of Stage 2 as a function of the Stage 1 training conditions (Scavio, Marshall, & Gormezano, in preparation).

squads for Groups S–W, W–S, U, and N given NMR conditioning performed. The right panel depicts the performances of the remaining rabbit squads for groups S–W, W–S, U, and N that received JMR conditioning. Turning to the left panel, Group W–S exceeded the NMR conditioning rate shown by Group N. Therefore, prior water-shock pairings, having produced NM CR acquisition in Stage 1, facilitated another acquisition of the NMR on tone-shock pairings. Groups S–W and U had similar NM CR performances that were below the level of Group N. Consequently, paired and unpaired presentations of shock and water in Stage 1 were equivalent in reducing the reinforcing value of shock for NMR conditioning to tone in Stage 2. Examination of the right panel of Fig. 12.4 reveals that Group N had the fastest JMR conditioning rate. Therefore, all manipulations of water and shock in Stage 1 contributed negative transfer effects upon JMR conditioning in Stage 2. Because Groups S–W and U had lower JM CR performances than did Group N in Stage 2, the prior conditioning (Group S–W) and pseudoconditioning (Group U) of the JMR in Stage 1 provided no advantage for JM CR acquisition on the tone-water pairings of Stage 2. Finally, Group W–S had the slowest JMR conditioning rate in the second stage. Thus, the water-shock pairings of Stage 1 had unique effects in reducing the reinforcing capacity of water for JM CR acquisition in Stage 2.

Evaluation of Appetitive-Aversive Interactions for USs

The previous experiment has revealed asymmetrical appetitive-aversive interactions for USs. Forward water-shock pairings were more effective than their unpaired deliveries in reducing the reinforcing capacity of water for later JMR conditioning. In contrast, forward shock-water presentations yielded the same degree of interference as their unpaired deliveries upon the reinforcing value of shock for subsequent NMR conditioning. The unique contribution of water-shock pairings for the retardation of the reinforcing value of water without any reciprocation in the ability of water-shock pairings to provide unique decrements in the reinforcing value of shock is consistent with the earlier proposal that inhibition is transferred from aversive to appetitive stimuli but not vise versa. The reduction in the reinforcing power of shock that did occur appears to be due to the consequences of prior US exposure (e.g., Holmes, 1971; Siegal & Domjan, 1971) given the equivalence in the negative transfer effects of paired and unpaired shock-water presentations upon NMR conditioning.

Another contrast between appetitive and aversive conditioning was observed in the previous experiment. Prior NMR conditioning on water-shock pairings was followed by accelerated NM CR acquisition on tone-shock pairings. However, prior JMR conditioning on shock-water pairings interfered with the subsequent JM CR acquisition on tone-water pairings. This difference implies that shock, as the first event in the pairing sequence, is also able to reduce the reinforcing capacity of water. Because appetitive stimuli apparently cannot return inhibition, no complementary reductions in the reinforcing value of shock occurred when water was the first event in the pairing relationship. Consequently, the positive consequences of the prior use of shock to condition the NMR to water were allowed to accelerate NM CR acquisitions to tone.

IMPLICATIONS FOR PAVLOVIAN MEDIATIONAL THEORIES

The use of classical-classical transfer experiments with the NMR and JMR preparations has yielded valuable information regarding the possible mechanisms for Pavlovian mediation. The most salient findings of the current research are the asymmetrical appetitive-aversive interactions. Thus, the aversive CS and US decremented appetitive JMR conditioning and the appetitive CS facilitated aversive NMR conditioning. These differential transfer effects question the opponent process (cf. Dickinson & Pearce, 1977) and associative (Trapold & Overmier, 1972) mediational theories both of which expected symmetrical appetitive-aversive interactions. Nevertheless, a compromise position between the alternative mediational views can be suggested to explain the data. The opponent-process theory correctly predicted the retardation of appetitive conditioning by aversive stimuli, and the associative theory was accurate in forcasting the enhancement of aversive conditioning by the appetitive CS. Consequently, only the aversive stimuli had the ability to inhibit behavior maintained by reward. Because the appetitive stimuli did not have complementary inhibitory consequences, the appetitive CS relied upon its associate properties to control aversive conditioning.

The asymmetrical transfer effects also force a reconsideration how the opponent-process model treats the interrelationship between appetite and aversive stimuli. According to the model, appetitive and aversive stimuli induce reciprocal inhibition through their motivational consequences. However, Hull (1951) hypothesized that aversive, but not appetitive, stimuli are motivators. Appetitive stimuli serve as reinforcers owing to their drive-reducing potential. If Hull's view is accepted, then the logic of the opponent-process model must acknowledge that appetitive stimuli cannot inhibit aversive behaviors. Because rewards remove excitation in the appetitive motivational system, the reciprocal inhibition of the aversive system is precluded. Therefore, appetitive CSs must utilize other mediational influences, such as their associative properties, to determine aversive conditioning. Consequently, the asymmetrical transfer outcomes support a revision of the opponent-process model that maintains that inhibition proceeds from aversive to appetitive stimuli but not vise versa.

The appetitive CS in the current work appeared to have associative properties in the mediation of aversive conditioning. However, the existing associative accounts of mediation (e.g., Ghiselli & Fowler, 1976; Trapold & Overmier, 1972) do not include specific mechanisms by which CSs control behavior. Therefore, a consideration of current theories of classical conditioning may be helpful in clarifying associative principles of mediation. For example, in Mackintosh's (1975) explanation of classical conditioning, a claim is made that a CS gains in "associability" as a result of the pairing operation. Consequently, the ability of prior tone-water pairings to increase NMR conditioning may have been tied to the greater facilitation of the tone for entering into associative connections. Moreover, Mackintosh's associability parameter may even extend to USs. This possibility is implied by the positive transfer effect of prior water-shock pairings upon subsequent NMR conditioning on tone-shock pairings. The potential for USs to have associability values has yet to be recognized in contemporary theories of classical conditioning.

ACKNOWLEDGMENTS

The author wishes to thank I. Gormezano who made available the conditioning laboratory at the University of Iowa for the conduct of the reported research. The research was supported by NSF grants to I. Gormezano and by a Partners-in-Excellence grant to the author.

REFERENCES

Amsel, A. (1958). The role of frustrative nonreward in noncontinuous reward situations. *Psychological Bulletin, 55,* 102–119.

Amsel, A. (1962). Frustrative nonreward in partial reinforcement and discrimination learning: Some recent history and a theoretical extension. *Psychological Review, 69,* 306–328.

Amsel, A. (1967). Partial reinforcement effect on vigor and persistence: Advances in frustration theory derived from a variety of within-subject experiments. In W. K. Spence & J. T. Spence (Eds.), *The psychology of learning and motivation: Advances in research and theory* (Vol. 1). New York: Academic Press.

Bacon, W. E., & Bindra, D. (1967). The generality of the incentive-motivational effects of classical conditioned stimuli in instrumental learning. *Acta Biologiae Experimentalis, 27,* 185–197.

Bersch, P. J., Notterman, J. M., & Schoenfield, W. N. (1956). Extinction of a human cardiac response during avoidance conditioning. *American Journal of Psychology, 69,* 244–251.

Black, A. H. (1959). Heart rate changes during avoidance conditioning in dogs. *Canadian Journal of Psychology, 13,* 229–242.

Carlson, N. J. (1960). Primary and secondary reward in traumatic avoidance learning. *Journal of Comparative and Physiological Psychology, 35,* 336–340.

Crespi, L. P. (1944) Amount of reinforcement and the level of performance. *Psychological Review, 51,* 341–357.

Dickinson, A., & Pearce, J. M. (1977). Inhibitory interactions between appetitive and aversive stimuli. *Psychological Bulletin, 84,* 690–711.

Ellison, G. D., & Konorski, J. (1964). Separation of the salivary and motor responses in instrumental conditioning. *Science, 146,* 1071–1072.

Ellison, G. D., & Konorski, J. (1966). Salivation and instrumental responding to an instrument CS pretrained using the classical conditioning paradigm. *Acta Biologicae Experimentalis, 26,* 159–165.

Erofeeva, M. N. (1916). Contributions a l'étude des réflexes conditionnels destructifs. *Compte Rendu de la Societé de Biologie, 79,* 239–240.

Estes, W. K., & Skinner, B. F. (1941). Some quantitative properties of anxiety. *Journal of Experimental Psychology, 29,* 390–400.

Gantt, W. H., & Dykman, R. A. (1957). Experimental psychogenic tachycardia. In P. H. Hock & J. Zubin (Eds.), *Experimental psychopathology.* New York: Grune & Stratton.

Ghiselli, W. B., & Fowler, H. (1976). Signaling and affective functions of conditioned aversive stimuli in an appetitive choice discrimination: US intensity effects. *Learning and Motivation, 7,* 1–16.

Goodkin, F. (1976). Rats learn the relationship between responding and environmental events: An expansion of the learned helplessness hypothesis. *Learning and Motivation, 7,* 382–393.

Gormezano, I., & Kehoe, E. J. (1975). Classical conditioning: Some methodological-conceptual issues. In W. K. Estes (Ed.), *Handbook of learning and cognitive processes* (Vol. 2). Hillsdale, NJ: Lawrence Erlbaum Associates.

Gormezano, I., & Moore, J. W. (1969). Classical conditioning. In M. H. Marx (Ed.), *Learning: Processes.* New York: MacMillan.

Gormezano, I., Schneiderman, N., Deaux, E. G., & Fuentes, I. (1962). Nictitating membrane: Classical conditioning and extinction in the albino rabbit. *Science, 138,* 33–34.

Gray, J. A. (1975). *Elements of a two-process theory of learning.* London: Academic Press.

Holmes, J. D. (1971). *Effects of backward pairings of the CS and US on classical conditioning of the nictitating membrane response in the rabbit.* Unpublished doctoral dissertation, The University of Iowa.

Hull, C. L. (1929). A functional interpretation of the conditioned reflex. *Psychological Review, 36,* 498–511.

Hull, C. L. (1930). Knowledge and purpose as habit mechanisms. *Psychological Review, 37* 511–525.

Hull, C. L. (1931). Goal attraction and directing ideas conceived as habit phenomena. *Psychological Review, 38,* 487–506.

Hull, C. L. (1934). The rat's speed-of-locomotion gradient in the approach to food. *Journal of Comparative Psychology, 17,* 393–422.

Hull, C. L. (1943). *Principles of behavior.* New York: Appleton–Century–Crofts.

Hull, C. L. (1951). *Essentials of behavior.* New Haven: Yale University Press.

Hull, C. L. (1952). *A behavior system.* New Haven: Yale University Press.

Kamin, L. J. (1965). Temporal and intensity characteristics of the conditioned stimulus. In W. F. Prokasy (Ed.), *Classical conditioning: A symposium.* New York: Appleton–Century–Crofts.

Kintsch, W., & Witte, R. S. (1962). Concurrent conditioning of bar press and salivation responses. *Journal of Comparative and Physiological Psychology, 55,* 963–968.

Konorski, J. (1967). *Integrative activity of the brain: An interdisciplinary approach.* Chicago: University of Chicago Press.

Konorski, J., & Szwejkowska, G. (1956). Reciprocal transformations of heterogeneous conditioned reflexes. *Acta Biologiae Experimentalis, 16,* 95–113.

Lewis, D. J., & Kent, N. D. (1961). Attempted direct activation and deactivation of the fractioned anticipatory goal response. *Psychological Reports, 8,* 107–110.

Mackintosh, N. J. (1975). A theory of attention: Variation in the associability of stimuli with reinforcement. *Psychological Review, 82,* 276–298.

Mellgren, R. L., Hunsicker, J. P., & Dyck, D. G. (1975). Conditions of preexposure and passive avoidance behavior in rats. *Animal Learning & Behavior, 3,* 147–151.

Miller, N. E. (1963). Some reflections on the law of effect produce a new alternative to drive reduction. In M. A. Jones (Ed.), *Nebraska Symposium on Motivation.* Lincoln: University of Nebraska Press.

Miller, S., & Konorski, J. (1928). Sur une forme particuliere des reflexes conditionnels. *Compte Rendy Hebdemadaire des Seances et Memoires de la Societe de Biologie, 99,* 1155–1158.

Mowrer, O. H. (1960). Learning theory and behavior. New York: Wiley.

Mowrer, O. H. (1947). On the dual nature of learning – A reinterpretation of "conditioning" and "problem solving." *Harvard Educational Review, 17,* 102–148.

O'Neill, W., & Biederman, G. B. (1974). Avoidance conditioning as a function of appetitive stimulus pretraining: Response and stimulus transfer effects. *Learning and Motivation, 5,* 195–208.

Overmier, J. B., & Payne, R. J. (1971). Facilitation of instrumental avoidance conditioning to the cue. *Acta Neurobiologiae Experimentalis, 31,* 231–249.

Parzen, E. (1960). *Modern probability theory and its applications.* New York: Wiley.

Rescorla, R. A. (1967). Pavlovian conditioning and its proper control procedures. *Psychological Review, 74,* 71–80.

Rescorla, R. A., & Solomon, R. L. (1967). Two-process learning theory: Relationships between Pavlovian conditioning and instrumental learning. *Psychological Review, 74,* 151–182.

Scavio, M. J., Jr. (1972) *Classical-classical transfer: Effects of prior classical aversive conditioning upon classical appetitive conditioning.* Unpublished doctoral dissertation. The University of Iowa.

Scavio, M. J., Jr. (1974). Classical-classical transfer: Effects of prior aversive conditioning in the rabbit. *Journal of Comparative and Physiological Psychology, 86,* 107–115.

Scavio, M. J., Jr., & Gormezano, I. (1980). Classical-classical transfer: Effects of prior appetitive conditioning upon aversive conditioning in rabbits. *Animal Learning & Behavior, 8,* 218–224.

Scavio, M. J., Jr., Marshall, B. S., & Gormezano, I. (In preparation). *Classical-classical transfer: Changes in the reflexive, associative, and reinforcing properties of hedonically opposite USs.*

Schlosberg, H. (1937). The relationship between success and the laws of conditioning. *Psychological Review, 44*, 379–394.

Shapiro, M. M. (1962). Temporal relationship between salivation and lever pressing with differential reinforcement of low rates. *Journal of Comparative and Physiological Psychology, 55*, 567–571.

Sheafor, P. (1975). "Pseudoconditioned" jaw movements of the rabbit reflect associations conditioned to contextual background cues. *Journal of Experimental Psychology: Animal Behavior Processes, 104*, 245–260.

Sheafor, P., & Gormezano, I. (1972). Conditioning the rabbit's (*Oryctolagus cuniculus*) jaw movement response: US magnitude effects on URs, CRs, and pseudo-CRs. *Journal of Comparative and Physiological Psychology, 81*, 449–456.

Sheffield, F. D. (1966). New evidence on the driver-induction theory of reinforcement. In R. N. Haber (Ed.), *Current research in motivation*. New York: Holt, Rinehart, & Winston.

Siegal, S., & Domjan, M. (1971). Backward conditioning as an inhibitory procedure. *Learning and Motivation, 2*, 1–11.

Skinner, B. F. (1938). *The behavior of organisms: An experimental analysis*. New York: Appleton–Century–Crofts.

Solomon, R. L., & Corbit, J. D. (1974). An opponent-process theory of motivation. I. Temporal dynamics of affect. *Psychological Review, 81*, 119–145.

Soltysik, S., & Kowalska, M. (1960). Studies on the avoidance conditioning: I. Relations between cardiac (Type I) and motor (Type II) effects in the avoidance reflex. *Acta Biologiae Experimentalis, 20*, 157–170.

Spence, K. W. (1956). *Behavior theory and conditioning*. New Haven: Yale University Press.

Trapold, M. A., & Overmier, J. B. (1972). The second learning process in instrumental conditioning. In A. H. Black & W. F. Prokasy (Eds.), *Classical conditioning II: Current theory and research*. New York: Appleton–Century–Crofts.

Williams, D. R. (1965). Classical conditioning and incentive motivation. In W. F. Proskasy (Ed.), *Classical conditioning: A symposium*. New York: Appleton–Century–Crofts.

13

Conditioned Diminution and Facilitation of the UR: A Sometimes Opponent-Process Interpretation

Nelson H. Donegan
Allan R. Wagner
Yale University

The research and theorizing reported in this chapter were instigated by prior studies in the rabbit that were remarkable in *not* reproducing a well-accepted phenomenon of Pavlovian conditioning. The phenomenon of interest is the so-called conditioned diminution of the UR (Kimble & Ost, 1961), which is a reduction in the amplitude of the response to a US that may be specifically attributed to preceding the US by an associated CS. Although the phenomenon has been widely observed in many different subject populations and conditioning preparations (e.g., Fanselow & Bolles, 1979; Fitzgerald, 1966; Kimble & Ost, 1961; Kimmel, 1966), Hupka, Kwaterski, and Moore (1970, Exp. 1) and Grevert and Moore (1970) reported that, in a nictitating-membrane conditioning preparation with the rabbit, preceding the US by an associated CS *increased*, rather than decreased, the amplitude of response, compared to US-alone occasions.

The conditioned diminution of the UR has been granted considerable theoretical significance as a basic witness to the diminished processing of "expected" versus "unexpected" stimuli and, moreover, has been proposed to be prototypical of context-specific "long-term" habituation effects (Wagner, 1976, 1978). That a conditioned diminution should not have been seen in the aforementioned studies in the rabbit challenges our understanding of the variables that determine it as well as the soundness of any generalizations to apparently similar behavioral phenomena. We have thus sought to ellucidate the conditions under which a conditioned diminution of the UR is more or less likely to occur and to formulate a theoretical model, embracing the apparent regularities, that can guide extrapolation. What we report is our progress in these directions.

In the following sections of the chapter we first review the available literature on the conditioned modulation of the UR, as well as certain related phenomena, to suggest some tentative generalizations. Then we summarize the results of a set of studies in Pavlovian conditioning with the rabbit that appear to support the anticipated importance of two variables in determining whether one observes a conditioned diminution or a conditioned facilitation of the UR. Finally, we present a quantitative model that may be viewed as an extension and formalization of Wagner's (1976, 1978) priming theory specifically designed to address the data domain.

CONDITIONED DIMINUTION OF THE UR AND ITS ASSOCIATIVE BASIS

The notion that a signaled US may have less of an effect than it otherwise would is hardly new. In the nineteenth century, Sechenov (1935) remarked that "when the impression (of a stimulus) is absolutely unexpected the reflex movement is effected exclusively through the nervous center connecting sensory and motor nerve. But if the stimulation is expected, a new mechanism interferes with the phenomenon seeking to suppress and inhibit the reflex movement." Pavlov (1927, pp. 239, 241) also noted that if dogs were given extensive training with the same CS consistently signaling a food US, the CS might eventually inhibit the usual alimentary reaction to the following US.

The modern experimental analysis of the phenomenon, however, began with the work of Kimble and Ost (1961). Using human subjects in an eyelid conditioning situation they observed that (1) at the start of training the amplitude of the eyelid closure UR was equivalent on CS→US and US-alone trials; (2) with repeated CS→US trials, anticipatory eyelid closures (CRs) developed to the CS whereas the closure response to the US, as indexed on trials without a measurable CR, decreased; so that (3) at the completion of 50 conditioning trials the amplitude of the eyelid UR was substantially reduced on CS→US trials as compared to US-alone occasions.

Additional research with human subjects in eyelid and GSR conditioning has further supported the interpretation that the diminished UR seen in the presence versus absence of a training CS depends upon the *associative* integrity of the CS. For example, in addition to documenting changes in US effectiveness over the course of training, Kimble and Ost (1961) arranged to systematically vary a training parameter known to affect the rate at which the CS becomes associated with the US, namely, the interstimulus interval (ISI). The authors report that conditioned diminution of the UR was greatest at ISIs optimal for associative learning (as indexed by the development of CRs), compared to less optimal ISIs. For example, subjects receiving CS→US pairings at a favorable, .5 sec, ISI showed a higher level of conditioned responding to the CS and a more diminished response to the US, compared to subjects receiving CS→US pairings with a less favorable, 2 sec, ISI. Similar results were obtained by Kimmel and Pennypacker (described in Kimmel, 1966) using a GSR preparation.

Other attempts to demonstrate the associative basis of the conditioned diminution of the UR have assessed the consequences of delayed- versus trace-conditioning procedures—the former typically being more effective in promoting associative learning than the latter. Baxter (1966) and Kimmel (1967), using a GSR conditioning preparation, reported that the level of conditioned responding to the CS and the level of conditioned diminution of the UR were greater in delayed- as compared to trace-conditioning groups when each was contrasted with its respective comparison group, which received unpaired presentations of the CS and US. However, the results of Baxter (1966) are problematic in that the differences between training procedures are attributable to differences in US amplitude between the two unpaired control groups; the differences in UR amplitude between the paired groups receiving the delayed or trace procedure were negligible. Furthermore, Baxter (1966) and Kimmel's (1967) reports have been challenged by other investigators who have not been able to replicate their findings (Grings & Schell, 1969, 1971).

One of the basic criteria by which one evaluates the associative basis of an effect is to show that it can be reversed with extinction training. If the conditioned diminution of the UR depends on the association of the CS with the US, then it should be attenuated by extinguishing the CS. Consistent with this procedure, Morrow (1966), having demonstrated that responding (GSR) to a US (shock) on CS→US trials decreased during acquisition, found that extinguishing the CS led to a recovery of US effectiveness on postextinction CS→US test trials. However, the results of Morrow (1966) need to be accepted with some caution as the amount of recovery was the same for groups receiving different numbers of extinction trials.[1]

The clearest demonstration that the conditioned diminution of the UR has an associative basis would be a demonstration of discriminative control over the phenomenon; that is, showing that preceding the US by a CS with which it has been previously paired (CS[+]) produces a more diminished UR, compared to a CS explicitly unpaired with the US (CS[-]). To our knowledge, such results have not been reported with human subjects.

---

[1]More generally, the results of experiments using the GSR preparation are problematic in that UR amplitude is conventionally determined from a pre-US (or post-US) baseline instead of a pre-CS baseline. To the degree that the CS is effective in eliciting a CR, the baseline level of responding will be different on CS→US compared to US-alone trials. Therefore, it may be the case that the reduced UR amplitude on CS→US trials is the consequence of changes in pre-US baseline rather than a reduced US effectiveness in such preparations.

Demonstrations of the dependence of UR diminution on the associative integrity of the CS are important because they make it clear that the phenomenon cannot be attributed solely to a general loss of sensitivity to the US (adaptation) or unlearned reflex modulating influences in responding to the US such as "prepulse inhibition effects" (e.g., Hoffman & Ison, 1980; Young, Cegavske, & Thompson, 1976). At the same time the possibility of such effects make it crucial that any presumed conditioned modulation of the UR be evaluated in comparisons such as those that have been described, in which the integrity of the CS→US association is manipulated.

Species Differences

Having failed to observe a conditioned diminution of the UR in the nictitating membrane response of the rabbit, but having instead observed the opposite—an apparent conditioned facilitation—Hupka et al. (1970) suggested that whereas a conditioned diminution of the UR may be characteristic of human eyeblink conditioning, it is not a similar feature of conditioning in the rabbit. Kimble (1971) echoed these sentiments in supposing that there may be "greater cognitive involvement of human subjects in experiments of this type" (p. 82).

There are several reasons to be dissatisfied with this reasoning. First there have been numerous reports of a conditioned diminution of the UR in nonhuman animals other than the rabbit. It is unlikely that the rabbit is unique in these matters. Indeed, the second point is that there is considerable evidence from investigations with the rabbit, apart from assessment of the conditioned modulation of the UR, to indicate that a signaled US is less effective than it otherwise would be. Finally, experiments using human subjects, again apart from assessment of the conditioned modulation of the UR, often show a *facilitating* effect of preceding a target stimulus by an associated stimulus. Each of these points, which we document in turn, encourages one to look to other than species differences to account for the variability in conditioned modulation of the UR observed by Hupka et al. (1970).

With regard to the first point, a conditioned diminution of the UR has been demonstrated in a variety of infrahuman subjects. Using dogs, Fitzgerald (1966) found that when a CS was consistently paired with a shock US, the likelihood of the CS eliciting a mimicking CR increased and the ability of the US to elicit a UR (tachycardia) decreased. Wagner, Thomas, and Norton (1967), also using dogs as subjects but cortical stimulation as the US, observed following conditioning that the training US elicited a less vigorous leg flexion UR when it was preceded by the CS than it did on occasional test trials in which it was presented alone. Using rats as subjects, Fanselow and Bolles (1979) observed a conditioned diminution of shock-elicited freezing behavior, that is, when the US (shock) was preceded by a CS, subjects who had previously received forward, CS→US pairings, showed less freezing behavior compared to subjects who had previously received backward, US→CS pairings. A conditioned diminution in the effectiveness of a variety of pharmacological USs has been found in numerous reports using rats as subjects (e.g., Siegel, 1975, 1976, 1977). The prototypical design involves pairing drug injections with one stimulus context and placebo injections with a second, discriminably different, stimulus context. When the drug US is preceded by stimuli with which it has been previously paired, it is typically less effective than when it is preceded by stimuli previously paired with the placebo. Such demonstrations of a conditioned diminution of drug URs have been found in rats using morphine (e.g., Siegel, 1975, 1976, 1977), ethanol (e.g., Crowell, Hinson, & Siegel, 1980; Lê, Poulos, & Cappell, 1979; Mansfield & Cunningham, 1980), and pentobarbital (Cappell, Roach, & Poulos, 1981).

With regard to the second point, there are several experiments using rabbit subjects in the context of eyelid conditioning, but measures other than UR amplitude, which suggest that signaling the occurrence of a US acts to diminish its effectiveness. It has been demonstrated that a US produces less association with a paired CS when it is announced by another, previously trained CS than by a nontrained CS (Marchant & Moore, 1973; Solomon, 1977; Wagner & Terry, 1975)—the so-called blocking effect (Kamin, 1969). It has been demonstrated that a post-trial US produces less of a disruption of conditioning when announced by a separately trained CS+ than by a CS- (Wagner, Rudy, & Whitlow, 1973). It has been demonstrated that a US employed as a discriminative stimulus for delayed responding has less persistent control over behavior when announced by a separately trained CS+ than by a CS- (Terry & Wagner, 1975). This pattern of signal-produced decrements in the learning and performance of rabbits in the context of eyelid conditioning has, in fact, provided a major portion of the impetus for assuming that signaled events may be less effectively processed than unsignaled events. According to Wagner's (e.g., 1976, 1978) priming theory, which incorporated this assumption, the several variations in the effects of US presentation are mediated by the variable activation of a US representation in short-term memory (STM).

The core assumption of the priming model is that when a stimulus representation is prerepresented (primed) in STM, presentation of the stimulus will produce a diminished level of representational activation, compared to presentation of the stimulus when not primed. Priming a stimulus can presumably be accomplished by prior presentation of the corresponding stimulus, or by presentation of a retrieval cue, i.e., an associated stimulus. It would be consistent with such an account to assume in the case of the conditioned diminution of the UR, that presentation of CS+, by acting to retrieve a representation of the US into STM, would result in the subsequently presented US being less successful in promoting activation of its representation in STM and therefore be less effective in producing a UR. Unlike the proposal of Hupka et al. (1970), the priming model and its supporting data would encourage the anticipation that a conditioned diminution of the UR would be observed in infrahuman as well as human subjects.

With regard to the third point, in the literature on associative priming in simple human information-processing tasks (e.g., lexical decision and naming tasks), preceding a target stimulus by an associated stimulus (prime) typically facilitates subjects' response to the target, compared to preceding the target by an associatively neutral stimulus. In such tasks, subjects are typically required to make an immediate response (e.g., naming) to a target stimulus, and the response can be considered UR-like in the sense that it is relatively automatic and based upon a prompt recognition of the stimulus. The measure of principal interest is subjects' reaction time. For example, in lexical decision and naming tasks, subjects are presented with target stimuli comprising letter strings and are required to judge whether or not the target is a word or nonword (lexical decision) or to pronounce the target (naming). In such tasks, preceding a target word (e.g., butter) by an associatively related word (e.g., bread) typically facilitates responding (results in shorter reaction times) compared to preceding the target by a nonrelated word (e.g., iron) (e.g., Becker & Killion, 1977; Meyer, Schvaneveldt, & Ruddy, 1975; Neely, 1977; Posner & Snyder, 1975a; Schvaneveldt & Meyer, 1973). Other tasks in which priming-produced facilitation has been observed are choice-reaction-time tasks, tasks, in which subjects are required to classify a target stimulus as a member of one of several categories as quickly as possible (e.g., LaBerge, vanGelder, & Yellot, 1970) and matching tasks, in which subjects are presented with a target comprising a pair of stimuli and are asked to judge whether or not the two stimuli are the same or different (e.g., Posner & Snyder, 1975a,b).

Alternative Variables

Antagonistic CRs.   Siegel has interpreted the conditioned diminution of URs to a variety of pharmacological USs as the result of antagonistic CRs (e.g., Siegel, 1977). For example, one initial response to morphine is analgesia, yet stimuli associated with morphine administration have been demonstrated to elicit a conditioned hyperalgesic response (e.g., Siegel, 1975, 1976, 1977). Antagonistic CRs have also been found to the thermic responses to morphine (Siegel, 1978) and ethanol (Crowell et al., 1981; Lê et al., 1979; Mansfield & Cunningham, 1980). Siegel proposes that if the conditioned response tendencies under the control of CS^+ persist into the US period and if the measure of responding reflects the combined responses under the control of the CS and US, then one should always expect to observe a conditioned diminution of the UR whenever the CR is antagonistic to the UR. Conversely, such a proposal leads one to expect a conditioned facilitation of responding whenever the CR mimics the UR, e.g., the findings of Hupka et al. (1970, Exp. 1) of a conditioned facilitation of the rabbit nictitating membrane response at the time of the US.

The major point of this reasoning is that any post-US response should not necessarily be interpreted as a simple "UR." It may reflect a CR tendency, under the control of the CS, that may either mimic or antagonize the UR and thus variously facilitate or diminish the post-US measure. However, this reasoning alone does not allow one to anticipate the findings of a conditioned diminution of the UR in response systems such as the eyeblink or GSR, in which the CR mimics the UR (e.g., Hupka et al., 1970, Exp. 2; Kimble & Ost, 1961; Kimmel, 1966).

US Intensity.   Other findings in the Pavlovian conditioning literature suggest that the intensity of the US is another variable that can influence the outcome of signaling the US on responding during the US period. Wagner, Thomas, and Norton (1967), in limb flexion conditioning in dogs with stimulation of the motor cortex serving as the US, reported that preceding a threshold value of the US by CS⁺ increased the probability of a detectable UR relative to preceding the US by CS⁻ or no CS. Similar observations of a conditioned facilitation when testing with threshold values of a US (cortical or hypothalamic stimulation) have been reported by Tchilingaryan (1963) and Thomas (1971), measuring limb flexion in dogs, and by Kogan (1960), Nikolayeva (1955), and Thomas and Basbaum (1972), measuring body movement in cats. However, when Wagner et al. (1967) signaled the high intensity, training US, they observed a *diminished* UR, relative to occasional presentations of the US-alone. With suprathreshold values of a US, Hupka et al. (1970, Exp. 1) found a signal produced facilitation of responding at the time of the US, but that facilitation was greater with a 2-mA compared to a 4-mA shock US, that is, as US intensity was increased, the facilitation observed on CS⁺US relative to US-alone trials decreased. Assuming that threshold and suprathreshold values of US intensity can be treated as lying on a continuum, the results of the preceding experiments suggest the following generalization: Signaling the occurrence of a US is more likely to result in facilitated responding at low US intensities but is more likely to result in diminished responding at high US intensities, compared to unsignaled presentations of the US. Consistent with this generalization are the findings in the human literature of Becker and Killion (1977) showing that priming-produced facilitation in lexical decision and naming tasks was greatest at the lowest target stimulus intensity employed. Similar relationships have been observed in lexical decision tasks in which the salience of the target stimulus was reduced by embedding the letter string in a random dot array (e.g., Meyer, Schvaneveldt, & Ruddy, 1975) or by rotating the target word 180° (Massaro, Jones, Lipscomb, & Scholz, 1978).

In addressing the literature on conditioned facilitation and conditioned diminution of responding following a US, Wagner (1979) proposed that signaling a US generally results in a diminished UR (UR′) and that the UR′ will be added to, or subtracted from, by the CR; that is, on CS⁺US trials, the measure of responding following the US will be a combination of a conditioned response and a diminished unconditioned response ($CS^+US \rightarrow CR + UR'$). Given this reasoning, we can speculate about the ways in which US intensity and conditioned responding interact to determine when one observes a conditioned diminution or conditioned facilitation of responding on CS⁺US relative to US-alone trials. If the contribution of the CR to the measure of responding following the US increases as the ratio of CR amplitude to UR amplitude increases, then variation of US intensity in testing should influence the relative contribution of the CR. In the case of a mimicking CR, a reduction in US intensity at the time of testing should increase the relative contribution of the CR, thereby offsetting the decremental effects of signaling the UR to a greater extent and increasing the likelihood of observing facilitation. Conversely, as US intensity increases, the relative contribution of the CR should decrease, thereby reducing the opportunity for the CR to offset the signal produced decrements in the UR and making a conditioned diminution a more likely outcome. For measures of responding in which CS⁺ produces no CRs or antagonistic CRs, one should consistently observe a diminished response following the US on CS⁺US, compared to US-alone, trials.

EXPERIMENTAL ANALYSIS

The preceding characterization of the available literature leads to some obvious suggestions as to how one might modify the particular features of the Hupka et al. (1970) experiment to produce a conditioned diminution of the UR, rather than a conditioned facilitation, in the rabbit. Restricting oneself to the same eyeblink response measure, in which the CR mimics the UR, it is likely that conditioned diminution would be favored by using a more intense US than employed by Hupka et al. Considering the full spectrum of URs that might be observed to the US, it is likely that conditioned diminution would be favored by selecting a response measure that was not so vigorously mimicked in the anticipatory CRs. These predictions were evaluated in a recent set of studies (Donegan, 1981) in our laboratory that also allowed an appraisal of the interaction of the variation of US intensity and response measure.

US Intensity Variation

An initial evaluation of the effect of US intensity upon the conditioned modulation of the eyeblink response was made in a cross-experiment comparison. Experiment 1 employed a 1.0-mA shock US, less intense than that employed by Hupka et al. (1970), calculated to produce substantial conditioned facilitation. Experiment 2 employed a 5.0-mA shock US, more intense than that employed by Hupka et al., to determine whether conditioned diminution would then result.

The general procedures common to the two experiments were as follows. In each experiment eight naive rabbits received conditioned stimuli that were always 1050 msec in duration and, when reinforced, overlapped and terminated with a 50-msec shock US applied to the area surrounding the eye. Eyeblink closures of .5 mm or greater were scored as CRs when they occurred between 140 and 1000 msec from CS onset. The amplitude of the eyeblink response following US occurrence was defined as the maximum extent of eyelid closure, from the pre-CS baseline, during a prespecified window beginning with US onset (which uniformly captured the maximum "UR"). Subjects initially received discrimination training in which one CS was reinforced (CS$^+$US) and a second CS was nonreinforced (CS$^-$). Fifty CS$^+$US and 50 CS$^-$ trials were presented in each session. After the discrimination training phase, subjects were tested by introducing five presentations of the US-alone and five presentations of CS$^-$ followed by the US (CS$^-$US) during the course of discrimination training sessions.

The major difference between the two experiments was in the aforementioned intensity of the US, which was consistently 1.0 mA in Experiment 1 and 5.0 mA in Experiment 2. However, the experiments also differed in several other ways that should be noted. In Experiment 1, a 3.5-kHz tone served as CS$^+$ and a 60-Hz vibratory stimulus in contact with the animal's chest served as CS$^-$ for half of the subjects, with the cue designations being reversed for the other half. In Experiment 2, an interrupted light CS produced by a strobe lamp located behind the subject was substituted for the vibratory CS because the latter interfered with the measurement of movement responses that were monitored in the experiment (see p. 350). In Experiment 1, the window during which the UR amplitude was determined was 175 msec in duration whereas in Experiment 2 the window was 250 msec because a longer time period was required to consistently capture the peak response amplitude at the higher shock intensity. A third difference was the amount of discrimination training given prior to testing. In Experiment 1 subjects received eight sessions of discrimination training whereas in Experiment 2 subjects received only four sessions because acquisition was more rapid with the more intense US. Also, subjects received two sessions of testing in Experiment 1 but only one in Experiment 2.

Discrimination training in Experiment 1 produced a gradual acquisition of conditioned eyelid closures to CS⁺ with few responses to CS⁻. Over the test sessions 49.4% of the CS⁺US and 12.5% of the CS⁻US trials involved a measurable CR, with mean amplitudes of approximately 2 mm and .3 mm, respectively, prior to the application of the US.

The UR measurements from the test sessions of Experiment 1 are summarized in Fig. 13.1. As can be seen, preceding the US by CS⁺ facilitated responding during the US period relative to preceding the US by CS⁻ or neither CS. Statistical analyses showed that the peak amplitude of responding during the US period was reliably greater on CS⁺US trials than on CS⁻US and US-alone trials and that responding on CS⁻US trials was reliably greater than on US-alone trials.

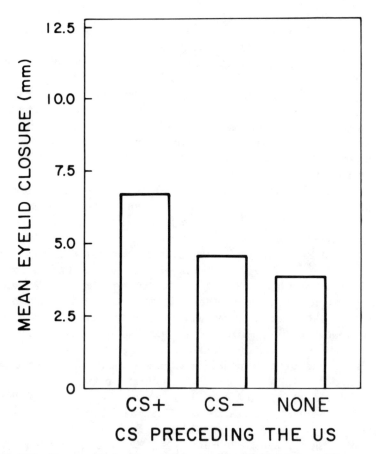

FIG. 13.1   Mean amplitude of the eyeblink response at the time of a 1-mA US presentation when the US was preceded by CS⁺, CS⁻, or neither CS in Experiment 1. Reprinted from Donegan (1981).

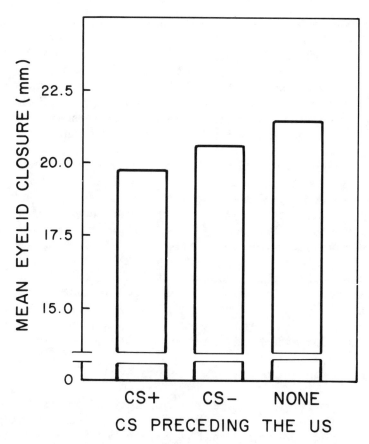

FIG. 13.2 Mean amplitude of the eyeblink response at the time of a 5-mA US presentation when the US was preceded by CS⁺, CS⁻, or neither CS in Experiment 2. Reprinted from Donegan (1981).

In Experiment 2, discrimination training produced a greater level of conditioned responding to both CS⁺ and CS⁻, but just as clear a differentiation between the two. Over the test session 87.5% of the CS⁺US and 26.3% of the CS⁻ trials involved a measurable CR, with mean amplitudes of 5.6 mm and 2.1 mm, respectively, prior to application of the US.

The UR measurements from the test session of Experiment 2 are summarized in Fig. 13.2. As can be seen, the results are the opposite of the results of Experiment 1; with a 5-mA US, the peak response amplitude was smallest on CS⁺US trials, at an intermediate level on CS⁻US trials, and greatest on US-alone trials. Statistical analyses showed that responding on CS⁺US trials was reliably less than responding on US-alone trials and that differences between the remaining paired comparisons were not reliable.

The results of Experiments 1 and 2, as depicted in Fig. 13.1 and 13.2, are consistent with the empirical generalization that UR diminution is more likely to be observed with an intense US than with a weak US. One way to rationalize these differences is to assume that what is measured in the post-US period is some combination of a CR initiated or not by a preceding CS and the UR initiated by the US. When the US is more intense, the UR becomes a larger component of the measured response so that its conditioned diminution on CS$^+$US trials as compared to US-alone trials is more detectable, in spite of the added CR component on the former occasions.

This reasoning need not necessarily hold, however, when different US intensities are used in *training* as well as in testing, as was the case in Experiments 1 and 2. Larger CRs were observed in Experiment 2 than in Experiment 1, and these should have the more obscured any diminution of the UR. It can only be noted that mean pre-US CR amplitudes to CS$^+$ were more constant (5.6 mm vs 2.0 mm during the test sessions) in the two experiments than were the mean UR amplitudes to the US-alone (21.5 mm vs 3.6 mm).

To determine whether or not conditioned facilitation and conditioned diminution could each be observed depending only upon the intensity of the US during testing, independent of any difference in the US (and CR tendencies) during training, a further test was conducted using the subjects of Experiment 2. The test included the measurement of an additional UR.

Different Response Measures

In the previously described Experiment 2, measures of subjects' gross body movement were taken via a phonograph cartridge transducer mounted on the floor of the restraining box in which subjects were conditioned. Any sudden gross body movement of a subject resulted in the movement transducer producing a rapidly damped voltage oscillation that was graphically recorded as a pattern of upward and downward pen deflections.[2] A notable feature of the measure was that, whereas it revealed a substantial UR to the shock US, it showed *no detectable CR* to CS$^+$ or CS$^-$, either in an increase in activity or a decrease in activity. It thus provided a good candidate for contrasts with the eyeblink response. In the absence of a mimicking CR it would be anticipated to evidence a more profound conditioned diminution of the UR.

After the initial session of testing with the 5-mA US (the results shown in Fig. 13.2), subjects received a series of three test sessions in which eyeblink

---

[2]The amplitude of subjects' movement response was defined as log (mm pen deflection + 1) where mm pen deflection was determined by measuring the distance between the maximum upward and downward pen deflections from the pre-CS baseline, in the 250 msec period beginning with US onset. The movement response was defined as a log transform of the mm pen deflection measure because, with such a transform, the movement response grew in a fashion more similar to the eyeblink response as the US intensity was increased.

and movement responses were assessed following three different US intensities under three cue conditions. In each of the three sessions, subjects received CS⁺US, CS⁻US, and US-alone test trials on which the US intensity was 1, 2, or 5 mA, for a total of nine different trial types. Test trials were introduced during the course of discrimination training with the eyeblink and movement responses being simultaneously recorded on each trial, i.e., the data from the eyeblink and movement response measures were obtained from the same test trials.

The mean amplitudes of subjects' eyeblink responses on CS⁺US, CS⁻US, and US-alone trials on which the test US was 1, 2, or 5 mA are shown in Fig. 13.3. As can be seen, with a 1-mA US the ordering of the trial types is comparable to the results of Experiment 1: The amplitude of the response on CS⁺ trials was reliably greater than the amplitude of the response on CS⁻ and US-

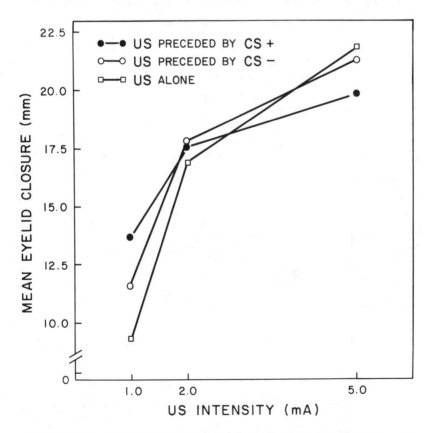

FIG. 13.3   Mean amplitude of the eyeblink response to 1-, 2-, and 5-mA USs when each US was preceded by CS⁺, CS⁻, or neither CS. Reprinted from Donegan (1981, Experiment 2).

alone trials. However, at the 5-mA intensity, the ordering of the trial types was reversed: Response amplitudes were reliably smaller on CS⁺ trials than on CS⁻ and US-alone trials. At the intermediate US intensity, 2 mA, the differences in the response amplitude on the different trial types were less apparent. It is notable that, just as the ordering of trial types was reversed from Experiment 1 (Fig. 13.1) to Experiment 2 (Fig. 13.2) when the training and testing intensity of the US was 1 versus 5 mA, respectively, an identical reversal was seen within subjects when the test intensity of the US was varied between 1 and 5 mA (Fig. 13.3).

The effects of preceding low-, intermediate-, and high-intensity USs by CS⁺, CS⁻, or neither CS on the amplitude of subjects' movement responses are shown in Fig. 13.4. Preceding the US by CS⁺ acted to decrease the amplitude of responding at all US intensities, with diminution being greatest at the 5-mA intensity. The diminished responding on CS⁺US, relative to CS⁻US and

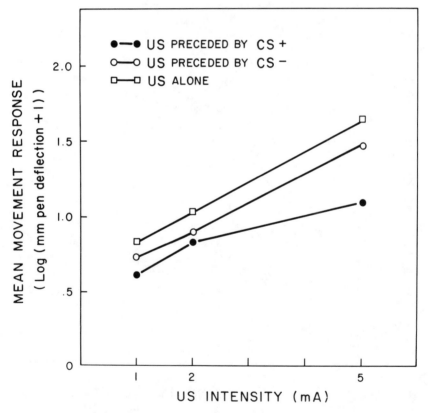

FIG. 13.4   Mean amplitude of the movement response to 1-, 2-, and 5-mA USs when each US was preceded by CS⁺, CS⁻, or neither CS. Reprinted from Donegan (1981, Experiment 2).

US-alone trials, was reliable at the 5-mA US intensity but not at the two lower intensities.

Contrary to the proposal of Hupka et al. (1970), that a conditioned diminution of the UR is not a feature of conditioning in the rabbit, the results of Donegan's (1981) experiments indicate that signaling the occurrence of a US can result in a diminished UR (e.g., Fig. 13.2, 13.3, & 13.4) and are in agreement with reports of a conditioned diminution of the UR in other species and response measures (e.g., Kimble & Ost, 1961; Kimmel, 1966). However, the findings of both facilitated and diminished responding on CS⁺US trials indicates that preceding the US by CS⁺ involves something more than a diminished UR processing.

In the preceding section, we speculated, *on the basis of the available literature* (e.g., Hupka et al., 1970, Exp. 1; Siegel, 1977; Wagner et al., 1967), about the ways in which US intensity variation and conditioned responding might interact to determine when responding following the US on CS⁺US trials would be greater or less than responding on US-alone trials. Assuming that responding following the US on CS⁺US trials reflects a combination of conditioned response tendencies and a diminished UR (Wagner, 1979), we proposed that the detection of conditioned facilitation should be more likely in response measures for which CS⁺ produces mimicking CRs compared to response measures for which CS⁺ produces nondetectable or antagonistic CRs. In addition, we proposed that the higher the intensity of the US, the less should be the relative contribution of the CR to the measured response following the US, and the more likely one should observe the decremental effects of signaling the US on the UR. These speculations were nicely supported by the data of Donegan (1981) that present clear evidence of (1) a correlation between CR type and the appearance of a conditioned facilitation (when different responses were measured after the same US, conditioned diminution was more apparent in that measure [gross movement] in which there was otherwise no evidence of a UR-mimicking CR, than in the measure [eyeblink] in which there was substantial evidence of a UR-mimicking CR); but (2) a main effect of US intensity in either response measure (1) a conditioned diminution was more likely to be seen the greater the intensity of the US at the time of testing.

THEORETICAL ANALYSIS

The Donegan (1981) data that have been presented are agreeable in their overall pattern with Wagner's (e.g., 1976, 1978, 1979) theoretical proposals; that is, they are consistent with the notion that a signaled US is generally less effective than an unsignaled US and thus likely to produce a diminished UR (Wagner, 1978), if it is also acknowledged that the signaling CS can evoke

CRs that persist into the UR-measurement period and can thus add to or oppose the UR diminution (Wagner, 1979).

At the same time, the data present a theoretical challenge. Consider the findings reported in Fig. 13.3 and 13.4. The figures commonly describe responding on the same occasions to the same US, at each of three intensities, when preceded or not by the same CS, with a presumably constant association with the US. The figures differ only in the nature of the response measure. If one assumes that the two response measures each reflects the general tendencies (1) for the US to be more effective the greater its intensity and less effective when signaled than when unsignaled and (2) for the CS to produce a CR, dependent on the degree of CS–US association, it should be possible to construe the two sets of data as equivalent except for the differential mapping of these general tendencies into the particular response measures.

This is, at least, the presumption of any theory such as Wagner's (e.g., 1976, 1978, 1979) that begins from the general view that responding to a Pavlovian US and any associated CS is mediated by the activation of a "US representation" in the memory system, either directly by the US or indirectly by a CS via associative linkages. Such a theory can be called upon to specify how different states of representational activation result from different patterns of stimulation and then specify how the states of representational activation that are produced result in different observed responding depending on the response measure employed.

In order to respond to this challenge, we have developed a more formal, quantitative rendering of Wagner's priming theory. The general model, dubbed "SOP," that followed from this effort has been described in overview by Wagner (1981). Mazur and Wagner (1982) may also be consulted for discussion of the learning rules included. Here we describe the approach for specific application to the data of Fig. 13.3 and 13.4.

The SOP Model

The Nature of Stimulus Representation. We begin with a popular view, that an organism's memory system can be usefully conceptualized as a general graph structure in which the nodes are representations of environmental events and the interconnections are associative linkages succeptible to modification (e.g., Anderson & Bower, 1973; Norman, 1968; Shiffrin & Schneider, 1977). Each node is, itself, conceived as consisting of a set of informational elements. Our use of this notion is in the spirit of stimulus-sampling theory (e.g., Estes, 1955a,b) to allow description of variation in nodal "activation" (see later) in terms of the proportion of like elements that are in theoretically discriminable states. Hence, we assume that there exists for each experimental stimulus a set of elements such that certain events that would provoke a state change in one element of that set have equal (probabilistic) effects upon all elements of the set that are in the same state.

In our assumptions about the activity dynamics of representational nodes, we distinguish between two different active states beyond inactivity that each nodal element can take on. We refer to the several states as a state of inactivity (I), a state of primary activity (A1), and a state of secondary activity (A2). Given this account, the momentary activity state of any representational node may be described by the proportional distribution of its elements among the three states, i.e., by the vector, (p_I, p_{A1}, p_{A2}). The activity dynamics can then be described by the regular changes in such a vector over time, under specified conditions of stimulation.

Rules of Activation Dynamics. Figure 13.5 presents a schematization around which several of our assumptions concerning activity dynamics may be made more concrete. It depicts a memorial representation (node) of an unconditioned stimulus (US). The connected circles, labeled I, A1, and A2, indicate the aforementioned states of activation in which individual elements may reside and can each be conceived as containing some proportion of the nodal elements. The permissible transitions among states are delineated by the connecting arrows. The adjoining *p*s refer to the transitional probabilities for individual elements in any moment (defined as an arbitrarily small unit of time) that will depend on the conditions of stimulation at that moment.

Consider with reference to Fig. 13.5 the assumed consequences of CS⁺ and US presentation on a US nodal element. We assume that for each moment the US is presented, there is a constant probability, p_1, that any element of the US node that is in the I state will transfer to the A1 state, with the value of p_1 being an increasing monotonic function of stimulus intensity. This is the only assumed direct effect of the US upon its node. However, once an element is in the A1 state, it is assumed that it may "decay" to the A2 state in any moment according to the probability p_{A1} and from the A2 state may correspondingly "decay" back to the I state with the probability p_{A2}. Thus, it should be apparent that a usual consequence of a brief US presentation will be a transient increase in proportion of US elements in the A1 state, followed by a delayed increase in the proportion of US elements in the A2 state, followed by a return of the elements to inactivity. From this account, it should be noticed that a US presentation may have differential magnitudes of effect depending upon the existing distribution of elements among the several states; that is, because the only effect that is assumed of US presentation is via p_1, a US will have greater influence the greater is the proportion of then inactive elements, p_I, and correspondingly the lesser is the proportion of already active elements, i.e., p_{A1} and p_{A2}. This characteristic of SOP parallels an essential thesis of Wagner's priming theory (Wagner, 1976, 1978), that a stimulus will be differentially effective if it is "prerepresented" or not in active memory.

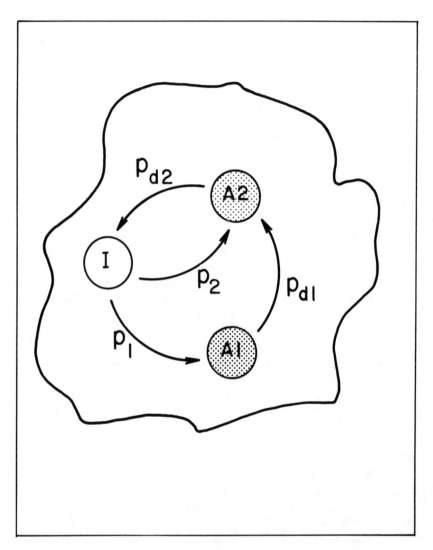

FIG. 13.5   An individual US node that depicts the states of activation that nodal elements may enter into and the permissible transitions among states assumed by the SOP model. The connected circles represent proportions of nodal elements that may be in the inactive state (I), the primary state of activation (A1), or the secondary state of activation (A2). The arrows illustrate the allowable transitions among states and the four parameters describe the probability of an element making the indicated transition during some unit of time. The values that the parameters take on will depend on the conditions of stimulation (see text for details).

With regard to CS presentation, the SOP model assumes that the influence of an associated CS (CS⁺) upon a US node is different than the influence of the US itself: It is assumed that CS⁺ can have the effect of causing inactive elements of the US node to be activated to the A2 state, according to the momentary probability p_2 (with the value of p_2 taken to be proportional to the signaling value of CS⁺ for the US, e.g., p_2 would be expected to increase as the number of CS⁺US pairings increases). This characteristic of SOP again parallels an essential thesis of Wagner's priming theory (Wagner 1976, 1978), that associatively activated representations do not enjoy the same state of activation (A1) as do directly activated representations. What is explicit in SOP is the supposition that the state of an associatively activated representation is the same as the secondary state (A2) of a directly activated representation. This includes the assumption that elements will decay from A2 back to I according to the probability p_{d2}, independent of the route by which they reach A2.

Rules for Response Generation. A necessary requirement for the model to address experimental performance is a specification of the relationship between nodal activation and responding. The general assumption is that a US will provoke its usual response by directly activating its representational node and that a CS may come to influence the same response by changing the activity of the US node via associative linkages.

It should be recalled, however, that, according to the previously specified activity dynamics of representational nodes, a CS is not presumed simply to come to act as a substitute for a US. Whereas a US is assumed to influence US-nodal activity by transfering inactive elements to the A1 state (according to the momentary probability, p_1), a CS is assumed to influence US-nodal activity by transferring inactive elements to the A2 state (according to the momentary probability, p_2). Consequently, we propose that the relationship between the activity of a "US" node and certain responses that it controls takes the general form of Equation 1:

$$R_j = f_j(W_{1,j}p_{A1} + W_{2,j}p_{A2}). \tag{1}$$

That is, if the activity of some "US" node can be presumed to control some response, j, then it is also assumed that the magnitude of the response will be some function (f_j) of the weighted proportion of nodal elements in the A1 state ($W_{1,j}p_{A1}$) plus the weighted proportion of nodal elements in the A2 state ($W_{2,j}p_{A2}$).

Equation 1, in concert with the previous assumptions concerning the activity dynamics of representational nodes, allows for a number of interesting relationships between the products of USs and CSs. A response to an excitatory CS should most consistently mimic the *secondary* effects of a US, as both are attributable to US-nodal elements in the A2 state. Whether or not the effect of an excitatory CS will mimic the immediate effects of a US will depend on the relationships between $W_{2,j}$ and $W_{1,j}$. It is possible that a CR will appear antagonistic to the prominent *initial* consequences of the US with which it has been reinforced (see, e.g., Siegel, 1978), which would be attributed to W_2 and W_1 having different algebraic signs. In such cases we should also expect to see antagonistic relationships between the initial component of the UR, primarily described by the product $(W_{1,j}, p_{A1})$ and the later component of the UR, primarily described by the product $(W_{2,j}, p_{A2})$. In this description, the A1 and A2 states of SOP resemble the *a* and *b* states of Solomon's Opponent-Process Model (e.g., Solomon, 1980). Because W_2 must sometimes be assumed to take on the same algebraic sign as W_1 (as in the case of mimicking eyeblink CRs to a shock US) and sometimes to take on an opposing algebraic sign to W_1 (as in the case of a hyperalgesic CR to stimuli paired with a morphine US) we have dubbed our model a "Sometimes Opponent-Process model," and hence the acronym "SOP."

With regard to differences in responding during the post-US period on CS$\rightarrow$US trials, in comparison to US-alone trials, what is presumed to be different is the proportion of nodal elements in the A1 and A2 states immediately following the US. This difference is what must be responsible for the conditioned facilitation or conditioned diminution that is observed.

Evaluation of Qualitative Relationships in Responding on CS$^+$US and US-Alone Trials

To appreciate the way SOP makes contact with Donegan's (1981) findings for the eyeblink and movement response systems, as seen in Fig. 13.3 and 13.4, first, consider a US-alone trial. Prior to US occurrence, it may be assumed that all elements of a US node are in an inactive state, i.e., the vector describing the proportion of elements in the three states, (p_I, p_{A1}, p_{A2}), is $(1,0,0)$. When the US is presented, elements make a transition from the I to the A1 state with some probability, p_1. The immediate consequences of US presentation can be described by the consequent vector, (p_I', p_{A1}', p_{A2}'), which is, $(1 - p_1, p_1, 0)$. Substituting the relevant vector values into Equation 1, we see that responding on US-alone trials can be described as

$$R_j | \ US \ = \ f_j(W_{1,j}, p_1). \tag{2}$$

On CS$^+$US trials the state of the US node will be different at the time of US occurrence. As a result of the action of CS$^+$, we must assume that some proportion of the US nodal elements will be in the A2 state at the time of US presentation, i.e., the pre-US vector, (p_I, p_{A1}, p_{A2}), will be $(1 - p_{A2}, 0, p_{A2})$. Immediately upon application of the US, p_1 of the elements in the I state will be activated to the A1 state so that the resulting post-US vector, (p_I', p_{A1}', p_{A2}')

will be $[(1 - p_{A2})(1 - p_{A1}), p_1(1 - p_{A2}), (p_{A2})]$. Substituting the relevant values from this vector into the response generation rule (Equation 1), we see that on CS⁺US trials,

$$R_j \mid CS^+US = f_j[W_{1,j}p_1(1 - p_{A2}) + W_{2,j}p_{A2}]. \tag{3}$$

In general, statements about conditioned "diminution," i.e., $R_j \mid$ CS⁺US $< R_j \mid$ US, or conditioned "facilitation," i.e., $R_j \mid$ CS⁺US $> R_j \mid$ US, are understood to refer to the designated directional effects upon a response measure that is construed to increase with increasing US intensity, i.e., in which f_j in Equation 2 (and Equation 3) is a monotonically increasing function. According to Equations 2 and 3, whether one then sees diminution or facilitation depends upon the combined contribution of two effects of signaling: There will be fewer elements in the A1 state on CS⁺US trials than on US-alone trials, which, because W_1 is positive, will favor diminution; there will be more elements in the A2 state on CS⁺US trials than on US-alone trials, which if W_2 is positive will favor facilitation or if W_2 is negative will favor diminution.

A more specific characterization of the conditions that favor conditioned diminution or conditioned facilitation may be seen by rewriting Equation 3 for the expected response on CS⁺US trials:

$$R_j \mid CS^+US = f_j \; [W_{1,j}p_1 - p_{A2}(W_{1,j}p_1 - W_{2,j})]. \tag{4}$$

The first term in this Equation is identical to the single term in Equation 2 for the expected response on US-alone trials. Thus, it may be appreciated that the expected response will be comparatively less on CS⁺US trials when the subtractive second term in Equation 4, $p_{A2}(W_{1,j}p_1 - W_{2,j})$, is positive, whereas the expected response will be comparatively greater on CS⁺US trials when the term is negative. Furthermore, we can see that the latter term will be positive (predicting a conditioned diminution) when $p_1 > W_{2,j}/W_{1,j}$. Correspondingly, we can see that the latter term will be negative (predicting a conditioned facilitation) when $p_1 < W_{2,j}/W_{1,j}$. The quantity, p_{A2}, determined by the degree of conditioning to CS⁺, will simply influence the size of these differences.

In terms of SOP, the finding of a conditioned facilitation in the eyeblink but a conditioned diminution in the movement response measure at the low-US intensity can be understood in terms of differences in the ratio $W_{2,e}/W_{1,e}$ for the eyeblink and $W_{2,m}/W_{1,m}$ for the movement response systems. The two ratios are expected to differ for the following reasons. If the CR mimics the immediate UR, we must assume that W_2 is positive. In addition, the greater the *maximum* CR in relationship to the maximum UR, the greater is the ratio W_2/W_1 (assuming the maxima are determined, respectively, by (W_2p_{A2}) and (W_1p_{A1}) when p_{A2} and p_{A1} both equal 1). As previously noted, the value of W_2 for the movement response should take on a much smaller value than W_2 for the eyeblink response given that the CS$^+$ evoked sizable eyeblink CRs but no detectable movement CR. Therefore, the ratio of $W_{2,m}/W_{1,m}$ should be less than the ratio $W_{2,e}/W_{1,e}$. If the value of p_1 for the 1-mA US was such that $W_{2,m}/W_{1,m} < p_1 < W_{2,e}/W_{1,e}$, then one should expect the results shown in Fig. 13.4 and 13.3, that is, a conditioned diminution of the movement response and a conditioned facilitation of the eyeblink response.

In summary, the differential likelihood of observing a conditioned facilitation in the eyeblink and movement response measures is captured by differences in the ratios $W_{2,e}/W_{1,e}$ and $W_{2,m}/W_{1,m}$. Within a response system, the likelihood of seeing a conditioned diminution or facilitation is influenced by the value of p_1 (US intensity): the higher the value of p_1, the greater the likelihood of observing signal-produced decrements in responding during the US period. The *magnitude* of signal-produced increments or decrements in responding will be determined by the value of p_{A2}, which indexes the success of the CS$^+$ to recruit elements from the I to the A2 state.

Quantitative Evaluation of SOP

Having considered the way in which the SOP model was designed to make contact with the global features of Donegan's (1981) data, we can evaluate its ability to fit the systematic quantitative relationships depicted in Fig. 13.3 and 13.4. With the aid of the model can we, in fact, view Fig. 13.3 and 13.4 as describing the same general behavioral tendencies, differing only in the mapping of these tendencies into the specific measures? To assume so is to assume that the two functions[3] in Fig. 13.3 depicting the eyelid response amplitude on US-alone trials, $R_e | US$, and on CS$^+$US trials, $R_e | CS^+US$, can be well described by the theoretical functions,

$$R_e | US_{(x)} = f_e[W_{1,e}p_{1(x)}] \tag{5}$$
$$\text{and}$$
$$R_e | CS^+US_{(x)} = f_e[W_{1,e}(1 - p_{A2})p_{1(x)} + W_{2,e}p_{A2}], \tag{6}$$

whereas the two functions in Fig. 13.4 depicting the gross movement amplitude on the same US-alone trials, $R_m | US$, and CS$^+$US trials, $R_m | CS^+US$, can be as well described by the theoretical functions,

$$R_m | US_{(x)} = f_m[W_{1,m}p_{1(x)}] \tag{7}$$
$$\text{and}$$
$$R_m | CS^+US_{(x)} = f_m[W_{1,m}(1 - p_{A2})p_{1(x)} + W_{2,m}p_{A2}]. \tag{8}$$

---

[3]We have chosen to ignore the data from CS$^-$US trials for expository simplification. These data could be addressed by assuming that p_{A2} is less on CS$^-$US than on CS$^+$US trials.

Comparing the preceding equations for the eyeblink and movement response measures, it can be noted that under identical conditions of testing, values of R_e and R_m are determined by identical values of p_{A2} (a constant on all CS^+US trials) and $p_{1(x)}$ (varying with the intensity of the US, X, to take on the three experimental values $p_{1(1)}, p_{1(2)},$ and $p_{1(5)}$). Therefore, any differences in observed values of R_e and R_m must be understood solely in terms of the weighting factors, $W_{1,j}$ and $W_{2,j}$, and mapping functions, f_j, taken to be invariant features of the respective response systems. And, because any absolute values of $W_{1,j}$ and $W_{2,j}$ can be accommodated via the specification of f_j, $W_{1,e}$ and $W_{1,m}$ may be treated as constants of arbitrary values leaving the ratio $W_{2,e}/W_{1,e}$ versus $W_{2,m}/W_{1,m}$ as the single differential weighting parameter for the two responses.

Thus, the question we raise is this: Can we specify a set of values for the parameters that are common to Equations 5 and 6 for the eyeblink response and Equations 7 and 8 for the movement response, i.e., $p_{1(1)}, p_{1(2)}, p_{1(5)}$ and p_{A2}, so that, when taken along with estimated values of the weighting parameter, $W_{2,j}/W_{1,j}$, and mapping function, f_j, that are allowed to differ in the two cases, Equations 5–8 will lead to predicted levels of responding in R_e and R_m that are equally congruent with the observed data in Fig. 13.3 and 13.4?

If viewed as a question of curve fitting, the challenge may not appear very demanding. There are only 12 data points in the US-alone and CS^+US functions involving R_e (Fig. 13.3) and R_m (Fig. 13.4). And they are to be approached via 6 parameters and two mapping functions of unspecified complexity. However, there are substantial theoretical constraints (e.g., that $P_{1(x)}$ monotonically increase with the intensity of the US within the bounds, $0 \leq p_{1(x)} \leq 1$) and a number of additional empirical criteria, as will be indicated, against which any solution may be evaluated. In fact, we have made no attempt to arrive at a "best-fitting" solution, being satisfied with the fact that we could use the 12 data points, restricting assumptions, and a variety of approximative analytical procedures to specify a sensible set of values with which the model appears to closely approximate the obtained findings.

It should be possible to gain an adequate appreciation of the general heuristics we followed in arriving at a set of parameter estimations by reference to Fig. 13.6. There we plot by the solid line *predicted* variation in the eyelid measure (see left-hand ordinate) on US-alone trials as a continuous function of variation in the theoretical quantity p_1, assuming that $R_e | US_{(x)}$ = .245(100$p_{1(x)}$), i.e., by letting $W_{1,e}$ be an arbitrary constant, 100, and treating f_e as a simple multiplicative constant, .245. With a shift in scale, the solid line in Fig. 13.6 also represents the predicted variation in the movement response (see right-hand ordinate) on US-alone trials, assuming that $R_m | US_{(x)}$ = .017(100$p_{1(x)}$), i.e., that when letting $W_{1,m} = W_{1,e}$, that f_m is also a simple multiplicative constant, .017. The simplifying assumption is that to a first approximation the two measures can be expressed on identical scales by the linear transform $R_e = R_m/.07$.[4]

If the predicted eyelid and movement measures on US-alone trials can both be expressed as linear functions of p_1, and are rendered in equivalent units as in Fig. 13.6, then according to Equations 5–8, the predicted eyelid and movement measures on CS⁺US trials should also be linear functions of p_1 with equivalent slopes, determined by $W_1(1 - p_{A2})$, but different intercepts, determined by $W_2(p_{A2})$. The dashed line in Fig. 13.6 presents a theoretical function for the predicted variation in the eyelid measure on CS⁺US trials with variation in p_1, whereas the broken line presents a similar function for predicted variation in the movement measure on the same trials, assuming that the slope determining parameter is commonly $100(1 - .44)$, i.e., that $p_{A2} = .44$. The two functions are allowed to differ only in that the slope determining variable is $73(.44)$ in the case of the eyelid function and $22(.44)$ in the case of the movement function, i.e., that $W_{2,e} = 73$ and $W_{2,m} = 22.5$.[5]

To evaluate the adequacy of the theoretical functions to accommodate the data from Fig. 13.3 and 13.4 representing test responding on US-alone and CS⁺US trials with different US intensities, it remains to identify the values of p_1 that correspond to the 1-mA, 2-mA, and 5-mA occasions. Estimated values are indicated on the abcissa of Fig. 13.6 as $p_{1(1)} = .41$, $p_{1(2)} = .63$, and $p_{1(5)} = .92$. With these assignments, it may be seen that the data points presented for comparison are closely approximated in all cases. Indeed, the predicted response amplitudes for the designated 1-, 2-, and 5-mA tests account for 96.8% of the variance in the observed mean values of R_e and R_m.

The essential point of this exercise is that the SOP model is capable of dealing equally with the data from the two response measures. According to the theoretical functions presented in Fig. 13.6, the single important difference between the eyelid measure and the movement measure in respect to the comparison of responding on CS⁺US versus US-alone trials is that the point of intersection of the respective functions is shifted along the p_1 continuum. And this is rationalized in terms of the greater additive contribution of the CR to the post-US measure in the case of the eyelid response, via the greater $W_{2,j}/W_{1,j}$ value.

---

[4]The specific values for f_e and f_m were selected following a graphical analysis of the function for each subject relating R_e and R_m to the intensity of the US on US-alone trials. Because these functions were uniformly negatively accelerated, it was possible to estimate the asymptomatic response level that would be produced by a maximally intense US, i.e., when $p_1 = 1.0$. The mean estimated asymptotic response levels were 24.5 for the eyelid response and 1.7 for the movement response, which would define slopes of .245 and .017 for the linear functions supposed, that are also constrained to go through the origin.

[5]Whereas for expository purposes we describe these theoretical functions prior to identifying the estimates of $p_{1(x)}$, in fact the estimates of $p_{1(1)}$, $p_{1(2)}$, and $p_{1(5)}$ were made solely on the basis of the US-alone data and were then used to provide algabraic solutions for p_{A2}, $W_{2,e}$, and $W_{2,m}$, given the relationships indicated.

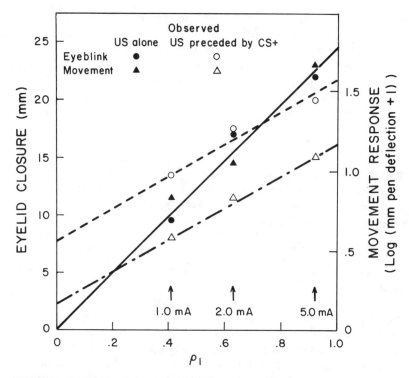

FIG. 13.6   Predicted and observed amplitudes of the eyeblink and movement responses on CS⁺US and US-alone trials as a function of p_1. The solid line (———) describes the predicted amplitude of the eyeblink and movement responses on US-alone trials, the dashed line (— —-) describes the predicted amplitude of the eyeblink response on CS⁺US trials, and the broken line (—·—) describes the predicted movement response amplitude on CS⁺US trials. The arrows along the abscissa indicate the values of p_1 estimated for the 1-, 2-, and 5-mA USs in tests of US intensity variation. Values on the theoretical functions directly above the arrow designate the predicted amplitude of the response at the three US intensities under the designated conditions of testing. The filled and open circles describe the observed amplitudes of the eyeblink and movement responses on CS⁺US and US-alone trials at each of the three US intensities from the tests of US intensity variation reported in Fig. 13.3 and 13.4.

In this light, it is of interest to follow the implications of the theoretical functions for the CS⁺US trials presented in Fig. 13.6. The theoretical function for the eyelid response predicts that when $p_1 = 0$, as it would be on CS⁺ alone trials, the amplitude of the eyeblink response should be 7.9 mm. Although no CS⁺ alone trials were administered in the sessions from which the data of Fig. 13.3 and 13.4 were collected, it is notable that the observed mean amplitude of the eyeblink CR just prior to the time of US onset on CS⁺US trials in these sessions was 7.6 mm. Considering the theoretical function for the movement response on CS⁺US trials, it may be seen that it also predicts a movement CR: When $p_1 = 0$, the predicted value of R_m is .17. Because we detected no movement CRs this could be viewed as a theoretical embarrassment. However, it should be noted that such predicted value (corresponding to a pen deflection of .47 mm) is less than the resolution of the measurement system employed and thus consistent with our observations.

CONCLUDING COMMENTS

In the present chapter we have indicated how two variables, namely US intensity and the relationship between the response tendencies controlled by the CS and US, influence the observance of a conditioned diminution or a conditioned facilitation of the UR. And we have taken pains to indicate how the effects of these variables can be accommodated in a quantitative model, SOP, in the spirit of Wagner's (1976, 1978) priming theory. The effort has seemed appropriate in so much as the conditioned modulation of the UR is not only of interest in its own right but may be representative of a larger class of phenomena.

For example, consider the aforementioned experiment of Terry and Wagner (1975) in which it was found that a signaled US was less effective than an unsignaled US as a discriminative stimulus for controlling subjects' responding to another stimulus presented some seconds later. The authors concluded that an "expected" US was less memorable than a "surprising" US. What we would now suppose is that evidence of this effect should vary, just as in the case of the conditioned diminution of the UR, with the intensity of the US and the relationship between the behavioral tendencies to the CS and US. It is notable in this regard that Terry and Wagner (1975) reported that a CS⁺ alone acted like the US as a discriminative stimulus, only less effectively so. Given this tendency of the CS⁺ to mimic the US, we would expect that with lower US intensities than the 4.8-mA US employed by Terry and Wagner, that a CS⁺US pairing would have *greater* discriminative control over responding than a US-alone presentation.

This may explain the variable results of several recent experiments using procedures similar to Terry and Wagner (1975). Maki (1979), using a delayed-symbolic-matching-to-sample task with pigeons and a food sample, found that signaling the food reduced its effectiveness as a sample, compared to unsignaled presentations of the food — an outcome consistent with the findings of Terry and Wagner. However, Bottjer and Hearst (1979), in a study similar to that of Maki, observed no consistent difference attributable to the surprisingness of the sample. Finally, Colwill and Dickinson (1980) found that performance could be superior when the sample food was preceded by CS⁺ than when not (although this occurred only under procedures that allowed prefood signals potentially to be *directly* trained as discriminative samples). The SOP model suggests that such variability in the apparent memorability of signaled versus unsignaled USs (samples) is perhaps due to effective variation in US intensity across the several experiments.

The same reasoning of SOP can be applied to the literature on subjects' preference for signaled versus unsignaled motivationally-significant events, a phenomenon first noted by Lockard (1963). Considerable data indicate that animals will elect to expose themselves to a situation in which they receive signaled shocks over one in which they receive the same shocks unsignaled, suggesting that signaling reduces the judged intensity or aversiveness of the shocks (e.g., Badia, Culbertson, & Harsh, 1973).[6] Here it is notable that a CS+ alone can act like the US insofar as both can be aversive. Given such a mimicking relationship, we would again anticipate variable outcomes when subjects are required to evaluate CS+US episodes against US-alone episodes, e.g., the recent finding of Miller and Balaz (1981) that rats classified shocks as though they were *more* intense when signaled than when unsignaled. By the reasoning of SOP — similar to that which has been drawn out in the case of the conditioned diminution of the UR and the decreased memorability of a signaled shock — we would expect that (1) decreasing the intensity of a shock at testing (reducing the value of p_1) should increase the likelihood of CS+US episodes being judged more intense (or aversive) than US-alone episodes and, conversely, (2) that increasing the intensity of the shock at testing (increasing the value of p_1) should decrease the likelihood that CS+US episodes will be judged to be more intense (or aversive) than US-alone episodes.

Another data domain that might profit from such analysis is that of long-term habituation (e.g., Davis, 1970). Wagner (1976, 1979) has proposed that long-term habituation of responding to punctate target stimuli is, in part, the result of associations between the target stimuli and the stimulus context in which they have been presented. The contextual stimuli and the target stimulus are in effect said to act like the CS+ and US, respectively, in Pavlovian conditioning, so that in the presence of the former there may be a conditioned diminution of the response to the latter. We would now expect, on the basis of SOP, that repeated presentations of a target stimulus in a particular context could produce more variable results in subjects' responding to the target. Depending on the "CR" tendencies accruing to the contextual stimuli and the intensity of the target stimulus at the time of testing, we might, in

---

[6]Most experiments that report that subjects prefer "signaled over unsignaled shocks" have not, in fact, so definitely identified the basis of subjects' choice behavior. Fanselow (1980), for example, has presented evidence that subjects may be selecting the *context* in which signaled shocks have previously occurred versus the context in which unsignaled shocks have occurred (a choice explicable in terms of differential "blocking" of fear acquisition a la Rescorla & Wagner, 1972). For expository reasons we here ignore this important fact, but the interested experimentalist should not.

some circumstances expect to see a context-specific, conditioned-facilitation-like effect (sensitization?) as compared to the more common habituation decrement.

ACKNOWLEDGMENTS

The research reported and preparation of the chapter were supported in part by National Science Foundation grants BNS77-16886 and BNS80-23399 to Allan R. Wagner.

REFERENCES

Anderson, J. R., & Bower, G. (1973). *Human associative memory*. New York: Winston.

Badia, P., Culbertson, S., & Harsh, J. (1973). Choice of longer or stronger signalled shock over shorter or weaker shock. *Journal of the Experimental Analysis of Behavior, 19*, 25–32.

Baxter, R. (1966). Diminution and recovery of the UCR in delayed and trace classical GSR conditioning. *Journal of Experimental Psychology, 71*, 447–451.

Becker, C. A., & Killion, T. H. (1977). Interaction of visual and cognitive effects in word recognition. *Journal of Experimental Psychology: Human Perception and Performance, 3*, 389–401.

Bottjer, S. W., & Hearst, E. (1979). Food delivery as a conditional stimulus: Feature learning and memory in pigeons. *Journal of the Experimental Analysis of Behavior, 31*, 189–207.

Cappell, H., Roach, C., & Poulos, C. X. (1981). Pavlovian control of cross-tolerance between pentobarbital and ethanol. *Psychopharmacology, 74*, 54–57.

Colwill, R. M., & Dickinson, A. (1980). Short-term retention of "surprising" events by pigeons. *Quarterly Journal of Experimental Psychology, 32*, 539–556.

Crowell, C. R., Hinson, R. E., & Siegel, S. (1981). The role of conditioning in tolerance to the thermic effects of ethanol. *Psychopharmacology, 73*, 51–54.

Davis, M. (1970). Effects of interstimulus interval length and variability on startle response habituation. *Journal of Comparative and Physiological Psychology, 72*, 177–192.

Donegan, N. H. (1981). Priming-produced facilitation or diminution of responding to a Pavlovian unconditioned stimulus. *Journal of Experimental Psychology: Animal Behavior Processes, 7*, 295–312.

Estes, W. K. (1955a). Statistical theory of spontaneous recovery and regression. *Psychological Review, 62*, 145–154.

Estes, W. K. (1955b). Statistical theory of distributional phenomena in learning. *Psychological Review, 62*, 369–377.

Fanselow, M. S. (1980). Signaled shock-free periods and preference for signaled shock. *Journal of Experimental Psychology: Animal Behavior Processes, 6*, 65–80.

Fanselow, M. S., & Bolles, R. C. (1979). Triggering of the endorphin analgesic reaction by a cue previously associated with shock: Reversal naloxone. *Bulletin of the Psychonomic Society, 14*, 88–90.

Fitzgerald, R. D. (1966). Some effects of partial reinforcement with shock on classically conditioned heart rate in dogs. *American Journal of Psychology, 79*, 242–249.

Grevert, P., & Moore, J. W. (1970). The effects of unpaired US presentations on conditioning of the rabbits' nictitating membrane response: Consolidation or contingency. *Psychonomic Science, 20*, 177–179.

Grings, W. W., & Schell, A. M. (1969). UCR diminution in trace and delay conditioning. *Journal of Experimental Psychology, 79,* 246–248.

Grings, W. W., & Schell, A. M. (1971). Effects of trace versus delay conditioning, interstimulus interval variability, and instructions on UCR diminution. *Journal of Experimental Psychology, 90,* 136–140.

Hoffman, H. S., & Ison, J. R. (1980). Reflex modification in the domain of the startle: I. Some empirical findings and their implications for how the nervous system processes sensory input. *Psychological Review, 87* 175–189.

Hupka, R. B., Kwaterski, S. E., & Moore, J. W. (1970). Conditioned diminution of the UCR: Differences between the human eyeblink and the rabbit nictitating membrane response. *Journal of Experimental Psychology, 83,* 45–51.

Kamin, L. J. (1969). Predictability, surprise, attention and conditioning. In B. Campbell & R. Church (Eds.), *Punishment and aversive behavior.* New York: Appleton–Century–Crofts.

Kimble, G. A. (1971). Cognitive inhibition in classical conditioning. In H. H. Kendler & J. T. Spence (Eds.), *Essays in neobehaviorism: A memorial volume to Kenneth W. Spence.* New York: Appleton–Century–Crofts.

Kimble, G. A., & Ost, J. W. P. (1961). A conditioned inhibitory process in eyelid conditioning. *Journal of Experimental Psychology, 61,* 150–156.

Kimmel, E. (1967). Judgments of UCS intensity and diminution of the UCR in classical GSR conditioning. *Journal of Experimental Psychology, 73,* 532–543.

Kimmel, H. D. (1966). Inhibition of the unconditioned response in classical conditioning. *Psychological Review, 73,* 232–240.

Kogan, A. B. (1960). The manifestations of processes of higher nervous activity in the electrical potentials of the cortex during free behavior of animals. *EEG Clinical Neurophysiology,* suppl. 13, 51–64.

LaBerge, D., vanGelder, P., & Yellot, J. J. (1970). A cueing technique in choice reaction time. *Perception and Psychophysics, 7,* 57–62.

Lê, A. D., Poulos, C. X., & Cappell, H. (1979). Conditioned tolerance to the hypothermic effect of ethyl alcohol. *Science, 206,* 1109–1110.

Lockard, J. S. (1963). Choice of warning signal or no warning signal in an unavoidable shock situation. *Journal of Comparative and Physiological Psychology, 56,* 526–530.

Maki, W. S. (1979). Pigeons' short-term memories for surprising vs. expected reinforcement and nonreinforcement. *Animal Learning and Behavior, 7,* 31–37.

Mansfield, J. G., & Cunningham, C. (1980). Conditioned tolerance to the hypothermic effect of ethanol. *Journal of Comparative and Physiological Psychology, 94,* 962–969.

Marchant, H. R., III, & Moore, J. W. (1973). Blocking of the rabbit's conditioned nictitating membrane response in Kamin's two-stage paradigm. *Journal of Experimental Psychology, 101,* 155–158.

Massero, D. W., Jones, R. D., Lipscomb, C., & Scholz, R. (1978). Role of prior knowledge on naming and lexical decisions with good or poor stimulus information. *Journal of Experimental Psychology: Human Learning and Memory, 4,* 498–512.

Mazur, J., & Wagner, A. R. (1982). An episodic model of associative learning. In M. Commons, R. Herrnstein, & A. R. Wagner (Eds.), *Quantitative analyses of behavior, Vol. 3: Acquisition.* Cambridge: Ballinger.

Meyer, D. W., Schvaneveldt, R. W., & Ruddy, M. G. (1975). Loci of contextual effects on visual word-recognition. In P. M. A. Rabbit & S. Dornic (Eds.), *Attention and performance.* New York: Academic Press.

Miller, R. R., & Balaz, M. A. (1981). The evolutionary difference between classical conditioning and instrumental learning. In N. E. Spear & R. R. Miller (Eds.), *Information processing in animals: Memory mechanisms.* Hillsdale, NJ: Lawrence Erlbaum Associates.

Morrow, M. C. (1966). Recovery of conditioned UCR diminution following extinction. *Journal of Experimental Psychology, 71,* 884–888.

Neely, J. H. (1977). Semantic priming and retrieval from lexical memory: The roles of inhibitionless spreading activation and limited capacity attention. *Journal of Experimental Psychology: General, 3*, 226–254.

Nikolayeva, N. I. (1955). Changes in the excitability of various regions of the cerebral cortex in the presence of the formation of motor conditioned reflexes. *Fiziologicheskii zhurnal SSSR, 41*, 19–24. (Report No. 62-15057, Office of Technical Services, United States Department of Commerce, Washington, DC).

Norman, D. A. (1968). Toward a theory of memory and attention. *Psychological Review, 75*, 522–536.

Pavlov, I. P. (1927). *Conditioned reflexes*. London: Oxford University Press.

Posner, M. I., & Snyder, C. R. R. (1975a). Attention and cognitive control. In R. L. Solso (Ed.), *Information processing and cognition: The Loyola Symposium*. Hillsdale, NJ: Lawrence Erlbaum Associates.

Posner, M. I., & Snyder, C. R. R. (1975b). Facilitation and inhibition in the processing of signals. In P. M. A. Rabbit & S. Dornic (Eds.), *Attention and performance*. New York: Academic Press.

Rescorla, R. A., & Wagner, A. R. (1972). A theory of Pavlovian conditioning: Variations in the effectiveness of reinforcement and nonreinforcement. In A. H. Black & W. G. Prokasy (Eds.), *Classical conditioning* II. New York: Appleton–Century–Crofts.

Schvaneveldt, R. W., & Meyer, D. E. (1973). Retrieval and comparison processes in semantic memory. In S. Kornblum (Ed.), *Attention and performance*. New York: Academic Press.

Sechenov, I. (1935). *Selected works*. Moscow: State Publishing House.

Shiffrin, R. M., & Schneider, W. (1977). Controlled and automatic information processing: II. Perceptual learning, automatic attending, and a general theory. *Psychological Review, 84*, 127–190.

Siegel, S. (1975). Evidence from rats that morphine tolerance is a learned response. *Journal of Comparative and Physiological Psychology, 89*, 498–506.

Siegel, S. (1976). Morphine analgesic tolerance: Its situation specificity supports a Pavlovian conditioning model. *Science, 193*, 323–325.

Siegel, S. (1977). Morphine tolerance acquisition as an associative process. *Journal of Experimental Psychology: Animal Behavior Processes, 3*, 1–13.

Siegel, S. (1978). Tolerance to the hyperthermic effect of morphine in the rat is a learned response. *Journal of Comparative and Physiological Psychology, 92*, 1137–1149.

Solomon, P. R. (1977). Role of the hippocampus in blocking and conditioned inhibition of the rabbits nictitating membrane response. *Journal of Comparative and Physiological Psychology, 91*, 407–417.

Solomon, R. L. (1980). The opponent-process theory of acquired motivation. *American Psychologist, 35*, 691–712.

Tchilingaryan, L. I. (1963). Changes in excitability of the motor area of the cerebral cortex during extinction of a conditioned reflex elaborated to direct electric stimulation of that area. In E. Gutman & P. Hnik (Eds.), *Central and peripheral mechanisms of motor functions: Proceedings of the conference* (pp. 167–175). Prague: Czechoslovak Academy of Sciences.

Terry, W. S., & Wagner, A. R. (1975). Short-term memory for "surprising" versus "expected" unconditioned stimuli in Pavlovian conditioning. *Journal of Experimental Psychology: Animal Behavior Processes, 1*, 122–133.

Thomas, E. (1971). Role of postural adjustments in conditioning of dogs with electrical stimulation of the motor cortex as the unconditioned stimulus. *Journal of Comparative and Physiological Psychology, 76*, 1 87–198.

Thomas, E., & Basbaum, C. (1972). Excitatory and inhibitory processes in hypothalamic conditioning in cats: Role of the history of the negative stimulus. *Journal of Comparative and Physiological Psychology, 79*, 419–424.

Wagner, A. R. (1976). Priming in STM: An information-processing mechanism for self-generated or retrieval-generated depression in performance. In T. J. Tighe & R. N. Leaton (Eds.), *Habituation: Perspectives from child development, animal behavior, and neurophysiology.* Hillsdale, NJ: Lawrence Erlbaum Associates.

Wagner, A. R. (1978). Expectancies and the priming of STM. In S. H. Hulse, H. Fowler, & W. K. Honig (Eds.), *Cognitive processes in animal behavior.* Hillsdale, NJ: Lawrence Erlbaum Associates.

Wagner, A. R. (1979). Habituation and memory. In A. Dickinson & R. A. Boakes (Eds.), *Mechanisms of learning and motivation: A memorial to Jerzy Konorski.* Hillsdale, NJ: Lawrence Erlbaum Associates.

Wagner, A. R. (1981). A model of automatic memory processing in animal behavior. In N. E. Spear & R. R. Miller (Eds.), *Information processing in animals: Memory mechanisms.* Hillsdale, NJ: Lawrence Erlbaum Associates.

Wagner, A. R., Rudy, J. W., & Whitlow, J. W. (1973). Rehearsal in animal conditioning. *Journal of Experimental Psychology, 97,* 407–426.

Wagner, A. R., & Terry, W. S. (1975). Backward conditioning to a CS following an expected vs. a surprising UCS. *Animal Learning and Behavior, 3,* 370–374.

Wagner, A. R., Thomas, E., & Norton, T. (1967). Conditioning with electrical stimulation of motor cortex: Evidence of a possible source of motivation. *Journal of Comparative and Physiological Psychology, 64,* 191–199.

Young, R. A., Cegavske, C. F., & Thompson, R. F. (1976). Tone-induced changes in excitability of abducens motoneurons and of the reflex path of nictitating membrane response in rabbit (Oryctolagus cuniculus). *Journal of Comparative and Physiological Psychology, 90,* 424–434.

14

Neuronal Substrates of Discrete, Defensive Conditioned Reflexes, Conditioned Fear States, and Their Interactions in the Rabbit

Richard F. Thompson, Nelson H. Donegan,
Gregory A. Clark, David G. Lavond, Jann S. Lincoln,
John Madden, IV, Laura A. Mamounas,
Michael D. Mauk, and David A. McCormick
Stanford University

About 1970 the first author decided to devote the future efforts of his laboratory to the study of the substrates of associative learning and memory in the mammalian brain — to continue Lashley's search for the engram. Selection of the best and most appropriate behavioral paradigm was of critical importance. Many were considered and a few explored in more detail. Thanks in significant part to the elegant and extensive behavioral studies by Gormezano and his associates on classical conditioning of the rabbit nictitating membrane (NM) response, we selected it as our basic paradigm. Special thanks are due M. M. Patterson, who received his Ph.D. with Gormezano in 1969 and then held a postdoctoral fellowship in our laboratory. He proselytized the rabbit NM paradigm most persuasively. The conditioned eyelid response in the rabbit (both eyelid and NM become conditioned together in an essentially identical fashion, as described later) has also been used to very good effect in analysis of basic theoretical issues in learning (e. g., Donegan & Wagner, Chapter 13; Wagner, 1969, 1971, 1981).

Classical conditioning of the rabbit NM/eyelid response has a number of advantages for analysis of brain substrates of learning and memory, which have been detailed elsewhere (Thompson, Berger, Cegavske, Patterson, Roemer, Teyler, & Young, 1976; Disterhoft & Stuart, 1977). Perhaps the greatest single advantage of this, and classical conditioning paradigms in general, is that the effects of experimental manipulations on learning versus performance can be more easily evaluated than in instrumental procedures. This problem of learning versus performance has plagued the study of brain substrates of learning from the beginning. For example, does a brain lesion or the administration of pharmacological agents impair a learned behavior because it damages the memory trace or because it alters the animal's ability to respond or perhaps because it alters the animal's motivation to respond? By using Pavlovian procedures, one can estimate the effects of such manipulations on learning and performance by comparing the subject's ability to generate the conditioned response (CR) and unconditioned response (UR) before and after making a lesion or administering a drug. If the CR is affected and the UR is unaffected, one can reasonably assume that memory processes are being affected rather than response generation processes per se. (Heyman, in press, has recently made ingenious use of Herrnstein's matching law to distinguish between learning and performance effects in instrumental conditioning). In general, far too little attention has been paid to the behavioral paradigms in brain studies of learning — to what can and cannot be demonstrated about the biological substrates of learning with a given behavioral learning paradigm. Other advantages of the rabbit NM preparation include the absence of alpha conditioning or sensitization, the simple and discrete phasic character of the NM response and its ease of measurement, and the fact that use of a corneal airpuff unconditioned stimulus (US) permits recording of neuronal activity during delivery of the US.

One final advantage of the conditioned NM/eyelid response is the fact that eyelid conditioning has become perhaps the most widely used paradigm for the study of basic properties of classical or Pavlovian conditioning of striated muscle responses in both humans and infrahuman subjects. It displays the same basic laws of learning in humans and other animals (Hilgard & Marquis, 1940). Consequently, it seems highly likely that neuronal mechanisms found to underly conditioning of the NM/eyelid response in rabbits will hold for all mammals, including humans. We view the conditioned NM/eyelid response as an instance of the general class of conditioned striated muscle responses learned with an aversive US and adopt the working assumption that neuronal mechanisms underlying learning of the NM/eyelid response will in fact be general for all aversive conditioning of striated muscle responses.

It should be noted that over the course of NM training, considerably more than just NM extension becomes conditioned. Gormezano and associates first showed that eyelid closure, eyeball retraction, and NM extension all develop during conditioning in essentially the same manner (Deaux & Gormezano, 1963; Gormezano, 1962; Schneiderman, Fuentes, & Gormezano, 1962). The efferent limb thus involves several cranial nerve nuclei. The primary response that produces NM extension is retraction of the eyeball (Cegavske, Thompson, Patterson, & Gormezano, 1976). A major muscle action producing this response is contraction of the retractor bulbus, which in rabbit is innervated by motoneurons of the abducens and accessory abducens nuclei (Cegavske et al., 1986; Gray, McMaster, Harvey & Gormezano, 1981). However, it appears that most of the extrinsic eye muscles may contract synchronously to some extent with the retractor bulbus (Berthier & Moore, 1980). In addition, the external eyelid (which is normally held open in NM conditioning) extends, under control of motoneurons in the seventh nucleus. Finally, there is a variable degree of contraction of facial muscles in the vicinity of the eye. In sum, the total response is a coordinated defense of the eye involving primarily eyeball retraction (NM extension) and eyelid closure with some contraction of periorbital facial musculature (see McCormick, Clark, Lavond, & Thompson, 1982a). Simultaneous recordings from one NM and both eyelids during conditioning of the left eye show essentially perfect correlations in both amplitude and latency of the conditioned responses they develop over the course of training (see Fig. 14.1). Although CRs are typically much smaller in the eye opposite to the trained eye and show marked interanimal differences in amplitude, the pattern of response, when clearly present, is on the average highly correlated with those of the eye being trained (McCormick, Lavond, & Thompson, 1982c).

Recordings of neural activity from the abducens nucleus simultaneously with measurement of NM extension show that the pattern of increased neural unit response precedes and closely parallels the amplitude-time course of the behavioral NM response (see Fig. 14.2). The cross correlation between the two responses is very high — typically over 0.90 (Cegavske et al., 1976). Eyelid closure shows a very similar time course to NM extension although the onset latency is somewhat shorter. In current work we have found that the patterns of increased neural unit activity in the accessory abducens nucleus and in the seventh cranial nucleus (eyelid control) during performance of the learned response are essentially identical to that seen in the abducens nucleus. In terms of amount of increase in neural unit activity, the response in the seventh nucleus is largest.

The amplitude-time course of the NM extension response mirrors the pattern of increased neuronal unit activity in the relevant motor nuclei with considerable precision on a trial-by-trial basis (except of course for onset latency differences). This is a great convenience. The extension of the NM across the eye reflects the change in neural unit activity in the final common path — a learned neuronal response that has the same properties in several motor nuclei. We can assume that the neuronal system responsible for generation of the learned NM/eyelid response will exhibit this same pattern of increased neuronal activity. Something must drive the several motor nuclei in a synchronous fashion.

In this seemingly simple paradigm, higher regions of the brain play important roles. Indeed, under certain conditions they are critically important (Thompson et al., 1984; Thompson et al., 1983b — see also Chapters by

Berger & Berry in this volume). However, in the standard short delay conditioning paradigm, animals with the cerebral neocortex or hippocampus removed are able to learn, as are animals with all brain tissue above the level of the thalamus or midbrain removed (Esner, 1976; Oakley & Russell, 1972). Although several inferences are possible from these findings, we have adopted the simple working hypothesis that the essential or "primary" mem-

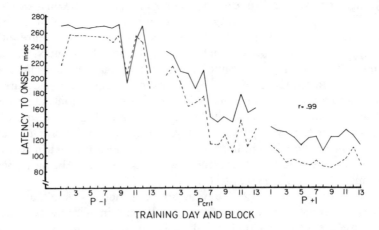

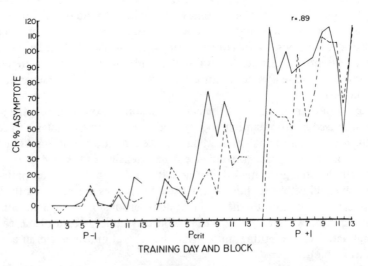

FIG. 14.1   The upper figure shows the latencies to onset of the left eyelid (--) and left NM (—) responses to a tone CS paired with an airpuff US delivered to the left eye. The bottom figure shows the development of conditioned responding of the *right* eyelid (—) and left NM (—) over the same period of training on the left eye.

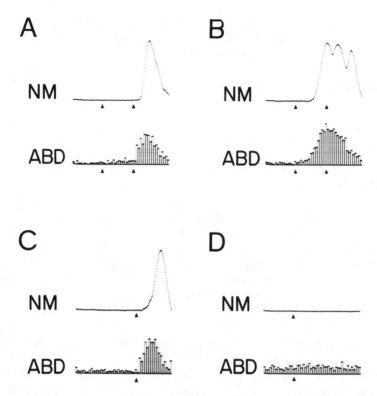

FIG. 14.2   Examples of eight-trial averaged behavioral nictitating membrane (NM) responses and associated multiple-unit histograms of abducens nucleus activity (15 msec time bins) for a conditioning animal at the beginning and end of training (A,B) and a control animal at the beginning of training for the airpuff UCS (C) and the tone CS (D). Note the close correspondence between the histogram of unit activity recorded from the final common path and the temporal form of the behavioral NM response in all cases. (Cegavske, Patterson, & Thompson, 1979. Reproduced by permission.)

ory trace for delay classical conditioning of the NM (and other striated muscle responses conditioned with an aversive US as well) is localized below the level of the thalamus.

In addition to conditioning of the NM/eyeblink response, it seems very likely that conditioned emotional states, such as fear, as indexed by autonomic responses and perhaps activity of the pituitary-adrenal axis, will become conditioned as well, given that NM conditioning involves presentation of an aversive US. For example, conditioned heart-rate slowing develops robustly in the NM conditioning paradigm when a periorbital shock US is used with appropriate parametric conditions. In the following sections we discuss recent research commenting on the neural substrates of conditioned NM/eyeblink responses and conditioned fear, and the ways that the two systems might interact.

LOCALIZATION OF THE MEMORY TRACE FOR DISCRETE, ADAPTIVE, LEARNED BEHAVIORAL RESPONSES

Brain Systems Where the Primary Memory Trace is Not Located

We have developed evidence arguing against localization of the primary memory trace for the NM CR to several brain systems. We have detailed these arguments elsewhere (Thompson et al., 1983a,b,c,d) and only summarize them here.

The Conditioned Stimulus (CS) Channel—the Auditory System. During acquisition of the classically conditioned NM eyelid response to an acoustic CS there are no changes in evoked neuronal unit activity in the mainline auditory relay nuclei (Thompson et al., 1983a). Using a signal detection paradigm with a staircase procedure so that the animal gives learned behavioral NM/eyelid responses 50% of the time to a constant intensity threshold level acoustic stimulus, there are clear evoked neuronal unit responses that are identical on both detection and nondetection trials in the anteroventreal cochlear nucleus, the central nucleus of the inferior colliculus, and the ventral division of the medial geniculate body (Kettner, Shannon, Nguyen, & Thompson, 1980; Kettner & Thompson, 1982). Because there must be differential activity or activation of the primary memory trace on detection and nondetection trials, the mainline auditory relay nuclei cannot be a part of the essential primary memory trace system. Some parts of them are obviously essential to convey the information that the CS has occurred but the memory is not there.

Reflex Pathways and Motor Neurons. The virtually perfect correspondence between the NM and both eyelids and with activity in the relevant motor nuclei (see Cegavske, Patterson, & Thompson, 1979; McCormick et al., 1982c & Fig. 14.1) over the course of learning implies that the primary memory trace is unlikely to develop independently in each motor nucleus. It can most easily be accounted for by assuming a common central system that acts upon the reflex pathways and/or simultaneously on all the relevant motor nuclei (see aforementioned). If manipulations of the brain can abolish the conditioned response but have no effect at all on the unconditioned reflex response (UR), it is prima facia evidence against the possibility that an essential component of the primary memory trace is in the reflex pathways and/or motor neurons. Morphine has just such an effect on the conditioned NM/eyelid response (Mauk, Warren, & Thompson, 1982b) as does spreading depression of the motor cortex (Megirian & Bures, 1969; Papsdorf, Longman, & Gormezano, 1965) and lesions of the cerebellum (McCormick, Clark, Lavond, & Thompson, 1982a).

The "Alpha Response" Pathway.   A sufficiently intense acoustic CS can elicit an alpha eyelid response that has a latency of about 20 msec in the cat (Woody & Brozek, 1969). There are thus fairly direct pathways from the primary auditory system to the seventh motor nucleus. However, the minimum onset latency of the conditioned NM/eyelid response is about 80 msec, much too long for the memory trace to be localized to the acoustic alpha response pathway.

In summary, the essential primary memory trace for standard delay classical conditioning of the NM/eyelid response is below the level of the thalamus and does not appear to be localized in the primary sensory component of the CS channel (here the auditory system), the motor neurons, the reflex pathways, or the acoustic alpha response pathways.

Cerebellum, Brain Stem, and Midbrain Structures.

From the previous findings, the circuitry that might serve to code the primary memory trace for the NM CR in the standard delay paradigm could include much of the midbrain and brain stem and the cerebellum excluding the primary CS channel (here the auditory relay nuclei), the reflex pathways, and the motor neurons. Because there was no a priori way of determining which regions and structures are involved in the memory trace, we undertook, beginning about 4 years ago, to map the entire midbrain, brain stem, and cerebellum by systematically recording neuronal unit activity (unit cluster recording) in already trained animals (McCormick et al., 1982c). For this purpose we developed a chronic micromanipulator system that permits mapping of unit activity in substantial number of neural loci per animal. Increases in unit activity that form a temporal model within a trial of the learned behavioral response were prominent in certain regions of the cerebellum, both in cortex and deep nuclei, certain regions of the pontine nuclei and the red nucleus. Such unit activity is also seen in certain regions of the reticular formation and of course in the cranial motor nuclei engaged in generation of the behavioral response — portions of the 3rd, 6th, accessory 6th, and 7th nuclei. The distribution of "learned motor program" responses in the brain stem is shown in Fig. 14.3. The results to date of the mapping study thus point to substantial engagement of the cerebellar system in the generation of the conditioned response.

Current studies in which we have recorded the neuronal unit activity from the deep cerebellar nuclei (dentate and interpositus nuclei) over the course of training have in some locations revealed a striking pattern of learning-related growth in activity (McCormick et al., 1982a). In the example shown in Fig.

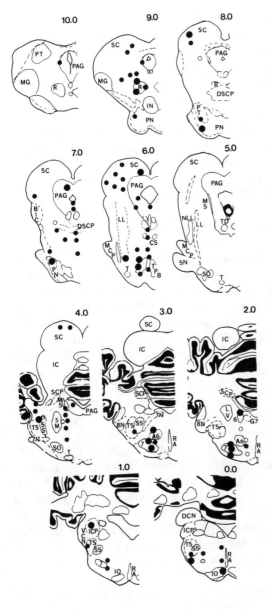

FIG. 14.3 Location of recording sites that revealed neuronal responses that related to the onset and/or topography of the learned eyeblink response. The larger dots represent the points where large responses were found. The number above each figure denotes the number of millimeters that the section is anterior to lambda. Note that the superior colliculus, periaqueductal gray, pontine nuclei, red nucleus, reticular tegmental nucleus of the pons (Bechterew), and the inferior olive possess these types of responses. Abbreviations are as follows: A6 — Accessory sixth (abducens), DCN — dorsal cochlear nucleus, DSCP — decussation of the superior cerebellar peduncle, G7 — genu of the seventh nerve, IC — inferior colliculus, ICP — inferior cerebellar peduncle, IN — interpeduncular nucleus, IO — inferior olive, LL — lateral lemniscus, LV — lateral vestibular nuclei, M5 — mesencephalic fifth nucleus, MF — medial longitudinal fasciculus, MG — medial geniculate, NLL — nuclei of the lateral lemniscus, PAG — periaqueductal gray, PN — pontine nuclei, PT — pretectal nuclei, R — red nucleus, RA — median raphe, S5 — spinal nucleus of the fifth, SC — superior colliculus, SCP — superior cerebellar peduncle, SO — superior olive, T — trapezoid nucleus, T5 — tract of the fifth, TD — dorsal tegmental nucleus, TPB — tegmental reticular nucleus (Bechterew), VCN — ventral cochlear nucleus, 5M — motor nucleus of the fifth, 5N — fifth nerve, 5S — principle sensory nucleus of the fifth, 6 — sixth (adbucens) nucleus, 7 — seventh (facial) nucleus, 7N — seventh nerve, 8N — eighth nerve.

14.4, the animal did not learn on Day 1 of training. Unit activity showed evoked responses to tone and airpuff onsets but no response in association with the unconditioned NM response, in marked contrast to unit recordings from the cranial motor nuclei. On Day 2 the animal began showing CRs and the unit activity in the dentate nucleus developed a model of the conditioned response. On Day 3 the learned behavioral response and the cerebellar model of the learned response are well developed but there is still no clear model of the reflex behavioral response. A second example of learning related changes in neural responding in the dentate-interpositus nuclei is presented in Fig. 14.5. This subject received initial training with unpaired presentations of the CS and US followed by paired training. In these animals, a neuronal model of the *learned* behavioral response appears to develop *de novo* in the cerebellum. (Note the contrast between these responses and the learning-induced response in the hippocampus that models the entire behavioral response – see Fig. 14.6.)

In current work, we have found that lesions ipsilateral to the trained eye in several locations in the neocerebellum – large ablations of the lateral portion of the hemisphere, localized electrolytic lesions of the dentate/interpositus

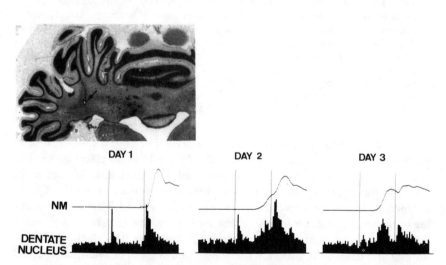

FIG. 14.4   Histograms of unit cluster recordings obtained from the medial dentate nucleus during classical conditioning of NM/eyelid response. The recording site is indicated by the arrow. Each histogram bar is 9 milliseconds in width and each histogram is summed over an entire day of training. The first vertical line represents the onset of the tone and the second vertical line represents the onset of the airpuff. The trace above each histogram represents the averaged movement of the animal's NM for the same day, with up being extension of the NM across the cornea. The total duration of each histogram and trace is 750 msec. The pattern of increased discharges of cerebellar neurons appears to develop a neuronal "model" of the amplitude-time course of the learned behavioral response (McCormick et al., 1982a).

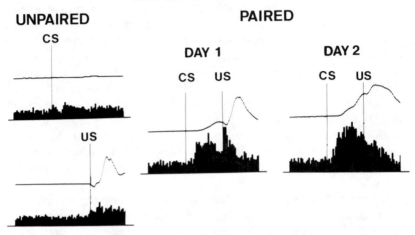

FIG. 14.5   Histograms of unit recordings obtained from a chronic electrode implanted on the border of the dentate/interpositus nuclei in one animal. The animal was first given random, unpaired presentations of the tone and airpuff (104 trials of each stimulus) and then trained with 2 days of paired training (117 trials each day). Each histogram is an average over the entire day of training indicated. The upper trace represents movement of the NM with up being closure. The first vertical line represents the onset of the conditioning stimulus, whereas the second line represents the onset of the unconditioned stimulus. Each histogram bar is 9 milliseconds in duration. Notice that these neurons develop a model of the conditioned, but not unconditioned, response during learning.

nuclei and surrounding fibers and small, discrete lesions of the superior cerebellar peduncle—permanently abolish the CR but have no effect on the UR and do not prevent learning by the contralateral eye (Clark, McCormick, Lavond, Baxter, Gray, & Thompson, 1982; McCormick, Lavond, Clark, Kettner, Rising, & Thompson, 1981, 1982a,b) (see Fig. 14.7 to 14.9). If training is given only after unilateral cerebellar lesions, the ipsilateral eye cannot learn but the contralateral eye subsequently learns as though the animal is normal and new to the situation (Lincoln, McCormick, & Thompson, 1982) (see Fig. 14.10). If training is given before unilateral cerebellar lesion the contralateral eye learns rapidly, with significant savings (McCormick et al., 1981, 1982a). In recent studies we have trained animals with both eyes and made bilateral ablations of the lateral cerebellum. These lesions permanently abolish the conditioned NM/eyelid response on both sides. One such animal, who shows no clear signs of motor dysfunction, has been trained repeatedly postoperatively over a period of 3 months and shows no relearning or recovery at all of the learned response in either eye. Lesions in several locations in the ipsilateral pontine brain stem produce a similar selective abolition of the CR (Desmond & Moore, 1982; Lavond, McCormick, Clark, Holmes, & Thompson, 1981; Moore, Desmond, & Berthier, 1982). Although some uncertainty still exists, the learning-effective lesions sites in the pontine brain stem appear to track the course of the superior cerebellar peduncle.

Additionally, in current works we have found that microinjection of as little as 2 nmol of bicuculline methiodide (a GABA antagonist) directly into the region of the medial dentate/lateral interpositus nuclei causes a selective and reversible abolition of both the behavioral CR and the neuronal model of the CR (recorded with a microelectrode 0.75 mm ventral to the tip of the microinfusion cannula) (see Fig. 14.11). This selective bicuculline abolition of the learned response occurs regardless of how well trained or overtrained

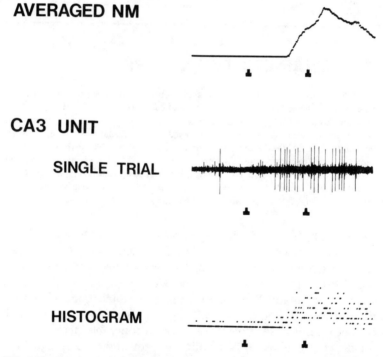

AVERAGED NM

CA3 UNIT

SINGLE TRIAL

HISTOGRAM

FIG. 14.6 Examples of the discharge pattern of an identified hippocampal pyramidal neuron responding during trial periods in a rabbit well-trained in the conditioned NM/eyelid response. Upper trace, NM response averaged over a number of trials. Center trace, single trial example of the discharge pattern of the pyramidal neuron. Lower trace, histogram (3 msec time bins) of the cell discharge over the same number of trials as for the NM response shown above. First cursor, tone CS onset, second cursor, airpuff UCS onset. Total trace duration 750 msec. Note that the pattern of increased frequency of cell discharge closely models the amplitude-time course of the behavioral NM response (Berger & Thompson, 1978b).

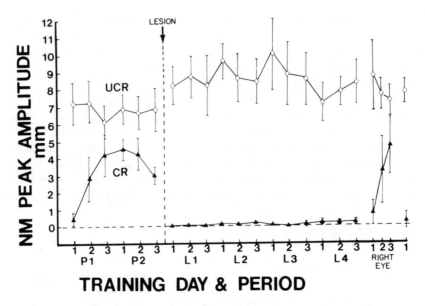

FIG. 14.7   Effects of ablation of left lateral cerebellum on the learned NM/eyelid response (six animals). Solid triangles, amplitude of conditioned response (CR); open diamonds, amplitude of unconditioned response (UCR). All training was to left eye (ipsilateral to lesion) except where labeled "right eye." The cerebellar lesion completely and permanently abolished the CR of the ipsilateral eye but had no effect on the UCR. P_1 and P_2 indicate initial learning on the 2 days prior to the lesion. L_1-L_2 are 4 days of postoperative training to the left eye. The right eye was then trained and learned rapidly (R1). The left eye was again trained and showed no learning. Numbers on abscissa indicate 40-trial periods, except for "right eye," which are 24 trial periods (McCormick et al., 1982a).

the animal is. The fact that high concentrations of GABA have been localized to these nuclear regions (Okada, Nitsch-Hassler, Kim, Bak, & Hassler, 1971), coupled with the observations by Chan–Palay (1977, 1978) demonstrating autoradiographic localization of GABA receptors in this region provides a basis for tentatively postulating that bicuculline produces its selective abolition of the CR in a traditional way—through blockage of inhibitory GABAergic transmission. Note that there is no noticeable increase in spontaneous unit activity following bicuculline infusion in the recordings shown in Fig. 14.11—thus the abolition of the CR seems not to be due to abnormally increased cellular activity. Instead, it seems more likely to be blocking inhibitory synaptic transmission that is in some way essential for the generation of the CR. One calls to mind Eugene Roberts' notion of GABAergic processes playing a key role in learning (Roberts, 1976, 1980). This result also demonstrates that abolition of the CR by lesions in this region cannot be due to nonspecific persisting effects of the lesion. The bicuculline abolition of the

CR dissipates over time — with CRs returning to baseline levels by the end of the test session (see Fig. 14.11).

Taken together, these results indicate that the cerebellum is an obligatory part of the learned response circuit for eyelid/NM conditioning. Because decerebrate animals can learn the response, this would seem to localize an essential component of the memory trace to the ipsilateral cerebellum and/or its major afferent–efferent systems. The fact that a neuronal unit "model" of the learned behavioral response develops in the cerebellar deep nuclei and may precede the behavioral response by as much as 50 msec would seem to localize the process to the cerebellum or its afferents. This time period, interestingly, is not too much less than the minimum onset latency for CRs in well-

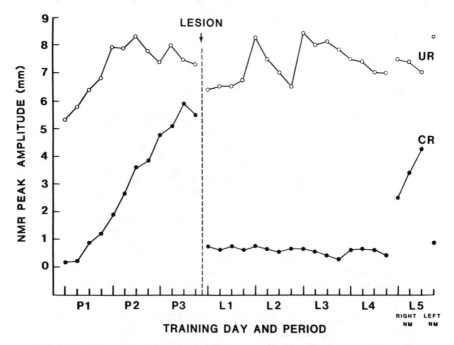

FIG. 14.8 Effects of unilateral lesions of cerebellar nuclei on conditioned and unconditioned nictitating membrane (NM) responses (mean amplitude, $n = 14$). Animals received 3 days of training (P_{1-3}) on the left eye prior to lesioning. After lesioning, (left cerebellar nuclei), animals were trained for 4 days (L_{1-4}) to test for retention and recovery of the conditioned responses. On the fifth postlesion session (L_5), training was switched to the right (nonlesioned) side, then returned to the left eye ($n = 13$). Results of each training day are represented in four periods of trials, approximately 27 trials per period. Note that CR amplitude was almost completely abolished by the lesion, but UR amplitude was unaffected. Note also the right (nonlesioned) side learned quickly, controlling for nonspecific lesion effects, but that conditioned responding on the left side showed essentially no recovery.

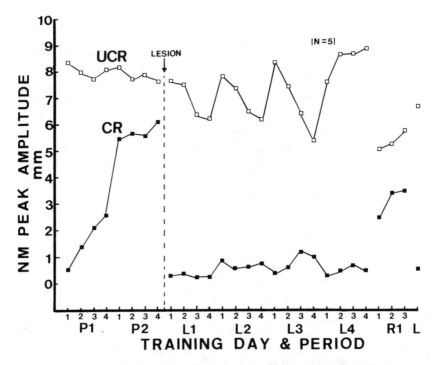

FIG. 14.9   Effect of lesion of the ipsilateral superior cerebellar peduncle (SCP) on retention and reacquisition of the nictitating membrane (and eyelid) responses, averaged for five animals. Solid squares, amplitude of conditioned respons (CR); open squares, amplitude of unconditioned response (UCR). All training was to the left side except where labeled R1. The lesion abolished or severely impaired the ipsilateral CR with no effect upon the UCR. P1–P2 indicate the 2 days of training prior to the lesion. L1–L4 indicate the 4 days of training after the lesion. The contralateral (righy) eye was then trained and learned quite rapidly (R1). The left eye was again trained (L) and still showed only very small responses. Numbers on abscissa represent approximately 27 trial blocks.

trained animals (about 80 msec) and is very close to the minimum CS–US interval that can support learning.

The possibility that unilateral cerebellar lesions produce a modulatory disruption of a memory trace localized elsewhere in the brain seems unlikely. If so, it must be efferent from the cerebellum, because discrete lesions of the superior cerebellar peduncle abolish the behavioral learned response. Yet the neuronal model of the learned NM/eyelid response is present within the ipsilateral cerebellum.

In current work Donegan, Lowry, and Thompson (unpublished observations) have obtained evidence that the cerebellum is also essential for classical conditioning of the hind limb flexion reflex. Rabbits are initally trained with a 2.0 mA shock (60 Hz 100 msec) to the left hind paw using the same tone CS as in NM/eyelid conditioning (350 msec, 1 KHz, 85 db, ISI 250 msec). Animals are given 45 trials per day with a 90 sec ITI. EMG activity is recorded from flexor muscles of both hind limbs. Interestingly, in the rabbit both hind limbs develop an equivalent conditioned flexor response, consistant with the fact that rabbits typically move their hind limbs synchronously when they locomote.

Ablation of the left lateral cerebellum including the deep nuclei substantially impairs this conditioned flexor response in both hind limbs when training is continued to the left hind limb (see Fig. 14.12). Training was then given to the right hind limb and both hind limbs developed clear conditioned responses (Fig. 14.12). Training was then shifted back to the left hind limb and the conditioned responses in both hind limbs extinguished, even though reinforced training continued to the left hind limb. These results demonstrate that the cerebellar lesion does not simply prevent the animal from making the

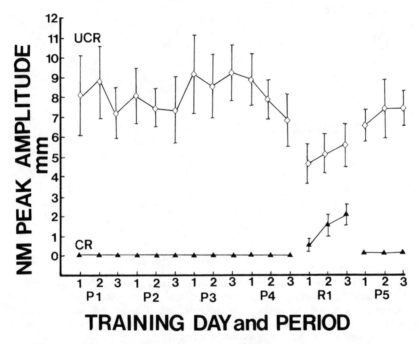

FIG. 14.10   Effects of ablation of left lateral cerebellum on learning of the nictitating membrane (and eyelid) responses (six animals). Solid triangles, amplitude of conditioned response (CR); open diamonds, amplitude of unconditioned response (UCR). All training was to left eye (ipsilateral to lesion) except where labeled R1. The cerebellar lesion prevented conditioning of the ipsilateral eye but had no effect on the UCR. P1–P4 indicate the 4 days of postlesion training to the left eye. The right eye was then trained and learned at a rate comparable to that of initial learning of nonlesioned animals. The left eye was again trained (P5) and showed no learning. Numbers on abscissa indicate 40-trial blocks.

conditioned response in the left hind limb — normal CRs are given by the left hind limb when training is given to the right hind limb. Interestingly, there is an earlier Soviet report indicating that in dogs well trained in leg-flexion conditioning, complete removal of the cerebellum apparently permanently abolished the ability of the animals to make a discrete leg-flexion response but did not abolish conditioned generalized motor activity (see description by Karamaian, Fanardjian, & Kosareva, 1969).

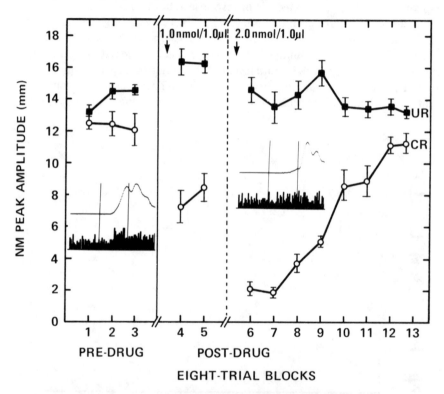

FIG. 14.11   Effects of localized microinjection of bicuculline methiodide into the medial dentate/lateral interpositus region on the well-learned NM/eyelid response. Closed squares and ○ open circles represent the peak amplitude of the unconditioned response (UR) and conditioned response (CR), respectively. Each training block consists of eight averaged trials with a variable 30 second intertrial interval. Left panel: mean NM response amplitude during three blocks of predrug baseline conditioning. Center panel: mean NM response amplitude for two blocks following microinjection of 1 nmol bicuculline methiodide into dentate/interpositus. Right panel: mean NM response amplitude for eight blocks following micorinjection of 2 nmol of bicuculline methiodide. Note inserts within left and right panels: Upper trace in each histogram represents the averaged NM response; lower trace depicts the corresponding dentate/interpositus multiple-unit peristimulus histogram. The bin width is 9 msec. The first vertical line in each histogram indicates tone onset; the second vertical line indicates airpuff onset. The predrug histogram is an average of blocks 2 and 3; the postdrug histogram is an average of blocks 6 and 7.

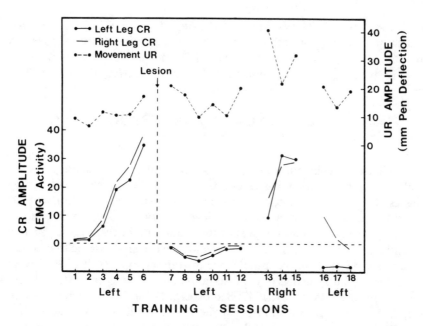

FIG. 14.12   Example of the results of a particularly effective lesion in the cerebellar deep nuclei ipsilateral to the side of training on leg-flexion conditioned responses (CRs) and unconditioned responses (CRs) in the rabbit, using a tone CS and a shock UCS delivered to the left or right hind paw. As can be seen, initial learning with left paw-shock is bilateral. Lesioning the left cerebellar deep nuclei resulted in an abolition of CRs in both legs but had no effect on UR amplitude. Switching the shock UCS to the paw contralateral to the lesion (right side) resulted in reacquisition of bilateral CRs. Switching the UCS back to the lesioned side resulted in a loss of the CR.

The possibility that the cerebellum is a locus for the coding of learned motor responses has been suggested by several authors (Albus, 1971; Eccles et al., 1967; Ito, 1970; Marr, 1969). Cerebellar lesions impair a variety of skilled movements in animals (Brooks, 1979; Brooks, Koslovskaya, Atkin, Horvath, & Uno, 1973). In addition, neuronal recordings from Purkinje cells of the cerebellar cortex have implicated these cells in the plasticity of various responses (Dufosse, Jastreboff, & Miyashita, 1978; Gilbert & Thach, 1977).

Recent evidence from our laboratory strongly supports a cerebellar locus for the essential memory trace. We have defined the efferent pathway from the trace, superior cerebellar peduncle, magnacellular red nucleus, descending rubral pathway (Chapman et al., *Neurosci. Abs.*, 1985, *11*, 835; Lavond et al., 1981; McCormick et al., 1982b; Haley et al., *Neurosci. Abs.*, 1983, *9*, 643; Madden et al., *Neurosci. Abs.*, 1983, *9*, 830); shown that the dorsal accessory olive-climbing fiber projection is the necessary and sufficient US pathway (Steinmetz et al., *Neurosci. Abs.*, 1984, *10*, 122; Mauk & Thompson, *Neurosci. Abs.*, 1984, *10*, 122); shown that the mossy fiber projection is the necessary and sufficient CS pathway (Steinmetz et al., *Bull. Psychonom.*

Soc., 1985, *23,* 245-248; Solomon et al., *Bull. Psychonom. Soc.,* in press); and shown that appropriately timed conjoint activation of mossy fibers as the CS and climbing fibers as the US yields normal learning of discrete, adaptive behavioral CRs (Steinmetz et al., *Neurosci. Abs.,* 1985, *11,* 982).

AVERSIVE LEARNING — TWO PROCESSES AND TWO MEMORY TRACES?

On the basis of behavioral analysis, a number of theorists have proposed that conditioning with aversive events results in the development of two classes of learned behavior, conditioned emotional states (conditioned fear) and discrete, skeletal responses, which develop in two phases, the first importantly influencing the development of the second. In the case of instrumental conditioning, two process models of avoidance learning assume that conditioned fear develops in the initial stage of training as a result of Pavlovian conditioning, i.e., pairings of the discriminative and other local stimuli with the noxious event (Mowrer, 1947; Schlosberg, 1937). With continued training, the subject learns a response that allows it to avoid the noxious stimulus. One line of research has focused on the role of conditioned drives (fear) on the acquisition of avoidance responses (e.g., Brown & Jacobs, 1949; Miller, 1948). These investigators proposed that subjects learn to escape from the stimulus context producing the conditioned fear (the context in which shock occurs) and thereby avoid the aversive event. (Escape behavior was said to be reinforced by a reduction in conditioned fear.) A second approach has focused on how Pavlovianly conditioned drives such as fear influence performance of the learned avoidance responses (e.g., May, 1948; Overmeir & Lawry, 1979; Rescorla & Solomon, 1967). Such studies generally show that Pavlovian procedures that act to increase the level of conditioned fear elevate levels of avoidance responding and that Pavlovian procedures that decrease the fear state diminish levels of responding.

In addressing the findings of Pavlovian conditioning with aversive USs, Konorski (1967) proposed that pairing a CS with a noxious US initially results in the development of associations between context cues (and to a lesser extent the CS) and an emotive system that produces the fear drive. These associations develop rapidly and are responsible for the occurrence of fear CRs as indexed by a number of autonomic responses (e.g., GSR, heart rate, pupil diameter) and motor arousal (or on the contrary, freezing). The conditioned fear state is assumed to play an important role in the development and expression of discrete conditioned reflexes (in Konorski's termonology, conditioned consummatory responses). The discrete conditioned responses, e.g., leg flexion or eyelid closure, are said to develop against a background of arousal produced by the fear state and require much more extensive training relative to the "fear CRs." (It should be noted that in Konorski's model of conditioned defensive reflexes drive induction is critical for acquisition, as opposed to reinforcement by drive reduction that is stressed in two process models of avoidance learning.)

Weinberger (1982) has made similar distinctions between the early and late products of conditioning, which he designates as "nonspecific" and "specific" responses (Konorski's preparatory CRs and consummatory CRs, respectively; also see Schlosberg, 1937). Most "nonspecific" responses are autonomic but some have skeletal muscular components (e.g., respiration and generalized motor activity), develop rapidly, and are adaptive in the sense that they prepare the animal to do something. The specific responses are discrete striated muscle responses elicited by the specific aversive stimulus, e.g., eyelid closure and eyeball retraction to a corneal airpuff, and usually require about 100 or more trials to become well conditioned, depending on the parameters of training (Weinberger, 1982). They are specifically adaptive in that they are precisely targeted to deal with the particular US. The key distinction we make, then, is between nonspecific responses and specific responses, not between autonomic and skeletal responses (even though most studies of nonspecific response learning have used autonomic and cardiovascular responses).

At a descriptive level, Prokasy (1972) has developed a two-phase model of classical conditioning that addresses the data of the conditioned NM/eyelid preparation. The two phases are defined operationally to be the time from the beginning of training to the occurrence of the first CR and the time from this point until the CR is well learned. Manipulation of variables that might be expected to influence "motivation" or "state," e.g., US intensity, lesions of the medial septum (see Berry, Chapter 9), influence Phase I but not Phase II.

Considering Konorski's proposal that conditioned fear influences the expression of discrete, defensive CRs, it should be noted that the role of conditioned fear in CR generation is less well documented than is its role in the generation of avoidance behavior. Most of the research addressing the issue of response generation has focused upon the ability of a fear eliciting CS to potentiate a defensive reflex elicited by an aversive US. For example, Brown, Kalish, and Farber (1951) observed that rats' startle response to a loud noise was potentiated when the noise was preceded by a conditioned stimulus (e.g., light) that had been previously paired with a shock US. That conditioned fear is what modulates amplitude in such procedures is supported by the elegant work of Davis (1979a,b; Davis et al., 1979). These studies show that pharmacological manipulations that reduce states of fear or anxiety selectively abolish the ability of a CS paired with shock to potentiate startle; the startle response to the noise alone is unaffected. Conversely, administration of drugs known to increase anxiety in humans increases the level of potentiated startle produced by the aversive CS (Davis, Redmond, & Barabam, 1979).

To further evaluate the role that conditioned fear might play in the generation of discrete CRs, one would want to determine whether or not the stimuli available to the subject during training acquire the ability to elicit fear, and if they do so over appropriate intervals of time. Ross (1961) and Spence and Rundquist (1958) addressed these issues by giving groups of human subjects CS-shock pairings at different interstimulus intervals. The ability of the CS to potentiate subjects' eyeblink response to a corneal airpuff probe stimulus was then assessed across several CS-probe stimulus intervals. Their findings suggest (1) that brief duration CSs (one second or less) that are typically used in the human eyeblink conditioning preparation do not acquire fear eliciting properties but that longer duration CSs do, and (2) that the latency of the conditioned fear response is much longer than the latency of the eyeblink CR, that is, too long to influence the generation of the eyeblink CR on a trial-by-trial basis. In contrast, Berg and Davis (1982) have shown that pairing a brief light CS with a shock (0.6 sec CS–US interval) results in the light acquiring the ability to dramatically increase the startle response to a loud tone in rats. In fact, having the light CS precede the startle eliciting tone by as little as 30 msec can result in a large elevation in startle amplitude, compared to groups having the tone preceded by a light that had been presented randomly in relation to the shock. Potentiation of startle by the light becomes asymptotic at about 80 msec (Davis, personal communication). Related observations of Gold and Cohen (1981) show that sympathetic cardiac neurons, i.e., neurons controling cardiac response to fear stimuli, respond to the fear eliciting stimulus with a latency of about 100 msec in the pigeon. Whether or not the short duration CSs used in the rabbit NM/eyeblink conditioning preparation acquire the ability to elicit conditioned fear, and do so at appropriately short latencies to influence NM/eyeblink CRs, remains to be determined. Recent observations from our lab suggest that in early stages of acquisition, conditioned fear plays an important role in the generation of NM/eyelid CRs (see below).

The Memory Trace System for Nonspecific Responses/ Conditional Emotional States

As noted earlier, conditioned emotional states such as fear and anxiety can potentiate defensive reflexive behavior (Brown, Kalish, & Farber, 1951; Davis, 1979a,b) and the ability of the fear eliciting stimulus to potentiate the reflex response can be selectively abolished by administration of anxiolytic drugs (Davis, 1979a,b). To the degree that conditioned fear has similar effects on the generation of discrete *conditioned* defensive reflexes, such as the eyeblink/NM, we might expect that reducing the level of conditioned fear elicited by the CS or context cues would correspondingly reduce the vigor of the discrete, defensive CR. We recently reported findings supporting this expectation: Systematic injection of 5 mg/Kg of morphine selectively abolishes the conditioned NM/eyelid response (it has no effect on the unconditioned

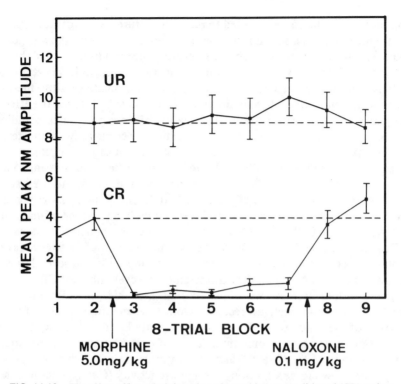

FIG. 14.13   The effect of i.v. administration of morphine on conditioned (CR) and un-conditioned (UCR) NM responses. Scores for the CR and UCR were determined by the peak amplitude of the NM extension during the CS and UCS periods, respectively. Dot-ted lines indicate baseline response amplitudes prior to morphine injection (Mauk et al., 1982).

response) and that naloxone reverses this effect (Mauk et al., 1982b, see Fig. 14.13). The CR is abolished on the first trial after injection, before the next aversive US is presented, thus ruling out the possibility that the action of morphine is related simply to a reduction in the aversiveness of the corneal airpuff US. The same dose of morphine has no effect at all on CS-evoked multiple-unit activity in the central nucleus of the inferior colliculus, arguing against possible action on the CS channel. In short, morphine appears to be exerting a selective action on some part of the neuronal circuitry essential for the learned response, excluding the CS channel, the reflex pathway, and the final common motor pathway.

As a first step in the localization and characterization of the opiate-sensitive circuit in question, we felt that it was necessary to determine the rel-ative contributions of peripheral and central opiate-sensitive sites in the me-diation of the opiate-induced abolition of the CR. The rationale behind this approach stemmed from observations implicating possible sites of opiate action on fear conditioning reported in recent literature. Among these reports are findings that microadministration of opiate agonists into the amygdala complex can alter the retention of passive-avoidance conditioning and the acquisition of fear-motivated conditioned heart rate (e.g., Gallagher & Kapp, 1981). Such findings have led to the speculation that opiate-sensitive mechanisms within the amygdala may provide a common substrate for the effects of opiates on memory processes and regulation of emotional states including fear (Gallagher & Kapp, 1981). On the other hand, peripherally administered opioid peptides have been reported to affect both acquisition and consolidation of avoidance responses (e.g., Rigter, Jensen, Martinez, Messing, Vasquez, Liang, & McGaugh, 1980). Such effects are time dependent, suggesting that these peptides acted to alter some aspect of learning and memory processes. Moreover, these effects occur at doses that indicate that the primary site of action may be in the peripheral rather than the central nervous system.

To this end we performed a series of experiments designed to determine the relative effects of both central and systemic administration of several opiate agonists and antogonists on the expression of the eyeblink/NM CR.

In our initial studies, we observed that morphiceptin (Tyr-Pro-Phe-Pro-NH$_2$), a highly selective μ-receptor agonist, when infused into the fourth ventricle of the brain, produced a pronounced abolition of the CR. This effect was prevented by concomitant infusion of opiate antagonist naltrexone. Administration of the (D-Pro^2) analogue of morphiceptin, which has previously been shown to be void of opiate agonist activity (Chang, Cuatrecasas, & Chang, 1982; Chang, Killian, Hazum, & Cuatrecasas, 1981) was ineffective in the present study in abolishing the CR. The fact that this isomer was ineffective supports the steric specificity of the morphiceptin-receptor interaction.

In a separate experiment central administration of as little as 12 nmol of the potent long-lasting analogue (N-MePhe^3, D-Pro^4) morphiceptin similarly produced a marked abolition of the CR. This effect was dose dependent and could be completely reversed by subsequent administration of the opiate antagonist naloxone. When viewed in concert, the effects of these substances on the expression of the CR are consistent with the known pharmacological properties that opiate agonists display through binding at recognition sites characterized as opiate receptors—i.e., high affinity, reversibility, stereospecificity, and the blockage or reversibility of such agonist-receptor interaction by opiate antagonists.

Preliminary analysis indicates that the periaqueductal gray/periventricular region of the fourth ventricle is a particularly sensitive site for producing this opiate-receptor-mediated abolition of the CR, relative to other sites studied. Microinfusion of comparable amounts of morphiceptin into the lateral ventricles produced an abolition of the CR; however, this effect typically had a delayed onset and a considerably shorter and more variable action. Moreover, bilateral microadministration of this peptide into either the medial septal region or the amygdaloid complex had no effect on the CR.

In spite of these observations, it could be argued that, although administered centrally, these opiate agonists are being transported from the cerebrospinal fluid to the circulation and ultimately acting at opiate-sensitive sites in the periphery. However, the results from our systemic studies argue against this position. First, i.v. administration of (N-MePhe³, D-Pro⁴) morphiceptin in doses ranging from 0.1 to 10 times those effective via central infusion had no effect on the CR. Second, serial systemic administration of the opiate antagonist quaternary naloxone, which does not cross the blood-brain barrier in any appreciable amount, had no effect on morphine-induced abolition of the CR. The range of doses used was comparable in potency with the dose of naloxone subsequently used to reverse completely the effect of morphine.

Collectively, these observations are consistent with the position that the effects of opiates on learned responses are mediated by activiation of μ-receptor-mediated processes within the central nervous system. Furthermore, this effect was selective to the CR. None of the opiate agonists tested affected the performance of the unconditioned reflex response. It may be argued that opiates are acting on some critical component(s) of the circuitry mediating conditioned fear, possibly localized to the periaqueductal gray/periventricular region of the fourth ventricle, that is necessary for the generation of the conditioned NM response. This region has also been shown to be a particularly sensitive site in the production of opiate-induced analgesia in the rabbit (Herz, Albus, Metys, Schubert, & Teschemacher, 1970). It is possible that opiate abolition of the CR shares a neural substrate common to that involved in modulation of slow pain and the production of analgesia.

Having more precisely characterized and localized a site where the opiate can selectively abolish the NM/eyelid CRs, and having proposed this effect was due to an action on conditioned fear, we were compelled to test the effects of (N-MePHe³, D-Pro⁴) morphiceptin on a conditioned response thought to index conditioned fear more directly. In current work we have found that infusion of the small amount of (N-MePhe³, D-Pro⁴) morphiceptin (12 nmol) into the fourth ventricle that abolishes the just-learned NM/eyelid response also abolishes the conditioned deceleration of the heart rate elicited by a CS previously paired with a shock US (Lavond, Mauk, Madden, Barchas, & Thompson, 1982, 1983). This effect is blocked by concomitant infusion of naltrexone (10 nmol). It is tempting to suggest that one and the same neuronal system in the vicinity of the fourth ventricle codes the learned fear that is indexed by conditioned heart-rate slowing and modulates the generation of the discrete, adaptive NM/eyelid response. However, this is at present only a speculation.

INTERRELATIONS OF THE TWO MEMORY TRACE
SYSTEMS

We suggest, in the spirit of Konorski (1967), the following modest theory concerning the brain substrates of aversive learning. When training is given with an aversive US, an initial associative process develops—the CS (and contextual cues) enter into association with the aversive aspect of the US. This basic associative process of "conditioned fear" develops rapidly and influences a number of brain systems, e.g., autonomic nervous system, motor control systems, pituitary-adrenal axis, that exhibit nonspecific conditioned responses. We assume that this basic associative process has a particular neuronal substrate, probably involving brain stem-hypothalamic circuitry. We further assume a different neuronal system codes the memory trace for the learning of specific striated muscle CRs and that learning and performance in this neuronal system is modulated by the brain stem-hypothalamic system. In short, we suggest that aversive learning involves two memory trace systems that have distinct neuronal substrates. The first influences the development of the second but once the second memory trace system, the neuronal substrate of the specific response, has developed it can function to some degree independently. However, the specific response does not become completely autonomous, as evidenced by the fact that if the US is omitted, it extinguishes.

That discrete responses can become somewhat autonomous of conditioned emotional states is indicated by findings that autonomic/nonspecific CRs often fade as the specific,, adaptive CRs develop (e.g., Powell, Lipkin, & Milligan, 1974; Schneiderman, 1972; Yehle, 1968). Similarly, Mineka and Gino (1980), using a signaled avoidance training procedure, observed that, with prolonged training, the strength of the avoidance response elicited by the signal increased (resistance to extinction grew) but the ability of the signal to elicit a conditioned emotional response (suppression of appetitively motivated behavior) decreased. Consistent with these observations, we have shown, using the rabbit conditioned NM/eyeblink preparation, that the ability of opiates to prevent the generation of NM/eyelid CRs is markedly reduced by overtraining (Mauk et al., 1983), compared to the effects observed early in training (Mauk, Madden, Barchas, & Thompson, 1982, Mauk, Warren, & Thompson, 1982).

Another implication of this reasoning is that manipulations that affect neural circuits responsible for the discrete, adaptive response should have no effect on conditioned emotional responses. We have recently evaluated this proposal by performing bilateral lesions of the dentate and interpositus nuclei of the cerebellum in the rabbit (i.e., lesions that have been shown to prevent the acquisition of the NM/eyelid CR; Lincoln et al., 1982) and assessing the effects on the development of conditioned fear and the conditioned NM/

eyelid response (Lavond, Lincoln, & Thompson, unpublished observations). Lesioned subjects readily learned a conditioned heart-rate deceleration to a CS paired with a shock US but failed to develop CRs to a CS paired with an airpuff delivered to the left or right eye. Thus these cerebellar lesions selectively prevented the development of a discrete CR (NM) although having no effect on the development of a conditioned fear response (heart-rate deceleration).

The findings of our laboratory over the last several years are especially encouraging in that (1) they reflect progress in localizing the neural substrates of two products of associative conditioning with aversive USs (conditioned fear and discrete adaptive responses), and (2) that these neural systems appear to interact in ways consistent with earlier theoretical formulations based on behavioral analyses (e.g., Konorski, 1967; Rescorla & Solomon, 1967). The task before us is to characterize more fully the neural circuitry responsible for the development and expression of these two classes of conditioned responses and to determine the extent to which the conditioned fear system influences the development and expression of discrete, conditioned skeletal responses.

ACKNOWLEDGMENTS

The work reported here was supported in part by research grants from the National Science Foundation (BNS 81-17115), the National Institutes of Health (NS23368), the National Institute of Mental Health (MH26530), and the McKnight Foundation and the Office of Naval Research to R. F. Thompson; the National Institute of Mental Health #MH23861 (John Madden, IV), Predoctoral Fellowships from the National Institute of Mental Health #1F31 MH08513-01 (Gregory A. Clark) and #5F31 MH08673-02 (David A. McCormick); Neuroscience Training Grant #1T32 MH17047-01 (Laura A. Mamounas); Postdoctoral Fellowships from the National Institute of Mental Health #1F32 MH08576-01 (Nelson H. Donegan) and #2F32 MH08233-03 (David G. Lavond). We would like to extend our gratitude to Jack Barchas for his support and guidance in our collaborative efforts.

REFERENCES

Albus, J. S. (1971). A theory of cerebellar function. *Math. Biosci., 10,* 25–61.

Berg, W. K., & Davis, M. (1982). A neural locus where a conditioned stimulus alters behavior (acoustic startle): Selective effects of stimulation site and diazepam. *Society for Neuroscience Abstracts, 8,* 42.5-147.

Berthier, N. E., & Moore, J. W. (1980). Role of extrocular muscles in the rabbit (*Oryctolagus cuniculus*) nictitating membrane response. *Physiology and Behavior, 2,* 931–937.

Brooks, V. B. (1979). Control of intended limb movements by the lateral and intermediate cerebellum. In H. Asanuma & V. J. Wilson (Eds.), *Integration in the nervous system* (pp. 321–356). New York: Igaku–Shoin Press.

Brooks, V. B. Kozlovskaya, I. B., Atkin, A., Horvath, F. E., & Uno, M. (1973). Effects of cooling dentate nucleus on tracking-task performance in monkeys. *Journal of Neurophysiology, 36,* 974–995.

Brown, J. S., & Jacobs, A. (1949). The role of fear in the motivation and acquisition of responses. *Journal of Experimental Psychology, 39,* 747–759.

Brown, J. S., Kalish, H. I., & Farber, I. E. (1951). Conditioned fear as revealed by magnitude of startle response to an auditory stimulus. *Journal of Experimental Psychology, 41,* 317–328.

Cegavske, C. F., Patterson, M. M., & Thompson, R. F. (1979). Neuronal unit activity in the abducens nucleus during classical conditioning of the nictitating membrane response in the rabbit *Oryctolagus cuniculus. Journal of Comparative and Physiological Psychology, 93,* 595–609.

Cegavske, C. F., Thompson, R. F., Patterson, M. M., & Gormezano, I. (1976). Mechanisms of efferent neuronal control of the reflex nictitating membrane response in the rabbit. *Journal of Comparative and Physiological Psychology, 90,* 411–423.

Chang, K.-J., Cuatrecasas, P., Wei, E. T., & Chang, J.-K. (1982). Analgesic activity of intraceberoventricular administration of morphiceptin and -casomorphins: Correlation with the morphine ( ) receptor binding affinity. *Life Sciences, 30,* 1547–1551.

Chang, K.-J., Killian, A., Hazum, E., & Cuatrecasas, P. (1981). Morphiceptin (NH₄-TYR-PRO-PHE-PRO-CONH₂): A potent and specific agonist for morphine (M) receptors. *Science, 212,* 75–77.

Chan-Palay, V. (1977). *Cerebellar dentate nucleus, organization, cytology, and transmitters.* Berlin: Springer-Verlag.

Chan-Palay, V. (1978). Autoradiographic localization of -aminobutyric acid receptors in the rat central nervous system by using [₃H]muscimol. *Proceedings of the National Academy of Sciences USA, 75*(2), 1024–1028.

Clark, G. A., McCormick, D. A., Lavond, D. G., Baxter, K., Gray, J., & Thompson, R. F. (1982). Effects of electrolytic lesions of cerebellar nuclei on conditioned behavioral and hippocampal responses. *Society for Neuroscience Abstracts, 8,* 22.

Davis, M. (1979a). Morphine and naloxone: Effects on conditioned fear as measured with the potentiated startle paradigm. *European Journal of Pharmacology, 54,* 341–347.

Davis, M. (1979b). Diazepam and flurozepam: Effects on conditioned fear as measured with the potentiated startle paradigm. *Psychopharmacology, 62,* 1–7.

Davis, M., Redmond, D. E., & Barabam, J. M. (1979). Noradrenergic agonists and antagonists: Effects on conditioned fear as measured by the potentiated startle paradigm. *Psychopharmacology, 65,* 111–118.

Deaux, E. G., & Gormezano, I. (1963). Eyeball retraction: Classical conditioning and extinction in the albino rabbit. *Science, 141,* 630–631.

Desmond, J. E., & Moore, J. W. (1982). Brain stem elements essential for classically conditioned but not unconditioned nictitating membrane responses. *Physiology and Behavior, 28,* 1029–1033.

Disterhoft, J. F., & Stuart, D. K. (1977). Differentiated short latency responnse increases after conditioning in inferior colliculus neurons of alert rat. *Brain Research, 130,* 315–33.

Dufosse, M., Ito, M., Jastreboff, P. J., & Miyashita, Y. (1978). A neuronal correlate in rabbit's cerebellum to adaptive modification of the vestibulo-ocular reflex. *Brain Research, 195,* 611–616.

Eccles, J. C., Ito, M., & Szentagothai, J. (1967). *The cerebellum as a neuronal machine.* New York: Springer-Verlag.

Esner, D. (1976). *Doctoral Thesis.* University of Iowa.

Gallagher, M., & Kapp, B. S. (1981). Influence of amygdala opiate-sensitive mechanisms, fear-motivated responses, and memory processes for aversive-experiences. In J. L. Martinez, R. A. Jensen, R. B. Messing, H. Rigter, & J. L. McCaugh (Eds.), *Endogenous peptides and learning and memory processes.* New York: Academic Press.

Gilbert, P. F. C., & Thach, W. T. (1977). Purkinje cell activity during motor learning. *Brain Res., 128,* 309–328.

Gold, M. R., & Cohen, D. H. (1981). Modification of the discharge of vagal cardiac neurons during learned heart rate change. *Science, 214,* 345–347.

Gormezano, I., Schneiderman, N., Deaux, E., & Fuentes, I. (1962). Nictitating membrane: Classical conditioning and extinction in the albino rabbit. *Science, 138,* 33–34.

Gray, T. S., McMaster, S. E., Harvey, J. A., & Gormezano, I. (1981). Localization of retractor bulbi motoneurons in the rabbit. *Brain Research, 226,* 93–106.

Herz, A., Albus, K., Metys, J., Schubert, P., & Teschemacher, Hj. (1970). On the central sites for the antinociceptive action of morphine and fentanyl. *Neuropharmacol., 9,* 539–551.

Heyman, G. M. (1983). A parametric evaluation of the hedonic and motoric effects of drugs: Pimozide and amphetamine. *Journal of the Experimental Analysis of Behavior.*

Hilgard, E. R., & Marquis, D. G. (1940). *Conditioning and learning.* New York: Appleton-Century-Crofts.

Ito, M. (1970). Neurphysiological aspects of the cerebellar motor control system. *International Journal of Neurology, 7,* 162–76.

Karamian, A. I., Fanardjian, V. V., & Kosareva, A. A. (1969). The functional and morphological evolution of the cerebellum and its role in behavior. In R. Llinas (Ed.), *Neurobiology of cerebellar evolution and development, First International Symposium.* Chicago: American Medical Association.

Kettner, R. N., Shannon, R. V., Nguyen, T. M., & Thompson, R. F. (1980). Simultaneous behavioral and neural (Cochlear Nucleus) measurement during signal detection in the rabbit. *Perception and Psychophysics, 28*(6), 504–13.

Kettner, R. E., & Thompson, R. F. (1982). Auditory signal detection and decision processes in the nervous system. *Journal of Comparative and Physiological Psychology, 96,* 328–331.

Konorski, J. (1967). *Integrative activity of the brain.* Chicago: University of Chicago Press.

Lavond, D. G., Mauk, M. D., Madden, IV, J., Barchas, J. D., & Thompson, R. F. (1983). Abolition of conditioned heart-rate response in rabbits following central administration of [N-MePhe³, D-Pro⁴] morphiceptin. *Pharmacology, Biochemistry, and Behavior, 19,* 379–382.

Lavond, D. G., Mauk, M. D., Madden, IV, J., Barchas, J. D., & Thompson, R. F. (1982). Central opiate effect on heart-rate conditioning. *Society for Neuroscience Abstracts, 8,* 319.

Lavond, D. G., McCormick, D. A., Clark, G. A., Holmes, D. T., & Thompson, R. F. (1981). Effects of ipsilateral rostral pontine reticular lesions on retention of classically conditioned nictitating membrane and eyelid responses. *Physiological Psychology, 9,* 335–339.

Lincoln, J. S., McCormick, D. A., & Thompson, R. F. (1982). Ipsilateral cerebellar lesions prevent learning of the classically conditioned nictitating membrane/eyelid response. *Brain Research, 242,* 190–193.

Marr, D. (1969). A theory of cerebellar cortex. *Research Journal of Physiology, 202,* 437–470.

Mauk, M. D., Castellano, J. G., Rideout, J. A., Madden, IV, J., Barchas, J. D., & Thompson, R. F. (1983). Overtraining reduces opiate abolition of classically conditioned responses. *Physiology and Behavior, 30,* 493–495.

Mauk, M. D., Madden, IV, J., Barchas, J. D., & Thompson, R. F. (1982). Opiates and classical conditioning: Selective abolition of conditioned responses by activation of opiate receptors within the central nervous system. *Proceedings of the National Academy of Sciences USA, 79,* 7598–7602.

Mauk, M. D., Warren, J. T., & Thompson, R. F. (1982). Selective, naloxone-reversible morphine depression of learned behavioral and hippocampal responses. *Science, 216,* 434–435.

May, M. A. (1948). Experimentally acquired drives. *Journal of Experimental Psychology, 38,* 66–77.

McCormick, D. A., Lavond, D. G., Clark, G. A., Kettner, R. E., Rising, C. E., & Thompson, R. F. (1981). The engram found? Role of the cerebellum in classical conditioning of nictitating membrane and eyelid response. *Bulletin of the Psychonomic Society, 18,* 103–105.

McCormick, D. A., Clark, G. A., Lavond, D. G., & Thompson, R. F. (1982a). Initial localization of the memory trace for a basic form of learning. *Proceedings of the National Academy of Sciences USA, 79,* 2731–2735.

McCormick, D. A., Guyer, P. E., & Thompson, R. F. (1982b). Superior cerebellar peduncle lesions selectively abolish the ipsilateral classically conditioned nictitating membrane/eyelid response of the rabbit. *Brain Research, 244,* 347–350.

McCormick, D. A., Lavond, D. G., & Thompson, R. F. (1982c). Concommitant classical conditioning of the rabbit nictitating membrane and eyelid response: Correlations and implications. *Physiology and Behavior, 28,* 769–775.

Megirian, D., & Bures, J. (1969). Unilateral cortical spreading depression and conditioned eyeblink responses in the rabbit. *Experimental Neurology, 27,* 34–45.

Miller, N. E. (1948). Studies of fear as an acquirable drive. I. Fear as motivation and fear-reduction as reinforcement in learning of new responses. *Journal of Experimental Psychology, 38,* 89–101.

Mineka, S., & Gino, A. (1980). Dissociation between conditioned emotional response and extended avoidance performance. *Learning and Motivation, 11,* 476–502.

Moore, J. W., Desmond, J. E., & Berthier, N. E. (1982). The metencephalic basis of the conditioned nictitating membrane response. In C. D. Woody (Ed.), *Conditioning: Representation of involved neural functions.* New York: Plenum Press.

Mowrer, O. H. (1947). On the dual nature of learning—a reinterpretation of "conditioning" and "problem-solving." *Harvard Educational Review, 17,* 102–48.

Oakley, D. A., & Russell, I. S. (1972). Neocortical lesions and classical conditioning. *Physiology and Behavior, 8,* 915–926.

Okada, Y., Nitsch-Hassler, C., Kim, J. S., Bak, I. J., & Hassler, R. (1971). Role of gamma-aminobutyric acid (GABA) in the extrapyramidal motor system. I. Regional distribution of GABA in rabbit, rat, guinea pig, and baboon NCS. *Experimental Brain Research, 13,* 514–518.

Overmeir, J. B., & Lawry, J. A. (1979). Pavlovian conditioning and the mediation of behavior. In G. A. Bower (Ed.), *Theories of learning and motivation* (Vol. 13). New York: Academic Press.

Papsdorf, J. D., Longman, D., & Gormezano, I. (1965). Spreading depression: Effects of applying KCl to the dura of the rabbit on the conditioned nictitating membrane response. *Psychonomic Science, 2,* 125–126.

Powell, D. A., Lipkin, M., & Milligan, W. L. (1974). Concomitant changes in classically conditioned heart rate and corneoretinal potential discrimination in the rabbit (Oryctolagus cuniculus). *Learning and Motivation, 5,* 532–547.

Prokasy, W. F. (1972). Developments with the two-phase model applied to human eyelid conditioning. In A. H. Black & W. F. Prokasy (Eds.), *Classical conditioning II: Current research and theory* (pp. 199–147). New York: Appleton–Century–Crofts.

Rescorla, R. A., & Solomon, R. L. (1967). Two-process learning theory: Relationships between Pavlovian conditioning and instrumental learning. *Psychological Review, 74,* 151–182.

Rigter, H., Jensen, R. A., Martinez, J. L., Messing, R. B., Vasquez, B. J., Liang, K. C., & McGaugh, J. L. (1980). Enkephalin and fear-motivated behavior. *Proceedings of the National Academy of Sciences, 77,* 3729–3732.

Roberts, E. (1976). Disinhibition as an organizing principle in the nervous system—the role of the GABA system. In E. Roberts, T. N. Chase, & D. B. Tower (Eds.), *GABA in nervous system function* (pp. 515–539). New York: Raven Press.

Roberts, E. (1980). Epilepsy and antiepileptic drugs: A speculative synthesis. In G. H. Glaser, J. K. Penny, & D. M. Woodbury (Eds.), *Antiepileptic drugs: Mechanisms of action* (pp. 667–713). New York: Raven Press.

Ross, L. E. (1961). Conditioned fear as a function of CS–UCS and probe stimulus intervals. *Journal of Experimental Psychology, 61,* 265–273.

Schlosberg, H. (1937). The relationship between success and the laws of conditioning. *Psychological Review, 44,* 379–394.

Schneiderman, N. (1972). Response system divergencies in aversive classical conditioning. In A. H. Black, & W. F. Prokasy (Eds.), *Classical conditioning II: Current research and theory.* New York: Appleton–Century–Crofts.

Schneiderman, N., Fuentes, I., & Gormezano, I. (1962). Acquisition and extinction of the classically conditioned eyelid response in the albino rabbit. *Science, 136,* 650–652.

Spence, K. W., & Rundquist, W. N. (1958). Temporal effects of conditioned fear on the eyelid reflex. *Journal of Experimental Psychology, 55,* 613–616.

Thompson, R. F., Barchas, J. D., Clark, G. A., Donegan, N. H., Kettner, R. E., Lavond, D. G., Madden IV, J., Mauk, M. D., & McCormick, D. A. (1985). Neuronal substrates of associative learning in the mammalian brain. In D. L. Alkon & J. Farley (Eds.), *Primary neural substrates of learning and behavioral change.* Princeton, NJ: Princeton University Press.

Thompson, R. F., Berger, T. W., Berry, S. D., Clark, G. A., Kettner, R. D., Lavond, D. G., Mauk, M. D., McCormick, D. A., Solomon, P. R., & Weisz, D. J. (1982). Neuronal substrates of learning and memory: Hippocampus and other structures. In D. C. Woody (Ed.), *Conditioning: Representation of involved neural functions* (pp. 115–130). New York: Plenum Press.

Thompson, R. F., Berger, T. W., Cegavske, C. F., Patterson, M. M., Roemer, R. A., Teyler, T. J., & Young, R. A. (1976). The search for the engram. *American Psychologist, 31,* 209–27.

Thompson, R. F., Berger, T. W., & Madden IV, J. (1983a). Cellular processes of learning and memory in the mammalian CNS. *Annual Review of Neuroscience, 6.*

Thompson, R. F., Clark, G. A., Donegan, N. H., Lavond, D. G., Madden IV, J., Mamounas, L. A., Mauk, M. D., & McCormick, D. A. (1983b). Neuronal substrates of basic associative learning. In L. Squire & N. Butters (Eds.), *Neuropsychology of memory* (pp. 424–442.) New York: Guilford Press.

Thompson, R. F., McCormick, D. A., Lavond, D. G., Clark, G. A., Kettner, R. E., & Mauk, M. D. (1983c). The engram found? Initial localization of the memory trace for a basic form of associative learning. In J. M. Sprague & A. N. Epstein (Ed.), *Progress in psychobiology and physiological psychology* (pp. 167–197). New York: Academic Press.

Wagner, A. R. (1969). Stimulus selection and "modified continuity theory." In G. H. Bower & J. T. Spence (Eds.), *Psychology of learning and motivation* (Vol. 3). New York: Academic Press.

Wagner, A. R. (1971). Elementary associations. In H. H. Kendler & J. T. Spence (Eds.), *Essays in neobehaviorism: A memorial volume to Kenneth W. Spence.* New York: Appleton–Century–Crofts.

Wagner, A. R. (1981). SOP: A model of automatic memory processing in animal behavior. In N. E. Spear & R. R. Miller (Eds.), *Information processing in animals: Memory mechanisms.* Hillsdale, NJ: Lawrence Erlbaum Associates.

Weinberger, N. M. (1982). Effects of conditioned arousal on the auditory system. In A. L. Bechman (Ed.), *The neural basis of behavior* (pp. 63–91). New York: Spectrum.

Woody, C. D., & Brozek, G. (1969). Changes in evoked responses from facial nucleus of cat with conditioning and extinction of an eye blink. *Journal of Neurophysiology, 32,* 717–726.

Yehle, A. L. (1968). Divergencies among rabbit response systems during three-tone classical discrimination conditioning. *Journal of Experimental Psychology, 77,* 468–473.

Author Index

Subject Index